Provence
& the Côte d'Azur

Nicola Williams
Catherine Le Nevez

On the Road

NICOLA WILLIAMS Coordinating Author

For Nicola, an English journalist living and working in France for the past 10 years (home today is a hillside house with a Lake Geneva view in Haute Savoie), it is an easy getaway to France's hot south. She has spent endless years eating her way around the region and revelling in its extraordinary art heritage and vibrant landscapes. When she's not working for Lonely Planet, she can be found in the Alps skiing or hiking, strolling around Florence or flitting between family in Britain and Germany. Nicola wrote the 1st edition of *Provence & the Côte d'Azur* in 1999 and has worked on numerous other Lonely Planet titles, including *The Loire* and *France*.

CATHERINE LE NEVEZ Catherine first lived and travelled in France aged four and has been hitting the road at every opportunity since, completing postgrad qualifications in editing, writing and publishing along the way. She's previously scoured Provence and the Côte d'Azur for Lonely Planet's *France* guidebook and online reviews across the region including Nice and Marseille – for which she's also authored European city break guides. She loves rambling across the wildflower-strewn countryside of Pays de Forcalquier, sipping pastis in Marseille's sweltering backblocks bars, driving among the vineyards during the *vendage,* and scrambling through the Gorges du Verdon in snow… and lingering in the Provençal markets, any time of year.

Provence & the Côte d'Azur

There's much more to Provence than pastis, *pétanque* and hilltop villages glinting gold and amber in the midday sun. Roughly wedged between rough-cut Marseille, with its urban art scene, and megalomaniacal Monte Carlo with its skyscraper skyline, this sunny spot on the sky blue Med screams action, glamour and a hint of the ridiculous. Where else do cowboys herd black bulls, while Roma blaze flamenco beneath flamingo-filled skies?

This seductive corner of southern France was made for gorging. Be it ancient Roman arches and amphitheatres, modern art, vineyards, almond blossoms, blue and purple lavender fields or pig-ugly truffles, the orgy of hues, scents and tastes to feast on is, quite simply, electrifying.

Beaches

Cats on leads, dogs in handbags and prima donnas dusting sand from their toes with shaving brushes are madcap sights to savour on the glorious beach-riddled Côte d'Azur, where anything goes. But it pays to know your *plage*. Beaches in and east of Nice are piled with porcelain-smooth pebbles (bum-numbing? *never*); beaches west of Nice are sumptuously sandy, soft and gold. Around Marseille – a *bouillabaisse* mix of both.

Author tip

When a yellow or red flag is flying, skip the dip and have lunch instead. Beach dining to remember, each kissed with a different hint of exoticism: Marseille's Le Petit Nice-Passédat, linked to a dramatic rock-ledge beach by a little path; chic Z Plage in Cannes; laid-back Chez Jo in Cavalière; hip Couleurs du Jardin on Gigaro and Kaï Largo on Pampelonne.

① Calanque d'En Vau

Sail a boat and scramble across rocks to savour sky-soaring rock sculptures and clear emerald waters on this exquisite, pocket-sized shingle beach (p116), slipped inside a *calanque* (rocky inlet). Heavenly any time other than body-jammed July and August.

② Plage de Notre-Dame

Pedalling along pot-holed trails between pines to this beach paradise (p368) on Île de Porquerolles' northern coast is as much an experience as playing Robinson Crusoe on the beach's gorgeous fine white sand.

③ Plage de Gigaro

Gigaro's golden-sand beach (p353), backed by peninsula vineyards, feels god-given. So does its coastal path, which dances around rocky capes to several quieter cove-hugged beaches, each more idyllic than the last.

④ Plage de Piémanson

Far from Riviera-manicured, this cowboy-wild plain of wind-sculpted sand (p152), stretching for several kilometres sits on the edge of world in the Camargue. Motor past salt pans and pink flamingos to get to it.

⑤ Plage de Pampelonne

Topless sunbathing, the G-string bikini, an erotically breathless Bardot... They all debuted on St-Tropez' hottest sands, 9km long, where the jet-set party never stops (p352).

⑥ Plage du Layet

A deeply bronzed, moneyed set with a penchant for baring all hangs out on Cavalière's most sizzling sands (p364), tucked in a cove with legendary Jo at the helm.

1

Lavender

Lavender is the soul of Provence, with no image better evoking this sweetly scented part of southern France than flowering fields of the aromatic purple flower. To see it at its blooming best, visit in late June or early July when spring-green fields blaze blue. With the short harvest over by mid-August, the serried sun-baked plants sit out autumn in a cropped wash of pale grey-blue.

2

Author tip
Whether you want to paint lavender landscapes, romp through them or fly above them, visit a lavender farm or distillery, help hand-harvest lavender, learn how to cook it, buy lavender bath salts or splash out in a lavender spa, make **Les Routes de la Lavande** (www.routes-lavande.com) your key information source.

❶ Plateau de Valensole

One of the region's greatest concentrations of lavender farms sweeps magnificently across this vast plateau (p244) of wheat fields and lavender squares – although 99% of what you see is lavendin (p244).

❷ Plateau de Claparèdes

Mooch away the day touring this stunning chequered landscape of gold (wheat), red (poppies) and purple (lavender). End it with dinner *à la lavande* in one of the area's idyllic *chambres d'hôtes* (p227).

❸ Abbaye de Sénanque

Get cameras at the ready. This 12th-century Cistercian abbey (p217; above) in Gordes is framed with a quintessentially Provence, picture-postcard-perfect surround of purple lavender fields. The 1980s Benedictine Abbaye Ste-Madeleine (p177) in Le Barroux is equally photogenic.

❹ Prieuré de Salagon

Ramble around lavender-laden gardens at this beautiful medieval priory (p246) in Provence's rural heart and learn about the lilac bloom in its Musée de Lavande.

❺ Château du Bois

Frolic along footpaths that wend their way through fields of lavender at this idyllic lavender farm in the Luberon – one of the few to still produce real lavender (p226).

❻ Lavender Spa

Fragrant, soothing lavender is a natural ingredient in Mediterranean body care. Bliss out with lavender and luxury in a top spa (p88).

Artist Portfolio

With its designer chapels, cutting-edge architecture and avant-garde art museums, Provence and the Côte d'Azur is a living art museum, with world-famous pieces to revel in. Provence's weighty artist portfolio bursts with 20th-century greats who were lured to the region, especially the Riviera, by a warmth and intensity of light absolutely unknown elsewhere in Europe. See it immortalised in their work.

❶ Cézanne

Derive inspiration from the atelier (p126; above left) where Cézanne worked – then marvel at the mountains that he painted (p131) and drink where he drank (p129) in Aix-en-Provence.

❷ Picasso

Antibes (p312; left) is a key stop on any Picasso-inspired itinerary. Nearby Vallauris (p310), where the artist painted war and peace inside a chapel, is another Pablovian highlight.

❸ Renoir

Although 66 years old and crippled with arthritis, Renoir was still painting during his time in Cagnes-sur-Mer – as a trip around his old studio and home, the Musée Renoir (p319), proves.

❹ Van Gogh

Arles (p138; above) is full of reminders of the 19th century's maddest artist. His work is everywhere but this town, where he painted 200-odd canvases and chopped off a chunk of his ear. You can also track him down in St-Rémy de Provence (p189).

❺ Matisse

Matisse was a Nice man. He slept at Hôtel Beau Rivage (p272), painted a wedge of works strung in the Musée Matisse (p266) and designed a one-off chapel in Vence for his nun friend (p321).

❻ Vasarely

An original Vasarely inside and out, the Fondation Vasarely in Aix-en-Provence (p126) woos lovers of 1970s op art with 16 hexagons showcasing a mesmerising collection of Vasarely works.

Hilltop Villages

There's no escaping *villages perchés* (hilltop villages) in Provence. Round a corner and – whoa – another cluster of old stone houses teetering precariously atop a crag peers down at you (watch that hairpin!). A particular speciality of the Luberon and less-explored back-country Var, these villages cropped up from the 10th century, as villagers from the plains to rocky crags tried to better defend themselves against Saracen attacks.

① Bonnieux & Ménerbes

This twinset of Luberon classics doesn't lose its edge despite the Mayle-inspired madding crowd. With real villages and real sights, Bonnieux (p219; right) boasts a bread-making museum and cedar forest, while Ménerbes (p221; above left) has a truffle house and a corkscrew museum.

② Gordes

Another serious classic. Approach from the south for a full frontal of it tumbling down the hillside. Early evening, the play of light – amber, gold, rust – is soul-soaring (p216).

③ Oppède-le-Vieux

No village is quite as fantastically left to ruin as Oppède 'the old' (not to be confused with the new village where everyone actually lives). Olive groves, cherry orchards and vineyards amble around its feet (p222).

④ Ste-Agnès & Gorbio

A 2km path links these two refreshingly quiet villages. It's best to start in St-Agnès, Europe's highest seaside village, then go down to Gorbio for lunch beneath jasmine in its quintessential village inn (p294).

⑤ Fox Amphoux

Lap up a glorious vision of unspoilt Provence between ruined ramparts and a 13th-century chateau at Fox Amphoux (p358), one of several remarkable villages to slumber in splendid isolation in the Pays Draçenois.

⑥ Seillans

Cobbled lanes coil to the crown of this northern Var village, which is irresistibly pretty and gloriously quiet. Lunch is a must at the *bastide* of Scipion, knight of the Flotte d'Agout (p357).

Riviera Legends

La Baie des Anges, promenade des Anglais, La Croisette, Eden Roc… Every name on this celebrated stretch of coastline, known the world over, is loaded with legend, myth and celebrity scandal. From bottle-top-covered nipples to cleavage-inspired architecture, billion-dollar real estate and champagne-toasted hedonism aboard monumental yachts, there is no disputing the sheer glitz, glam and racy razzmatazz of the French Riviera.

Author tip
After a hard day dabbling with fame, consider dining at La Réserve de Nice – a luxury hotel in 1878, it's now a ground-breaking dining space, courtesy of the most exciting young chef on the Riviera.

③ Le Club 55
Paparazzi just love this sexy St-Tropez beach club where many a sarong-clad star has been caught belly out. Book a table well ahead and be as famous as possible (p346).

① Fairy-Tale Land
A Hollywood queen weds a Monégasque prince: visit the palace (p387), flutter in the world's most famous *belle époque* casino (p388; above) and cruise along the same *corniches* as Grace Kelly did – to her peril.

④ Pétanque
Immortalised on film innumerable times, the gravel *pétanque* pitch in St-Paul de Vence (p320) and the pitch beneath plane trees on place des Lices in St-Tropez (p343) are hot spots to spin with stars.

② La Croisette
Trail world stars of cinema along Cannes' fabled seaside promenade: pose on the bunker steps (p302), match a celebrity handprint to yours and lunch on the sand of the Art Deco Martinez (p305; left).

⑤ Eden Roc
Sizzling stuff since the 1920s, the Med-side pool at this seaside beauty on Cap d'Antibes is a legend in its own right: lunch at the Eden Roc Grill to see why (p317).

⑥ Grand Hôtel du Cap Ferrat
Ride an air-conditioned teak-clad funicular down the cliff face for a day of self-pampering by the pool at the beach club of this Riviera legend on Cap Ferrat (p284).

Roman Provence

Ancient Roman ruins transport travellers to a very different Provence. Gloriously intact, carefully preserved amphitheatres, triumphal arches, baths and other public buildings evoke the very period in its rich history that gave Provence – a Roman *provincia* – its name. Throw the region's gregarious festive spirit into the arena and Roman Provence suddenly becomes really rather fun.

Author tip

Watch out for Les Chorégies d'Orange at Orange's Roman amphitheatre and the two-week Festival de Vaison-la-Romaine in Puymin's Théâtre Antique, both in July or August; the year-round plays, concerts and bullfights at Les Arènes in Nîmes and the bullfights and *courses Camarguaises* in Arles.

2 Pont du Gard

Its sheer size impresses. For a different perspective on this awe-inspiring three-tiered aqueduct above the River Gard, skip on top of it or paddle beneath it in a canoe (p200).

1 Glanum

This vast archaeological site is a walk through history from the 3rd century BC to 3rd century AD. Top it off with a Roman drink in the Taberna Romana and a snap-happy moment at Les Antiques (p189).

3 Les Arènes & Maison Carré

A thrill-filled evening at a *féria* is the most intoxicating way of viewing Nîmes' resplendent amphitheatre (p195). The Maison Carré (p195; above) is its other Roman thrill.

Contents

On the Road 2

Highlights 3

Getting Started 20

Snapshot 23

History 24

The Culture 34

Food & Drink 42

The Arts 58

Environment 72

Outdoor Activities 80

Marseille Area 90

ITINERARIES	91
MARSEILLE	93
History	93
Orientation	95
Information	96
Dangers & Annoyances	96
Sights	97
Activities	102
Tours	104
Festivals & Events	104
Sleeping	104
Eating	108
Drinking	111
Entertainment	111
Shopping	113
Getting Around	114
AROUND MARSEILLE	115
Les Calanques	115
Cassis	116

Pays de Pagnol	119
Côte Bleue	119
Salon de Provence	121
PAYS D'AIX	123
Aix-en-Provence	123
Around Aix	131

The Camargue 133

ITINERARIES	134
ARLES	138
Orientation	139
Information	140
Sights	140
Tours	142
Festivals & Events	142
Sleeping	143
Eating	144
Shopping	145
Getting There & Away	145
Getting Around	146
STES-MARIES DE LA MER	146
Orientation & Information	146
Sights & Activities	147
Tours	147
Festivals & Events	147
Sleeping	148
Eating	149
Getting There & Away	149
Getting Around	149
AIGUES-MORTES	149
Information	149
Sights	150
Boat Trips	150
Sleeping & Eating	150
Getting There & Away	150
SOUTHEASTERN CAMARGUE	150
Arles to Digue à la Mer	150
Salin de Giraud & Beyond	151
Back to Arles	152

Avignon Area 154

ITINERARIES	155
AVIGNON & AROUND	157
Avignon	157
Villeneuve-lès-Avignon	168
NORTH OF AVIGNON	169

Châteauneuf du Pape 169
Orange 171
Vaison-la-Romaine 173
Enclave des Papes
& Around 176
Dentelles de Montmirail
& Around 177
Mont Ventoux 180
Carpentras 182
Around Carpentras 185
LES ALPILLES **189**
St-Rémy de Provence 189
Around St-Rémy de
Provence 192
Tarascon & Beaucaire 194
ACROSS THE RIVER RHÔNE 194
Nîmes 194
Around Nîmes 199

The Luberon 209

ITINERARIES **210**
NORTH OF THE N100 **212**
Apt 212
Around Apt 215
SOUTH OF THE N100 **219**
Le Petit Luberon 219
Cavaillon 223
Cavaillon to Cadenet 225
Le Grand Luberon 226
Manosque & Around 229

Haute-Provence 231

ITINERARIES **232**
GORGES DU VERDON **234**
Orientation 234
Information 234
Dangers & Annoyances 234
Sights & Activities 235
Sleeping & Eating 237
Getting There & Around 239
LACS DU VERDON **239**
Sights & Activities 239
Sleeping & Eating 241
**RÉSERVE GÉOLOGIQUE
DE HAUTE-PROVENCE** **241**
Digne-les-Bains 242
VALLÉE DE LA DURANCE **245**
Sisteron 245
Around Sisteron 246
Pays de Forcalquier 246
**PARC NATIONAL DU
MERCANTOUR** **248**

Orientation 249
Information 249
Vallée de l'Ubaye 249
Vallée du Haut Verdon 251
Vallée de la Tinée 252
Vallée de la Vésubie 253
Vallée des Merveilles 254
Vallée de la Roya 255

Nice to Menton 257

ITINERARIES **258**
NICE **260**
Orientation 260
Information 261
Sights 265
Activities 268
Nice for Children 269
Tours 269
Festivals & Events 270
Sleeping 270
Eating 272
Drinking 275
Entertainment 276
Shopping 277
Getting There & Away 278
Getting Around 279
THE THREE CORNICHES **279**
Corniche Inférieure 280
Moyenne Corniche 285
Grande Corniche 286
ARRIÈRE-PAYS NIÇOIS **288**
Contes to Coaraze 288
Peille & Peillon 289
MENTON & AROUND **290**
Menton 290
Around Menton 294

Cannes Area 296

ITINERARIES **297**
CANNES TO NICE **299**
Cannes 299
Îles de Lérins 310
Vallauris & Golfe-Juan 310
Antibes 312
Biot 318
Cagnes-Sur-Mer 318
St-Paul de Vence 319
Vence 321
Around Vence 322
INLAND TO GRASSE **324**

Mougins 324
Grasse 325
MASSIF DE L'ESTÉREL **328**
Corniche de l'Estérel 328
St-Raphaël 331
Fréjus 333

St-Tropez to Toulon 338

ITINERARIES **339**
PRESQU'ÎLE DE ST-TROPEZ 341
St-Tropez 341
The Peninsula 352
Golfe de St-Tropez 354
NORTHERN VAR **356**
Draguignan 357
Around Draguignan 357
MASSIF DES MAURES **360**
Collobrières 360
Chartreuse de la Verne 361
La Garde Freinet 362
Cogolin 363
La Môle & Around 363
Forêt du Dom
& Bormes-les-Mimosas 363
Corniche des Maures 364
Le Lavandou 365
**ÎLES D'HYÈRES & ÎLES
DU FUN** **366**
Île de Porquerolles 366
Île de Port-Cros 369
Île du Levant 370
Île de Bendor 371
Îles des Embiez 371
TOULON & AROUND **371**
Hyères 372
Cap de Carqueiranne 376
Toulon 376
Towards Marseille 380

Monaco 382

Orientation 383
Information 385
Sights 386
Activities 390
Festivals & Events 390
Sleeping 390
Eating 391
Drinking 392
Shopping 395
Getting There & Away 395
Getting Around 396

Directory   398

Accommodation   398
Activities   400
Business Hours   400
Children   401
Climate Charts   401
Courses   402
Customs   402
Dangers & Annoyances   402
Discount Cards   403
Embassies & Consulates   404
Festivals & Events   405
Food & Drink   405
Gay & Lesbian Travellers   407
Holidays   407
Insurance   408
Internet Access   408
Legal Matters   408
Local Government   409
Maps   409
Money   410
Photography & Video   410
Post   410
Shopping   411
Solo Travellers   411
Telephone   411
Time   412
Toilets   412

Tourist Information   412
Tours   413
Travellers with Disabilities   413
Visas   414
Volunteering   415
Women Travellers   415
Work   415

Transport   417

GETTING THERE & AWAY   417
Entering the Country   417
Air   417
Land   419
River   421
Sea   421
GETTING AROUND   422
Air   422
Bicycle   422
Boat   423
Bus   424
Car & Motorcycle   424
Train   427

Health   428

BEFORE YOU GO   428
Insurance   428
Recommended Vaccinations   428

IN TRANSIT   428
Deep Vein Thrombosis (Dvt)   428
Jet Lag   428
IN PROVENCE & THE CÔTE D'AZUR   429
Availability & Cost of Health Care   429
Diarrhoea   429
Environmental Hazards   429
Sexual Health   429
Travelling with Children   429
Women's Health   430

Language   431

Glossary   437

Behind the Scenes   439

Index   446

World Time Zones   454

Map Legend   456

Regional Map Contents

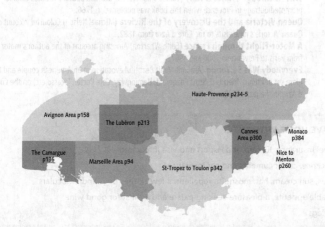

Haute-Provence p234-5

Avignon Area p158

The Lubéron p213

Cannes Area p300

Monaco p384

The Camargue p136

Marseille Area p94

St-Tropez to Toulon p342

Nice to Menton p260

Getting Started

Planning a trip to the region is as straightforward or as tricky as you make it: razz around Riviera hot spots in July and August and you need to book everything months in advance to make it affordable. But hop south to Marseille for an autumnal city break and planning time hovers close to zero.

WHEN TO GO

See Climate Charts (p401) for more information.

Not in hot-and-bothered July and August when holiday-makers hog the region, clogging up roads and hotels and making life in the blistering heat unbearable.

May and June are the best times, followed by September and October. Spring is a cocktail of flowering poppy fields and almond trees. In September vines sag with plump red grapes, pumpkin fields glow orange and the first olives turn black in van Gogh's silver-branched olive groves. The *vendange* (grape harvest) starts around 15 September, followed by the *cueillette des olives* (olive harvest) from 15 November through to early January.

If you ski, late December to March is your season. Lavender fields blaze purple for two or three weeks any time between late June and mid-July.

HOW MUCH?

Filled baguette €4

Croissant and *café au lait* €3

Local/foreign newspaper €1/3

Ten-minute taxi ride €15

Metro, tram or city bus ticket €1.40

COSTS & MONEY

Accommodation will be your biggest expense: count on €70 minimum a night for a midrange double with bathroom in a hotel or *chambre d'hôte*. Hostel-sleeping, bread-and-cheese-eating backpackers can survive on €40 a day; those opting for midrange hotels, restaurants and museums will easily spend €120.

TRAVEL LITERATURE

Provence and the Côte d'Azur inspired writers two centuries ago –and still inspires today. Literature evoking specific places is listed in destination chapters. For books on history, culture and gastronomy, see the History, Culture and Food & Drink chapters.

Essential reading for a general overview:

Travels through France & Italy (Tobias Smollett) The Scottish author's ruthless candour prompted outrage in Provence when this book was published in 1766.

Queen Victoria and the Discovery of the Riviera (Michael Nelson) Colourful account of Queen Victoria's nine visits to the Côte d'Azur from 1882.

A Motor-Flight through France (Edith Wharton) Amusing account of the author's motor trip from Paris to Provence in 1906 and 1907.

Everybody Was So Young (Amanda Vaill) Beautiful evocation of an American couple and their glam set of literary friends (F Scott Fitzgerald, Hemingway, Cole Porter, Picasso etc) on the Côte d'Azur in the jazzy 1920s.

LONELY PLANET INDEX

Litre of petrol €1.30

50cl bottle of Evian next to Monaco's Oceanographic Museum/elsewhere €3/1

Cheap/expensive bottle of wine €4/25

Souvenir T-shirt €25

Ice cream (two-scoop cone) €2.50 to €3.70

DON'T LEAVE HOME WITHOUT...

- Valid travel insurance, ID card or passport and visa if required
- Driving licence, car documents and car insurance
- Sunglasses, sun cream, hat, mosquito repellent, a few clothes pegs and binoculars
- An insatiable appetite, a pleasure-seeking palate and a thirst for good wine
- Your sea legs

TOP TENS

Festivals & Events

The region loves to party. Proof of the pudding: legendary *fêtes* are a dime a dozen. See p405 for regional festivals and the respective destination chapters for town-specific festivals.

- Carnaval de Nice, February (Nice; p270)
- Pélerinage des Gitans, May & October (Stes-Maries de la Mer; p147)
- Fête des Gardians, May (Arles; p148)
- Cannes International Film Festival, May (Cannes; p302)
- Formula One Grand Prix, May (Monaco; p396)
- Fête de la Transhumance, June (St-Rémy de Provence; p190)
- Les Chorégies d'Orange, late July to early August (Orange; p172)
- Festival de Marseille, July (Marseille; p104)
- Festival International d'Art Lyrique d'Aix-en-Provence, July (Aix-en-Provence; p126)
- Festival d'Avignon & Festival Off, July (Avignon; p163)

Thrills

- Paddle by moonlight through emerald waters in Les Calanques (p115)
- Bathe like a Roman in Aquae Sextiae (p127)
- Skip across the top tier of the Pont du Gard (p200)
- Feast on *bouillabaisse* at Chez Jo on the sand; no obligation to strip (p365)
- Be a gorge explorer (p232)
- Hunt truffles with Dominique, Eric and Mirette, *le chien truffier* (p178)
- Canoe from Fontaine de Vaucluse to L'Isle sur la Sorgue (p188)
- Lap up luxury and legend around the pool for a day at the Cap Ferrat hotel of Lebanese diamond dealer Robert Mouawad (p284)
- Play the hedonist in millionaire Monaco (p387)
- Catch a Roma band during Stes-Maries de la Mer's astonishing May and October pilgrimages (p142)

Chambres d'Hôtes

Simply the best to sleep, dream, eat and experience picture-postcard Provence.

- La Bastide des Papes (p164)
- La Forge (p218)
- La Bastide de l'Adrech (p230)
- Le Mas des Câpriers (p229)
- Relais d'Elle (p248)
- La Bastide aux Camélias (p286)
- La Parare (p290)
- Les Cabanes d'Orion (p320)
- Villa Ste-Maxime (p320)
- La Grande Maison des Campaux (p364)

Dramatic Drives

- Col de Canadel, Corniche des Maures (p364)
- D36B from south of Arles to Salin de Giraud (p150) then D36D to Plage de Piémanson, Southeastern Camargue (p151)
- D39 from Collobrières to Gonfaron, Massif des Maures (p360)
- Moyenne Corniche, Nice to Beausoleil (p285)
- Col de l'Espigouler, Gémenos to Plan d'Aups (p120)
- Rte des Crêtes, Cassis to La Ciotat (p118)
- Formula One Grand Prix circuit, Monaco (p396)
- Europe's highest mountain pass, the Col de Restefond la Bonette, Vallée de la Tinée (p252)
- Rte des Crêtes and Corniche Sublime, Gorges du Verdon (p235)
- Grand Corniche, Nice to Roquebrune (p286)

Provence A – Z (Peter Mayle) The best, the quirkiest, the most curious, the funniest and indeed, the most bizarre moments of the 20-odd years this best-selling author has spent in Provence – organised alphabetically.

The Collected Traveller: Provence (Barrie Kerper) 'Inspired anthology and travel resource' comprising hundreds of Provence-related magazine- and newspaper-published articles collected by the author over a couple of decades.

Words in a French Life: Lessons in Love and Language from the South of France (Kristen Espinasse) Excerpts from the author's blog (p38), capturing daily life in Provence through a series of day-to-day French words.

INTERNET RESOURCES

AngloINFO Riviera (www.angloinfo.com) Life on the Côte d'Azur in English; lots of predeparture planning links.

Avignon & Provence (www.avignon-et-provence.com) Provence and French Riviera accommodation guide oozing charming *chambres d'hôtes*.

Comité Régional de Tourisme Provence-Alpes-Côte d'Azur (www.decouverte-paca.fr) Fabulous regional tourist board website.

Comité Régional du Tourisme Riviera Côte d'Azur (www.guideriviera.com) Exceptional online guide to the coast, crammed with unusual discovery ideas alongside solid practical information.

Lonely Planet (www.lonelyplanet.com) Notes and posts on travel in Provence.

Provence Beyond (www.beyond.fr) Comprehensive tourist guide.

Provence-Hideaways (www.provence-hideaway.com) Exceptionally well-written travel guide covering inland western Provence.

Provence Web (www.provenceweb.fr) Comprehensive tourist guide.

TER-SNCF (www.ter-sncf.com/paca) Regional train tickets, fares and schedules.

Snapshot

The blanket ban on smoking in public places, coming up for France in 2008, will go down with little fuss in affluent fat-cat Provence and the Côte d'Azur, where the living is laid-back and easy – and wholly outside in the shade of the hot Mediterranean sun for a handsome chunk of the year. Not that the chic, avant-garde clubs and café terraces on the Côte d'Azur won't feel it – this is, after all, where Jean-Paul Sartre scrolled parts of *Roads to Freedom* (p350), cigarette in hand, and where a sultry Brigitte Bardot (a Gitanes woman through and through) set the trend for gals to smoke Cuban cigars. This privileged stretch of celebrity-studded coastline smacks of everything the cigarette in France embodies: sex, scandal, cinema, more sex and Gallic chic.

Rebel-yells in rough-cut Marseille might have something to say about it. Not ones to hold back (just look at that head butt, gone down in the annals of unforgettable sporting moments, by the port city's biggest hero Zinedine Zidane – it had the city, not to mention the world, talking for days!), born-and-bred Marseillais are the first to speak their mind – in theatrical torrents of thick sing-song and wild gesticulations. Or maybe IAM, Massilia Sound System or another of Marseille's cutting-edge sounds (p68) will simply bemoan the death of public smoking in a rhapsody of chart-topping rap. Incidentally, to anyone who read in the international press in mid-2006 about the gangster shoot-out in a bar in the east of Marseille (an armed gang burst in and sprayed it with bullets, killing three), there is no need for alarm: the city's underworld generates a murderous story every decade or so to ensure Provence's most diverse and completely addictive city doesn't lose its magnificently gritty edge. No wonder Europe plumped for the region's largest urban conglomeration and biggest trendsetter as the stage for its first street-art school (p58).

Of course there is no chance of stumbling across a fag end (or gunfire for that matter) in squeaky-clean Monaco where the living is extra easy (should you have an excess of cash) – and strictly by the rules. The recently crowned prince, in this land of fairy-tale princesses, grapples with making financial affairs more transparent in this legendary tax haven, while millionaire members of Monaco's exclusive yacht club are revelling in the fabulous design Sir Norman Foster is drawing up for their new portside clubhouse. Should you want to move into Monégasque circles, a one-bedroom apartment costs around €1 million – add another €1 million for each additional bedroom you fancy. Better perhaps to do what a sizable wedge of the working population does: commute to Monaco by train from France where a dreamy 140-sq-metre converted *bergerie* (sheepfold) with 7882 sq metres of land near Fayence is on the market for €742,000 and an old stone 70-sq-metre house in Murs with two hectares of land, water but no electricity and *beaucoup de charme* (bags of Provençal charm) costs €299,000.

Of course, if current talks on extending France's superspeedy, state-of-the-art TGV service from Marseille along the sparkling azure coast to Nice ever come to fruition – placing Paris a quicker-than-lightening 3½ hours away – there's no saying where one could end up.

FAST FACTS

Population: 4.74 million

Area: 31,399 sq km

GDP: €21,020 per inhabitant

GDP growth: 0.5%

Unemployment: 11.8%

Monthly net salary: €1225

Population density: 145 people per sq km

Life expectation: men 76yr, women 83yr

Largest cities: Marseille, Nice & Toulon

Percentage of *résidences secondaires* (second homes): 17.2% of all homes

History

PREHISTORIC MAN

Provence was inhabited from an exceptionally early age and has a bounty of prehistoric sights to prove it. In Monaco the Grottes de l'Observatoire (p390) showcase brilliant prehistoric rock scratchings, carved one million years ago and among the world's oldest. Around 400,000 BC, prehistoric man settled in Terra Amata (present-day Nice): the archaeological site's Musée de Paléontologie Humaine de Terra Amata (p268) explores prehistoric man and his movements at this time.

Neanderthal hunters occupied the Mediterranean coast during the Middle Palaeolithic period (about 90,000 to 40,000 BC), living in caves. Provence's leading prehistory museum, the Musée de la Préhistoire des Gorges du Verdon (p240) in Quinson, runs visits to one such cave, the Grotte de la Baume Bonne (p240).

Modern man arrived with creative flair in 30,000 BC. The ornate wall paintings of bison, seals, ibex and other animals inside the decorated Grotte Cosquer in the Calanque de Sormiou (p116), near Marseille, date to 20,000 BC.

The Neolithic period (about 6000 to 4500 years ago) witnessed the earliest domestication of sheep and the cultivation of lands. The first dwellings to be built (around 3500 BC) were *bories:* learn about life inside these one- or two-storey beehive-shaped huts at the Village des Bories (p217) near Gordes.

The star of Provence's prehistoric show is the collection of 30,000 Bronze Age petroglyphs decorating Mont Bégo in the Vallée des Merveilles (p254). Marked walking trails lead to the rock drawings, which date to between 1800 and 1500 BC.

GREEKS TO ROMANS

Massalia (Marseille) was colonised around 600 BC by Greeks from Phocaea in Asia Minor; from the 4th century BC they established more trading posts along the coast at Antipolis (Antibes), Olbia (Hyères), Athenopolis (St-Tropez), Nikaia (Nice), Monoïkos (Monaco) and Glanum (near St-Rémy de Provence). With them, the Greeks brought olives and grapevines.

While Hellenic civilisation was developing on the coast, the Celts penetrated northern Provence. They mingled with ancient Ligurians to create a Celto-Ligurian stronghold around Entremont; its influence extended as far south as Draguignan.

In 125 BC the Romans helped the Greeks defend Massalia against invading Celto-Ligurians from Entremont. Their subsequent victory marked the start of the Gallo-Roman era and the creation of Provincia Gallia Transalpina, the first Roman *provincia* (province), from which the name Provence is derived.

THE GALLO-ROMANS

Provincia Gallia Transalpina, which quickly became Provincia Narbonensis, embraced all of southern France from the Alps to the Mediterranean Sea and as far west as the Pyrenees. In 122 BC the Romans destroyed the Ligurian capital of Entremont and established the Roman stronghold of Aquae Sextiae Salluviorum (Aix-en-Provence) at its foot.

Enjoy a different twist on the region's classic Roman and medieval sights with *Old Provence* by hugely successful journalist and travel writer Theodore Andrea Cook (1867–1928), penned in 1905, now republished and as fascinating as ever.

TIMELINE	c90,000–30,000 BC	600 BC
	Neanderthal hunters occupy the Mediterranean coast; around 30,000 BC Cro-Magnons start decorating their caves	The Greeks colonise Massalia and establish trading posts along the coast, bringing olives and grapevines

During this period the Romans built roads to secure the route between Italy and Spain. The Via Aurelia linked Rome to Fréjus, Aix-en-Provence, Arles and Nîmes; the northbound Via Agrippa followed the River Rhône from Arles to Avignon, Orange and Lyons; and the Via Domitia linked the Alps with the Pyrenees by way of Sisteron, the Luberon, Beaucaire and Nîmes. Vestiges of these roads – the Pont Julien (p220) from 3 BC at Bonnieux and an arch in Cavaillon (p223) – remain.

The Roman influence on Provence was tremendous, though it was only after Julius Caesar's conquest of Gaul (58–51 BC) and its consequent integration into the Roman Empire that the region flourished. Massalia, which had retained its independence following the creation of Provincia, was incorporated by Caesar in 49 BC. In 14 BC the still-rebellious Ligurians were defeated by Augustus, who celebrated by building a monument at La Turbie (p287) in 6 BC. Arelate (Arles) became the chosen regional capital.

Under the emperor Augustus, vast amphitheatres were built at Arelate (Arles), Nemausus (Nîmes), Forum Julii (Fréjus) and Vasio Vocontiorum (Vaison-la-Romaine). Triumphal arches were raised at Arausio (Orange), Cabelio (Cavaillon), Carpentorate (Carpentras) and Glanum, and a series of aqueducts was constructed. The 275m-long Pont du Gard (p200), with its impressive multimedia museum, was part of a 50km-long system of canals built around 19 BC by Agrippa, Augustus' deputy, to bring water from Uzès to Nîmes. All these ancient public buildings remain exceptionally well preserved and lure sightseers year-round.

The end of the 3rd century saw the reorganisation of the Roman Empire. Provincia Narbonensis was split into two provinces in AD 284. The land on the right bank of the Rhône (Languedoc-Roussillon today) remained Narbonensis, and the land on the left bank (today's Provence) became Provincia Viennoise. Christianity – brought to the region according to Provençal legend by Mary Magdalene, Mary Jacob and Mary Salome who sailed into Stes-Maries de la Mer (p146) in AD 40 – penetrated the region and was adopted by the Romans.

MEDIEVAL PROVENCE

After the collapse of the Roman Empire in AD 476, Provence was invaded by various Germanic tribes: the Visigoths (West Goths, from the Danube delta region in Transylvania), the Ostrogoths (East Goths, from the Black Sea region) and the Burgundians of Scandinavian origin. In the 6th century it was ceded to the Germanic Franks.

In the early 9th century the Saracens (an umbrella term adopted locally to describe Muslim invaders such as Turks, Moors and Arabs) emerged as a warrior force to be reckoned with. Attacks along the Maures coast, Niçois hinterland and more northern Alps persuaded villagers to take refuge in the hills. Many of Provence's perched, hilltop villages date from this chaotic period. In AD 974 the Saracen fortress at La Garde Freinet was defeated by William the Liberator (Guillaume Le Libérateur), count of Arles, who consequently extended his feudal control over the entire region, marking a return of peace and unity to Provence, which became a marquisate. In 1032 it joined the Holy Roman Empire.

The marquisate of Provence was later split in two: the north fell to the counts of Toulouse from 1125 and the Catalan counts of Barcelona gained

Provence Beyond has an excellent section on the general history of Provence, not to mention almost every Provençal village. Read it at www .beyond.fr.

control of the southern part, which stretched from the River Rhône to the River Durance and from the Alps to the sea. This became the county of Provence (Comté de Provence). Raymond Bérenger V (1209–45) was the first Catalan count to reside permanently in Aix (the capital since 1186). In 1229 he conquered Nice and in 1232 he founded Barcelonnette. After Bérenger's death the county passed to the House of Anjou, under which it enjoyed great prosperity.

THE POPES

In 1274 Comtat Venaissin (Carpentras and its Vaucluse hinterland) was ceded to Pope Gregory X in Rome. In 1309 French-born Clement V (r 1305–14) moved the papal headquarters from feud-riven Rome to Avignon. A tour of the Papal palace (p161) illustrates how resplendent a period this was for the city, which hosted nine pontiffs between 1309 and 1376.

The death of Pope Gregory XI led to the Great Schism (1378–1417), during which rival popes resided at Rome and Avignon and spent most of their energies denouncing and excommunicating each other. Even after the schism was settled and a pope established in Rome, Avignon and the Comtat Venaissin remained under papal rule until 1792.

The arts in Provence flourished (see p59). A university was established in Avignon as early as 1303, followed by a university in Aix a century later. In 1327 Italian poet Petrarch (1304–74) encountered his muse, Laura: visit Fontaine de Vaucluse's Musée Pétrarque (p187) for the full story. During the reign of Good King René, king of Naples (1434–80), French became the courtly language.

FRENCH PROVENCE

In 1481 René's successor, his nephew Charles III, died heirless and Provence was ceded to Louis XI of France. In 1486 the state of Aix ratified Provence's union with France and the centralist policies of the French kings saw the region's autonomy greatly reduced. Aix Parliament, a French administrative body, was created in 1501.

In 1560 Nîmes native Jean Nicot (1530–1600) was the first to import tobacco into France from Portugal, hence the word 'nicotine'.

This new addition to the French kingdom did not include Nice, Barcelonnette, Puget-Théniers and their hinterlands that, in 1388, had become incorporated into the lands of the House of Savoy. The County of Nice, with Nice as its capital, did not become part of French Provence until 1860.

A period of instability ensued, as a visit to the synagogue in Carpentras (p183) testifies: Jews living in French Provence fled to ghettos in Carpentras, Pernes-les-Fontaines, L'Isle-sur-la-Sorgue, Cavaillon or Avignon – all were part of the pontifical enclave of Comtat Venaissin, where papal protection remained assured until 1570.

An early victim of the Reformation that swept Europe in the 1530s and the consequent Wars of Religion (1562–98) was the Luberon. In April 1545 the population of 11 Waldensian (Vaudois) villages in the Luberon were massacred (see the boxed text, p227). Numerous clashes followed between the staunchly Catholic Comtat Venaissin and its Huguenot (Protestant) neighbours to the north around Orange.

In 1580 the plague immobilised the region. Treatments first used by the prophetic Nostradamus (1503–66) in St-Rémy de Provence were administered to plague victims. The Edict of Nantes in 1598 (which recognised

William the Liberator extends his feudal control over Provence, which becomes a marquisate and joins the Holy Roman Empire
The Holy See moves from feud-riven Rome to Avignon, and nine pontiffs head the Roman Catholic church from the city

Protestant control of certain areas, including Lourmarin in the Luberon) brought an uneasy peace to the region – until its revocation by Louis XIV in 1685. Full-scale persecution of Protestants ensued. Visit Aigues-Mortes's Tour de Constance (p150) and Château d'If (p102) to see where Huguenots were killed or imprisoned.

The close of the century was marked by the French Revolution in 1789: as the National Guard from Marseille marched north to defend the Revolution, a merry tune composed in Strasbourg several months earlier for the war against Prussia – *Chant de Guerre de l'Armée du Rhin* (War Song of the Rhine Army) – sprang from their lips. France's stirring national anthem, *La Marseillaise*, was born.

LA ROUTE NAPOLÉON

Provence was divided into three *départements* in 1790: Var, Bouches du Rhône and the Basse-Alpes. Two years later papal Avignon and Comtat Venaissin were annexed by France, making way for the creation of Vaucluse.

In 1793 the Armée du Midi marched into Nice and declared it French territory. France also captured Monaco, until now a recognised independent state ruled by the Grimaldi family (see p388). When Toulon was besieged by the English, it was thanks to the efforts of a dashing young Corsican general named Napoleon Bonaparte (Napoleon I) that France recaptured it.

The Reign of Terror that swept through France between September 1793 and July 1794 saw religious freedoms revoked, churches desecrated and cathedrals turned into 'Temples of Reason'. In the secrecy of their homes, people handcrafted thumbnail-sized, biblical figurines, hence the inglorious creation of the *santon* (p100).

In 1814 France lost the territories it had seized in 1793. The County of Nice was ceded to Victor Emmanuel I, king of Sardinia. It remained under Sardinian protectorship until 1860, when an agreement between Napoleon III and the House of Savoy helped drive the Austrians from northern Italy, prompting France to repossess Savoy and the area around Nice. In Monaco the Treaty of Paris restored the rights of the Grimaldi royal family; from 1817 until 1860 the principality also fell under the protection of the Sardinian king.

Meanwhile the Allied restoration of the House of Bourbon to the French throne at the Congress of Vienna (1814–15), following Napoleon I's abdication and exile to Elba, was rudely interrupted by the return of the emperor. Following his escape from Elba in 1815, Napoleon landed at Golfe-Juan on 1 March with a 1200-strong army. He proceeded northwards, passing through Cannes, Grasse, Castellane, Digne-les-Bains and Sisteron en route to his triumphal return to Paris on 20 May. Unfortunately Napoleon's glorious 'Hundred Days' back in power ended with the Battle of Waterloo and his return to exile. He died in 1821.

THE BELLE ÉPOQUE

The Second Empire (1852–70) brought to the region a revival in all things Provençal, a movement spearheaded by Maillane-born poet Frédéric Mistral; the house-museum in his home town (p194) looks at his life. Rapid economic growth was another hallmark: Nice, which had become part of France in 1860, was among Europe's first cities to have a purely tourist-based economy.

In 1848 French revolutionaries adopted the red, white and blue tricolour of Martigues near Marseille as their own. This became France's national flag.

1481	1539
Good King René's successor dies heirless and Provence falls to Louis XI of France	French (rather than Provençal) is made the official administrative language of Provence

Between 1860 and 1911 it was Europe's fastest-growing city. In the Victorian period the city became particularly popular with the English aristocracy, who followed their queen's example of wintering in mild Nice. European royalty followed soon after. The train line reached Toulon in 1856, followed by Nice and Draguignan, and in 1864 work started on a coastal road from Nice to Monaco. Nice Opera House (p277) and the city's neoclassical Palais de Justice (p265) were built in fine Second Empire architectural style.

In neighbouring Monaco the Grimaldi family gave up its claim over its former territories of Menton and Roquebrune (which has been under Monégasque rule until 1848) in 1861 in exchange for France's recognition of its status as an independent principality. Four years later Casino du Monte Carlo – a stunning place, still operational, that should not be missed (see the boxed text, p389) – opened and Monaco leapt from being Europe's poorest state to one of its richest.

The Third Republic ushered in the glittering *belle époque*, with Art Nouveau architecture, a whole field of artistic 'isms' including impressionism, and advances in science and engineering. Wealthy French, English, American and Russian tourists and tuberculosis sufferers (for whom the only cure was sunlight and sea air) discovered the coast. The intensity and clarity of the region's colours and light appealed to many painters; and in 1887 the first guidebook to the French coast was published.

WWI & THE ROARING '20S

No blood was spilled on southern French soil during WWI. Soldiers were conscripted from the region, however, and the human losses included two out of every 10 Frenchmen between 20 and 45 years of age. With its primarily tourist-based economy, the Côte d'Azur recovered quickly from the postwar financial crisis that lingered in France's more industrial north.

The Côte d'Azur sparkled as an avant-garde centre in the 1920s and 1930s, with artists pushing into the new fields of cubism and surrealism, Le Corbusier rewriting the architectural textbook and foreign writers attracted by the coast's liberal atmosphere: Ernest Hemingway, F Scott Fitzgerald, Aldous Huxley, Katherine Mansfield, DH Lawrence and Thomas Mann were among the scores to seek solace in the sun. Guests at Somerset Maugham's villa on Cap Ferrat included innumerable literary names, from TS Eliot and Arnold Bennett to Noël Coward, Evelyn Waugh and Ian Fleming.

The coast's nightlife gained a reputation for being cutting edge, with everything from jazz clubs to striptease. Rail and road access to the south improved: the railway line between Digne-les-Bains and Nice was completed and in 1922 the luxurious *Train Bleu* made its first run from Calais, via Paris, to the coast. The train only had 1st-class carriages and was quickly dubbed the 'train to paradise'.

The roaring '20s hailed the start of the summer season on the Côte d'Azur. Outdoor swimming pools were built, seashores were cleared of seaweed to uncover sandy beaches, and sunbathing sprang into fashion after a bronzed Coco Chanel appeared on the coast in 1923, draped over the arm of the duke of Westminster. France lifted its ban on gambling, prompting the first casino to open on the coast in the Palais de la Méditerranée (today a hotel; p272) on Nice's promenade des Anglais in 1927. The first Formula One Grand Prix (p396) sped around Monaco in 1929, while the early 1930s saw

Twinkling with glamour, *Côte d'Azur: Inventing the French Riviera* by Mary Blume is a fascinating and colourful study of the glamorous rise and fall of the modern Côte d'Azur.

1790–92	1860
Provence is divided into three *départements*; Papal Avignon and Comtat Venaissin are annexed by France and Vaucluse is mapped	The County of Nice becomes part of French Provence; European royalty winters in Nice, Europe's fastest-growing city

---

THE SKY BLUE COAST

The Côte d'Azur (literally 'Azure Coast') gained its name from a 19th-century guidebook.

La Côte d'Azur, published in 1887, was the work of Stéphane Liégeard (1830–1925), a lawyer-cum–aspiring poet from Burgundy who lived in Cannes. The guide covered the coast from Menton to Hyères and was an instant hit.

Its title, a reflection of the coast's clear blue cloudless skies, became the hottest buzz word in town. And it never tired. The Côte d'Azur is known as the French Riviera by most Anglophones.

---

wide pyjama-style beach trousers and the opening of a nudist colony on Île du Levant. With the advent of paid holidays for all French workers in 1936, even more tourists flocked to the region. Second- and 3rd-class seating was added to the *Train Bleu*, which had begun running daily in 1929.

WWII

With the onset of war, the Côte d'Azur's glory days turned grey. Depression set in and on 3 September 1939 France and Britain declared war on Germany. But following the armistice treaty agreed with Hitler on 22 June 1940, southern France fell into the 'free' Vichy France zone, although Menton and the Vallée de Roya were occupied by Italians. The Côte d'Azur – particularly Nice – immediately became a safe haven from war-torn occupied France; by 1942 some 43,000 Jews had descended on the coast to seek refuge. Monaco remained neutral for the duration of WWII.

On 11 November 1942 Nazi Germany invaded Vichy France. Provence was at war. At Toulon 73 ships, cruisers, destroyers and submarines – the major part of the French fleet – were scuttled by their crews to prevent the Germans seizing them. Almost immediately, Toulon was overcome by the Germans and Nice was occupied by the Italians. In January 1943 the Marseille quarter of Le Panier was razed, its 40,000 inhabitants being given less than a day's notice to pack up and leave. Those who didn't were sent to Nazi concentration camps. The Resistance movement, particularly strong in Provence, was known in the region as *maquis* after the Provençal scrub in which people hid.

Two months after D-Day, on 15 August 1944, Allied forces landed on the southern coast. They arrived at beaches – all open for bronzing and bathing today – along the Côte d'Azur, including Le Dramont near St-Raphaël, Cavalaire, Pampelonne and the St-Tropez peninsula. St-Tropez and Provence's hinterland were almost immediately liberated, but it was only after five days of heavy fighting that Allied troops freed Marseille on 28 August (three days after the liberation of Paris). Toulon was liberated on 26 August, a week after French troops first attacked the port.

Italian-occupied areas in the Vallée de Roya were only returned to France in 1947.

MODERN PROVENCE

The first international film festival (see the boxed text, p302) at Cannes in 1946 heralded the return to party madness. The coast's intellectuals reopened their abandoned seaside villas, and Picasso set up studio in Golfe-Juan. The 1950s and 1960s saw a succession of society events: the fairy-tale marriage

A brilliant and true read, Rosemary Sullivan's *Villa Air-Bel: World War II, Escape and a House in Marseille* is the story of a chateau outside Marseille and the 'safe' haven it provided for some of Europe's most prominent artists, writers and cultural elite stranded in France when WWII broke out.

1920s	1939–45
The Côte d'Azur sparkles as Europe's avant-garde centre	Nazi Germany occupies France and the Vichy regime is established; Provence is liberated two months after D-Day

THE BIRTH OF THE BIKINI

Almost called *atome* (French for atom) rather than bikini after its pinprick size, the scanty little two-piece bathing suit was the 1946 creation of Cannes fashion designer Jacques Heim and automotive engineer Louis Réard.

Top-and-bottom swimsuits had existed for centuries, but it was the French duo who plumped for the name bikini – after Bikini, an atoll in the Marshall Islands chosen by the USA in 1946 as a testing ground for atomic bombs.

Once wrapped around the curvaceous buttocks of 1950s sex-bomb Brigitte Bardot on St-Tropez's Plage de Pampelonne, there was no looking back. The bikini was born.

of a Grimaldi prince to Hollywood film legend Grace Kelly in 1956; Vadim's filming of *Et Dieu Créa la Femme* (And God Created Woman) with Brigitte Bardot in St-Tropez the same year; the creation of the bikini (see the boxed text, above); the advent of topless sunbathing (and consequent nipple-covering with bottle tops to prevent arrest for indecent exposure); and Miles Davis, Ella Fitzgerald and Ray Charles appearing at the 1961 Juan-les-Pins jazz festival.

In 1962 the French colony of Algeria negotiated its independence with President Charles de Gaulle. During this time some 750,000 *pieds noirs* (literally 'black feet', as Algerian-born French people are known in France) flooded into France, many settling in large urban centres such as Marseille and Toulon.

Rapid industrialisation marked the 1960s. A string of five hydroelectric plants was constructed on the banks of the River Durance and in 1964 Électricité de France (EDF), the French electricity company, dug a canal from Manosque to the Étang de Berre. The following year construction work began on a 100-sq-km petrochemical zone and an industrial port at Fos-sur-Mer, southern Europe's most important. The first metro line opened in Marseille in 1977 and TGV high-speed trains reached the city in 1981.

From the 1970s mainstream tourism started making inroads into Provence's rural heart. While a concrete marina was being constructed at Villeneuve-Lourbet-Plage (west of Nice), the region's first purpose-built ski resort popped up inland at Isola 2000 (p252). The small flow of foreigners that had trickled into Provence backwaters to buy crumbling old *mas* (Provençal farmhouses) at dirt-cheap prices in the late 1970s had become an uncontrollable torrent by the 1980s. By the turn of the new millennium, the region was welcoming nine million tourists annually.

Corruption cast a shady cloud over France's hot south in the 1980s and early 1990s. Nice's mayor, the corrupt right-wing Jacques Médecin (son of another former mayor, Jean Médecin, who governed Nice for 38 years), was twice found guilty of income-tax evasion during his 24-year mayorship (1966–90). In 1990 King Jacques – as the flamboyant mayor was dubbed – fled to Uruguay, following which he was convicted *in absentia* of the misuse of public funds (including accepting four million francs in bribes and stealing two million francs from the Nice opera). Médecin was extradited in 1994 and imprisoned in Grenoble where he served two years of a 3½-year sentence. Upon being released the ex-mayor, who died in 1998 aged 70, returned to Uruguay to sell handpainted T-shirts.

1946	1956
The first international film festival opens at Cannes	Prince Rainier of Monaco weds his fairy-tale princess, Hollywood film legend Grace Kelly

During 1994 Yann Piat became the only member of France's National Assembly (parliament) since WWII to be assassinated while in office. Following her public denunciation of the Riviera Mafia, the French *député* (member of parliament) was shot in her Hyères constituency. Her assassins, dubbed the 'baby killers' by the press after their conviction in 1998, were local Mafia kingpins barely in their 20s.

THE FN

In the mid-1990s blatant corruption, coupled with economic recession and growing unemployment, fuelled the rise of the extreme-right Front National (FN). Nowhere else in France did the xenophobic party gain such a stronghold as in Provence, where it stormed to victory in municipal elections in Toulon, Orange and Marignane in 1995, and Vitrolles in 1997.

Yet the FN, led by racist demagogue Jean Marie Le Pen, never made any real headway in the national arena. Party support for the FN rose from 1% in 1981 to 15% – a level it has pretty much stayed at ever since – in the 1995 presidential elections, yet the FN never secured any seats in the National Assembly. And despite gaining 15.5% of votes in regional elections in 1998 and 14.7% in 2004, the FN never succeeded in securing the presidency of the Provence-Alpes-Côte d'Azur *région*.

A deadly blow was dealt to the FN in 1998 when second-in-command Bruno Mégret split from Le Pen to create his own breakaway faction. In subsequent European parliamentary elections in 1999, Le Pen and the FN won just 5.7% of the national vote (enough to secure just five of the 87 French parliamentary seats), while Mégret's splinter group, the Mouvement National Républican (MNR) party, trailed with 3.28% (and no seats). This was in contrast to the Socialists, Rassemblement pour la République (RPR), communists and extreme left who won the backing of 21.95%, 12.7%, 6.8% and 5.2% of the electorate, respectively.

> Lose yourself in regional politics at the prefecture, online at www.paca.pref .gouv.fr (in French).

The next blow came in 2000 when Le Pen was suspended from the European Parliament after physically assaulting a Socialist politician three years previously. A year later the extreme right lost the mayorship of Toulon. Extreme-right mayors Jacques Bompard (FN) and Daniel Simonpiéri (MNR) clung onto Orange and Marignane, but in Vitrolles elections were declared invalid, only for the last bastion of MNR power to be smashed to smithereens by left-wing candidate Guy Obino in repeat elections in 2001.

Le Pen's incredible success in the first round of presidential elections in 2002 – he landed 16.86% of votes – shocked the world. More than one million protestors took to the streets across France in the days preceding the second round of voting in which the FN politician was up against incumbent president Jacques Chirac. Fortunately 80% of the electorate turned out to vote (compared with 41.41% in the first round) and Chirac won by a massive majority.

Never to be defeated, Le Pen pulled out his final trump card – his blonde daughter, Marine (dubbed 'the clone' because of the uncanny likeness to her father). Despite accusations of nepotism following her appointment as party vice-chairman at the FN party congress in Nice in 2003, Marine Le Pen stoically pushed forth in her drive to inject youthful zest into an otherwise ageing party (Jean Marie Le Pen is in his 70s), and was rewarded with relative success in the 2004 European elections.

ANOTHER MILLENNIUM

Nowhere was the startling newfound optimism sweeping through France at the start of the new millennium more pronounced than in multicultural Marseille, France's third-largest city that stood at the cutting edge of hip-hop, rap and football (p38).

France's sea-blue south sped into the 21st century with the opening of the high-speed TGV Méditerranée railway line (p420) and a booming information technology sector. In Marseille, Euroméditerranée laid the foundations for a massive 15-year rejuvenation project in the port city (see the boxed text, p112); while the arrival by sea of the world's largest floating dike (see the boxed text, p386) in Monaco doubled the capacity of the already thriving port. The €2 million purchase of a vast 19th-century estate near Bargemon (p357) by the Beckhams (footballer David and ex–Spice Girl Victoria) was mere confirmation that the Côte d'Azur had not lost its sex appeal.

Yet two years on, the tide started to turn. Flash floods devastated northwestern Provence in September 2002, killing 26. A year later floodwaters rose again, this time in Marseille, Avignon, Arles and other Rhône Valley cities, where several died and thousands lost their homes after the river burst its banks. The floods topped off a year that had seen the Festival d'Avignon (p163) – Europe's premier cultural event with an annual revenue of €15 million – paralysed by striking artists, furious at government proposals to tighten unemployment benefits for arts workers. Strikes peppered much of 2004 and 2005.

Regional elections in March 2004 reflected the national trend, socialist Michel Vauzelle (b 1944) staving off the government-backed centre-right UMP (Union pour un Movement Populaire) candidate to secure a second term in office as president of the 123-strong, Marseille-based Provence-Alpes-Côte d'Azur *conseil régional* (regional council; p409). Among other things, the staunchly left politician – a former justice minister, Bouches du Rhône MP and mayor of Arles – was a very loud voice in the *'Non'* campaign to the proposed EU constitution that an overwhelmingly disgruntled French electorate rejected in a referendum in May 2005.

Urban violence across the country – including in Marseille, Cannes, Nice and dozens of other Provençal towns – in response to the death of two teenagers of North African origin in October 2005 who, apparently running from the police, were electrocuted after hiding in an electricity substation in a northeast Paris suburb, capped off these terrible times for a desperate government and France. Just a year before in multicultural Marseille, part of the city's sizable ethnic population had resorted to street protests following the government's national ban of the Islamic headscarf, Jewish skullcap, Sikh

Keep in the loop with current affairs in the region with the Provence-Alpes-Côte d'Azur region website at www.regionpaca.fr (in French).

THE TREATY OF NICE

No pan-European agreement has been more influential on the future map of Europe than the Treaty of Nice, a landmark treaty thrashed out by the-then-15 EU member states in the seaside city of Nice in late December 2000. Enforced from February 2003, the treaty laid the foundations for EU enlargement starting in 2004, determined the institutions necessary for its smooth running and – not without controversy – established a new system of voting in the Council of Ministers for the 25 EU countries from 1 November 2004.

2001	2004
The high-speed TGV Méditerranée railway line puts Marseille just 3½ hours away from Paris by train	The National Assembly bans overtly religious symbols, including the Islamic headscarf and Jewish skullcap, in state schools

---

LAID TO REST

It was in the turquoise depths of the Mediterranean between Marseille and Cassis that the book was closed on one of aviation's greatest mysteries: in 2004 a local diver uncovered the wreckage of the plane of Antoine de Saint-Exupéry, thus identifying the spot where the legendary author of one of the world's most enchanting tales, *Le Petit Prince* (The Little Prince), plunged to his death in July 1944.

---

turban, crucifix and other religious symbols in French schools. The law, as Marie-Josée Roig – France's minister for the family and Avignon city's mayor – explained to a UN committee for child rights, might well be intended to place schoolchildren on an equal footing in the republican French classroom, but for many Muslims it merely confirmed that the French state was not prepared to fully integrate Muslims into French society. For a deeper look at contemporary multicultural affairs, see p40.

Meanwhile, in a privileged pocket of coastal paradise, well away from all this modern-day mayhem, the bachelor son of a Hollywood queen was crowned monarch following the death of his aged father (see the boxed text, p388). A new era, albeit one peppered with a couple of out-of-wedlock kids, was born.

2005	**2006**
Prince Albert I of Monaco is crowned monarch of the world's second-smallest country	Zinadine Zidane retires from football after the 2006 World Cup Final

The Culture

I AM PROVENÇAL

'No I'm not!', shrieks a modish chunk of 20-somethings. 'It's too folkloric. Things like the tablecloths (fussy flowery motifs, sky blue and sunflower yellow, tomato red), the costumes (traditional long skirts and stiff white hats) – they're cute and amusing, but they're not contemporary,' asserts 28-year-old Aix-en-Provence gal Claire Tourette who, as communications manager at one of Marseille's most cutting-edge radio stations, is in tune with modern vibes. 'They belong to an older generation, my grandparents' generation,' she continues, adding 'I am French. But more than French, I am from the south…the weather, the sea…it's different to the rest of France.'

Indeed, in a part of the country where foreigners have always come and gone (and invariably stayed), regional identity is not clear cut. Less than a smidgen of born-and-bred Provençaux understands or speaks Prouvènço (below), rendering the region's traditional mother tongue useless as a fair expression of regional identity.

Young, old or salt-and-pepper-haired in between, people do share a staunch loyalty to the hamlet, village, town or city in which where they live. 'People in Marseille have a real identity that is attached to the place, they love this town,' says Claire, whose smile betrays her own fondness for the port city and its stereotyped rough-and-tumble inhabitants, famed throughout France for their blatant exaggerations and imaginative fancies such as the tale about the sardine that blocked Marseille port.

Markedly more Latin in outlook and temperament, the Niçois exhibit a common zest for the good life with their Italian neighbours; while St-Tropez's colourful community is a trendy mix of bronzed-year-round glamour queens, reborn hippies and old-time art-lovers. Law-abiding Monégasques (p394) dress up to the nines, don't break the law or gossip, and only cross the road on a zebra crossing.

For many, particularly in rural pastures where family trees go back several generations and occupations remain firmly implanted in the soil, identity is deeply rooted in tradition. Truffle hunter Jean François Tourrette explains: 'Truffles are part of my family's traditions. My father, my grandfather and many of my relatives (at least four generations, maybe more) did the same thing before me. But they are also part of the regional patrimony, which makes me proud', adding 'I am and feel Provençal, but I am also French and European'. Monsieur Tourrette is clearly at ease with life.

> 'Unless you're born and bred in Provence, you have little hope of adjusting to the mistral's menacing climes'

Three-quarters of the population is wedged into the region's three key urban hubs: Marseille, Toulon and Avignon.

I SPEAK PROVENÇAL

Should you wish to dip into Provençal culture and bone up on the rich lyrics and poetry of Prouvènço (Provençal), the region's age-old dialect of *langue d'Oc* (Occitan; p431), the Frédéric Mistral house-museum in Maillane (p194) runs writing workshops in Provençal.

In Nice, birthplace of subdialect Niçois, **La Remembrança Nissarda** (☎ 04 93 88 32 03; felixmacri@ yahoo.fr; 1 rue des Combattants) runs weekly lessons in the Niçois language and *chants niçois* (traditional Niçois songs and chants), and cultural workshops on Niçois history, carnival traditions and *cuisine nissarde* (local cooking).

Online, pick up useful Provençal phrases and old proverbs such as *'fai pas bon travaia quand la cigalo canto'* (it is not good to work when the cicada chants) at the portal of Provençal culture, **Lou Pourtau de la Culturo Prouvençalo** (http://prouvenco.presso.free.fr in French). For an online Provençal–French dictionary see www.lexilogos.com/provencal_langue_dictionnaires.htm.

RIVIERA HIGH LIFE

From the giddy days of the *belle époque* to the start of the summer season during the avant-garde 1920s, the Côte d'Azur has always glittered as Europe's most glamorous holiday spot: the Beckhams own a 15-bedroom mansion in Bargemon ('is it haunted?' splashed the *Daily Mail* in 2006, claiming Posh and Becks hadn't stayed in it once since making the €2.2-million purchase in 2003); their old pal Elton John and film-producer partner David Furnish live next door with 15 dogs (who have a daily swim in the pool) and a constant turnover of showbiz friends at Castel Mont-Alban, a lemon-coloured 600-sq-m villa on Mont Boron near Nice; American film star John Malkovich lives in the Luberon; a €5.3 million wine-producing chateau near St-Raphael is F1 superstar Michael Schumacher's cup of tea; and Tina Turner, Leonardo DiCaprio, Claudia Schiffer and Bono of U2 are long-term seasonal residents.

Hidden behind high stone walls it might be, but voyeurs can peep in on Riviera high-life during a sunlit stroll between dream mansions on Cap Martin and Cap Ferrat, over an apéritif on Pampelonne beach or at St-Tropez's yacht-filled old port where yachtsmen pay €90,000 a week to moor; or in Monaco where heli-pads on pleasure boats are the norm. In Cannes, meanwhile, millionaires congregate once a year at the celebrity city's Millionaire Fair (www.milionairefair .com), an overtly brash celebration of wealth where the world's most luxurious limousines, jewels, homes, private jets, wine, fashions and living concepts are showcased. Target audience: 'consumers in the high-end luxury segment, the rich and famous, CEOs, entrepreneurs and internet-workers, bon vivants, the media, VIPs, business and cultural elite,' quotes its website, footnoting that the 'spiritually rich' can also join in (sort of) the fun. Dress code: *tenue de ville* (jacket and tie) – a key phrase to know should you intend moving in luxury-lifestyle circles.

Places to do precisely that include several star-loved legends in hedonist Monaco (p387); Grand Hôtel du Cap Ferrat and Michael Powell's La Voile d'Or in St-Jean-Cap Ferrat (p283); the Martinez, Majestic, Carlton and Hilton hotels (p305) in Cannes; Cap d'Antibes' twinset of Riviera legends (p317); La Colombe d'Or (p321) in St-Paul de Vence; St-Tropez's top five beach legends (p346), Hôtel Byblos (p348) and Spoon Byblos (p349). Celebrity-studded bars and clubs to guzzle outrageous amounts of champagne include those on Pampelonne beach and pretty much any club in St-Tropez (p350) or Cannes' 'magic square' (p308).

Affluent outsiders buying up the region are prompting some traditional village communities to question their own (shifting) identities: 'Les Nouveaux clash with the locals' screeched the headline of a Luberon-village portrait, published in the *International Herald Tribune* in 2006. Property prices spiralling out the reach of local salaries, farmers being deprived of livelihoods and English heard more than French were symptoms of the dramatic influx of foreigners in recent years, the piece rallied. It painted Bonnieux's Socialist mayor as 'a champion of the native-born…[who] chides the village's new co-citizens'. Indeed, within the region, 20% of privately owned homes are *résidences secondaires* (second homes).

Propped against age-old yellow stone, one hand fondling the water of Châteauneuf du Pape's village fountain, a born-and-bred Provence man ponders this 'them and us' notion: 'I don't see myself or the people living here today as French or Provençal, but as being 'from the south'. People in Provence today have vastly different origins, Italian, African and so on, but we are all from the south. More than a culture, it is a certain way of life here that defines us.'

> 'I've lived in Cannes for years but still have the head of a Marseillais. People from Marseille are more natural than the Cannois. Marseillais are simpler, easier to understand. In Cannes there's a lot of money but little culture; in Marseille it is one's *metier* (trade) that is still important.'
>
> MARSEILLE-BORN DJ MAX FROM CANNES

LIFESTYLE PARADE

Lifestyles are as dazzlingly different as those out-of-vogue tablecloth designs.

Enter Jeanine Squarzoni, market-stall holder at Marseille's garlic market: 'I've been here 20 years; my mother, Thérèse, has been here for 40 years. I

10 FACES TO SPOT

Intrinsic to its rich, multifaceted identity, the region wouldn't be the same without these larger-than-life personalities, dead easy to see in one form or another.

- Jimmy McKissic (pianist, Hôtel Martinez, Cannes) has played in the piano bar (p307) of this celebrity-studded 1920s Art Deco hotel since 1985; he's in his 60s; and he's hot. The black American was born in Little Rock, Arkansas, and still plays at New York's Carnegie Hall when he's not wooing punters in Cannes with his incredible finger-work, voice and radiant, indiscriminate smile. Joe Bloggs or Joe Superstar, he oozes warmth: 'For Jimmy the only thing that counts is giving pleasure and sharing his good humour with the audience,' says the press officer at the hotel.

- Zinedine Zidane (retired footballer, Marseille) is football's most expensive player, Christian Dior's first male model, a Lego minifigure, FIFA's 2006 player of the year and Golden Ball winner and France captain in the last two World Cups: everyone knows this Marseille footballer (b 1972), the youngest of five children, born in La Castellane to Algerian parents. Career-defining moment: head-butting Italian opponent Matarazzi 10 minutes before the close of his career in the 2006 World Cup final against Italy (play the Zidane Head Butt Game online). Spot him in gigantic form (p103) in his home town.

- Dany Lartigue (artist, St-Tropez): 'always surrounded by ladies', octogenarian Dany (b 1921), son of the famous Riviera photographer Jacques Lartigue (1894–1986), until recently cruised around St-Tropez on his bicycle. He can still be spotted, basket in hand, shopping at the Place des Lices market. Painter in his own right, Lartigue spent his heyday (1948–70) in Montmartre but lives where his mother did in St-Tropez (p345) today.

- Jeanine Vernet (fishmonger, Marseille): Marseille wouldn't be Marseille without its early-morning fish market. 'Twenty years I've worked here. My husband and sons fish every day and I come here every morning year-round to sell the fish they catch', explains the fisherman's wife, merrily dressed in blue-and-white striped top and gumboots as eels writhe and fish flap in buckets around her. She brings the fish by van from Soumaty, 10.5km north of the Vieux Port in Marseille's 16e, where the family fishing boat is moored.

- Jenifer Bartoli (*Star Academy* winner, Nice): young wannabe' stars have come and gone on France's pioneering reality-TV show *Star Academy*, but fame seems to have stuck to Jenifer,

---

'Wild gesticulations, passionate cheek kissing and fervent handshaking are a part of daily life'

Cut to the heart of business at www.business riviera.com

used to help her on the stall, but now I run it.' And will her children continue the family tradition? 'No, they work in an office. It's hard for young people to make a living from farming these days; traditions are no longer being passed on. When my mother started on the market there were 42 stalls. A decade ago there were 14; now there are five', said Jeanine, who reckons the market will have folded within five years.

Next up, what a character! Frédéric Bon, full-time *guardian* (Camargue cowboy) on the family *manade* (bull farm), traditionally assisted at busy times of the year by 'freelance' or 'amateur' *guardians* who work in exchange for a place to stable their horses, meals etc. But with many a young local lad firmly implanted behind a desk Monday to Friday in Arles these days, casual cowboys are becoming hard to find. Moreover, people are less willing to trade their services and be flexible since the work week was slashed from 39 to 35 hours in 2000, according to the Bon family, who see the shift in work hours as 'spirit changing'. Frédéric's father Jacques was born on the farm in 1926, farmed sheep until 1979 when changes in the-then EEC rendered it less profitable, and still rides every day.

Avoiding the midday heat means a 5.30am start for viticulturer Michel Vivet who grabs a coffee for breakfast and works in the vineyards until noon when the sun drives him in for *une bonne sieste* – a good two-hour snooze.

the dark-haired, good-looking singer from Nice who won the 1st series of *Star Academy* (it's now in its 6th) in 2001 and has released three albums since.

■ Thérèsa (*socca* queen, Cours Saleya market, Nice): fully made-up with blood red lips, super-long lashes and dripping gold jewellery, 56-year-old Theresa steals the show on cours Saleya. 'The market is my life – I love it, the people, the restaurants, We all know each other', laughs the hard-working daughter of a Spanish mother and Israeli father who's cooked up *socca* (chickpea and olive-oil cake) at the market for 20 years. Six days out of seven start at 6am and end around 2pm with a *pastis* on one of cours Saleya's many café terraces.

■ Hans Silvester (globe-trotting photographer, Lioux, 15km north of Apt): you might not snag sight of him, but you'll certainly run into the subjects his world-famous lens zooms in on. Camargue horses, cats, dogs and lavender fields in every season are among the quintessential elements of local life the German-born photographer, at home in the Luberon since 1962, has immortalised in his stunning coffee-table books. You don't need to understand French to appreciate his 250 nostalgic B&W photos of Provence between 1957 and 1964, published in *C'était Hier* (It was Yesterday; 2004).

■ Noëlle Perna (comic actress, Nice): better known as 'Mado la Niçoise', a comic music-hall dame of cult standing with indiscreet blue eye-shadow, bright pink lipstick and heavy Niçois accent, this actress is being tipped across France as the next best thing since sliced bread. It started in 1999 when Perna opened the one-man Théâtre des Oiseaux in Vieux Nice, drawing on characters from her parent's adjoining bar as the inspiration for her comic sketches. Buy the DVD.

■ Olivier Baussan (entrepreneur, Mane): the man behind two of Provence's best-known brands remains true to his Haute-Provence roots. He grew up on a farm in Ganagobie and the headquarters of L'Occitane en Provence (www.loccitane.com), his hugely successful luxury bath, body and skincare product company with 470-odd shops worldwide is in Mane. Founded by the then 23-year-old in 1976, L'Occitane uses essential oils from Provence as the natural basis for its creams, shampoos and so on. Not content to sit on his laurels; Baussan created Oliviers & Co (www.oliviersandco.com) in 1993, wooing eager punters with olive oil from Provence and elsewhere. Watch out for whatever the region's most incredible entrepreneur does next.

'Afternoons are spent in the *cave* (cellar) where it's cooler', explains Michel who describes local lifestyle as a mix of 'outside living and siestas' (as we sit around a tree-shaded table behind the sage green shuttered farmhouse, cicadas making an absolute din in the July heat). Michel runs Domaine Valette in Les Arcs with his father, mother and wife. Bar September's grape harvest (p54), the Vevets do everything themselves on the small 15-hectare holding.

Enter Haute-Provence organic sheep farmers, Luisella and Pierre Bellot. May to November they tend 130 to 180 sheep, chickens and vegetable garden on their 11-hectare farm and are ski instructors in winter. 'We dream of just having the farm, but we don't make enough money from it. Many people in the mountains have to do this to make a living', says father-of-three Pierre, who grew up on his parent's farm down the road, bought his own farm when he was 18 and laments the decline of mountain farms like his: 'It's why villagers complain about the mess and the smell when they see sheep walking on the village roads. They've forgotten the farming traditions of the region.' Their lifestyle in a nutshell: 'We live with the rhythm of the animals – when days are shorter, we go inside earlier.' And in summer when the sheep are grazing on higher pastures (2000m) with a shepherd? 'We cut dry grass and grow corn.'

Peep into homes in Provence and at lifestyles led inside them with Lisa Lovett-Smith's lavish image-driven *Provence Interiors* and Johanna Thornycroft's *The Provençal House*.

Hone into Anglophone life on the Riviera with AngloINFO Riviera at http://riviera.angloinfo .com.

TALK OF THE TOWN

Tune into the underbelly of what people are really thinking NOW, with these locally generated, voice-of-the-moment blogs:

Blogs Nice Matin (http://blogs.nice-matin.com in French) French-language blogosphere of daily newspaper *Nice Matin*, lots of local politics and current affairs.

Chez mistral (http://chezmistral.vrbx.com) 'Wine, food and other adventures' by a New Yorker with Italian-Irish roots married to an Avignon lad, living in Avignon; particularly strong restaurant reviews.

French Word-a-Day (http://french-word-a-day.typepad.com) Well-established blog, from which three books have been published (p20); thrice-weekly entries are inspired by a French word and tell a tale of life in the region as well as teaching fairly advanced colloquial French.

Life on Marseille (www.lifeonmarseille.canalblog.com in French) French-language photoblog from Marseille.

Marseille Forum (www.marseilleforum.com in French) Chat to Marseillais online and find out what's happening in the region's most buzzing city.

Provence Blog (www.residencelesmarronniers.com) News-driven blog compiled in La Croix Valmer; pulls together articles on the region from the international press.

Provence Blog by Provence Beyond (www.provenceblog.typepad.com) Travel stories.

Provence from Fayence outwards (www.go-provence.com) Brilliant, on-the-button, Fayence-generated blog loaded with news, chat, hot links and celebrity scoops.

Tongue in Cheek (http://willows95988.typepad.com) The latest word on the ground from the markets, written by a *marché aux puces*–addicted, antique-loving American, resident in Marseille since the 1980s.

Shift to the wealthy Luberon where many a foreigner lives the Provençal dream. Enter Englishwoman Sally Faverot de Kerbrech who traded in the London smog for a Luberon vineyard in 2000: 'There is everything you could want here … quality of life, music, opera, theatre and art all around,' explained Sally, who tends the vines at Domaine Faverot (p225) with husband François, a Frenchman. And with their 'more than abundant' social life, there's a 50% French-/English-speaking split: 'We love going to local markets and to restaurants. There are all sorts of other activities (apart from meeting all sorts of friends and having dinner and musical evenings in all our homes) like walking, cycling, horse riding, tennis, golf. We do a bit of all that. The next thing I'd like to do is to take up painting', says an exuberant Sally, clearly high on life.

Then, of course, there's the razzmatazz of Riviera high life (p35).

'Football isn't just a religion in Marseille, it crosses religions'

SPORT

Be it bullfighting – revered as a sport and a celebration of Provençal tradition by those who do it (p148) – or the hottest date on the Formula One calendar (p396) that tears around regular town streets rather than a racetrack – sport here is dramatic and entertaining.

Football

'Merci les bleues!' was the slogan emblazoned on Paris' Arc de Triomphe when the national team captained by Marseille's beloved Zizou came home after the dramatic final of the 2006 World Cup: high drama indeed, thanks to Zinedane Zidane's head-butt (p36) 10 minutes before the end of the match – and a brilliant career that saw the Marseille-born midfielder of North African origin captain France to victory in the 1998 World Cup and transfer from Juventus (Italy) to Real Madrid (Spain) for a record-breaking €75.1 million.

The splendid documentary *Zidane: A 21st Century Portrait* (2006) is not only for football fans; watch it on DVD.

Long the stronghold – not to mention heart and soul – of French football, Marseille at club level was national champion for four consecutive years between 1989 and 1992, and in 1991 Olympique de Marseilles (OM) became the first French team to win the European Champions League. It reached the UEFA Cup final in 2004 but hasn't qualified since. Club colours are white at home, turquoise away. To witness the side in action, see p103. Arsenal manager Arsène Wenger and star striker Thierry Henry both began their careers with the region's other strong club, AS Monaco (ASM).

Tied Feet

Despite its quintessential image of a bunch of old men throwing balls on a dusty patch of gravel beneath trees, Provence's national pastime is a serious sport with its own world championships and a museum to prove it.

Pétanque (Provençal *boules*) was invented in La Ciotat, near Marseille, in 1910 when arthritis-crippled Jules Le Noir could no longer take the running strides prior to aiming demanded by the *longue boule* game. The local champion thus stood with his feet firmly on the ground – a style that became known as *pieds tanqués* (Provençal for 'tied feet', from which '*pétanque*' emerged).

Big dates on the *pétanque* calendar include France's largest tournament, La Marseillaise, held each year in Parc Borély in Marseille in early July; and the annual celebrity tournament organised in Avignon on the banks of the River Rhône.

Keep abreast with cultural affairs in the region with www.culture.gouv .fr/paca (in French).

Nautical Jousting

Joutes nautiques is typical only to southern France. Spurred on by bands and a captive audience, participants (usually male and traditionally dressed in white) knock each other into the water from rival boats with 2.60m-long lances. The jouster stands balanced at the tip of a *tintaine*, a wooden gangplank protruding from the wooden boat where the rest of his team members spur him on.

The sport is particularly strong in St-Raphaël, where the annual jousting championships are invariably held. In the Vaucluse, river jousters set L'Isle-sur-la-Sorgue ablaze with colour on 14 and 26 July.

THE RULES OF BOULES

Should you wish to play the game:

Two to six people, split into two teams, can play. Each player has three solid metal *boules* (balls), weighing 650g to 800g and stamped with the hallmark of a licensed *boule* maker. Initials, a name or a family coat of arms can be crafted on to made-to-measure *boules*. The earliest *boules*, scrapped in 1930, comprised a wooden ball studded with hundreds of hammered-in steel nails.

Each team takes it in turn to aim a *boule* at a tiny wooden ball called a *cochonnet* (jack), the idea being to land the *boule* as close as possible to it. The team with the closest *boule* wins the round; points are allocated by totting up how many *boules* the winner's team has closest to the marker (one point for each *boule*). The first to notch up 13 wins the match.

The team throwing the *cochonnet* (initially decided by a coin toss) has to throw it from a small circle, 30cm to 50cm in diameter, scratched in the gravel. It must be hurled 6m to 10m away. Each player aiming a *boule* must likewise stand in this circle, with both feet planted firmly on the ground. At the end of a round, a new circle is drawn around the *cochonnet*, determining the spot where the next round will start.

Underarm throwing is compulsory. Beyond that, players can dribble the *boule* along the ground (known as *pointer*, literally 'to point') or hurl it high in the air in the hope of it landing smack-bang on top of an opponent's *boule*, sending it flying out of position. This flamboyant tactic, called *tirer* (literally 'to shoot'), can turn an entire game around in seconds.

Throughout matches *boules* are polished with a soft white cloth. Players unable to stoop to pick up their *boules* can lift them up with a magnet attached to a piece of string.

ZOOM IN: AIX-BORN TUNISIAN GRAFFITI ARTIST

Medhi's parents moved from Tunis to Provence in their early 20s, ushering a kind and sincere Medhi into the world in Aix-en-Provence. Since 1999 he has lived in Marseille where he musters a living as a web designer in between tags. Catherine Le Nevez caught up with the charismatic, short, dark-haired 20-something, dressed in the latest street fashion, in Marseille.

In Marseille do you have a sense of Tunisian community?
I have Tunisian friends, but not exclusively. I am a graffiti artist and my 'community' comprises people who do the same thing, share the same passion. The graffiti-art community is a big mix – I have friends from Martinique, Korea, Laos, China and many other places.

Is your Tunisian heritage an integral part of daily life?
Now it's a mix of French culture and Tunisian culture. I don't want to lose my Tunisian roots. My double culture creates my identity; it's very important for me.

And graffiti?
When I was younger I did graffiti art every day; now I have other commitments in life it's about one time per week. There are places where you can tag legally in Marseille. I choose places where a lot of people can see the tags. The walls along the train tracks are best because a lot of people can see my art from the train.

Do you encounter racism?
Every day – it's normal. Well, maybe not *every* day, but frequently. It's OK, because Marseille is cosmopolitan. It happens more often in Aix. Aix is a town with lots of money. Rich people are in the majority, but not only rich people live there (which creates tension).

What sort of racism do you encounter?
Things like a grandmother sees you and clutches her handbag tighter or changes it to the other arm, away from you. Or if I go in a shop, the guy in the shop will be watching me all the time. People are more afraid since terrorism. But I don't care (about encountering racism), I've got friends (who aren't racist), I don't feel marginalised. Look at the French side in the 2006 World Cup – it was multicoloured and went far because of that, more than if there had been only one (religious/ethnic) community of French people playing.

How important is religion to you?
Religious observations like Ramadan and Aïd El Kebir are very important to my parents; it's a way for the family to be together, something to share with family. I don't have children yet, but I hope to have them, when I can afford them – it's expensive! I want them to know their Tunisian roots, and I will take them to Tunisia. But afterwards, whether they want to be Muslim, or any other religion like Christian, it's no problem; they will be free to choose. My girlfriend is French; she's not religious at all.

MULTICULTURALISM

In Didier van Cauwe- leart's *One Way*, a French boy orphaned in a crash in multicultural Marseille is pulled from the burn- ing car by Roma people and given false ID papers making him Moroccan.

For creative souls in particular, the region's substantial multicultural mix is energising and gives the region its razor-sharp edge: 'Marseille's richness attracts artists like musician David Walters who is from a French/West Indies/English-speaking Caribbean background, and has come to live here to express every aspect of himself', explains Radio Grenouille musical director Stephane Galland, himself the Marseille-born son of a French father and mother from Guadeloupe. 'The rhythm of life is more human here than other parts of France (because of this multicultural mix)', he continues, adding with a laugh: 'My mother has a very, very strong Marseille accent, almost from the day she arrived'.

Immigrants form around 9.5% (430,000) of the regional population, a constant since 1975 when France implemented its first immigration law. The largest foreign communities are European (31.4%), Algerian (19%), Moroccan (19%), Tunisian (13.8%) and Turkish (1.7%). The vast majority of this ethnic community do have French citizenship, which is subject to various administrative requirements rather than being conferred at birth.

The Algerian community originates from the 1950s and 1960s, when over one million French settlers returned to metropolitan France from Algeria, other parts of Africa and Indochina. At the same time millions of non-French immigrants from these places were welcomed as much-needed manpower. A 1974 law banning all new foreign workers ended large-scale immigration.

Racial tensions are fuelled by the National Front whose leader makes no bones about his party's antiforeigner stance. The French republican code, meanwhile, does little to accommodate a multicultural society. While the government's banning of the Islamic headscarf, Jewish skullcap, Sikh turban, crucifix and other religious symbols in French schools in 2004 was meant to place all schoolchildren on an equal footing, Muslims slammed it as intolerant and yet more proof that the French state is not prepared to properly integrate them into French society.

A large chunk of Marseille's sizable Muslim and Jewish populations lives in depressed city suburbs, unemployment among immigrants being 12% higher than the regional average.

RELIGION

Countrywide, 80% of people identify themselves as Catholic, although few attend Mass. Catholicism is the official state religion in neighbouring Monaco, which marks a number of religious feasts with public holidays. Protestants account for less than 2% of today's population.

Many of France's four to five million nominally Muslim residents live in the south of France, comprising the second-largest religious group. Marseille's notable 200,000-strong Muslim community is served by 62 mosques and places of worship – although, somewhat controversially, the port city still lacks a grand mosque it can call its own. In mid-2006 the city council, after years of bickering among local Muslims who couldn't agree on a site, bit the bullet and allocated an 8000-sq-metre plot of land to its Muslims for the project. But building work won't start until the local Muslim community has found the €10 million needed to build the 2500 sq m edifice.

France's Jewish community – Europe's largest – numbers 650,000, some 80,000 of whom live in Marseille. There are several synagogues in the latter, as well as in Avignon, Cavaillon and Carpentras.

Claire Messud's second novel, *The Last Life*, is the dramatic portrayal of one family who fled Algeria in the 1960s and settled in the south of France.

'The essence of Nice for me is its mix of cultures…the city is like a very well-done *ratatouille*, full of flavours and savours.'

MARCO FOLICALDI, LA ZUCCA MAGICA, NICE

Food & Drink

Thinking, dreaming and living food is the norm in Provence, where most peoples' days are geared around satisfying their passionate appetite for dining well. And not without good cause: Provençal cuisine is reputed the world over. Lazing over lunch with friends, leaving one vowing never to eat that much again (until tomorrow), is an integral part of the Provençal experience.

Some culinary traditions are upheld everywhere: oodles of olive oil, garlic and tomatoes invariably find their way into many a dish; anything *à la Provençal* involves garlic-seasoned tomatoes. Yet there are exciting regional differences, rooted in geography and history, which see fishermen return with the catch of the day in seafaring Marseille; herds of bulls grazing and paddy fields in the Camargue; lambs in the Alpilles; black truffles in the Vaucluse; cheese made from cows milk in alpine pastures and an irresistible Italianate accent to Niçois cooking (p273).

Ultimately, the secret of Provençal cuisine lies not in elaborate preparation techniques or state-of-the-art presentation but in the use of fresh ingredients produced locally. There are top-dog chefs and pioneering food designers (p44), yes; but when in Provence it is the humble rhythm and natural cycle of the land and the seasons that really drive what you eat, and when.

NUTS & BOLTS

What is a *ferme auberge*? Are there menus for kids? For the practical nuts and bolts of dining and drinking in Provence, see p405. For table etiquette see p49.

JANUARY: PIG OUT ON TRUFFLES

Break and beat three eggs, season with salt, pepper and 15g of grated truffle. Leave to rest for 30 minutes, then cook slowly in a *bain-mairie* with

---

DINING DIARY

So what precisely is the dining order of the day for people in Provence? 'My father would start work at 5.30am, stopping around 9am or 10am for a plate of ham, *saucisson* (sausage), radishes from the garden … but breakfast for me is a coffee,' says third-generation wine producer Michel Vivet, at home amid 15 hectares of vines in Les Arcs. 'At lunchtime it is too hot; our evening meal is the most important,' he says, looking at his wife who reels off their previous evening's menu: courgette omelette and *saucisson*, bought from neighbouring farms.

While *petit déjeuner* (breakfast) for urban folk generally entails a short, sharp, black *café* (coffee) or milky *café au lait* and a croissant (no jam or butter) grabbed at a café on the way to work, *petit déj* in agricultural circles is a more imaginative affair, albeit one that is never cooked, and generally fresh from the farm: 'I get up at 3.45am to take my melons to the wholesale markets, have a coffee and when I get back at 8am, I have breakfast with my wife,' says Bernard Meyssard (p51) who kick-starts his dining day several hours after getting up with a feast of *jambon cru* (uncooked ham) and melon.

While *déjeuner* (lunch) is the traditional main meal of the day (and an inevitable highlight for those visiting Provence), people who work actually dine quite lightly at midday and save the ritual feast of apéritif followed by a hot meal with wine for the evening when it is cooler and the day's work is done. 'For lunch I have melon, ham and a tomato salad,' says Bernard, adding, 'A healthy appetite, I always have one,' eyes dancing, when asked which meal – lunch or *dîner* (dinner) – was the more important to him.

The same pattern is echoed in urban climes where restaurants get packed out from noon with regulars lunching on a light(er) *plat du jour* (dish of the day), *formule menu* (fixed main course plus starter or dessert) or lunch *menu* (choice of two-course meal) – saving the heavier, three- or four-course *menu* for the evening when several hours can be devoted to appreciating an *entrée* (starter), *plat* (main course), *fromage* (cheese) and dessert. Many top-end restaurants serve an *amuse-bouche* (complimentary morsel of something very delicious) between the starter and main course; some also serve a sweet equivalent before dessert, plus petit fours with coffee.

THE TRUFFLE MASS

The truffle mass pays homage to St-Antoine, the patron saint of truffle growers, and venerates the 'black diamond': the truffle. All of the festivities, in one way or another, honour truffles. After mass, the truffles – offered primarily by truffle growers – are collected in the same baskets used during truffle hunts and weighed on the square in front of the church by members of the Confrérie du Diamant Noir et de la Gastronomie (Black Diamond & Gastronomy Brotherhood; www.conf-truffe.com in French). The brotherhood – dressed in long black capes, black hats and yellow-ribboned medals – then proceeds to the place de la Mairie (town hall square) where the *Grand Chambellan* (Great Chamberlain) auctions the truffles – a particularly powerful moment. The money raised is used by the parish to restore religious monuments in the village. After the truffle auction, an apéritif is offered to everyone, followed at 1pm by the *repas des confrères* – a great meal of excellent quality/price ratio (€50 per person) composed entirely of truffles.

Visitors are charmed by the folklore ... these days the festivities are geared more to the tourists than locals; people of the village prefer not to take part to let others experience it.

Mylène Savoye, Point Tourisme, Richerenches

a drizzle of olive oil or a knob of butter. Stir regularly, adding a spoon of crème fraîche if necessary. Sprinkle with 15g of grated truffle, stir and serve immediately.

Christian Etienne's (p44) recipe for *brouillade de truffes* – a Provençal classic included in many a lavish three- and four-course *menu aux truffes* (truffle menu) served by several restaurants in season – is nothing more than scrambled eggs with truffle shavings. Simplicity laces many truffle dishes, allowing the palate to revel in the flavour (it's subtle) of Provence's most luxurious and elusive culinary product. A fungus that takes root underground at the foot of a tree, usually in symbiosis with the roots of an elm or oak tree, the black truffle *(tuber melanosporum)* is snouted out in modest amounts in the Vaucluse, especially around Carpentras, Vaison-la-Romaine and in the Enclave des Papes, from November to March. January is the height of the season, which climaxes midmonth with Richerenches' sacred Messe des Truffes (above). Dubbed *diamants noir* (black diamonds) and at €500 to €1000 per kg, truffles are as precious as gold dust.

Traditionally snouted out by pigs, these days it's dogs that hunt truffles. 'Dog training is a long activity and requires an enormous amount of patience,' explains fourth-generation *trufficulteur* (truffle farmer) Jean-François Tourrette from Vénasque who hunts black truffles with Youcan, his 10-year-old mongrel, in winter and the cheaper, lesser-known and not nearly-as-precious white truffle – often called *truffe d'été* (summer truffle; *tuber aestivum*) – between May and August. 'It has to be a game for the dog – not work. You have to make it understand that it gets a reward when it finds a truffle,' says Monsieur Tourrette who rewards Youcan with a lump of gruyère cheese or – should the black truffles be abundant that day – a less fatty biscuit. Planting oak trees, picking acorns and guarding his oak plantation against 'spring's water excess, summer dryness, autumn's water excess, winter frost and wild boars' are other daily *trufficulteur* tasks.

Truffles form an integral part of the traditional New Year's Day feast in Provence. Families pig out on the biggest *coq* (chicken, rooster; symbolising the coming year) they can find, either stuffed with sausage meat and truffles or chestnuts or – in wealthier circles – served alongside 12 partridges (one for each month of the year), truffles (symbolising the nights) and eggs (the day).

For more on truffle culture see p178, www.la-truffe.com (in French) and www.truffle-and-truffe.com. The ultimate truffle dining experience? Chez Bruno (p360).

The Provence of Alain Ducasse by Alain Ducasse is not just a book: it is an essential listing of 'insider' markets, food shops and addresses frequented by one of Provence's biggest chefs.

From the 5th century AD until the French revolution, the kings of France were baptised with olive oil from St-Rémy de Provence.

FEBRUARY: A FISHY AFFAIR

Slice off the bottom of the spiny ball, deep purple in colour and serve like oysters by the dozen or half. Scrape off the foul-looking guts and brown grit to uncover the pale-orange ambrosia – the roe of the sea urchin, exquisitely arranged by nature in six delicate sweet–salty strips. This is what you eat.

Savouring *oursin* (sea urchin) – a delicacy that falls in the same love-it-or-hate sphere as oysters and foie gras – is reason enough to be in Carry-le-Rouet in February when the quaint fishing port west of Marseille celebrates its *oursin* festival (p119). *Oursins* can be fished September to April and are best served with a white Cassis, chilled.

'It's only a true authentic *bouillabaisse* if it's made in Marseille by a Marseillais.'

CHRISTIAN BUFFA, CHEF, MIRAMAR, MARSEILLE

Other catches worth a bite include clamlike *violets* (sea squirts), another fishy affair whose iodine-infused yellow flesh tastes like the sea; *supions frits* (squid pan-fried with fresh garlic and parsley (sample it at Pizzaria Etienne in Marseille; p109). There are shoals of Mediterranean fish – *merlan* (whiting), *St-Pierre* (John Dory), *galinette* (tub gurnard), *maquereau* (mackerel), *chapon de mer* (chapon), *congre* (conger eel) and *rascasse* (scorpion fish) – sold straight from the sea at the region's premier fish market.

Assessing whether a fish is fresh hardly takes a genius, says fishmonger Jeanine Vernet with a smile, pointing to the slithering eels and fish flapping noisily in buckets on her market stall at Marseille's Vieux Port. 'You can also tell by the colour; it should be clear,' she continues, citing her favourite way of preparing the day's catch as 'sprinkled with fresh herbs, wrapped in aluminium and baked in the oven'.

Marseillais chef Christian Buffa buys the fish he needs for his highly regarded fish restaurant, Miramar (p108), each morning at the Vieux Port market and a wholesale fish market 10km out of town. For him, essential purchases are scorpion fish, white scorpion fish, *vive* (weever), conger eel, chapon and tub gurnard – the six fish types he would not consider making his famous *bouillabaisse* without. King of regional dishes, *bouillabaisse* is a pungent yellow fish stew, brewed by Marseillais for centuries and requiring a minimum of four types of fresh fish cooked in a rockfish stock with onions, tomatoes, garlic, saffron (hence its colour), parsley, bay leaves, thyme and other herbs. Its name is derived from the French *bouillir* (to boil) and *baisser* (to lower, as in a flame), reflecting the cooking method required: bring it to the boil, let it bubble ferociously for 15 minutes, then serve it: the *bouillon* (broth) first as a soup, followed by the fish flesh in the company of a local wine. Try it with a white Cassis or dry Bandol rosé.

No two cooks make an identical *bouillabaisse* and the debates about which fish constitute a true *bouillabaisse* are endless. '*St-Pierre* or *lotte* (John Dory or monkfish) are optional,' says Christian Buffa, who also throws in a *cigale de mer* (sand lobster), *langouste* (crayfish) or *langoustine* (small saltwater lobster) sometimes to transform a bog-standard *bouillabaisse* into *bouillabaisse royale*. In Toulon – shock horror – Toulonnais throw potatoes into the pot (taste it at

CHEFS & LEGENDS

The two tend to go hand in hand: the region's dynamic dining scene is charted by a mix of big-name chefs heading historic eating venues and young, rising stars busy making a name for themselves with more cutting-edge dining concepts.

Names well worth the €50-plus that their *menus* command include Alain Ducasse (p393 and p359), Christian Etienne (p166), Bruno Clément (p359 and p360), Alain Lorca (p325), Jacques Chibois (p328), Franck Cerutti (p392), Édouard Loubet (p221), Olivier Teissedre (p173), Bruno Sohn (p274), Christian Buffa (p108) and last but far from least, with a huge round of applause for innovation, Jouni (p274).

DIY BOUILLABAISSE

Learn how to do it yourself – the authentic way. Marseille tourist office takes bookings for half-day *bouillabaisse* workshops (€110) comprising a chef-accompanied trip to the fish market, a cooking lesson, an apéritif around the kitchen table, lunch (no guessing what) and a copy of the real McCoy Marseille recipe to share with your friends.

L'Oursinado atop a cliff on Cap de Carqueiranne; p377); while *bourride* is a cheaper version of *bouillabaisse* – it contains no saffron, features cheaper white-fleshed fish, and is served with white *aïoli* instead of pink *rouille* (p46).

Seafood dining standouts: Marseille's *bouillabaisse* restaurants (p108); Le Sloop, St-Jean-Cap Ferrat (p282); Bacon, Cap d'Antibes (p317); La Table du Mareyeur, Port Grimaud (p355); Chez Jo (p365) in Cavalière.

MARCH: OLIVE-OIL SHOP

Drink water first. Pour a drop of oil onto a plastic teaspoon, raise it to your lips and taste it. It can have a varying degree of sweetness or acidity; be peppery or fruity and 'green' or it can be clear or murky (which means the oil has not been filtered). Once opened, consume within six months, don't cook with it and keep out of direct sunlight.

The secret behind many a Provençal dish, olive oil is a key ingredient in every Provençal sauce; essential for *socca*, the Niçois chickpea-flour pancake (p273); and best tasted in March with asparagus, the month's seasonal speciality – steam the slender green tips, sprinkle with *fleur de sel* (salt crystals) and drizzle with olive oil.

March is, in fact, the last chance to shop for *huile d'olive* at the *moulin* (mill) – by far the most interesting place to buy it – before the mill runs out. Most open soon after the winter harvest (p50) until March or April. Sold in glass bottles or plastic containers, olive oil costs around €20 per litre and degustation is an integral part of buying.

Some mills are listed in the regional chapters: in the northern Vaucluse around Nyons (p176), the Vallée des Baux and the Alpilles (p189), *oléiculteurs* (olive growers) adhere to a rigid set of rules to have their bottles stamped with a quality-guaranteed *appellation d'origine contrôlée* (AOC) mark. Generally, 5kg of olives yield 1L of oil. Markets and olive-oil shops sell oil year-round and several restaurants serve olive-oil *menus*.

APRIL: SPRING CHEESE

Take a round of fresh *chèvre*, drizzle it with local olive oil or honey and bite into what goatherds say is the finest goat cheese of the year. Serve with bread.

'Our cheese is best in spring because of the lush new grass; the milk tastes the best,' says farm-born, 25-year-old Emanuelle Marbezy, technical manager of a small *fromagerie* (cheese dairy) in Banon (p249), Haute-Provence, where the milk from 12 mountain goat farms is brought down to the plain and turned into Provence's best-known cheese, Banon.

Instantly recognisable by the autumnal chestnut leaves it comes wrapped in, Banon cheese has been protected by its own AOC since 2003, the strict rules of which require goats to graze for a minimum of 210 days on the prairies; their milk to stay unpasteurised; and the cheese produced from it to ripen for at least 15 days after being pressed into delicate 7cm-to-8cm-diameter rounds.

Banon aside, *chèvre* comes in heart shapes, pyramids, logs and squares. It can be eaten young and *frais* (fresh) – a mild creamy taste – or matured into a tangy, stronger tasting *demi-sec* (semidry) or *sec* (dry) cheese.It can be plain, raisin-studded or coated in crushed pepper corns, *herbes de Provence* (p48)

Learn more about *oléi-culture* (olive culture) at www.olivierdeprovence .com and www.olei culture.com (in French).

'Everything uses olive oil. It is the base of Provençal cuisine. For lunch today I prepared a filet mignon with fresh rosemary and olive oil – simple but magnificent.'

NICOLE BÉRENGUIER, OLIVE FARMER, NORTHERN VAR

or black ash. Or you can dip the round in egg and breadcrumbs, fry it and serve it with sweet *miel de Provence* (local honey) or a fruit chutney.

MAY: LAMBS & BULLS

Sprinkle fresh garlic, rosemary and wild thyme over a *gigot d'agneau* (leg of spring lamb), pour over three tablespoons of olive oil and bake in the oven. Or try *pieds et paquets* – sheep trotters wrapped in tripe and cooked with wine and tomatoes.

It is in early May during the traditional transhumance that sheep farmers move their flocks – by truck, in many places, since the 1950s – to higher mountain pastures to fatten up on summer's cool, lush grass under the watchful eye of a shepherd. 'My sheep graze on the mountain for 120 days or so. Their return depends on the weather, but it is invariably in October before the first mountain snow,' says Alpilles sheep farmer René Tramier, adding, 'I belong to the 'Lamb of Sisteron' red label which requires me to kill them when they're 70 to 150 days old.' No wonder lamb from Sisteron alongside the Alpilles de la Crau is so tender.

It is a bullish affair in the Camargue where three- or four-year-old bulls who have failed to prove their worth in the arena are slaughtered for their meat instead to make *guardianne de taureau* (bull-meat stew) and *saucission d'Arles* (air-dried bull sausage). Bull calves reared specifically for their meat are born in early spring, fattened all summer and sent packing to the abattoir in October 'so we don't have to feed them in winter' according to Camargue *guardian* Frédéric Bon (p152).

JUNE: RED & GREEN GARLIC

'Crunch a few coffee beans or parsley stems afterwards if your breath smells too aggressively of garlic, or better still, share the aïoli with your friends': wise words of legendary 'cuisine of the sun' chef, Roger Vergé, one of Provence's biggest names from the late 1960s until his new-millennium retirement.

Garlic – harvested and piled high in woven garlands at the markets in June – gives Provençal cuisine its kick, letting rip in a clutch of fantastic strong-tasting sauces, traditionally served to complement *crudités* (raw vegetables), soups and fish dishes. *Anchoïade* is a strong, anchovy paste laced with garlic and olive oil (try it at La Taca d'Oli in Nice with *bagna cauda* (raw mixed veg dipped into a pot of warm tangy anchovy paste known as *anchoïade*);

'Each cheese is wrapped in five chestnut leaves and hand-tied with a sticker and raffia. Six people just do this job all day; each cheese takes one minute to wrap'.

EMANUELLE MARBEZY, FROMAGERIE DE BANON

TOP 10 EATS

The 'best' in terms of Michelin stars, no. An extremely tasty cross-section of long, lazy, lunch choices to remember, yes.

L'Épuisette (see p108) Bountiful *bouillabaisse* in a magical setting: Marseille's most picturesque fishing harbour.

Le Cilantro (see p144) Dine well in Arles on Jêrome Laurant's contemporary Camargaise cuisine and learn how to cook it (see p52).

Le Bistrot de l'Eygalières (see p193) This unassuming village restaurant in Eygalières has twin-Michelin-starred cuisine.

L'Olivier (see p173) One to watch; headed by Olivier Teissedre (see p44).

La Bastide de Capelongue (see p221) Fine countryside dining, not for the faint-of-wallet but worth every centime.

Atelier du Goût (see p393) Simple but stunning palate creations in Nice by Jouni.

Beau Séjour (see p294) A must-try village inn for the quintessential Provence lunch experience. In Gorbio.

Z Plage (see p307) Lunch with the smart set on the beach in Cannes.

Restaurant des Arcades (see p318) Bistro lunch between art, from a bygone era. In Biot.

Couleurs du Jardin (see p354) Hip, romantic dining above the sand on the St-Tropez peninsula, in Gigaro.

Ferme de Peïgros (see p361) Lunch on a farm at the top of mountain pass in Collobrières.

THE OIL MILL

Siblings Anne and Gilles Brun make a formidable team at the family mill, Moulin à Huile du Calanquet, 4.5km southwest of St-Rémy de Provence. Stopped in its tracks following the great frost of 1956, the oil press started turning again in 2001 – to the joy of Anne and Giles' grandmother, now in her 80s, who can still be found between bottles at the mill. Lonely Planet author Catherine Le Nevez met the family.

Tell me about a little bit more about the mill and its past.

Our family have farmed this property for five generations. Our grandparents ran the oil mill and olive farm but after 1956 production stopped and they grew cauliflowers and potatoes instead. Before 1956 there were five mills in the area; one traded for 10 years afterwards then stopped too, meaning there was nowhere in the northern Alpilles to mill oil.

Provençal and local traditions are important to us. (The mill's name comes from the Provençal word 'calan', a rock used as shelter from the mistral.) After we reopened the mill, we also replanted olive trees where our grandparents' trees were.

What sort of oil do you produce and how much?

We cultivate five traditional Alpilles olive varieties which give five types of oil, as well as a blend. Our speciality is separating the different varieties for mono-varietals. Our oils have 0% to 8% acidity which means they go well with sweet dishes as well as fish. Our 5000 trees produce 100,000kg of olives and 20,000 litres of oil a year.

When is olive oil at its best?

When it's new; the taste and flavour is good.

---

p273); *brandade de morue* is a don't-mess-with-me mix of crushed salt cod, garlic and olive oil; and *tapenade* is a sharp, black-olive-based dip seasoned with garlic, capers, anchovies and olive oil.

Then there is handsome *pistou*, a green crushed-up mix of garlic, basil, pine kernels and olive oil that the Provençal stir into *soupe au pistou* (a vegetable, three- or four-bean and basil soup) or paste on toast. On the coast, *aïoli* (a potent garlic mayonnaise) is smeared over many a fish dish and is an essential component of aïoli *Provençal complet* – a mountain of vegetables (including artichokes), boiled potatoes, a boiled egg and *coquillages* (small shellfish), all of which are dunked into the pot of aïoli. Fiery pink *rouille* (a garlic mayonnaise with breadcrumbs and crushed chilli peppers, hence its wild colour) is best friend to *soupe de poisson* (fish soup), served with bite-sized toasts, a pot of *rouille* – *and* a garlic clove. Rub the garlic over the toast, spread the *rouille* on top, bite it and breathe fire.

JULY: YELLOW & BLACK TOMATOES

Slice six red tomatoes. Grate two *cébettes* (small white onions) and sprinkle on top. Dress with a vinaigrette of balsamic vinegar, olive oil, salt and pepper; sprinkle with chopped basil or parmesan shavings and *voilà* – *salade de tomates*.

The humble tomato salad remains a firm favourite of Provençal chef Christian Etienne who conjures up a magnificent four-course *menu de tomates* (tomato feast; €60) at his Avignon restaurant in July when the region's most quintessential vegetable is at its noble best. 'Tomatoes remind me of my childhood – there were always tomatoes in our garden,' says the burly Avignon-born chef as he waves enthusiastically at the line-up of potted tomato plants on his restaurant terrace.

Tomatoes in this fertile neck of the woods are not all red. Of the region's 2500 known varieties, some are white, some are burgundy, some black, green, orange, yellow and so on. **René Caramela** (☎ 04 90 47 58 40, ☎ 06 03 48 52 69; Mas du Bout des Vignes, chemin des Poissoniers) grows 30 to 40 different types in her exceptional tomato garden in Mouriès, 15km south of St-Rémy de Provence.

Tapenade combines the favourite flavours of Provence: the tang of the home-cured black olives in brine, the saltiness of the tiny anchovy, the briny flavour of the caper, the vibrant sharpness of garlic, the heady scent of thyme, the unifying quality of a haunting olive oil.'

PATRICIA WELLS

Long and skinny, smooth or crinkled, shape also differs dramatically – as does the vital difference between '*une belle tomate et une bonne tomate* (a beautiful tomato and a good tomato)'. 'My tomatoes are not beautiful but I know they are good,' explains the tomato-mad chef, taking me through his steely kitchen to the sun-flooded balcony out back where the 40kg of far-from-uniform tomatoes he will use in two days are stacked in crates. 'Never keep tomatoes in a fridge,' says Monsieur Etienne with horror, 'it dulls their taste'. He adds that there is little point smelling a tomato to check quality: it's the green branch, not the flesh, that exudes that lovely fresh-from-the-garden tomato scent – '*Quel bonheur!*' (What joy!) – familiar to too few these days.

The Provence Cookbook by Patricia Wells is the recipe-book bible for anyone keen to try their hand at Provençal cooking.

Like every chef in the region, Monsieur Etienne buys his fruit and vegetables at the market and directly from local producers. A stroll through the Provençal market in July is a particularly succulent affair: July is the month for melons (p51), apricots, pomegranates, the first fleshy black figs of the year and the last of the cherries. Francis et Jacqueline Honoré grow 150 different fig varieties at **Les Figuières** (☎ 04 90 95 72 03; www.lesfiguieres.com; Mas de Luquet), an organic fig farm in Graveson.

The artichoke, another July vegetable, is eaten young and can be stuffed with a salted pork, onion and herb mix, then baked, to become *petits légumes farcis* (little stuffed vegetables); stuffed courgette flowers make an enchanting variation. Most vegetables that grow under the Provençal sun can be thrown into a *tian* (vegetable-and-rice gratin) or eaten as *crudités*, that is, chopped up and served raw with *anchoïade, tapenade* or *brandade de morue* with an apéritif.

Staples like onions, aubergines (eggplant) and courgettes (summer squash or zucchini) are stewed alongside green peppers, garlic and various aromatic herbs to produce that perennial Provençal favourite known the world over, *ratatouille*.

AUGUST: HERBAL SCRUB

Distinctive to Provençal cuisine is the use of lavender (p244), harvested during the hot dry days of August when the aromatic purple flower is still in bloom. Its flowers flavour herbal tea, tart up desserts and spice grilled meats. Its leaves float in soups.

Provence's titillating array of aromatic herbs and plants is a legacy of the heavily scented garrigue that grows with vigour in the region. While

---

STRAIGHT FROM THE HORSE'S MOUTH

Tomates à la Provençale (tomatoes cut in two, sprinkled with crushed garlic and oven-baked), potatoes cooked in the oven with loads of garlic and herbs, and *bœuf boulettes ail persil* (garlic and parsley-spiced beef balls) are typical dishes eaten in the family home of garlic-farmer Jeanine Squarzoni, a regular at Marseille's seasonal garlic market:

'The market opens on 24 June (midsummer and the feast day of St-John) and runs for a month. People buy garlic to keep for the whole year,' explains Jeanine who farms near Aix-en-Provence. Garlic is planted in August, plucked from the soil the following June and strewn across the fields to dry for a few days before harvesting.

'I farm two types of garlic: violet (€2.40 per kg) which keeps 10 months and is particularly good raw in salads as it's less strong; and Moulinin or *rouge* (red; €2.80 per kg) which keeps 12 months,' continues Jeanine, stressing that both garlic taste the same after cooking. The strongest-tasting garlic is *vert* (green) garlic, harvested in May when it is not fully ripened. Eat it quickly; it doesn't keep.

Any other tips for avoiding 'garlic breath'? 'Chewing gum,' she says with a grin, pulling out a packet from her apron pocket.

TABLE MANNERS

The Provençal book of etiquette:

- Cardinal sins – skipping lunch, turning down a *dégustation* (wine-tasting) session or expressing a dislike of regional specialities *pieds et paquets* (sheep tripe) or *testicules de mouton* (sheep testicles).

- Don't even try to balance your bread on your main-course plate (side plates are only provided in formal, multistarred, gastronomic restaurants); a liberal sprinkling of crumbs on the table is fine.

- Using the same knife and fork for your starter and main course is common in many *fermes auberges* and bistros. Don't be surprised if the waiter adds up your *addition* (bill) on the paper tablecloth.

- Feel free to order *une carafe d'eau* (a jug of tap water) in any type of restaurant, formal or otherwise, rather than a €5 to €10 bottle of *plate* (still) or *gazeuse* (fizzy) mineral water.

- *Santé* (cheers!) is the toast used for alcoholic drinks; raise a full glass and chink it lightly against those of fellow drinkers before taking a sip. *Bon appetite* (or simply *'bon app'* between families and very good friends) is the thing to say before eating.

- End your meal with a short, sharp *café* (espresso); ordering anything else (a tea, milky coffee) is just not on.

---

the classic *herbes de Provence* mix of dried basil, thyme, oregano, rosemary (which was a natural ingredient for eternal youth in medieval Provence) and savory seasons dishes throughout Europe, culinary creations in the region rely more on fresh herbs. Fresh basil lends its pea green colour and strong fragrance to *pistou* (pesto) but the herb is used dried to flavour *soupe au pistou*. Sage is another *pistou* ingredient, while aromatic rosemary brings flavour meat dishes. Chervil leaves are used in omelettes and meat dishes, and the tender young shoots of tarragon flavour delicate sauces accompanying seafood.

Particularly rife is the sensual aniseed scent of the bulbous fennel. While its leaves are picked in spring and finely chopped for use in fish dishes and marinades, its potent seeds are plucked in late August to form the basis of several herbal liqueurs, including pastis (p50).

SEPTEMBER: RED RICE

Gourmets rave about the red rice harvested in September in Europe's most northerly rice-growing region – the Camargue. Nutty in taste and borne out of a cross-pollination of wild red and cultivated short-grain rice, the russet-coloured grains are best shown off in a salad or pilaf. They are also quite delicious simply served with olive oil, salt and herbs or almonds; and marry beautifully with the region's other big product, bull (p46). Risotto-style white and other brown-rice varieties are also cultivated in this wet westerly corner of Provence where paddies cover 10,000 hectares and conditions can be quite unique.

'Flamingos try to eat our rice so we have an automatic gun-sound machine to scare them off,' says Camargue rice farmer Lucille Bon, whose 500-hectare rice plantation – strictly organic – yields just 2000kg to 5000kg of rice per hectare (compared to up to 8000kg per hectare on a traditional nonorganic farm).

'Because we're organic, turning the fields is important otherwise the earth becomes too poor,' she explains, adding that 'this year we have lentils and alfalfa; but next year we'll plant red rice again'.

Search by product, establishment or village to track down a tasty of choice of fabulous and authentic *fromageries* (cheese shops), farmhouse kitchens and so on with the annual *Guide Gantié Provence & Côte d'Azur* at www .guidegantie.com (in French).

Rice is planted in a pancake-flat field at the end of April and flooded with water from the Rhône, remaining submerged until 15 days before the September harvest when the water is drained off. Harvesting is just like harvesting wheat, after which the field is burned and the rice sent to the cooperative to have its outer husk machine-removed, thus becoming brown rice. White rice is stripped of its second husk too – making red rice a type of brown rice.

Since 2003 Provence's classical dried herbal mix has been protected by a Label Rouge (Red Label), which requires *herbes de Provence* to contain 26% rosemary, 26% savory, 26% oregano, 19% thyme and 3% basil.

OCTOBER: SWEET CHESTNUTS

Roast chestnuts hot off the coals brighten darker days in October when the first fresh fruits of the *châtaignier* (chestnut tree) fall – *marrons* (the larger fruits packed singularly in the prickly chestnuts burs) and *châtaignes* (the smaller fruits, packed two or more per bur) in culinary terms.

In Collobrières (p360), chestnut capital in the Massif des Maures, the autumnal fruit is made into *marrons glacés, crème de marrons* (sickly sweet chestnut spread, much loved on crepes) and *liqueur de châtaignes* (chestnut liqueur). The tree's aromatic flowers flavour *gelée de fleurs de châtaignes* (chestnut flower jelly).

If it's savoury you're after, Grasse-based chef Jacques Chibois at the Bastide St-Antoine (p328) cooks a mean roast partridge with juniper berries and chestnuts.

NOVEMBER: THE OLIVE HARVEST

In November, the bulk of the region's succulent, sunbaked black olives – born from clusters of white flowers that blossom on the knotty old trees in May and June – are harvested. The harvest continues in some parts until January, olives destined for the oil press (p45) usually being the last to be picked.

A ramekin of olives marinated in olive oil and spices or tangy *tapenade* (an olive-based dip fusing the region's quintessential edibles; p46) are classic

---

THE MILK OF PROVENCE

When in Provence, do as the Provençaux do: drink pastis. The aniseed-flavoured alcoholic drink is a classic apéritif in the region, although it can be drunk any time of day.

Amber-coloured in the bottle, it turns milky white when mixed with water. Bars and cafés serve it straight, allowing you to add the water (roughly five parts water to one part pastis). It's best drunk before lunch or as the sun sets – and never on the rocks.

A dash of *sirop de menthe* (mint syrup diluted with water) transforms a regular pastis into a *perroquet* (literally 'parrot'). A *tomate* (tomato) is tarted up with one part grenadine, while the sweet Mauresque is dressed with *orgeat* (a sweet-orange and almond syrup).

Pastis was invented in 1932 in Marseille by industrialist Paul Ricard (1909–97). The earliest aniseed liqueur to hit the market was absinthe, a dangerous and potent liqueur distilled with wormwood oil that, from the early 1800s, was manufactured in France by Henri-Louis Pernod. The drink – which boasted an astonishing 72% alcohol content – was banned in 1915, paving the way for Ricard's 45% alcohol pastis and other harmless (except for the alcohol) aniseed and liquorice liqueurs, such as the modern-day Pernod. Leading pastis brands are Pastis 51 and Ricard, both owned by the Ricard empire (in addition to Pernod, taken over by Ricard in 1974).

Taste these and others at Marseille's Maison du Pastis (see the boxed text, p113). Tasting tips from locals not quite rolling under the table include (a) never order simply 'a pastis' at the bar; ask for it by the brand name such as Ricard, Janot or Casanis etc (b) if you find it too strong, add sugar (c) bars in Marseille serve it in four sizes of glass: in a *momie* or *mominette* (a dinky shot glass), a *bock* (double-height shot glass), a *tube* (tall thin juice glass) and a *ballon* (like a brandy balloon).

HERB 'N' SPICE WIZARDS

Gem up on herbs, spices, their mixes and uses – from Provence and elsewhere – for a morning or weekend at the inventive *atelier de créations culinaires* (culinary creations workshop) of herb 'n' spice whiz Gérard Vives in Forcalquier (p246). In Mane, 4km south, see every herb growing under the Provençal sun at the Prieuré de Salagon (p246) and ask the local priest to concoct a herbal remedy for you.

---

apéritif accompaniments. Table olives are the first to be harvested and can be black, round and fleshy *(grossane)*; green and pointed *(picholine)* or pear-shaped with yellow tints *(salonenque)*. *Olives de Nice* (the Cailletier grape variety) are small, firm and lime, wine, brown or aubergine in colour.

With son Anthony, Nicole and Serge Bérenguier cultivate four different varieties of olives at their 10-hectare olive farm and mill in Callas (p357), a four-generation family business founded in 1928 by grandfather Félix and revived by grandson Serge in the 1970s after the 1956 frost froze most olive trees to death. 'October, just before the harvest when the olives change colour, is a magnificent moment. The olives stay green, but they become paler, promising *une belle recolte* (beautiful harvest),' says Nicole, adding that 'early November when the olives fall is also magical'. Just two extra people are taken on to help harvest: green nets are laid out beneath the trees to catch the falling olives, loosened from the tree with special scissors. Annual yield: around 350 tons.

THE MELON FARM

Charismatic Bernard Meyssard has plenty of passions in life: 'melons, *la chasse* (hunting), *pétanque*, my wife,' says the 58-year-old melon producer and French *pétanque* champ. Monsieur Meyssard zips around his melon farm in Cheval Blanc, 6km south of Cavaillon, on a quad like a kid, eyes popping out of sockets, frizzy grey locks flying behind him as he revs between greenhouses side-saddle.

A bus driver when he wed Martine in 1969, Bernard traded in the road for agriculture in 1982, quickly establishing himself as one of the largest of the dozen or so small melon-producers farming around Cavaillon. His greenhouses span 20,000 sq m and yield 2kg to 3.5kg per sq metre of Charentais melons a year (Galia is the other variety rife in these parts). The gentle-hued, sweet-fleshed fruit is harvested and sold at the market late June to early September, although July is the best month. About 90% of melon flesh is water.

But life on the melon farm is not a bed of roses: 'It is not as good as it was. The last 10 years have been catastrophic. There are areas now that grow melons like fields of corn while the big buyers fix the prices months before melons are harvested. For us small producers, it is finished,' explains Bernard, bemoaning the industrialisation of the melon trade between sweet mouthfuls of his lovingly grown melon: we are all savouring it around his kitchen table between restrained sips (we *are* all driving) of Beaumes de Venise. 'Melon is my passion – I won't abandon it. But now I grow lettuces November to March and strawberries in spring to make ends meet,' says the man who holidays twice a year ('two weeks in August with my wife on the coast and a gastronomy week in Le Gers with my friends in September before planting the lettuces'). 'Chin chin, *c'est bon*, huh?' Murmurings of contentment rumble around the table as the bottle of Beaumes is drained (we *are* six).

Should you want to meet Bernard in the middle of a melon field and learn more about his trade, ask at Cavaillon or Cheval Blanc tourist offices about their July and August **melon-farm visits** (adult/child under 12 €6/free). Otherwise, stop at his roadside stall in front of his farm, 2km south of Cheval Blanc towards Merindol, and buy a Meyssard melon.

For the ultimate melon-dining experience, try Prévôt (p225).

DECEMBER: A DOZEN & ONE DESSERTS

December in Provence sees families rush home after Mass on Christmas Eve for Caleno vo Careno, a traditional feast of 13 desserts symbolising Jesus and the 12 apostles. Among the culinary delights are *pompe à huile* (leavened cake baked in olive oil and flavoured with orange blossom), sweet black-and-white nougat (homemade from honey and almonds), nuts and an assortment of dried and fresh fruits.

Not that there's not plenty to keep sweet-tooths appeased year-round. Lavender and thyme flavour milk-based dishes such as *crème brûlée* as well as jams and honey. Anise and orange blossoms give *navettes* (canoe-shaped biscuits from Marseille) and *fougassettes* (sweet bread) their distinctive flavours. A secret 60 different Mont Ventoux herbs are used to make the liqueur that laces *papalines d'Avignon* (pink liqueur-laced chocolate balls). Almonds are turned into *gâteaux secs aux amandes* (snappy almond biscuits) around Nîmes; *calissons* (almond biscuit frosted with icing sugar) in Aix-en-Provence; and black honey nougat everywhere. Countrywide, christening and wedding guests receive *dragées* – porcelain-smooth sugared almonds tinted pink for a girl, blue for a boy and white for a blushing bride.

TOP 10 COOKING COURSES

Cooking courses are a big business. Many *chambres d'hôtes* also host cooking workshops; see the regional chapters for details.

At Home with Patricia Wells (www.patriciawells.com; c/o Judith Jones, 708 Sandown Place, Raleigh NC 27615, USA) Four- and five-day general Provence, truffle, fish and wine courses with Patricia Wells, the only wholly foreign cook considered to have truly embraced the soul of Provençal cooking. Courses upwards of US$4000 (excluding accommodation); most take place in Wells' 18th-century farmhouse kitchen near Vaison-la-Romaine.

Le Cilantro (☎ 04 90 18 25 05; 29 rue Porte de Laure, Arles) Learn the tricks of the trade in the restaurant kitchen of Arlésian chef Jérôme Laurant; seasonally themed classes with lunch (€45), once a month March to December.

École de Cuisine du Soleil (☎ 04 93 75 35 70; www.moulindemougins.com; av Notre Dame de Vie, Mougins) Thematic 2½-hour sessions (Riviera flavours, snails, Sunday in the country etc), June to August, with well-known Provençal chef Alain Llorca cost €58/265 for one/five sessions.

L'Estocaficada (☎ 04 93 80 21 64; brigitte.autier@wanadoo.fr; 7 rue de l'Hôtel de Ville, Nice) Atmospheric Niçois cooking workshops (September to June) by third-generation female chef Brigitte Autier, in the open kitchen of family restaurant L'Estocaficada, where stockfish, *tourte de blette* and other staunchly Niçois dishes have been boiled up in since 1958. Three-hour workshop with lunch costs €55, with lunch and market and producer visits €70.

Hostellerie de Crillon le Brave (☎ 04 90 65 61 61; www.crillonlebrave.com; place de l'Église, Crillon le Brave) Five-day courses in October with French chef Philippe Monti; €2900 per person per week, including hotel accommodation.

Jean-Jacques Prévôt (☎ 04 90 71 39 43; www.restaurant-prevot.com in French; 353 av de Verdun, Cavaillon) Half-day thematic sessions (€120/110 with/without market visit) focusing on a seasonal product – melons, clams, truffles, asparagus, chocolate – with Provence's melon-mad chef.

Le Marmiton (☎ 04 90 85 93 93; www.la-mirande.fr in French; Hôtel de la Mirande, 4 place de la Mirande, F-84000 Avignon) Morning/evening classes for €80/135 and afternoon pastry sessions in the *atelier de cuisine* (cooking studio)of Avignon's loveliest hotel, a 14th-century cardinal's palace; truffle weekend €460. Course calendar online.

Christophe Leroy (☎ 04 94 97 87 20; www.christophe-leroy.com; 38 rue Georges Clemenceau, St-Tropez) Three-hour *ateliers* (workshops) cost €100 and include coffee and *viennoiseries* (Viennese pastries). They each cover four recipes with inventive St-Tropez chef Christophe Leroy at La Table du Marché (p348).

L'Oustau de Baumanière (☎ 04 90 54 33 07; www.oustaudebaumaniere.com; Les Baux de Provence) Indulge in a three-hour *atelier* followed by lunch (€165) with chef Jean-André Charial or a patisserie and confectionery sessions (€110 including meal) with this prestigious hotel's pastry chef.

Les Petits Farcis (☎ 06 81 67 41 22; www.petitsfarcis.com; 7 rue du Jésus. Nice) Niçois cooking sessions built around the cours Saleya market by long-time Nice resident Rosa Jackson. A market tour, cooking class and lunch costs €200 or throw in a postlunch gourmet stroll (€290) to make a day of it; three-hour gourmet walks (€100), early-morning market tours with breakfast (€120) and full-day meet-the-producers tours (€290).

TOP FIVE SPECIALIST FOOD MARKETS

Market days are listed at the start of regional chapters. Photogenic highlights:

- Farmers Market on Tuesdays from April to December in Apt
- Fresh Fish Market on mornings year-round in quai des Belges, Marseille
- Garlic Market daily from late June and July in cours Belsunce, Marseille
- Melon Market on mornings from May to September in Cavaillon
- Truffle Market on Saturdays from November to March in Richerenches

---

Nice and Apt excel at *fruits confits* (crystallised or glazed fruits); see them made in Apt (p212), Pont du Loup and Nice. *Berlingots* are hard caramels originating in Carpentras, and *tarte Tropézienne* is a cream-filled sandwich cake from St-Tropez. A popular dessert in the Vaucluse is cantaloupe melon from Carpentras doused in Muscat de Beaumes de Venise, a sweet dessert wine made in a village nearby.

EAT YOUR WORDS
Useful Phrases

I'd like to reserve a table.
    J'aimerais resérver une table.   zhay·mer·ray ray·zair·vay ewn ta·bler

A table for two, please.
    Une table pour deux, s'il vous plaît.   ewn ta·bler poor der seel voo play

Do you have a menu in English?
    Est-ce que vous avez la carte en anglais?   es·ker voo a·vay la kart on ong·glay

Could you recommend something?
    Est-ce que vous pouvez recommender quelque chose?   es·ker voo poo·vay re·ko·mon·day kel·ker shoz

I'd like a local speciality.
    J'aimerais une spécialité régionale.   zhay·mer·ray ewn spay·sya·lee·tay ray·zhyo·nal

I'd like the set menu.
    Je prends le menu.   zher pron ler mer·new

I'd like today's special.
    Je voudrais avoir le plat du jour.   zher voo·dray a·vwar ler pla doo zhoor

I'm a vegetarian.
    Je suis végétarien/végétarienne. (m/f)   zher swee vay·zhay·ta·ryun/vay·zhay·ta·ryen

I don't eat meat/fish/seafood.
    Je ne mange pas de viande/poisson/ fruits de mer.   je ne monzh pa de vee·and/pwa·so/ fwee·de·mair

I'd like to order the ...
    Je voudrais commander ...   zher voo·dray ko·mon·day

Is service included in the bill?
    Est-ce que le service est inclu?   es·ker ler sair·vees ay un·klew

The bill, please.
    La note, s'il vous plaît.   la not seel voo play

Food Glossary
STARTERS

anchoïade	on·sho·yad	anchovy puree laced with garlic and olive oil
assiette anglaise	a·syet ong·glayz	plate of cold mixed meats and sausages
assiette de crudités	a·syet de krew·dee·tay	plate of raw vegetables with dressings
banon à la feuille	ba·no a la fer·yer	goats cheese dipped in eau de vie and wrapped in a chestnut leaf
bouillon	boo·yon	broth or stock

REPAS DES VENDANGES

Harvesting the grapes is all very well but for *vendangeur* (grape picker) and *vigneron* (wine grower), it is the *repas des vendanges* marking the end of the harvest's end that is the most memorable feast.

The 'harvest meal' is the culmination of three long weeks spent working hard in the heat of late summer – from around 7.30am to 2am in the case of small-scale wine producer Michel Vivet in Les Arcs who pretty much works around the clock despite the extra eight *coupeurs* and additional *porteur* he takes on to help him pick and carry grapes on his 15-hectare estate.

The day after the harvest, everyone who's helped harvest joins Michel and his family around 11am on the terrace of their green-shuttered farmhouse overlooking vines for an apéritif and lunch which carries on well into the night: 'It is a fabulous affair. We eat *petit gris de Provence* (snails in tomato sauce), a huge aïoli and plenty of wine.'

For Michel the *repas des vendanges* evokes the free spirit of his childhood growing up in Les Arcs: 'I looked for mushrooms, I hunted truffles, I took my bike and built tree houses, I walked wherever I wanted to and no one worried about fires. Everyone knew everyone and helped each other. Now, with more and more large industrial *domaines* run by people who don't actually work on the land, this contact between *paysans* (farmers, country folk) is being lost'.

bourride	boo·reed	fish soup; often eaten as a main course
brandade de morue	bron·dad der mo·rew	mix of crushed salted cod, olive oil and garlic
brebis	brer·bee	sheeps milk dairy product
fromage de chèvre	fro·mazh der shev·rer	goats cheese (also called *brousse*)
pissala	pee·sa·la	Niçois paste mixed from pureed anchovies
pissaladière	pee·sa·la·dyair	anchovy, onion and black olive 'pizza' from Nice
soupe au pistou	soop o pees·too	vegetable soup made with basil and garlic
soupe de poisson	soop der pwa·son	fish soup
tapenade	ta·per·nad	sharp, olive-based dip
tomme arlesienne	tom ar·ler·syen	moulded goats cheese from Arles

MEAT, CHICKEN & POULTRY

Visit the Comité Interprofessionnel des Vins Côtes de Provence and learn more about Côtes de Provence wine at www.cotes-de-provence.fr.

agneau	a·nyo	lamb
bœuf	berf	beef
bœuf haché	berf ha·shay	minced beef
canard	ka·nar	duck
chèvre	shev·rer	goat
chevreau	sher·vro	kid (baby goat)
daube de bœuf à la Provençale	dob der berf a la pro·von·sal	beef stew
entrecôte	on·trer·cot	rib steak
épaule d'agneau	e·pol da·nyo	shoulder of lamb
estouffade de bœuf	es·too·fad der berf	Carmargais beef stew with tomatoes and olives
filet	fee·lay	tenderloin
jambon	zham·bon	ham
lardons	lar·don	pieces of chopped bacon
pieds de porc	pyay der pork	pig trotters
pieds et paquets	pyay ay pa·kay	sheep tripe; literally 'feet and packages'
poulet	poo·lay	chicken
saucisson d'Arles	so·see·son darl	sausage made from pork, beef, wine and spices
taureau de Camargue	to·ro der ka·marg	Camargais beef

PROVENÇAL WINE

Provençal wines are by no means France's most sought after, but making and tasting them is an art and tradition that bears its own unique and tasty trademark. Each AOC possess a common trait: an exceptionally cold mistral wind and an equally exceptional, hot, ripening sun. Most carry the name of the chateau or *domaine* (wine-growing estate) they are produced on – unlike **Fat Bastard** (www .fatbastard.com), a label created by Gigondas oenologist Thierry Boudinaud ('*now zat iz what you call eh phet bast-ard*,' said Thierry allegedly to his English partner Guy Anderson upon tasting the wine, hence the ground-breaking hip name). Using grapes from neighbouring Languedoc, the Gigondas-born wine is the French sensation of the moment since breaking into the US market.

Wine can be bought direct from the *producteur* (wine producer) or *vigneron* (wine grower), most of whom offer degustation, allowing you to sample two or three vintages with no obligation to buy. For cheap plonk *(vin de table)* costing €2 or so per litre; fill up your own container at the local wine cooperative; every wine-producing village has one. Lists of estates, *caves* (wine cellars) and cooperatives are available from tourist offices and *maisons des vins* (wine houses) in Avignon (p163), Les Arcs-sur-Argens (p359) and elsewhere.

Côtes du Rhône

The most renowned vintage in this respected appellation established in 1937 is Châteauneuf du Pape, a full-bodied wine bequeathed to Provence by the Avignon popes who planted the vineyards 10km south of Orange.

Châteauneuf du Pape reds are strong (minimum alcohol content 12.5%) and well-structured masters in their field. Whites account for 7% of total annual production. Châteauneuf du Pape wine growers, obliged to pick their grapes by hand, say it is the *galets* (large smooth, yellowish stones) covering their vineyards that distinguish them from others. Both whites and reds can be drunk young (two to three years) or old (seven years or more). Irrespective of age, whites should be served at 12°C; reds at 16°C to 18°C.

The Tavel rosé is another popular Rhône Valley *grand cru* (literally 'great growth'). The vineyards around the Dentelles de Montmirail, some 15km east of Orange, produce notable red and rosé Gigondas, and the sweet dessert wine, Muscat de Beaumes de Venise.

Côtes de Provence

The 18 hectares of vineyards sandwiched between Nice and Aix-en-Provence produce red, rosé and white Côtes de Provence, France's sixth largest appellation, dating from 1977. The *terroir* (land) ranges from sandy coastal soils around St-Tropez to chalky soils covering subalpine slopes around Les Arcs-sur-Argens.

The appellation is the largest in Provence, with an annual production of 100 million bottles; 75% are rosé. Côtes de Provence rosé is drunk young and served at a crisp 8° to 10°C. Reds drunk young should be served at 14° to 16°C, while older red *vins de garde* – a traditional accompaniment to game, sauced meats and cheese – are best drunk at 16° to 18°C.

Côtes de Provence whites, a golden friend to fish, should be chilled to 8°C.

Others

Six other pocket-sized appellations are dotted along or near the coast: Bandol, Cassis, Coteaux Varois, Coteaux d'Aix-en-Provence, Bellet and Palette. Of these, Bandol is the most respected, known for its deep-flavoured reds produced from the dark-berried *mourvèdre* grape, which needs oodles of sun to ripen (hence its rarity). In neighbouring Cassis, crisp whites (75% of its production) are drunk with gusto.

Those who like a dry rosé should try Coteaux d'Aix-en-Provence. Palette, east of Aix, is just 20 hectares, dates from 1948 and produces well-structured reds from its old vines. Four of every five Palette bottles come from Château Simone. Wines from the Bellet AOC are rare outside Nice.

Vast areas of the region's interior are carpeted with Côtes du Ventoux (6900 hectares established in 1973) and Côtes du Lubéron (3500 hectares dating from 1988) vineyards.

FISH & SEAFOOD

aïoli Provençale complet	a-ee-o-lee pro-von-sal kom-play	shellfish, vegetables, boiled egg and aïoli
anchois	on-shwa	anchovy
coquillage	ko-kee-lazh	shellfish
coquille St-Jacques	ko-keel san zhak	scallop
crevette grise	kre-vet grees	shrimp
crevette rose	kre-vet ros	prawn
fruits de mer	frwee der mair	seafood
gambas	gom-ba	king prawns
homard	o-mar	lobster
langouste	lang-goost	crayfish
langoustine	lang-goos-teen	small saltwater 'lobster'
oursin	oor-san	sea urchin
paella	pa-ay-a	rice dish with saffron, vegetables and shellfish
palourde	pa-loord	clam
rouget	roo-zhay	red mullet
estocaficada (in Niçois)	es-to-ka-fee-ka-da	stockfish, dried salt fish soaked in water for four to five days, stewed for two hours with onion, tomato and white wine, then laced with anchovies and black olives

VEGETABLES, HERBS & SPICES

aïl	ai	garlic
artichaut	ar-tee-sho	artichoke
asperge	a-spairzh	asparagus
basilic	ba-see-leek	basil
blette de Nice	blet der nees	white beet
cèpe	sep	cepe (boletus mushroom)
estragon	es-tra-zhon	tarragon
fleur de courgette	fler der coor-zhet	courgette (zucchini) flower
légumes farcis	lay-goom far-see	stuffed vegetables
mesclun	mes-kloo	Niçois mix of lettuce

TOP 10 APÉRITIFS & DIGESTIVES

Lounging over a pre- or postdinner drink is one of the region's great sensual delights; most are loaded with herbs, plants and spices of Provence

- Pastis (p50) – quintessential Provençal drink

- Côtes de Provence rosé (p55) – crisp and chill

- Beaumes de Venise (p177) – sweet muscat wine, popular apéritif

- Liqueur de châtaignes – chestnut liqueur; mixed with white wine in the Massif des Maures to make a sweet apéritif

- Rinquinquin de pêche – peach liqueur mixed with chilled white wine, distilled at the Distilleries et Domaines de Provence in Forcalquier (p246)

- Amandine – almond liqueur from Haute-Provence

- La Farigoule – thyme liqueur from Haute-Provence

- Reverend Father Gaucher's Elixir – sweet, yellow chartreuse blended from 30 aromatic herbs in Tarascon

- Marc – fiery spirit distilled from grape skins and pulp left over from wine-making; digestive

- Eau de vie – generic name for brandies distilled from the region's fruits; digestive

TOP FIVE FOOD FESTIVALS

Food itself is a reason to celebrate: practically every harvest (grapes, olives, cherries, chestnuts, melons, lemons and so on) is honoured with its own festival. Our favourites:

- Messe de la Truffe (Truffle Mass) in Richerenches in January (see p43)
- Fête des Citrons (Lemon Festival) in Menton in February (see p292)
- Fête du Melon (Melon Festival) in Cavaillon in July (see p223)
- Fête des Prémices du Riz (Rice Harvest Festival) in Arles in mid-September (see p142)
- Fête de la Châtaigne (Chestnut Festival) in Collobrières in October (see p361)

ratatouille	ra·ta·too·yer	casserole of aubergines, tomatoes, peppers and garlic
riz de Camargue	ree der ka·marg	Camargais rice
romarin	ro·ma·ran	rosemary
salade Niçoise	sa·lad nee·swa	green salad featuring tuna, egg and anchovy
thym	teem	thyme
tian	tyan	vegetable-and-rice gratin served in a dish called a *tian*
tourta de bléa	toor·ta de blay·a	Niçois white beetroot and pine-kernel pie
truffe	trewf	black truffle

SAUCES

aïoli	ay·o·lee	garlicky sauce to accompany *bouillabaisse*
huile d'olive	weel do·leev	olive oil
pistou	pees·too	pesto (pounded mix of basil, hard cheese, olive oil and garlic)
Provençale	pro·von·sal	tomato, garlic, herb and olive-oil dressing or sauce
rouille	roo·yer	aïoli-based sauce spiced with chilli pepper; served with *bourride*
vinaigrette	vun·ay·gret	salad dressing made with oil, vinegar, mustard and garlic

BREAD & SWEETS

chichi freggi	shee·shee·fre·gee	sugar-coated doughnuts from around Marseille
fougasse	foo·gas	elongated Niçois bread stuffed with olives, chopped bacon or anchovies
fougassette	foo·gas·set	brioche perfumed with orange flower
gâteaux secs aux amandes	ga·to sek o a·mond	crisp almond biscuits
michettes	mee·shet	Niçois bread stuffed with cheese, olives, anchovies and onions
navettes	na·vet	canoe-shaped, orange-blossom-flavoured biscuits from Marseille
pain aux noix	pan o nwa	walnut bread
pain aux raisins	pan o ray·son	sultana bread
pan-bagnat	pan·ba·nya	Niçois bread soaked in olive oil and filled with anchovy, olives and green peppers
panisses	pa·nees	chickpea flour patties from in and around Marseille
socca	so·ka	Niçois chickpea flour and olive-oil pancake

The Arts

Artists and their Museums on the Riviera by Barbara Freed is an essential art-driven read for anyone touring the region for its art.

'Artistic dynamo' sums up the region pretty well. 'It's important to have a place for everybody. If you don't like it, you can always shut your eyes,' believes Nathalie Duchayne (see the boxed text, p349), who receives requests daily from artists all over the world keen to have their work shown in her gallery – a mixed-medium cocktail of wall and floor art (painting, drawing, sculpture, designer furniture, ceramics etc) – in St-Tropez, the old fishing village on the Mediterranean where it all started.

But those dreamy bohemian days of impoverished artists sharing studio and sleeping space, using their artistic creations as a form of currency to drink and dine very well – St-Paul de Vence's La Colombe d'Or (see the boxed text, p321) and Biot's Restaurant des Arcades (p318) have fabulous collections as a result – are over. The artistic pace today is fast and furious, fuelled by a frenetic creative energy that finds expression in an orgy of diverse and often ground-breaking artistic mediums, as one look at the portfolio of **Documents d'Artistes** (www.documentsdartistes.org), a Marseille-based association that catalogues and diffuses the work of contemporary regional artists on an international circuit, proves: be it tracing a line along the surface of the planet, creating sound installations, inflatable or mechanical art, it is happening here.

The high profile attributed to undiscovered younger artists echoes the region's natural leaning towards the avant-garde: Avignon has its theatre-driven Festival Off (p163) and La Manutention (p167); Marseille has La Friche la Belle de Mai (see the boxed text, p112 and opposite) and La Cité des Arts de la Rue (see the boxed text, below); while legendary art centres on the Côte d'Azur – Nice, Vence, St-Paul de Vence, Vallauris and Mougins – are rich in one-person *ateliers* (workshops). In 2005 urban art scored a major coup with the opening of Europe's first further-education establishment dedicated solely to street art, FAI AR. Venue: cutting-edge Marseille.

ART TALK

Nowhere is the contemporary-art dialogue sparkier than in Marseille where a potent cocktail of street-art projects, artists' residencies and public forums keeps the debate raging.

On the 5th floor of La Tour at La Friche, **Astérides** (www.asterides.org) – an association committed to launching young unknown artists – invites a contemporary artist to present his/her work to an audience of local artists and art-lovers. On top of these twice-monthly vibrant Garage Hermétique sessions, Astérides provides short-term studio space for young artists and hosts two or three contemporary art exhibitions a year at Galerie de la Friche. Installation artist Gilles Barbier (b 1965) is one of the well-known local artists behind the Astérides group; see his work at Nîmes' Carrée d'Art (p195).

In a rejuvenated soap and oil factory complex, 'theatrical laboratory' **La Cité des Arts de la Rue** (☎ 04 91 03 20 75; 225 rue des Aygalades, Marseille) generates further art talk: emerging artists temporarily reside in studios on the industrial site alongside arts and culture 'diffuser' **Karwan** (hugely informative website in French at www.karwan.info); musical street-theatre 'like public transport' **Generik Vapeur** (www.generikvapeur.com); mechanical workshop **Ateliers Sud Side** (www.sudside.org in French) where urban installations, stage sets and furniture are created; **Lézarap'art** (http://perso.orange.fr/lezarapart in French) which, among other things, runs a brilliant mechanical-art workshop in its multimedia garage; and national centre for the creation of street art **Lieux Publics** (www.lieuxpublics.com).

At the other end of the coast, in Nice, it is **Villa Arson** (www.villa-arson.org in French; p268) that fires up dialogue and encourages artistic activity with artists' residencies, exhibitions, workshops etc.

ZOOM IN: LA FRICHE LA BELLE DE MAI

From 1868 until 1990 tobacco was manufactured at La Belle de Mai, a vast factory complex in a run-down urban quarter northwest of Marseille's central train station. Since 1992 the industrial dinosaur has been the hub of creative life in Provence, providing cheap or free work space for experimental artists. Author Catherine Le Nevez spoke to Séverine Cappiello, international relations manager at La Friche, about its ground-breaking concept.

How did it all start?

It started 15 years ago with a one-year contract, when the government suggested using the abandoned factory to make a cultural space to extend the downtown area of Marseille into the poor neighbourhoods. Fifteen years later it's still here, with no contract. The space is smaller now; some areas are used by other companies, such as the studios where Plus Belle La Vie (a soap opera broadcast nationally on FR3) is filmed.

How many people are involved?

There are 60 to 70 independent artistic organisations, with 300 people working on the site, ranging from short residencies to long-term artists, some here from the beginning.

What are its basic tenets?

It's multidisciplinary, with music venues (hip-hop, electronic and reggae), dance and theatre venues, galleries for contemporary visual artists, as well as film studios and radio stations. It's independent, not lucrative, and politicised; focusing on emerging artists. It's definitely not mainstream. Artists pay cheap or no rent.

How accessible is it to artists and the general public?

Artists arrive but often don't leave, so space is very limited. Artists work outside in summer; the public can come in and walk around. There's a restaurant here and a shop to buy music, discover new artists. Our season runs September to the end of June. There's something to see four or five days a week – music, dance, theatre… Most of it is free for the public, but some nights there are big shows people pay to enter. It's random, there's no specific programming; the rule here is that there is no rule.

PAINTINGS & VISUAL ARTS

Contemporary art in the region rides on the back of an extraordinary artistic legacy. 'People who come to St-Trop already have a fantasy of St-Tropez in their head. With my painting, I let people live out that fantasy,' says Cica, a street artist in Vieux Port, St-Tropez.

Papal Pleasures to Rococo Silliness

In the 14th century Sienese, French and Spanish artists working at the papal court in Avignon created an influential style of mural painting, examples of which can be seen in the city's Palais des Papes – or rather on postcards featuring the paintings that once adorned the palace's now very bare interior.

While the rest of France found itself preoccupied with the Hundred Years' War, art flourished in Nice county, where the School of Nice emerged, led by Louis Bréa. Much exalted as the 'Fra Angelico Provençal', Louis Bréa created the burgundy colour known as *rouge bréa*. View his works at Nice's Église Notre Dame (p268) and Menton's Musée des Beaux-Arts (p291). In the Vallée de la Roya, meanwhile, a pair of artists from northern Italy set to work on what has since been dubbed the 'Sistine Chapel of the southern Alps', Notre Dame des Fontaines (p255).

Blind-man's bluff, stolen kisses and other courtly frivolities were the focus of Enlightenment artists. One of the most influential was Avignon-born Joseph Vernet (1714–89), who left a series depicting French ports. Rococo influences brushed the landscapes of Jean-Honoré Fragonard (1732–1806), whose playful and often licentious scenes immortalised his native Grasse.

Marseille's ground-breaking Art-cade, Galerie des Grands Bains Douches de la Plaine, online at www.art-cade .org, provides gallery space for rapidly rising contemporary artists.

Find out about FAI AR (Formation Avancée et Itinerante des Arts de la Rue), Marseille's pioneering performing street-arts school at www.faiar.org/anglais.

The elevated style of Nice-born Carle van Loo (1705–65) represented rococo's more serious 'grand style'; good examples hang in Nice's Musée des Beaux-Arts (p267) and Avignon's Musée Calvet (p162).

19th Century

The strong empathy with nature expressed in watercolour by François Marius Granet (1775–1849), a born-and-bred Aix-en-Provence artist, was a trademark of early-19th-century Provençal painters.

Landscape painting further evolved under Gustave Courbet (1819–77), a frequent visitor to southern France where he taught Provençal realist Paul Guigou (1834–71). A native of Villars in the Vaucluse, Guigou painted the Durance plains overdrenched in bright sunlight.

Provence's intensity of light drew the impressionists, among them Alfred Sisley and Pierre-Auguste Renoir (1841–1919). Renoir lived in Cagnes-sur-Mer from 1903 until his death. Many of his works are displayed in the Musée Renoir (p319), his former home and studio.

Paul Cézanne (1839–1906), celebrated for his still-life and landscape works, spent his entire life in Aix-en-Provence and painted numerous canvases in and around the fountain city; the tourist-office trail traces what he painted where.

Southern France was also immortalised by Paul Gauguin (1848–1904). In Arles Gauguin worked with Vincent van Gogh (1854–90), who spent most of his painting life in Paris and Arles. A brilliant and innovative artist, van Gogh produced haunting self-portraits and landscapes, in which colour assumes an expressive and emotive quality. Unfortunately, van Gogh's talent was largely unrecognised during his lifetime (see the boxed text, p143) and just one of his paintings remains in the region (in Avignon's Musée Angladon; p162).

Pointillism was developed by Georges Seurat (1859–91), who applied paint in small dots or with uniform brush strokes of unmixed colour. His most

> Xavier Girard's photo-biography, *French Riviera: Living Well Was the Best Revenge*, captures the incredible artistic creativity of the Riviera during the 1920s and 1930s. Equally captivating on the same subject is Pari Stave's *Making Paradise: Art, Modernity and the Myth of the French Riviera*.

PAINTING & DRAWING COURSES

Our pick of the plethora of painting courses run within the region:

■ The painting atelier of Jean-Claude Lorber in an 18th-century *mas* (farmhouse), **L'Atelier Doré** (☎ 04 90 06 29 60; www.mas-des-amandiers.com in French; 48 chemin des Puits Neufs, Cavaillon), offers workshops for adults/children covering all media (oil, watercolour, acrylic, pastel etc). The cost is €20.50/17 per two-hour session (20 hours €195/140). *Chambre d'hôte* accommodation is available at Mas des Amandiers (p224).

■ Resident painting courses are run from June to September with semiabstract/modern painter Camille Monnier in a forest overlooking lavender fields at **Technique & Creation** (☎ 04 90 75 48 81; www.lestavannes.com; Les Tavannes, St-Saturnin-les-Apt). One week costs €580 per person including 5½ hours of painting a day, meals and accommodation.

■ **L'Art et la Manière** (☎ 04 42 01 80 04; www.peindreacassis.com in French; Les Hauts Cépages, Euvezin, Cassis) offers one-day painting oil or acrylic workshops (€90) along the route des Crêtes and other fabulous coastal spots around Cassis; four-day workshops (€350 plus €50 for materials excluding brushes) with two days' studio work; three-day portrait/live model workshops cost €260/270 (excluding materials).

■ English–French one-week painting/drawing courses at **Maison des Arts** (☎ 04 93 32 32 50; www.maisondesarts.com; 10 rue Maréchal Foch, La Colle sur Loup) cover several media (acrylic, charcoal, watercolour, oil). The cost is €1450/1630 for a single/shared twin room including five days' tuition, seven nights' full board and materials. Venue: an 18th-century *maison de village* in the heart of a medieval Var village.

devout pupil was Paul Signac (1863–1935), who settled in St-Tropez from 1892. Part of the Musée de l'Annonciade (p343) in St-Tropez is devoted to pointillist works and includes *Étude pour le Chenal de Gravelines* (Study for the Channel at Gravelines), painted by Seurat in 1890, as well as numerous works by Signac.

20th Century

On the Côte d'Azur, leading fauvist exponent Henri Matisse (1869–1954) spent his most creative years lapping up the sunlight and vivacity of the coast in and around Nice. While in St-Tropez with Signac, Matisse began sketches that produced *Luxe, Calme et Volupté* (Luxury, Calm and Tranquillity). Pointillism's signature uniform brush strokes were still evident, but were also intermingled with splashes of violent colour. His subsequent painting, *La Gitane* (1906) – displayed in St-Tropez's Musée de l'Annonciade – is the embodiment of fauvism.

Cubism was launched in 1907 by Spanish prodigy Pablo Picasso (1881–1973), for whom Provence had a tremendous importance. As demonstrated in his pioneering *Les Demoiselles d'Avignon*, cubism deconstructed the subject into a system of intersecting planes and presented various aspects of it simultaneously. The collage, incorporating bits of cloth, wood, string, newspaper and anything lying around, was a cubist speciality.

After WWI the School of Paris was formed by a group of expressionists, mostly foreign, such as Belarusian Marc Chagall (1887–1985) who lived in France from 1922 and spent his last few years in St-Paul de Vence; his grave can be visited at the town's cemetery (p320). The largest collection of Chagall's works is at Nice's Musée National Message Biblique Marc Chagall (p267).

With the onset of WWII many artists left, and although some later returned the region never regained its old magnetism. Picasso moved permanently to the Côte d'Azur, settling first in Golfe-Juan, then Vallauris and finally Mougins, where he died. In 1946 he set up his studio in An tibes' Château Grimaldi (now the Musée Picasso; p313) and later painted a chapel, which is now the Musée National Picasso at Château Musée De Vallauris (p311).

The 1960s ushered in new realists Arman, Yves Klein and César and art generated from recycled trash, dirty crockery, crushed cars and scrap metal. Marseille-born César Baldaccini (1921–98), after whom the French cinema awards, the Césars, are named (he created the little statue handed to actors at the awards) was greatly inspired by Michelangelo. He started out using wrought iron and scrap metals, but later graduated to pliable plastics. From 1960 he crushed motor cars.

In 1960 Nice-born Klein (1928–62) produced *Anthropométrie de l'Époque Bleue*, a series of blue imprints made by two naked women (covered from head to toe in blue paint) rolling around on a white canvas – in front of an orchestra of violins and an audience in evening dress. Nice-born Arman (b 1928) became known for his trash-can portraits, made by framing the litter found in the subject's rubbish bin. Another influential realist from the School of Nice was Martial Rayasse, born in Golfe-Juan in 1936, and renowned for pioneering the use of neon in art. Most notable is his 1964 portrait of *Nissa Bella* (Beautiful Nice) – a flashing blue heart on a human face.

Another influential artist was Hungarian-born Victor Vasarely (1908–97). In Gordes from 1948, the avant-gardist turned his attention to geometrical forms, juxtaposed in contrasting colours to create shifting perspectives. Forty-two works by Vasarely are displayed in the Fondation Vasarely – designed and funded by the artist himself – in Aix-en-Provence.

In his candid, kiss-and-tell memoir, *The Sorcerer's Apprentice*, acclaimed Picasso biographer John Richardson recounts the 12 years he spent living the high life with cubist art collector Douglas Cooper and their wide circle of famous artist friends in 1950s Provence.

Roussillon served as a refuge to playwright Samuel Beckett during WWII; he stayed until April 1945 and wrote *Watt* there.

The 1970s supports-surfaces movement focused on deconstructing the traditional concept of a painting and transforming one of its structural components – such as the frame or canvas – into a work of art instead. The Groupe 70, specific to Nice, expressed an intellectual agitation, typical to Vivien Isnard's 1987 *Sans Titre* (Without Title) and Louis Chacallis' *Tension* (1978). In the 1990s bold paintings of naked angels brought world fame to Arles-born Louis Feraud (1921–99), an artist and couturier who dressed Brigitte Bardot and Ingrid Bergman in the 1950s.

It was in Nice that modern-dance icon Isadora Duncan (1878–1927), Paris resident from 1900, died. Her neck was broken in a freak motoring accident on the Riviera when the customary scarf that trailed behind her got caught in the car wheels.

ARCHITECTURE

Nothing competes with Mouans-Sartoux's lime green building designed by Swiss-based architects Annette Gigon and Mike Guyer to complement its 16th-century chateau museum (see the boxed text, p326) or Sacha Sosno's square head in Nice (p266) in which the city's public library offices are housed. Other striking examples of contemporary architecture include French architect Rudi Ricciotti's Pavillon Noir in Aix-en-Provence (see the boxed text, p129); the Grimaldi Forum (2000; p389) in Monaco, two-thirds of which sits beneath sea level; and MAMAC (1990; p266) and Fondation Maeght (1964; p320) in Nice. Nîmes' steel-and-glass Carrée d'Art (1993; p195) and the Musée de la Préhistoire des Gorges du Verdon in Quinson (p240) are the work of British architect Sir Norman Foster, who is to design a new building for Monaco Yacht Club.

Italian architect Vittorio Gregotti's theatre in Aix-en-Provence and the future hotel extension of Riviera legend Grand Hôtel du Cap Ferrat (see the boxed text, p284) by Nice-based hot-shot architect Luc Svetchine (www.lucsvetchine.com) will be guaranteed stunners.

VISUAL ARTS COURSES

From ceramics, mosaics and sculpture to photography, pottery and installation art, art-mad Provence sports courses to suit every creative taste.

- Summer installation-art workshops in the grounds of Mouans-Sartoux's cutting-edge Centre of Concrete Art with **Espace de l'Art Concret** (see the boxed text, p326).

- Learn the art of opiocolour mosaics and ceramic decoration in the ceramic workshop of a Greek-inspired villa, looking out to sea in Beaulieu-sur-Mer, with **Atelier de Céramique – Villa Grecque Kérylos** (p284).

- Study pottery, sculpture and the art of decoration – as Picasso did – in Vallauris at **École Municipal des Beaux-Arts** (☎ 04 93 63 07 61; blvd des Deux Vallons, Vallauris). Courses – a joint venture between Vallauris tourist office and School of Fine Arts – cost €140/185/250 for 12/20/30 hours of tuition over four/five/five days.

- Tailor-made photography, sculpture, landscape design courses and workshops hosted by the coast's wackiest art venue are available at **Chateau La Napoule** (p328).

- **Les Ateliers de l'Image** (p190) offers English and French half-day to one-week residential photography courses (digital and film) at this design-driven photography hotel with on-site dark rooms, studios and artsy grounds to inspire in St-Rémy de Provence.

- Paper dying, wall-mural painting and wood-craft workshops are offered by **Usine Mathieu Okhra** (see the boxed text, p220) and cost €110/99/88/77 for the first/second/third/fourth day. You'll use traditional techniques and natural dyes and pigments, extracted from the ochre earth in Roussillon.

- **Atelier de Sculpture Martine Wehrel** (☎ 04 92 00 13 84; martinewehrel@hotmail.com; 900 chemin des Espinets, St-Paul de Vence) offers twice-weekly sculpture classes with live model and skilled sculptor Martine Wehrel, best known for her voluptuous nudes in bronze.

SLEEP EAT DESIGN

Top 10 addresses for discerning design-lovers:

- 3.14 Hôtel, Cannes (p305)
- Bar & bœuf, Monaco (see the boxed text, p393)
- Chambre de Séjour avec Vue, Saignon (p227)
- Columbus Monaco, Monaco (p391)
- Domaine des Andéols, St-Saturnin-lès-Apt (see the boxed text, p219)
- Hôtel Burrhus, Vaison la Romaine (p175)
- Hôtel Hi, Nice (p272)
- Hôtel Les Ateliers de l'Image, St-Rémy de Provence (p190)
- La Maison du Frêne, St-Paul de Vence (see the boxed text, p323)
- Palm Beach Marseille, Marseille (p107)

Urban 20th-century architecture is the focus of Patrimoine XXème, a national government-funded project protecting 33 edifices in the Provence-Alpes-Côte d'Azur region: a 1920s Marseille silo, a dazzling white 1930s summerhouse in Antibes, Toulon port and a hydroelectric power plant. Read all about it www.culture.gouv.fr/paca/dossiers/xxeme.

Prehistoric to Villages Perchés

See remnants of stone megaliths at Marseille's Musée d'Archéologie Méditerranéenne (in the Centre de la Vieille Charité; p97), Monaco's Musée d'Anthropologie Préhistorique (p390) and Quinson's Musée de la Préhistoire des Gorges du Verdon (p240). Numerous petroglyphs are evident in the Vallée des Merveilles (p254) and examples of the region's earliest habitats – beehive-shaped huts built from dry limestone called *bories* – can be seen near Gordes (p216).

To view the Romans' colossal architectural legacy look no further than Pont du Gard, amphitheatres in Nîmes and Arles, the theatres at Orange and Fréjus, Nîmes' Maison Carrée and the triumphal arches at Orange and Carpentras.

Bar the octagonal 5th-century baptistry that can be visited in Fréjus, few churches constructed between the 5th and 10th centuries remain.

Romanesque to Renaissance

A religious revival in the 11th century ushered in Romanesque architecture, so-called because of the Gallo-Roman architectural elements it adopted. Round arches, heavy walls with few windows and a lack of ornamentation were characteristics of this style, Provence's most famous examples being the 12th-century abbeys in Sénanque (p217), Le Thoronet (p359) and Silvacane (p226). You can visit all three.

Fortresslike sacred buildings also marked this era, as the majestic Chartreuse de la Verne (p361), the older monastery on Île St-Honorat (p310) and the church at Stes-Maries de la Mer (p147) demonstrate. The exceptional dimensions of Digne-les-Bains cathedral (p242) are typical of the late Provençal-Romanesque style.

Provence's most important examples of Gothic architecture are Avignon's Palais des Papes (p161), the Chartreuse du Val de Bénédiction (p168) in Villeneuve-lès-Avignon and Carpentras' Cathédrale St-Siffrein (p183). Look for ribbed vaults carved with great precision, pointed arches, slender

Ted Jones' *The French Riviera: A Literary Guide for Travellers* is the essential companion for – the literary traveller.

verticals, chapels along the nave and chancel, refined decoration and large stained-glass windows.

The French Renaissance scarcely touched the region – unlike mighty citadel architect Sébastien Le Prestre de Vauban (1633–1707), who thundered in with Antibes' star-shaped Fort Carré, hilltop Entrevaux and constructions at Toulon.

Classical to Modern

Classical architecture fused with painting and sculpture from the end of the 16th to late 18th centuries to create stunning baroque structures with interiors of great subtlety, refinement and elegance: Chapelle de la Miséricorde in Nice, Menton's Italianate Basilique St-Michel Archange and Marseille's Centre de la Vieille Charité are classics.

Neoclassicism came into its own under Napoleon III, the Palais de Justice and Palais Masséna in Nice demonstrating the renewed interest in classical forms that it exhibited. The true showcase of this era, though, is 1878 Monte Carlo Casino (p388), designed by French architect Charles Garnier (1825–98). In 1887 Garnier, together with Gustave Eiffel (1832–1923) of tower fame, who lived in Beaulieu-sur-Mer, came up with the Observatoire de Nice. Elegant Aix-en-Provence's fountains and *hôtels particuliers* (private residences) date from this period; as do the intricate wrought-iron campaniles.

The *belle époque* heralded an eclecticism of decorative stucco friezes, trompe l'œil paintings, glittering wall mosaics, brightly coloured Moorish minarets and Turkish towers. Anything went.

Hyères' 1920s concrete-and-glass Villa Noailles is a stark expression of the cubist movement that gained momentum in the interwar period. Examples of surrealist interiors designed by Jean Cocteau, who lived in Menton at this time, include Menton's Salles des Mariages, Chapelle St-Pierre in Villefranche-sur-Mer and Cap d'Ail's amphitheatre.

Aix-en-Provence's Fondation Vasarely, designed by Victor Vasarely (1908–97), was an architectural coup when unveiled in 1976. Its 14 giant monumental hexagons reflected what he had already achieved in art: the creation of optical illusion and changing perspective through the juxtposi-

Born in L'Estaque near Marseille to an Armenian mother and German docker father, fiercely successful experimental film-maker Robert Guédiguian (b 1953) is your typical Marseillais. Working with the same actors – including his beautiful actress wife and muse Ariane Ascaride (who won Best Actress award at the 2003 Césars) – is his trademark, as is his commitment to a realist portrayal of Marseille and its inhabitants on screen. Of his many films, *Marius et Jeannette* (1997) and *Marie-Jo et ses deux amours* (2002; Marie-Jo and her Two Loves) are the best known.

ZOOM IN: LE CINÉMA DU CÔTÉ DES AUTEURS

Making flicks needs money and the industry in Provence could do with more, as Matthieu Colotte, manager of Le Cinéma du Côté des Auteurs, the film centre committed to helping first-time and/or low-budget filmmakers in La Friche La Belle de Mai, explains to Lonely Planet author Catherine Le Nevez.

What film activities take place at La Friche?
We cover every dimension of cinema – teaching, technical skills, acting and screenwriting. We also have programmes working in prisons, and art fairs and screenings. Residencies are long term as well as short term (one day to three weeks).

Do you have public screenings?
Yes, we try to have one screening a month (€5) covering a different theme. But we receive our funding from the government, meaning we don't know if we'll have enough money to continue the screenings. So far they have been a success – 80% to 90% full.

How do you see your organisation's role in cinema today?
The next revolution of cinema could be here (because of the creativity and technical ability of the centre's film-makers), but to make a revolution you need money now and Marseille is not 'la Provence' but 'la Province' – film is done in Paris. Our president, film-maker Robert Guédiguian, has put his back office here for artistic and social fights, but the money (the business end) is in Paris.

TRAILING LE CORBUSIER

Le Corbusier rewrote the architectural stylebook in southern France: track him down in Marseille (where he built the ground-breaking Unité d'Habitation), Cap Martin (where he had a studio) and Roquebrune (where he's buried).

It was the latter part of his life that saw Swiss-born Charles Édouard Jeanneret (1887–1965), alias Le Corbusier, turn to Provence. Of all his architectural achievements, it was the concrete apartment block he designed in Marseille that was the most revolutionary. Built between 1947 and 1952 as a low-cost housing project, the **Unitè d'Habitation** saw 337 apartments arranged inside an elongated block on stilts. Considered a coup by architects worldwide, the façade, communal corridors and rooftop terrace of the block has been protected as an historical monument since 1986. Apartments on the 7th and 8th floors function as a hotel (p105); the rest are private flats.

Le Corbusier frequently visited the coast from the 1930s, often staying with his architect friends, Irish Eileen Gray and Romanian-born Jean Badovici, in their 1920s seaside villa, **E-1027** (www .e1027.com), on Cap Martin. In 1938 Le Corbusier painted a trio of wall frescoes in E-1027, one of which featured three entangled women and offended Gray (a proclaimed lesbian) so much that she broke off her friendship with Le Corbusier and moved to Menton.

After WWII, Le Corbusier befriended Thomas Rebutato who ran L'Étoile de Mer, a neighbouring shack restaurant. He bought a plot of land from Rebutato and in 1951 created Le Cabanon, a cabin containing everything needed for holiday living in 13 sq metres, which he gave to his wife, Monégasque model Yvonne Gallis, as a birthday present. It remained their summer home until 1965 when Le Corbusier had a heart attack while swimming in the sea.

Future plans for Le Cabanon will see the site developed as a museum and architectural research centre, incorporating the cabin, L'Étoile de Mer (still owned by the Rebutato family) and E-1027 (inhabited by squatters from 1990 until 1999). The coastal footpath promenade Le Corbusier leads from Roquebrune-Cap Martin train station to the site; exit the station and bear left along the *sentier littoral* (coastal path; signposted 'Plage de Carnolés').

Le Corbusier is buried with his wife in section J of Roquebrune cemetery. His grave (he designed it before his death) is adorned by a cactus and the epitaph, painted in Le Corbusier's cursive hand on a small yellow, red and blue ceramic tile: *ici repose Charles Édouard Jeanneret (1887–1965)*.

tion of geometrical shapes and colours. This 'father of Op Art' went on to design the town hall in La Seyne-sur-Mer, near Toulon, and the stained-glass windows inside Port Grimaud's church.

Roquebrune's Vista Palace (see the boxed text, p289) is the other gawp-worthy piece of 1970s architecture.

CINEMA

Posing on the steps where many a silver-screen star has stood during the glitzy glam Festival International du Film (see the boxed text, p302) or viewing cinema personified on Cannes' bus-station wall (p301) are film-buff musts. To sense the grit of regional film-making, tour the film studios at Marseille's La Friche La Belle de Mai (see the boxed text, opposite).

One film studio at La Friche la Belle de Mai, Marseille, touts a 17m-high ceiling, making it among the highest sets in Europe.

History

With its spectacular light and subtle shadows, southern France was inspirational to cinema: the world's first motion picture by the Lumière brothers premiered in Château Lumière in La Ciotat in September 1895. The series of two-minute reels, entitled *L'Arrivée d'un Train en Gare de La Ciotat* (The Arrival of a Train at La Ciotat Station), made the audience leap out of their seats as the steam train rocketed forward. In March 1899 the brothers opened Eden Théâtre (p118) in La Ciotat.

French film flourished in the 1920s, Nice being catapulted to stardom by Hollywood director Rex Ingram, who bought the city's Victorine film studios in 1925 and transformed them overnight into the hub of European film-making.

A big name was Aubagne-born writer Marcel Pagnol, whose career kicked off in 1931 with *Marius*, the first part of his *Fanny* trilogy portraying prewar Marseille. Pagnol filmed *La Femme du Boulanger* (The Baker's Wife; 1938) in Castellet. These films launched the career of France's earliest silver-screen heroes, Toulon-born comic actor Raimu, alias Jules Auguste César Muraire (1883–1946), and 'horse face' Fernandel (1903–71), an honorary citizen of Carry-le-Rouet where he summered most years. Throughout his career Pagnol stuck to depicting what he knew best: Provence and its ordinary people.

Portraits of ordinary people dominated film until the 1950s when surrealist Jean Cocteau (1889–1963) eschewed realism in two masterpieces of cinematic fantasy: *La Belle et la Bête* (Beauty and the Beast; 1945) and *Orphée* (Orpheus; 1950). Both starred beautiful blonde-haired Vallauris-born actor Jean Marais (1914–98), who met Cocteau in 1937 and remained his lover until Cocteau's death in 1963. Find out more about the film-maker at Menton's Musée Jean Cocteau (p290).

Nouvelle Vague (New Wave) directors made films without big budgets, extravagant sets or big-name stars. Roger Vadim turned St-Tropez overnight into the hot spot to be with *Et Dieu Créa la Femme* (And God Created Woman; 1956) starring Brigitte Bardot. Several French classics filmed in the region followed, among them François Truffaut's *Les Mistons* (1958), filmed exclusively in Nîmes; Jacques Démy's *La Baie des Anges* (The Bay of Angels; 1962); Henri Decoin's *Masque de Fer* (Iron Mask; 1962), parts of which were filmed in Sospel; and Rohmer's *La Collectionneuse* (The Collectors; 1966), again shot in St-Tropez. In 1972 Truffaut filmed part of *La Nuit Américaine* (The American Night; 1972) in the Victorine studios, the Niçois hinterland and the Vésubie Valley.

Generous state subsidies to film-makers focused on costume dramas and heritage movies in the 1980s, prompting a renewed interest in Pagnol's great Provençal classics. Parts of Claude Berri's *Jean de Florette* and *Manon des Sources* were shot in the Massif de la Ste-Baume and in 1990 Yves Robert directed film versions of Pagnol's *La Gloire de Mon Père* (My Father's Glory) and *Le Château de Ma Mère* (My Mother's Castle). Big-name stars, slick production values and a strong sense of nostalgia were dominant motifs of the 1998 Hollywood box office hit *The Man in the Iron Mask* set on Île Ste-Marguerite near Cannes in the late 17th century.

LITERATURE
Courtly Love to Sadism

Lyric poems of courtly love, written solely in Occitan *langue d'oc* by troubadours, dominated medieval Provençal literature.

Provençal life featured in the works of Italian poet Petrarch (1304–74), exiled to Avignon in 1327 where he met Laura, to whom he dedicated his life's works. Petrarch lived in Fontaine de Vaucluse from 1337 to 1353, where he composed his song book *Canzonière* and wrote poems and letters about local shepherds, fishermen he met on the banks of the Sorgue and his pioneering ascent up Mont Ventoux. The village's Musée Pétrarque (p187) tells his life story.

Bellaud de la Bellaudière (1533–88), a Grasse native, wrote *Oeuvres et Rîmes* in Occitan. The literary landmark is a book of 160 sonnets drawing on influences by Petrarch and French epic writer Rabelais.

Cocteau's best-known novel, *Les Enfants Terribles* (1955), portrays the intellectual rebellion of the postwar era.

British novelist and travel writer Lawrence Durrell (1912–90) settled in Somières, near Nîmes, and dedicated the last 33 years of his literary career to writing about Provençal life.

TOP 10 FILMS STARRING PROVENCE

- *To Catch a Thief* (1956) Classic Hitchcock suspense starring Cary Grant and Grace Kelly.

- *Et Dieu Créa la Femme* (And God Created Woman; 1956) Roger Vadim's tale of the amorality of modern youth set in St-Tropez made a star out of Bardot and St-Tropez.

- *Le Gendarme de St-Tropez* (1964) Fast-paced, farcical and utterly French film in which an ambitious but incompetent police officer is transferred to St-Tropez and makes it his mission to crack down on the local nudists. Meanwhile, daughter Nicole fibs her way into high society by pretending her dad's a high-rolling yacht owner.

- *Herbie goes to Monte Carlo* (1977) Disney lovable starring Herbie the Volkswagen Beetle and his race to Monte Carlo to take part in the Monte Carlo Rally (p395).

- *Taxi 3* (2003) Comedy guaranteed to raise a giggle; filmed and set in Marseille.

- *Swimming Pool* (2002) A dispirited middle-aged English novelist seeks repose and inspiration in the Luberon at the summerhouse of her publisher, only for the latter's high-spirited, sexy and very French daughter to show up. Directed by François Ozon.

- *The Statement* (2004) Norman Jewison film set in Vichy France and starring Michael Caine; shot on location in Marseille and in the village of Ste-Anne d'Evenos, northwest of Toulon.

- *Brice de Nice* (2005) Hilarious take of cult surfing movie *Point Break* in which surfing dude and poseur Brice, aka charismatic French comic actor Jean Dujardin, waits for *sa vague* (his wave) to come in waveless Nice (great shots of the town).

- *A Good Year* (2006) Ridley Scott's adaptation of the Peter Mayle novel, filmed at Château La Canorgue in Bonnieux (p219); London financier May Skinner inherits his uncle's wine-producing chateau in the Luberon and, all too predictably, falls in love with the place after hard-heartedly vowing to sell it for the cash.

- *French Bean* (Bean II; 2007) The lovable Mini Cooper–mad, teddy bear–loving buffoon, Mr Bean, holidays on the Côte d'Azur and somehow gets his video diary entered into the Cannes film festival. The second, and allegedly last, Bean movie.

In 1555 the philosopher and visionary writer from St-Rémy de Provence, Nostradamus (1503–66), published (in Latin) his prophetic *Centuries* in Salon de Provence, where he lived until his death (from gout, as he had predicted). Find out why the papal authorities banned his work as blasphemous at Salon de Provence's Maison de Nostradamus (p121).

The 17th-century *grand siècle* yielded Nicolas Saboly's the *Noëls Provençaux*, poems encapsulating a nativity scene, the pious tone typical of the strait-laced fervour dominating baroque Provençal literature.

Mistral to Mayle

The 19th century witnessed a revival in Provençal literature, thanks to Frédéric Mistral (1830–1914), the only minority-language writer so far to be awarded a Nobel Prize for Literature (1904). A native of Maillane, Mistral's passion for Provence and its culture, history and language was awakened by his Avignon tutor Joseph Roumanille (1818–91), who published *Li Margarideto* in 1847. In 1851 Mistral began his most momentous work, *Mirèio*. Three years later Le Félibrige was founded by seven young Provençal poets who pledged to revive Provençal and codify the language's orthography.

Between 1878 and 1886 Mistral's most influential work on Provençal culture was published, the monumental *Trésor du Félibrige*. The 1890s saw Le Félibrige popularise his work with the opening of the Museon Arlaten (p141) and the publication of the *L'Aïoli* journal.

Imagist poet Ezra Pound took traditional Provençal songs and troubadour ballads and adapted them to suit modern tastes in his two poetry collections, *Provença* (1910) and *Cantos* (1919).

Another outstanding Provençal writer was Nîmes-born Alphonse Daudet (1840–97) who wrote *Lettres de Mon Moulin* (Letters from My Windmill; 1869) from a windmill, a replica of which can be visited (p193) in Fontvieille.

Parisian novelist Émile Zola (1840–1902) lived in Aix-en-Provence from the age of three to 18. Zola aimed to convert novel writing from an art to a science by the application of experimentation – a theory that, though naive, produced powerful works. Aix-en-Provence is evoked in *La Conquête de Plassans* (1874), and his friendship with Cézanne is the focus of *L'Oeuvre* (The Masterpiece; 1886).

Early-20th-century Provençal literature is dominated by writers depicting their homeland. Jean Giono (1895–1970) from Manosque blended myth with reality in novels that remain a celebration of the Provençal Alps and their people.

Surrealism was expressed by Jean Cocteau (1889–1963), French poet and film-maker who ran away from home to the Côte d'Azur at the age of 15, returned in 1924 and is buried in Menton. Colette (1873–1954), who thoroughly enjoyed tweaking the nose of conventional readers with titillating novels that detailed the amorous exploits of such heroines as the schoolgirl Claudine, lived in St-Tropez from 1927 until 1938. *La Naissance du Jour* evokes an unspoilt St-Tropez.

The post-WWII years saw the existentialist literary movement develop around Jean-Paul Sartre (1905–80), Simone de Beauvoir (1908–86) and Albert Camus (1913–60). The latter moved to Lourmarin (where he is buried) in 1957; he started his unfinished autobiographical novel *Le Premier Homme* (The First Man) there. The manuscript was found in the car wreckage when the Algerian-born writer – son of an illiterate mother – died in a car accident three years later.

Writers who settled in the region in the latter part of their careers include Lawrence Durrell, Dirk Bogarde, James Baldwin, Anthony Burgess and Peter Mayle. Provence-inspired novels written by foreign writers are listed at the start of regional chapters.

MUSIC

Contemporary music is pretty much a one-stop shop, immigrant life in Marseille *banlieue* (suburbs) proving the inspiration behind a diverse and influential scene enjoyed by an audience far further flung than the beat-hot port city.

The hip-hop lyrics of the 1991 smash-hit first album, *de la Planète Mars* ('from Planet Mars', Mars being short for Marseille) by rapping supergroup IAM – France's best-known rap group from Marseille – nudged rap into the mainstream. A decade on, the city's music scene has transcended its rap roots. 'It has exploded, in all styles. Marseille is a rich place for music; it's not pigeonholed into rap and hip-hop any more', says Stéphane Galland, music director of alternative Marseillais radio station, **Radio Grenouille** (Radio Frog; www .grenouille888.org in French), on air 24/7 since 1981 and famed across France for broadcasting tomorrow's music. Ten to 15 demo CDs land on Stéphane's

Sidebar notes (left margin)

Mistral's epic poem *Mirèio* (1859) tells the story of a beauty who flees to Stes-Maries de la Mer when her parents forbid her to marry her true love, only to die of a broken heart on the beach.

Daudet is best remembered for his comic novels evoking small-town Tarascon through the eyes of antihero Tartarin: his *Tartarin de Tarascon* trilogy was published between 1872 and 1890.

Government funded and wholly independent, with no on-air advertising, Radio Grenouille has a full-time staff of 12 assisted by 70 volunteers and a daily audience of around 60,000. Tune in on 88.8FM.

DANCE ROOTS

The *farandole* is a Provençal dance, performed at the close of village festivals in and around Arles since the Middle Ages. Men and women take their partner by the hand or remain linked with a cord or handkerchief as they briskly jig, accompanied by a tambourine and *galoubet* (shrill flute with three holes).

STÉPHANE GALLAND: TOP 10 PLAYLIST

Asked who his favourite Marseille artists were by Lonely Planet's Catherine Le Nevez, Stéphane Galland revealed his top 10 bands. And his hot tips on tomorrow's sounds to listen for: Anais, a solo female artist singing in the melodic Chanson Française style; new pop-rock outfit, Heidi; and Rosa, a band playing 'jazz-rock-contemporary music with energy and groove', which recorded its first album in 2006.

- **Alif Tree** (http://alif.tree.free.fr in French) Down-tempo, electronic music; very moody, cinematic sound.
- **Cheb Mami** (www.chebmami.net) and **Cheb Khaled** (http://khaled-lesite.artistes.universalmusic.fr in French) Rai solo artists internationally well known.
- **David Walters** (www.davidwalters.fr) Very fresh, Marseille-based artist from France and the West Indies. Sound: world-electro incorporating lots of instruments like drums and guitar. Presents weekly mix on-air for Radio Grenouille.
- **Dupain** 'Trad-innovation' style. First album exclusively in Occitan, subsequent albums a mix of French and Occitan featuring work songs and lyrics from political poets; one of the best bands to see live.
- **IAM** (www.iam.tm.fr in French) Symbolic Marseillais hip-hop outfit, active for more than 15 years.
- **Jack de Marseille** (http://w4-web160.nordnet.fr) One of Europe's top DJs. Initiated electronic music scene in Marseille 15 years ago and formed the record label Wicked Music. Returned to Marseille in 2004 after performing club raves and festivals worldwide.
- **Kabbalah** Modern yet traditional five-person Jewish band, formed in 2003 and blending jazz, contemporary Mediterranean folk and klezmer (traditional Eastern European music).
- **Massilia Sound Systeme** (www.massilia-soundsystem.com in French) Legendary reggae band incorporating a Marseille accent with Provençal and typical Marseillais slang that 'Parisians often can't understand. Another legend from the same generation and genre is Jo Corbeau'.
- **Raphael Imbert** Saxophonist and composer playing classic jazz and sacred music; listen out for him solo and as part of the Newtopia Quintet.
- **Troublemaker** Electro-funk trio comprising Lionel Corsini aka DJ Oil (himself the son of a famous DJ), Arnaud Taillefer and Fred Berthet; present in weekly mix on-air on Radio Grenouille.

---

desk every day, not to mention a clutch of CDs from record labels, all angling for air space. Postlucky break, many artists return to the Grenouille studios to jam live on the station that launched them.

Massilia Sound Systeme is another Marseille-born band: 'They initiated reggae in France,' explains Stéphane, 'using a south-of-France sound as a vehicle for their own identity.' The Rub a Dub trio is involved in dozens of side projects too: Moussu-T performs blues, calypso, south of France and acoustic music and heads up **Moussu-T e lei jouvants** (http://moussut.ohaime.com in French), a trio that draws on the musical melting pot of 1930s Marseille – a mix of traditional Provençal, local operettas and imported black music – for inspiration. Its latest album, *Foreover Polida* (2006), promises to be as huge as its previous, *Mademoiselle Marseille* (2005).

In world music, 20-something Iranian percussionist Bijan Chemirani stuns with rhythmic playing of the *zarb* (Persian goblet drum), and his debut solo album *Eos* (2002) is hot. Cheb Khaled, Cheb Aïssa and Cheb Mami – all from the same multicultural portside city – have contributed hugely to the development of Algerian rai. 'You can't do rai without passing through Marseille', says Stéphane (whose music knowledge is encyclopedic). 'Marseille is a mecca, but the scene is underground, very community based, in small, low-budget venues, not very visible. You'll always hear guys playing it in cars

For a handle on performing arts in the region, surf ARACDE, the Agence Régionale des Arts du Spectacle (Regional Agency for Performing Arts) at http://arcade-paca.com.

on the streets, though,' he adds. And on jazz: 'Marseille has a lot of very good jazz – traditional, modern, electro jazz… the whole spectrum.'

Traditional Provençal chants form the root of the powerful percussion-accompanied polyphony sung by Lo Còr de la Plana, a six-voice male choir born in 2001 in La Plaine, Marseille. Its album *Chants à Danser*, which was planned for release in 2007, is one to buy.

DANCE

The Centre Chorégraphique National (CNN; see the boxed text, p129) in Aix-en-Provence, one of 21 national choreographic centres in France, drives contemporary dance. At its front end is **Ballet Preljocaj** (www.preljocaj.org) and French-Albanian-born choreographer, Angelin Preljocaj (b 1957), known for pushing dance to its limits. Ballet Preljocaj and the CNN are deemed the likely benefactors of additional funding created by the decision of Aix city mayor, Maryse Joissans-Masini, in late 2005 to scrap Aix-en-Provence's annual dance festival, Danse à Aix, after 29 years. As a longtime platform for the discovery of new talent and innovation, the festival's loss was a major blow to contemporary dance; Avignon's annual dance festival, **Les Hivernales** (www.hivernales-avignon.com) hosted each February by Hivernales (the other big choreography centre in the region) provides little consolation.

As part of its local awareness dance programme, Ballet Preljocaj occasionally performs on public squares and hosts open rehearsals, dance workshops and evening *apéritif-danse* events. See www.preljocaj.org for details.

ELIZABETH LEWIS: TOP 10 PLAYLIST

Vastly different kettle of fish, yes, but on the Riviera, it is Nice that is music queen. Touting a great range of live-music venues, including a rash of Brit-style bars where bands play most nights, it is the hot spot to party. Nicola Williams caught up with former Kiss FM DJ and Riviera Radio presenter, Elizabeth Lewis, at Monaco's Star 'n Bars to find out which gigs she looks out for in her adopted hometown, Nice.

'**Scott Allen**, a black guy from America who sings soul, funk and jazz; and **Ronnie Rae Junior** (www.raefamilyjazz.com), a Scottish jazz-keyboard player from a big Scottish musical dynasty. Ronnie Rae Senior is a very well-known bass player in Scotland, one of the top bass players in Britain in fact. Then there's **Donal Corcoran**, an Irish singer and songwriter, very talented, a lovely charismatic man, who writes the most amazing songs that already sound like hits (see www.myspace.com).

'The **Boogie Men** are good; that's my mate Brice. They do swing, jazz and play at Wayne's new place, La Cave (see the boxed text, p324), in Tourettes-sur-Loup. Wayne plays drums with them, although they work with other drummers too. If you prefer heavy rock, Aerosmith/Rolling Stones–style, you need to see **The Running Birds**. They're Italian, but sing in English. They're heavier, they've got the hair.

'The **Philip Jones Orchestra**: Phil's an American who taught me how to busk; he's a very accomplished musician who plays double bass and guitar. He tends to do more private parties these days, on yachts etc, although you still occasionally hear him on cours Saleya. For true jazz, **Jean-Marc Jafet**, a bass player, is extremely good and for a more eclectic, folky, Bob Dylanish–REM–Rolling Stones mix, there's **Joe Danger** (http://joe.danger.free.fr). He plays in bars, is Austrian but sounds like he's from east London.

'Another excellent local band is **Medi and the Medicine Men** (www.mediandthemedicineshow .com). Medi is the (multi-instrumentalist) figurehead and has a record deal; Dave Stewart from the Eurythmics took him under his wing and produced his album (*Medi and the Medicine Show;* 2006). He works mainly in Paris but comes to Nice from time to time. He's the local star – a beautiful-looking man (LP: his website says he looks like Jesus), only about 27.

'**Anthony Caligagan** (www.caligagan.com), an Afro-Swede with Bob Marley dreadlocks, is very enjoyable. He sings reggae.

'And then there's **Fat Cat**, a cross between Barry White and Marvin Gaye; he's even recorded a Barry White tribute album.'

WATCH OUT

... for these young, vibrant, dead-exciting contemporary dance companies:

Al Masîra (http://almasira.free.fr in French) French-Arabic fusion of contemporary and oriental dance from Marseille, with choreography by dancer Virginie Recolin.

Compagnie Lézards Bleus Apt-based company known for its architectural choreography, vertical dance performances being staged on building façades.

Kubilai Khan Investigations (www.kubilai-khan-investigations.com) Marseillais mixed-media urban dance company; heavy accent on hip-hop, photography and video-art.

Onstap (www.onstap.com) *Percussions corporelles* (body percussion; step) is the beat of this Avignon company who clap out their dance rhythm with their feet, on thighs etc.

Pascal Montrouge (www.pascalmontrouge.fr) Company split between Hyères (catch a performance at Villa Noailles) and Réunion Island, headed by Pascal Montrouge.

Provence's innovative spirit in contemporary dance echoes the role France played in the development of 19th-century classical ballet – until the centre for innovation shifted to Russia in 1847, taking France's leading talent, Marius Petipa (1818–1910), a native of Marseille, with it. The **Ballet National de Marseille** (www.ballet-de-marseille.com) continues in a classical vein today.

Environment

THE LAND

Provence and the Côte d'Azur – an elongated oval in southeast France – is bordered by the southern Alps (to the northeast), which form a natural frontier with Italy, and by the River Rhône to the west. The Grand Rhône (east) and Petit Rhône (west) form the delta of the Rhône, a triangular alluvial plain called the Camargue.

The Mediterranean Sea washes the region's southern boundary – a 250-odd-km coastline (Côte d'Azur in French, French Riviera in English) stretching from Marseille to Menton. Offshore lie several islands: the Îles du Frioul (Marseille), the Îles des Embiez (Toulon) and the Îles de Lérins (Cannes). The most southern, the Îles d'Hyères (Hyères), are inhabited. A chain of calcareous rocks, Les Calanques, forms the coastline around Marseille, and France's highest cliff (406m) crowns Cap Canaille in nearby Cassis.

Three mountain ranges cut off the coast from the vast interior: the red volcanic Massif de l'Estérel, the limestone Massif des Maures and the foothills of the Alps north of Nice. Hills dominate the interior, peaking with stone-capped Mont Ventoux (1912m). Lower-lying ranges include (west to east) the Alpilles, Montagne Ste-Victoire, Massif Ste-Baume, the Vaucluse hills and the Luberon. Further east is the Gorges du Verdon, Europe's largest and most spectacular canyon.

WILDLIFE
Animals

The Camargue shelters 400 land and water birds including the kingfisher, bee-eater, stork, shelduck, white egret, purple heron and more than 160 migratory species. It is also home to native horse and bull populations, and 10% of the world's greater flamingos (see the boxed text, p137).

Port-Cros is a key autumn stopover for migratory birds, the puffin, ash-grey shearwater and yelkouan shearwater among the many species in its diverse seabird population.

Nowhere do more mammals romp than in the Parc National du Mercantour (p248), home to 8000 chamois (mountain antelopes) with their dark-striped heads, 1100 *bouquetin* (Alpine ibex) and the mouflon, which hangs out on stony sunlit scree slopes in the mountains. At higher altitudes the alpine chough – a type of crow with black plumage, red feet and a yellow beak (that appears white from a distance) – can be seen. Other treats include

---

THE MUD-EATING MISTRAL

Folklore claims it can drive people crazy. Its namesake, Provençal poet Frédéric Mistral, cursed it. And peasants in their dried-out fields dubbed the damaging wind *mange fange* (*manjo fango* in Provençal), meaning 'mud eater'.

The legendary mistral, a cold, dry northwesterly wind, whips across Provence for several days at a time. Its furious gusts, reaching over 100km/h, destroy crops, rip off roofs, dry the land and drive tempers round the bend. It chills the bones for 100 days a year and is at its fiercest in winter and spring.

The mistral's intense and relentless rage is caused by high atmospheric pressure over central France, between the Alps and the Pyrenees, which is then blown southwards through the funnel of the narrow Rhône Valley to an area of low pressure over the Mediterranean Sea. On the upside, skies are blue and clear of clouds when the mistral is in town.

TOP 10: NATURE WATCH

Precious opportunities to peer close-up at Mediterranean wildlife:

- Camargue 4WD safari tours (p138) – see bulls, horses, flamingos and other typical Camargue fauna roam wild, from the back of a jeep.
- Cetacean-spotting boat trips (Villefranche-sur-Mer, p281) – watch dolphins leap from the Med; bring binoculars and plenty of luck.
- Half-day forest walks – discover chestnuts, learn how cork is harvested (see the boxed text, p78) or trace transhumant trails with **Conservatoire du Patrimoine et du Traditions du Freinet** (☎ 04 94 43 08 57; www.conservatoiredufreinet.org; Chapelle St-Jean, place de la Mairie, La Garde Freinet).
- Var nature walks – tourist offices in the Var (see p356) take bookings for balades nature accompagnées (adult/under 10yr €5 to €9/free). Themes include salt-pan bird-watching; man, plants and health; orchids; the forest and its mushrooms; 'fire' plants; cicadas and insects; mimosas and exotic plants. See www.webvds.com/sorties in French for info.
- Kayaking and canoeing river expeditions – paddle through peaceful waters and observe river wildlife at play along the Petit Rhône (p137), the Sorgue (p187), the River Gard (p200) and the Ubaye (p250).
- Wildlife photography – Fréderic Larrey and Thomas Roger of **Regard du Vivant** (☎ 06 10 57 17 11; www.regard-du-vivant.fr; 26 blvd Henri Fabre, Marseillle) run nature-photography workshops (€200/day), bird-watching treks (p136) and nine-hour dolphin-observation expeditions (€70 for adults and €55 for children 7 to 12 years old).
- Underwater nature trails (Domaine du Rayol, p364; Île de Port-Cros, p369; La Londe, see the boxed text, p373; Parc Régional Marin de la Côte Bleue, p119) – view underwater marine flora through a snorkeller's mask.
- Tortoise sanctuary – view the rare Hermann tortoise at Village des Tortues (see the boxed text, p362).
- Vulture culture (see the boxed text, p236) – spot the griffon vulture during half-day vulture treks, departing from Castellane and Rougon in the Gorges du Verdon.
- Wolf-watching – learn how man is learning to live with the wolf and watch wolves roam wild at **Wolf Watch at Alpha** (☎ 04 93 02 33 69; www.alpha-loup.com; Le Boréon, St-Martin de Vésubie) in the Mercantour.

the ermine, the green lizard, the viper, the rare Alexanor butterfly and 19 of Europe's 29 bat species.

ENDANGERED SPECIES

The Hermann tortoise (see the boxed text, p362), a yellow-and-black creature once indigenous to Mediterranean Europe, is now found only in the Massif des Maures (and Corsica). Forest fires threaten it.

The Bonnelli eagle swoops above Les Calanques (p115) and 40 pairs of golden eagles nest in the Mercantour alongside the buzzard and short-toed eagle. The griffon vulture and the bearded vulture, with its unsavoury bone-breaking habits and awe-inspiring wing span of 3m, only remain in the wild thanks to reintroduction programmes instigated in protected areas such as the Gorges du Verdon and the Parc National du Mercantour.

The Parc National de Port-Cros (p369) safeguards the monk seal, a 3m-long mammal in danger of extinction due to its natural food supply (of plaice, mackerel and flounder) being gobbled up by intensive fishing and pollution.

To sheep farmers' horror, wolves roam the Parc National du Mercantour.

SIZE DOESN'T MATTERS FOR GARDENERS   Louisa Jones

The Riviera's legendary *belle époque* gardens are essential viewing for garden-lovers visiting southern France.

But as long-standing gardening authority and best-selling author Louisa Jones told Nicola Williams, it is the smaller, lesser-known gardens in western Provence where the real horticultural excitement is.

What is the difference between gardens in Provence and on the Riviera?
The agricultural roots are the same but what is going on now is quite different. Most Northern Mediterranean gardens were working farms and everything was built and planted for practical reasons, to provide shade, produce food… When I started writing about this in the 1970s, people told me there were no gardens in Provence because they meant summer floral gardens, ornamental gardens, mixed borders…

Gardens in western Provence are also very mineral. Bare rock and stone construction lend themselves to what people think of today as a new kind of land art – involving the landscape in the garden. There is also a lot of unbuilt space and many different kinds of landscapes in a very small area, giving garden designers the opportunity to do very original and interesting gardens involving the landscape. You can't really do that on the Riviera. It's very rare.

Why not?
Because there's hardly any landscape left! The gardens are completely enclosed, for security reasons and because there is such ugly stuff built everywhere.

When you say 'western Provence', where exactly do you mean?
The two fashionable areas are the Luberon and the Alpilles, but they're now filling up and people who really want to be away from others are going further out. [Jones herself lives well away from the madding crowds in a village in northwestern Provence.]

The Var is beginning to develop as a garden area too – not St-Tropez which is very fashionable as it always is: I mean back-country Var.

What are the current trends in contemporary garden design?
One very important aspect of gardens in Provence is how foreground connects to distant landscape. A traditional garden will have a foreground, then the view, but nothing in between. But here, there are people who've planted a gradually modulated progression – a whole sequence of framing and partial framing – in the middle ground.

What's going on here is much more art gardening: architecture, sculpture, land art, an interest in living space and form whether it's the structure of trees or of landscape with terracing.

Which gardens best reflect these trends?
One of the best is the Garden of the Alchemist (alchemy gardens and botanic gardens of magic plants designed by Arnaud Maurières and Eric Ossart, two of France's most original young designers; p193).

Plants

Take a springtime stroll along any of the 600km of walking trails in the Parc National du Mercantour and you'll see dozens of different species of plants. Particularly enchanting are the 63 types of orchids, 30 endemic plants and 200 rare species: wild blueberry bushes, rhododendrons, fuchsias and geraniums are abundant.

Rare or threatened species visible during coastal walks in the Parc National du Port-Cros include the *ail petit moly,* a type of garlic that sprouts in early autumn, flowers in January and lingers until spring – look for six white petals. The Powis Castle artemisia, typical to stony, sun-baked soils, is identified by its lacy, silver grey leaves and small yellow flowers. Jupiter's beard, a cloverlike plant resistant to sea spray, thrives on the coastline where it breaks out in a riot of small white flowers in spring.

Forest covers 40% of the region; the most heavily forested areas (predominantly oak and pine) are northeastern Provence and the Var. Cork oak (see the boxed text, p78) and chestnut trees dominate the Massif des Maures;

Visit an organic farm in Provence and chat with the local farmer about organic farming: a list of *fermes bio* welcoming visitors is online at www .bio-provence.org (in French).

Another is **Aux Fleurs de l'Eau** (☎ 04 90 95 85 02; Quartier Cassoulen, rte de St-Rémy) in Graveson. It was made by a professional builder who used to help farmers lay out fields. Agriculture declining as it is, he used his rock-lifting machinery to create a huge rockery garden in his back yard and it has turned into a really interesting garden. It is a water garden essentially, a grass-roots project done with great care and a very good eye. The planting was done by **Braun Nurseries** (☎ 04 90 92 89 56; pepbraun@aol.com; 1016 rte de St-Rémy, Eyragues) so it's sophisticated, interesting planting.

There's also a brand-new garden, a **Roman garden** (Jardin Romain; ☎ 04 90 22 00 22; www.jardin -romain.fr; adult/under 7yr €3/free; ☿ 10am-12.30pm & 3-7pm Easter-Sep, noon-4pm Mon-Fri, 10am-4pm Sat & Sun Oct-Easter), in Caumont-sur-Durance, 15km southeast of Avignon, which is very interesting (gardens evoking Roman gods, labyrinth, Roman games); it is designed around Roman archaeological digs found quite recently.

And the famous Riviera gardens?
They are all very different, all very historic but there's little contemporary creation. They're living monuments in a sense. There is a definite English influence, which is one reason why they are very plant-orientated.

One of my favourites is Jardins de la Serre de la Madone (see the boxed text, p293). Lawrence Johnston was a genius and he did something on the Riviera he didn't do at all in his English garden, which was take really great advantage of the site, the setting…And that was done in the 1920s and 1930s.

Clos du Peyronnet (see the boxed text, p293) is one of the best gardens on the Riviera. It is very much a live garden. The owner is heavily involved and keeps an avid interest in the garden. It is not just a monument; it is an ongoing project.

What are the big names in Provençal garden design?
There are two: landscape architect **Michel Semini** (☎ 04 90 72 38 50; rue St-Frusquin, Goult) whose work can be seen at the **Château de Brantes** (☎ 04 90 39 11 73; www.jardinez.com/jardindebrantes; Sorgues; adult/under 14yr €5/free; ☿ by appointment 10am-noon & 2-6pm Easter-early Nov) in Sorgues, 12km north of Avignon; and **Dominique Lafourcade** (☎ 04 90 92 10 14; www.architecture-lafourcade.com; 10 blvd Victor Hugo, St-Rémy de Provence), a family enterprise; she does the gardens and her husband and stepson restore old homes. Both designers are very deeply rooted in the almost-Roman tradition, but at the same time they're very playful, inventive and imaginative.

Canadian garden critic Louisa Jones (www.gardeninprovence.com/louisajones) has lived in Provence since 1975. She has written 21 books on gardens (in English and French), including The French Country Garden (2000), Gardens of the French Riviera (2001), Provence Harvest (2005) and most recently New Gardens of Provence (2006), in which she examines current gardening trends. Her six-day 'Garden Week in Provence', the third week in April (€3800 incl seven nights' accommodation at Avignon's Hôtel de la Mirande; p165), takes a small group of garden lovers around gardens in Provence no one else can take them to. A new updated itinerary is available each year in November; email her at ljones@wanadoo.fr.

maritime, Aleppo and umbrella pines provide shade along the coast; and plane trees stud village squares.

Maquis is a vegetation whose low, dense shrubs provide many of the spices used in Provençal cooking. Garrigue is typified by aromatic Mediterranean plants such as juniper, broom and fern growing on predominantly chalky soil.

NATIONAL & REGIONAL PARKS
Two national parks protect 2.6% of the region and another 16% of the region is protected to a lesser degree by three *parcs naturals régionaux*. Nature reserves offer protection of sorts, as do the three Unesco-backed *réserves de biosphère* (biosphere reserves) – the Camargue, Luberon and Mont Ventoux.

Parks and reserves strive to maintain local ecosystems: in the Parc Régional Marin de la Côte Bleue, artificial reefs were submerged in the sea in the 1980s to encourage sea life to grow and prevent illegal fishing.

Precious pockets of coast fall within the realm of the **Conservatoire du Littoral** (Coastal Protection Agency; ☎ 05 46 84 72 50; www.conservatoire-du-littoral.fr; Corderie Royale, BP 13 7, F-17306 Rochefort Cedex), an association that acquires threatened natural areas by the sea to restore, rejuvenate and protect.

Among the Conservatoire's rich pageant of *espaces naturels protégés* (protected natural areas) are the Archipel de Riou, which is a cluster of uninhabited limestone islands offshore from Marseille, sheltering 30% of France's cory's shearwater population; the *calanques*-laced Presqu'île de Port-Miou; the Côte Bleue (p119); a twinset of wildlife-rich capes (Cap Lardier and Cap Taillat; p352) on the St-Tropez peninsula and the former salt marshes on La Capte in Hyères (p372). There's also the red-rock Massif de l'Estérel (p328); Corniche des Maures (p364), which is neighboured

NATIONAL & REGIONAL PARKS

Park	Features	Activities	Best Time to Visit	Page Ref
Parc National du Mercantour (1979; 685 sq km)	majestic 3000m-plus peaks, uninhabited valleys; mouflon, chamois, ibex, wolves, eagles & vultures	skiing (alpine), white-water sports, mountain biking, walking & donkey trekking	spring, summer & winter	p248
Parc National de Port-Cros (1963; 7 sq km plus 13 sq km of water)	island marine park; puffins, shearwaters & migratory birds	snorkelling, bird-watching, swimming, gentle strolling & sunbathing	summer (water activities) & autumn (bird-watching)	p369
Parc Naturel Régional du Verdon (1997; 1769.6 sq km)	Europe's most spectacular canyon, 5 green-water lakes & prealpine massifs; griffon vultures	white-water sports, swimming, horse riding, walking & cycling	summer	p234
Parc Naturel Régional du Luberon (1977; 1650 sq km)	hilltop villages & limestone gorges; eagles, Egyptian vultures & European greater horned owls	walking, cycling, rock climbing & paragliding	spring, late summer & autumn	p218
Parc Naturel Régional de Camargue (1970; 863 sq km)	paddy fields, salt pans & marshes; horses, bulls, boars, flamingos, egrets & herons	horse riding, cycling, bird-watching, botany & walking	spring & autumn	p136
Parc Régional Marin de la Côte Bleue (1983; 2.95 sq km)	marine reserve protecting Cap Couronne & surrounding waters; marine flora & fauna	guided snorkelling expeditions & boat tours	spring & summer	p119
Réserve Géologique de Haute-Provence (1900 sq km)	geological reserve; 185-million-year-old fossilised ichthyosaur skeleton & fossils from 300-million-year-old tropical forests	geology & walking	year-round	p241
Réserve de Biosphère du Mont Ventoux (1990; 810 sq km)	1912m-high mountain; 60 rare flora species, Lebanese cedars, mouflon & chamois	cycling, walking, skiing & snowboarding	spring & summer (cycling & walking) & winter (skiing)	p180

RENDEZ-VOUS AUX JARDINS

For four days in early June dozens of exceptional private gardens, otherwise inaccessible, welcome visitors, among them **La Chèvre d'Or** (www.lachevredor.com), lovingly created with the help of English botanist Basil Leng in Biot in 1950. Find a complete garden list at www.rendezvous auxjardins.culture.fr.

Year-round, Nice-based **Société Centrale d'Agriculture et d'Horticulture de Nice et des Alpes-Maritimes** (☎ 04 93 86 58 44; http://perso.orange.fr/scanice/index.htm; 113 promenade des Anglais; visits €4-10) organises visits to some superb, lesser-known gardens, including Dirk Bogarde's former garden–olive grove in Châteauneuf du Grasse and a private garden designed by another of the region's top garden designers, Cabris-based **Jean Mus** (www.jeanmus.com).

La Pomme d'Ambre (☎ 04 94 53 25 47; www.gardeninprovence.com; impasse ancienne rte d'Italie, La Tour de Mare, Fréjus; d incl breakfast €90; ⏰ mid-Sep–mid-Jul; ✖) is a *chambre d'hôte* with gardening and botany library, a luxuriant Riviera garden and half-day gardening workshops (€95 per person).

---

by Domaine du Rayol (p364); and several soggy chunks of the Camargue (p133).

ENVIRONMENTAL ISSUES

Forest fires are the hottest issue: 3000 fires destroy 150 sq km of forest a year, eight out of 10 being caused by careless day-trippers or arsonists seeking to get licences to build on the damaged lands. A concerted fire-prevention effort by local authorities in the 1990s paid off in the early years of the new millennium (the number of forest fires fell by 45%), but it was back to square one in 2003 when a freakishly hot summer sparked off the worst fires for 15 years: 2500 hectares sizzled. Only 8.5% of forests in Provence are protected; 70% are privately owned.

Provence has a pivotal role to play in the world quest to develop fusion power: Cadarache, 40km northeast of Aix-en-Provence, is the chosen hot spot for a thermonuclear experimental reactor. Assuming it succeeds, the ambitious US$5 billion engineering project between the EU, the USA, China and Japan will revolutionise the production of world power. Unlike conventional nuclear power plants, fusion reactors produce energy through the fusion of light atom nuclei and produce dramatically less radioactive waste. The cleaner, new-generation reactor in Cadarache will start churning out energy in 2014.

Marine life between Toulon and Menton is being choked by *Caulerpa taxifolia*, a pea green seaweed that starves native flora of sunlight; originating in the Pacific it's been found in the Med since 1984.

RESPONSIBLE TRAVEL

Training rather than flying to Provence scores instant Brownie points in the campaign to limit global warming; see p418 for more on climate change

---

BLUE FLAG BEACHES

No green label says more about a beach than the **Blue Flag** (www.blueflag.org), a recommendation of quality awarded to clean, safe and well-maintained beaches, ports and marinas Europe-wide. Clean bathing water, sanitary facilities and litter bins are among criteria needed to fly a Blue Flag.

Beaches clean enough to do so for the 2006 season (beaches are reassessed seasonally) included those in Antibes, Cap d'Ail, Cavalière, Ste-Maxime, Six Four les Plages, La Londe les Maures, Hyères, Plage de Gigaro in La Croix Valmer and Le Lavandou. Of the 92 beaches in Bouches du Rhône, just seven – in Port de Bouc, Fos-sur-Mer and Martigues – scored a Blue Flag.

Beaches in Marseille, Nice and St-Tropez haven't been flagged for years.

and travel. Within the region, shopping at markets, roadside stalls and farms rather than supermarkets is environmentally responsible.

Otherwise, don't litter; minimise waste; don't use detergents or toothpaste, even if they are biodegradable, in or near watercourses; stick to designated walking paths; and obey the 'no dogs, tents and motorised vehicles' rule in national parks.

THE CORK HARVESTER   Nicola Williams

Call me old-fashioned but there's a definite appeal to watching a man wield an axe. Or maybe it had more to do with the earthy good looks and gentle humour of forest technician Fabien Tamboloni, whose unreserved passion for, and extraordinary ease in, the forest had us all spellbound.

'I grew up in the forest, in the Jura, not far from Switzerland. The forest is my home,' he explained, adding: 'for me this is not a tree, it's a plane tree' pointing to the *platane* we were standing under on a village square in La Garde Freinet. Born-and-bred forest stock, at home in Collobrières today, Fabien leads guided hikes in the chestnut- and cork-rich forests around La Garde Freinet for the Conservatoire du Patrimoine (p362). When he's not captivating cork-curious minds with his axe-chopping, cork-harvesting prowess, he is a tree surgeon and researcher at an experimental plantation for France's Centre de Formation Professionnelle Forestière (www .cfpf.prg in French). Introductions done, the long-haired 30-something naturalist with well-used walking boots and a hole in his trousers (don't ask where) lopped his Catalan axe, straight blade protected by pea green felt, over his shoulder and off we strode up the street, around the corner and 'gosh, here already', into the forest.

Cork-oak *(chêne-liège)* trees have grown in the western Mediterranean basin for 60 million years, but it was not until the 17th century when a Benedictine monk called Dom Pérignon started bottling sparkling wine in glass that a cork industry emerged. Cutting out cylindrical wedges from the tree's honeycomb-textured bark – cork – and stuffing them in the bottles was quickly found to be the best means of conserving wine.

'Cork is impermeable, lightweight, soft and a great thermal insulator. More importantly, it protects the tree against sun and fire; it doesn't burn,' says Fabien, quick to explain that a cork-oak tree – once stripped of its bark – is unprotected from fire for two years. In tracts of forest affected by fire, trunks are charred black but the tree lives.

Harvesting cork is a delicate business. It is only allowed mid-June to mid-August when the tree is physiologically active. The bark must be at least 3cm thick, making the tree a minimum of 40 to 60 years old. One wrong move and *la mère* (the mother), the amber-coloured layer beneath the cork, is damaged and the tree's internal balance turned upside-down. 'Cork should only be harvested in the morning – the afternoon is too hot,' Fabien tells us, at this point on his knees, as he deftly pushes his spat-on-and-sharpened axe into the vertical crack of around 1m that he has cut from the foot of the tree up. The cork creaks and groans as, inch by inch, he prises it loose from the tree. He has already cut the bevelled '*couronne*' (crown) at the top of the section he is harvesting.

With a macho yank and a flick of the ponytail, the cork comes away in two half-pipe sheets. The suddenly-skinny trunk is a gentle ginger in colour, wet, warm and wrinkly. Within a couple of months it will turn brick red; within 12 months, brown; and within 13 years, be ready for the next harvest. But it is the fresh, heady mineral scent it exudes that is the most extraordinary.

Today's cork industry has annual revenue of approximately €1.5 billion: 'No one has ever been able to live only on cork in the Massif des Maures' says Fabien, who spent three years working at France's Institut Méditerranéen du Liège (Mediterranean Institute of Cork; www .institutduliege.com in French) where cork-oak cultivation is studied, researched and developed. France produces just 1.6% of the world's cork, all of which comes from the Mediterranean, primarily Portugal and Spain. A bumper harvest in 2006 yielded 110,000 tons of raw cork in Portugal, 30,000 tons in Spain and between 3500 and 5500 tons in France – of which the Var produced some 50%.

ENERGY WATCH

Learn about renewable energy and see for yourself what this sun-rich region is doing, with a free tour of a solar-energy plant in St-Raphaël, Draguignan, La Garde Freinet, Hyères and other towns and villages in the Var. Contact the **Espace Info Energie** (☎ Eastern Var 04 94 51 41 36, Massif des Maures 04 94 55 70 49, Toulon 04 94 92 35 76) for information and reservations.

If you want to take environmentally responsible travel a step futher, you can immerse yourself in the environment with a *chantier vert* (green work-shop) or other volunteering opportunity. Fancy restoring a village, clearing a forest or mothering a tortoise? See p415 for a detailed listing.

Outdoor Activities

Despite its compact size, Provence has a vast array of landscapes, from alpine mountains to cavernous gorges, wetlands and a world-famous coastline scattered with offshore islands. There are outdoor activities for all energy levels.

ASTRONOMY

Provence's infamous mistral might bite, but on the bright side the wind blows away cloud cover, resulting in sunny days and, for stargazers, clear, star-filled night skies. Large tracts of protected areas, especially across the Luberon and Haute-Provence, give off little artificial light, allowing stars to shine at their brightest.

Observatories welcoming stargazers include the Observatoire de Haute-Provence (p248), a national research centre in St-Michel l'Observatoire, west of Manosque, and the nearby Centre d'Astronomie (p248). Amid the Luberon's lavender fields in Lagarde d'Apt you can stay up all night to watch the stars at the Observatoire Sirene (p217). On the star-studded Côte d'Azur, see stars at the Observatoire de Nice (p286) in La Trinité and nearby at Astrorama (p286), east of Nice.

Young astronomers will be enthralled by the Parc d'Astronomie, du Soleil et du Cosmos (p163) near Avignon.

BALLOONING

Inspiring ideas for outdoor activities throughout the entire region are listed on the regional tourist board's website www.crt-paca.fr.

Drifting across Provence's patchwork fields in a hot-air balloon is an uplifting and romantic way to take in the captivating countryside. Balloon flights last one to 1½ hours (allow three to four hours in all for getting to/from the launch pad, inflating the balloon etc) and cost from €230 per person (€305 for a sunrise flight). Flights run year-round but are subject to weather forecasts. Operators include **Hot-Air Ballooning Provence** (☎ 04 90 05 74 39; www.avignon-et-provence.com/ballooning; Joucas), just outside Gordes (p216), with flights in the Avignon and Luberon area; and **Les Montgolfières du Sud** (☎ 04 66 37 28 02; www.sudmontgolfiere.com in French; 64 rue Sigalon, Uzès), west of Nîmes, floating over the Pont du Gard.

BEACH VOLLEYBALL

Baywatch types can set, spike and dig at nets set up along Marseille's beaches; see p102.

BIRD-WATCHING

Ornithologists flock to see clouds of pink flamingos in the protected Camargue delta (p137) and the Presqu'île de Giens (p372) near Hyères, and majestic birds of prey in the Parc National du Mercantour (p248). The national **Ligue pour la Protection des Oiseaux** (LPO; League for the Protection of Birds; www.lpo.fr in French) has a regional branch, **LPO PACA** (☎ 04 94 12 79 52; paca@lpo.fr; Villa la Paix, rond-point Beauregard, F-83400 Hyères), which organises guided bird-watching expeditions, can tell you where to spot what and can put you in touch with LPO-affiliated bird-watching groups in the region.

BUNGEE JUMPING

The daring and downright fearless can leap off Europe's highest bridge (182m) in the Gorges du Verdon (p235) or from a (slightly) less daunting 80m-high equivalent in the red-rock Gorges de Dalius (p252), near Guillaumes in the Vallée de la Tinée. Prices for *saut en élastique* (bungee jumping) range from €60 to €98 for an initial jump (cheaper for subsequent jumps).

CANOEING

Glide on a peaceful paddling expedition beneath the Pont du Gard (see p200), along the bird-filled Camargue waterways (p137) or along the River Sorgue from Fontaine de Vaucluse to L'Isle-sur-la-Sorgue (p187 and p188).

CANYONING

Provence has Europe's biggest canyon, the gaping Gorges du Verdon (p236) in its backyard, so a guided canyoning expedition, involving a combination of scrambling, swimming and hiking through the gorges' depths (wetsuits provided) is a high point of any trip to the region. Convivial English-speaking operators include **Guides Aventure** (☎ 06 85 94 46 61; www.guidesaventure.com).

CYCLING

Pedalling is practically synonymous with Provence. With near-endless sunshine and few killing hills to climb, not to mention storybook scenery and enchanting villages en route, the region is ideal two-wheeling territory for professionals and amateurs, adults and kids alike. On the Côte d'Azur the noisy motorway is never far away, making cycling a less tranquil affair: coastal cyclists often base themselves in Nice, from where they take a train along the coast each morning with their bicycles to avoid the stress of cycling out of the city. Some GR trails (see p88) are open to mountain bikes, and those keen to tackle the region's roughest mountain terrain should hightail it to Haute-Provence.

Road and mountain bikes can be easily hired for around €15 a day including helmet, puncture-repair kit and suggested itineraries. Many rental outlets, especially on the coast and in the Luberon, have tandems (€20 to €30 per day), children's bikes (around €12 per day), toddler seats (around €5 per day) and two-seater trailers (*remorques* or *carrioles*; up to €15 per day) to tow little kids and babies along. Some deliver to your door for free. Rental outlets are listed under Getting Around in the respective regional chapters.

Both on- and off-road cycling itineraries of various lengths and difficulties, compiled by local experts, can be picked up at most tourist offices. The **Conseil Général du Var** (www.cg83.fr in French) publishes an excellent cycling *topoguide* for the St-Tropez to Toulon area containing 22 detailed itineraries. For Nice, its coast and hinterland, *Rando VTT: Guide RandOxygène*, published by the **Conseil Général des Alpes-Maritimes** (www.cg06.fr in French), maps out 30 cycling routes ranging from a gentle 7km (1½ hours) to a sporty 22km (four hours). And for the Avignon area, there are the 13 routes suggested by the Vaucluse **département** (www.vaucluse.fr in French) in its *VTT: Loisirs de Plein Air* booklet. These free guides (in French only) can all be ordered online.

Otherwise, the **Ligue Provence Alpes de Cyclotourisme** (☎ 04 90 29 64 80; perso .wanadoo.fr/cyclo-provence-alpes in French; Hôtel de Ville, Espace Acampado, BP 27, F-84220 Piolenc) publishes a clutch of excellent French-only guides, some free; while Didier-Richard publishes *Les Guides VTT* series of cyclists' *topoguides*, sold in bookshops. Outside France, Lonely Planet's *Cycling France* details six cycling itineraries in the region.

Following are seven free and easy (and not-so-easy) cycling itineraries.

Le Luberon en Vélo

Nearest towns Apt & Cavaillon **Difficulty** easy to hard **Information** ☎ Maison du Parc 04 90 04 42 00, Vélo Loisir en Luberon 04 92 79 05 82; www.parcduluberon.fr in French, www .veloloisirluberon.com

Cyclists can cross the Parc Naturel Régional du Luberon by following a circular 230km-long itinerary. Roads – steep in places – have little traffic and

> 'Those keen to tackle the region's roughest mountain terrain should hightail it to Haute-Provence'

saunter up, down and around photogenic hilltop villages, vineyards, olive groves, lavender fields and fruit farms. Cyclists taking the northern route pedal 111km from Forcalquier to Cavaillon via Apt, Bonnieux, Lacoste and Ménerbes; the southern route links the two towns by way of Lourmarin, Vaugines, Cucuron and Manosque.

Those who enjoy a stiff climb should tackle the northern route east to west (signposted with white markers). Freewheelers should opt for the easier westbound route, which is marked by orange signs. For day-trippers in Cavaillon, the 40km round trip to Ménerbes makes for an exhilarating bike ride.

Information boards posted along both routes provide details on accommodation, eating and sightseeing.

At press time, the first section of a car-free cycleway utilising disused railway tracks had opened for cyclists from Apt. By 2008 it is expected to span Cavaillon to Forcalquier; and ultimately it will extend east to Italy; see p216 for details.

Les Ocres en Vélo

Nearest town Apt **Difficulty** easy **Information** ☎ Maison du Parc 04 90 04 42 00, Vélo Loisir en Luberon 04 92 79 05 82; www.parcduluberon.fr in French, www.veloloisirluberon.com

This colourful itinerary forms a 50km circular route around the land of Luberon ochre (see p220), linking rocky-red Roussillon with Villars (to the north), Rustrel (to the east), Apt (to the south) and Gargas (to the west). The route can be followed in either direction; green signs mark the westbound way from Apt and ochre markers flag its eastbound counterpart.

Le Pays de Forcalquier et Montagne de Lure en Vélo

Nearest town Forcalquier **Difficulty** easy to hard **Information** ☎ 04 92 75 10 02; www .velopaysforcalquier.com in French

The rough-cut plains of rough 'n' ready Haute-Provence star on the agenda of this mountainous-in-parts, 78km-long route that can be followed in either direction from Forcalquier; ochre signs mark the eastbound route, blue the west, and brown the 6km *boucle* (loop) that can be picked up in Lurs. Villages passed en route include Aubenas les Alpes, St-Michel de l'Observatoire and Mane.

Île de Porquerolles

Only town Porquerolles **Difficulty** easy **Information** ☎ 04 94 58 33 76; www.porquerolles.com

The only means of transport on the national park–protected island of Porquerolles – bar one's feet – is bicycle. Sights are few and distances between beaches are small, making it a hassle-free cycling choice for families happy to spend the day sauntering about by pedal power. In all, 70km of unpaved biking trails zigzag across the island and there are seven rental companies; some provide picnic hampers (€14 per person) for cyclists.

Toulon–St-Raphaël

Nearest towns Toulon, Hyères & Cavalaire-sur-Mer **Difficulty** ultraeasy **Information** ☎ 04 94 18 53 00, 04 94 01 84 50, 04 94 01 92 10; www.cg83.fr in French

Between 1905 and 1949 a steam train (poetically named *le macaron* after a local almond cake containing pine kernels extracted from the same pine cones that fuelled the locomotive) huffed and puffed between Toulon and St-Raphaël. Today the same 101km-long coastal stretch is covered by a smooth-as-silk two-lane cycling path *(piste cyclable)* instead. The track winds from Toulon to Hyères via Cap de Carqueiranne (a great lunch spot; see p377) past Cavalaire-sur-Mer and St-Tropez to St-Raphaël.

Mont Ventoux
Nearest towns Malaucène & Sault **Difficulty** brutal **Information** ☎ 04 90 65 22 59, 04 90 64 01 21; www.lemontventoux.net in French

Many cyclists who make it to the summit of the mighty Mont Ventoux do it as something of a tribute to British world-champion cyclist Tommy Simpson (1937–67), who suffered a fatal heart attack on the mountain during the 1967 Tour de France. A moving roadside memorial to Simpson 1km east of the summit reads 'There is no mountain too high'. The road ascent from Chalet Reynard on the westbound D974 to the summit is six painful kilometres, but a good many cycling enthusiasts only pedal part of the road, often just to see how hard it is!

Tourist offices have information on guided bike rides on the mountain, including night descents by road and daytime mountain-bike descents.

Brevet des 7 Cols Ubayens
Nearest towns Barcelonnette **Difficulty** ultrahard **Information** ☎ 04 92 81 03 68; www .ubaye.com

The seven cols – Allos (2250m), Restefond la Bonette (2802m), Larche (1991m), Vars (2109m), Cayolle (2326m), Pontis (1301m) and St-Jean (1333m) – linking the remote Vallée de l'Ubaye in Haute-Provence with civilisation form the region's most challenging bike rides. The series of loop rides from Barcelonnette involves 207km of power-pedalling and can only be done May to September when the passes aren't blocked by snow. Cyclists who do all seven get a medal (to prove it, participants have to punch a special card in punch-machines installed on each mountain pass). Local tourist offices sell a map of the route (€6.10).

'The seven cols form the region's most challenging bike rides'

DIVING & SNORKELLING
The coastline and its offshore islands – Porquerolles and Embiez particularly – offer enticing diving opportunities. Experienced divers enjoy the waters around Hyères and the Presqu'île du Giens, where the sea beds are littered with shipwrecks. Military WWII wrecks can be explored from St-Raphaël.

Spectacular dive sites in and around Marseille include the Rade de Marseille (a bay with a far-from-flat bottom) and its offshore islands. Diving is also spectacular around Les Calanques, where Henri Cosquer discovered prehistoric paintings in an underwater cave; the school in Cassis he formerly headed up (see p117) organises a variety of dives including night and wreck dives.

The diving season generally runs mid-March to mid-November. Irrespective of whether you're a first-timer about to embark on a *baptême de plongée* (baptism dive) or a highly experienced diver, you will need to show a medical certificate. You should automatically be covered by the diving school's own insurance, but always check. Prices for a half-day baptism/explorative dive start from €48/37 including full equipment hire, and a 10-dive course starts from €396/247.50 with/without equipment hire and without an instructor, or €450/297 with an instructor.

In summer underwater nature trails encourage the aquatically curious to discover marine life at Domaine du Rayol (p364) on the Corniche des Maures, on Île de Port-Cros (p369) and on Plage d'Argentière near La Londe (p373).

Park authorities on Cap Couronne near Marseille organise one-hour guided snorkelling sessions in the Parc Régional Marin de la Côte Bleue (p119).

Diving shops and clubs are listed in the relevant regional chapters.

DONKEY RAMBLING

To ramble amid steep gorges and mountain slopes unencumbered by the weight of a pack on your back, engage a gentle-natured donkey to accompany you on your journey. Farms renting donkeys include Les Ânes des Abeilles (p188), near the Gorges de Nesque, and a couple of other options in Thoard in Haute-Provence (see p243).

FISHING

Provence's crystal-clear rivers and lakes offer excellent fishing. Local restrictions dictate which fish can be caught and which must be thrown back. Cafés and *tabacs* situated close to fishing spots sell licences for a few euros (depending on the area and the catch), and can often provide tips about local sweet spots. Tourist offices throughout Provence stock detailed information.

For private trout fishing in the Avignon area, including rod rental and bait, contact **Maurice Paris** (☎ 04 75 28 07 66; ⊙ Jul & Aug, Sat & Sun Apr-Jun & Sep). Prices vary according to the weight of the fish caught.

FLYING & GLIDING

Fabulous views of Mont Ventoux can be seen from above with **Air Ventoux** (☎ 04 90 66 35 81; monsite.wanadoo.fr/airventoux in French). Half-hour flights (adult/child under 12 €72/36; minimum two passengers) take off from airstrips in Montfavet (near Avignon) and Pernes les Fonatines (near Carpentras).

'Take to the skies above Salon-de-Provence'

Alternatively, you can take to the skies above Salon-de-Provence (famed as the home of France's military flying school, the École de l'Air et École Militaire de l'Air) in a glider. Baptism flights with **Centre de Vol à Voile de la Crau** (☎ 04 90 42 15 38) lasting 20 minutes cost €60.

GOLF

A total of 15 golf courses across Provence participate in the **Golf Pass Provence** (www.golfpass-provence.com) network, offering savings on green fees. A pass for three/five green fees in high season (April to October) costs €150/250, and can be purchased online. Individual rounds must be booked 48 hours in advance.

Marseille's tourist office organises golf lessons from 10am to 11.30am on Sunday at the Marseille Borély Golf School costing €10 including equipment, where beginners and intermediate players aged over eight years are given technical advice by qualified instructors. See p96.

One of the most memorable places to tee off is **Golf de Digne La Lavande** (☎ 04 92 30 58 00; www.golfdigne.com; 57 rte du Chaffaute; 18 holes low/high season from €34/48), amid the lavender fields in Haute-Provence. The course also has an on-site restaurant and hotel; see p243.

GRASS-SKIING

Come the melting snow of spring, off go the sleek snow skis and on go the grass skis, which – for those not familiar with this fringe sport, invented in Germany in the 1960s to help Alpine skiers train year-round – resemble short clunky skis with a caterpillar tread like a bulldozer.

Popular spots in France for *le ski sur herbe* (grass-skiing) are the Mont Serein ski station (p181) on Mont Ventoux's slopes, and La Foux d'Allos and Sauze in Haute-Provence. Ski and boot hire costs around €15 a day and a one-day drag-lift pass is likewise around €15. The season – July and August in the main – is supershort and face-first wipeouts can be frequent (and fierce). As with other types of skiing, grass-skiing has its own world championship, world cup and European cup. For more information, see http://grass-ski.alpes provence.net.

HORSE RIDING

With its famous cowboys, creamy white horses and expansive sandy beaches to gallop along, the Camargue (see p137) is a wonderful – if windswept – spot to ride. Aspiring cowboys and gals can learn the ropes on week-long *stages de monte gardiane* (Camargue cowboy courses); see p148.

Elsewhere in Provence, tourist offices have lists of stables and riding centres where you can saddle up, and the national **Fédération Française des Relais d'Etape de Tourisme Équestre** (☎ 03 86 20 08 04; www.chevalfrance.org in French; Mairie, F-58800 Corbigny) arranges riding itineraries and accommodation.

> A swag of information on horse riding, schools, tours and other equestrian activities in the Provence-Côte d'Azur region is linked to www .terre-equestre.com (in French).

ICE DIVING

James Bond wannabes who find themselves high and dry in Provence in winter can plunge into the chilly but extraordinarily crystal-clear depths of an iced-over lake. See p251 for the full ice-diving brief.

JEEP TOURS

A range of 4WD tours setting out from Arles or Stes-Maries de la Mer take you well off the beaten bitumen in the wild Camargue wetlands; see p138 for info.

NATURISM

The Côte d'Azur has long embraced a let-it-all-hang-out attitude. Nudist spots – known as *aires naturistes*, not to be confused with *aires naturelles*, which are primitive farm camp sites – range from small rural camp sites to large chalet villages with cinemas, tennis courts and shops. Most open April to October; visitors need an International Naturist Federation (INF) *passeport naturiste*, available at naturist centres.

If you're not a fan of tan lines, the coastline between Le Lavandou and the St-Tropez peninsula is well endowed with nudist beaches. Héliopolis on Île du Levant – one of a trio of islands off the coast between Le Lavandou and Hyères – is the region's oldest and largest nudist colony, dating from the 1930s and easily visited on a day trip by boat. See p370 for details.

The **Fédération Française de Naturisme** (☎ 08 92 69 32 82; www.ffn-naturisme.com in French; 5 rue Regnault, F-93500 Pantin) can tell you precisely where in Provence you can roam in the buff.

PARACHUTING

To *saut en parachute* (skydive) above the dramatic Provençal countryside, Marseille-based Latitude Challenge (p235) organises solo/tandem jumps starting from €221/236.

PARAGLIDING

St-André-les-Alpes (p241), 20km north of Castellane in Haute-Provence, is the French capital of *parapente* (paragliding). If the thermals are good – as in St-André – you can stay up for hours circling the area and enjoying breathtaking aerial views. Paragliding schools in St-André and St-Dalmas-Valdeblore (p254) typically charge €445/475 in low/high season for a five-day initiation course and €60/85 for a 10-/20-minute tandem flight (with instructor) for those who'd rather not brave it alone.

In the Luberon paragliders can soar with the birds over Provence's russet red Colorado in Rustrel (p217).

QUADING

Razzing around by quad bike is an exhilarating way of exploring the great outdoors. Mont Ventoux and the Alpilles in the Avignon area are hot quad spots, as is the Camargue; see the Activities sections of the regional chapters and check with local tourist offices for details.

ROCK CLIMBING & VIA FERRATA

Via Ferrata: A Complete Guide to France by Philipe Poulet is a bible for anyone intending to tackle the elevated *via ferrata* climbing trails across the mountains of Haute-Provence.

The Gorges du Verdon, the *calanques* around Marseille, the lacy Dentelles de Montmirail in the Vaucluse, Buoux in the Luberon and the Vallée des Merveilles in the Parc National du Mercantour are but a handful of the region's *sites d'escalade* (climbing sites). Most tourist offices stock lists of spots to climb, guides and climbing schools, as well as information on branches of Club Alpin Français (CAF; located in most major towns). Local Luberon climbing club Améthyste (p226) runs a packed programme of climbs in the Buoux area.

Crisscrossing the dizzying peaks of Haute-Provence are four heart-lurching *via ferrata* (a type of rock climbing using pre-attached cables bolted into the mountainside) courses; see p253 for details and locations.

INLINE SKATING & SKATEBOARDING

Inline skating is still one of the chicest ways to cruise around town. Blades (and usually boards) can be hired in any of the larger cities as well as most resorts on the Côte d'Azur for around €10 to €20 per day. Top inline skating spots on the Riviera include Nice's promenade des Anglais and La Croisette in Cannes. Marseille's La Canebière (once the tramway construction's completed), the coastal corniches and the legendary bowl at Marseille Skatepark (p103) are also prime skating terrain. Year-round, Marseille's tourist office organises lessons for beginner bladers over the age of 11 years from 10am to noon Sunday at Parc Borély (€12 plus €2 for blade hire), where you'll learn how to stop, glide and turn. Bookings must be made in advance through the tourist office (p96).

Hundreds of inline skaters meet each week for a police-escorted evening blade around town in Avignon (p163). Marseille's mass blade had been cancelled by the authorities at press time, but strong local support may yet see it reinstated. Nice also hosts an en masse blade (p269).

Skating and boarding are forbidden in Monaco.

SAILING & SEA SPORTS

Sailing is big business on the French Riviera: Antibes, Cannes, Mandelieu-La Napoule and St-Raphaël as well as Marseille are large water-sports centres where those without their own boat can hire a set of sails. Tourist offices have a list of sailing centres *(stations violes)* that rent gear and run courses. Count on paying around €40/70 to rent a catamaran for 1½/three hours and €40 for a one-hour sailing lesson.

Marseille's tourist office organises three-hour sailing courses from 2pm to 5pm on Saturday for €36 for start-up sailors aged over six years; book with the tourist office (p96).

Other sea sports readily available on the beach include windsurfing (around €30 per hour to rent a board), water-skiing and wake-boarding (€25 for around 15 minutes), jet-skiing (around €50 for 30 minutes) and rides from the back of a boat in a parachute (€45/60 for one/two people for a 10-minute ride), hair-raising rubber ring (€20 per person for a 10-minute ride) or fly fish (€30 per person for a 10-minute ride).

Surfing the waves with a kite is rapidly taking off all along the coast. March to November, surfers can ride the best winds of the day on a board propelled by a kite with **Air'X Kite** (☎ 06 60 41 87 34; www.airxkite.com; St-Laurent du Var **Centre Nautique**, 416 av Eugène Donadeï; Mandelieu-La Napoule Centre Nautique, av Général de Gaulle), a kite-surf school that surfs from its bases at St-Laurent du Var and Manedelieu-La Napoule. Four-hour private lessons cost €180 and a 20/32-hour group-lesson pass is available for €590/840, both including equipment hire.

Among the emerging kite-surfing and windsurfing hot spots are the beaches at L'Almanarre in Hyères, home to **Funboard Center** (☎ 04 94 57 95 33; www.funboardcenter.com; route l'Almanarre) which runs lessons year-round costing up-wards of €23 per hour for windsurfing and €70 for a maiden kite-surf; several other places are open in summer. The Camargue is another up-and-coming kite-surfing spot, both for kite-boarding the wind-whipped seas and speeding along the flat sands on a kite-powered buggy; see p138 for details.

The Atlantic it ain't, but Marseille's beaches often get enough of a swell to satisfy regular board-riders, at least briefly, with short, zippy rides in to shore. For surfing info, see p103.

From Marseille you can also paddle out in a sea kayak; see p103 for in-formation about all-day and moonlight paddles.

To get a marine weather forecast before setting sail, call ☎ 3250 or visit www.meteo.fr/marine in French.

SKIING & SNOWBOARDING

The few ski resorts in Haute-Provence are refreshingly low-key, with little of the glitz and glamour attached to the Alps' better-known centres such as Chamonix. Provence's pistes are best suited to beginner and intermediate skiiers and are marginally cheaper than their northern neighbours.

Resorts include the larger Pra Loup (straddled between 1500m and 1600m) and La Foux d'Allos (1800m), which share 230km of downhill pistes and 110km of cross-country trails. Smaller sister resorts of Le Sauze (1400m) and Super-Sauze (1700m) in the Vallée de l'Ubaye tend to attract domestic tourists. The concrete-block Isola 2000 (2450m) is the largest of the resorts, and the least attractive.

TOP FIVE ACTIVITY TOURS FROM ABROAD

Signing up for an activity tour before you leave home allows you to hit the ground running. Most cycling- and walking-tour operators lighten the load by transporting baggage by minibus between hotels. Tours take in hilltop villages and other sights en route.

Andante on Foot (☎ 01722-713813; www.andanteonfoot.co.uk; The Old Barn, Old Rd, Alderbury, Salisbury SP5 3AR, UK) You only need book your own transport to/from Nice and let Andante on Foot do the rest, ie organise 11km to 17km (four to seven hours) a day of scenic walking from the hilltop villages of the Roya Valley to *belle époque* Menton, seven nights' B&B accommodation (including two evening meals and three picnics) and luggage transfer, costing UK£540.

ATG Oxford (☎ 01865-315678; www.atg-oxford.co.uk; 69-71 Banbury Rd, Oxford OX2 6PJ, UK) Escorted and independent walking holidays, including a guided eight-day Luberon trip (UK£1795 excluding flights) with five days of walking through the colour-rich countryside.

Europeds (☎ 800-321 9552, 831-646 4920; www.europeds.com; 761 Lighthouse Ave, Monterey CA 93940, USA) This friendly California-based Europe specialist runs seven-day 'Provence Loops' circuits incorporating five full days of cycling costing US$2400.

Susi Madron's Cycling for Softies (☎ 01612-488282; www.cycling-for-softies.co.uk; 2 & 4 Birch Polygon, Rusholme Manchester M14 5HX, UK) Gourmet restaurants, charming hotels and itineraries catering to all cycling abilities have made this 'soft' approach to cycling Provence perennially popular. Three- to 14-day self-guided tours cost from UK£428 to UK£1579.

Top Yacht (☎ 01243-520950; www.top-yacht.com; Southgate, Chichester, West Sussex PO19 8DN, UK) Yachts com-plete with experienced crews can sail you around the Mediterranean from US$8000 per week (excluding dinner, drinks, marina fees and port taxes) for one or two people. Skippered and unskippered yachts are also available for charter.

These resorts – all in the Parc National du Mercantour (p248) – open for the ski season from December to March/April/May (depending on the snow conditions), and for a short period in July and August for summer walkers. Buying a package is the cheapest way to ski and/or snowboard. For information on lift passes, equipment hire and the like, see the relevant sections in the Parc National du Mercantour section.

North of Dignes-les-Bains, near the western edge of the Parc National du Mercantour in the Vallée de la Blanche, the locally patronised resort of St-Jean Montclar (p244) is well set up for families.

Mont Ventoux offers limited downhill and cross-country skiing; Chalet Reynard in Bédoin and Mont Serein are the two ski stations. See p181 for details.

Snow-bunnies can get the scoop on skiing or surfing the region's slopes on www.skifrance .com.

SPELUNKING

The harsh moonscape of the Plateau d'Albion (p182) is riddled with natural potholes and caverns, inviting nonclaustrophobic adventurers to explore underground. The **Association Spéléologique du Plateau d'Albion** (☎ 04 90 76 08 33; www.aspanet.net in French; 2 rue de l'Église, St-Christol d'Albion) runs spelunking trips from €60 per day.

Before setting off on a trek, pop Lonely Planet's *Walking in France* or the English-language *Walks in Provence: Lubéron Regional Nature Park*, a *topoguide* by the Fédération Française de Randonnée Pédestre in your backpack.

WALKING

The region is crisscrossed by a maze of *sentiers balisés* (marked walking paths) and *sentiers de grande randonnée* (long-distance paths with alphanumeric names beginning 'GR'). Some of the latter are many hundreds of kilometres long, including the GR5, which travels from the Netherlands through Belgium, Luxembourg and the spectacular Alpine scenery of eastern France before ending up in Nice. The GR4 (which crosses the Dentelles de Montmirail before climbing up the northern face of Mont Ventoux and winding east to the Gorges du Verdon), GR6 and their various diversions also traverse the region. Provence's most spectacular trail, the GR9, takes walkers to most of the area's ranges, including Mont du Vaucluse and Montagne du Luberon.

No permits are needed but there are restrictions on where you can camp, especially in the Parc National du Mercantour, Les Calanques and the Gorges du Verdon. Between 1 July and 15 September paths in heavily

---

BLISS OUT

Lavender and algae baths, shiatsu and Ayurvedic massages, Mediterranean mudpacks and lots of other pampering pleasures soothe and rejuvenate weary feet and souls at a handful of spas.

A supersoak in a bubbling thermal bath laced with essential lavender oil at Établissement Thermal (p242) in Digne-les-Bains costs €45.

Thermes Sextius (p127), a Roman spa in Aix-en-Provence, hits the spot with Zen massages, Camargue-salt skin scrubs and dozens of other blissful treatments, starting from €37.

Aromatherapy, *oshiboris* (Japanese hot towels) and shiatsu prove a potent cocktail at the Shiseido Spa at Le Mas Candille (p325) in Mougins, near Cannes. Surrounded by Japanese gardens and all things Zen, the spa practises the Qi method; test it out with a 45-minute body polish (€90), 30-minute quick tension release (€65), an ultimate pampering day (€445) or the men-only energising antistress day (€420).

At Monaco's Thermes Marins de Monte-Carlo (p390), the region's (and quite possibly the world's) most exclusive and luxurious spa, the truly decadent can splurge on a Monte Carlo diamond massage (€398 for 90 minutes) – a body scrub with diamond powder, followed by a massage with rose-scented lotion and topped off with a 'gold and light of Monte Carlo' cream for the ultimate sparkle – or a star massage (€110 for one hour) to relax each of the body's five 'star-shape' points (head, arms and legs).

WALKING WITH A FARMER

No-one knows the lay of the land better than those who tirelessly farm it. For a wonderful introduction to a Provençal farm, sign up for an *itineraire paysan* (farmer's itinerary): a two- to three-hour walk with a local farmer across their property. These thematic walks take you through fruit orchards and Alpine pastures, past beehives, along canals, around goat farms and in search of black diamonds (truffles); ending with a small sample of the farm's produce.

Itineraires paysans take place on farms and agricultural land in Haute-Provence (including the area around Manosque in the Luberon), and in the Var to the east from June to September. They cost €7/3 for an adult/six to 16 year old and must be booked directly with the farmer at least 24 hours in advance. Walks are cancelled if there are fewer than eight participants. A calendar covering the season's walks is online at www.itineraires-paysans.com. Alternatively, contact the **Centre Permanent d'Initiatives pour l'Environnement Alpes de Provence** (☎ 04 92 87 58 81; www.cpie04.com in French; Château de Drouille, F-04100 Manosque).

---

forested areas – such as the section of the GR98 that follows Les Calanques between Cap Croisette (immediately south of Marseille) and Cassis – are closed completely due to the high risk of forest fire. The GR51 crossing the Massif des Maures, paths in the Montagne de Ste-Victoire east of Aix-en-Provence and numerous trails in Haute-Provence are likewise closed in summer due to fire risk.

Many walking guides – predominantly in French – cover the region. The *Guides RandOxygène* walking guides published by the Conseil Général des Alpes-Maritimes (Alpes-Maritimes General Council) are outstanding. The guides detail 60 walks of varying lengths – for seaside amblers to serious walkers – in the Alpes-Maritimes *département*: *Rando Haut-Pays* covers the Parc National du Mercantour, *Rando Moyen-Pays* tackles the hilltop villages north of Nice and *Rando Pays Côtier* features invigorating coastal walks. Tourist offices have information, as does the jam-packed website www.randoxygene.org (in French).

Almost every tourist office takes bookings for short two- to three-hour guided nature walks in their areas during summer; many are organised by the local branch of the Office National des Forêts (ONF, National Forests Office) or by a local mountain guide. Several companies, both within and outside the region, organise longer treks; see p87.

The Manosque-based branch (☎ 04 92 70 54 54; centre. giono@wanadoo.fr; Centre Giono 3, blvd 'Elémir Bourges F-04100) of Handi Cap Évasion (☎ 04 78 22 71 02; www.hce.asso.fr in French) organises nature walks for travellers with disabilities (including those in wheelchairs).

WHITE-WATER SPORTS

Between April and September Haute-Provence (p231) promises thrills and spills galore with a torrent of opportunities for white-water rafting, canoeing, kayaking, hot-dogging (bombing in an inflatable canoe), canyoning (scaling waterfalls and rivers with ropes), hydrospeed (bombing on a body-board), 'floating' (like rafting minus the raft, with a buoyancy bag strapped to your back) and water-rambling (navigating rivers with or without a mountain bike).

The Rivers Verdon, Vésubie, Roya and Ubaye are easily the region's most dramatic waterways; leading centres where you can sign up for guided half- and full-day expeditions are Castellane (for the Gorges du Verdon), St-Martin-Vésubie (for the Vésubie descent), Breil-sur-Roya (for the Vallée de la Roya) and Barcelonnette (for the Vallée de l'Ubaye). Expect to pay around €50/75 for a half-/full-day group expedition with guide. Full details are listed in the Haute-Provence chapter.

MARSEILLE AREA

Marseille Area

Provence's seething, sultry metropolis of Marseille and its surrounds fly in the face of the region's typically tranquil images. The pulsating port city itself is an exhilarating hub, bubbling over with history, a host of cutting-edge creative spaces, and a hip, multicultural urban style. Since Greek settlers came ashore more than 2½ millennia ago, waves of immigrants have made Marseille home. Among today's Marseillais are descendants of Armenians, Spaniards, Italians, Greeks, Arabs, Russians, Jews and North Africans, as well as those of Provençal origin, making the city as much a melange as its fabled *bouillabaisse*.

From Marseille, the craggy coast jags southeast around the translucent aquamarine waters lapping Les Calanques – rocky, white-limestone inlets gashed during the Ice Age's rising seas – to the cliff-crowned fishing village of Cassis, and the former shipyards of La Ciotat, where cinematic history began.

Salt (and pollution) tangs the air west of Marseille. Europe's largest brine lake, the Étang de Berre, is home to one of the continent's biggest petrochemical plants, but also harbours highlights such as the canal-straddled town Martigues. Nearby, the clear coves and cluster of townships along the Côte Bleue (Blue Coast) are a seaside haven little touched by tourism.

Heading north, Marseille's barren, sea- and wind-scoured backdrops soften to the green and purple hues of Provence's picturesque landscapes. Pays d'Aix (Aix Country), with the elegant plane-shaded boulevards, filigreed fountains and mansions of Aix-en-Provence at its gateway, unfold west to Salon de Provence's olive groves.

HIGHLIGHTS

- Shop for artisanal specialities in the atmospheric jumble of streets winding through Marseille's **Le Panier quarter** (p113)

- Follow the footsteps of writer/film-maker Marcel Pagnol in and around **Aubagne** (p119)

- From Cassis, hike the precipitous cliffs of **Les Calanques** (p116)

- Climb up to La Ciotat's panoramic botanical park, **Parc du Mugel** (p118)

- Indulge in a heavenly hydrotherapy treatment at Aix-en-Provence's Roman thermal spa, **Thermes Sextius** (p127)

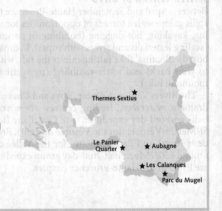

★ Thermes Sextius

★ Le Panier Quarter   ★ Aubagne

★ Les Calanques

★ Parc du Mugel

ITINERARIES

MAX OUT MARSEILLE   Two Days / Marseille

Despite its sprawling layout, greater Marseille has corners crammed with a frenzy of sights, sounds, smells and flavours. To experience the city's sensory overload, weave through the narrow streets of its oldest quarter, **Le Panier** (**1**; see the boxed text, p113), and get into the Marseille mode at the **Musée de la Mode** (p99). Follow the African drums, accordions and clinking masts to the yacht-filled **Vieux Port** (**2**; p97) and the clamour of the daily **fish market** (p110). Savour the city's signature **bouillabaisse** (p180) and a fiery **pastis** (p113).

Afterwards, stroll, cycle or skate along the **coast** (p100), stopping by the fairy-tale fishing village of **Vallon des Auffes** (**3**; p100). Hang out with local hipsters at **La Maronnaise** (p111) and dance until dawn. Or take the open-topped **Le Grand Tour** (p104) bus back to the city centre, jumping off at **Basilique Notre Dame de la Garde** (p99) for celestial views. Dine at the open-air cafés on **place Thiars** (**4**; p97) then head to the bohemian **cours Julien** (**5**; p110) quarter for **live music** (p111).

Put a slower spin on the city the next day with a blissful boat ride from the Vieux Port to **Château d'If** (p102). Then, depending on your passion, make an architectural pilgrimage to Le Corbusier's urban masterpiece, **Unité d'Habitation** (p102); a sporting pilgrimage to the **Stade Vélodrome** (p103); a cultural pilgrimage to Marseille's **museums** (p97); or worship the sun, wind and waves at the **Prado beaches** (p102). On a Sunday, don't miss mooching the Moroccan-style market **Marché aux Puces** (p113).

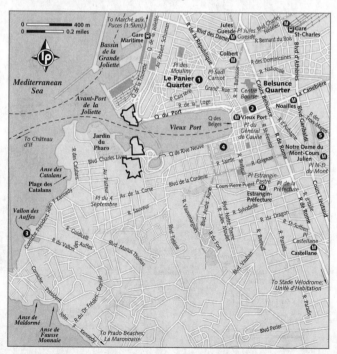

MOUNTAINS TO THE SEA   Two Days / Montagne Ste-Victoire to L'Estaque

Marvel at the mountainscapes that inspired Cézanne at **Montagne Ste-Victoire** (**1**; p131), then retrace his steps around his home town, **Aix-en-Provence** (**2**; p126) and visit his last studio, the **Atelier Paul Cézanne** (p126). Linger over lunch on the pavement terrace of Aix's legendary café (and former Cézanne haunt) **Les Deux Garçons** (p130) on Aix's beautiful boulevard, cours Mirabeau. Afterwards, admire Cézanne's works at Aix's magnificent new museum, **Musée Granet** (p126).

Whiz west to medieval **Salon de Provence** (**3**; p121) to ponder Nostradamus' prophecies at his former-home-turned-museum, the **Maison de Nostradamus** (p121) and stop by the antiquated, aromatic soap factory, **Savonnerie Marius Fabre** (p122). Stroll through the olive groves massed around **Mas des Bories** (p122) on a free guided tour; and depending on the time of year, help with the harvest. Come nightfall, dine on Francis Robin's celebrated, sun-inspired cuisine at **Mas du Soleil** (p123) and spend the night in one of the garden-view rooms of the *mas* (farmhouse), or tuck yourself up in the **Grand Hôtel de la Poste** (p122) with a view over Salon's moss-covered, mushroom-shaped **Fontaine Moussue** (p121).

The next day, skirt the western edge of the industrialised brine lake **Étang de Berre** (**4**; p120) to the brightly coloured fishermen's houses clustered around the canals of **Martigues** (**5**; p120). Continue south to **Cap Couronne** (**6**; p119) for a summertime snorkel in its marine-life-rich waters, then carry on along the **Côte Bleue** (p119) east to **Carry-le-Rouet** (**7**; p119) to sample its sea urchins. Keep heading east to the picturesque port of **L'Estaque** (**8**; p119) to pick up Cézanne's trail once more.

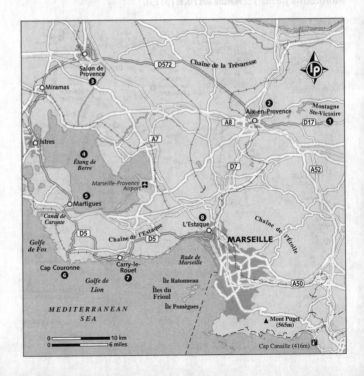

MARSEILLE

pop 1.5 million

With buildings in hues of ripened apricot, cracked wheat and blanched almond scattered along the seashore, Marseille is infused with a perceptible and irrepressible energy. This gritty, grimy and gloriously real city – France's oldest, and largest after Paris – isn't gentrified like its Provençal counterparts. But its rough-and-tumble, litter-swirled streets and its coastal corniches chicaning around sun-scorched coves and beaches are filled with treasures. Pulsing to a sultry southern European tempo, Marseille also beats to the drum of neighbouring North Africa. Its maritime heritage thrives at its vibrant Vieux Port (Old Port), where fresh-off-the-boat catches are displayed along the docks at its centuries-old fish market.

Unlike Paris, London and other mondial cities, this heady, heated melting pot has no China Town, Little Italy, Mini Morocco or Tiny Tunisia. Instead, cuisines, shops, music and cultural celebrations are strewn throughout the city like confetti blown by the mistral wind. Locals are unified by their high-spirited accent – and by their cherished football team, Olympique de Marseille (OM), when matches see a myriad of nationalities sing as one: '*Nous sommes les Marseillais!*' (We are the Marseillais!)

The city's cutting-edge music scene, warehouses-turned-nightclubs, cultural centres and museums are among the hippest and most happening of any in the country. Its seaport

---

MARKET DAY

Marseille and Aix-en-Provence have daily food markets; see p110, p113 and p130 for details. Morning market days elsewhere:
Tuesday La Ciotat
Wednesday Cassis, Salon de Provence
Friday Cassis
Sunday La Ciotat

---

remains the most important in France, handling a quarter of all external trade, and is the third-largest in Europe, while high-speed rail now puts Paris just three hours from Marseille. (The English spelling, Marseilles – pronounced the same – is passing out of use.)

In part because of Marseille's unfounded (or at least outdated) reputation as a dangerous city, tourism, for now, is yet to temper this unique urban undercurrent of Provence.

HISTORY

Around 600 BC, Greek mariners founded Massilia, a trading post at what is now Marseille's Vieux Port. In the 1st century BC, the city lost out by backing Pompey the Great rather than Julius Caesar, whose forces captured Massilia in 49 BC and exacted revenge by confiscating the city's fleet and directing Roman trade elsewhere. Massilia stayed a free port, remaining the last Western centre of Greek learning before falling into ruin. It was revived in the early 10th century by the counts of Provence, and became part of France in the 1480s. Calamity struck in 1720 when the plague, carried on a merchant ship

---

LITERARY MARSEILLE

Marseille has long inspired the literary to be literary.

▪ *Little Dorrit* (Charles Dickens) Classic novel, opens with Marseille 'burning in the sun'.

▪ *The Count of Monte Cristo & The Three Musketeers* (Alexandre Dumas) Nineteenth-century Marseille features in these classics by the French novelist (1802–70).

▪ *Two Towns in Provence* (MFK Fisher) Street-by-street, fountain-by-fountain celebration of Aix-en-Provence and Marseille, penned in 1964.

▪ *The Arrow of Gold* (Joseph Conrad) 'Certain streets have an atmosphere of their own, a sort of universal fame… One such street is the Canebière'. So begins Conrad's tale (1919) of swashbuckling love and adventure, opening in Marseille.

▪ *Marseille Taxi* (Peter Child) Contemporary tale of a married Marseillais taxi driver with too many mistresses and dodgy dealings with the underworld; great beach reading.

▪ *To Die in Provence* (Norman Bogner) Late 1990s thriller set in Aix-en-Provence.

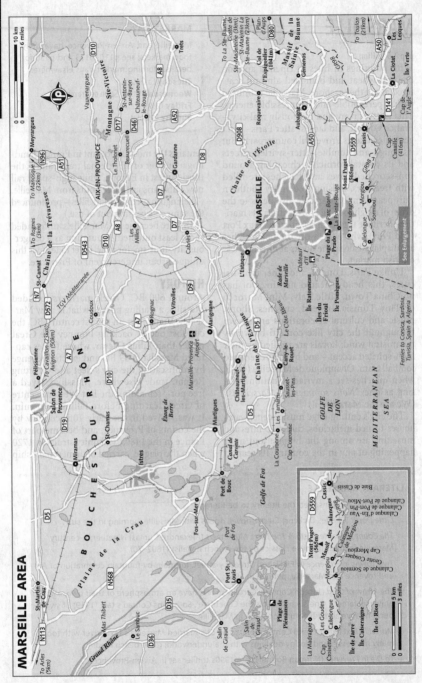

MARSEILLE AREA

RHYTHM OF THE CITY

Ask almost anyone in this sun-drenched city where they're from, and the answer's not France or other country of origin, but simply 'Marseille'. Even if you didn't know where they were from, though, chances are the city's distinctive accent would be a dead giveaway. The Marseille accent has a singsong cadence that originated in large part from early-19th-century Italian émigrés, and is now citywide and adopted by new arrivals.

The accent stands out even to foreigners, particularly the twang on the final syllable. The word *porte* (door; pronounced 'port' elsewhere in France), for example, sounds something like 'por-tay' in Marseille, and *matin* (morning; pronounced 'ma-tun' elsewhere) sounds more like 'ma-tang'; adding a theatrical flair to even the most run-of-the-mill storytelling (much less the entertainingly tall stories for which Marseille locals are renowned).

As an artistic technical director who divides his time between Marseille and Paris describes it: 'The way of speaking here is like a badge, which people wear with pride. Parisians will ask, in a low, serious voice, '*Comment allez-vous?*' (How are you?). In Marseille, it's '*COMMENT VAS-TU?*' with arms waving wildly. People are very open and passionate here; and very proud to be Marseillais.'

Music director of Marseille radio station Radio Grenouille, Stéphane Galland, agrees. Stéphane believes the accent is a way of asserting identity because it's all that's remaining from the original Provençal language. The government forced people to speak French, and a strong accent is a form of rebellion to retain individual identity; which musicians like Jo Corbeau and Massilia Sound System reinforce by singing in the Marseille accent.

from Syria, wiped out more than half of the city's 90,000 inhabitants.

Marseille's citizens embraced the Revolution, sending 500 volunteers to defend Paris in 1792. Heading north, they sang a rousing march recently composed in Strasbourg and ever after dubbed *La Marseillaise* – now France's national anthem. Trade with North Africa escalated after France occupied Algeria in 1830. In 1869 the Suez Canal was opened; growing work opportunities saw the number

of inhabitants escalate by more than a quarter of a million. The population rose again following Tunisia's independence in 1956 and Algeria's in 1962, with residents of these two former French colonies increasing Marseille's population by 50%.

The economic downturn of the 1990s bred poverty and widespread unemployment. The extreme-right politicians rode the wave of discontent, and morale remained low until a myriad of expansion projects (see the boxed text, p112) and a boom in employment (now nearly double the national average) saw the city's spirits soar. Today Marseille is arguably the city most on the rise in France.

DOWN-TEMPO

One of the creative forces behind Marseille's alternative radio station Radio Grenouille, Claire Tourette, says, 'There's a saying in Marseille that sums up the Mediterranean tempo:

Pas trop vite le matin,
Pas trop vite le soir
(Not too fast in the morning,
Not too fast in the evening)

So it's never fast. It can be frustrating working in the music industry in Marseille, because it takes so long to make something happen… You call someone and they ask you to call back the next day, and the next… But it's a good way of life here. You've got time to enjoy it.'

ORIENTATION

The city's main thoroughfare, the wide boulevard La Canebière, stretches eastwards from the Vieux Port. To the north of the Vieux Port is the labyrinth of narrow streets weaving through Le Panier, Marseille's most historic quarter. Heading southwest of the Vieux Port brings you to the start of the seaside corniches. The city's commercial heart is around rue Paradis.

From the central Gare St-Charles (St-Charles train station), north of La Canebière at the northern end of blvd d'Athènes, it's a 10-minute walk or two metro stops to the Vieux Port. Shuttle buses link Marseille airport, 28km northwest, with the station. The ferry terminal is west of place de la Joliette, or a 10-minute walk or two-minute metro ride to the Vieux Port.

Greater Marseille is divided into 16 arrondissements (districts). In this chapter, arrondissements are noted in addresses: 1er for first arrondissement and so on.

Maps

The tourist office distributes a decent, free city map (note that its eastern point is at the top of the page where you'd normally find north).

INFORMATION
Bookshops

Librairie de la Bourse (Map p106; ☎ 04 91 33 63 06; 8 rue Paradis, 1er; metro Vieux Port) Extensive range of maps and guides, primarily in French.

Librairie Maritime et Outremer (Map p106; ☎ 04 91 54 79 26; 26 quai de Rive Neuve, 1er; metro Vieux Port) Seafaring books, maps and guides.

Maison de la Presse (Map p106; 29 quai des Belges, 1er; metro Vieux Port) Stocks English-language newspapers and magazines.

Emergency

Police headquarters (Préfecture de Police; Map p106; ☎ 04 91 39 80 00; place de la Préfecture, 1er; metro Estrangin-Préfecture; ☺ 24hr)

Internet Access

Get free wi-fi at Vieux Port on the *Marseille Sans Fils* (Marseille without wires) network.
Info Cafe (Map p106; ☎ 04 91 33 74 98; 1 quai du Rive Neuve, 1e; per 30 min/hr €2/3.60; ☺ 9am-10pm Mon-Sat, 2.30-7.30pm Sun) Right on the Vieux Port up a short flight of steps; has English keyboards.

Internet Resources

Mairie-Marseille (www.mairie-marseille.fr in French) Official city website.

Marseille-Tourisme (www.marseille-tourisme.com) Tourist office website.

Webcity Marseille (marseille.webcity.fr in French) City guide with particularly strong nightlife section.

Laundry

La Savonnerie (Map p106; 5 rue Breteuil, 1er; metro Vieux Port; ☺ 6.30am-8pm) A 7/10kg load costs €3.50/5; drying is €.40 per five minutes. Bring change.

Left Luggage

Gare St-Charles (Consignes; Map p98; small/medium/large locker €3.50/6/8; ☺ 7.30am-10pm) Next to Platform A.

Media

Mars Magazine Hip *The Face*–style 'magazine of the Marseillais' with short, sharp dining and nightlife city guide (€5, in French, published quarterly).

Medical Services

A list of pharmacies open at night and/or on Sunday is pinned outside the tourist office.
Hôpital de la Timone (☎ 04 91 49 91 91, 04 91 38 60 00; 264 rue St-Pierre, 5e; metro La Timone) Just over 1km southeast of place Jean Jaurès.

Money

Several banks and exchange bureaus dot La Canebière, 1er.
Canebière Change (Map p106; ☎ 04 91 13 71 26; 39 La Canebière, 1er; metro Vieux Port) Amex agent.

Post

Central post office (Map p106; 1 place de l'Hôtel des Postes, 1er; metro Colbert)

Tourist Information

Comité Départemental du Tourisme (Map p98; ☎ 04 91 13 84 13; www.visitprovence.com; Le Montesquieu bldg, 13 rue Roux de Brignoles, 6e; metro Estrangin-Préfecture) Tourist information on the Bouches-du-Rhône *département* (administrative area).

Tourist office annexe (Map p98; ☎ 04 91 50 59 18; Gare St-Charles, 1er; metro Gare St-Charles; ☺ 10am-noon & 1-5pm Mon-Fri); main branch (Map p106; ☎ 04 91 13 89 00; accueil@marseille-tourisme.com; 4 La Canebière, 1er; metro Vieux Port; ☺ 9am-7.30pm Mon-Sat, 10am-6pm Sun Jul-Sep, 9am-7pm Mon-Sat, 10am-5pm Sun Oct-Jun)

Travel Agencies

Voyages Wasteels (Map p106; ☎ 04 95 09 30 60; marseille@wasteels.fr; 67 La Canebière, 1er; metro Noailles; ☺ 9.30am-12.30pm & 2-6pm Mon-Fri, 9.30am-12.30pm Sat)

DANGERS & ANNOYANCES

Forget everything you may have heard about Marseille being a hotbed of crime: it's no more dangerous than other French cities. As with any big city, keep your wits about you and your valuables out of view. At night take extra care in the Belsunce area, southwest of the train station bounded by La Canebière, cours Belsunce and rue d'Aix, rue Bernard du Bois and blvd d'Athènes. Day and night keep car doors locked and windows up, especially when stationary at traffic lights; and *never* leave anything of value in a parked vehicle, even in the boot.

Taxi drivers departing from the train station and the ferry terminal are notoriously dishonest – you're usually better off preordering one (and arranging a meeting point), or picking one up in the street.

SIGHTS
Around the Vieux Port
VIEUX PORT & LE PANIER

Ships have docked for more than 26 centuries at the city's birthplace, the colourful Vieux Port. The main commercial docks were transferred to the Joliette area on the coast north of here in the 1840s, but the Vieux Port remains a thriving harbour for fishing boats and pleasure yachts.

Guarding the harbour are **Bas Fort St-Nicolas** (Map p98) on the southern side and, across the water, **Fort St-Jean** (Map p98), founded in the 13th century by the Knights Hospitaller of St John of Jerusalem. In 2008 a national Musée des Civilisations de l'Europe et de la Méditerranée (Museum of European & Mediterranean Civilisations) will open inside the latter as part of Marseille Euroméditerranée (see the boxed text, p112).

Marseille's 17th-century **town hall** (Map p106; quai du Port) dominates the port's northern quay. Behind it, the historic **Le Panier quarter** (Map p106), dubbed Marseille's Montmartre for its sloping streets as much as its artsy ambience, was the site of the Greek *agora* (marketplace), hence its name translates as 'the basket'. Dynamited during WWII and extensively rebuilt afterwards, today its mishmash of laneways is an atmospheric jumble of authentic artisan shops (see the boxed text, p113) and washing lines strung outside the terraced houses that evoke the area's past.

On the Vieux Port's southern side, late-night restaurants and cafés pack the **place Thiars** and **cours Honoré d'Estienne d'Orves** pedestrian zone (Map p106). Heading southwest of the Vieux Port brings you past the serene **Jardin du Pharo** (Map p98) overlooking the sea; continuing southwest leads you around to the coast.

EAST OF THE VIEUX PORT

From the Provençal word *canebe* (hemp) after the city's traditional rope industry, **La Canebière** (Map p106) stretches northeast from the old port to sq Léon Blum.

Bounded by La Canebière, cours Belsunce and rue d'Aix, rue Bernard du Bois and blvd d'Athènes, the ramshackle **Belsunce** (Map p106) quarter is slowly being rehabilitated. The **public library** (Map p106) on cours Belsunce was the legendary Alcazar music hall from 1857 until 1964.

North here lies the central train station area and La Friche la Belle de Mai (see the boxed text, p112), the hub of Marseille's underground arts scene.

A few blocks south of La Canebière is the student hang-out, **cours Julien** (Map p98), a bohemian, graffitied concourse with a water garden and palm trees, hip cafés, music venues and bars, and a Berlin vibe. Nearby, students and artists also gather around place Jean Jaurès in the quarter of **La Pleine** (Map p98). Aubagne-born Marcel Pagnol (1895–1974) spent his childhood here at 52 rue Terrusse.

Museums

Marseille has 30 museums; the tourist office has a comprehensive list.

Permanent exhibitions at municipal museums are free on Sunday mornings, and cost €2/1 for adult/child during the rest of the week. Temporary exhibitions usually cost €3/1.50. Unless otherwise indicated, museums listed here are open Tuesday to Sunday, 10am to 5pm October to May, and 11am to 6pm from June to September.

CENTRE DE LA VIEILLE CHARITÉ

Designed by Marseillais architect Pierre Puget, the arcaded courtyard of the **Centre de la Vieille Charité** (Old Charity Centre; Map p106; ☎ 04 91 14 58 80; 2 rue de la Charité, 2e) wraps around Provence's most imposing baroque church. Used variously as a barracks, a soldiers' rest home and, later,

MARSEILLE AREA

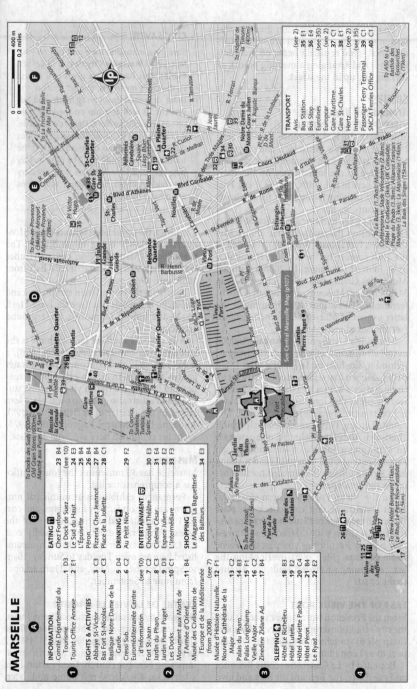

MARSEILLE

INFORMATION
Comité Départemental du
Tourisme....................................1 D3
Tourist Office Annexe....................2 E1

SIGHTS & ACTIVITIES
Abbaye St-Victor..........................3 C3
Bas Fort St-Nicolas......................4 C3
Basilique Notre Dame de la
Garde..5 D4
Cressi Sub..................................6 C2
Euroméditerranée Centre
d'Information...........................(see 10)
Fort St-Jean................................7 C2
Jardin du Pharo...........................8 C3
Jardin Pierre Puget......................9 D3
Les Docks..................................10 C1
Monument aux Morts de
l'Armée d'Orient.......................11 B4
Musée des Civilisations de
l'Europe et de la Méditerranée
(from 2008)...........................12 F1
Nouvelle Cathédrale de la
Major..13 C2
Palais du Pharo..........................14 B3
Palais Longchamp.......................15 F1
Vieille Major................................16 C2
Zinedine Zidane Ad....................17 B4

SLEEPING
Hôtel Le Richelieu.......................18 B3
Hôtel Lutetia..............................19 E2
Hôtel Mariette Pacha..................20 C4
Hôtel Péron................................21 B4
Le Ryad.....................................22 E2

EATING
Chez Fonfon..............................23 B4
Le Dock de Suez......................(see 10)
Le Sud du Haut.........................24 E3
L'Épuisette................................25 B4
Péron..26 B4
Pizzeria Chez Jeannot................27 B4
Place de la Joliette.....................28 C1

DRINKING
Au Petit Nice.............................29 F2

ENTERTAINMENT
Chocolat Théâtre.......................30 E3
Cinéma César............................31 E4
Espace Julien.............................32 E2
L'Intermédiaire...........................33 F3

SHOPPING
Le Magasin La Baguetterie
des Batteurs............................34 E3

TRANSPORT
Avis.......................................(see 2)
Bus Station...............................35 E1
Bus Stop..................................36 E4
Eurolines..............................(see 35)
Europcar...................................37 C1
Gare Maritime..........................(see 2)
Gare St-Charles..........................38 E1
Hertz....................................(see 2)
Intercars...............................(see 35)
Passenger Ferry Terminal.............39 C1
SNCM Ferries Office....................40 C1

low-cost housing for people who lost their homes during WWII, the centre now houses the **Musée d'Archéologie Mediterranéenne** (☎ 04 91 14 58 80) and the **Musée des Arts Africains, Océaniens & Amérindiens** (Museum of African, Oceanic & American Indian Art; ☎ 04 91 14 58 38), which has a diverse and often striking collection, including masks from the Americas, Africa and the Pacific.

A combined ticket for adult/student costs €5/2.50.

MUSÉE CANTINI

Recessed behind grand gates inside a 17th-century *hôtel particulier* (private mansion), the **Musée Cantini** (Map p106; ☎ 04 91 54 77 75; 19 rue Grignan, 6e; metro Estrangin-Préfecture; adult/child 10-16yr €3/1.50; ☺ 10am-5pm Tue-Sun Oct-May, 11am-6pm Tue-Sun Jun-Sep) has collections including 17th- and 18th-century Provençal ceramics and landscapes of the surrounding region including André Derain's *Pinède, Cassis* (1907) and Raoul Dufy's *Paysage de l'Estaque* (1908).

MUSÉE D'HISTOIRE DE MARSEILLE

For a fascinating insight into Marseille's composited history, the **Musée d'Histoire de Marseille** (History Museum of Marseille; Map p106; ☎ 04 91 90 42 22; ground fl, Centre Bourse shopping centre, 1er; ☺ noon-7pm Mon-Sat) has some extraordinary exhibits such as the remains of a merchant vessel discovered by chance in the Vieux Port in 1974, which plied the surrounding waters back in the early 3rd century AD.

Fragments of Roman buildings unearthed during the construction of the Centre Bourse shopping centre can be seen outside the museum in the **Jardin des Vestiges** (Garden of Ruins), which fronts rue Henri Barbusse (1er).

MUSÉE DES DOCKS ROMAINS

At the **Musée des Docks Romains** (Roman Docks Museum; Map p106; ☎ 04 91 91 24 62; place Vivaux, 2e; metro Vieux Port), displays include 1st-century Roman structures; with vast jars that held up to 2000L of wine or oil.

MUSÉE DE LA MODE

Avant-garde fashions take centre stage at the stylish **Musée de la Mode** (Fashion Museum; Map p106; ☎ 04 91 56 59 57; 11 La Canebière, 1er; adult/child €3/1), which features thousands of garments and accessories from 1945 onwards, and some striking temporary retrospectives such as 1920s beachwear.

MUSÉE DE LA MARINE ET DE L'ÉCONOMIE

The colonnaded Chamber of Commerce (also known as the Palais de la Bourse), built between 1854 and 1860, houses a **Musée de la Marine et de l'Économie** (Naval & Economy Museum; Map p106; ☎ 04 91 39 33 33; 9 La Canebiére, 1er; metro Vieux Port; adult/child under 12 €2/free; ☺ 10am-6pm Tue-Sun). The museum highlights Marseille's economic ties to the sea through a series of paintings, engravings, models and other exhibits.

PALAIS LONGCHAMP

Constructed in the 1860s, the colonnaded **Palais Longchamp** (Map p98; blvd Philippon, 4e; metro Cinq Avenues Longchamp) was designed in part to disguise a water tower built at the terminus of an aqueduct from the River Durance. Ponder prehistoric Provence in its **Musée d'Histoire Naturelle** (Natural History Museum; Map p98; ☎ 04 91 14 59 50; adult/child 10-16yr €3/1.50; ☺ 10am-5pm Tue-Sun Oct-May, 11am-6pm Tue-Sun Jun-Sep).

MUSÉE D'ART CONTEMPORAIN

Wild, off-the-wall creations of Marseille-born sculptor César (César Baldaccini; 1921–98) are displayed at the **Musée d'Art Contemporain** (Museum of Contemporary Art; MAC; ☎ 04 91 25 01 07; 69 blvd de Haïfa, 8e) as well as works by Christo, Nice new realists Ben and Klein, and pop artist Andy Warhol.

Take bus 44 from the Rond-Point du Prado (Prado roundabout) metro stop to the place Bonnefons stop, from where it is a short walk along av de Hambourg to rond-point Pierre Guerre, easily recognisable by a giant metal thumb – a classic César imprint – that sticks up from the middle of the roundabout.

Churches & Cathedrals

BASILIQUE NOTRE DAME DE LA GARDE

Everywhere you go in Marseille, you'll see the golden statue of the **Basilique Notre Dame de la Garde** (Map p98; ☎ 04 91 13 40 80; admission free; ☺ basilica & crypt 7am-7pm, longer hr in summer), the Romano-Byzantine basilica rising up from the city's highest hill, La Garde (162m). Built between 1853 and 1864, the domed basilica is ornamented with coloured marble, murals, and intricate mosaics, which were superbly restored in 2006; it gives you a 360-degree panorama of the city's sea of terracotta roofs below. Its bell tower is crowned by a 9.7m-tall gilded statue of the Virgin Mary on a 12m-high pedestal. Bullet marks and vivid shrapnel scars on the cathedral's northern façade mark the fierce fighting that took place during Marseille's Battle of Liberation in August 1944.

Bus 60 links the Vieux Port (from cours Jean Ballard) with the basilica. Otherwise, there's a **little train** (p104), which departs from the Vieux Port for the 20-minute trip up the steep hill. This gives you around 20 minutes to look around before catching the next one back down. By foot it's 1km south of the Vieux Port.

NOUVELLE CATHÉDRALE DE LA MAJOR

Cupolas, towers and turrets top the Romano-Byzantine **Nouvelle Cathédrale de la Major** (New Cathedral of the Major; Map p98; place de la Major, 2e; metro Joliette). Built between 1852 and 1893, the enormous 140m-long, 60m-high structure dwarfs the remains of the neighbouring 11th-century cathedral, **Vieille Major** (Old Major; Map p98; closed to visitors).

ABBAYE ST-VICTOR

The twin tombs of 4th-century martyrs and a 3rd-century sarcophagus are among the sacred objects inside imposing Romanesque 12th-century **Abbaye St-Victor** (Map p98; 3 rue de l'Abbaye, 7e; metro Vieux Port), set on a hill above the Vieux Port. The annual Pèlerinage de la Chandeleur and Marseille's annual sacred-music festival, Festival des Chants Sacrés en Méditerranée, also take place here (see p104).

The Coast

Mesmerising views of the Med – and of a whole other face of Marseille – unveil along **corniche Président John F Kennedy** (7e). Beginning 200m southwest of the Jardin du Pharo, Marseille's main coast road continues south past the small **Plage des Catalans** (Map p98) – the nearest beach to the city centre – to **Vallon des Auffes** (Map p98). Nestled around this picture-postcard fishing village are traditional *cabanons* (seaside cabins), built by fishermen to store tackle and cook traditional Sunday *bouillabaisse*. A narrow staircase (behind the bus stop) links corniche Président John F Kennedy with the harbour.

On the road above stands the 1922 **Monument aux Morts de l'Armée d'Orient** (Map p98), a WWI memorial statue.

LITTLE SAINTS

One of Provence's most enduring – and endearing – Christmas traditions is *santons*, tiny kiln-fired figures accompanying the nativity scene.

The custom of creating a crèche with figurines featuring Mary, Joseph, shepherds, kings, oxen and a donkey dates from the Avignon papacy of John XII (1319–34). But it was only after the 1789 Revolution and consequent Reign of Terror that these figures were cut down in size as the people of Provence handcrafted them in the secrecy of their homes: hence, the birth of the *santon* and the Provençal crèche.

Santons (from *santoùn* in Provençal, meaning 'little saint') stand between 2.5cm and 15cm high. The first colourfully painted terracotta figures were created by Marseillais artisan Jean-Louis Lagnel (1764–1822), who came up with the idea of crafting clay miniatures in a plaster mould and allowing them to dry before firing the figures at 950°C. *Santonniers* (*santon* makers) still stick to Lagnel's method today.

In a traditional Provençal crib – set up in churches and peoples' homes in early November and dismantled after the three kings have delivered their gifts during Epiphany – there are 55 *santons* ranging from the tambourine man, chestnut seller, fishwife and woman with aïoli, to the tinsmith, scissor grinder, a trumpet-blowing angel and the patron saint of *santonniers*, St Francis of Assisi.

Since 1803, *santonniers* have continued to visit Marseille each December to take part in the **Foire aux Santonniers**, which sees the length of La Canebière transformed into one great big *santon* fair. The same month, Aubagne (p119) holds its two-day **Biennale de l'Art Santonnier** incorporating *santon*-making workshops.

Marseille's magical **Musée du Santon** (Map p106; ☎ 04 91 54 26 58; 47 rue Neuve Ste-Catherine, 7e; admission free; ☾ 10am-noon & 2-6.30pm Tue-Sun) displays an enchanting private collection of 18th- and 19th-century *santons* belonging to *santonnier* Marcel Carbonnel. Entrance to the adjoining **ateliers** (workshops; ☾ 8am-1pm & 2-5.40pm Mon-Thu), where you can watch the figures being crafted, is also free.

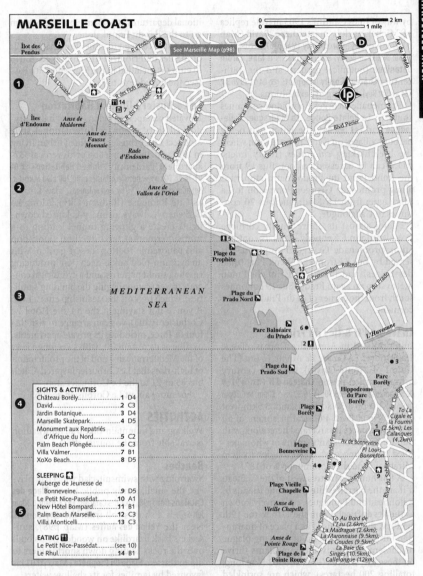

MARSEILLE COAST

SIGHTS & ACTIVITIES
Château Borély.....................1 D4
David.....................................2 C3
Jardin Botanique.................3 D4
Marseille Skatepark.............4 D5
Monument aux Repatriés
  d'Afrique du Nord............5 C2
Palm Beach Plongée...........6 C3
Villa Valmer.........................7 B1
XoXo Beach.........................8 D5

SLEEPING
Auberge de Jeunesse de
  Bonneveine.......................9 D5
Le Petit Nice-Passédat.......10 A1
New Hôtel Bompard...........11 B1
Palm Beach Marseille.........12 C3
Villa Monticelli...................13 C3

EATING
Le Petit Nice-Passédat.....(see 10)
Le Rhul...............................14 B1

The *jardins* (gardens) of **Villa Valmer** (Map p101; ☎ 04 91 31 32 49; 275 corniche Président John F Kennedy; admission free; ☽ gardens 8am-7pm) are a potent cocktail of pistachio, palm and pine trees shading one of the few surviving bourgeois villas that were built along the coast during the Second Empire. The villa is otherwise closed to visitors.

Sculpted in bronze by César in 1971, the enormous propeller of the **Monument aux Repatriés d'Afrique du Nord** (Map p101) honours those who returned from North Africa. Further south, in front of the body-packed Prado beaches (p102) on the intersection of av du Prado and promenade Georges Pompidou, Marseille's Italian connection is demonstrated by way of Jules Cantini's 1903 marble replica of Michelangelo's masterpiece, **David** (Map p101). Nearby, **Parc Borély** (Map p101; ☎ 04 91 76 59 38; av du Parc Borély) encompasses a **lake**, **jardin botanique** (botanical garden) and the 18th-century **Château Borély** (Map p101; ☎ 04 91 25 26 34; 134 av Clot Bey), hosting art exhibitions.

Promenade Georges Pompidou continues south to **La Pointe-Rouge**, **La Madrague**, **Callelongue** and **Les Goudes**, the latter two being harbour villages on Cap Croisette from where the breathtaking *calanques* (rocky inlets; p115) can be accessed on foot. Bus 19 from the Rond-Point du Prado metro stop runs along promenade Georges Pompidou to La Madrague; from La Madrague bus 20 continues to Callelongue.

Along almost its entire length, corniche Président John F Kennedy – and its continuation, promenade Georges Pompidou – is served by bus 83 from the Vieux Port (quai des Belges) and the Rond-Point du Prado metro stop on av du Prado. Bus 19 continues south from the corner of av du Prado and the corniche.

Château d'If & Îles du Frioul

Immortalised in Alexandre Dumas' classic 1840s novel *Le Comte de Monte Cristo* (The Count of Monte Cristo), the 16th-century fortress-turned-prison **Château d'If** (☎ 04 91 59 02 30; adult/student €5/3.50; ☉ 9.30am-5.30pm, to 6.30pm Jun-Aug) sits on a 30-sq-km island, 3.5km west of the Vieux Port. Political prisoners of all persuasions were incarcerated here, along with hundreds of Protestants (many of whom perished in the dungeons), the Revolutionary hero Mirabeau, and the Communards of 1871.

A few hundred metres west of the Château d'If are the barren white-limestone islands of Ratonneau and Pomègues, collectively known as the **Îles du Frioul**. From the 17th to the 19th century, they were used as a place of quarantine for people suspected of carrying plague or cholera. Sea birds and rare plants thrive on these tiny islands (each about 2.5km long, totalling 200 hectares), which are sprinkled with the ruins of the old quarantine hospital, Hôpital Caroline, and Fort Ratonneau (used by German troops during WWII).

Boats run by **GACM** (Map p106; ☎ 04 91 55 50 09; www.answeb.net/gacm in French) leave from quai des Belges at 9am, 10.30am, noon, 2pm and 3.30pm (€10 return, 20 minutes) to both the Château d'If and the Îles du Frioul, and add-itional departures at 6.45am, 5pm and 6.30pm go to the Îles du Frioul alone.

It costs €10 to go to either the Château d'If or the Îles du Frioul, or €15 combined. A trip to either is included in the Marseille City Pass (see the boxed text, p97).

Le Corbusier's Unité d'Habitation

Elevated on tapering pylons like a titanic dry-docked ship, visionary International-style architect Le Corbusier redefined urban living in 1952 with the completion of his vertical 337-apartment 'garden city', **Unité d'Habitation** (☎ 04 91 16 78 00; www.hotellecorbusier.com; 280 blvd Michelet, 8e; admission free; ☉ by appointment), also known as Cité Radieuse (Radiant City). Along its darkened hallways, primary-coloured downlights create a glowing tunnel leading to a minisupermarket, architectural bookshop and panoramic rooftop 'desert garden' with an avocado-tiled ankle-deep pool producing rippling sunlit patterns, and a cylindrical concrete tower (camouflaging the building's utilities), which tops off the steamship effect. Even if you're not staying at the on-site Hôtel Le Corbusier (p105), you can arrange to visit this tour de force, including its private apartments, or dine at its restaurant, with sweeping views of the Mediterranean – and of the proliferation of high-rises that Le Corbusier inspired. Catch bus 83 or 21 to the Le Corbusier stop.

For more about Le Corbusier, see p65.

ACTIVITIES

Walking and mountain-bike trail information is available from the tourist office.

Beaches

Swarming with swimsuit-clad volleyball players, the small, sandy public beach **Plage des Catalans** (Map p98; 3 rue des Catalans; ☉ 8.30am-6.30pm Jun-Sep) is a short stroll from the city centre. Near the **Vallon des Auffes** (Map p98), sun-seekers bask lizardlike on wooden decks built over the rocks, sliding down short ladders to dip in the sea. **Plage du Prophète** (Map p101) is favoured by families for its shallow waters.

Marseille's main beach area is the 1km-long **Parc Balnéaire du Prado** (Map p101; ☎ 04 91 29 30 40); created from backfill from the excavations for Marseille's metro. Beginning 5km south of the centre, it's split into five beaches (north to south): **Plage du Prado Nord** (also called Plage du Petit Roucas Blanc), **Plage du Prado Sud** (also called Plage de David), **Plage Borély, Plage Bon-**

FEVER PITCH

Nothing unites Marseillais from all backgrounds like their beloved football team, **Olympique de Marseille** (OM; www.olympiquedemarseille.com), established in 1899. The team's hallowed home ground, the **Stade Vélodrome** (3 blvd Michelet, 8e; metro Rond-Point du Prado) was built in the 1930s and initially held cycling fixtures (hence the name). Overhauled to host the 1998 World Cup, the stadium now seats up to 60,000 screaming spectators. One-hour **guided stadium tours** (€5) kick off in July and August – reserve at the tourist office.

In town, match tickets as well as shirts, scarves and other paraphernalia in the club's 'sky (blue) and white' colours are sold at OM's **Boutique Officielle** (Map p106; ☎ 04 91 33 52 28; 44 La Canebière, 1er; metro Noailles; ☯ 10am-7pm Mon-Sat), and **L'OM Café** (Map p106; ☎ 04 91 33 80 33; 3 quai des Belges, 1er; metro Vieux Port; ☯ 7am-1am), with soccer balls suspended from the ceiling and press clippings and posters plastering the walls. The bar – and especially its outdoor terrace – hosts a giant party when it screens every OM game. If you can't make it here, OM has its own pay-TV channel, **OMTV** (www.omnet-web.com/tv.html in French), which broadcasts daily from 5pm to 9pm.

Marseille's most famous footballer never to have played for OM is Midas-booted midfielder, Zinedine 'Zizou' Zidane, who struck gold for France in 1998's World Cup and captained the country to the 2006 World Cup final (losing to Italy after *that* head-butt)then retired as the word's highest-paid player. He's immortalised in gigantic Adidas-ad form on the side of 82b corniche Président John F Kennedy (Map p98).

---

neveine and **Plage Vieille Chapelle**. These beaches have public toilets, showers, first-aid posts with coastguards and free lockers to safeguard valuables. Prado du Nord and Sud are wheelchair accessible; Prado du Nord and Borély have a children's playground; and café-clad Borély and Bonneveine have sun-loungers/parasols to rent (€10/4 per day). **Plage de la Pointe Rouge**, further south again, is hot with windsurfers and water-skiers. And, even though it's the Med, the swell's often big enough (not Biarritz-big, but big enough!) to surf; you'll find board-hire shops on av du Prado.

Take bus 83 (583 at night) from quai des Belges to the Plage David or La Plage stop; or buses 19 or 72 from the Rond-Point du Prado metro stop. On foot, follow corniche Président John F Kennedy.

Boating

In addition to Château d'If and the Îles du Frioul (opposite), several more islands (some protected by the Conservatoire du Littoral; p76) are scattered offshore. Though it's not possible to visit them, you can rent a boat to sail around them. **AVP Location** (☎ 04 91 91 86 77; 96 quai du Port, 2e; metro Vieux Port) rents boats and yachts of all shapes and sizes.

Diving & Snorkelling

Spectacular diving and snorkelling abounds in the waters around Marseille and its offshore islands. Hire equipment from **Cressi Sub** (Map

p98; ☎ 04 91 90 95 74; 11 av de St-Jean, 1er; metro Vieux Port) or **Palm Beach Plongée** (Map p101; ☎ 04 91 22 10 38; www.airdive-provence.com; Hôtel Concorde Palm Beach, 2 promenade de la Plage, 8e). Dives start from €37 including gear; snorkelling is priced from €23.

From mid-June to mid-September, half-day baptism dives (€48) run by **Aqua 13** (www .aqua13.com in French) can be booked through the tourist office.

Kayaking

All-day sea-kayaking (€55; June to September) adventures with **Raskas Kayak** (www.raskas-kayak .com in French) are arranged by the tourist office.

For a moonlit paddle around the *calanques*, contact **Jean Christophe Fabre** (☎ 06 75 74 25 81) for times and prices.

Inline Skating & Skateboarding

Even if you're not a skater, you'll get a rush watching the death-defying tricks at the beachside **Marseille Skatepark** (Map p101; www .marseilleskatepark.fr.st; av Pierre Mendès, 8e), a giant bowl that's legendary on the international circuit. Take bus 19 from the Rond-Point du Prado metro stop on av du Prado to the Vieille Chapelle stop in front of Plage Vieille Chapelle. If you are a skater, you can hire blades and boards opposite the skate park from **XoXo Beach** (Map p101; ☎ 04 91 25 15 39; 197 av Pierre Mendès France, 8e; per hr/half-day/full-day €3.80/7.60/12; ☯ 10am-7pm). If you pick them up at 6.30pm and return them by noon you'll only pay for half a day. Some ID is required as a deposit.

At press time, Marseille's en-masse blade through the city streets, **Marseille en Roller** (MER; ☎ 06 26 50 34 76; www.marseilleenroller.com), had been cancelled by the authorities, but hopes were high for its resurrection.

TOURS

Marseille's tourist office runs several thematic **guided tours** a week, with at least a couple in English, spotlighting aspects of the city's art, architecture and artists such as writer-film-maker Marcel Pagnol. Walking tours start from €6.50, with coach tours from €14. Schedules are usually available one month ahead; advance bookings are essential.

The hop-on-hop-off, open-topped bus, **Le Grand Tour** (☎ 04 91 91 05 82; adult/student/child €17/14/8; ☻ 10am-at least 4pm) travels between key sights and museums, taking in the Vieux Port, the corniche and Notre Dame de la Garde, accompanied by a five-language audio guide. Tickets are available from the tourist office or on the bus.

For a DIY walking tour, the free city map handed out by the tourist office outlines three **walking circuits**. The one around Le Panier corresponds with a red-painted line on the pavement, though once in a while it dead-ends (and at one point runs straight into a concrete-bound tree).

Two **little trains** (Les Petits Trains; Map p106; ☎ 04 91 25 24 69; www.petit-train-marseille.com; adult/child €5/3), offer a great, calf-friendly way to see some of the steeper parts of the city. One circuit runs up to the Basilique Notre Dame de la Garde (p99) year-round; the other tootles around Le Panier (p97) from April to October. Recorded commentary is in several languages, but because of the open-air 'carriages' and chattering groups aboard, it's difficult to hear. Check at the ticket office for departure times. Note that trains only depart when they have enough passengers.

In July and August, **GACM** (p102) runs boat trips (commentary in French) from the Vieux Port to Cassis and back (€20), which pass by the *calanques'* clear turquoise coves.

FESTIVALS & EVENTS

Pèlerinage de la Chandeleur (Candlemas Pilgrimage) Each year on 2 February, the statue of the Black Virgin inside the Abbaye St-Victor (p100) is carried through the streets in this candlelit procession.
Carnaval de Marseille A street carnival with decorated floats, held in March.
Beach volleyball world championships Hosted by Plage du Prado; in July.
Festival de Marseille (www.festivaldemarseille.com in French) The city's frenetic energy peaks in July, with 21 days of contemporary international dance, theatre, music and art.
Five Continents Jazz Festival (www.festival-jazz-cinq -continents.com in French) Fired up with acid jazz, funk and folk; in July.
Ciné Plein Air festival In July and August, watch French-language films for free under open skies – look for posters or ask at the tourist office.
Fête de l'Assomption On 15 August; honours the city's traditional protector with a Mass in the Nouvelle Cathédrale de la Major (p100) and a procession through Le Panier.
Festival des Chants Sacrés en Méditerranée In October; brings sacred-music concerts to Marseillais churches.
Fiesta des Suds Celebrates world music; held at the Docks des Suds (p112) in October.

SLEEPING

Because Marseille's not geared to tourists (in the way that Nice is), rooms are in short supply – book ahead.

Chambres d'Hôtes

Le Ryad (Map p98; ☎ 04 91 47 74 54; www.leryad.fr; 16 rue Sénac de Meilhan, 1er; metro Vieux Port; s €65-90, d €75-100, mini-ste €110-120; ✖ ♿) Stepping inside the richly coloured, tapered arches of this *chambre d'hôte* (bed and breakfast accommodation) half a block off La Canebière feels like

---

AUTHOR'S CHOICE

Hôtel Péron (Map p98; ☎ 04 91 31 01 41; www.hotel-peron.com; 119 corniche President John F Kennedy, 7e; s €66-76, d €70-79, tw €90-106; ℗ 🖳) Wow. In the same family for four generations, this utterly unassuming 1920s period piece has a faded exterior that conceals museumlike rooms preserving original Art Deco turquoise-and-black ceramic bathrooms (some only partly partitioned) and parquet floors inlaid with Provençal olive-picking scenes. Many rooms are set at an angle to accentuate the sea views, and all have balconies. Breakfast (€8) isn't a meal so much as an event, when the family plays traditional Marseille music. Bonus: free parking.

setting foot in Casablanca, home town of its artist-owner. Rates include breakfast in the sculpture-strewn garden; book ahead for a festive table d'hôte meal (€35) featuring North African specialities such as plum-and-apricot-flavoured lamb *tajines* (Moroccan stew). Kids under 10 stay free; baby cots cost €10.

La Bastide des Escourches (☎ 04 91 27 08 47; www .bastidedesescourches.com; 6 chemin des Escourches, Village d'Eoures, 11e; d €67; P ⊠ �🐾) *Just* inside Marseille's city limits – about 19km east of the centre via the zippy A50 but close to Les Calanques and Aubagne – this late-19th-century mansion has five flowing rooms (two with private external bathrooms) painted in soothing tones of green and blue to reflect the *calanques*, after which each room takes its name. The property also has two separate, spacious, self-contained houses (from €550 per week; breakfast, sheets and cleaning extra)

Villa Monticelli (Map p101; ☎ 04 91 22 15 20; www .villamonticelli.com; 96 rue du Commandant Rolland, 8e; d €80-95; P ⊠ 🐾 🖳 ♿) Secluded within sprawling, shady gardens amid similarly grand early-20th-century mansions, this elegant Italianate villa run by Colette and Jean Paranque has five impeccable rooms inspired by Provençal luminaries like Mistral and Pagnol. You can cook up a meal in the guest kitchen or pack a picnic for the nearby beaches. Included in the rates (which drop for longer stays) are wi-fi and crispy, flaky breakfast pastries. Parking's free; for a seaside spin, bike hire costs €8 per day.

Hotels
BUDGET

Hôtel Le Richelieu (Map p98; ☎ 04 91 31 01 92; www .lerichelieu-marseille.com; 52 corniche Président John F Kennedy, 7e; d €40-88; ♿) With a breezy, beach-house vibe and marine-motif rooms, most opening to balconies, this artists' haven and adjoining atelier-gallery is built onto the rocks next to the plage des Catalans. Bathrooms are mostly tiny and tucked behind shower curtains. Jutting over the water, the sundrenched terrace is idyllic for breakfast (€7) with a backdrop of island views.

Hôtel St-Louis (Map p106; ☎ 04 91 54 02 74; www .hotel-st-louis.com; 2 rue des Récollettes, 1er; metro Noailles; s €38, d €47-49, tw €54, tr €59-65) This charmingly simple pied-à-terre is in the heart of Marseille's chic shopping district. Double sets of French doors open to Juliet balconies in many of the 22 rooms, which have towering ceilings,

French-washed walls and hexagonal-tiled terracotta floors.

MIDRANGE

Hôtel Relax (Map p106; ☎ 04 91 33 15 87; 4 rue Corneille, 1er; metro Vieux Port; s €35, d €50-55; 🐾) In a dress-circle location overlooking Marseille's Art Deco Opera House, this *chambre d'hôte*–feel 20-room hotel is framed by sunflower yellow awnings above geranium-filled window boxes. Some rooms are itty-bitty but button-cute with Provençal fabrics, TVs, telephones and an in-room fridge to stash your pre-opera champagne.

Hôtel Hermes (Map p106; ☎ 04 96 11 63 63; www .hotelmarseille.com; 2 rue de la Bonneterie, 2e, metro Vieux Port; s €47, d €63-79, nuptial ste €90; P 🐾) Adjoining the Vieux Port, Hôtel Hermes' cosy rooms are a steal. The communal rooftop terrace with tables and chairs is perfect for a sunset picnic. Perched above it, up a metal stairway-to-heaven, you'll find the ship's-cabin-style nuptial suite: it feels like you're on top of the world. Rooms on the 1st or 2nd floors are your best bet for picking up the free wi-fi. Parking costs €6.

Hôtel Belle-vue (Map p106; ☎ 04 96 17 05 40; www.hotel bellevue.fr; 34 quai du Port, 2e; metro Vieux Port; s €68-115, d €68-122, tr €137; 🐾) Inside this classical cream building cased in duck-egg blue shutters on the Vieux Port you'll find the very funky jazz bar La Caravelle (p111) and above it, the Hôtel Belle-vue's artistic rooms. Wrapping around a wrought-iron staircase (no lift, unfortunately), claret-coloured walls create a dramatic backdrop for up-and-coming painters who exhibit their work in the de facto gallery formed by the hotel's public spaces.

New Hôtel Bompard (Map p101; ☎ 04 91 99 22 22; www.new-hotel.com; 2 rue des Flots Bleues, 7e; s €75-125, d €75-140, Mas des Genêts d €180/250; P ⊠ 🐾 🖳 ⍟ ♿) From the secreted garden of this oasis near the sea, the city's commotion is a world away. Through a grand Victorian arched hallway hung with oil paintings, classically appointed rooms have dark timber furniture; or for something a bit more this century, rooms in the slate-and-olive Mas de Genêts come with glass-brick bathrooms. A guest-only restaurant opens daily for lunch and dinner in summer (Monday to Friday only in winter), with mains from €13 to €18; breakfast (€11) is served daily. Parking is free.

Hôtel Le Corbusier (☎ 04 91 16 78 00; www.hotel lecorbusier.com; 280 blvd Michelet, 8e; d €85-95; ⊠ 🐾) Staying at the restored 20-room hotel within

MARSEILLE AREA

CENTRAL MARSEILLE

this iconic concrete monolith (see p102) gives architectural aficionados the opportunity to absorb Le Corbusier's legacy from the inside out. A few extra euros get you a sublime sea view, and some rooms have balconies framed by distinctive bold colour panels.

Also recommended:

Hôtel Mariette Pacha (Map p98; ☎ 04 91 52 30 77; www.mariettepacha.fr; 5 place du 4 Septembre, 7e; s €49-54, d €59-70, q €94-99; P 🖳 🐬) Close to the city and just 200m from the sea; creatively configured to adapt to a range of accommodation including family rooms. Free online computer and wi-fi; private parking costs €10.

Hôtel Lutetia (Map p98; ☎ 04 91 50 81 78; www .hotelmarseille.com; 38 allées Léon Gambetta, 1er; metro Réformés-Canabière; s/d/tr from €55/60/69) You'll awaken to church bells ringing out from Les Réformés, the twin-

steepled church up the street from this sweet, petite place with a thimble-size lift whisking you to neat-as-a-pin rooms. Wi-fi is free.

Hôtel Saint-Ferréol (Map p106; ☎ 04 91 33 12 21; www.hotel-stferreol.com; 19 rue Pisançon, 6e; metro Vieux Port; s €72-82, d €77-92; 🖳) On the corner of the city's most beautiful lamp-lit pedestrian shopping street. Wi-fi's free; breakfast (€8.50) includes fresh-squeezed OJ.

Hôtel du Palais (☎ 04 91 37 78 86; www.hotel marseille.com; 26 rue Breteuil, 6e; metro Estrangin-Préfecture; d €80-100; ✂ ✂ 🖳) Chic place of 22 rooms done out in designer shades, with chrome-and-glass minibars, free wi-fi, a sleek red lobby and cachet to spare.

Hôtel Résidence du Vieux Port (Map p106; ☎ 04 91 91 91 22; www.hotelmarseille.com; 18 quai du Port, 2e; metro Vieux Port; s €91-105, d €91-135, apt €162; P ✂ 🖳) Most rooms in this shipping-crate-styled

INFORMATION		
Canebière Change	1	C2
Central Post Office	2	B2
Info Café	3	C3
La Savonnerie	4	C4
Librairie de la Bourse	5	C3
Librairie Maritime et Outremer	6	A4
Main Tourist Office	7	C3
Maison de la Presse	8	C3
Police Headquarters	9	D4
US Consulate	10	D4
Voyages Wasteels	11	D2

SIGHTS & ACTIVITIES		
AVP Location	12	B3
Centre de la Vieille Charité	13	A1
Jardins des Vestiges	14	C2
Le Grand Tour Bus Stop	15	B3
Les Petits Trains	16	B3
Musee d'Archéologie Méditerranéenne	(see 13)	
Musée Cantini	17	C4
Musée d'Histoire de Marseille	18	C2
Musée de la Marine et de l'Économie	19	C3
Musée de la Mode	20	C3
Musée des Arts Africains, Océaniens & Amérindiens	(see 13)	
Musée des Docks Romains	21	A2
Musée du Santon	22	A4
Pl Thiars	23	B4
Public Library	24	C2
Santon Workshop	25	A4
Town Hall	26	A2

SLEEPING		
Hôtel Belle-vue	27	B3
Hôtel Hermes	28	B2
Hôtel Mercure Beauvau Vieux Port	29	C3
Hôtel Relax	30	C4
Hôtel Résidence du Vieux Port	31	B2
Hôtel Saint-Ferréol	32	D3
Hôtel St-Louis	33	D3

EATING		
Ardamone	34	A2
Centre Bourse	35	C2
Chez Madie Les Galinettes	36	A3
Fresh Fish Market	37	B3
Garlic Market	38	C2
La Fabrique	39	A3
Le Bistro à Vin	40	A3
Le Café Parisien	41	B2
Le Femina	42	D3
Le Mas	43	C4
Le Miramar	44	B2
Le Pain Quotidien	45	B4
Le Souk	46	A3
Lemongrass	47	B4
Les Arcenaulx	48	B4
Lina's Sandwiches	(see 20)	
Marché des Capucins	49	D2
Monoprix	50	C3
Pizzaria Étienne	51	A1
Restaurant O'Stop	52	C3
Une Table Au Sud	53	B2

DRINKING		
Bar de la Marine	54	B4
Cup of Tea	55	A2

L'Exit Café	56	B4

ENTERTAINMENT		
Boutique Officielle de OM	(see 64)	
FNAC	(see 18)	
L'OM Café	57	C3
La Caravelle	(see 27)	
Le Quai du Rire	(see 63)	
Le Trolleybus	58	B4
Les Variétes	59	D2
Metal Café	60	C4
MP Bar	61	C3
Opéra de Marseille	62	C3
Passage des Arts	63	C2
Pelle Mêle	64	B4
Théâtre Badaboum	(see 63)	
Théâtre National de Marseille	65	A4
Théâtre Off	(see 63)	
Virgin Megastore	66	D4

SHOPPING		
72% Pétanque	67	A1
Au Cochon Dingue	68	A1
La Chocolatière du Panier	69	A2
La Cie de Provence	70	A2
La Maison du Pastis	71	A3
Le Comptoir du Panier	72	A2
Le Goût de l'Enfance	73	A1
Les Navettes des Accoules	74	A2

TRANSPORT		
Algérie Ferries	75	A1
Cross-Port Ferry	76	B3
Cross-Port Ferry	77	A3
Espace Infos RTM	78	C2
GACM Boats	79	B3

building give onto the port, with a small loggia to lap up the views. Parking costs €6.

TOP END

Le Petit Nice-Passédat (Map p101; ☎ 04 91 59 25 92; www.petitnicepassedat.com; Anse de Maldormé, 7e; d €150-470, ste €590-810; P X □ □ □) Nestled into the rocks above a petite cove and rock-ledge beach, this intimate little hideaway of just 16 individually and exquisitely appointed rooms overlooks an orchid-mosaic-tiled saltwater pool; and is also home to Gerald Passédat's virtuoso restaurant (p110); with half-board from €100. Guest parking's free.

Hôtel Mercure Beauvau Vieux Port (Map p106; ☎ 04 91 54 91 00; www.mercure.com; 4, rue Beauvau, 1er; metro Vieux Port; s €158-263, d €170-275, ste €400; X □ □) First opened in 1816, and receiving luminaries like Frédéric Chopin and George Sand, Marseille's most historic hotel houses antique Louis-Philippe and Napoléon III furniture. Above down-quilted beds, suspended embroideries give rooms a regal feel. Sleep under the stars in six mezzanine rooms beneath retractable shuttered skylights. The Beauvau's one

of Marseille's best bets for wheelchair access. Wi-fi starts from €10 for two hours.

Palm Beach Marseille (Map p101; ☎ 04 91 16 19 00; h3485@accor-hotels.com; 200 corniche Président John F Kennedy, 7e; s/d/ste from €249/275/495; P X □ □) You can specify if you want your views of the sea from your bathtub or bed at this cool, streamlined hotel built into the rocks. Flanked by palms, the reception area is on the 3rd floor; below it, looking a bit like a modish furniture showroom, a flowing art-gallery space has an exposed rockface gushing water from the Roucas Blanc springs, which also fills the pool. Parking costs €15.

Hostels

Frustratingly, France's second-biggest city has no central hostel.

Auberge de Jeunesse de Bonneveine (Map p101; ☎ 04 91 17 63 30; fax 04 91 73 97 23; impasse du Docteur Bonfils, 8e; dm incl sheets & breakfast €14.60-15.60, d €33.70-35.70; meals €3-8; ⏰ Feb-Dec; P □) Handy for the *calanques*, this functional HI (Hostelling International) is an easy stroll to the expansive beaches opposite Parc Borély – or just kick

CULINARY CAST-OFFS

Fish, *huîtres* (oysters), *moules* (mussels) and mounds of other shellfish are predominant and plentiful in Marseille, but nothing stands out like the city's signature dish, *bouillabaisse*. Originally it was a means for fishermen to feed their families by salvaging scraps after they'd sold the best of their catch. Despite its humble origins, today it's Marseille's most sought-after meal, prepared by pedigreed chefs including signatories to the *Charte de la Bouillabaisse Marseille* – an international charter for quality control.

Though some restaurants trap unsuspecting diners by touting it for as little as €15 (invariably meaning the fish is frozen), expect to pay about €35 to €50 per person for a true *bouillabaisse*, dished up in two parts with the soup and fish served separately. Many of the better places require you to order up to 48 hours ahead, and may require a minimum of two diners. For more on *bouillabaisse*, see p44.

Marseille subscribers to the *charte:*

Le Rhul (Map p101; ☎ 04 91 52 54 54; 269 corniche Président John F Kennedy, 7e; menus €20-50; ❂ lunch & dinner) This stalwart has been brewing *bouillabaisse* for over half a century. The views of the sea, and cuisine from it, are indubitable. And the welcome? Well, two out of three ain't bad.

Le Miramar (Map p106; ☎ 04 91 90 10 40; 12 quai du Port, 2e; metro Vieux Port; mains €25-50; ❂ lunch & dinner Tue-Sat) The white-clothed tables and burgundy velveteen settees gracing Miramar's quayside terrace and glowing lamplit interior create a fine ambience for dining on Christian Buffa's celebrated creations in style.

Chez Fonfon (Map p98; ☎ 04 91 52 14 38; 140 rue du Vallon des Auffes; menus €40 & €55, mains €15-46; ❂ lunch & dinner Tue-Sat, dinner Mon) Overlooking the quaint fishing harbour of Vallon des Auffes from an apricot-hued dining room, this third-generation-run peach of a place also specialises in *poisson à l'argile* (fresh clay-cooked fish, flavoured with aniseed).

L'Épuisette (Map p98; ☎ 04 91 52 17 82; rue du Vallon des Auffes, 7e; menus €45, €65 & €95; ❂ lunch & dinner Tue-Sat) Chef Guillaume Sourrieu's culinary wizardry conjures up desserts such as pan-fried mango doused with balsamic vinegar and sprinkled with sherbet as well as a breathtaking *bouillabaisse*.

back at the hostel bar's balmy terrace. Take bus 44 from the Rond-Point du Prado metro station to the place Bonnefons stop.

La Cigale et la Fourmi (☎ 04 91 40 05 12; 19 rue Théophile Boudier, Mazargues, 9e; dm €15, d €30) A quirky guesthouse of miniature twisting staircases and *Being John Malkovich*–like, loft-style rooms, the tiny, independent 'Cicada and the Ant' is run by Jean Chesnaud, who grew up in the house and expanded it room by room, spilling over to another little house up the road. Freebies include wi-fi and bikes; there are self-catering facilities, but no breakfast. From the Rond Point du Prado metro stop, take bus 21 to the Obelisque stop or bus 22 to the Robespierre stop.

EATING
Vieux Port & Around

The quai de Rive Neuve (1er) teems with restaurants and cafés; those along quai du Port (2e) are generally better but pricier. Behind quai de Rive Neuve, the pedestrian streets around place Thiars, cours Honoré d'Estienne d'Orves and place aux Huiles brim with umbrella-filled dining terraces in the warmer months.

Chez Madie Les Galinettes (Map p106; ☎ 04 91 90 40 87; 138 quai du Port, 2e; metro Vieux Port; mains €10-28, bouillabaisse €35; ❂ lunch & dinner Mon-Sat, closed Sat lunch in summer) Decked out with colourful original pop art and mural panels, this *très* Marseille place produces an authentic *bouillabaisse* (you'll need to order before Mme Roux's expedition to the fish markets around 3pm, so order the day before if you're headed here for lunch). Other standouts include the house specialty fish, *Les Galinettes;* marinated capsicums with anchovy tapenade; and chestnut ice cream.

Le Bistro à Vin (Map p106; ☎ 04 91 54 02 20; 17 rue Sainte, 6e; metro Vieux Port; dishes €12; ❂ closed Sun & Sat lunch) Fronted by a scrubbed claret-coloured wooden façade and filled with timber tables, this rustic beamed-ceiling wine bistro has some top drops, accompanied by Provençal fare like tapenade, an *assiette garrigue* (a mix of warm goats cheese, dried ham, fresh figs and melon), and a mouthwatering selection of artisanal cheeses.

Lemongrass (Map p106; ☎ 04 91 33 97 65; 8 rue Fort-Notre-Dame, 1er; metro Vieux Port; menus €30; ❂ closed Sun) Spice up your Marseille dining experience at this refreshing place serving succulent Asian-French fusion creations such as peeled local lobsters in curry with tart Granny Smith apples, and coconut rice pudding in banana leaf.

Le Souk (Map p106; ☎ 04 91 91 29 29; 98 quai du Port, 2e; metro Vieux Port; menus €20-30; ☉ lunch Tue-Sun & dinner Tue-Sat Sep-Jun, lunch Sat & Sun & dinner Sun Jul & Aug) Enhanced by exotic décor of orange-and-red mosaic walls, wrought-iron furniture, and tiny tea-light candles, Le Souk is an atmospheric place to savour a Moroccan *tajine* – a heaping slow-cooked meat and vegetable stew elegantly delivered in a conical covered earthenware dish that takes its name from the Greek *teganon* (frying pan).

Le Mas (Map p106; ☎ 04 91 33 25 90; 4 rue Lulli, 1er; metro Vieux Port; menu €25; ☉ 11am-4am, ☉ closed Sun Oct-Apr) Its name might mean Provençal farmhouse, but this little late-night place is snugly at home amid the urban tumult. Lining its walls are photographs of the stars, show-biz types and other insomniac artists who dine here on fab French-Provençal fare. Wine is included in *menu* prices.

Les Arcenaulx (Map p106; ☎ 04 91 54 85 38; 27 cours Honoré d'Estienne d'Orves, 1er; metro Vieux Port; menus €30-50; ☉ Mon-Sat) Wrapped around cours des Arcenaulx, this cavernous former Louis XIV warehouse contains an antiquarian and contemporary bookshop and publishing house with a specialist interest in gastronomy; as well as a grand, airy restaurant turning out taste sensations such as whole pigeon with caramelised quinces; and a *salon de thé* (tearoom) serving ice creams named after literary classics.

Une Table au Sud (Map p106; ☎ 04 91 90 63 53; 2 quai du Port, 2e; metro Vieux Port; lunch menu €34, dinner menus €48-88; ☉ closed Sun & Mon) Chef Lionel Lévy continues to break the Modern Mediterranean mould at his Michelin-starred restaurant with picture windows framing the port. Utilising local ingredients in inventive ways, you (and he) will be surprised every time by his 'surprise menu'. It comprises four imaginative courses in addition to cheese and dessert – which could be anything from a chocolate-and-avocado creation to olive-oil-and-lemon sorbet. A glass lift provides wheelchair access.

Le Panier

The area of Le Panier contains some dining legends. For artisanal specialities, see p113.

Ardamone (Map p106; ☎ 04 91 90 18 09; 28 rue Caisserie, 2e; metro Vieux Port; menus €14-20, mains €9.50-18; ☉ 10am-7pm Tue-Sat) Avocado and salmon sushi, green chicken curry with fragrant rice, and tofu and carrots marinaded in ginger are among the world-influenced dishes at Marseille's only *resto bio* (organic restaurant). A couple of vegan dishes are included on the strictly organic menu, which also features scrumptious desserts such as chocolate and split-almond brownies and blueberry crumble with raspberry coulis.

Pizzaria Étienne (Map p106; 43 rue de Lorette, 2e; metro Colbert; mains €7-13.50; ☉ lunch & dinner Mon-Sat) This old Marseillais haunt has the best pizza in town as well as succulent *pavé de boeuf* (beef steak) and scrumptious *supions frits* (pan-fried squid with garlic and parsley), but it's not just the food that packs the place out. Because Pizzaria Étienne is a convivial meeting point for the entire neighbourhood, you'll need to pop in beforehand to reserve in person (there's no phone), though you will get a free aperitif while you wait for a table. Credit cards aren't accepted. From rue de la République, cut down passage de Lorette and walk up the staircase.

Le Café Parisien (Map p106; ☎ 04 91 90 05 77; 1 place Sadi Carnot, 2e; metro Colbert; mains €14.90-24.60;

KICK STARTS & QUICK FIXES TO REV YOU UP

Le Pain Quotidien (Map p106; ☎ 04 91 33 55 00; 18 place Aux Huiles, 1er; metro Vieux Port; dishes €5-8; ☉ 8am-6pm Sun-Wed, to 10pm Thu-Sat) Locals tuck into eggs for breakfast along with their daily *bio* (organic) bread, smothered in finger-licking chocolate spread.

Lina's Sandwiches (Map p106; ☎ 04 96 11 54 16; 11 La Canebière, 1er; metro Vieux Port; lunch formule €7.50, sandwiches €3.50-6.85; ☉ 9.30am-5pm Mon-Sat) Adjoining the Musée de la Mode, this spiffy home of the 'beautiful sandwich' sports cranberry, orange and mustard décor and stylish desserts such as lemon-meringue pie.

La Caravelle (Map p106; ☎ 04 96 17 05 40; www.hotelbellevue.fr; 34 quai du Port, 2e; metro Vieux Port; breakfast €8, mains €11.50-12.50; ☉ breakfast & lunch) Top-notch breakfasts and lunches that hit the spot come with tip-top views of the port. Also a live-music venue (p111).

Restaurant O'Stop (Map p106; ☎ 04 91 33 85 34; 15 rue St-Saëns, 1er; metro Vieux Port; menu €10; ☉ 24hr) Simple regional specialities are dished up this little hole-in-the-wall round the clock.

⊗ 7.30am-4pm Mon-Sat Jul-Aug, to 4pm Mon-Wed, to 2am Thu-Sat Sep-Jun) Le Café Parisien's sculpted plaster walls have been a theatrical backdrop for Marseillais diners for over a century. The brasserie's once-faded glamour has recently been restored to its former heyday splendour, serving elegant fare such as squid drizzled in olive oil and a richer-than-rich risotto. Post-repas, play boules on the café's indoor pitch downstairs, or have a pastis at the adjacent underground bar.

La Fabrique (Map p106; ☎ 04 91 91 40 48; 3 place Jules Verne, 2e; metro Vieux Port; mains around €15; ⊗ 7.30pm-2am Wed-Fri, noon-2am Sat & Sun) The concrete bar and loungy retro vibe is a magnet for hipsters, as is the Mediterranean menu.

Le Panier's western fringe flows into the commercial port area (metro Joliette, 8e), where dining spots at the London-docks-like complex, Les Docks, include the voluminous **Le Dock de Suez** (Map p98; ☎ 04 91 56 07 56; 10 place de la Joliette, 2e; metro Joliette; mains around €25; ⊗ lunch Mon-Fri; dinner & weekends by reservation). Business high flyers rub shoulders as chef Richard Tucita greases the wheeling and dealing with sophisticated dishes such as supions à la Provençale (squid with garlic and tomatoes) and braised ox cheek.

Cours Julien & Around

For fare as diverse as Marseille itself, head to cours Julien and its surrounding streets like rue des Trois Mages for a staggering array of cuisines, including Greek, Indian, Lebanese, Spanish and North African.

Le Femina (Map p106; ☎ 04 91 54 03 56l 1 rue Musée, 1er, metro Noailles; menus €8-18; ⊗ lunch & dinner Tue-Sat) East from the Vieux Port towards cours Julien, Le Femina is a great and eminently affordable traditional Algerian place for couscous. This dish has been cooked to perfection by five generations of the same welcoming family since 1921.

Le Sud du Haut (Map p98; ☎ 04 91 92 66 64; 80 cours Julien, 6e; metro Notre Dame du Mont-Cours Julien; mains around €10; ⊗ lunch Tue-Sat, dinner Thu-Sat) Dine on the sky-topped terrace or amid the contemporary sculptures and artworks at this offbeat place. The chef prepares local faves such as stuffed Provençal vegetables.

By the Sea

Beach cafés, restaurants and bars overlooking Plage Borély and Plage Bonneveine all give you a chance to dine with sand between your toes; there are also a couple of eateries where you can wear your bikini, around Plage des Catalans.

Several bouillabaisse specialists (see p108) also serve up sea views.

Pizzeria Chez Jeannot (Map p98; ☎ 04 91 52 11 28; 129 rue du Vallon des Auffes, 7e; dishes from €6; ⊗ lunch & dinner Tue-Sun) With a magical setting overlooking the storybook Vallon des Auffes, this affable, affordable joint has fresh-as-it-gets salads, pasta and shellfish, plus piping-hot pizzas.

La Baie des Singes (The Bay of Monkeys; ☎ 04 91 73 68 87; Cap Croisette; mains €12-25; ⊗ lunch & dinner Apr-Sep) Stunningly located on a cape 15km south of the centre. Select your seafood prior to its preparation, and afterwards collapse on a comfy deck chair overlooking Île Maïre. From Les Goudes follow the signs to the Cap Croisette car park then walk 500m along the narrow path through rocks. Ask when booking about getting here by boat.

Au Bord de l'Eau (☎ 04 91 72 68 04; 15 rue des Arapèdes, port de la Madrague Montredon, 8e; menus €25-30; ⊗ daily Jul & Aug, closed Tue & lunch Sun, Dec & Jan) Promise you won't tell too many people about this little harbourside haven literally 'at the water's edge'. Chances are, you can thank the fishing boats moored below the sun-drenched terrace for catching the fish on your plate just hours before. To get here, catch bus 83 to the statue of David at av du Prado, then continue south on bus 19.

Péron (Map p98; ☎ 04 91 52 15 22; 56 corniche Président John F Kennedy, 7e; menu €60; ⊗ lunch & dinner) This designer, truffle-coloured place set out over the sea is one of the premier destinations in Marseille for a no-holds-barred gastronomic extravaganza. Stunning views unfold over the Med – and your plate, with highlights including lobster risotto.

Le Petit Nice-Passédat (Map p101; menus €90-150, mains €50-95; ⊗ lunch Tue-Sat & dinner daily summer, lunch & dinner daily winter) Maestro Gerald Passédat creates twin-Michelin-starred seafood- and meat-based masterpieces inspired by the slow southern tempo – and by Nénette the turtle, who has roamed Le Petit Nice-Passédat's terrace for over 30 years. For more on accommodation here, see p107.

Self-Catering

Marseille's most aromatic markets are its **fresh fish market** (Map p106; quai des Belges, 1er; metro Vieux Port; ⊗ 8am-noon), at the old port, circled by hungry seagulls; and its **garlic market** (Map p106; cours Belsunce, 1er; metro Vieux Port; ⊗ late Jun-late Jul).

Fruit, vegetables, fish and dried products are sold at the **Marché des Capucins** (Map p106; place des Capucins, 1er; metro Noailles; 🕑 8am-7pm) and the morning market on **place de la Joliette** (Map p98; place de la Joliette, 2e; metro Joliette; 🕑 Mon-Fri). For more markets, see p113.

Central supermarkets include **Monoprix** (Map p106; 36 La Canebière, 1er; metro Noailles; 🕑 8.30am-8.30pm Mon-Sat) and a couple inside the concrete bunker Centre Bourse (Map p106).

DRINKING

Drinking tends to be laid-back in Marseille, stretching languorously from the daytime into the night. Many bars double as *glaciers* (ice creameries). You can't go wrong heading for the café-ringed Vieux Port, which also has a couple of Guinness-serving Irish pubs along quai de Rive Neuve. Students and artists congregate at the alternative cafés and bars on and around cours Julien and place Jean Jaurès.

Bar de la Marine (Map p106; ☎ 04 91 54 95 42; 15 quai de Rive Neuve, 1er; 🕑 7am-1am) Marcel Pagnol filmed the card-party scenes in *Marius* – the first of his early-20th-century cult-classic trilogy – here. Today it draws in people from every walk of life, from grizzled sailors to high-powered business types. There's a terrace overlooking the port, but to really experience this institution, take a seat in the 1930s interior lined with photographs and caricatures. The bar made another big screen appearance in 2003's *Love Actually*.

L'Exit Café (Map p106; 12 quai de Rive Neuve, 7e; metro Vieux Port; 🕑 7am-1am) Close to Bar de la Marine, L'Exit Café buzzes during its nightly buy-one-get-one-free happy hour from 6pm to 9pm.

Cup of Tea (Map p106; ☎ 04 91 90 84 02; 1 rue Caisserie, 2e; metro Vieux Port; 🕑 8.30am-7pm Mon-Fri, 9.30am-7pm Sat) Just behind the northern side in Le Panier is a clutch of chic spots like this hip bookshop-café – a soothing stop if you're craving a cuppa after all that pastis. Writers' workshops and poetry slams are regular events.

Au Petit Nice (Map p98; ☎ 04 91 48 43 04; 28 place Jean Jaurès; 🕑 6am-2am) This local favourite sees shoppers stop in for a morning espresso and diners drop by for a sunset aperitif on the terrace; by nightfall its eclectic interior gets packed.

ENTERTAINMENT

Cultural events are covered in Wednesday's *L'Hebdo* (in French; €1) available around town. The website www.marseillebynight

.com (in French) also has listings. *Billetteries* (ticket counters) include **FNAC** (Map p106; ☎ 04 91 39 94 00; Centre Bourse, 1er; metro Vieux Port) and **Virgin Megastore** (Map p106; ☎ 04 91 55 84 11; 75 rue St-Ferréol, 6e; metro Estrangin-Préfecture), as well as the tourist office.

The cutting-edge cultural centre La Friche la Belle de Mai (see the boxed text, p112) embraces the entire cultural spectrum – from theatre, ballet and contemporary music to installation and video art. See p34 for more information.

Nightclubs

Marseille's club scene is burgeoning along with the rest of the city, with some of the hottest spots spread outside the city centre.

La Maronnaise (☎ 04 91 73 98 58, 04 91 72 42 65; rte de la Maronnaise, 8e; admission €10; 🕑 9am-4am Wed-Sat early May-early Sep) This hipsters' hangout at Les Goudes on Cap Croisette is a day-night event. You'll need to arrive early to snag a sun lounge or earlier still for a patch of sand on the tiny beach, before dancing under the stars till dawn. To keep you going, you can have lunch (€15) and dinner (€30) on the seaside terrace. Take bus 19 from the Rond Point du Prado metro stop on av du Prado.

Le Trolleybus (Map p106; ☎ 04 91 54 30 45; 24 quai Rive Neuve, 1er; metro Vieux Port; admission varies; 🕑 11pm-dawn Wed-Sat) Booty-shaking, tunnel-like harbourside club in a 17th-century arsenal. Top DJs spin groove, soul, funk, acid jazz, hip-hop and salsa in the Terminus and pop and rock in the Trolleybar. There's also a whisky bar and a wicked sound system.

Other happenin' haunts:

Le Bazar (☎ 04 91 79 08 88; 90 blvd Rabatau, 8e; admission €15; 🕑 midnight-6am Thu-Sun) This is a vast Moroccan-style space with bungalows and palms; DJs play techno and house.

Le Millenium (☎ 08 92 88 80 13; route de Cassis, 9e; admission free; 🕑 11pm-6am Thu-Sun) Five kinds of music across five gyrating floors, and a record-producer/rock-star-type crowd aged 20 to 50; about 6km from the centre.

Metal Café (Map p106; ☎ 04 91 54 03 03; 20 rue Fortia, 1er; metro Vieux Port; admission €5; 🕑 until late Thu-Sun) Look for the steely grey door at the foot of the staircase linking cours Honoré d'Estienne d'Orves with rue Sainte.

Live Music

La Caravelle (Map p106; ☎ 04 96 17 05 40; www.hotel bellevue.fr; 34 quai du Port, 2e; metro Vieux Port; 🕑 7am-2am; 🎵) Legendary jazz sessions take place on Friday and Saturday nights from September to May at the Hôtel Bellevue's funky 1st-floor bar. It's lined by timber walls with black-and-red-vinyl upholstered chairs, theatrical murals, and a sky blue ceiling. Free tapas is served during happy hour (6pm to 9pm) every night. On balmy nights, the balcony is a prized portside perch.

Dock des Suds (☎ 04 91 99 00 00, 08 25 83 38 33; www .dock-des-suds.org in French; 12 rue Urbain V, 2e) World music is among the genres performed at this sprawling venue near the commercial port. Hours are variable, as are admission prices.

Espace Julien (Map p98; ☎ 04 91 24 34 10; www .espace-julien.com in French; 39 cours Julien, 6e; metro Notre Dame du Mont-Cours Julien; ☺ variable) Rock, *opérock*, alternative theatre, reggae, hip-hop, Afro-groove and other cutting-edge entertainment are on the bill here; the website lists upcoming gigs and cover charges. Hours are variable.

L'Intermédiare (Map p98; ☎ 04 91 47 01 25; 63 place Jean Jaurès, 6e; metro Notre Dame du Mont-Cours Julien; admission free; ☺ 6.30pm-2am Mon-Sat) Famed for its free live-music sessions ranging from blues to breaking new bands (from 10.30pm most nights), the intimate L'Intermédiare is a gathering spot for Marseille's artists, musos and writers.

Pelle Mêle (Map p106; ☎ 04 91 54 85 26; 8 place aux Huiles, 1er; metro Vieux Port; admission €2; ☺ 5pm-2am Tue-Sat) Swing to live jazz from 10pm most nights.

Gay & Lesbian Venues

The website www.petitfute-gay.com (in French) has comprehensive coverage of Marseille's gay and lesbian scene, which revolves around the perennial favourite, **MP Bar** (Map p106; ☎ 04 91 33 64 79; 10 rue Beauvau, 1e, metro Vieux Port; ☺ until sunrise).

Opera & Ballet

Opéra de Marseille (Map p106; ☎ 04 91 55 11 10; http://opera .mairie-marseille.fr in French; 2 rue Molière, 1er; metro Vieux Port; tickets €8-35) Housed in an Art Deco building built in 1921; enter on place Ernest Reyer.

Marseille-based dance companies include the **Ballet National de Marseille** (www.ballet-de-marseille .com), which performs at various venues.

Theatre

Théâtre National de Marseille (Map p106; ☎ 04 96 17 80 00; www.theatre-lacriee.com in French; 30 quai de Rive Neuve, 7e; metro Vieux Port) Mainstream dramas are staged in Marseille's old fish-auction house, built in 1909.

Alternative performance venues include **Chocolat Théâtre** (Map p98; ☎ 04 91 42 19 29; www .chocolattheatre.com in French; 59 cours Julien, 6e; metro Notre Dame du Mont-Cours Julien); and three pocket-sized places in the **Passage des Arts** (Map p106; 16 quai de Rive Neuve, 7e; metro Vieux Port):

Le Quai du Rire (Map p106; ☎ 04 91 54 95 00)

Théâtre Badaboum (Map p106; ☎ 04 91 54 40 71)

Théâtre Off (Map p106; ☎ 04 91 33 12 92)

MARSEILLE'S RENAISSANCE

The city was slammed as a flash point for crime and corruption a few years ago, but the 21st century has heralded the rebirth of Marseille, particularly its docklands (La Joliette quarter) and central train-station area (St-Charles quarter). Marseille Euroméditerranée (Euromed) is pouring €3.05 billion into these two high-unemployment districts. By the project's completion in 2010, it will have delivered 15,000 to 20,000 new jobs, 4000 brand-new and 6000 renovated homes, and 800,000 sq metres of commercial real estate, as well as doubling the precincts' green recreational areas in size.

State-of-the-art offices and trendy restaurants are up and running in the enormous former warehouse **Les Docks** (Map p98; 10 place de la Joliette), the project showcase. Quai d'Arenc's old grain silos now contain a 2000-seat cinema, a business centre and panoramic restaurant; and in 2008 Fort St-Jean will house a **Musée des Civilisations de l'Europe et de la Méditerranée** (Museum of European & Mediterranean Civilisations; Map p98), replacing the National Museum of Arts & Popular Traditions, in Paris since 1937.

The St-Charles quarter will be the site of a new **Grand Halle** (Grand Hall), designed by French architect Jean-Marie Duthilleul, at the central train station. In the adjoining Belle de Mai district, **La Friche la Belle de Mai** (☎ 04 95 04 95 04; www.lafriche.org in French; 23 rue Guibal), a former tobacco factory and sugar-refining plant, houses theatrical and artists' workshops, cinema studios (see p65), a couple of radio stations, multimedia displays and exhibition halls.

A scale model of the future face of Marseille is on display at **Euroméditerranée Centre d'Informations** (Map p98; ☎ 0 800 111 114; www.euromediterranee.fr; Atrium 103, Les Docks, 10 place de la Joliette, 2e; metro Joliette; ☺ 10am-1pm & 2-6pm Mon-Thu, 10am-1pm & 2-5pm Fri).

MARSEILLE'S BASKET

In Le Panier's history-woven streets you can get your fill of its past, and fill your shopping basket with artisan products handmade in Marseille.

Sniff Marseille's scented handmade soaps at **La Cie de Provence** (Map p106; ☎ 04 91 56 20 94; 1 rue Caisserie), and pick up bathroom accoutrements such as colourful towels at the neighbouring **Le Comptoir du Panier** (Map p106; ☎ 04 91 56 20 94; 1 rue Caisserie). Olive-wood carvings, olive soaps and olive oils fill **72% Pétanque** (Map p106; ☎ 04 91 91 14 57; 10 rue du Petit Puits). Nearby is a clutch of ceramic ateliers with shops attached to their workshops, including **Le Transfo** (Map p106; ☎ 04 91 56 21 93; 3 rue du Petit Puits). Squeal over the cute **Au Cochon Dingue** (The Mad Pig; Map p106; ☎ 06 71 39 96 16; 6 place de Lorette), selling handmade pig ornaments.

To fill your picnic basket, try **La Chocolatière du Panier** (Map p106; ☎ 04 91 91 67 66; 4 place des 13 Cantons), with weird-and-wonderful flavours of handmade chocolates like onion and lavender; and **Les Navettes des Accoules** (Map p106; ☎ 04 91 90 99 42; 68 rue Caisserie) for traditional biscuits made from orange flour and shaped like torpedos. At **Le Goût de l'Enfance** (Map p106; ☎ 04 91 54 11 25; 6 place des Pistoles; ☿ Tue-Sat 9am-6pm) you can buy by Le Panier legend Mme Brigitte Garelli's homemade jam (it's also served by cafés in the quarter). Wash it down with the local firewater at **La Maison du Pastis** (Map p106; ☎ 04 91 90 86 77; 108 quai du Port) where you can sample more than 60 varieties of pastis or splash out on absinthe.

Then cross the port and climb up to the sculpted stone benches of the **Jardin du Pharo** (p97) to empty your picnic basket as the sunset sizzles over the water.

Cinema

Les Variétés (Map p106; ☎ 04 96 11 61 61; cesarvarietes@ wanadoo.fr; 37 rue Vincent Scotto, 1er; metro Noailles) and **Cinéma César** (Map p98; ☎ 04 91 37 12 80; 4 place Castellane, 6e; metro Castellane) screen nondubbed films.

SHOPPING

Shops around town sell the *Tarot de Marseille*, today the most commonly used tarot deck, which was originally created in Marseille to play the local version of the *tarocchi* card game before its (oc)cult following.

Music shops are massed around cours Julien, including the specialist drum shop, **Le Magasin La Baguetterie des Batteurs** (Map p98; ☎ 04 91 36 55 55; 42 cours Julien, 6; metro Notre Dame du Mont-Cours Julien; ☿ closed Sun & Mon), jam-packed with *djembes* (West African hand drums), kits, sticks and more.

Live chickens killed to order and African carved animals are among the many colourful sights at the Moroccan-style markets, **Marché aux Puces** (av du Cap Pinède, 15e; ☿ 9am-7pm Sun). To get there, take buses 35 or 70 from rue des Fabres, which is in front of Espace Infos RTM.

Cours Julien (Map p98; 6e; metro Notre Dame du Mont-Cours Julien) hosts various morning markets: fresh flowers on Wednesday and Saturday, antique books alternate Saturdays, and stamps or antique books on Sunday.

GETTING THERE & AWAY

Air

Aéroport Marseille-Provence (Marseille-Provence airport; ☎ 04 42 14 14 14; www.marseille.aeroport.fr) is in Marignane, 28km northwest of Marseille.

Boat

From two terminals at Marseille's **Gare Maritime** (Passenger ferry terminal; Map p98; ☎ 04 91 39 45 66; 23 place de la Joliette & blvd des Dames, 2e; metro Joliette), **SNCM** (Map p98; ☎ 0 891 701 801; www.sncm.fr; 61 blvd des Dames, 2e; metro Joliette; ☿ 8am-6pm Mon-Fri, 8.30am-noon & 2-5.30pm Sat) operates ferries to and from Corsica, Sardinia, Tunisia and Algeria. **Algérie Ferries** (Map p98; ☎ 04 91 90 89 28; 29 blvd des Dames, 2e; metro Joliette; ☿ 9-11.45am & 1-4.45pm Mon-Fri) operates boats to and from Algeria.

For more information about boat travel to and from Marseille, see p421.

Bus

Most buses use the **bus station** (Map p106; ☎ 04 91 08 16 40; 3 place Victor Hugo, 3e; metro Gare St-Charles) next to the train station, but some services to and from Bandol, La Ciotat and Cassis use the stop on **place Castellane** (Map p98; ☎ 04 91 79 81 82; 6e; metro Castellane), south of the centre. Bus drivers sell tickets.

Buses travel to Aix-en-Provence (€4.40, 35 minutes via the autoroute or one hour via the N8, every five to 10 minutes), Avignon (€17.20, two hours, one daily), Cannes (€23.50, two hours, four daily), Carpentras (€12, two hours), Cavaillon (€10.20, one hour), Orange and other destinations. **Phocéens Cars** (☎ 04 93 85 66 61) travels to Nice (€25, 2¾ hours, up to three daily).

Year-round services going to and from Digne-les-Bains (€15.10, 2¼ hours) and ski-season buses to and from Barcelonnette (€24.10, four hours) are operated by the Gap-based **Société des Cars Alpes Littoral** (SCAL; ☎ 08 20 83 38 33).

International routes are covered by **Eurolines** (☎ 04 91 50 57 55) and **Intercars** (☎ 04 91 50 08 66), both at Marseille bus station.

Car & Motorcycle

Car-hire agencies at the train station:

Avis (Map p98; ☎ 04 91 64 71 00; Gare St-Charles, 1er)

Europcar (Map p98; ☎ 04 91 99 09 32; 7 blvd Maurice Bourdet, 1er)

Hertz (Map p98; ☎ 04 91 14 04 24; 21 blvd Maurice Bourdet, 1er)

Train

From **Gare St-Charles** (Map p106; metro Gare St-Charles, 1er), which is Marseille's central passenger train station, there are direct services to and from Aix-en-Provence centre (€6.40, 38 minutes, 16 to 24 daily), Avignon centre (€16.80, one hour, hourly), Nîmes (€17.60, 1¼ hours, 12 daily), Arles (€12.40, 50 minutes), Orange (€19.90, 1½ hours, 10 daily) and other destinations.

More than two dozen trains a day chug east along the coast on the Marseille–Vintimille (Ventimiglia in English and Italian) line, linking Marseille with Toulon (€10.20, 45 minutes to one hour), Cannes (€24.20, two hours), Antibes (€25.20, 2¼ hours), Nice (€27, 2½ hours), Monaco (€28.50, three hours via Nice) and Menton (€29.20, 3¼ hours via Nice). Most Marseille–Hyères trains (€12.60, 1¼ hours, four daily) stop at Cassis, La Ciotat, Bandol, Ollioules, Sanary-sur-Mer and Toulon.

For trains to other parts of France and Europe see p420.

GETTING AROUND
To/From the Airport

Navette (airport ☎ 04 42 14 31 27; Marseille ☎ 04 91 50 59 34) shuttle buses link Marseille-Provence airport (adult/child €8.50/5, one hour) with Marseille's train station. Buses heading to the airport leave from outside the station's main entrance every 20 minutes between 5.30am and 9.50pm, and buses to the train station depart from the airport between 6.10am and 10.50pm.

Bicycle

Motorists parked with Vinci Park (below) can pick up a free bicycle to pedal around town. **Tandem** (Map p101; ☎ 04 91 22 64 80; 6 av du Parc Borély; ☼ 9am-6.30pm) hires out wheels near the beach.

Boat

A ferry yo-yos between the town hall on quai du Port and place aux Huiles on quai de Rive Neuve 8am to 6.30pm daily. An adult single/return fare costs €0.50/0.80 (under seven years free). Sailing time is three minutes. Tickets are available on the ferry.

Car & Motorcycle

Dead-central underground car parks run by **Vinci Park** (www.vincipark.com in French):

Bourse (Map p106; rue Reine Elisabeth, 1er; metro Vieux Port; per hr/day €1.80/13) Underneath the shopping centre.

De Gaulle (Map p106; 22 place du Général de Gaulle, 1er; metro Vieux Port; per hr/day €2/14.50; ☼ 24hr) Just off La Canebière.

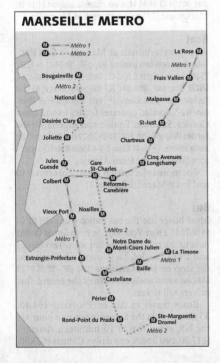

MARSEILLE METRO

Ⓜ ——— Métro 1
Ⓜ ---- Métro 2

La Rose Ⓜ

Métro 1

Bougainville Ⓜ
Frais Vallon Ⓜ

Métro 2

National Ⓜ
Malpasse Ⓜ

Désirée Clary Ⓜ
St-Just Ⓜ

Joliette Ⓜ
Chartreux Ⓜ

Jules Guesde Ⓜ   Gare St-Charles Ⓜ   Cinq Avenues Longchamp Ⓜ

Colbert Ⓜ   Réformés-Canebière Ⓜ

Vieux Port Ⓜ   Noailles Ⓜ

Métro 2

Métro 1   Notre Dame du Mont-Cours Julien Ⓜ   La Timone Ⓜ

Estrangin-Préfecture Ⓜ   Métro 1

Baille Ⓜ

Castellane Ⓜ

Périer Ⓜ

Rond-Point du Prado Ⓜ   Ste-Marguerite Dromel Ⓜ

Métro 2

Public Transport

Marseille has two metro lines (Métro 1 and Métro 2) and an extensive bus network.

The metro and most buses run from 5am until 9pm. From 9.25pm to 12.30am, metro and tram routes are covered every 15 minutes by buses M1 and M2; stops are marked with the fluorescent green signs reading *métro en bus* (metro by bus). Most night buses begin their runs in front of the **Espace Infos RTM** (Map p106; ☎ 04 91 91 92 10; 6 rue des Fabres, 1er; ☒ 8.30am-6pm Mon-Fri, 9am-12.30pm & 2-5.30pm Sat).

Bus/metro tickets (€1.70) can be used on any combination of metros and buses for one hour after they've been time-stamped. A pass for one/three days costs €4.50/10.

By the time you're reading this, sections of Marseille's new **tramway** (www.metro-tram way-marseille.com in French) *should* be operational, though construction has been hampered by delays. Check the website for updates and route maps.

Taxi

Marseille Taxi (☎ 04 91 02 20 20) and **Taxis France** (☎ 04 91 49 91 00) run taxis 24 hours a day.

AROUND MARSEILLE

Butting up against Marseille's built-up environs are spectacular stretches of rocky coast hiding crystalline coves, charming towns and celebrated vineyards.

LES CALANQUES

Skirting 20km of pristine turquoise coves, Les Calanques (including the 500 sq km of the rugged inland Massif des Calanques) have been protected since 1975. The three main gateways are Marseille's southern hemline, and the coastal towns of Cassis and La Ciotat to the east.

Despite its barren, windswept landscape, the massif shelters an extraordinary wealth of flora and fauna – including 900 plant species, of which 15 are protected, such as the dwarf red behen, Marseille astragalus and tartonraire sparrow wort. The Bonnelli eagle is a frequent visitor to Les Calanques, which are also home to Europe's largest lizard (the 60cm eyed lizard) and longest snake (the 2m Montpellier snake) in its darker cracks and crevices.

Although largely inaccessible by car, Les Calanques offer ample walking opportunities

---

NO ENTRY

The threat of forest fire to the semiarid flora skirting Marseille's limestone coastline prompts the Office National des Forêts (National Forests Office) to close Les Calanques each year from 1 July until the second Saturday in September – as well as any time when conditions are too dry. From April to June, they're also closed on Saturday and Sunday. At other times walkers can usually access footpaths between 6am and 11am only (reduced hours in high-risk conditions) – check with the Marseille, Cassis or La Ciotat tourist offices for updates. On-the-spot fines are issued for breaching the strictly enforced rules.

(of varying degrees of difficulty, including some rock clambering). The coastal GR98 leads south from the Marseille suburb of La Madrague to Callelongue on Cap Croisette, and then east along the coast to Cassis. Count on 11 to 12 hours at least to walk the full 28km stretch across the cliffs. A head for heights is a definite advantage. Lonely Planet's *Walking in France* includes step-by-step coverage along Les Calanques west from Cassis to Morgiou.

Marseille's tourist office runs guided walks (€13) from 2pm to 5pm on Friday between early January and late June, and again from mid-September to the end of December. Participants must be aged over eight years; sturdy shoes are a must.

Les Calanques are spectacular when viewed aboard a boat. You can hire your own boat in Marseille or Cassis for your own explorations (see p103 and p116 for details). Otherwise, a myriad of boat excursions to Les Calanques leave from Marseille (see p102), Cassis (see p116) and La Ciotat (p118) in the Marseille area, and from Bandol (p380) and Sanary-sur-Mer (p380) further east.

For information about Les Calanque,s including maps and aerial photographs, check out www.gipcalanques.fr (in French).

Sormiou & Morgiou

The largest *calanque* (rocky inlet), **Sormiou**, hit the headlines in October 1991 when Henri Cosquer, a diver from Cassis, swam through a narrow, 150m-long passage 36m underwater into an underwater cave to find its interior adorned with prehistoric wall paintings from around 20,000 BC. Now named the **Grotte Cosquer**, the cave is a historical monument and, to protect both it and divers' safety, is closed to the public. Many more are believed to exist.

To get here by car from place Louis Bonnefon (next to Château Borély) in Marseille, follow the southbound av de Hambourg past César's thumb on rond-point Pierre Guerre to chemin de Sormiou. From the end of this road, the rte du Feu forest track (a 45-minute walk) leads to Sormiou's small, isolated fishing port and beach. Or, take bus 23 from the Rond-Point du Prado metro stop to La Cayolle stop, from where it is a 3km walk to Sormiou.

Sormiou and Morgiou are separated by Cap Morgiou. **Calanque de Morgiou** nestles on the eastern side of the cape, which has a pretty little port bobbing with a handful of fishing boats, and a restaurant. From av de Hambourg, follow the Morgiou road signs past Marseille's prison in Les Beaumettes. Morgiou beach is one hour's walk from the car park. Alternatively, you could catch bus 23 and continue past La Cayolle to get off at the Morgiou-Beauvallon bus stop.

En-Vau, Port-Pin & Port-Miou

Continuing east along the stone-sculptured coast brings you to **Calanque d'En-Vau**, with emerald waters encased by cliffs where climbers sometimes dangle precariously, and a pebbly beach. Its entrance is guarded by the **Doigt de Dieu** (God's Finger), a giant rock pinnacle. The car park on the Col de la Gardiole (south off the D559), 5km west along a dirt road from Cassis, is closed from July to the second Saturday of September and when the fire risk is too great. When the car park is open, a *steep* three-hour marked trail leads from here to En-Vau. The slippery limestone surface and sheer descents into En-Vau are for the truly hardcore only; and definitely not for those prone to vertigo. Approaching from the east, it is a solid 1½-hour walk on the GR98 from **Calanque de Port-Miou**, immediately west of Cassis. En route you pass the neighbouring **Calanque de Port-Pin**, a 30-minute walk from Port-Miou. In summer, boats sail from Cassis to En-Vau (see right).

Cassis' tourist office distributes free maps of the walking trails leading to these three *calanques*.

CASSIS
pop 8070

Cascading down the rock face to its St-Tropez-like little fishing port, Cassis (pronounced 'ca-see') isn't related to the blackcurrant liqueur (pronounced 'ca-sees'), which is used to create a kir apéritif – but it is famed for kir's other ingredient, producing sweet whites from its terraced vines. The town's name comes from the Roman *Carsicis Portus*, meaning 'crowned port', so christened for the imperial rock now known as the Couronne de Charlemagne (Crown of Charlemagne) presiding above, which is visible from far out to sea.

Peering down on the port from a rocky outcrop is Cassis' 14th-century chateau, now a hotel (www.chateaudecassis.com) visitable only by guests of its five rarefied suites. In high season, holidaymakers pour into this petite port to frolic along its waterfront and sip its fabled wines.

Orientation

Cassis train station is 3.5km east of the centre on av de la Gare. Buses stop at rond-point du Pressoir, five minutes' walk along av du Professeur René Leriche and rue de l'Arène to the port. The old town surrounds the port. Quai St-Pierre, from where boat trips depart, runs alongside the port to the beach, the sandy Plage de la Grande Mer. Pebbly Plage de Bestouan is 700m northwest of the port.

Information

Tourist office (☎ 08 92 25 98 92; www.ot-cassis.fr; quai des Moulins; ⏰ 9am-7pm Mon-Fri, 9.30am-12.30pm & 3-6pm Sat & Sun Jul & Aug, 9am-12.30pm & 2-6.30pm Mon-Fri, 9.30am-12.30pm & 2-5.30pm Sat, 10am-12.30pm Sun Mar-Jun & Sep-Oct, 9.30am-12.30pm & 2-5.30pm Mon-Fri, 10am-12.30pm & 2-5pm Sat, 10am-12.30pm Sun Nov-Feb) On the port.

Activities
BOATING

Year-round, more than a dozen boats sail around Les Calanques daily. Tickets are sold at the portside **kiosk** (☎ 04 42 01 90 83; www .cassis-calanques.com; sq Gilbert Savon) on quai St-Pierre. A 45-minute trip to three *calanques* (Port-Miou, Port-Pin and En-Vau) costs €12/6.50 per adult/child two to 10 years; a 65-minute trip covering these three *calanques* plus Oule and Devenson *calanques* is €14/9; and a 1½-hour trip covering eight *calanques* (including Morgiou) costs €17/12.50. Credit cards aren't accepted.

In addition to the circular boat trips, you can disembark at En-Vau (return adult/child two to 10 years €16/10.50), spend a couple of hours on the beach, and return to Cassis on a later boat. The walk from the boat to the beach is a 200m scramble across rocks, not recommended for young children.

Boats of all shapes and sizes can be hired with or without a permit from **Loca'Bato** (☎ 04 42 01 27 04; impasse du Grand Carnot) starting from €90 for a morning, up to €2000 for a week (plus a hefty deposit).

DIVING

Diving expeditions are organised by the **Cassis Services Plongée** (☎ 04 42 01 89 16; www.cassis-services -plongee.fr; 3 rue Michel Arnaud; ☺ daily mid-Mar–mid-Nov), also known as Centre Cassidain de Plongée. Baptism dives cost €60 including gear. Regular dives including gear with/without an instructor start at €50/44. The company also runs night dives and shipwreck expeditions.

WINE TASTING

Twelve estates producing the Cassis appellation (*appellation d'origine côntrolée*; AOC) wines ribbon the surrounding hillsides; the tourist office has a list of suggested itineraries.

In town, the bottle-lined wine bar **Le Chai Cassidain** (☎ 04 42 01 99 80; 7 rue Séverin Icard; ☺ 11am-1pm & 4-10pm Apr-Oct, 11am-1pm & 4-8pm Tue-Sun Nov-Mar) sells locals wines by the glass (€4 to €6) and often has free tastings.

On the first Sunday in September, the **Fête des Vendanges et du Vin Cassis** heralds the annual grape harvest.

Sleeping & Eating

Auberge de Jeunesse (☎ 04 42 01 02 72; dm €11; ☺ mid-Mar–Dec; **P**) BYO provisions for this 60-bed hostel isolated in the heart of the Massif des Calanques, 4km west of Cassis' centre; this place relies on the sun and wind for electricity and has no running water or public transport. By car, follow the signs off the D559 from Marseille then follow the trail from av des Calanques. Kids aged under seven aren't allowed to stay here. Parking's allowed, but hours of access may be restricted – check ahead.

Le Clos des Arômes (☎ 04 42 01 71 84; www.le-clos -des-aromes.com; 10 rue Abbé Paul Mouton; s €49, d €65-75; ☺ Mar-Dec; **P** ♿) A short stroll from the port, this intimate hotel houses comfortable, cosy rooms (with phones but no TVs). It's fronted

by a flowering restaurant terrace (menus €24 to €36; closed Tuesday lunch and Wednesday), which is a favourite with Cassidians. Limited garaged parking (€11) is available.

La Bastidaine (☎ 04 42 98 83 09; www.labastidaine.com; 6b av des Albizzi; B&B €75-95; **P** ♿) This centuries-old wine grower's house, 1.5km from the centre, contains a delightful four-room *chambre d'hôte*, but if you're looking to ensconce yourself for a while, there's also a *cabanon* (apartment; €420 to €570 per week) with a self-catering kitchen and private terrace.

Le Jardin d'Émile (☎ 04 42 01 80 55; www .lejardindemile.fr; d low season €82-107, high season €102-132; **P** ♿) Nestled beneath leafy trees opposite Plage de Bestouan, Émile's Garden has seven rooms in a bouquet of colours (some with sea views), and a restaurant serving Provençal classics. Menus €30 to €50.

La Table du Boucher (☎ 04 42 01 70 95; 6 rue Adolphe Thiers; menus from €15; ☺ lunch & dinner summer, closed Mon & lunch Tue winter) Run by a former butcher (as evident from the beef-butchering layouts on the placemats), La Table du Boucher has a candlelit terrace that's an appealing spot to enjoy specialist meat dishes, and, this being Cassis, seafood too, including a mouthwatering *marmite* (not the yeast spread, but a subtly spiced 'cooking pot' of fish, tropical fruit and vegetables).

La Poissonerie (☎ 04 42 01 71 56; 5 quai JJ Barthélemy; menu €20; ☺ closed Mon, lunch Thu & Jan) Fish is guaranteed to be at its freshest at this locals' favourite and its adjoining fish shop, owned by two brothers, one who catches the fish, the other who cooks it.

Getting There & Around

Cassis is on the Bandol–Marseille (five daily) and La Ciotat–Aix-en-Provence (three to 12 daily) bus routes; see www.lepilote.com (in French) for schedules. Two to four buses daily serve Marseille (1¼ hours, €2.70).

Cassis train station is on the Marseille–Hyères rail line and there are regular daily trains in both directions including to and from La Ciotat (€2.20, six minutes), Bandol (€4.40, 18 minutes), Marseille (€4.90, 22 minutes) and Toulon (€6.80, 34 minutes).

Buses 2, 3 and 4 link Cassis train station with the town centre (€1.30, 10 minutes, at least hourly).

Free minibuses shuttle motorists from free car parks on the edge of town to the centre from June to mid-September.

CLIFFTOP VISTAS

Europe's highest maritime cliff, the hollow limestone **Cap Canaille** (399m) towers above the southwestern side of **Baie de Cassis** (Cassis Bay). From the top, captivating views unfold across Cassis and **Mt Puget** (565m), the highest peak in the Massif des Calanques.

An equally heart-stopping panorama unfurls along the **rte des Crêtes** (Road of Crests; closed during high winds), wiggling 16km along the clifftops from Cassis to La Ciotat.

LA CIOTAT

pop 35,000

La Ciotat, 16km east of Cassis, crackles with the promise of a town whose charms are yet to be 'discovered' by tourists. Not that La Ciotat is any stranger to influential visitors – it was a favourite of Georges Braque (1892–1963), who painted its quaint old port; and it was where the Lumière brothers (see p65) shot the world's first motion picture, *L'Arrivée d'un Train en Gare de La Ciotat* (The Arrival of a Train at La Ciotat Station). Shipyards dominated La Ciotat's economy until their closure in 1989. Today the rusty cranes cranked up over this seaside town add a filmic effect, with the waterfront now a marina specialising in yacht maintenance and repairs.

Information

Tourist office (☎ 04 42 08 61 32; www.laciotatourisme .com in French; blvd Anatole France; 🕒 9am-8pm Mon-Fri, 10am-1pm Sun mid-Jun–Sep, 9am-noon & 2-6pm Mon-Sat, 10am-1pm Sun May–mid-Jun, 9am-noon & 2-6pm Mon-Sat Oct-Apr) On the headland separating the old port and marina.

Sights & Activities

La Ciotat's **film festival** takes to the screens in June, showcasing up-and-coming talent. Year-round, cinema is celebrated at the **Espace Simon-Lumière** (☎ 04 42 71 61 70; 20 rue du Maréchal Foch; admission free; 🕒 3-6pm Tue-Sat), which has an exhibition hall dedicated to filmography and the Swiss-born film icon Michel Simon (1895–1975), who lived in La Ciotat. Restoration is underway of the world's oldest cinema, the grand Eden Théâtre (blvd Georges Clemenceau), where the Lumières screened many films from 1899; the modern **Cinéma Lumière**

(place Evariste Gras) screens a mix of Hollywood and art-house fare. The pioneering Lumière brothers also feature at La Ciotat's history museum, **Musée du Vieux Ciotat** (☎ 04 42 71 40 99; 1 quai Ganteaume; adult/child €3.20/1.60; 🕒 4-7pm Wed-Mon Jun-Sep, 3-6pm Wed-Mon Oct-May), as does local champion boules player, Jules Le Noir, who invented Provence's favourite game (see p39).

Soaring 155m above the town is the wind- and sea-sculpted Bec d'Aigle (Eagle's Beak) on Cap de l'Aigle. Climbing from the sea to the cape's peak, the rambling 12-hectare botanic gardens **Parc du Mugel** (av du Mugel; admission free; 🕒 8am-8pm Apr-Sep, 9am-6pm Oct-Mar) proliferate with exotic plants, a bamboo forest and palms, as well as a peaceful picnic area.

Affording a superb panorama of the town and cape is the tiny **Île Verte** (Green Island). **Boats** (☎ 04 42 83 11 44, 06 63 59 16 35; adult/child under 10yr return €8/4; 🕒 departures hourly 10am-noon & -5pm May, Jun & Sep, every 30min 9am-7pm Jul & Aug) depart from quai Général de Gaulle at the old port. On weekends a boat departs at 7am for fishermen; book in advance. From the same departure point but with a different boat company, you can also cruise from La Ciotat's old port around the nearby *calanques* (☎ 06 09 35 25 68; cruises from €17; 🕒 Mar-Oct).

Summer days can be lazed away on La Ciotat's wide sandy **beaches**.

In addition to food markets (see p93), an evening **arts & crafts market** is held on Saturdays from late June to early September.

Sleeping & Eating

A clutch of simple but appealing hotels clusters in the town centre; more rustic options dot the cliffside corniches.

Auberge du Revestel (☎ 04 42 83 11 06; www.revestel .com in French; corniche du Liouquet; d €55; 🕒 closed Nov & Feb; 🅿 🐕) Overlooking the sea 6km east of town, this inn has six breezy guest rooms, and a lime-painted restaurant (with stylised geckos climbing its walls) where chef Michel Siepen serves delights such as lamb with spring vegetables and potato gratin.

Yachtclub Chez Michel et Baya (☎ 04 42 83 64 69; av Wilson; mains around €45; 🕒 lunch & dinner daily Jul–mid-Sep, lunch & dinner Tue-Sun mid-Sep–Dec & Mar-Jun) La Ciotat's prize dining catch is this increasingly buzzy place on the marina, which has just signed the *Charte de la Bouillabaisse Marseille* (see the boxed text, p108). Book two days ahead.

Getting There & Around

From La Ciotat train station, a 5km trek from the centre, there are trains on the Marseille–Hyères line (see p114).

The **bus station** (☎ 04 42 08 90 90; blvd Anatole France) adjoins the tourist office. Information is available from **Ciotàbus** (☎ 04 42 08 41 05; 9am-12.30pm & 1.30-7pm Mon-Fri, 8.45am-12.30pm & 1.30-7pm Sat) or www.lepilote.com (in French). Two to four buses daily serve Marseille (1½ hours, €2.40).

PAYS DE PAGNOL

North of La Ciotat and Cassis, on Marseille's easternmost fringe, the area around **Aubagne** (population 43,083) is affectionately known as Pays de Pagnol (Pagnol Country) after its much-loved son, Marcel Pagnol (see p66). The writer-film-maker moved to Marseille proper when he was two but evoked Aubagne's brick-and-tile factories and colourful Provençal characters in many of his works. Aubagne's **tourist office** (☎ 04 42 03 49 98; www.aubagne.com/tourisme; av Antide Boyur; 9am-noon & 2-6pm Mon-Sat) arranges Pagnol-themed **guided tours** (adult €10-18, child €6-13) and hands out maps plotting his trail.

Buried deep amid Aubagne's modern-day sprawl is its quaint, restored **Vieille Ville** (old town), where you'll find *santonniers* workshops (see the boxed text, p100).

About 5km east in **Gémenos** (population 5048), the outdoor **Théâtre de Verdure** (☎ 04 42 32 89 00; rte de St-Pons) hosts the world-music festival Les Arts Verts from June to July. Nearby is the beautiful *bastide* (country house) **Relais de la Magdeleine** (☎ 04 42 32 20 16; www.relais-magdeleine.com; rond-point de la Fontaine; s €85-100, d €95-185, tr €150-225, q €160-235; closed mid-Nov–mid-Mar;). Run by the same family since 1932, this hotel lets you sleep on canopied beds, stroll gardens graced with century-old trees, curl up by the fireplace in the book-lined lounge, and – even if you're not staying here – dine on gastronomic cuisine such as Alpilles lamb at the exquisite restaurant (menus €30 to €55; open for lunch and dinner).

On the village's eastern edge, the rambling stone mill **Le Moulin de Gémenos** (☎ 04 42 32 22 26; rte de St-Pons; weekday menus €13-17, Sunday menu €26; lunch Tue-Fri & Sun) makes a picturesque stop before setting off on a pilgrimage to the nearby Massif de la Ste-Baume (p120).

CÔTE BLEUE

The contrast between the Côte d'Azur and the Côte Bleue is summed up by their very names. Infinitely more down-to-earth than its romanticised counterpart, the rocky Côte Bleue, clambering from Marseille's western edge to Cap Couronne, has a string of rustic fishing villages and is a favourite with Marseillais at weekends.

L'Estaque

A once-untouched fishing village now butting onto Marseille's northern suburbs, **L'Estaque** (www.estaque.com) lured artists from the impressionist, fauvist and cubist movements. A fascinating artists' trail links the footsteps of Renoir, Cézanne, Dufy and Braque around L'Estaque's sheltered port, along its beach, and passes distinctive houses on blvd de la Falaise set back from the beach's western end, which Braque painted in both fauvist and cubist styles.

Around the water's edge, kiosks sell local specialities *chichi frégi* (sugar-coated doughnuts) and *panisses* (chickpea-flour cakes).

From June to August, Marseille's tourist office (p96) runs two-hour guided tours departing from 122 plage de l'Estaque at 10am on Tuesday (€6.50), and one-hour tours at 2pm on Sunday (€3).

Carry-le-Rouet & Cap Couronne

Delectable *oursins* (sea urchins) can be sampled in **Carry-le-Rouet** (population 6200), a harbour town lying 17km west of L'Estaque. The prickly critters can be caught only between September and April; fishing for them in summer when they reproduce is forbidden. These *châtaignes de mer* (sea chestnuts) are exquisite accompanied by chilled Cassis white wine.

Each year, on the first three Sundays of February, Carry-le-Rouet's sea-urchin festival **L'Oursinade** sees a giant open-air picnic spill across the old-port quays. Restaurants and hotels set up stalls selling urchins, allowing everyone to taste the delicacy around shared tables. For more details contact the **tourist office** (☎ 04 42 13 20 36; www.carry-lerouet.com in French; av Aristide Briand; 10am-noon & 2-5pm Tue-Sat).

West along the coast, the marine-life-rich waters around the sandy **Cap Couronne** are protected by the **Parc Régional Marin de la Côte Bleue** (☎ 04 42 45 45 07, 06 83 09 38 42; perso.wanadoo .fr/parcmarin in French), marked by yellow buoys topped with St Andrew's crosses. In July and August the park authority organises one-hour **snorkelling** sessions (free), open to anyone aged

A PILGRIM'S DETOUR

From Gémenos, take the D2 east, following the signs for 'Vallée St-Pons & La Ste-Baume' for a couple of kilometres. The going soon gets green and dramatic, the smooth tarmac road snaking uphill through the **Parc Départemental de St-Pons**, whose dry scrubby terrain is protected by the same fire regulations as Les Calanques. After 8km, just as the sea pops up on the horizon, the road narrows and loses its smooth surface. A kilometre and several hairpins later, the road markings return for the final 2km climb to the **Col de l'Espigouler** (725m), a mountain pass with dramatic coastline views.

The winding descent is dominated by the **Massif de la Ste-Baume**, a hulk of a mountain with rolling ridged sides topped by a 12km-long shelf. After a couple of kilometres signs of habitation start to appear. At the D45a/D2 junction, continue on the D2 through **Plan d 'Aups** (2km) to **La Ste-Baume** (8km), home to the **Ecomusée de la Ste-Baume** (☎ 04 42 62 56 46; ☻ various), where local flora, fauna and geology can be discovered; and the **Hôtellerie de la Ste-Baume** (☎ 04 42 04 54 85), where pilgrims stay. From La Ste-Baume, a 40-minute path through forest leads to the **Grotte de Ste-Madeleine** (950m), a cave in the mountain where Mary Magdalene is said to have spent the last years of her life. Daily Mass is celebrated here at 10.30am. Its entrance offers a breathtaking panorama of Provence's peaks Montagne Ste-Victoire, Mont Ventoux and the Alps.

For a fitting finish, take the D80 northeast via Nans-les-Pins then turn right on the N560 (about 20km all up) to reach **St-Maximin La Ste-Baume** (www.la-provence-verte.net). The pastel-hued town (population 9594) congregates around the Gothic **Ste-Madeleine Basilica** (☎ 04 94 59 84 59; place Jean Salusse; ☻ welcome office 9am-7pm except during religious services), built in 1295 as the home of the relics of Mary Magdalene, which were discovered in a crypt on the site around 1279. Should you feel like indulging in a gastronomic lunch or dinner, or need a place to rest your head, the adjacent convent now houses the sumptuous **Hôtellerie du Couvent Royal** (☎ 04 94 86 55 66; www.hotelfp-saintmaximin.com; place Jean Salusse; menus €26-35; ☻ lunch daily, dinner Mon-Sat; Ⓟ). Doubles are €80 to €140; guest parking costs €8.

eight or over, aimed at discovering marine fauna and flora.

Étang de Berre

Buffering the Côte Bleue from the industrialised 6m-deep, 155-sq-km brine lake **Étang de Berre**, the uninhabitable massif **Chaîne de l'Estaque** protects the clear coastal waters from the pollution of some 24 million tons (30% of French production) of petrol produced per year at the lake's oil refineries.

The **Canal de Caronte**, at the Étang de Berre's southwestern corner (10km north from Cap Couronne along the D5), connects the Mediterranean's Golfe de Fos with one of the area's gems, the fishing port of **Martigues** (population 44,256).

Martigues' mostly pedestrianised old town sits on a little island crisscrossed by bridges, giving the town its nickname, the 'Venice of Provence' (its wines are under the AOC de la Venise Provençale). The old town's rainbow of brightly coloured houses is a legacy of the ancient tradition of fishermen using leftover paint from their boats on their homes. Medi

eval jousting aboard boats is still a lively and popular sport – you'll see teams training on Tuesdays, Wednesdays and Fridays from around 4pm in summer on the Canal Gallifet on the island's southern side. The French tricolour (no, not red, white and rosé, but the national flag) originates from the town. It's also where Marseille-born Henri Fabre (1882–1984) invented, tested and took off in a hydroplane in 1910.

As elsewhere along the Côte Bleue, Martigues is blessed with bountiful seafood. Summer sees *sardinades*, during which sardines are grilled outdoors along the canals. Other specialities include *poutargue* (the 'caviar of the Provence', made with mullet eggs, which are salted, dried and pressed into lumps, costing a hefty €150 per kilo), *mêlets* (anchovies prepared with fennel) and *perles de l'étang* (pearls of the lake; cherries macerated in alcohol, coated in marzipan and covered with chocolate).

Martigues' **tourist office** (☎ 04 42 42 31 10; www.martigues-tourisme.com; rond-point de l'Hôtel de Ville; ☻ 9am-7pm Mon-Sat, 10am-1pm & 3-7pm Sun Jul & Aug,

9am-6.30pm Mon-Sat, 9.30am-1pm Sun Sep & Easter-Jun, 9am-6.30pm Mon-Sat & 10am-12.30pm Sun Oct-Easter) has information on *chambres d'hôtes* and hotels.

On the Étang's de Berre's southeastern edge, **Marignane** (population 34,238), is dominated by Marseille-Provence airport. A reproduction of Henri Fabre's wooden hydroplane hangs in its hall. Five kilometres north, the *étang's* vast industrial landscape can be surveyed from the ruins of an 11th-century Saracen tower, teetering on top of a rock in **Vitrolles** (population 37,087).

Getting There & Away

Bus 34 links Marseille's bus station with Martigues (€6.20, one hour, hourly). A couple of buses a day continue to the industrial helm, Fos-sur-Mer. Bus 35 from Marseille's Vieux Port drops you at L'Estaque's port.

More than a dozen daily trains (fewer in winter) trundle from Marseille along La Côte Bleue stopping at L'Estaque (€2.10, eight minutes), Carry-le-Rouet (€4.30, 25 minutes), La Couronne (€5.70, 35 minutes) and Port de Bouc (€7.20, 55 minutes), from where the line heads inland to Miramas (€7.90, 1¼ hours), on the northern shore of the Étang de Berre.

SALON DE PROVENCE

pop 40,000

Shrouded by olive groves around 15km north of the Étang de Berre and 35km west of Aix, Salon de Provence is famed for its *savon de Marseille* (Marseille soap), made from the trees' oil, and as the place where the philosopher Nostradamus (1503–66) wrote his prophecies.

Against the atmospheric backdrop of its walled city, this former Arles bishops' residence celebrates its medieval heritage most years in July with street festivities, elaborate costumes and traditional music. The town's many Art Deco façades are a legacy of an earthquake that struck in 1909.

Engines roar in the skies above Salon on Thursdays between noon and 2pm from September to April when France's military flying school, the École de l'Air et École Militaire de l'Air, stationed here since 1936, take to the air when not on tour. The **tourist office** (☎ 04 90 56 27 60; 56 cours Gimon; ☒ 9.30am-12.30pm & 2-6.30pm Mon-Sat, 9.30am-12.30pm Sun Jul & Aug, 9.30am-12.30pm & 2-6pm Mon-Sat Sep-Jun) runs guided tours (€46) taking in training sessions along with a gourmet lunch – book several months ahead.

Sights & Activities

FLYING

To take to the skies yourself in a glider, contact **Centre de Vol à Voile de la Crau** (☎ 04 90 42 15 38; 20min baptism flights €60).

MUSEUMS & MONUMENTS

A mushroom-shaped, moss-covered fountain, **Fontaine Moussue**, is the centrepiece of Salon's prettiest square, place Crousillat, just outside the walled old city opposite the **Tour de l'Horloge** (Clock Tower; 1626).

Inside the pedestrian Vieille Ville is the **Maison de Nostradamus** (☎ 04 90 56 64 31; 11 rue Nostradamus; adult/student €3.05/2.30; ☒ 9am-noon & 2-6pm Mon-Fri, 2-6pm Sat & Sun), where the philosopher lived from 1547 until his death in 1566. Scrolls of Nostradamus' prophecies line the walls, while often-macabre wax figures recreate key scenes from his life accompanied by piped commentary in several languages (tell the front desk what language you'd like and they'll run it on the next available loop). Nostradamus' remains lie behind a plaque inside the **Collégiale St-Laurent** (place St-Laurent; built in 1344.

More wax figures – some 56 – depict local legend and lore at the **Musée Grévin de la Provence** (☎ 04 90 56 36 30; place des Centuries; adult/student €3.05/2.30; ☒ 9am-noon & 2-6pm Mon-Fri, 2-6pm Sat & Sun).

Immense medieval halls within the **Château-Musée de l'Empéri** (☎ 04 90 56 22 36; place du Château; adult/child 7-18yr €3.05/2.30; ☒ 10am-noon & 2-6pm Wed-Mon Dec-May, Sep & Oct, 10am-6pm Wed-Mon Jul & Aug), home to the archbishops of Arles from the 9th to the 18th centuries, display more than 10,000 exhibits dedicated to French military history up to WWI.

Peer up inside the **Tour du Bourg Neuf**, part of the fortified ramparts built around the city in the 12th century, to see the statue of the Black Virgin. The ebony colour is said to come from the smoke of candles held by women who venerated the statue in the 13th century hoping to conceive.

Recalling the town's medieval past, Gregorian chants are sung at Sunday Mass (9am) in the 13th-century **Église St-Michel** (place St-Michel) on the first and third Sunday of the month, September to June. The **statue of Adam de Craponne** on place de l'Hôtel de Ville commemorates the designer of a canal channelling water from the River Durance to irrigate the Crau Plain in 1559, allowing Salon's olive groves to flourish.

SALON DE PROVENCE

0 — 200 m
0 — 0.1 miles

INFORMATION	
Tourist Office	1 B3

SIGHTS & ACTIVITIES	
Château-Musée de l'Empéri	2 B3
Collégiale St-Laurent	3 C1
Église St-Michel	4 B3
Fontaine Moussue	5 B2
Maison de Nostradamus	6 B2
Musée Grévin de la Provence	7 B2
Rampal-Patou	8 A1
Statue of Adam de Craponne	9 C3
Tour de l'Horloge	10 B2
Tour du Bourg Neuf	11 C3

SLEEPING	
Ghyslaine Martin-Castellino	12 A2
Grand Hôtel de la Poste	13 B2

EATING	
Au Péché Mignon	14 B3
Café des Arts	15 B2
La Salle à Manger	16 C2
La Table du Roy	17 B2
Mas du Soleil	18 D3

TRANSPORT	
Bus Station	19 A2

SOAP FACTORIES

Just two traditional *savonneries* (soap factories) remain in Salon today.

Run by three generations of the same family, the **Savonnerie Marius Fabre** (☎ 04 90 53 24 77; www.marius-fabre.fr; 148 av Paul Borret; adult/15-18yr/under 15yr €3.85/1.95/free; 9.30-11.30am & 2-5pm Mon-Thu, 9.30-11.30am & 2-4pm Fri, guided tours 10.30am Mon & Thu) incorporates a museum displaying wooden stamps and old advertising posters and also runs tours including a film (in French). The factory produces 80 tonnes of soap a year.

The inner workings of the **Rampal-Patou** (☎ 04 90 56 07 28; 71 rue Félix Pyat, 8am-noon & 2-6pm Mon-Fri) factory are closed to visitors, but you can stock up cheaply at its beautiful 1907 boutique.

OLIVE FARM

The working olive farm **Mas des Bories** (☎ 04 90 56 03 65; www.masdesbories.com; Vieille rte de Pélissanne) conducts enthusiastic, extensive tours of its groves, often with a tasting of the farm's AOC oils (which you can buy on-site) inside one of the property's stone *bories* (primitive beehive-shaped dwellings, built from dry

limestone around 3500 BC). The free tours are conducted in English and/or French by appointment. Owners Nico and Roxanne also offer green-fingered guests an informal place to kip in exchange for helping with the harvest in November and December. Year-round, there's a self-contained guest apartment sleeping up to seven people (€85 to €100; weekly rates available). It's about 4km northwest of Salon down a series of signed tracks.

Sleeping & Eating

Grand Hôtel de la Poste (☎ 04 90 56 01 94; grandhotel.provence.free.fr; 1 rue des Frères J & R Kennedy; d €40-47, q €47-53;) With an old fashioned charm and spruced up, two-star rooms, this 19th-century townhouse overlooks Salon's mossy fountain. Parking costs €5.50.

Ghyslaine Martin-Castellino (☎ 04 90 56 99 81; perso.wanadoo.fr/ghyslaine.castellino; 68 rue Auguste Girad; d €90) You'll find three welcoming rooms in this triple-decker townhouse *chambre d'hôte*, but the best reason to stay here is Ghyslaine's sumptuous cooking courses (also available to nonguests). Courses start from €110 for the preparation and feast of a three-course meal; you'll be involved in everything from peeling potatoes to picking out the perfect wines to accompany them. Longer courses (from €140) include a trip to local village markets.

Mas du Soleil (☎ 04 90 56 06 53; www.lemasdusoleil.com in French; 38 chemin St-Côme; d €106-267; P ⊠ ⊑ ⌂) The pride and joy of Maîtres Cuisiniers de France chef Francis Robin, this haven of a hotel is a five-minute stroll from the town centre. Ranging around a rambling garden are flowing modern rooms, a beautiful pool, and destination restaurant (menus €38 to €62; closed Sunday dinner; Monday by reservation only) where you can savour Francis' sun-inspired cuisine such as herb-fragranced rabbit.

Abbaye de Sainte Croix (☎ 04 90 56 24 55; www.relais -chateaux.com/saintecroix; Val de Cuech; d €130-453, ste €422-453; ⌂ closed Nov-Mar; P ⊠ ⊑ ⌂) Within the towering stone walls of this 12th-century abbey are 21 heavenly rooms and a restaurant (menus €45 to €95; closed lunch Monday to Friday April, May, and October) serving exalted contemporary/classic cuisine. The abbey's 20-hectare grounds sprawl 2km east of Salon (with, should you need it, a helipad on the lawn).

Café des Arts (☎ 04 90 56 00 07; place des Arts; lunch formule €14; ⌂ lunch & dinner; ⌂) Everything at this delightful café, which cascades onto a terrace in front of Salon's famous fountain, is cooked in front of you – be it lamb grilled *au feu de bois* (over a wood fire) in the dining room, served with honey and sesame; or tapas turned out at the outdoor open kitchen.

La Table du Roy (☎ 04 90 56 53 42; 35 rue Moulin d'Isnard; menus €23-29, mains €13-25; ⌂ lunch & dinner Wed-Sun) Diagonally opposite one of Salon's oldest, crumbling buildings from which pigeons peep at you from its broken windows, this atmospheric old-town restaurant, much loved by locals, opens to an internal vine-draped courtyard. Be tempted by treats such as a symphony of sea bass and salmon with thyme and lavender.

La Salle à Manger (☎ 04 90 56 28 01; 6 rue du Maréchal Joffre; menu €27, desserts from €5; ⌂ lunch & dinner Tue-Sat) Wrapped around a secret garden, 'the dining room' of this 19th-century *hôtel particulier* serves aperitifs accompanied by a lavender dip, Asian-inspired mains, and – the icing on the cake – a choice of 40 desserts such as thyme, lavender and rosemary sorbet.

For a self-catering option, find foie gras, fine chocolates and other fine treats at **Au Péché Mignon** (☎ 04 90 59 19 76; place St-Michel).

Getting There & Away

From the **bus station** (☎ 04 90 56 50 98; cnr blvd Maréchal Foch & blvd Victor Joly) there are daily services to and from Aix-en-Provence (€5, 35 minutes, up to 12 daily) and Arles (€5, 1¼ hours, eight daily Monday to Saturday, two a day Sunday).

The **train station** (av Émile Zola) is a 1km walk from town. There are eight or so trains a day to and from Marseille (€9.80, one hour) and Avignon (€8.50, one hour).

PAYS D'AIX

It's hard to believe oh-so-elegant Aix-en-Provence, ensconced within picturesque Pays d'Aix (Aix Country), is just 25km or so from chaotic, exotic Marseille.

AIX-EN-PROVENCE

pop 137,067 / elev 206m

A pocket of left-bank Parisian chic deep in Provence, Aix (pronounced like the letter X) is all class: its leafy boulevards and public squares are lined with 17th- and 18th-century mansions, and punctuated by gurgling, moss-covered fountains. The city's grandest avenue, cours Mirabeau, is guarded by haughty stone lions – and by fashionable Aixois sipping espresso on wicker chairs on elegant café terraces.

Like Paris' left bank, Aix is a prestigious student hub (and like Paris' left bank, it's expensive, too). First established in 1409, the Université de Provence Aix-Marseille has a 30,000-strong campus here, including many French-language foreign students. But for all its polish, Aix is still a laid-back Provençal town at heart.

History

Aix marks the spot where, under the proconsul Sextius Calvinus, Roman forces enslaved the inhabitants of the Ligurian Celtic stronghold of Entremont, 3km to the north. In 123 BC the military camp was named Aquae Sextiae (Waters of Sextius) for the thermal springs that still flow today. In the 12th century the counts of Provence proclaimed Aix their capital, which it remained until the Revolution when it was supplanted by Marseille. The city became a centre of culture under arts patron King René (1409–80); two of its most famous sons are painter Paul Cézanne and novelist Émile Zola.

MARSEILLE AREA

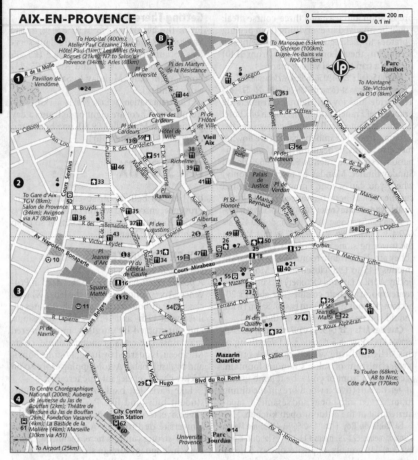

AIX-EN-PROVENCE

Orientation

Cours Mirabeau extends eastwards to place Forbin from place du Général de Gaulle, a roundabout with a huge fountain commonly referred to as La Rotonde. The city's mostly pedestrianised old town, Vieil Aix, is north of cours Mirabeau. Radiating from La Rotonde, av des Belges leads southwest to the bus station; while av Victor Hugo brings you southeast to the train station – the tourist office is on the southern edge of La Rotonde between the two. The TGV station is 8km from the city centre, linked by shuttle buses.

South of cours Mirabeau is the Mazarin Quartier, with a street grid laid out in the 17th century. The city centre is ringed by a series of maddening one-way boulevards.

Information

Book in Bar (☎ 04 42 26 60 07; 1bis rue Cabassol) Secondhand and new English-language books; with a bohemian reading café out the back.

Librairie Goulard (☎ 04 42 27 66 47; 37 cours Mirabeau; ⏰ 10.30am-7.30pm Mon, 9am-7.30pm Tue-Sat) Provence's best selection of Lonely Planet guides in English.

Paradox Librairie Internationale (☎ 04 42 26 47 99; 15 rue du Quatre Septembre) Dublin-style shop paradoxically stocking foreign books and groceries.

EMERGENCY

Police (☎ 04 42 91 91 11; place B Niollon)

INTERNET ACCESS

Virtualis (☎ 04 42 26 02 30; 40 rue Cordeliers; per

INFORMATION
Book in Bar............................**1** C3
Change Nazareth......................**2** B2
Laundrette.............................**3** A2
Laundrette.............................**4** A2
Laundrette.............................**5** C1
Laundrette.............................**6** D2
Librairie Goulard.....................**7** C3
Maison de la Nature et de
  l'Environnement................**8** B3
Paradox Librairie Internationale...**9** C3
Police.................................**10** A3
Post Office............................**11** A3
Tourist Office.........................**12** B3
Virtualis..............................**13** B2

SIGHTS & ACTIVITIES
Boulodrome Municipal.............**14** C4
Cathédrale St-Sauveur.............**15** B1
Fontaine de la Rotonde............**17** B3
Fontaine de Roi René..............**18** C3
Fontaine d'Eau Thermale.........**16** C3
Galerie d'Art du Conseil Général des
  Bouches du Rhône.............**19** B3
Hôtel d'Espargnet.................**20** C3
Hôtel d'Isoard de Vauvenarges..**21** C3
Musée Granet.......................**22** D3
Musée Paul Arbaud...............**23** C3

Thermes Sextius......................**24** A1

SLEEPING 🛏
Bastide du Cours.....................**25** C3
Grand Hôtel Nègre Coste.........**26** C3
Hôtel Cardinal.......................**27** C3
Hôtel Cardinal (Annexe)............**28** D3
Hôtel Cèzanne.......................**30** B4
Hôtel Concorde......................**29** D4
Hôtel des Augustins.................**31** B3
Hôtel des Quatre Dauphins......**32** C3
Hôtel Le Manoir.....................**33** A2

EATING 🍴
Amphityron...........................**34** B3
Bistro Latin...........................**35** B2
Charlotte.............................**36** A2
Chez Grand Mère...................**37** B2
Food Market.........................**38** B2
Food Market.........................**39** B2
Icône..................................**40** C3
Jacquèmes...........................**41** B2
La Boulangerie du Coin............**42** C1
L'Aixquis.............................**43** A3
Le Comptoir des Oliviers..........**44** B1
Le Formal.............................**45** B2
Le Zinc d'Hugo......................**46** B2
Monoprix.............................**47** B3

Place aux Huiles......................**48** D3
Roy René..............................**49** C2

DRINKING 🍷
Les Deux Garçons...................**50** C3
L'Orienthé............................**51** B2

ENTERTAINMENT 🎭
Bar Sextius...........................**52** A2
Chapelle de Ste-Catherine.......**53** C1
Ciné Mazarin........................**54** B3
Cinéma Renoir.......................**55** C3
Église Ste-Marie Madeleine.....**56** C2
La Belle Époque.....................**57** C3
Théâtre de l'Archevêché........(see 15)
Théâtre du Jeu de Paume.......**58** D2

SHOPPING 🛍
Cave du Felibrige....................**59** B2

TRANSPORT
Avis...................................**60** B4
Bus Station...........................**61** A4
City Centre Train Station..........**62** B4
Europcar............................(see 60)
Hertz................................(see 60)
National Citer.......................(see 60)
Relais Aix en Vélo.................(see 12)

15min/hr €0.15/€3.80; ⏱ 9am-midnight Mon-Fri, noon-midnight Sat & Sun) Central and state of the art.

LAUNDRY
Laundrettes (open 7am or 8am to 8pm) include those at 3 rue de la Fontaine, 34 cours Sextius, 3 rue de la Fonderie and 60 rue Boulegon.

MEDICAL SERVICES
Hospital (Centre Hospitalier Général du Pays d'Aix; ☎ 04 42 33 50 00; av des Tamaris)

MONEY
Commercial banks mass along cours Mirabeau and cours Sextius, which runs north–south to the west of La Rotonde.
Change Nazareth (7 rue Nazareth; ⏱ 9am-7pm Mon-Sat, to 5pm Sun Jul & Aug)

POST
Post office (place de l'Hôtel de Ville)

TOURIST INFORMATION
Maison de la Nature et de l'Environnement
(☎ 04 42 93 15 80; 2 place Jeanne d'Arc; ⏱ 10am-12.30pm & 2-6pm Mon-Fri, 10am-1pm Sat) Green source for information on the environment and ways to explore it (nature walks, discovering Mediterranean flora and so on).
Tourist office (☎ 04 42 16 11 61; www.aixenprovence tourism.com; 2 place du Général de Gaulle; ⏱ 8.30am-7pm Mon-Sat, 10am-1pm & 2-6pm Sun) Extended hours in summer.

Sights & Activities
Art, culture and architecture abound in Aix. The city's literal and spiritual heart is the graceful **cours Mirabeau**, laid out during the latter half of the 1600s and named after the revolutionary hero Comte de Mirabeau. Cafés spill out onto the sunny northern footpaths. The southern side shelters a string of elegant Renaissance *hôtels particuliers*; **Hôtel d'Espargnet** (1647) at No 38 is among the most impressive (today it houses the university's economics department). The Marquis of Entrecasteaux murdered his wife in their family home, **Hôtel d'Isoard de Vauvenarges**, at No 10, built in 1710.

Cours Mirabeau is bookended to the west by the cast-iron fountain **Fontaine de la Rotonde**, dating from 1860; at its eastern end, the fountain by place Forbin, **fontaine du Roi René**, is decorated with a 19th-century statue of King René clasping a bunch of Muscat grapes, which he's said to have introduced to the region. The mossy **Fontaine d'Eau Thermale**, at the intersection of cours Mirabeau and rue du Quatre Septembre, spouts 34°C water, as the name suggests.

Rue Mazarine, one block south of cours Mirabeau, also has some splendid buildings. Two blocks further south again, the fountain at **place des Quatre Dauphins** dates from 1667. More fine architectural examples are found at the eastern continuation of cours Mirabeau,

VISA FOR AIX

Buy a €2 Visa pour le Pays d'Aix from any tourist office for a stack of discounts on admission fees, transport tickets, guided tours and the like, in and around Aix.

rue de l'Opéra (at Nos 18, 24 and 26); and the pretty, fountain-clad place d'Albertas, just west of place St-Honoré, where musicians often play on midsummer nights.

South of Aix's historic centre is the peaceful Parc Jourdan, dominated by Aix's largest fountain and home to the town's Bouldodrome Municipal (municipal bowling pitch) where locals gather to play *pétanque* under the plane trees.

MUSEUMS

Coinciding with the centenary of Cézanne's death, Aix's exceptional Muse Granet (☎ 04 42 52 88 32; place St-Jean de Malte; ☺ 11am-6pm Wed-Mon) reopened in 2006 after nearly three years of works, tripling it in size. Housed in a 17th-century priory of the Knights of Malta, its collections include 16th- to 20th-century Italian, Flemish and French paintings, including the museum's pride and joy, eight of Cézanne's works. Ongoing admission prices not yet finalised at the time of writing.

Musée Paul Arbaud (☎ 04 42 38 38 95; 2a rue du Quatre Septembre; adult/student €3/1.50; ☺ 2-5pm Mon-Sat) connects you to Aix's literary heritage with displays of books and manuscripts. It also exhibits Provençal faïence (tin-glazed earthenware).

Galérie d'Art du Conseil Général des Bouches du Rhône(☎ 04 42 93 03 67; 21bis cours Mirabeau; admission free; ☺ 10.15am-12.45pm & 1.30-6.30pm Mon-Sat) showcases photography and contemporary art.

The Bauhaus-style edifice Fondation Vasarely (☎ 04 42 20 01 09; 1 av Marcel Pagnol; adult/child under 7 €7/4; ☺ 10am-6pm Mon-Sat) is 4km west of town. Built in 1976, its 16 hexagonal spaces house vast architecture-meets-art works by Victor Vasarely, the 'father of optical art'. Take bus 4 from La Rotonde to the Vasarely stop.

CATHÉDRALE ST-SAUVEUR

A potpourri of architectural styles, the Cathédrale St-Sauveur (rue J de Laroque; ☺ 8am-noon & 2-6pm) was primarily built between 1285 and 1350. A Romanesque 12th-century nave is incorporated in its southern aisle, the chapels were added in the 14th and 15th centuries,

and there's a 5th-century sarcophagus in the apse. More recent additions include the 18th-century gilt baroque organ. The acoustics make the Gregorian chants (usually sung at 4.30pm on Sunday) an unforgettable experience.

CÉZANNE SIGHTS

His star may not have reached its giddiest heights until after his death, but the life of local lad Paul Cézanne (1839–1906) is treasured in Aix. To see where he ate, drank, studied and painted, you can follow the Circuit de Cézanne (Cézanne trail), marked by footpath-embedded bronze plaques inscribed with the letter C. Corresponding with the plaques is an informative English-language guide *Cézanne's Footsteps*, available free from the tourist office, where the circuit begins.

Cézanne's last studio (Atelier Paul Cézanne; ☎ 04 42 21 06 53; www.atelier-cezanne.com; 9 av Paul Cézanne; adult/student €5.50/2; ☺ 10am-noon & 2-5pm, to 6pm Apr-Jun & Sep, 10am-6pm Jul & Aug), while it doesn't hold any of his works, is painstakingly preserved as it was at the time of his death, strewn with his tools and still-life models, giving the impression he's just popped out to the shops and will be back any moment. The atelier is 1.5km north of the tourist office on a hilltop; take bus 1 to the Cézanne stop.

See p131 for information about trailing Cézanne further afield in the countryside where he painted his landscapes.

Tours

Between April and October the tourist office runs a packed schedule of guided bus tours throughout the region, in English and in French. Literary buffs can take a guided Émile Zola literary walk, or follow the free, self-guided *Literary Walk* brochure. Ask for the free *Guide Map* at the tourist office for details of all tours or check its website. Prices start from around €28.

Festivals & Events

Aix's sumptuous cultural calendar is capped by the month-long Festival International d'Art Lyrique d'Aix-en-Provence (International Festival of Lyrical Art; www.festival-aix.com) in July. It brings classical music, opera and ballet to city venues such as the Théâtre de l'Archevêché, outside the Cathédrale St-Sauveur, while buskers keep cours Mirabeau's festive spirits high.

Comic books, animation and cartoon art feature during the Rencontres du 9ème Art (www

.bd-aix.com in French) festival in March. Other highlights are the two-day **Festival du Tambourin** (Tambourine Festival) in mid-April and the **Fête Mistralienne**, marking the birthday of Provençal troubadour, Frédéric Mistral, on 13 September.

Sleeping

The city centre fills up fast in summer and during busy conference and exam times. The tourist office has extensive accommodation lists including farmhouses for longer stays. Hotel and *chambre d'hôte* bookings are coordinated through the email address resaix@aixenprovencetourism.com.

CHAMBRES D'HÔTES

La Bastide de la Molière (☎ 04 42 52 36 04; www .bastidelamoliere.com; 3797 rte de Galice; s €65-100, d €70-105; P ℞) This rambling *bastide* outside the town centre amid Romanesque gardens has four graceful and surprisingly affordable guest rooms. It's (understandably) popular for weddings so you'll need to reserve ahead. Breakfast is an extra €6.50. From town, continue past the Jas de Bouffan stadium through three roundabouts; it's about 1km ahead on your left.

Bastide du Cours (☎ 04 42 26 10 06; www.cafebastide ducours.com; 43-47 cours Mirabeau; d €171-245; ℞) In the beating heart of Aix, this café right on cours Mirabeau has a delightful interior garden where you can get a culinary taste of Provence with dishes such as slow-roasted lamb shank with wild thyme and locally grown tomatoes (mains €16.50 to €28). It also has four richly adorned *chambre d'hôte* rooms with a visual taste of Provence's striped, flowered and checked fabrics. Rates jump about 30% in July. Breakfast is an additional €13 to €19.

OLD-FASHIONED PAMPERING

When in Aix, do as the Romans did when they were here back in the 1st century BC and bliss out at the thermal spas. Built on the site of Roman Aquae Sextiae's thermal springs, the excavated remains of the Roman spa are displayed beneath glass in the lobby of **Thermes Sextius** (☎ 04 42 23 81 82; www.thermes-sextius.com; 55 cours Sextius). Decadent hydrotherapy treatments include a 'Zen spray massage'. A day's access to the fitness centre or a massage starts at €37; all-day pampering packages are available.

HOTELS
Budget

Hôtel Paul (☎ 04 42 23 23 89; hotel.paul@wanadoo.fr; 10 av Pasteur; d €39-49, tr €60) Close to Cézanne's atelier and the thermal spa, the single-star Hôtel Paul is a bright and cheery little bargain, with a sweet garden, telephones in its 24 rooms, and a salon to watch TV.

Hôtel Concorde (☎ 04 42 26 03 95; fax 04 42 27 38 90; 68 blvd du Roi René; d €43-69; P ℞) Definitely ask for a room with views over the hills at this 50-room place just on the southeastern edge of the city centre. Some have small balconies, and higher-priced rooms come with air-con and minibars; but skip the dark ground-floor rooms out the back. Parking costs €7.50.

Midrange

Hôtel Le Manoir (☎ 04 42 26 27 20; www.hotelmanoir .com; 8 rue d'Entrecasteux; d €57-85, tr €78-85, q €93; ☽ closed Jan; P ♿) Elegantly set within a 14th-century cloister reconstructed in the 16th century, Le Manoir has 40 antique-furnished rooms in a secluded but central wedge of the old town; with a lovely, leafy garden and free private parking.

Hôtel Cardinal (☎ 04 42 38 32 30; fax 04 42 26 39 05; 24 rue Cardinale; s/d €58/68, self-catering ste €80; ♿) Beneath stratospheric ceilings, the Hôtel Cardinal's 29 romantic rooms are beautifully furnished with antiques, tasselled curtains, and newly tiled bathrooms. Try for room 8, with double sets of French doors opening to a narrow street-facing balcony. Small self-catering suites are annexed half-a-dozen doors up.

Hôtel des Quatre Dauphins (☎ 04 42 38 16 39; fax 04 42 38 60 19; 54 rue Roux Alpheran; s €55, d €65-85; ℞) Close to cours Mirabeau, a skylit central staircase gives on to 13 coir-carpeted rooms with freshly laundered Wedgwood-blue and pale-pink quilts and curtains. Four quaint attic rooms have sloped beamed ceilings (maybe not ideal if you're pushing 6ft). Wi-fi is available for €5 per 24 hours.

Grand Hôtel Nègre Coste (☎ 04 42 27 74 22; www .hotelnegrecoste.com; 33 cours Mirabeau; d €70-140; P ℞) The only hotel right on cours Mirabeau isn't as grand as it was when Louis XIV stayed here in 1660. It has musty corridors and blasé service, but rooms are cheered up with Provençal colours, and there aren't many spots more central than this. Garage parking is €10.

Top End

Hôtel des Augustins (☎ 04 42 27 28 59; www.hotel -augustins.com; 3 rue de la Masse; d €97-240; ℞) A heartbeat from the hub of Aixois life, this former 15th-century convent has volumes of history: for example, Martin Luther stayed here after his excommunication from Rome. Decorated with hand-painted furniture, the largest, most luxurious abodes have Jacuzzis; and two have private terraces beneath the filigreed bell tower. The stained-glass foyer has free wi-fi.

Hôtel Cézanne (☎ 04 42 91 11 11; www.hotelaix.com; 40 av Victor Hugo; d €140-155; 🔊 🖥 🕭) In an elegant white building with royal purple canvas awnings and interiors, this place has personalised touches including monogrammed towels, free stamped postcards, and free (nonalcoholic) minibars. Downstairs, the open bar is lit by designer lamps and strewn with purple glass pebbles and bowls of seasonal nuts and fruits such as cherries and clementines – just as Cézanne himself would have painted.

HOSTELS

Auberge de Jeunesse du Jas de Bouffan (☎ 04 42 20 15 99; fax 04 42 59 36 12; 3 av Marcel Pagnol; dm incl breakfast & sheets €15.70; 🕑 7am-1pm & 5pm-midnight, closed 20 Dec-9 Feb) This cyclist-friendly HI, with a fun bar and tennis courts, is a landing pad for many of Aix's foreign-language students. The hostel's 2km west of the centre; take bus 4 from La Rotonde to the Vasarely stop.

Eating

Aix excels at Provençal cuisine. Terraces spill across dozens of backstreet squares, including place des Cardeurs, forum des Cardeurs, place de Verdun, place Richelme and place de l'Hôtel de Ville. Place Ramus, off pedestrianised rue Annonciade, is a restaurant-filled square where buskers often play.

RESTAURANTS

Charlotte (☎ 04 42 26 77 56; 32 rue des Bernardines; 2-/3-course menu €13/16; 🕑 lunch & dinner Tue-Sat) Townspeople congregate like a big extended family at this bustling place turning out delicious, simple home cooking, including incredible *crème brûlée* (a cream or custard dessert covered with caramelised sugar) from the open kitchen. In summer, feasting takes place outdoors in the garden, and there's a comfy lounge room to unwind pre- or post-*repas*.

Chez Grand Mère (☎ 04 42 53 33 47; 1 rue des Bernardines; mains €12.50-21.50; 🕑 closed Sun dinner & Mon) In the old town, this friendly place, characterised by colourful murals, serves French fare in-

cluding frogs' legs and the like. If you missed out on *bouillabaisse* in Marseille, this is your chance to make up for it (minimum of two diners; order two days before).

Bistro Latin (☎ 04 42 38 22 88; 18 rue de la Couronne; menu €21; 🕑 lunch & dinner Tue-Sat) Readers rave about this bistro and with good reason. Engaging and affordable (it's definitely worth booking ahead), Bistro Latin has extensive *menu* choices spanning cod, scampi risotto and a myriad of meat dishes cooked with saffron, spinach and cream.

Le Zinc d'Hugo (☎ 04 42 27 69 69; 22 rue Lieutaud; mains €14-18; 🕑 lunch & dinner Tue-Sat) Outside this rustic bistro of stone walls and chunky wooden tables, a blackboard chalks up daily specials such as a terrine of foie gras with confit of vegetables, as well as highlights from its 80-strong wine list.

Icône (☎ 04 42 27 59 82; 3 rue Frédéric Mistral; 2-/3-course menu €17/25; 🕑 lunch & dinner Mon-Sat) The designer Italian-Mediterranean fare matches the designer boxlike teal armchairs and dark timber lining this glam place just off cours Mirabeau; with a stainless-steel bar and DJ spinning electro lounge beats.

L'Aixquis (☎ 04 42 27 76 16; 22 rue Victor Leydet; mains €18-25; 🕑 lunch & dinner Tue-Sat) You'll probably be tempted to whip out your camera to photograph elaborately presented *plats* such as truffle-infused St-Jacques scallops at this small peach-coloured restaurant, which has a way of giving even the most humble vegetables panache. The *carte* (no *menus*) changes seasonally, but the magical *minute chocolat noir* (a tray of petite desserts) is a year-round fixture.

Le Formal (☎ 04 42 27 08 31; 32 rue Espariat; mains from €14; ☯ lunch & dinner Tue-Fri, dinner Sat) Actually the namesake of its chef, Jean-Luc Le Formal, who's gaining a reputation in France's foodie circles, this first-class establishment has impeccably mannered service both at its whitewashed-stone lounge/reception area at street level and in its vaulted-cellar dining rooms.

SELF-CATERING
Aix is blessed with bountiful **markets** (see p130).

There are around 20 *calisson* makers in town (see p130), as well as plenty of patisseries. Fresh, often still-warm loaves cram the shelves of **La Boulangerie du Coin** (4 rue Boulegon; ☯ Tue-Sun). It's also one of the few *boulangeries* to bake on Sunday, along with the **boulangerie** (5 rue Tournefort) that never closes.

Pick up gourmet goodies at **Jacquèmes** (☎ 04 42 23 48 64; 9 rue Méjanes; ☯ closed Mon am & Sun), a fantastic *épicerie* (grocery) that sells cheese, cold meats, sausages and 500 types of whisky. **Le Comptoir des Oliviers** (14 rue Gaston de Saporta; ☯ closed Mon) sells olive oil, as does **Place aux Huiles** (59 rue d'Italie), which also dispenses chocolates, coffees and teas, and culinary advice.

Staples are on hand at **Monoprix** (cours Mirabeau; ☯ 8.30am-9pm Mon-Sat).

Drinking
Pavement cafés gracing cours Mirabeau provide a plethora of people-watching and posing ops. Open-air cafés also saturate the city's squares, especially place des Cardeurs, forum des Cardeurs, place de Verdun and place de l'Hôtel de Ville.

Les Deux Garçons (☎ 04 42 26 00 51; 53 cours Mirabeau) The best – since 1792 and still resplend-

ent – is the legendary café where Cézanne and Zola used to hang out. Be waited on by white-aproned waiters in the gilded olive-painted salon and outdoor terrace, or head upstairs to the jazz club–piano bar.

L'Orienthé (5 rue de Félibre Gaut; ☯ 1pm-1am) For a mellow change of pace, smoke a *shisha* (Turkish water pipe) and soak up the Buddha atmosphere, along with more than 50 different flavours of tea.

Entertainment
Flip though a copy of the monthly *In Aix* (free from the tourist office) to find out what's on where.

THEATRE, OPERA & CLASSICAL MUSIC
August brings open-air performances (theatre, cinema, cabaret, circus, video projections etc; tickets €1) to Parc Jourdan (p126), **Théâtre de Verdure du Jas de Bouffan** (av St-John Perse), and the Carrières d'Ocre in Rognes (p131) during the month-long Les Instants d'Été.

Théâtre du Jeu de Paume (☎ 04 42 99 12 00; 17-21 rue de l'Opéra) was built in 1756 on the site of a royal tennis court; the curtain rises in the ornate Italianate auditorium most evenings from June to September.

Classical concerts (☎ 04 42 99 37 11) are held in two enchanting churches, **Église Ste-Marie Madeleine** (place des Prêcheurs) and the 17th-century chapel **Chapelle de Ste-Catherine** (20 rue Mignet).

Aix will imminently be graced with a stunning new 1300-seat theatre, designed by Italian architect Vittorio Gregotti – check with the tourist office for updates.

LIVE MUSIC & DJS
Like all good student cities, the scene in Aix is fun, but fickle. The areas on and around

---

DANCE IN AIX
Long at the forefront of contemporary dance, Aix is now home to France's first purpose-built choreography centre, the **Centre Chorégraphique National** (CNN, National Choreographic Centre; rue des Allummettes). Opened in October 2006, this glass, steel and black-concrete box, Pavillon Noir, houses a 378-seat auditorium, roof deck and glass-walled rehearsal studios. The skeletal building, masterminded by French architect Rudi Ricciotti, allows passers-by to peer into the illuminated studios to watch the agile artistry of dancers, including resident dance company **Ballet Preljocaj** (☎ 04 42 93 48 00; www.preljocaj.org). The cutting-edge Preljocaj, founded in 1984, presents some of Europe's most creative – and at times shocking – works. Performance schedules are posted on the company's website; its other programmes (when not on tour) include dance workshops for adults and children.

For more on dance in Aix – and Provence – see p70.

rue de la Verrerie and place Richelme are prime for nightlife. Listings on the website www.marseillebynight.com (in French) also cover Aix.

La Belle Époque (☎ 04 42 27 65 66; 29 cours Mirabeau) Many a 'beautiful time' has been had at this place, which sees DJs spinning Latino, house and funk every evening. Opening hours vary.

Bar Sextius (☎ 04 42 26 07 21; 13 cours Sextius; ☻7am-2am Mon-Sat) With live music and DJs playing house, reggae and raga, depending on the night, Bar Sextius is *le* local gathering spot – ask the in-the-know crowd here about Aix's latest in-spots.

CINEMA

Aix's arty-intellectual student population makes for great cinema offerings, from Oscar contenders to cult flicks, very often in English:

Ciné Mazarin (cinemazarin@wanadoo.fr; 6 rue Laroque; adult/student €7.50/6.50)

Cinéma Renoir (☎ 08 92 68 72 70; 24 cours Mirabeau; adult/student €7.50/6.50)

Le Cézanne (☎ 0 892 687 270; www.lecezanne.com in French; 1 rue Marcel Guillaume; adult/student €8.50/6.70)

Shopping

Shopping is at its most chic along pedestrian rue Marius Reinaud, which winds behind the Palais de Justice on place de Verdun. Elegant boutiques also grace cours Mirabeau.

Local wine vendors include **Cave du Felibrige** (18 rue des Cordeliers), which has a splendid array – some *very* expensive.

SWEET TREAT

Aix's sweetest treat since King René's wedding banquet in 1473 is the marzipan-like local speciality, *calisson*, a small, diamond-shaped chewy delicacy comprising 40% ground almonds and 60% fruit syrup, wrapped in a communion wafer and glazed with white icing sugar. When the Great Plague came into town in 1630, *calissons* supposedly staved off the disease. Traditional *calissonniers* still make the sweets, including **Roy René** (☎ 04 42 26 67 86; www.calisson.com; 10 rue Clémenceau), which also runs guided tours for €1 at its out-of-town factory/museum (at 10am on Tuesday and Thursday; book at the shop in town). Eight or nine plainly wrapped *calissons* (100g) cost around €3 to €4.

Trestle tables set up each morning for the **produce market** on place Richelme, selling olives, goats cheese, garlic, lavender, honey, peaches, melons and other sun-kissed products. Another **food market** (place des Prêcheurs) takes place on Tuesday, Thursday and Saturday morning.

Rainbows of flowers fill place des Prêcheurs during the Sunday morning **flower market**; and place de l'Hôtel de Ville (Tuesday, Thursday and Saturday mornings). Quirky vintage items can also be found at the **flea market** (Tuesday, Thursday and Saturday mornings) on place de Verdun.

Getting There & Away

BUS

Aix's **bus station** (☎ information office 08 91 02 40 25; av de l'Europe) is a 10-minute walk southwest from La Rotonde. Numerous companies' services include buses to Marseille (€4.40, 35 minutes, every 10 minutes, every 20 minutes on Sunday), Arles (€10, 1¾ hours, five daily), Avignon (€13.90, one hour, six daily) and Toulon (€10, one hour, six daily Monday to Saturday).

Buses serve the Gorges du Verdon – see p239 for details.

CAR & MOTORCYCLE

Circumnavigating the one-way, three-lane orbital system encircling the old town is nightmarish in heavy traffic. Street parking spaces are like hens' teeth, but secure, pricier covered parking is plentiful.

The following car-hire agencies also have offices adjacent to the Gare d'Aix TGV train station:

Avis (☎ 04 42 21 64 16; 11 blvd Gambetta)

Europcar (☎ 04 42 27 83 00; 55 blvd de la République)

Hertz (☎ 04 42 27 91 32; 43 av Victor Hugo)

National Citer (☎ 04 42 93 07 85; 42 av Victor Hugo)

TRAIN

Non-TGV trains chug between Aix's **City Centre Train Station**(☻ 5am-9.15pm Mon-Fri, 6am-9.15pm Sat & Sun, information office 9am-7pm) and Marseille (€6.20, 35 minutes, at least 18 daily), while TGV services use Gare d'Aix TGV, 8km west. Within the region the only destinations served by TGV are Marseille (€7.80, 15 minutes), Avignon (€25, 20 minutes) and Nice (€32.50, 3¼ hours).

Getting Around

TO/FROM THE AIRPORT & TGV STATION

A half-hourly **Navette** (☎ 04 42 93 59 13) links Aix's bus station with both the TGV station (€3.90)

A HORRIBLE DETOUR

Drive 6km west of Aix along the D9 to reach **Tuileries des Milles**, a red-brick tile factory in Les Milles that manufactured 30,000 tonnes of bricks and tiles a year from 1882 until 31 August 1939, when it was turned into a WWII concentration camp. By June 1940 some 3500 artists and intellectuals – predominantly Germans living in the Marseille region, including surrealist painters Max Ernst (1891–1976) and Hans Bellmer (1902–75) – were interned at **Camp des Milles**. Poignant paintings and prose inscribed on the walls by the prisoners in the refectory remain untouched, as does one of the wagons used to transport prisoners by rail from Les Milles to Auschwitz.

Unnervingly almost intact, since 1993 the camp has been preserved as a **memorial** (☎ 04 42 24 34 68; admission free; ☽ 9am-noon & 1-4pm Mon-Fri); the wagon can be visited by appointment only.

---

and the Marseille-Provence airport (€7.90), 25km away, from around 5am to 11.30pm.

BICYCLE

Those with a used public-transport ticket for that day can get a discount on their wheels from **Relais Aix en Vélo** (☎ 04 42 26 78 92; La Rotonde, 2 av des Belges; ☽ 9.30am-noon & 12.30-6pm Mon-Sat).

BUS

The city's 14 bus and three minibus lines are operated by **Aix en Bus** (☎ 04 42 26 37 28; ☽ 8.30am-7pm Mon-Sat). The information desk is inside the tourist office.

La Rotonde is the main bus hub. Most services run until 8pm. A single/carnet of 10 tickets costs €1.10/7.70; a day pass costs €3.50. Minibus 1 links the bus station with La Rotonde and cours Mirabeau. Minibus 2, starting at the train station, follows much the same route.

TAXI

You can usually find taxis outside the bus station. To order one, call **Taxi Radio Aixois** (☎ 04 42 27 71 11) or **Taxi Mirabeau** (☎ 04 42 21 61 61).

AROUND AIX

Mountains painted by Cézanne, a truffle kingdom and a chilling WWII concentration camp are a short drive from Aix.

Montagne Ste-Victoire

Before leaving Aix, make sure you pick up a copy of the tourist office's *In Cezanne's Footsteps*. Between 1902 and 1906 Cézanne produced 11 oil and 17 watercolour paintings in the surrounding countryside, including *La Montagne Ste-Victoire au Grand Pin* (1887).

Heading east on the D17 from Aix, you pass local artists at their easels in the roadside pine forests recreating Cézanne's favourite haunt, the magnificent mountain ridge Montagne Ste-Victoire. Garrigue covers the mountain's dry slopes, which are skirted by 32 sq km of vineyards producing Coteaux d'Aix-en-Provence wine.

Cézanne's cubist works *Les Baigneurs* and *Les Baigneuses* (The Bathers) were painted in the **Vallée de l'Arc** around the small mining town of **Gardanne** (population 19,679), 10km south off the D6.

Mountain flora and fauna can be found at **Écomusée de la Forêt Méditerranéenne** (☎ 04 42 51 41 00; www.institut-foret.com in French; chemin de Roman; adult/child under 15 €5.30/3; ☽ 10am-12.30pm & 1.30-6.45pm Sun-Fri Jul–mid-Aug, 9am-12.30 & 1-5.45pm Sun-Fri early Sep-Jun, closed mid-Aug–early Sep) in Gardanne; and along the *sentier de découverte* (discovery path) at the **Maison de Ste-Victoire** (☎ 04 42 66 84 40; ☽ 10am-6pm) in St-Antonin-sur-Bayon. The latter, in converted stables, shelters fauna and flora exhibits and has mountains of information on **walking** and **mountain-biking** around Montagne Ste-Victoire. The entire mountain, save the roads that cross it, is closed between 1 July and 1 September due to the threat of forest fire.

Returning to Aix via the westbound D10, you pass Vauvenargues, with the 14th-century Château de Vauvenargues, in the grounds of which Picasso is buried. The red-brick castle, purchased by the artist in 1958, still belongs to the Picasso family and cannot be visited.

Rognes

pop 4191 / elev 311m

Originally built on the slopes of Foussa, part of the Chaîne de la Trévaresse, Rognes' little village tumbled down to the bottom of the hill in 1909 after an earthquake struck.

Almost 75% of Provence's black truffles are snouted out here. The village's **Grand Marché Truffes et Gastronomie** (Truffle & Gastronomy

Market), held the Sunday before Christmas, opens with a Bénédiction des Truffes (truffle blessing) in the church. Rognes' **tourist office** (☎ 04 42 50 13 36; www.ville-rognes.fr in French; 5 cours St-Étienne; ☒ 3.30-6.30pm Mon, 10am-noon & 3.30-6.30pm Tue-Sat, 10am-noon Sun) knows what's on at the **Carrières d'Ocre** (rte de St-Cannat), a theatre in a former quarry; and has information on *chambres d'hôtes* in the area.

Truffle ice cream, lamb roasted in truffle juice and *foie gras de canard* (duck foie gras) are among the creations of Chef Paul Dietrich at his gorgeous countryside manor, **Les Olivarelles** (☎ 04 42 50 24 27; chemin Font de Vabre; menu €32; ☒ lunch Tue-Sun, dinner Tue-Sat Jun-Aug, lunch & dinner Fri & Sat, lunch Sun Sep-1 Jan & 15 Jan-May; ☒), 6km northwest of Rognes along the D66 amid scented garrigue.

The Camargue

Provence's vividly hued landscapes become bleached out in the haunting, desolate beauty of the Camargue. Roamed by black bulls herded by cowboys on white horses, this 'wild west' is a sparsely populated wetland wilderness interspersed with glinting saltpans and waterlogged paddies producing up to 70% of France's annual rice yield.

Formed over the ages by sediment deposited by the Rhône flowing to the Mediterranean, this triangular 780-sq-km delta lies within the Petit Rhône and Grand Rhône Rivers. Most of its wetlands are protected by the 850-sq-km Parc Naturel Régional de Camargue. On the periphery, the Étang de Vaccarès and nearby peninsulas and islands form the 135-sq-km nature reserve, Réserve Nationale de Camargue. Delving into this delta by bicycle, jeep, boat or horseback is a buzz – literally, when mosquitoes in their multitudes swarm in the summer months.

Birds flock to this remote part of the world. Pale pink flamingos wade in marshes strewn with wild irises in spring and summer, and migratory birds from both the north and the south visit each year, with the area home (at least temporarily) to more than 500 species.

The main stepping stone to the region, Arles, memorably rendered by former resident Vincent Van Gogh, is rich with Roman treasures and a festive atmosphere that reaches a crescendo during bullfights. Isolated townships include Aigues Mortes, encircled entirely by walls amid flat marshland, and the seaside pilgrim's outpost, Stes-Maries de la Mer, filled with feisty flamenco dancers and fiery guitarists.

Its shifting waters steeped in legends and lore, Provence's *enfant sauvage* (wild child) has a soul all its own.

HIGHLIGHTS

- Kite-surf on the wind-whipped waters or across flat, expansive sands around **Stes-Maries de la Mer** (p138)

- Watch rose pink flamingos take to the skies at the **Parc Ornithologique du Pont de Gau** (p136)

- Connect with Provençal culture at the Frédéric Mistral–founded museum, Museon Arlaten, in **Arles** (p141)

- Clip-clop through the bulrush-filled marshes on a horse-drawn carriage ride through the **Marais du Vigueirat** (p153)

- Wince at the chilling instruments displayed at the Musée de la Torture in **Aigues Mortes** (p150)

THE CAMARGUE

ITINERARIES

JOURNEY TO THE EDGE OF THE WORLD (& BACK)

One to Two Days / Southeastern Camargue

Pack your hiking boots and binoculars (and your insect repellent) for a wild ride through the southeastern Camargue. Leaving **Arles** (**1**; p138), catch an initial glimpse of the wetlands' incredible flora and fauna at **La Capelière** (**2**; p150), then continue to **Salin de Badon** (**3**; p151) for breathtaking bird-watching (to catch the earliest birds, doss down at the on-site *gîte*; guesthouse).

The see-forever sea dike of **Digue à la Mer** (**4**; p151) offers idyllic strolling and cycling. Past the salt pans of **Salin de Giraud** (**5**; p151) and the flamingos flocking around the **Domaine de la Palissade** (**6**; p151) and bliss out on the **Plage de Piémanson** (**7**; p152).

Swing back towards Arles and saddle up for a **horse ride** (p152). Stop by the **Musée du Riz du Petit Manusclat** (p152) to learn about rice, then have it for lunch at the authentic bull farm **Le Mas de Peint** (p152). To fully explore the rambling property, stay overnight in countrified comfort. Doing so gives you the chance for an organic feast the next day in the 19th-century sheepfold **La Chassagnette** (see the boxed text, p151) before returning to Arles.

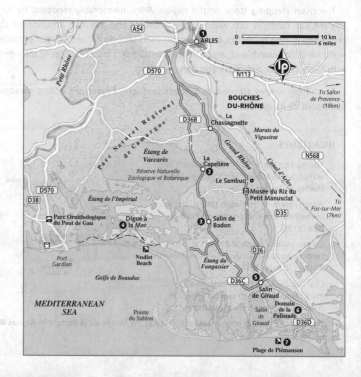

VAN GOGH'S ARLES   One Day / Arles & Around

Celts, Greeks and Romans all shaped this colourful city over the centuries, but the most indelible legacy in recent times is that of Vincent Van Gogh. Follow the streets he walked and gaze out from where he set up his easel along the emotive **Van Gogh trail** (p142); be awed by mighty Roman monuments including the necropolis **Les Alyscamps** (p141) and the magnificent amphitheatre **Les Arènes** (**1**; p140), both of which he portrayed.

Just near Les Arènes are two very different tributes to Van Gogh's art – a re-creation of his 'bedroom in Arles', **La Chambre de Vincent** (**2**; p142); and the impressive **Fondation Vincent Van Gogh** (**3**; p141) gallery, where modern-day greats emulate his vibrant style.

Lunch at local favourite **Jardin des Arts** (**4**; p145), whose cloister terrace backs onto the **Espace Van Gogh** (**5**; 142), host of regular art exhibitions; and study up at the adjoining art bookshop, **Librairie Van Gogh** (**6**; p140).

Tootling past meadows of sunflowers brings Van Gogh's canvases to life aboard **Le Train des Alpilles** (see the boxed text, p146). And, back in Arles, where he painted *Starry Night over the Rhône* (**7**; p142), if you stand by the river at twilight as the sky deepens to midnight blue with the yellow moon rising in a sea of fiery stars, the painter's presence seems hauntingly palpable.

THE CAMARGUE

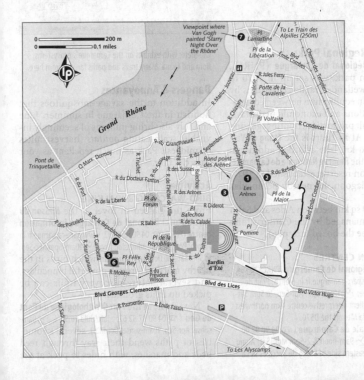

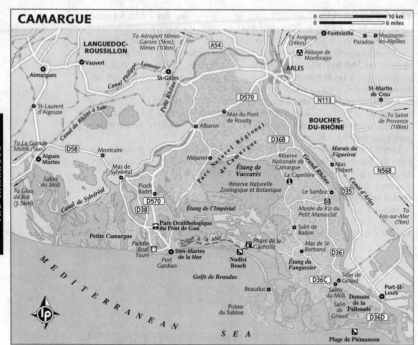

National & Regional Parks

Parc Naturel Régional de Camargue (PNRC), an 863-sq-km park, was set up in 1970 to preserve the wetlands' fragile ecosystems by maintaining an equilibrium between ecological considerations and economic mainstays: agriculture, salt production, hunting, grazing and tourism. At its heart is the **Étang de Vaccarès**, a 600-sq-km lake has afforded additional protection by the **Réserve Nationale de Camargue**. This 135-sq-km reserve, established in 1927, protects the lagoon, its nearby peninsulas and islands.

Another 20 sq km between Arles and Salin de Giraud is managed by the Conservatoire du Littoral (see the boxed text, p76).

INFORMATION CENTRES
Parc Naturel Régional de Camargue (PNRC; ☎ 04 90 97 86 32; www.parc-camargue.fr in French; Pont de Gau; admission free; ☀ 10am-6pm Apr-Sep, to 5pm Sat-Thu Oct-Mar) Excellent interpretive centre 4km northwest of Stes-Maries de la Mer off the D570.

Réserve Nationale de Camargue (☎ 04 90 97 00 97; La Capelière; ☀ 9am-noon & 2-5pm Mon-Sat) Along the D36B, on the eastern side of Étang de Vaccarès in La

Capelière; with exhibits on the Camargue's ecosystems, flora and fauna. Many trails and paths fan out from here.

Dangers & Annoyances
In addition to the savage mosquitoes that flourish in the Camargue in summer, June and July also bring millions of seemingly invisible, scalp-eating *aoûtats* (harvest mites or midges). Pack as much repellent as your bags can take.

Activities
BIRD-WATCHING & WALKING
From the glassed-in foyer at the **Maison du Parc Naturel Régional de Camargue information centre** (PNRC; ☎ 04 90 97 86 32; www.parc-camargue.fr in French; Pont de Gau; admission free; ☀ 10am-6pm Apr-Sep, to 5pm Sat-Thu Oct-Mar) you can watch birds in the nearby marshes through powerful binoculars, and several nature-discovery trails can be picked up in its grounds.

Next door, in the **Parc Ornithologique du Pont de Gau** (☎ 04 90 97 82 62; adult/child €6.50/4; ☀ 9am-sunset Apr-Sep, 10am-sunset Oct-Mar), several kilometres of paths wend their way through reed beds and marshes, with hides to peek at the

PRETTY IN PINK

The pink or greater flamingo *(Phoenicopterus ruber)* in flight is a breathtaking sight. Equally majestic is the catwalk stance – neck high, breast out – adopted by this elegant, long-legged creature when strutting through shallow waters.

Flamingo courtship starts in January, with mating taking place from March to May. The single egg laid by the female in April or May is incubated in a mud-caked nest for one month by both parents. The young chicks shakily take to the skies when they are about three months old. By the time they reach adulthood (around five years old), their soft grey down has become a fine feather coat of brilliant white or pretty rose-pink.

This well-dressed bird lives to the grand old age of 34 (longer if kept in captivity). It stands between 1.5m and 2m tall and has an average wing span of 1.9m. When the flamingo feels threatened, its loud hiss is similar to the warning sound made by a goose. It feeds on plankton, sucking in water and draining it off with its disproportionately heavy, curved bill.

Some flamingos remain in the Rhône delta year-round. Come September, several thousand take flight to Spain, Tunisia and Senegal where they winter in warmer climes before returning to the Camargue in February in time for early spring.

area's dazzling array of bird life. Pink flamingos fly overhead or stalk the watery landscape. Guided walks around the park are available. Salin de Badon in southeastern Camargue is another prime bird-watching spot.

Numerous other walking trails traverse the sea embankments and the coast in the PNRC. One of the most dramatic paths, the Digue à la Mer (p151), is atop the dike between Stes-Maries de la Mer and Salin de Giraud. Shorter nature trails start from the Musée Camarguais (p141) southwest of Arles; and La Capelière (p150), Salin de Badon (p151) and Domaine de la Palissade (p151) in the southeastern Camargue.

Many trails also fan out from the Parc Naturel Régional de Camargue (opposite).

Park offices sell detailed maps of the area, including the 1:25,000 IGN Série Bleue maps, Nos 2944E and 2944O.

CANOEING

Kayak Vert (☎ 04 66 73 57 17; www.kayak.camargue .fr; Mas de Sylvéréal), 14km north of Stes-Maries de la Mer off the picturesque D38C, rents canoes to explore Camargue waterways by paddle power for €9.50 per hour. The canoeing centre also runs half-/one-/two-/three-day guided expeditions for €18/24/48/72 and offers a combined canoe (10km) and bicycle trip (16km) departing from Stes-Maries de la Mer (€30).

CYCLING

Pancake-flat, with little traffic, the Camargue is ideal for cycling (insects and stiff sea breezes notwithstanding). East of Stes-Maries de la Mer, areas along the seafront and further inland are reserved for walkers and cyclists. Cycling is forbidden on beaches, but you can bike along the Digue à la Mer.

Le Vélo Saintois and Le Vélociste in Stes-Maries de la Mer (see p149), both open Easter to early October, distribute cycling itineraries (20km to 70km long) with route descriptions in English and deliver bicycles to your door for free.

Arles' **tourist office** (☎ 04 90 18 41 20; www.arles -tourism.com; esplanade Charles de Gaulle; ☿ 9am-6.45pm Apr-Sep, to 4.45pm Mon-Sat, 10am-1pm Sun Oct-Mar) sells a packet of brochures (in French) with maps outlining cycling itineraries (€4.50).

HORSE RIDING

Heaps of roadside farms along the D570 into Stes-Maries de la Mer offer *promenades à*

SEA CHANGE

At some places along the coast, the delta continues to grow, sweeping one-time seaside towns kilometres from the Mediterranean. Elsewhere, sea currents and storms have, in recent centuries, washed away land that had been around long enough for construction to take place. The course of the Rhône has changed repeatedly over the millennia, but the Grand Rhône (which carries 90% of the river's flow) and the Petit Rhône have followed their present channels for about 500 years.

LITERARY CAMARGUE

Immerse yourself in the region with the best of Camargue-inspired travel literature.

- *Garden of Eden* (Ernest Hemingway) Two honeymooners pursue a hedonistic life in the sun in 1920s Le-Grau du Roi, near Aigues-Mortes.

- *Taurine Provence* (Roy Campbell) The history of the Provençal bullfight told by a 1930s matador.

- *The Bull that Thought* (Rudyard Kipling) Short story with a twist about bullfighting in Arles, written in 1924 by the 1907 Nobel Prize for Literature winner.

- *A Little Tour in France* (Henry James) Vivid portrait of Van Gogh's 19th-century Arles, first visited by James in 1882.

- *A Spell in Wild France* (Bill and Laurel Cooper) Life aboard a boat moored near Aigues-Mortes. *Watersteps to France* recounts the couple's canal journey to Provence.

---

cheval (horse riding), including **L'Auberge Cavaliere** (☎ 04 90 97 88 88; www.aubergecavaliere.com; rte d'Arles) for around €30 for two hours and around €60 for daylong rides on the beach.

For short rides, as well as longer treks of two to seven days, contact **Promenades des Rieges** (☎ 04 90 97 91 38; www.promenadedesrieges.com in French; rte de Cacharel), just north of Stes-Maries de la Mer.

The **Domaine Paul Ricard de Méjanes** (☎ 04 90 97 10 62; mejanes@camargue.fr; ☒ Apr–mid-Oct), on the northwestern bank of the Étang de Vaccarès in Méjanes, 20km southwest of Arles, also has horses – as well as a train (adult/child €4/3) whose tracks take in a 3.5km loop of the property; and a 2.5km nature trail for amblers.

Scenic rides in the wild southeastern Camargue start out from **Domaine de la Palissade** (p151).

KITE-SURFING

The wind-whipped waters off Stes-Maries de la Mer are prime for kite-surfing – **HB Kite Academy** (☎ 06 16 29 47 42; www.hb-kite-academy.com) runs a variety of programmes from April to October starting from €45 for a 1½-hour discovery session – you'll find the academy on the eastern side of Stes-Maries' beach.

On land, **Gliss Kite** (☎ 06 61 43 54 23; www.gliss kite.com in French) teaches you to speed aboard kite-powered buggies across the sands of Beauduc. Two-day missions cost €205; bring camping gear to pitch up with the crew on the beach (there's a communal kitchen tent).

Tours

Boat tours depart from Aigues-Mortes (p150) and Stes-Maries de la Mer (p147).

La Maison du Guide en Camargue (☎ /fax 04 66 73 52 30, 06 12 44 73 52; www.maisonduguide.camargue.fr) in Montcalm, 10km northwest of Stes-Maries de la Mer on the D58, organises guided tours by foot, boat and bicycle.

Tour operators in Arles include **Safari Robert** (☎ 04 90 91 71 78; www.safari-robert.com in French; 1 rue Porte de Laure; ☒ 9am-6pm Mar-Oct), which runs English-language 4WD tours from March to October. Morning/afternoon 'safari-photo' tours last two/four hours and cost €25/38. **Camargue Découverte** (☎ 04 90 96 69 20; www .camargue-decouverte.com; 1 rue Émile Fassin) is another Arles-based Jeep-safari company. Stes-Maries de la Mer operators include **Camargue Safaris 4x4 Gallon** (☎ 04 90 97 86 93; camargue-safari .gallon@wanadoo.fr; 22 av Van Gogh).

ARLES

pop 52,000

If Arles' winding streets, stone squares, Roman relics and colourful houses baking in the sun evoke a sense of déjà vu for first-time visitors, it's invariably because they feature in Vincent Van Gogh's prolific outpouring of art here.

Long before Van Gogh captured this spot on the Grand Rhône River, just south of where the Petit Rhône diverges on canvas, the Romans had already been turned on to its charms. (Even before that, Arles was a Celtic settlement in the Bronze Age, before becoming a Greek colony known to the Romans as Arelate.)

In 49 BC, Arles' prosperity and political standing rose meteorically when it backed a winner in Julius Caesar (who would never meet defeat in his entire career). After Caesar

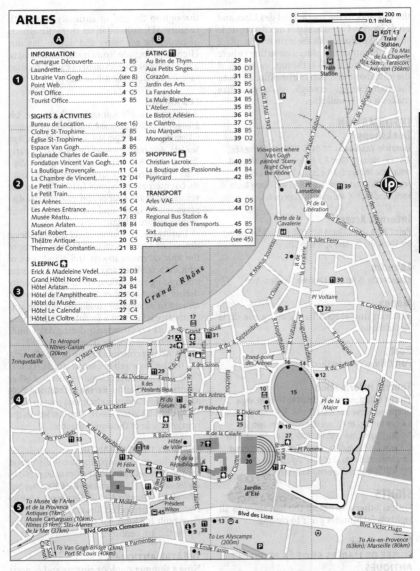

ARLES

INFORMATION
Camargue Découverte.................1 B5
Laundrette...............................2 C3
Librairie Van Gogh..............(see 8)
Point Web...............................3 C3
Post Office..............................4 C5
Tourist Office..........................5 B5

SIGHTS & ACTIVITIES
Bureau de Location.............(see 16)
Cloître St-Trophime...................6 B5
Église St-Trophime...................7 B4
Espace Van Gogh......................8 B5
Esplanade Charles de Gaulle......9 B5
Fondation Vincent Van Gogh....10 C4
La Boutique Provençale............11 C4
La Chambre de Vincent............12 D4
Le Petit Train..........................13 C5
Le Petit Train..........................14 C4
Les Arènes.............................15 C4
Les Arènes Entrance................16 C4
Musée Réattu.........................17 B3
Museon Arlaten......................18 B4
Safari Robert..........................19 C4
Théâtre Antique......................20 C5
Thermes de Constantin............21 B3

SLEEPING
Erick & Madeleine Vedel..........22 D3
Grand Hôtel Nord Pinus...........23 B4
Hôtel Arlatan..........................24 B4
Hôtel de l'Amphitheatre...........25 C4
Hôtel du Musée.......................26 B3
Hôtel Le Calendal....................27 C4
Hôtel Le Cloître.......................28 C5

EATING
Au Brin de Thym.....................29 B4
Aux Petits Singes....................30 D3
Corazón.................................31 B3
Jardin des Arts........................32 B5
La Farandole...........................33 A4
La Mule Blanche.....................34 B5
L'Atelier.................................35 B5
Le Bistrot Arlésien...................36 B4
Le Cilantro.............................37 C5
Lou Marques..........................38 B5
Monoprix...............................39 D2

SHOPPING
Christian Lacroix.....................40 B5
La Boutique des Passionnés......41 B4
Puyricard...............................42 B5

TRANSPORT
Arles VAE..............................43 D5
Avis.......................................44 D1
Regional Bus Station &
  Boutique des Transports........45 B5
Sixt.......................................46 C2
STAR................................(see 45)

---

seized and plundered Marseille, which had supported his rival, Pompey the Great, Arles eclipsed Marseille as the region's major port. Within a century and a half, it boasted a 12,000-seat theatre and a 20,000-seat amphitheatre to entertain its citizens with gruesome gladiatorial spectacles and chariot races. Still impressively intact, the structures now stage events including *corrida* (bullfighting) in Les Arènes, which sends the town into a frenzy of excitement when the season starts with fanfare each spring.

ORIENTATION

Arles is shoehorned between the Grand Rhône River to the northwest, blvd Émile Combes to the east and, to the south, blvd des Lices and blvd Georges Clemenceau. The city centre is shaped like a foot, with the train station, place de la Libération and place Lamartine (where Van Gogh once lived) at the top, les Arènes at the anklebone and the tourist office beneath the arch. Fittingly enough, its compact size makes it easily walkable.

INFORMATION
Bookshops
Librairie Van Gogh (☎ 04 90 49 39 39; 1 place Félix Rey; ☽ 10am-12.30pm & 2-6.30pm Tue-Sat) Wrapped around the courtyard of the Espace Van Gogh cultural centre, with an extensive range of art and history books in French and English, and regional travel guides.

Internet Access
Point Web (☎ 04 90 18 91 54; 10 rue du 4 Septembre; per 10min €1; ☽ 9am-7pm Mon-Sat)

Laundry
Laundrette (6 rue de la Cavalerie; ☽ 7am-7pm)

Money
You can find several banks along rue de la République.

Post
Post Office (5 blvd des Lices)

Tourist Information
Tourist Office main office (☎ 04 90 18 41 20; www .arlestourism.com; esplanade Charles de Gaulle; ☽ 9am-6.45pm Apr-Sep, to 4.45pm Mon-Sat, 10am-1pm Sun Oct-Mar); train station (☎ 04 90 49 36 90; ☽ 9am-1pm & 2-5pm Tue-Sat Apr-Sep) Both offices sell a discounted combination ticket to all of Arles' sights (adult/student €13.50/12). Note that opening hours may vary.

SIGHTS
Unless otherwise noted, the last entry to all sights is 30 minutes prior to closing.

Roman Arles
MUSÉE DE L'ARLES ET DE LA PROVENCE ANTIQUES
The fabulous story of Roman Arles takes centre stage at the state-of-the-art showpiece **Musée de l'Arles et de la Provence Antiques** (☎ 04 90 18 88 88; www.arles-antique.cg13.fr; av de la Première Division Française Libre; adult/12-18yr €5.50/4; ☽ 9am-7pm Mar-Oct, 10am-5pm Nov-Feb), fronted by a cobalt blue façade. Within the triangular structure you can trace the area's evolution from 2500 BC

through to the end of antiquity in the 6th century AD, or hone in on thematic aspects of trade, the economy and day-to-day life. Highlights include Roman statues, artefacts, and a renowned assortment of early Christian sarcophagi from the 4th century.

LES ARÈNES
Arles' remarkable Roman amphitheatre, **Les Arènes** (☎ 04 90 96 03 70; adult/student €5.50/4; ☽ 9am-6.30pm May-Sep, to 5.30pm Mar, Apr & Oct, 10am-4.30pm Nov-Feb), was built around the late 1st or early 2nd century AD. With a slightly smaller capacity but marginally larger dimensions than its counterpart in Nîmes (p195), it was the venue for chariot races and gladiatorial displays where slaves and criminals met their demise before jubilant crowds.

During the Arab invasions of early medieval times, Les Arènes became a fortress. Three of the four defensive towers still stand (one of which is accessible), and parts of Les Arènes are undergoing restoration, creating community debate about whether the structure should remain in its original condition. But the amphitheatre is far from a forgotten ruin – today it fills to its 12,000 capacity during Arles' bullfighting season (see the boxed text, p148).

Les Arènes crowns a hilltop in the city centre, reached by a web of narrow streets. Tickets for bullfights, *courses Camarguaises* and other events are sold at the **Bureau de Location** (☎ 04 90 96 03 70; arenes.arles@wanadoo.fr; Rond-point des Arènes; ☽ 9am-noon & 2.30-6pm Mon-Fri, 10am-1pm Sat) on the northern side of the amphitheatre.

THERMES DE CONSTANTIN
Admission to the amphitheatre is also good for the **Thermes de Constantin** (rue du Grand Prieuré; adult/student €3/2.20; ☽ 9am-noon & 2-6.30pm May-Sep, 9am-noon & 2-5.30pm Mar, Apr & Oct, 10am-noon & 2-5pm Feb & Nov), partly preserved Roman baths near the river built for Emperor Constantin's private use in the 4th century.

THÉÂTRE ANTIQUE
Now a summer outdoor cinema and concert venue, the **Théâtre Antique** (Roman theatre; ☎ 04 90 96 93 30; adult/student €3/2.20; ☽ 9am-6.30pm May-Sep, to noon & 2-6pm Mar, Apr & Oct, 10am-noon & 2-5pm Nov-Feb) dates from the end of the 1st century BC. For centuries it was used as a convenient source of construction materials, chipping away at the 102m diameter structure (the remaining column on the right-hand side

near the entrance indicates the height of the original arcade). Enter via the Jardin d'Été on blvd des Lices.

LES ALYSCAMPS

Van Gogh and Gauguin both painted this large **necropolis** (adult/student €3.50/2.60; ☺ 9am-7pm May-Sep, 9am-noon & 2-6pm Mar & Apr, 9am-noon Oct, 10am-noon & 2-5pm Nov-Feb). Founded by the Romans and taken over by Christians in the 4th century, it became a coveted resting place because of the apparent presence of miracle-working Christian martyrs among its dead.

OTHER ROMAN SITES

Under your feet as you stand on the place du Forum are the underground storerooms *Cryptoporticus du Forum*, carved out in the 1st century BC; and closed at press time for repairs – check with the tourist office for reopening dates.

Église St-Trophime

Arles was an archbishopric from the 4th century until 1790, and this Romanesque-style **church** was once a cathedral. Built in the late 11th and 12th centuries on the site of several earlier churches, it's named after St-Trophime, a late-2nd- or early-3rd-century bishop of Arles. On the western portal's intricately sculpted biblical scene façade (more spectacular than the interior), you will see on the far right of the left-hand side St-Trophime's depicted holding a spiral staff in his right hand. Inside the austere church, the most fascinating feature is the 'treasury', containing pieces of bone of Arles' bishops, who were later canonised. Many of the broken statues inside were decapitated during the French Revolution.

Across the courtyard, the **Cloître St-Trophime** (St-Trophime cloister; ☎ 04 90 49 36 36; adult/student €3.50/2.60; ☺ 9am-6.30pm May-Sep, to 6pm Mar, Apr & Oct, 10am-5pm Nov-Feb) is flanked by highly detailed stone and marble columns. Its two Romanesque galleries date from the 1100s, while the two Gothic galleries were added in the 14th century.

Museums

Museon Arlaten (☎ 04 90 93 58 11; 29 rue de la République; adult/student €4/3; ☺ 9.30am-1pm & 2-6.30pm Jul & Aug, 9.30am-12.30pm & 2-6pm Sep, 9.30am-1pm & 2-6.30pm Tue-Sun Jun, 9.30am-12.30pm & 2-6pm Tue-Sun Apr & May, 9.30am-12.30pm & 2-5pm Tue-Sun Oct-Mar) was founded

> ### ROMAN COMBO
>
> A **combination ticket** (adult/child €9/7) gives you access to Arles' Roman monuments: Les Arènes, the Thermes de Constantin, the Théâtre Antique, and Les Alyscamps.

by Nobel Prize–winning poet and dedicated Provençal preservationist Frédéric Mistral. Occupying a 16th-century townhouse, it has displays of traditional Provençal furniture, crafts, costumes, ceramics, wigs, and a model of the mythical people-eating amphibious monster, the Tarasque. Last entry is one hour prior to closing.

Muse Réattu (☎ 04 90 96 37 68; 10 rue du Grand Prieuré; adult/student €4/3; ☺ 10am-noon & 2-5pm Mar, Apr & Oct, 10am-noon & 2-6.30pm May-Sep, 1-5pm Nov-Feb) is housed in a former 15th-century priory. This splendid museum has two Picasso paintings and 57 of his sketches from the early 1970s, as well as works by 18th- and 19th-century Provençal artists; but it's best known for its cutting-edge photographic displays. Temporary exhibitions incur an additional admission fee depending on the exhibits.

Inside an 1812-built sheep shed, the **Musée Camarguais** (Camargue Museum; Museon Camarguen in Provençal; ☎ 04 90 97 10 82; Mas du Pont de Rousty; adult/student €5/2.50; ☺ 10am-6pm Wed-Sat Apr-Oct, 10.15am-4.45pm Wed-Sat Nov-Mar) is a fantastic introduction to this unique area, covering its history, ecosystems, flora and fauna, with a glimpse into traditional life in the region. From here, a 3.5km nature trail leads to an observation tower, with bird's-eye views. The museum is 10km southwest of Arles on the D570 to Stes-Maries de la Mer.

Van Gogh Sights

Although Van Gogh painted around 200 canvases in Arles, not one remains here today (the only Van Gogh canvas in Provence is in Avignon's Musée Angladon, p162). There's a certain poetic justice, considering that following his altercation with housemate Paul Gauguin in place Victor Hugo in which he threatened Gauguin with a cut-throat razor before using it to slice off part of his own left ear, a petition was raised by fearful neighbours, and Van Gogh was committed to hospital for one month on the mayor's orders.

But Arles has admirably made up for it. Fitting tributes to his art include **Fondation Vincent**

THE CAMARGUE

Van Gogh (☎ 04 90 49 94 04; 24bis Rond-point des Arènes; adult/student €7/5; ⏰ to 7pm Jul-Sep, 10am-6pm Apr-Jun, 11am-5pm Tue-Sun Oct-Mar), where celebrated artists, including David Hockney, Francis Bacon and Fernando Botero, have paid homage to the artist's distinctive style.

Van Gogh's little 'yellow house' on place Lamartine, which he painted in 1888, was wiped out during WWII. But to get a sense of stepping into his bedroom – which he sketched and painted several times (or least the sense of stepping into its brightly coloured canvas likeness, skewed perspective and all), **La Chambre de Vincent** (☎ 04 90 18 27 09; 25 Rond-point des Arènes; adult/child €3/2; ⏰ 9am-5pm Wed-Mon) re-creates a life-size approximation. Opening hours can be erratic.

Temporary art exhibitions regularly take place at **Espace Van Gogh** (☎ 04 90 49 39 39; place Félix Rey), housed in the former hospital where Van Gogh had his ear stitched and was later locked up.

Accompanied with a brochure (in English) handed out by the tourist office, the evocative **Van Gogh trail**, a walking circuit of the city marked by footpath-embedded plaques, takes in spots where Van Gogh set up his easel to paint canvases such as *Starry Night Over the Rhône* (1888). At each stop there's a lectern-style signboard with a reproduction of the painting and interpretative information (also in English).

See also the boxed text, opposite.

TOURS

In addition to the Van Gogh trail (above), several other **self-guided walking tours** are marked along Arles' footpaths in conjunction with an explanatory brochure.

From mid-June to mid-September the **tourist office** (☎ 04 90 18 41 20; www.arlestourism.com; esplanade Charles de Gaulle) runs thematic city tours for around €5 for two hours, usually with a couple of tours a week in English.

Jeep tours of the Camargue departing from Arles are organised by several companies, costing around €30/15 per adult/child for a half-day trip. The tourist office has information and seasonal schedules; reservations can also be made at **La Boutique Provençale** (☎ 04 90 49 84 31; 8 Rond-point des Arènes). For further operators, see p138.

Le Petit Train d'Arles (☎ 04 93 41 31 09; adult/under 10yr €6/3; ⏰ 10am-5pm Apr-Oct) is an easy way of glimpsing the main sights without wear and tear on your feet. Tours with English commentary take 35 minutes and depart from Les Arènes and blvd des Lices.

FESTIVALS & EVENTS

Arles heralds the beginning of the bullfighting season with the festive **Feria Pascale** around Easter. May sees Camargue cowboys parade through the streets of town, the crowning of the Queen of Arles and Camargue games in Les Arènes during the **Fête des Gardians**. Dance, theatre, music and poetry readings feature during the two-week **Fêtes d'Arles** (☎ 04 90 96 47 00) from around the end of June.

In early July, **Les Rencontres Internationales de la Photographie** (International Photography Festival; www.rencontres-arles.com) attracts photographers from around the world, with works displayed until September.

The **Festo Vierginenco** in mid-July, celebrated since 1904, honours young women wearing the traditional Arlésienne costume of a long full skirt, lacy shawl and cap (which takes more than two hours to don). Mid-July also brings the world music festival **Les Suds** (www.suds-arles.com in French) to venues around town. During **Un Été au Ciné** in July and August, films (free

---

STREET BEATS

Roma bands such as Los Reyes, Arles' own Gypsy Kings (discovered while busking in St-Tropez), Chico & the Gypsies (founded by former Gypsy King Chico Bouchikhi) and Manitas de Plata have all performed on the streets of Arles and Stes-Maries de la Mer at some point in their vibrant careers. For an outstanding collection of tracks by these and other artists, shop at **La Boutique des Passionnés** (☎ 04 90 96 59 93; www.passionnes.com in French; 14 rue Réattu; ⏰ 2-7pm Mon, 9am-7pm Tue-Sat). Stop by its website to check its gig guide. **Chico's website** (www.chico.fr) lists performances.

The best time to catch Roma bands perform on the streets is during Arles mid-July festivities and the Stes-Maries de la Mer pilgrimages (see the boxed text, p147) in May and October. The musicians (exclusively male) are usually encircled by Roma women dancing Camargue flamenco (reminiscent of Spanish flamenco).

THE CAMARGUE

VINCENT

Vincent Van Gogh may have been poor – he sold only one painting in his lifetime – but he wasn't old. It's easy to forget from his self-portraits, in which he appears much older (partly the effects of his poverty), that he was only 37 when he died. But his short life, especially his ephemeral time in Provence, continues to influence art to this day.

Born in 1853, the Dutch painter arrived in Arles in 1888 after living in Paris with his younger brother Theo, an art dealer, who financially supported him from his modest income. In Paris he became acquainted with seminal artists including Edgar Degas, Camille Pissarro, Henri de Toulouse-Lautrec and Paul Gauguin. Revelling in Arles' intense light and bright colours, Van Gogh painted sunflowers, irises and other vivid subjects with a burning fervour, unfazed by howling mistrals, during which he knelt on his canvases and painted horizontally or lashed his easel to iron stakes driven deep into the ground. He sent paintings to Theo in Paris to try and sell, and dreamed of founding an artists colony here, but only Gauguin followed up his invitation. Their differing artistic approaches – Gauguin believed in painting from imagination; Van Gogh painting what he saw – and their artistic temperaments, fuelled by absinthe, came to a head with the argument that led to Van Gogh lopping his ear and his subsequent committal. Gauguin left Provence immediately (at times he too suffered from mental illness and also attempted suicide).

During Van Gogh's hospitalisation in Arles, he produced, among other works, a portrait of his doctor, Dr Rey, which he presented as a gift. The doctor didn't throw it away, exactly; he used it to plug a hole in his chicken coop. It's now in Moscow's Pushkin Museum.

In May 1889, Van Gogh voluntarily entered an asylum in St-Rémy de Provence, 25km northeast of Arles over the Alpilles, where he painted another 150-odd canvases during his one-year, one-week and one-day confinement, including masterpieces like *Starry Night* (not to be confused with *Starry Night over the Rhône*, painted in Arles). A reconstruction of his room at the Monastère St-Paul de Mausole is open to visitors (p190). While there, Theo sent him a positive critique of his work that had appeared in the *Mercure de France* newspaper in January 1890. The following month, his 1888 Arles-painted work *The Red Vines* was bought by Anne Boch, sister of his friend Eugene Boch, for 400 francs (around €50 today). It also now hangs in the Pushkin Museum.

On 16 May 1890 Van Gogh moved to Auvers-sur-Oise, just outside Paris, to be closer to Theo, but on 27 July that year he shot himself, possibly to avoid further financial burden on his brother, whose wife had just had a baby son, named Vincent, and who was also supporting their ailing mother. Van Gogh died two days later with Theo at his side. Theo subsequently had a breakdown, and was also committed, prior to succumbing to physical illness. He died, aged 33, just six months after Van Gogh.

It would be less than a decade before Van Gogh's talent would start to achieve wide recognition, with major museums acquiring his works. By the early 1950s, he had become a household name. His tormented life is documented in countless books, films, and Don McLean's poignant song, 'Vincent '.

admission) are shown on giant screens rigged up in various outdoor venues around town.

Just some of Arles' other events include the **Festival Ame Gitane** in mid-August, which celebrates Gitane ('Gypsy' or 'Romany') culture; and September's week-long **Fête des Prémices du Riz**, marking the start of the rice harvest. The tourist office has detailed information.

SLEEPING

The city has plenty of reasonably priced accommodation (most of which shuts during January, if not the entire low season), which fills fast during festivals and bullfights.

Chambre d'Hôte

Erick & Madeleine Vedel (☎ 04 90 49 69 20; www .cuisineprovencale.com with English sections; 11 rue Portagnel; d €65; ☒ ⓖ) Three charming, colourful rooms including a mezzanine room that can accommodate families, are the result of the tireless work of hosts Erick and Madeleine Vedel at their *chambre d'hôte* (bed and breakfast accommodation) in the heart of the city. Chef Erick also runs a renowned cooking school, Association Cuisine et Tradition École de Cuisine Provençale, offering a range of programmes such as the five-day 'minigourmand' (€800) with visits including a wine *cave, fromagerie* (cheese shop), boulangerie (bakery) and the bustling market.

Hotels

BUDGET

Hôtel Le Cloître (☎ 04 90 96 29 50; members.aol.com /hotelcloitre; 16 rue du Cloître; d €42-65; ☑ mid-Mar–Oct) Atmospherically housed in a 12th-century former cloister and clerics residence, this pistachio -shuttered hotel's terrazzo lobby leads to 30 rooms with private glazed-tiled bathrooms. Especially coveted are rooms 1 and 2 with traces of 12th-century paint, which was revealed during renovations and left exposed; and rooms 18 and 20 looking into the stone and marble St-Trophime cloister.

MIDRANGE

Hôtel de l'Amphitheatre (☎ 04 90 96 10 30; www.hotel amphitheatre.fr; 5-7 rue Diderot; d €45-83; ☒ ▣) Deep crimson décor dresses the solid bones of this 1600s-built structure with contemporary flair. Right near its namesake Roman amphitheatre, have breakfast (€6.50) beneath the shadowed hands of the salon's slide-projected clock or in a high-walled, red-painted courtyard.

Hôtel du Musée (☎ 04 90 93 88 88; www.hotel dumusee.com.fr; 11 rue du Grand Prieuré; d €46-68; ☑ closed mid-Jan–mid-Feb; ℗ ☒) In a fine 12th- to 13th-century building, this impeccably maintained hotel has 28 beautifully furnished rooms, a checkerboard-tiled lobby, and tranquil terrace garden as well as its own 'museum' showcasing local painters, sculptors and photographers. Rooms with showers only are significantly cheaper than those with bath tubs. Parking is €7, pets are free.

Hôtel le Calendal (☎ 04 90 96 11 89; www.lecal endal.com; 5 rue Porte de Laure; d €64-104; ☑ closed Jan; ℗ ☒ ☒ ▣ ☒) Rendered in ochre with sky blue shutters, Hôtel Calendal is best known for its *salon de thé* (tearooms) serving a garden-fresh buffet lunch for €14. Its 38 quaint rooms, some grouped around a leafy courtyard, have beamed ceilings and bright Provençal fabrics, and are well equipped. Garage parking costs €10. Wi-fi is €10 per hour, but there's a free online computer.

Hôtel Arlatan (☎ 04 90 93 56 66; www.hotel-arlatan .fr; 26 rue du Sauvage; d €85-153; ☑ closed mid-Jan–mid-Feb; ℗ ☒ ☒) Swim in the heated pool set in flowering gardens at this three-star hotel, sections of which were once part of the palace of Emperor Constantin. Stylish stone-and-wood rooms are individually decorated in flowing,

subtly floral fabrics, with views over Arles' old town rooftops. Garaged parking (including help carrying your bags) is €14.

TOP END

Grand Hôtel Nord Pinus (☎ 04 90 93 44 44; www.nord pinus.com; place du Forum; r €145-190; ☒ ☒) On the café-clad place du Forum, and incorporating the only remaining chunk of the original Roman Forum wall in its façade, this 1927-established hotel is an intimate 26-room affair offering American breakfasts (€20) as well as classic Continental fare (€14). Even if you're not staying here, stop by the bar to view striking photography exhibitions.

EATING

Arles' restaurant terraces give even the most upmarket eating establishments a relaxed café atmosphere.

Restaurants

Aux Petits Singes (☎ 06 89 61 72 81; 11 place Voltaire; dishes €3-6, children's menu €6; ☑ 10.30am-7.30pm Tue-Sun; ☒) Little visitors will be delighted by this adorable 'children's restaurant' where they can sit at tiny tables, play with toys and games, and enjoy their own special *menu* of a drink, main dish and a 'surprise' (chocolate or similar). Grown-ups' choices range from *charcuterie* (cold meats) to *tartes*, salads and soup. Everything – including the cakes – is homemade.

AUTHOR'S CHOICE

Le Cilantro (☎ 04 90 18 25 05; 29 rue Porte de Laure; lunch menu €23, mains €18-23; ☑ lunch Tue-Fri & Sun, dinner Tue-Sat) Arles' most buzzing tables are a result of the homecoming of Arlésian chef Jêrome Laurant, cooking accomplished dishes like saddle of lamb in almond oil with mash and braised carrots. Children can be catered for by request.

To learn how to create Jêrome's feasts for yourself, cooking classes (lesson and lunch €45, lunch only €25 including wine and coffee) are held once a month from March to December, themed around seasonal produce – spring, for example, might have you preparing frittered sweetbread and lambs' brains, milk-fed lamb and vegetable pie, and a luscious red wine, strawberry and hibiscus sorbet.

La Mule Blanche (☎ 04 90 93 98 54; 9 rue du Président Wilson; mains €12.20-20; ☺ lunch Tue-Sun & dinner Wed-Sun summer, lunch Tue-Sat & dinner Wed-Sat winter; ⊛) Jazz is often performed at the piano in the 'White Mule's' domed interior, but the hottest tables are on the pavement terrace, which is the prettiest in town and gets packed in fine weather.

Au Brin de Thym (☎ 04 90 49 95 96; 22 rue du Docteur Fanton; menus €14-22; ☺ lunch Thu-Mon, dinner Wed-Mon) Market-fresh produce is made to look like a work of art at this pretty place fronted by a lavender and white awning and damask-clothed tables. The Provençal *menu* (€17) is a great way to sample creative dishes laced in local olive oil, and there's a strong wine list.

Corazón (☎ 04 90 96 32 53; 1bis rue Réattu; mains €16.50-24.50; ☺ lunch & dinner Tue-Sat) This funky, modern space in a recessed arcade combines a contemporary art gallery with elongated pink and red dining areas highlighted by quirky-chic lighting and furnishings. Modern Mediterranean fare includes warm goat's cheese drizzled with lavender honey.

Jardin des Arts (☎ 04 90 96 10 36; 38 rue de la République; lunch menu from €17, dinner menu from €26, mains €10-16; ☺ lunch Tue-Sat, dinner Sat; ⊛) Opening out to a leafy cloister courtyard adjoining the Espace Van Gogh, this fresh new establishment is popular with locals for light but luscious lunches, and is a hot spot on Saturday nights when it also swings its doors open for dinner. During July and August it doubles as an afternoon *salon de thé* from 2pm to 7pm; and artisan ice creams tempt passers-by (€1.80 per scoop).

L'Atelier (☎ 04 90 91 07 69; 7 rue des Carmes; menus €20-50; ☺ lunch Wed-Sun, dinner Tue-Sun) Ex–La Chassagnette (see the boxed text, p151) Jean-Luc Rabanel has now restrung his Michelin star in Arles' historic heart, where you can savour superbly crafted dishes like crumbed pigs' trotters and cuttlefish with fennel and coriander amid a striking interior of black tables and red flowers. Children's *menus* are available at lunch only.

Lou Marques (☎ 04 90 52 52 52; 9 blvd des Lices; lunch menus €21-28, dinner menus €40-75; ☺ lunch & dinner Mon-Sat; ⊛) Gastronomic treats at the Hôtel Jules César's sumptuous restaurant, within a former 17th-century Carmelite convent, include a fine variety of foie gras, a St-Jacques risotto with red Camargue rice, and a Grand Marnier soufflé served with cool chocolate sorbet.

> **MARKET DAY**
>
> Pack a perfect safari picnic from local produce fresh from the morning market:
>
> **Monday** Stes-Maries de la Mer
> **Wednesday** Aigues-Mortes, Arles
> **Friday** Stes-Maries de la Mer
> **Saturday** Arles
> **Sunday** Aigues-Mortes

Cafés

The Roman place du Forum, shaded by outstretched plane trees, turns into a giant dining table at lunch and dinner in summer. Here you'll find Café la Nuit, thought to be the café in Van Gogh's *Café Terrace at Night* (1888). Painted bright yellow to re-create the effect used by Van Gogh to indicate bright night-time lights, it's invariably packed with tourists dining in front of its famous façade. A few doors down, Le Bistrot Arlésien is the locals' pick of places on place du Forum.

Blvd Georges Clemenceau and blvd des Lices are also lined with plane trees and brasserie terraces, though depending on the time of day, you may find yourself dining à la traffic fumes.

Self-Catering

Amble the Saturday morning market, stretching the length of the main boulevard, selling strong cheese, Camargue salt, olive oil, and bull sausages. On Wednesday, market stalls set up along blvd Émile Combes.

Shops that specialise in *saucissons d'Arles* (local bull-meat sausages) include **La Farandole** (11 rue des Porcelets).

Pick up groceries at **Monoprix** (place Lamartine; ☺ 8.30am-7.25pm Mon-Sat).

SHOPPING

Next door to the first-ever boutique of home-grown fashion designer **Christian Lacroix** (52 rue de la République) is **Puyricard** (54 rue de la République), purveying exquisite handmade Provençal chocolates.

GETTING THERE & AWAY
Air

The **Aéroport Nîmes-Garons** (☎ 04 66 70 49 49) is 20km northwest of the city on the A54. There is no public transport to Arles; a taxi costs €45 to €60. See also p199 for more information on travel to/from the region.

THE CAMARGUE

TOOTLING AROUND

Taking a gentle 20km/h tootle aboard **Le Train des Alpilles** (☎ 04 90 18 81 31; www.rdt13.fr; return adult/4-12yr €9/6; ⊙ Wed & Thu early Jun–mid-Sep) offers an unfolding panorama of bird life, paddy fields and sunflower meadows.

Linking Arles with Fontvieille (best known for its windmill immortalised by Alphonse Daudet; see p193), 7km northeast, the scenic 40-minute trip is made by a 1950s diesel train departing 10am, 1.45pm and 3.30pm Wednesday and Thursday from Arles; and 10.50am, 2.30pm and 4.30pm Wednesday and Thursday from Fontvieille (making the last train of the day from Fontvieille a one-way ride). Fares include admission to the small railway museum at the **RDT13 train station** (17bis av de Hongrie, Arles), north of place Lamartine, from where trains arrive/depart.

For groups only, at the time of writing, the same organisation operates a steam train painted by Van Gogh in 1888.

Bus

The **regional bus station** (☎ information office 08 10 00 08 16; 24 blvd Georges Clemenceau; ⊙ 7.30am-4pm Mon-Sat) is served by companies including **Telleschi** (☎ 04 42 28 40 22), which runs services to Aix-en-Provence (€9.80, 1¾ hours). Buses also link Arles with various parts of the Camargue, including Stes-Maries de la Mer (€4.90, one hour).

Long-haul, international bus company **Eurolines** (☎ 04 90 96 94 78) stops here, though there's no ticket office.

Car & Motorcycle

Car-rental agencies:

Avis (☎ 04 90 96 82 42; av Paulin Talabot) In the train station.

Sixt (☎ 04 90 93 02 17; 4 av Paulin Talabot)

Train

Arles' **train station** (⊙ information office 9am-12.30pm & 2-6.30pm Mon-Sat) serves destinations including Nîmes (€7, 30 minutes), Marseille (€12.40, 45 minutes) and Avignon (€6.10, 20 minutes).

GETTING AROUND
Bicycle

Arles VAE (☎ 04 90 43 33 14; www.arles-vae.com in French; 65 blvd Émile Combes) rents regular bikes (€2 per hour) and electric bikes (€3 per hour) and also has a nifty *vélo et patrimoine* day package that incorporates a museum pass for €25 for classic bikes and €30 for electric wheels.

Bus

Local buses are operated by **STAR** (☎ 09 10 00 08 16; information office 24 blvd Georges Clemenceau; ⊙ 8am-12.30pm & 1.30-6pm Mon-Fri). This office, west of the tourist office, is the main bus hub, although most buses also stop at place Lamartine, a

short walk south of the train station. In general, STAR buses run from 7am to 7pm (5pm on Sunday). A single ticket costs €0.80. In addition to its 11 bus lines, STAR runs free minibuses called Starlets that circle most of the old city every 30 minutes from 7.15am to 7.40pm Monday to Saturday.

Taxi

For a taxi call ☎ 04 90 96 90 03.

STES-MARIES DE LA MER

pop 2478

You could be forgiven for thinking you'd crossed into Spain at this remote seaside outpost. With some of the most captivating light in Provence, especially in early spring and in autumn, the dusty village streets are lined with whitewashed buildings with pitched roofs thatched with bulrush reeds. Stes-Maries de la Mer bursts into life during festivals when flamenco dancers spin in its squares and horse riders trot into town, wearing traditional costumes and carrying flags; and during the summer months when guitarists and dancers (not to mention a legion of visitors) give the streets a chaotic carnival atmosphere (see the boxed text, opposite).

Away from the small pedestrian village, an ends-of-the-earth coastline of 30km of uninterrupted sandy beach basks in the sun.

ORIENTATION & INFORMATION

From the bus stop on av d'Arles (the southern end of the D570), head south along av Frédéric Mistral then east across place des Remparts and place Portalet to get to central place de l'Église.

Laundrette (24 av d'Arles) Near the tourist office.

Tourist office (☎ 04 90 97 82 55; www.saintesmaries
.com; 5 av Van Gogh; ☼ 9am-8pm Jul & Aug, to 7pm
May, Jun & Sep, to 6pm Apr & Oct, 9am-5pm Nov-Mar) Has
an ATM outside.

SIGHTS & ACTIVITIES

One of the best panoramas of the Camargue
is rolled out from the **rooftop terrace** (Terrasse de
l'Église; adult/child €2/1.30; ☼ 10am-8pm Jul & Aug, 10am-
12.30pm & 2-6.30pm Mon-Fri, 10am-7pm Sat & Sun Mar-Jun,
Sep & Oct, 10am-noon & 2-5pm Wed, Sat & Sun Nov-Feb) of
the **Église des Stes-Maries** (place de l'Église). In this
12th- to 15th-century-built church, the relics of
St Sara – the highly revered patron saint of the
Roma – were found in the crypt by King René
in 1448 and are enshrined in a wooden chest,
stashed in the stone wall above the choir.

Contact the tourist office for **bullfights**
scheduled in and around Stes-Maries.

Stes-Maries de la Mer is fringed by around
30km of uninterrupted fine-sand **beaches**. For
an all-over tan, you can bathe *sans* suit at the
area around **Phare de la Gacholle**, the lighthouse
11km east of town.

About 10km north of Stes-Maries is **Châ-
teau d'Avignon** (☎ 04 90 97 58 58; rte d'Arles; guided
tour adult/under 16yr €3/free; ☼ 10am-5pm Wed-Mon),
an 18th-century chateau furnished almost
exactly as it was by wealthy Marseille merchant Louis Noilly Prat, who used the place
as a hunting lodge in the 1890s. He kitted out
the castle with hot and cold running water,
central heating and other gadgets revolution-

ary at the time. Next door is the fascinating
Maison du Cheval Camargue (see the boxed
text, p148).

TOURS

You can travel 12km of the Parc Naturel
Régional de Camargue from Stes-Maries de
la Mer's tourist office on the electric train,
Le Petit Train Camarguais (☎ 06 09 96 02 65; adult/
child €6/4; ☼ Apr-Oct). Departure times for the
45-minute trip are irregular; ask at the Stes-
Maries de la Mer **tourist office** (☎ 04 90 97 82
55; www.saintesmaries.com; 5 av Van Gogh) for updates.

From March to November, several companies run boat trips from Port Gardian in
Stes-Maries de la Mer, including **Le Camargue**
(☎ 04 90 97 84 72; bateau.camargue@wanadoo.fr; 5 rue des
Launes) and **Les Quatre Maries** (☎ 04 90 97 70 10; www
.lesquatremaries.com in French; 36 av Théodore Aubanel). The
Tiki III (☎ 04 90 97 81 68; tiki3@wanadoo.fr) is docked
at the mouth of the Petit Rhône, 1.5km west
of Stes-Maries. All charge around €10/5 per
adult/under 16 years for a 1½-hour trip.

For walking, cycling and horse-riding tours
see p136.

FESTIVALS & EVENTS

Stes-Maries de la Mer bursts into life during the
Pélerinage des Gitans (Roma pilgrimages; see the
boxed text, below) on 24 and 25 May and the
Sunday closest to 22 October. Bullfights ani-
mate Les Arènes during Easter; most Sundays
in May and June; in mid-June for the village's
five-day **Fête Votive** when it celebrates traditional

A WASHED-UP LEGEND?

Catholicism first reached European shores in what is now the little township of Stes-Maries de
la Mer. So the stories go, Ste Marie-Salomé and Ste Marie-Jacobé (some say along with Lazarus,
Marie-Madeleine, Martha and Maximin) fled the Holy Land in a tiny boat and were caught in a
storm, drifting at sea until washing ashore here in AD 40.

Provençal and Catholic lore diverge at this point: Catholicism believes Sara (patron saint of the
Gitans, Romas also known as Gypsies), travelled with the Maries on the boat; Provençal legend
says Sara was already here, and was the first person to recognise their Holiness. (And if you
believe Dan Brown's ubiquitous blockbuster *The Da Vinci Code*, Sara was no other than Jesus'
and Marie-Madeleine's daughter.) In 1448 skeletal remains said to belong to Sara and the Maries
were found in a crypt in Stes-Maries.

Finer ficto-historical points aside, it's by no means a washed-up legend: Gitans continue to
make the Pélerinage des Gitans (Gitans pilgrimage) here on 24 May for three days (many staying
for up to three weeks), dancing and playing music in the streets, and parading a statue of Sara
through town. The Sunday in October closest to the 22nd sees a second pilgrimage, dedicated
to the Saintes Maries; when *Courses Camarguaises* (nonlethal bullfights) are also held.

The annual Festival Ame Gitane, a celebration of Gitane culture with theatre, music, film and
dance, is held in Arles in mid-August.

THE CAMARGUE

THE CAMARGUE

Camargue traditions; and in mid-August during the **Feria du Taureau** (bull festival).

SLEEPING

Low-rise 'ranch style' accommodation lines the D570 heading into Stes-Maries de la Mer, with atmospheric old *mas* (Provencal farmhouse) surrounding the town. Aspiring cowboys can rent a self-catering *cabane de gardian* (cowboy cabin); the tourist office has details. Most sleep up to five people and can be rented on a weekly basis from April to September. There is a cluster for hire on av Riquette Aubanel, a narrow lane (the D38) leading from Stes-Maries de la Mer past the port to Aigues-Mortes.

Accommodation is limited in the winter off-season; in summer places open and fill just as quickly.

Chambres d'Hôtes & Farmhouses

Mas de la Grenouillère (☎ 04 90 97 90 22; fax 04 90 97 08 58; d/tr incl breakfast from €60/80; P ✗ ✗) Be sung to sleep by an open field full of croaking frogs while tucked up in snug, cosy rooms at 'Frog Farm'. Horse-riding trips are organised by the farm's stables. The farm and its frogs are 1.5km down a dirt track signposted 1km north of Stes-Maries off the D570.

Mas de Bardouine (☎ 04 90 97 16 55, 06 21 05 05 09; www.mas-de-bardouine.com; d incl breakfast €70-180; P ▯) Housed in what was a hunting lodge in the 18th century, this exquisite five-room *chambre d'hôte* lets you get well away from it all with no telephones and, better yet, no TVs. Instead, borrow books from the library to read in the glorious sunshine. Tables d'hôtes (set courses) are possible by reservation. Credit cards aren't accepted.

Hotels

Hôtel Méditerranée (☎ 04 90 97 82 09; fax 04 90 97 76 31; 4 av Frédéric Mistral; r €39-52) Handily located in the centre of town, so a good bet if you don't have your own wheels, this place is one of the cheapest options around (book well ahead). With a homey, familial ambience, its pretty flower-decked terrace is a peaceful spot for a leisurely breakfast.

A BULLISH AFFAIR

Animal lovers fear not: not all types of bullfights end with deceased beasts. The local Camargue variation, *course Camarguaise,* sees amateur *razeteurs* (from the word 'shave'), wearing tight white shirts and trousers, get as close as they dare to the *taureau* (bull) to try and remove rosettes and ribbons tied to the bull's horns, using a *crochet* (a razor-sharp comb) held between their fingers – leaping over the arena's barrier as the bull charges, making spectators' hearts lurch.

Bulls are bred on a *manade* (bull farm) by *manadiers,* who are helped in their daily chores by *gardians* (Camargue cowboys who herd cattle on horseback). These mounted herdsmen are honoured by the **Fête des Gardians** in Arles in May, during which they parade through town on horseback clad in leather hats, checked shirts and boots. *Gardians* traditionally live in *cabanes de gardians* (whitewashed, thatched-roof cottages sealed with a strip of mortar).

Many *manades* also breed the cowboys' best friend: the creamy white *cheval de Camargue* (Camargue horse), recognised as a breed in its own right. **Maison du Cheval Camargue** (House of the Camargue Horse; ☎ 04 90 97 76 37; Mas de la Cure, chemin de la Bardouine, Stes-Maries de la Mer; ☼ by appointment), managed by the Conservatoire du Littoral (see p76), promotes and develops the robust, agile breed, which you can learn about on a guided visit (adult/child €3.50/2). Several *manades* open their doors to visitors; tourist offices in Arles and Stes-Maries de la Mer have seasonal information.

To get a taste of *gardian* life like Frédéric Bon's (see the boxed text, p152) you can sign on for one-week *stages de monte gardiane* (Camargue cowboy courses) run by the **Manade Salierène** (☎ 04 66 86 45 57; www.manadesalierene.com in French; Mas de Capellane), 11km west of Arles in Saliers. An initiation/perfection course (€600 including accommodation and meals with the *manadier*'s family) comprises up to six/seven hours a day on horseback learning how to ride the Camargue's rough terrain and herd bulls.

A calendar of *courses Camarguaises* is posted online by the **Fédération Française de la Course Camarguaise** (French Federation of Camargue Bullfights; ☎ 04 66 26 05 35; www.ffcc.info in French; 485 rue Aimé Orand, 3000 Nîmes). *Recortadores* (a type of bull-baiting with lots of bull-jumping and vaulting) can also be caught during the bullfighting season (Easter to September).

THE CAMARGUE

Hostels & Camping

Camping La Brise (☎ 04 90 97 84 67; fax 04 90 97 72 01; av Marcle Carrière; camping winter €13, summer €18-20; ☒ closed mid-Nov–mid-Dec; ☒) Right on the beach, this three-star campground northeast of the town centre has a refreshing pool and a friendly, family atmosphere.

Auberge de Jeunesse (☎ 04 90 97 51 72; fax 04 90 97 54 88; Pioch Badet; dm incl breakfast, dinner & sheets €27.30; ☒ reception 7.30-10.30am & 5-11pm, to midnight Jul & Aug) Half-pension is part of the package at this rural hostel 8km north of Stes-Maries de la Mer in an old schoolhouse where tables and chairs lounge beneath trees. The hostel is on the D570 to Arles in Pioch Badet; buses from Arles' bus station drop you at the door (see p146).

EATING

In summer the seafront sees outdoor diners in their multitudes. If you're self-catering, eye the day's catch at the early-morning fish market.

Le Delta (☎ 04 90 97 81 12; 1 place Mireille; menus €18-26) A local favourite, Le Delta is a great place to try Camargue specialities like *gardianne de taureau* (bull stew) and the area's teensy thumbnail-sized clams, *tellines*.

Hostellerie du Pont de Gau (☎ 04 90 97 81 53; rte d'Arles; menus €19.50-50; ☒ lunch & dinner daily mid-Feb–mid Nov, closed Jan–mid-Feb, closed Wed & some evenings mid-Nov–Dec; ☒) This intimate Logis de France hotel with just nine rooms (doubles €51) is best known for its excellent restaurant, a handy spot for lunch after visiting the neighbouring Parc Ornithologique du Pont de Gau (p136). Specialities span a host of crustaceans and a heavenly caramel cake.

Other accommodation options serving stand-out cuisine include **L'Auberge Cavaliere** (☎ 04 90 97 88 88; www.aubergecavaliere.com; route d'Arles/D570).

GETTING THERE & AWAY

Stes-Maries de la Mer has no bus station; buses use the shelter at the northern entrance to town on av d'Arles (the continuation of rte d'Arles and the D570).

For bus details to/from Arles (via Pont du Gau and Mas du Pont de Rousty), see p146.

GETTING AROUND

Le Vélociste (☎ 04 90 97 83 26; www.levelociste.com in French; place Mireille) charges €15/34 per day/three days for bicycle hire and distributes a

brochure with cycling routes. It also organises cycling, canoeing, and horse-riding trips. Bikes can be delivered to your hotel for free. Le Vélociste also packages up bike-riding and canoeing and bike-riding and horse-riding itineraries.

Le Vélo Saintois (☎ 04 90 97 74 56; 19 rue de la République) also rents bikes.

AIGUES-MORTES

pop 6084

Actually over the border from Provence in the Gard *département,* the town of Aigues Mortes (meaning, somewhat eerily, 'dead waters') sits 28km northwest of Stes-Maries de la Mer at the western extremity of the Camargue. Encircled entirely by walls, Aigues Mortes, unlike Provence's fortified hilltop villages, sits on flat marshland. The town was established in the mid-13th century by Louis IX to give the French crown a Mediterranean port under its direct control, and in 1248 Louis IX's flotilla of 1500 ships massed here before setting sail to the Holy Land for the Seventh Crusade.

To minimise traffic, parking within the walls costs €5 per hour.

INFORMATION

Tourist office (☎ 04 66 53 73 00; www.ot-aigues mortes.fr; place St-Louis; ☒ 9am-noon & 1-6pm Sep-Jun, 9am-8pm Jul & Aug) Inside the walled city.

THE CAMARGUE

SIGHTS

Scaling the ramparts rewards with a sweeping overview of the town's history; and of surrounding marshes. Head to the top of the tower, **Tour de Constance** (☎ 04 66 53 61 55; adult/under 17yr €6.50/free; ☼ 10am-5.30pm winter, to 7pm summer). The 1.6km walltop walk takes about 30 minutes. Inside the impregnable fortress, with its 6m-thick walls, you can visit the 32m-tall tower that served as a Huguenot womens prison after the revocation of the Edict of Nantes in 1685. From the southern ramparts are magnificent views of the surrounding salt pans (see the boxed text, below).

The grisly history of torture and the gruesome instruments used in its execution make for a horridly fascinating visit at the **Musée de la Torture** (☎ 06 11 97 70 83; 3 rue de la République, adult/child €7/5; ☼ 10am-7pm Jul & Aug, to 7pm Fri-Sun Sep-Jun).

BOAT TRIPS

Between March and November, boats docked at Aigues-Mortes port cruise the Camargue's wild waters; the **tourist office** (☎ 04 66 53 73 00; www.ot-aiguesmortes.fr; place St-Louis) has a list of operators. Tickets cost €7/4.50 per adult/three to 12 years for a 1½-hour safari and €10/6 for a 2½-hour trip.

SLEEPING & EATING

Within the walls, place St-Louis, at the southern foot of Grande Rue, is (in fine weather, at least) filled with open-air cafés and terrace restaurants. Grande Rue is also where picnick-

ers can find bakeries, groceries and butchers selling bull sausages.

Le Victoria (☎ 04 66 51 14 20; www.victoria.camargue.fr; place Anatole-France; d €49-58, tr €80-95, mains €15-21) Just opposite the Tour Constance, this elegant place with blue-toned rooms is at least as well known for its traditional restaurant serving local classics such as *soupe de poissons* (fish soup) and the ubiquitous Camargue bull stew, *gardienne de taureau*.

L'Hermitage de St-Antoine (☎ 06 03 04 34 05; www.hermitagesa.com; 9 blvd Intérieur Nord; d €50-60; P ⚹ ☐) Inside the walled town, this *chambre d'hôte* has just three rooms beautifully appointed with crisp linens, canopied beds, and a lovely courtyard garden for a relaxing – and filling – breakfast in the sunshine (€7). You won't be disturbed by littlies running around – L'Hermitage de St-Antoine only caters to children aged over 12. Get a pass for free parking.

L'Oustau Camarguais (☎ 04 66 53 79 69; 2 rue Alsace-Lorraine; mains €11-22; ☼ lunch & dinner high season, lunch & dinner Fri-Wed low season) Accompanied by rotating art exhibitions and often live music, this wood-beamed place in the old town is great for trying *tellines*, but the main event here is *civet de taureau aux saveurs de garrigue* (bull stew flavoured with Provence scrubland herbs).

GETTING THERE & AWAY

From Aigues-Mortes' tiny train station on route de Nîmes, there is a handful of trains and SNCF buses to/from Nîmes (€6.60, 45 minutes).

SOUTHEASTERN CAMARGUE

For a jaunt to what feels like the edge of the world (see p134), head for the Camargue's wild southeast. The wetland is at its most savage around the eastern shores of the Étang de Vaccarès. Much of this area is protected and off-limits to tourists.

ARLES TO DIGUE À LA MER

Midway along this 48km stretch – where the D36B skims Vaccarès' eastern shores – is **La Capelière**, a minuscule hamlet where the Réserve Nationale de Camargue runs its excellent **Centre d'Information Nature** (Nature Information Centre; ☎ 04 90 97 00 97; www.reserve-camargue.org in

---

A SALTY DETOUR

Following the lone D979 from Aigues Mortes takes you along the narrow land bar that cuts across the still pools of the **Salins du Midi** that stretch south from the town, glinting pink in the sun.

Alternatively, hop aboard the **salt train** (☎ 0466511710; www.salins.fr; adult/child €6.80/5; ☼ Mar-Oct), accompanied by commentary in English and a visit to the salt museum and shop. Heading towards the Salins du Midi, La Baleine train stop is clearly flagged on the left just before the bridge.

Between May and August **tours** of the salt works and marshes are possible. **Aigues Mortes' tourist office** (☎ 04 66 53 73 00; www.ot-aiguesmortes.fr; place St-Louis) has details.

French; adult/under 12yr €3/1.50; 9am-1pm & 2-6pm Apr-Sep, 9am-1pm & 2-5pm Wed-Mon Oct-Mar). As well as exhibitions, a 1.5km-long **Sentier des Rainettes** (Tree-frog Trail), studded with four wildlife observatories (two of which are wheelchair-accessible), enables you to discover flora and fauna native to freshwater marshes.

The centre runs three observatories and 4.5km of nature trails at **Salin de Badon**, former royal salt pans about 7km further south along the D36B. Unlike at La Capelière, the bird-watching towers fall within the Réserve Nationale de Camargue. Photography is forbidden and visitors need a permit (adult/under 12 years €3/1.50; issued at the Centre d'Information Nature in La Capelière) to enter. The site is accessible to permit holders from sunrise to sunset daily. To stay overnight, an onsite **gîte** (incl entry to reserve €12) offers 'rustic comfort' with solar electricity (including heating), a self-catering kitchen, and 20 beds between seven rooms – BYO drinking water, sheets and pillows.

Mas de St-Bertrand (☎ 04 42 48 80 69; rte du Vaccarès; d €35, menus €9-14.50; closed mid-Nov–Jan, restaurant closed Tue except Apr, Jul & Aug;), 80m past the Digue à la Mer turnoff on the D36C to Salin de Giraud, is where you'll find legendary restaurant Chez JuJu, previously camped at the former shantytown of Beauduc before the shacks were demolished by the authorities. It's now at home at this authentic *gîte* of three low-ceilinged chalets with sculptures from old rusty farm tools strewn on the grounds. You can arrange to ride horses and bikes, and the bar sells mozzie spray.

A beautiful stroll along what seems to be the edge of the world can be enjoyed on the **Digue à la Mer** (admission free; 9am-1pm & 2-6pm Apr-Sep, 9am-1pm & 2-5pm Oct-Mar), a dike built in the 19th century to cut the delta off from the sea. A 20km-long walking and cycling track runs along the length of the dike; there's also a shorter 10km circuit and a 2.3km footpath that cuts down to a lovely sandy beach. Walking on the fragile sand dunes is forbidden. Bird-watching is beyond belief: grey herons, little egrets, shelduck, avocet, the Kentish plover, oystercatcher and the yellow-legged gull are among the dozens of species to strut past.

To access the dike, follow the D36B for 17km southwest from La Capelière to Parking de la Gacholle where motorists must park; the final 3km is a second-gear drive along an unsealed, potholed road. From the car park,

a 1km-long footpath (a particularly popular cycle ride for families) leads to the **Phare de la Gacholle** (11am-5pm Sat, Sun & school holidays), a lighthouse with exhibitions about the coast, bird's-eye ocean views, and a panoramic picnic spot (note there's no drinking water).

SALIN DE GIRAUD & BEYOND

The chequered evaporation *marais salants* (salt pans) of **Salin de Giraud** cover 140 sq km and produce about one million tonnes of salt per year, making them one of Europe's largest. *Sel* (salt), which takes three years to produce, is harvested in September and stored in giant mountains. Pass the entrance to Salin de Giraud on the D36 and continue south along the D36D for a windswept panorama of the marsh village, the salt pans and the salt mountains. A couple of kilometres south is a **point de vue** (viewing point) where you can pull up and breathe in the salty sea air, and, between August and mid-October, watch salt being harvested.

Inside the **Les Salins de Giraud** (☎ 04 42 86 71 80; www.salins.fr; Salin de Giraud village; adult/4-13yr €6.80/5) village saltworks, a small **ecomuseum** (9.30am-12.30pm & 2-7pm Jul & Aug, 10.15am-12.15pm & 2.30-6pm Sep-Jun) displays old photographs and tools. Admission is good for an **electric tourist train** that departs two to five times daily between March and October, affording another panorama of the pans.

The final 12km leg of this southbound journey is unforgettable. Drive slowly to enjoy the views and stop to see pink **flamingos** wading through the water. About 8km south of Salin de Giraud is **Domaine de la Palissade** (☎ 04 42 86 81 28; rte de la Mer; adult/child €3/free; 9am-6pm mid-Jun–mid-Sep, 9am-5pm mid-Sep–mid-Nov & Mar–mid-Jun, 9am-5pm Wed-Sun mid-Nov–Feb), a nature centre run by the Conservatoire de l'Espace Littoral et des Rivages Lacustres, which organises for-ays into the marshes on foot and horseback. There are a couple of observation towers here for nature-spotting on the estate, a 1km-long **sentier de découverte** (discovery trail), and audio-visual displays in the main house interpreting local flora and fauna.

The road reaches the Mediterranean about 4km further south. Caravans and camper vans can park overnight in the camp site on the sand here, overlooking **Plage de Piémanson** – one of the few remaining free camping areas in France. Bear east (left) from the car park and walk 1400m to get to the nudist section of the very windy beach.

Salin de Giraud is 15km east of the Digue à la Mer via the winding D36C. The **tourist office** (☎ 04 42 86 80 87; rue Pasteur; ☼ 9am-12.30pm & 3-6pm Thu-Mon mid-Jun–mid-Sep) has information on the few other accommodation options in this isolated part of the world.

BACK TO ARLES

Some 8km north of Salin de Giraud on the D36 is the very informal **Musée du Riz du Petit Manusclat** (☎ 04 90 97 29 44; adult/under 12yr €3.50/free; ☼ 9am-noon & 1.30-5.30pm) in Petit Manusclat. The history of the Camargue rice industry, which dates from the 13th century, is explained in an informal setting (opening hours may fluctu-ate), detailing the working life of rice growers. Rice remains a key part of the Camarguais economy: 8 million quintals (400,000 tonnes) is produced here.

In **Le Sambuc**, 1km further north along the same road, there are a couple of places where you can **ride horses**, including the fabulous Manade Jacques Bon, a 500-hectare farm in-corporating **Le Mas de Peint** (☎ 04 90 97 20 62; www .masdepeint.com; d €205-265, ste €335-381; lunch/dinner menu €39/50; ☼ closed mid-Jan–mid-Mar & mid-Nov–mid-Dec; P ✶ ✷ ♿), in a restored 17th-century barn and pigeon house. Experience authentic farm life, with horse riding, jeep tours and cycling available, before retreating to your *Country Living*–style quarters beautifully

---

LIFELONG COWBOY

Frédèric Bon was practically born in the saddle. Of good Camargue stock – his father is bull breeder and local legend Jacques Bon, and his sister and aunt were both Queen of Arles – the affable 20-year-old lives and works as a *gardian* on his family's *manade* in the southeastern Camargue. Frédèric describes his daily routine thus:

'My day starts at 7am, feeding the *cocardiers* – they're bulls that are good and aggressive in the ring, and we keep about 20 of them separate to the others. If we have a branding and a bullfight on, I'll take the horses down to the stables, and put leather gloves on the *cocardiers'* horns so the *razeteurs* don't get injured. Then I'll take the young bulls we want to brand and put them in the paddock. I'll take a turn throughout the property, looking to see if there are broken fences, or if there's no grass then I'll move the bulls to a field that has grass. Everything's done on horses; I've been riding since I was two. After lunch, I'll repair fences or make feed by cutting alfalfa to dry to give to the bulls in the winter. If there's a branding, I'll do that. We put a number on each one when they're six months old, and when they're a year old we brand them. It's very strict since mad cow disease. You're not allowed to kill and eat bulls, even if they've been gored by another bull – they have to go to the abattoir, so branding's important.

'I'm lucky because my best friends live 20km to 30km from here. They come here to ride, and in summer, every week there's a *fiéria* in a different village 30 minutes by car, you always find one. My friends like the same thing I like – bulls.

'I'm not a *razeteur*. When you breed bulls, you're always running behind them, and a *razeteur* always runs in front, and you have to train hard to run fast to get out of the way. It's not the same; you don't see bulls the same way. You have to make a choice. I like being a *gardian* and breeding bulls, so I do that.

'I usually work every day, Sundays too. Here it's impossible to have a holiday, because there's always work to do, so if I have a holiday, I go away. Last year I went skiing in the Alps with my friends, and that was great.'

But despite the week-round workload, when asked how long Frédèric plans to stay on the farm he says, without hesitation, 'Forever, I hope.'

furnished with checked fabrics, antiques and stone-tiled floors. Even nonguests should stop by at the *mas'* restaurant (lunch Friday to Tuesday, dinner Thursday to Tuesday) to taste the farm's own organic red rice, and, of course, bull meat, cooked in front of you at an open island kitchen.

The **Station Biologique de la Tour du Valat** (☎ 04 90 97 20 13), just west of here, is a biology research station. It covers 25 sq km and opens to the public one day per year (in January). In 1970 the station instigated the construction of the artificial **Étang du Fangassier**. The 4000-sq-metre island serves as a flamingo-breeding colony, to counter previously falling levels of breeding in the area.

On the eastern bank of the Grand Rhône is the **Marais du Vigueirat** (☎ 04 90 98 70 91; www.marais -vigueirat.reserves-naturelles.org; ✆ 10am-5pm Tue-Sun

Feb-Nov), 10 sq km of extensive marshland protected by the Conservatoire du Littoral and frequented by eight species of heron and a wealth of other bird life. The family-friendly **Sentiers de l'Étourneau** nature trails (free) can be followed alone, or on a one-hour guided tour (adult/child €4/2) departing at 10am, 11am, noon, 2pm and 3pm daily April to May and July and August, and at the same hours on Wednesday, Sunday and public holidays in June and September. Two-hour horse-drawn carriage tours (adult/child €13/6.50) depart at 10am and 3pm daily in July and August, Tuesday and Sunday in April, May, June and September, and at 2.30pm on Saturday and Sunday in October and November – book ahead as places are limited. More active guided nature walks (some for older children and/or adults only) cost between €10 to €18 by reservation.

THE CAMARGUE

Avignon Area

Shaped like a fan, the *département* of the Vaucluse (from the Provençal Vau-Cluso, meaning 'closed valley') opens up across variegated landscapes of red poppies and bright yellow sunflowers, plane-shaded village squares, laden grapevines, olive groves, cloudlike almond blossoms, and deep purple lavender. Scattered throughout are golden-stone villages.

At its hinge the capital, Avignon, is resplendent thanks to its former popes, who left an architectural legacy of imposing palaces, a viticultural legacy in neighbouring Châteauneuf du Pape, and an artistic legacy that takes to the stage each July during Avignon's renowned performing arts festival. Skirted by soaring, superbly intact stone ramparts, its cobbled streets overflow with animated cafés, a wealth of museums within grand old mansions, and a spirited student population from the city's university.

Northwest of Avignon, Roman relics of imperial proportions rise up in Orange and across the River Rhône in Nîmes. To the northeast, Vaison-la-Romaine also has a rich Roman legacy, with the largest archaeological site in France. Nearby Carpentras' magnificent markets overflow with jars of lavender honey, loaves of oven-warm bread, a rainbow of hardboiled sweets, and, in season, elusive, earthy black truffles. East of Avignon, crystal-clear water surges from Fontaine de Vaucluse to the canals encircling the antique markets of Île-sur-la-Sorgue. To Avignon's south, the silvery ridge of the Alpilles shelters olive mills, sheepfolds, and some of the region's finest dining in and around St-Rémy de Provence.

Presiding over the region – and fanning it with up to 300km/h winds – Provence's highest peak, Mont Ventoux (1909m), is a snowy spectacle in winter and a maze of hiking trails in summer.

HIGHLIGHTS

- Sip wine amid the stone-crusted vineyards of **Châteauneuf du Pape** (see the boxed text, p170)
- Savour the exquisite flavours of the Alpilles in and around **St-Rémy de Provence** (p189)
- Stroll among shady olive groves at **Nyons** (p176)
- Paddle through sparkling spring water from its source at **Fontaine de Vaucluse** (p187)
- Catch a classical concert or bloodthirsty bullfight in the Roman arena, Les Arènes, in **Nîmes** (p195)

ITINERARIES

CYCLING CIRCUIT
One Day / Dentelles de Montmirail

Looping the lacy limestone **Dentelles de Montmirail** (p177) outcrop makes a spectacular, sensory day trip from **Vaison-la-Romaine** (**1**; p173). Gear up with a hearty breakfast at one of Vaison's charming **chambres d'hôtes** (private bed and breakfast accommodation; p175). Then pedal off on your bike (or cruise in your car) in the direction of Carpentras.

On the D938 wind around the Dentelles' eastern edge to the little hilltop village of **Le Barroux** (**2**; p177), where you can visit its **medieval chateau** (p177), and pick up a monk-made cake for morning coffee at its **abbey** (p177).

From Le Barroux, take the westbound D21 to **Beaumes de Venise** (**3**; p177) to taste its locally milled **olive oil** (p177) and liquid-gold **wine** (p179). And for a taste of life on a **working ecological farm** (p179) with vineyards of its own, scoot 7.5km southwest via the D21 and D52 to Sarrians.

Afterwards, follow the D52 north from Sarrians, and continue on the D7 via Vacqueyras, spearing east to **Gigondas** (**4**; p179) to set eyes on a striking set of **sculptures** (p179). It's just 2km further north on the D7 to Sablet, where your pedal-weary legs can rest over a languidly long lunch at a honey of a restaurant/*chambre d'hôte*, **Les Abeilles** (p179). Then make your way 3km north on the D23 to **Séguret** (**5**; see the boxed text, p179), guardian of Provençal Christmas traditions, and forge a final 9.5km northeast via the D88 and D977 back to Vaison-la-Romaine.

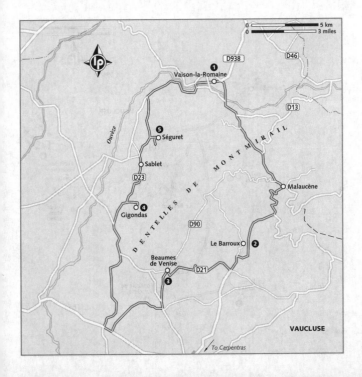

WATER WONDERLAND

One Day / Around Carpentras

Flowing from **Carpentras** (**1**; p182) is a water world of fountains, mossy water wheels, gushing springs and breathtaking gorges.

Travelling 5km south of Carpentras brings you to **Pernes-les-Fontaines** (**2**; p185), named for its 40 fountains burbling around town (Pernes' tourist office can provide a map to ferret them out). A further 11km south, canals ploughed by giant wooden water wheels completely surround the island-town of **L'Isle-sur-la-Sorgue** (**3**; p186). Take a gentle 1km stroll to the **partage des eaux** ('parting of the waters'; p186) where the River Sorgue splits in two, and where there are quaint cafés to stop for morning tea. Should you want to sleep down by the riverside, 5km west of L'Isle in the enchanting village of Le Thor, is **Moulin Font de Capelle** (p186), an old restored mill with its own dock.

The source of the Sorgue lies 7km east of L'Isle in **Fontaine de Vaucluse** (**4**; p187), France's most powerful spring, which is spectacular after rainfall. For a day trip within a day trip, bus up to Fontaine then **canoe** (p188) the crystalline waters back to L'Isle, where you'll find idyllic restaurants right on the water and ideal for lunch, including the impossibly charming **La Prévôté** (p186). Afterwards, make your way from Fontaine or L'Isle to the hilltop village of **Venasque** (**5**; p188), before spending the rest of the afternoon exploring the wild, rugged **Gorges de la Nesque** (**6**; p188). Back in Carpentras, unwind with a dip in its 1930 geometric **Art Deco swimming pool** (p184).

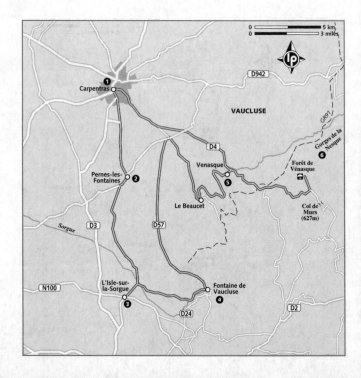

AVIGNON & AROUND

At the heart of the Avignon Area is the city itself. Across the river, villagelike Villeneuve-lès-Avignon offers respite from the city's bustle.

AVIGNON

pop 88,312

Hooped by 4.3km of superbly preserved stone ramparts, this graceful city is the belle of Provence's ball. Its time as the papal seat of power bestowed on Avignon a treasury of magnificent art and architecture, none grander than the massive medieval fortress and papal palace, the Palais des Papes.

Famed for its annual performing arts festival, these days Avignon is also an animated student city and an ideal spot from which to step out into the surrounding region. In France and beyond, Avignon is perhaps best known for its fabled bridge, the Pont St-Bénézet, aka the Pont d'Avignon.

History

Avignon first donned its ramparts and its reputation as a city of art and culture during the 14th century, when Pope Clement V and his court fled political turmoil in Rome. From 1309 to 1377, the seven French-born popes invested huge sums of money in building and decorating the papal palace in Avignon. Under the popes' rule, Jews and political dissidents took shelter here. Pope Gregory XI left Avignon in 1376, but his death two years later led to the Great Schism (1378–1417), during which rival popes – up to three at one time – resided at Rome and Avignon, denouncing and excommunicating one another. Even

after the schism was settled and an impartial pope, Martin V, established himself in Rome, Avignon remained under papal rule; and the city and Comtat Venaissin (now the Vaucluse *département*) were ruled by papal legates until 1791, when they were annexed to France.

Orientation

The main avenue within the *intra-muros* (walled city) runs northwards from the train station to place de l'Horloge. South of the tourist office it's called cours Jean Jaurès, north it's rue de la République.

LITERARY AVIGNON

Discover the Avignon area through literary eyes:

- *The Avignon Quintet* (Lawrence Durrell) This one-volume, 1367-page edition of five Durrell novels, written between 1974 and 1985, kicks off on a southbound train to Avignon.

- *Cesar's Vast Ghosts: Aspects of Provence* (Lawrence Durrell) Philosophical reflections on Provençal history and culture, published days before the author's death at his home in Somières, near Nîmes.

- *Letters from my Windmill* (Alphonse Daudet) Masterpiece evoking 1860s Fontvieille. Daudet's *Tartarin of Tarascon* is also in print in English.

- *The Red Cockade* (Stanley John Weyman) First published in 1896 and set in part against a backdrop of Nîmes, in the swashbuckling tradition of Dumas.

MARKET DAY

For porcine products in all their manifestations, along with a staggering array of fresh produce. Outdoor markets generally set up from around 8am to noon. Covered food markets in Avignon (p166) and Nîmes (p199) operate daily.

Monday Fontvieille
Tuesday Beaumes-des-Venise, Maussane-les- Alpilles, Tarascon, Vaison-la-Romaine
Wednesday Malaucène, Sault, St-Rémy de Provence, Valréas
Thursday Eryragues, L'Isle-sur-la-Sorgue, Maillane, Nyons, Orange, Vaison-la-Romaine, Villeneuve-lès-Avignon
Friday Carpentras, Châteauneuf du Pape, Fontvieille, Graveson (farmers' market; 4pm to 8pm May to October)
Saturday Orange (June to September), Pernes-les-Fontaines, Richerenches (truffles; November to March), Vaison-la-Romaine
Sunday L'Isle-sur-la-Sorgue, Vaison-la-Romaine (July and August)

The café-clad central square, place de l'Horloge, is 300m south of place du Palais, which abuts the Palais des Papes. The city gate nearest the train station is called Porte de la République, while the city gate next to Pont Édouard Daladier, which leads to Villeneuve-lès-Avignon, is Porte de l'Oulle. The Quartier des Teinturiers (dyers' quarter), which is centred on rue des Teinturiers, southeast of place Pie, is Avignon's bohemian artists' hang-out.

Villeneuve-lès-Avignon and Les Angles are adjacent suburbs on the west bank of the River Rhône, and are reached by crossing the two branches of the river as well as Île de la Barthelasse, the island that divides them.

Information

BOOKSHOPS

The tourist office (opposite) has a small boutique (open April to October) that sells maps and regional guides in French and English.

Shakespeare (☎ 04 90 27 38 50; 155 rue de la Carreterie; ⏰ 9.30am-12.30pm & 2-6.30pm Tue-Sat) Enjoy scones with your tomes at this English bookshop-tearoom.

EMERGENCY

Police station (☎ 04 90 16 81 00; blvd St-Roch)

INTERNET ACCESS

There are internet cafés around place Pie.

Chez W@M (☎ 04 90 86 19 03; www.chezwam.fr in French; 41 rue du Vieux Sextier; per 15/60min €1/3.50; ⏰ 8am-midnight Mon-Fri, noon-midnight Sat & Sun)

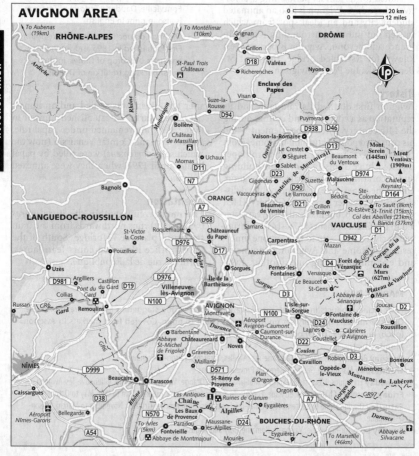

AVIGNON AREA

UNDER THE BRIDGE

This author doesn't quite remember dancing on Avignon's broken bridge as a pinafored four-year-old, but family snaps show that she did. The bridge continues to capture kids' imaginations everywhere with its namesake nursery rhyme, 'Sur le Pont d'Avignon'. All together now:

> *Sur le pont d'Avignon*
> *L'on y danse, l'on y danse*
> *Sur le pont d'Avignon*
> *L'on y danse tout en rond…*
>
> *(On the bridge of Avignon*
> *Everyone is dancing, everyone is dancing*
> *On the bridge of Avignon*
> *Everyone is dancing in a circle…)*

And so on. But actually, apart from rhyming better in French, because the bridge was too narrow for dancing (much less in a circle), people are believed to have danced *sous* (under) its arches, where it straddled the island Île de la Barthelasse. Previously pleasure gardens hosting folk dancing, the island is another prime spot for a bridge panorama today.

The 16th-century composer Pierre Certon penned the original song, albeit to a different tune, under the title of 'Sus le Pont d'Avignon'. In the mid-19th century, Adolphe Adam featured the present-day version in the 1853 operetta *l'Auberge Pleine*, but it wasn't until it was popularised in 1876 that it was inverted.

The alleged inspiration for the now Unesco-listed bridge is an even older tale. Construction is said to have begun in 1177 when Bénézet (Benedict the Bridge Builder), a pastor from Ardèche, was told in three visions to span the Rhône at any cost.

Regardless of the song's or bridge's origins, chances are you'll see kids (and maybe a Lonely Planet author) doing a jig on the bridge for posterity.

Webzone (☎ 04 32 76 29 47; 3 rue St Jean le Vieux; per 30/60min €2/3.50; ☼ 10am-10pm)

INTERNET RESOURCES
Avignon & Provence (www.avignon-et-provence.com) Sleeping and eating options in Avignon and Provence.
Provence Guide (www.provenceguide.com) Covers the Vaucluse region including B&Bs.
Visit Provence (www.visitprovence.com)

LAUNDRY
Laverie la Fontaine (27 rue du Portail Magnanen; ☼ 7am-7.30pm)

MEDICAL SERVICES
Hôpital Général Henri Duffaut (☎ 04 32 75 33 33; 305 rue Raoul Follereau) Marked on maps as Hôpital Sud (bus 1 or 3 to end of line); 2.5km south of the central train station.

MONEY
CIC is in the train station forecourt with a currency-changing machine and ATM.

POST
Main post office (cours Président Kennedy)

TOURIST INFORMATION
Tourist office (☎ 04 32 74 32 74; www.avignon-tourisme.com; 41 cours Jean Jaurès; ☼ 9am-6pm Mon-Sat & 10am-5pm Sun Apr-Jun & Aug-Oct, 9am-6pm Mon-Fri & 9am-5pm Sat & 10am-noon Sun Nov-Mar, 9am-7pm Mon-Sat & 10am-5pm Sun Jul) About 300m north of the train station.

Sights
Ticket offices for most sights close half to one hour before overall closing times.

PONT ST-BÉNÉZET (PONT D'AVIGNON)
The fabled **Pont St-Bénézet** (St Bénézet's Bridge; ☎ 04 90 27 51 16; full price/pass €4/3.30; ☼ 9am-9pm Jul, 9am-8pm Aug-Sep, 9am-7pm mid-Mar–Oct, 9.30am-5.45pm Nov–mid-Mar) was completed in 1185, linking Avignon with the settlement across the Rhône that later became Villeneuve-lès-Avignon (see the boxed text, above). The 900m-long wooden structure was repaired and rebuilt several times before all but four of its 22 spans were washed away in the mid-1600s.

At the entrance, via cours Châtelet, is the new **Musée du Pont St-Bénézet** (admission incl in bridge entry) where you can make your own DVD of

AVIGNON

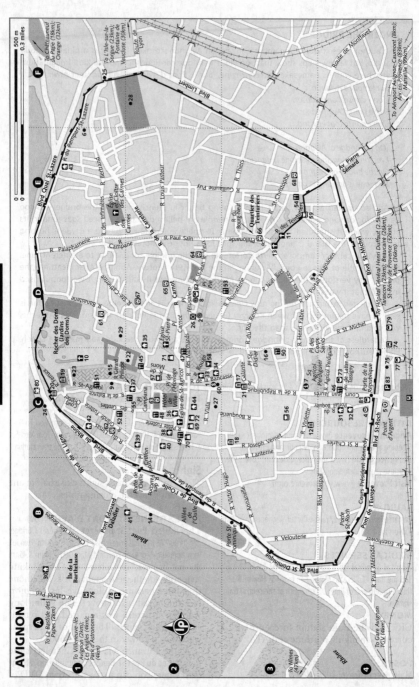

INFORMATION
Banque de Lyonnais...................**1** C2
Chez W@M...............................**2** D2
CIC..(see 84)
Laverie la Fontaine.....................**3** D3
Main Post Office........................**4** C4
Police Station............................**5** C4
Shakespeare..............................**6** E1
Tourist Office............................**7** C3
Webzone..................................**8** D2

SIGHTS & ACTIVITIES
Autocars Lieutaud.................(see 74)
Bureau du Festival..................(see 31)
Bureau du Off.........................**9** C1
Cathédrale Notre Dame des
   Doms.................................**10** C1
Chapelle des Pénitents Gris......**11** E3
Collection Lambert................**12** C3
Couvent des Cordeliers.......... **13** D3
Les Grands Bateaux de
   Provence.............................**14** B2
Les Trains Touristiques
   d'Avignon...........................**15** C1
Maison des Vins.....................**16** C3
Musée Angladon.....................**17** C3
Musée Calvet..........................**18** C3
Musée du Petit Palais..............**19** C1
Musée du Pont St-Bénézet.......**20** C1
Musée Lapidaire......................**21** C3
Palais des Papes......................**22** C2
Place du Palais........................**23** C1
Pont St-Bénézet......................**24** C1
Pont St-Bénézet Entrance........(see 24)
Porte St-Lazare........................**25** F1
Synagogue..............................**26** D2
Trompe l'Œil Painting of Popes..**27** C2

Université d'Avignon................**28** F2
Verger d'Urbain V....................**29** D1

SLEEPING
Auberge Bagatelle...................**30** A1
Cloître St-Louis.......................**31** C4
Hôtel Boquier.........................**32** C4
Hôtel de Blauvac....................**33** C2
Hôtel de Garlande...................**34** C2
Hôtel de la Mirande................**35** D2
Hôtel de l'Horloge...................**36** C2
Hôtel du Palais des Papes.........**37** C2
Hôtel Le Provençal..................**38** C2
Hôtel L'Europe........................**39** C2
Hôtel Mignon.........................**40** C2
La Péniche..............................**41** B2
Le Limas.................................**42** C1
Lumani...................................**43** E1
Villa Agapé.............................**44** C2

EATING
Christian Étienne.....................**45** C2
Erio Convert...........................**46** C4
La Cure Gourmande.................**47** C2
La Fourchette..........................**48** C2
La Tropézienne........................**49** C2
Le Caveau du Théâtre..............**50** C2
Le Grand Café.........................(see 61)
Le Moutardier.........................**51** C1
L'Echappée Belle.....................**52** C1
Les Halles & Food Market.........**53** D3
Numéro 75..............................**54** E3
Restaurant Brunel....................**55** C2

DRINKING
La Compagnie des Comptoirs...**56** C3
L'Opéra Café...........................**57** C2

Tapalocas...............................**58** C2
Woolloomooloo......................**59** E3

ENTERTAINMENT
AJMI......................................(see 61)
Cinéma Utopia........................(see 61)
FNAC.....................................**60** C2
La Manutention.......................**61** D1
L'Esclave................................**62** C1
Opéra Théâtre d'Avignon.........**63** C2
Red Lion.................................**64** D2
Red Zone................................**65** D2
Théâtre du Bourg Neuf.............**66** D3
Théâtre du Chêne Noir.............**67** D2
Théâtre du Chien qui Fume.......**68** E3

SHOPPING
Comtesse du Barry..................**69** C2
Covered Mall..........................**70** C2
Instant du Sud........................**71** C2
Oliviers & Co..........................**72** C2

TRANSPORT
Agence Commerciale TCRA......**73** C4
Avis.......................................(see 75)
Bus Station.............................**74** D4
Europcar................................**75** C4
La Barthelasse Bus Stop...........**76** A1
National Citer..........................**77** C4
Parking de l'Ile Piot.................**78** A1
Provence Bike.........................**79** D4
Shuttle Boat Embarkment
   Point..................................**80** C1
Shuttlebuses to/from Gare
   TGV....................................**81** C4
TCRA Office............................**82** D2
Vinci Park Gare Centre.............**83** C4

AVIGNON AREA

the song. Dreamy (if distant) bridge views unfold from the Rocher des Doms, Pont Édouard Daladier and across the river on the Île de la Barthelasse.

WALLED CITY
Wrapping around the city, Avignon's ramparts were built between 1359 and 1370. They were restored during the 19th century, minus their original moats – though even in the 14th century this defence system was hardly state-of-the-art, lacking machicolations (openings in the parapets for niceties like pouring boiling oil on attackers or shooting arrows at them).

To peek at Avignon's nine popes in their fashionable garbs of the day, seek out their **trompe l'œil portrait** on the side of the *conseil général* (general council) building, off rue Viala.

Université d'Avignon (Avignon University; www.univ-avignon.fr; 74 rue Louis Pasteur), founded by Pope Boniface VIII in 1303, resides in all its splendour inside **Porte St-Lazare**, the gate linking the eastern part of the walled city with the modern world.

Within the walls is a wealth of fine museums – the Avignon Passion booklet (see the boxed text, p162) lists the whole gamut.

Palais des Papes
Flanked by the sprawling courtyard cour d'Honneur, the **Palais des Papes** (Palace of the Popes; ☎ 04 90 27 50 00; place du Palais; full price/pass €9.50/7.50; ◷ 9am-9pm Jul, 9am-8pm Aug & Sep, 9am-7pm mid-Mar–Oct, 9.30am-5.45pm Nov–mid-Mar) is the largest Gothic palace in the world. Its cavernous stone halls and extensive grounds testify to the fortune amassed by the papacy during the 'Babylonian Captivity'. Papal banquets held here were of fitting proportions. A feast to celebrate Clement VI's coronation in 1342 included 118 oxen, 1033 spit-roasted sheep, 1195 geese, 7428 chickens, 50,000 sweet tarts, 39,980 eggs and 95,000 loaves of bread.

Palace admission includes an audioguide to direct you around 24 of the halls; the **Grande Chapelle** (Great Chapel), where temporary exhibitions are held; the **Musée de l'Oeuvre**, with its interactive maquettes, archaeological pieces, statues and other works illustrating medieval

---

AVIGNON PASSION

Anyone passionate about Avignon's rich cultural heritage will want to pick up a free Avignon Passion pass from the tourist office. This nifty pass entitles you to 20% to 50% discounted entry on your second and subsequent visits to museums and monuments (the equivalent of student prices), as well as reduced prices on the tourist office walking tours. It's good for 15 days in all the museums of Avignon as well as Villeneuve-lès-Avignon, and covers a family of five.

---

papal life; and a stroll around the wine boutique **La Bouteillerie**.

A two-hour **Visite Palais Secrét** (secret palace tour; French only; tours €30; ⊙ by reservation Sat & Sun Sep-May) takes you to unexplored parts of the palace (the baths, bedrooms where the popes kept caged nightingales, secret towers, rooftop walkways etc), followed by brunch (and a stunning panorama) on the **Great Dignitaries' Terrace**.

Combination tickets covering admission to the palace and Pont St-Bénézet (adult/eight to 17 years March to October €11.50/9, November to mid-March €9.50/7.50) are available.

Place du Palais

In the 14th and 15th centuries bishops and archbishops lived in the sizable **Petit Palace** (Little Palace; place du Palais). Today the **Musée du Petit Palais** (☎ 04 90 86 44 58; musee.petitpalais@wanadoo.fr; place du Palais; adult/under 12yr €6/free; ⊙ 10am-1pm & 2-6pm Wed-Mon Jun-Sep, 9.30am-1pm & 2-5.30pm Wed-Mon Oct-May), it houses a collection of 13th- to 16th-century Italian religious paintings from artists including Botticelli, Carpaccio and Giovanni di Paolo.

From the Romanesque **Cathédrale Notre Dame des Doms** (1671–72), the **Promenade des Papes** (signposted along rue de Mons) leads to the **Verger d'Urbain V** gardens – since gravelled over – where the popes grew plants and herbs and kept exotic animals in cages.

Musée Calvet

Impressive architecture and art intertwine at the 18th-century mansion housing the **Musée Calvet** (☎ 04 90 86 33 84; 65 rue Joseph Vernet; full price/pass €6/3; ⊙ 10am-1pm & 2-6pm Wed-Mon). Collections include 15th-century wrought-iron works and paintings from the 16th to 20th centuries.

Musée Lapidaire

Museum buffs on a budget will like the **Musée Lapidaire** (☎ 04 90 86 33 84; 27 rue de la République; full price/pass €2/1; ⊙ 10am-1pm & 2-6pm Wed-Mon), with an interesting collection of Egyptian, Roman, Etruscan and early Christian pieces ranging from large sections of statuary and hieroglyphics to delicate vases and bronze figurines.

Musée Angladon

From the private collection of couturier Jacques Doucet (1853–1929), the charming **Musée Angladon** (☎ 04 90 82 29 03; www.angladon.com; 5 rue Laboureur; full price/pass €6/4; ⊙ 1-6pm Wed-Sun Sep-Jun) holds the only Van Gogh painting in Provence, *Railway Wagons*. If you look closely you'll see the 'earth' isn't paint but the bare, underlying canvas. Also housed in this gracious mansion are works by Picasso, Cézanne, Sisley, Manet, Degas and others, and antiquities upstairs.

Collection Lambert

Avignon's contemporary art museum, **Collection Lambert** (☎ 04 90 16 56 20; www.collectionlambert.com; 5 rue Violette; adult/under 18yr €5.50/4; ⊙ 11am-6pm Tue-Sun Aug-Jun, 11am-7pm Tue-Sun Jul), showcases photography, video, and minimalist, conceptual and land art from the 1960s and '70s.

Quartier des Teinturiers

Rue des Teinturiers follows the River Sorgue through Avignon's old dyers' district, busy til the 19th century. Some water wheels still turn. Beneath plane trees stands the 16th-century **Chapelle des Pénitents Gris** (rue des Teinturiers) and the chapel and bell tower of the former **Couvent des Cordeliers** (rue des Teinturiers), Avignon's largest convent when it was founded in 1226. Inside lies the grave of Laura, muse of the poet Petrarch.

Synagogue

Avignon's neoclassical **synagogue** (☎ 04 90 85 21 24; 2 place Jérusalem; ⊙ 10am-noon & 3-5pm Mon-Thu, 10am-noon Fri) was built in 1221. A 13th-century oven used to bake unleavened bread for Passover can still be seen, but the rest of the present round, domed neoclassical structure dates from 1846; a fire destroyed the original edifice in 1845. Visitors must be modestly dressed and men's heads must be covered, as is the custom.

Activities

BOATING

Les Grands Bateaux de Provence (☎ 04 90 85 62 25; www
.avignon-et-provence.com/mireio; allées de l'Oulle), based at
the landing stage opposite Porte de l'Oulle, runs
cruises along the River Rhône from Avignon
to Arles and Châteauneuf du Pape (both four
to seven hours) including lunch prepared by
an on-board chef year-round (from €44), with
children's *menus* available. In summer you can
enjoy a candlelight dinner (adult/under 12 years
€23.50/12) aboard, or make a return trip (adult/
under 12 years €7/3.50, one hour, six daily,
mid-June to mid-September) on the company's
boat-bus around Île de la Barthelasse.

Avignon Passion pass holders get discounts.

INLINE SKATING

Avignon en Rollers (www.avignonenrollers.asso.fr in French)
meets for a weekly blade (7km to 10km, one
hour) on Friday at 8.30pm in front of the main
post office (see p159), and also arranges longer
trips into the surrounding countryside.

WINE TASTING

The **Maison des Vins** (☎ 04 90 27 24 00; www.vins-rhone
.com; 6 rue des Trois Faucons) doesn't have in-house
tastings, but it does hand out a series of free
booklets, detailing nine different colour-coded
routes touristiques (tourist trails) in the Côtes
du Rhône wine region, and lists dozens of
estates where you can taste, buy, eat, drink,
be merry and sleep.

Within the Palais des Papes (opposite) you
can pay for tastings and buy Côtes du Rhône
wines at cellar-door prices.

Avignon for Children

Trundling a 40-minute circuit around town, the
little tourist trains **Les Trains Touristiques d'Avignon**
(☎ 06 11 35 06 66; place du Palais; tickets €7; ☺ mid-Jun–mid-
Oct) are a winner with kids and adults alike.

A playground is situated in the hilltop gardens **Jardins des Doms** (see also p166). Avignon's
tourist office (☎ 04 32 74 32 74; www.avignon-tourisme
.com; 41 cours Jean Jaurès) often runs family-oriented
guided tours in English and French.

Across the river in Les Angles, planets loom
large at the **Parc d'Astronomie, du Soleil et du Cosmos** (☎ 04 90 25 62 82; www.parcducosmos.net in French;
av Charles de Gaulle), an astronomy park where
young masterminds can follow a 1½-hour
trail through garrigue to unravel the mysteries of the universe. Call ahead to check what
workshops/guided visits it has that day.

Tours

The **tourist office** (☎ 04 32 74 32 74; www.avignon-tourisme
.com; 41 cours Jean Jaurès) runs several city tours,
including English-language ones on foot. These
thematic tours regularly change, but include
highlights such as Avignon l'Italienne (Italian
Avignon), which departs from the tourist office
at 10am Thursday and Saturday April to October (adult €10, child under eight years €7); and
Avignon at the time of the Popes (including a
tour of the Palais des Papes), departing from the
tourist office at 10am Tuesday and Friday from
April to October (adult/child €15/7). From
November to March, a city tour in English and
French departs at 10am on Saturday.

Autocars Lieutaud (☎ 04 90 86 36 75; www.cars-lieutaud
.fr), based at the bus station, runs thematic
half- and full-day bus tours throughout the
Vaucluse between April and October.

Festivals & Events

More than 600 *spectacles* take to the stage
and streets during Avignon's **Festival d'Avignon**
(Bureau du Festival; ☎ 04 90 27 66 50; www.festival-avignon
.com; Espace St-Louis, 20 rue du Portail Boquier), founded
in 1946 and held every year from early July
to early August. Tickets for official festival
performances in the Palais des Papes' cour
d'Honneur cost around €30; reservations can
be made from mid-June.

Paralleling the official festival, the fringe
event, **Festival Off** (Avignon Public Off; ☎ 04 90 25 24 30;
www.avignon-off.org), has an eclectic – and cheaper –
programme of experimental performances. A
Carte Public Adhérent (€14) gives you a 30%
discount on all Festival Off performances.

Tickets for both festivals are also available
from FNAC branches. The tourist office has
annual ticket information.

Toast the first Côtes du Rhône wines of
the year at the **Fête des Côtes du Rhône Primeurs**
in mid-November.

Sleeping

Finding a room during the Festival d'Avignon
is all but impossible unless you've reserved
months ahead. Many places close for a few
weeks midwinter.

CHAMBRES D'HÔTES

Avignon's *chambres d'hôtes* are becoming something of a key attraction in their own right.

La Péniche (☎ 04 90 25 40 61; www.avignon-et
-provence.com/location-peniche/la-peniche; d incl breakfast
from €60; ☒) Be rocked to sleep by the gentle

River Rhône aboard Avignon's most unique *chambre d'hôte*. Permanently moored just outside the ramparts, this 1956 houseboat gleams with polished solid timber cabinetry, and incorporates a small self-catering kitchen. Free bikes are available for a spin around the city or Île de la Barthelasse.

Lumani (☎ 04 90 82 94 11; www.avignon-lumani .com; 37 rue du Rempart St-Lazare; d incl breakfast €85-150; ✗ ⊠) This fabulous *maison d'hôte* run by Elisabeth, whose artworks are hung throughout the stunning house, and her husband, Jean, a saxophonist, is a fount of inspiration for artists. Lumani's stone walls house five rooms (including two suites) and a soundproofed music atelier overlooking a fountained garden. Elisabeth and Jean offer a table d'hôte (set meal; €25; minimum four people). An adjacent artists' workshop is available for rent. Wi-fi is free.

Le Limas (☎ 04 90 14 67 19; www.le-limas-avignon.com; 51 rue du Limas; incl breakfast d €86-135, tr €139-165; ✗ ⊠) Behind its discreet (easily missed) entrance in a quiet side street 50m from the papal palace, this chic *chambre d'hôte* in an 18th-century mansion looks like it's been lifted from the pages of *Vogue Living*, with four white-on-white rooms with hardwood floors. Breakfast on homemade jam by the cosy fireplace or on the sun-drenched terrace.

La Bastide des Papes (☎ 04 90 86 09 42; www.bastide despapes.com; 352 chemin des Poiriers, Île de la Barthelasse; d incl breakfast €90-115; P ✗ ⊠ ♿) A five-minute drive from the hurdy-gurdy of Avignon and a quick flit across the river to Villeneuve, on the Île de la Barthelasse, the only sounds from this restored retreat's exquisitely decorated, airy rooms are the birds chirping in the century-old trees. A sumptuous breakfast is served poolside, there's a farm-style self-catering kitchen, and you can ride the *bastide*'s bikes around the little-trafficked island. Parking is free.

Villa Agapé (☎ 04 90 85 21 92; www.villa-agape.com; 13 rue St-Agricol; d incl breakfast €90-140; ☽ closed during Festival d'Avignon; ✗ ✗ ♿) Wrapped around a swimming pool in central Avignon, this sophisticated townhouse has a deep crimson lounge room lined with bookshelves and three delightful rooms. Two are named after multilingual host Mme de La Pommeraye's grown-up daughters, Caroline and Olivia, whose rooms they once were; and one, large enough to accommodate a family, opens to a sunny private terrace. Agapé's entrance is the inconspicuous wooden door next to the pharmacy.

HOTELS
Budget
Hôtel Mignon (☎ 04 90 82 17 30; www.hotel-mignon.com; 12 rue Joseph Vernet; s €36, d €40-55; ✗ ⊠) Cute and comfy, this 16-room place within the walled city is a favourite for its boutique rooms in a palette of Provençal colours like lavender, its friendly, helpful staff, wi-fi, and a decent breakfast of croissants and rolls (€5).

Hôtel le Provençal (☎ 04 90 85 25 24; www.hotelle provencal.com; 13 rue Joseph Vernet; s €41.15-60.15, d €43.30-60.30) In the northeastern corner of the walled city centre, 11 rooms painted the colour of sunshine are clean, cosy and welcoming, and all are equipped with telephones and TVs.

Hôtel Boquier (☎ 04 90 82 34 43; www.hotel-boquier .com; 6 rue du Portail Boquier; d €45-62) Handy for the train and bus stations, this 18th-century manor's attractive rooms are inspired by destinations like India and southern Africa. A wrought-iron gate opens to a 'café' (for guests only), with wood-beamed ceilings, serving breakfast (€7).

The Auberge Bagatelle (opposite) also has hotel rooms.

Midrange
Hôtel de Blauvac (☎ 04 90 86 34 11; www.hotel-blauvac .com; 11 rue de la Bancasse; s €52-72, d €57-87, tr €72-97) This graceful, twin-starred hotel was the town residence of the Marquis de Blauvac in the 17th century. Today it houses 16 individually adorned rooms (some with lofts) with sparkling contemporary bathrooms and exposed stone walls. Staff are a fount of information for your Avignon explorations.

Hôtel du Palais des Papes (☎ 04 90 86 04 13; www .hotel-avignon.com; 1 rue Gérard Philippe; d €65-75; menus €25-50) It's not taking the Palais' name in vain: this might be an old-fashioned abode with wrought-iron furniture, frescoed ceilings and exposed stone walls, but the pricier rooms indeed sport a view of the Palais des Papes opposite. There's also a wonderfully authentic, cavelike restaurant, Le Lutrin.

Hôtel de Garlande (☎ 04 90 80 08 85; www.hotel garlande.com; 20 rue Galante; d €70-110; ✗ ✗ ♿) Central for just about everything including the bus and train stations, the Hôtel de Garlande is a sweet, familial, 12-room place housed in a historic *hôtel particulier* (private mansion) overlooking a narrow street in the city's heart.

Hôtel de l'Horloge (☎ 04 90 16 42 00; www.hotels-ochre -azur.com; place de l'Horloge; s €72-122, d €82-132; ✗ ♿) On Avignon's main square, refined rooms are decorated in natural fabrics and fibres, with muslin curtains overlaid by stone-coloured checked linen drapes and lustrous chocolate-brown carpet. Even the sprayed concrete interiors manage to look stylish as well thanks to smart two-toned colour schemes. Breakfast (€13) is an impressive buffet banquet.

Top End

Cloître St-Louis (☎ 04 90 27 55 55; www.cloitre-saint -louis.com; 20 rue du Portail Boquier; d €100-170; **P** ✗ ✗ ⬛ ⬛ ⬛) This four-star hotel's 80 rooms are housed in a Jesuit school dating from 1589, as well as a contemporary wing with a rooftop pool designed by French architect Jean Nouvel. Most look over the namesake cloister, with some peering out to the private garden. Parking is free during the winter, and costs €10 in the busier months and €15 during the festival.

Hôtel L'Europe (☎ 04 90 14 76 76; www.heurope .com; 12 place Crillon; d €141-449; ✗ ✗) You're in good company at this antique-laden, 1799-established hotel: illustrious guests have included Napoleon, King Edward VII of England, Charles Dickens, Jackie Kennedy-Onassis and Jacques Chirac. All 44 rooms are befittingly resplendent, subtly incorporating mod cons including English and Japanese TV channels, with free wi-fi in about half the rooms. Gourmands can dine at chef Bruno d'Angelis' Michelin-starred restaurant (open Tuesday to Saturday for lunch and dinner).

Hôtel de la Mirande (☎ 04 90 14 20 2; www.la-mirande .fr; 4 place de la Mirande; d €295-475, ste from €570; **P** ✗ ✗ ⬛ ⬛) In a 14th-century cardinal's palace behind Palais des Papes, this exclusive hotel has rooms decorated to reflect the tapestries adorning its walls. Its restaurant (*menus* €34 to €105) is praiseworthy and innovative, and it's also home to the renowned cooking school, Le Marmiton. On Tuesday and Wednesday at 8pm, a table d'hôte (€85) is served in the 19th-century kitchen. Set around a pretty interior courtyard patio, a continental breakfast costs €24 (€29 for a buffet), and parking costs an even more impressive €22 per night.

HOSTEL & CAMPING

Auberge Bagatelle (☎ 04 90 85 78 45; auberge.bag atelle@wanadoo.fr; Île de la Barthelasse; dm €14.56, s €28.90-32.90, d €34.80-36.80; ⬛) Just north of Pont Édouard Daladier on Île de la Barthelasse, 850m from the walled city, this hostel has 180 beds in a mix of two- to eight-bed rooms, plus snazzier private digs including family rooms in

its adjoining hotel. All rates include breakfast; sheets are €2.50. Take bus 10 from the main post office to the La Barthelasse stop, then follow the river where you'll see the adjacent camping ground (camping €8.92 to €15.32).

Eating
RESTAURANTS

Place de l'Horloge is a riot of restaurants and cafés from Easter until mid-November. They're popular with tourists, but generally ambient and decent value. Most menus start at around €16.

Several hotels (opposite) have superb restaurants open to guests and nonguests.

Restaurant Brunel (☎ 04 90 27 16 00; 46 rue de la Balance; mains €10-18; ✉ lunch & dinner Tue-Sat) Brunel is a local favourite for authentic Provençal dishes such as aïoli (see p46), especially at lunch, when there are outstanding deals on main courses (which always include a fish of the day) and desserts. The handful of outdoor tables is hotly contested in warm weather.

Le Caveau du Théâtre (☎ 04 90 82 60 91; 16 rue des Trois Faucons; lunch/dinner menus €10.60/18; ✉ closed Sat lunch & Sun) Swing over to the south of the square for mellow, moody jazz and a monthly changing *carte* (menu) of traditional southern French fare with extra zip, such as butter-fried fish in a curry paste with sun-dried tomatoes.

Numéro 75 (☎ 04 90 27 16 00; 75 rue Guillaume Puy; menus from €16, mains from €10; ✉ lunch & dinner Mon-Sat, daily during Festival d'Avignon) This place in a lovely old house (where, incidentally, Pernod was concocted in 1870 by absinthe inventor Jules Pernod while he was living here) is now one of Avignon's in-spots for Mediterranean cuisine with succulent flavours like mango, and a fantastic €16 'chef's suggestion' *menu*.

Le Grand Café (☎ 04 90 27 04 96; 4 rue des Escaliers Ste-Anne; lunch/dinner menus from €18/30, mains from €13; ✉ lunch & dinner Tue-Sat, daily Jul) Within the arty Manutention cultural centre (p167), the duck breast/mushroom tart fare at Le Grand Café is endorsed by locals as 'almost gastronomic' (ie delectable but affordable).

La Fourchette (☎ 04 90 85 20 93; 17 rue Racine; menus from €28; ✉ lunch & dinner Mon-Fri) An enduring classical French bistro west of place de l'Horloge run by the same family for generations, La Fourchette offers a tempting choice of dishes on its fixed-price *menu* (prices are the same for lunch or dinner). Along with tender lamb, specialities include marinaded sardines, and a sinful meringue ice cream with praline.

Le Moutardier (☎ 04 90 85 34 76; moutardier@wanadoo .fr; 15 place du Palais; menus €28-50; 🕙 lunch & dinner, closed early-late Jan) In the medieval days of the Avignon popes, the *souffleur* blew the fire to get it going, the *rôtisseur* roasted the meat on it and the *moutardier* made the mustard – hence the name of this traditional restaurant lazing in the shade of the Palais des Papes with sweeping views from its terrace.

Christian Étienne (☎ 04 90 86 16 50; 10 rue de Mons; lunch menu €30, dinner menus €55-105; 🕙 lunch & dinner Tue-Sat, daily Jul) Extending from an elevated dining room to a leafy outdoor terrace in a 12th-century palace neighbouring the Palais des Papes, this is Avignon's top table. Seasonally varying signature specialities such as Avignonnaise wild boar stew, tomatoes prepared in an inordinate amount of ways, and truffle ice cream are created by its eponymous master chef.

SELF-CATERING

Pack a picnic basket from the 40-plus outlets filling Les Halles' **food market** (place Pie; 🕙 7am-1pm Tue-Sun); freshly baked breads, pastries and filled baguettes from **Erio Convert** (45 cours Jean Jaurès) and St-Tropez's famous cream-and-cake concoction at **La Tropézienne** (☎ 04 90 86 24 72; 22 rue St-Agricol; 🕙 8.30am-7.30pm Mon-Sat). Then make your way to Avignon's picturesque picnic spot, **Rocher des Doms**, a blufftop park with views spanning the Rhône, Pont St-Bénézet, Villeneuve-lès-Avignon and the Alpilles. Finish off with a *papaline d'Avignon*, a pink chocolate ball of potent Mont Ventoux herbal liqueur that packs a punch; it's available from speciality sweet shops in town such as **La Cure Gourmande** (☎ 04 90 82 65 35; 24 rue des Marchands; 🕙 10am-7pm daily).

Drinking

Tapalocas (☎ 04 90 82 56 84; 15 rue Galante; tapas from €2.50; 🕙 11.45am-1am) Tuck into an endless array of Spanish tapas over a sangria or two at this vivacious place in the pedestrian area.

La Compagnie des Comptoirs (☎ 04 90 85 99 04; 83 rue Joseph Vernet; mains €25-29; 🕙 doors close 1am) Also incorporating a snazzy restaurant wrapped around an 18th-century courtyard. Sink back on raised Moroccan-style beds beneath the arches of this former convent cloister. On weekends, cutting-edge DJs mix it up.

L'Opéra Café (☎ 04 90 86 17 43; 24 place de l'Horloge; lunch formule/plat du jour €13/9, menu €32; 🕙 10am-1.30am) DJs keep the beats coming at this contemporary café with a thespian bent on central place de l'Horloge. Open for lunch and dinner.

Woolloomooloo (☎ 04 90 85 28 44; 16bis rue des Teinturiers; menus from €15; 🕙 to 10.30pm winter, to 11.30pm summer) Inspired by the Australian bush, this eclectic Avignon institution, in a former printing house adjoining an old paper mill, embraces timber, antiques and a down-to-earth, authentic air that extends to its vegetarian-leaning menu. Get into to the spirit with a glass of the house speciality, Ti-Punch, packing Caribbean rum, lime juice, candied fruits, and spice-infused syrup.

L'Echappée Belle (☎ 04 90 82 52 61; 13 rue de la Balance; mains €14; 🕙 noon-10pm) For flavours of cumin, saffron and ginger infusing regional produce, or for a homemade pastry and tea, Avignon's newest restaurant/tearoom is a treat. Named after the Nicolas Bouvier novel of the same name (which translates as 'the beautiful escape'), it's a chic yet relaxed spot amid Avignon's architectural and artistic highlights.

Entertainment

The free *César* weekly magazine and the tourist office's fortnightly newsletter, *Rendez-vous d'Avignon* (both in French) carry events listings. Tickets for most events are sold at **FNAC** (☎ 04 90 14 35 35; 19 rue de la République; 🕙 10am-7pm Mon-Sat); the tourist office also sells tickets for many cultural fixtures.

NIGHTCLUBS & LIVE MUSIC

Avignon's entertainment scene tends to revolve more around its cultural offerings rather than party-hard nightlife, but there are some perennial favourites for a pint.

Red Lion (☎ 04 90 86 40 25; 21-23 rue St-Jean le Vieux; 🕙 8am-1am) Looking like someone picked it up from central London and plonked it down in Avignon, this cherry red English pub has gigs a couple of nights a week, and theme nights a couple of times a month.

Red Zone (☎ 04 90 27 02 44; 25 rue Carnot) A studenty crowd gathers here for its regular gigs and always-buzzing bar that's open late.

L'Esclave (☎ 04 90 85 14 91; 12 rue du Limas; 🕙 from 11pm Tue-Sun) Avignon's inner-city gay hot spot is tucked behind a blank backstreet façade.

CLASSICAL MUSIC, OPERA, BALLET & THEATRE

The season at the **Opéra Théâtre d'Avignon** (☎ 04 90 82 81 40; place de l'Horloge), built in 1847, runs October to June, presenting operas, operettas, plays, symphonic concerts, chamber-music concerts and ballet.

There are dozens of theatres, among them the mainstream **Théâtre du Bourg Neuf** (☎ 04 90 85 17 90; bourgneuf@wandoo.fr; 5bis rue du Bourg-Neuf) and **Théâtre du Chêne Noir** (☎ 04 90 86 58 11; www .theatreduchenenoir.asso.fr in French; 8bis rue Ste-Catherine). The **Théâtre du Chien qui Fume** (The Dog who Smokes; ☎ 04 90 85 89 49; www.chienquifume.com in French; 76 rue des Teinturiers) is an alternative venue in the dyers' district.

JAZZ

AJMI (Association pour Le Jazz & La Musique Improvisée; ☎ 04 90 86 08 61; www.jazzalajmi.com in French; 4 rue des Escaliers Ste-Anne) This a popular jazz club is inside the arts centre, La Manutention. Concert tickets cost around €15.

CINEMA

Cinéma Utopia (☎ 04 90 82 65 36; www.cinemas-utopia .org in French; 4 rue des Escaliers Ste-Anne; tickets day/evening €3.50/5.50) Catch nondubbed films, both classic and contemporary at Utopia, inside the La Manutention building.

Shopping

Place des Carmes buzzes with a flower market on Saturday and a flea market on Sunday. Avignon's smartest shopping streets are rue St-Agricol and rue Joseph Vernet, southwest of place de l'Horloge. Find art and antique galleries on rue du Limas and inside the **covered mall** (23 rue St-Agricol) beneath Hôtel du Petit Louvre.

Comtesse du Barry (☎ 04 90 82 62 92; 25 rue St-Agricol) Stock up on gourmet goodies like fine wine and foie gras.

Instant du Sud (☎ 04 90 82 24 48; 1 place Nicolas Saboly) Make your own perfume in an instant (well, a few).

Oliviers & Co (☎ 04 92 70 48 20; 19 rue St-Agricol) Olive oil and olive-oil-based products such as soap, hand cream and biscuits.

Getting There & Away

AIR

The **Aéroport Avignon-Caumont** (☎ 04 90 81 51 51) is 8km southeast of Avignon. Low-cost carrier Flybe flies three times per week from the UK between late May and late October.

There is no public transport into town; a taxi costs about €15.

BUS

The **bus station** (halte routière; ☎ 04 90 82 07 35; blvd St-Roch; ⏰ information window 10.15am-1pm & 2-6pm Mon-Fri) is in the basement of the building down the ramp to the right as you exit the train station. Tickets are sold on the buses.

Bus services include Aix-en-Provence (€13.90, one hour), Arles (€7.10, 1½ hours), Carpentras (€4.20, 45 minutes), Marseille (€20, 35 minutes), Nîmes (€7.60, 1¼ hours) and Orange (€5.60, 40 minutes). Most lines operate on Sunday at reduced frequency.

Long-haul bus companies **Linebus** (☎ 04 90 85 30 48) and **Eurolines** (☎ 04 90 85 27 60; www .eurolines.fr) have offices at the far end of the bus platforms.

CAR & MOTORCYCLE

To reduce traffic within the walls, the city has more than 900 free, monitored parking spaces at **Parking de L'Île Piot**, served by a free shuttle bus from the Porte de l'Oulle in the city centre.

Car-rental agencies:

Avis (☎ 08 20 61 16 50; Avignon Centre train station, 42 blvd St-Roch)

Europcar (☎ 04 90 85 01 40; Avignon Centre train station, 42 blvd St-Roch)

National Citer (☎ 04 90 85 96 47; 2a av Monclar)

TRAIN

Avignon has two train stations: **Gare Avignon TGV**, 4km southwest in the suburb of Courtine, and central **Gare Avignon Centre** (42 blvd St-Roch), where local trains to/from Orange (€5, 20 minutes), Arles (€6, 20 minutes) and Nîmes (€7.70, 30 minutes) arrive/depart.

Some TGVs to/from Paris stop at Gare Avignon Centre, but TGV services such as those to/from Marseille (€20.90, 30 minutes) and Nice (€47.80, 3¼ hours) only use Gare Avignon TGV.

From early July to early September, there's a direct **Eurostar** (www.eurostar.com) service on Saturdays to/from London (six hours) and Ashford (five hours) to Avignon Gare TGV.

Getting Around

BICYCLE & CAR

Motorists can park their cars in **Vinci Park Gare Centre** (☎ 04 90 80 74 40; blvd St-Roch & blvd St-Ruf; ⏰ 24hr) beneath the train station and borrow a bike for free to get around.

Provence Bike (☎ 04 90 27 92 61; www.provence-bike .com in French; 52 blvd St-Roch; ⏰ 9am-12.30pm & 3-6.30pm Apr-Jun, Sep & Oct, 9am-6.30pm Jul & Aug) rents city bikes for €9/39 per day/week, and mountain bikes for €15 to €25 per day or €75 to €125 per week including helmet, repair kit and road book with map and route description (in English). The shop also rents tandems, scooters and motorcycles. Out of season, arrange rental by telephone.

BOAT

A free **shuttle boat** (☺ 10am-12.30pm & 2-6.30pm Apr-Jun, 11am-9pm Jul & Aug, 2-5.30pm Wed, 10am-noon & 2-5.30pm Sat & Sun Oct-Dec) adjacent to Pont St-Bénézet connects the walled city with the Île de la Barthelasse.

BUS

Local **TCRA** (www.tcra.fr) bus tickets cost €1.10 each on board. Buses run from 7am to about 7.40pm (8am to 6pm and less frequently on Sunday). The most important transfer points are at the main post office and place Pie.

Carnets of 10 tickets (€9) and free *plans du réseau* (bus maps) are available at the **TCRA office** (Agence Commerciale TCRA; ☎ 04 32 74 18 32; av de Lattre de Tassigny; ☺ 8.30am-12.30pm & 1.30-6pm Mon-Fri).

Villeneuve-lès-Avignon is linked with Avignon by bus 10, which stops in front of the main post office and on the western side of the walled city near Porte de l'Oulle.

Navettes (shuttle buses) link Gare Avignon TGV with the centre (€1.10, 10 to 13 minutes, twice hourly between 6.15am and 11.30pm); buses use the bus stop in front of the main post office on cours Président Kennedy Monday to Saturday, and the Cité Administrative bus stop on cours Jean Jaurès on Sunday.

Bus 11 links Avignon with Villeneuve-lès-Avignon and bus 10 serves Les Angles.

VILLENEUVE-LÈS-AVIGNON

pop 12,078

Across the Rhône from Avignon (and in a different *département*), the 13th-century Villeneuve-lès-Avignon (sometimes written as Villeneuve-lez-Avignon, and almost always just called Villeneuve, meaning 'new city') became known as the City of Cardinals because many primates affiliated with the papal court built large residences in town. This was despite the fact that it was in territory ruled by the French crown, which in turn established a garrison here to keep an eye on events in the papal-controlled city across the river. Stroll over the bridge to see the dramatic tower and fortress and experience the tranquil township.

Information

Tourist office (☎ 04 90 25 61 33; www.villeneuveles avignon.fr; 1 place Charles David; ☺ 9am-12.30pm & 2-6pm Mon-Sat Sep-Jun, 10am-7pm Mon-Fri, 10am-1pm & 2-7pm Sat & Sun Jul, 9am-12.30pm & 2-6pm Aug) Runs guided city tours in English on Tuesday and Thursday in July and August.

Sights

The Avignon Passion museum pass (see the boxed text, p162) is valid in Villeneuve.

Crossing Pont Édouard Daladier from Avignon, looming on your left is **Tour Philippe le Bel** (☎ 04 32 70 08 57; full price/pass €1.80/1; ☺ 10am-12.30pm & 2-6.30pm, closed Mon mid-Sep–mid-Jun). If you're up for it, take the steep spiral steps to the top of this 14th-century defensive tower built at what was – then – the northwestern end of Pont St-Bénézet for awesome views of Avignon's walled city. Several **walking and cycling nature trails** start from the foot of the tower; the tourist office has details.

Provençal panoramas also unfold from the turreted, 14th-century **Fort St-André** (☎ 04 90 25 45 35; full price/pass €4.60/3.10; ☺ 10am-1pm & 2-6pm Apr-Sep, 10am-1pm & 2-5pm Oct-Mar).

Pope Innocent VI lived in a palatial *livrée* (livery) in Villeneuve-lès-Avignon which, once he became pontiff in 1352, became the **Chartreuse du Val de Bénédiction** (☎ 04 90 15 24 24; 60 rue de la République; full price/pass €6.10/4.10; ☺ 9am-6.30pm May-Aug, 9.30am-5.30pm Sep-Apr). It was once the largest and most significant Carthusian monastery in France and still looks it today.

During the French Revolution the monastery was shut down and its treasures stolen. Many are now displayed at the **Musée Pierre de Luxembourg** (☎ 04 90 27 49 66; rue de la République; full price/pass €3/2; ☺ 10am-12.30pm & 2-6.30pm, closed Mon mid-Sep–mid-Jun). If you're remotely interested in religious art, seek out Enguerrand Quarton's lavish and dramatic 1453 painting *The Crowning of the Virgin*, and ask for the accompanying notes about its commissioning and underpinning religious dogma.

Sleeping & Eating

Les Jardins de la Vivrée (☎ 04 90 26 05 05; www.la-livree .com in French; 4bis rue du Camp de Bataille; d incl breakfast €60-90; **P ☺**) In the centre of town, and handy for Avignon, beautiful high-walled gardens screen a serene swimming pool from the outside world, and each of these four *chambre d'hôte* rooms has tiled floors and natural sunlight. Parking is free.

Écuries des Chartreux (☎ 04 90 25 79 93; www.ecuries -des-chartreux.com; 66 rue de la République; d €60-115; ☺) This historic building was once part of the adjoining Chartreuse monastery (above) and has

VILLENEUVE–LÈS–AVIGNON

INFORMATION	
Tourist Office..............................1	B3

SIGHTS & ACTIVITIES	
Chartreuse du Val de Bénédiction..2	A2
Fort St-André..............................3	B2
Musée Pierre de Luxembourg......4	A3

SLEEPING	
Ecuries des Chartreux.................5	A2
Les Jardins de la Vivrée..............6	A3

NORTH OF AVIGNON

Unfolding northwest of Avignon are the vineyards of Châteauneuf du Pape and the Roman treasures of Orange. The region extends up to the rocky Dentelles de Montmirail, the slopes of Mont Ventoux and east to the harsh Plateau d'Albion (see the boxed text, p182).

CHÂTEAUNEUF DU PAPE
pop 2098

Eons ago the River Rhône extended up to the Alps. When it receded, it deposited large, smooth, pale, *calcaire* stones in its wake. Those stones now play an integral role in the production of Châteauneuf du Pape's renowned wines, retaining heat trapped during the day to keep the ground a constant temperature after sunset. In 1317 Pope John XXII (r 1316–34) built a pontifical summer residence 18km north of Avignon, Château des Papes, at a former mining hamlet, planting vineyards around the castle.

The best wines of the last *millésime* (vintage) are cracked with gusto around 25 April during the **Fête de la St-Marc**. Other festivities include the **Fête de la Véraison**, held over the first weekend of August (tickets €48), with horse jousting, a Sunday morning Mass in Provençal, a medieval market, and feasting in conical tents, washed down with papal wine.

Amid the vineyards, the dignified village of Châteauneuf du Pape is lorded over by the ruined **papal castle**. Burnt during both the Wars of Religion (1562–98) and WWII, its remains standing on a 118m hillock at the village's northern end, a 10-minute walk from the **tourist office** (☎ 04 90 83 71 08; http://perso.wanadoo.fr/ot-chato9-pape in French; place du Portail; ⏰ 9.30am-7pm Mon-Sat Jul & Aug, 9.30am-12.30pm & 2-6pm Mon-Sat Sep-Jun), with panoramic views over Avignon, the Plateau de Vaucluse, the Luberon, the Rhône and beyond.

Wine Tasting

Splashed around town are more than two dozen wine shops offering *dégustation gratuite* (free wine tasting).

Tastings are also free at the **Musée du Vin** (☎ 04 90 83 70 07; www.brotte.com; rte d'Avignon; admission free; ⏰ 9am-1pm & 2-7pm mid-May–mid-Oct, 9am-noon & 2-6pm mid-Oct–mid-May), which has a collection of old tools and extensive information about the area's soils, grape varieties and wine-making processes. Nearby, learn about the history

been impeccably and lovingly restored by hosts Pascale and Antoine. It now incorporates three exposed stone studios (two with lofts) opening onto the garden. The largest, sleeping up to four people, has free private parking by reservation, and all have free wi-fi. Breakfast costs €7, or nip out to the nearby village shops and whip something up yourself in your kitchenette.

La Magnaneraie (☎ 04 90 25 11 11; www.hostellerie-la-magnaneraie.com; 37 rue du Camp de Bataille; d €135-235, ste €240-450; menus €339-80; P ⏰ 🖥 🍷) White-clothed tables and wicker chairs clustered beneath a canopy of trees create a seductive setting to savour delights like foie gras marinated in peach wine. To prolong the experience, stay overnight in La Magnaneraie's four-star guest rooms in shades of cornflower blue, rose and violet. Higher-priced rooms open to a private balcony or terrace.

Getting There & Away

Villeneuve-lès-Avignon is an easy 15-minute stroll from Avignon's walls.

Bus 11 links Villeneuve-lès-Avignon with Avignon, from where there are extensive connections.

AN APPELLATION DETOUR

Meandering among the vineyards is the ultimate way to appreciate the Châteauneuf du Pape's celebrated grapes (followed, of course, by a taste).

Covering just 32 sq km between Avignon and Orange on the Rhône's left bank, the manually harvested vines of the coveted Châteauneuf du Pape appellation are rigidly controlled by regulations that predate any *appellation d'origine contrôlée* (AOC). In 1923, decorated WWI fighter pilot, lawyer and viticulturalist Baron Le Roy de Boiseaumarié defined the boundaries – literally and figuratively, establishing the region's first syndicate of wine-growers. AOCs became a national system in 1935.

The appellation's still-enforced rules stipulate a maximum output of 35 hectolitres comprising a maximum of 13 grapes, of which 60% to 70% are Grenache. The minimum alcohol level is 12½% (maximum 15%). Annual production is sold years in advance, commanding €300-odd a bottle, but a run-of-the-mill red from 2002/2000 sells for €14.60/18. Châteauneuf also produces some wonderful whites, though rosés are forbidden.

Follow av St-Joseph (the westbound D17) out of the village, then turn right (north) at the *'circuit touristique'* sign along chemin de l'Arnesque and chemin de Pradel, passing row upon stone-crusted row of vineyards. Stop at **Château Mont Redon** (☎ 04 90 83 72 75; www.chateaumontredon.fr in French; ☖ cellar 8am-7pm Thu-Tue, 8am-noon & 2-6pm Wed, closed Sun early Jan–mid-Feb) for a tipple (visits are by appointment) before rounding the corner for a mesmerising view of Mont Ventoux.

Returning to Châteauneuf, cross the village and head southeast along av Baron Le Roy and follow the signs to the right (south) for a final free tasting at **Château Fortia** (☎ 04 90 83 72 25; www.chateau-fortia.com; rte de Bedarrides; ☖ cellar 9am-noon & 2-6pm Mon-Sat, 2-6pm Sun) on the southern fringe of town, which is still held by Baron Le Roy de Boiseaumarié's family today.

of chocolate with artisan *chocolatier* **Bernard Castelain** (☎ 04 90 83 54 71; rte d'Avignon; admission free; 9am-noon & 2-7pm Mon-Sat, closed 1st week Jan).

The tourist office has details of producers in the area that allow cellar visits and offer free tastings by appointment (generally Monday to Friday). English tours are often available with advance notice. For more on Châteauneuf's seminal appellation see the boxed text, above.

Sleeping & Eating

La Mère Germaine (☎ 04 90 83 54 37; www.lamere germaine.com; place de la Fontaine; d €50-70; lunch menu €16, evening menus €22-85; ☐) Eight charming rooms slumber above this village restaurant (closed Tuesday night, all day Wednesday and Sunday night). The *menu pontifical* includes seven surprise courses accompanied by seven different glasses of papal wine.

La Sommellerie (☎ 04 90 83 50 00; www.hotel-la -sommellerie.com in French; d €70-107, ste €90-133; menus €30-80; ☐ ☒ ☒ ☖) This 17th-century former sheepfold is now a haven of peace and tranquility, situated in glorious countryside 3km out of the village along the westbound D17. There are to a dozen rooms (and two suites) with rustic beamed ceilings and classical colours. Chef Pierre Paumel creates mouthwatering *menus* at the on-site restaurant, and also offers cook-

ing courses (minimum of four participants) on demand (prices and dates vary).

Maison Felisa (☎ 04 66 39 99 84; www.maison-felisa .com; 6 rue des Barris, St-Laurent des Arbres; d €110-150; ☐ ☒ ☒ ☒) Across the River Rhône in the medieval village of St-Laurent des Arbres, 15km west of Châteauneuf and handy if you're visiting the Pont du Gard and Nîmes, this tranquil *maison d'hôte* rejuvenates the weariest of travellers. Bed linen is ironed with jasmine-scented water, on-site spa treatments include Ayurvedic massages, and cooking classes and a nourishing table d'hôte are available by reservation. There's a two-night minimum stay.

Hostellerie du Château des Fines Roches (☎ 04 90 83 70 23; www.chateaufinesroches.com; d €160-206; lunch menus €16-32, dinner menus €35-60; ☐ ☒ ☒ ☖) At the end of an elongated driveway through the vineyards, 2km south along the Avignon-bound D17, this fairy-tale 19th-century castle has a splendid restaurant with views extending from its terrace to the papal chateau. Above the library (where Mistral and Daudet debated literature), grand rooms have flourishes like poster beds, clawfoot baths, and in a couple, a shower in the turret. Outside May to October, Fines Roches closes each Sunday after lunch and accepts guests from Tuesday afternoon; it closes completely during November and two weeks of February.

Other dining recommendations:

La Marmite (☎ 04 90 83 78 45; 22 rue Joseph Ducos; menus €17-19; ☯ lunch & dinner Wed-Mon, lunch only mid-Nov–Mar; ♿) Refreshingly simple in such an upmarket village, cooking up regional cuisine.

Le Pistou (☎ 04 90 83 71 75; 15 rue Ducos; menus €15-30; ☯ lunch Tue-Sun, dinner Tue-Sat, closed Jan; ♿) A local favourite for its namesake summertime *pistou* (pesto) soup.

Le Verger des Papes (☎ 04 90 83 50 40; 4 rue du Château; menus €19-27; ☯ lunch & dinner Mar–mid-Dec; ♿) Touts a panoramic terrace perched at the pinnacle of the village and two brothers turning out traditional dishes paired with wines from the cavernous cellar.

Getting There & Away

Rapides du Sud-Est (☎ 04 90 34 15 59) operates buses to/from Orange (€2.70, 15 minutes, two or three daily). On school days, buses also run to Avignon (€3.70, 40 minutes, one or two daily). In Châteauneuf buses use the stop on av du Général de Gaulle.

ORANGE

pop 28,889

This friendly little city has a refreshingly down-to-earth ambience among its plazas, fountains and cobweb of pedestrian streets; and is generally more affordable than its Provençal neighbours too.

The House of Orange – the princely dynasty that had ruled Orange since the 12th century – made its mark on the history of the Netherlands through a 16th-century marriage with the German House of Nassau; and later on English history through William III (William of Orange). Known as Arenja in Provençal, it had earlier been a stronghold of the Reformation, and was ceded to France in 1713 by the Treaty of Utrecht. To this day many members of the royal house of the Netherlands are known as the princes and princesses of Orange-Nassau.

Orange is home to two of Provence's juiciest Roman treasures: a steep, spectacular theatre and a magnificent triumphal arch.

Orientation

Orange's train station is about 1.5km east of the city centre's place de la République, along av Frédéric Mistral then rue de la République. Rue St-Martin links place de la République and nearby place Georges Clemenceau with the tourist office, 250m to the west. Théâtre

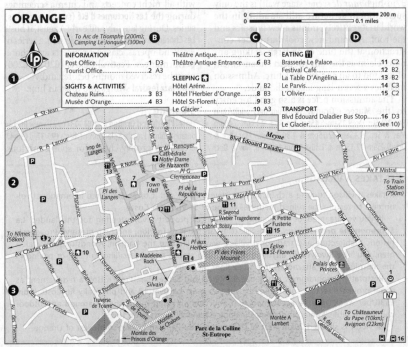

ORANGE

INFORMATION	Théâtre Antique...............5 C3	**EATING**
Post Office.......................1 D3	Théâtre Antique Entrance...6 B3	Brasserie Le Palace..............11 C2
Tourist Office....................2 A3		Festival Café......................12 B2
	SLEEPING	La Table D'Angélina.............13 B2
SIGHTS & ACTIVITIES	Hôtel Arène.....................7 B2	Le Parvis.........................14 C3
Chateau Ruins..................3 B3	Hôtel l'Herbier d'Orange.......8 B3	L'Olivier.........................15 C2
Musée d'Orange.................4 B3	Hôtel St-Florent.................9 B3	
	Le Glacier........................10 A3	**TRANSPORT**
		Blvd Édouard Daladier Bus Stop...16 D3
		Le Glacier....................(see 10)

To Arc de Triomphe (200m); Camping Le Jonquier (300m)

R. St-Jean

R. A Lacour

Imp de Langes

R du Renoyer

Notre Dame de Nazareth

Meyne

Blvd Édouard Daladier

Av H Fabre

Av F Mistral

To Train Station (750m)

Cathédrale

Pl G Clemenceau

Town Hall

Pl des Langes

R Notre Dame

R Victor Hugo

Pl de la République

R du Pont Neuf

Pont Neuf

R. du Noble

R. de la République

R. St-Martin

R Segond

Weber Tragedienne

R. des Avsnes

R des Fusterie

R Contrescarpe

To Nîmes (58km)

Av Charles de Gaulle

Cours Aristide Briand

R de Tourre

R Pontillac

R Madeleine Roch

Pl A BRY

R Courmand

Pl aux Herbes

R Gabriel Boissy

Pl des Frères Mounet

Eglise St-Florent

R de l'Hopital

R St-Florent

Palais des Princes

Blvd Édouard Daladier

Pl Silvain

Cours Pourtoules

N7

R de Tourre

Traverse de Tourre

R des Vieux Fossés

Av des Thèmes

Montée des Princes d'Orange

Parc de la Colline St-Eutrope

Montée A Lambert

R du Général Leclerc

To Châteauneuf du Pape (10km); Avignon (22km)

0............200 m
0............0.1 miles

Antique, Orange's magnificent Roman theatre, is two blocks south of place de la République. The tiny River Meyne lies north of the centre. From the train station, bus 1 from the École Mistral school goes to the centre of town; get off at Pourtoules for the Théâtre Antique.

Information

Post office (679 blvd Édouard Daladier) The only place in Orange that changes money.

Tourist office (☎ 04 90 34 70 88; www.otorange.fr; 5 cours Aristide Briand; ⏰ 9.30am-7pm Mon-Sat, 10am-4pm Sun Apr-Sep, 10am-1pm & 2-5pm Mon-Sat Oct-Mar) Closed mid-January, but phones are staffed.

Sights

THÉÂTRE ANTIQUE

For an unforgettable first ogle at Orange's **Roman theatre** (☎ 04 90 51 17 60; adult/student €7.70/5.60; ⏰ 9am-7pm Jun-Aug, 9am-6pm Apr, May & Sep, 9.30am-5.30pm Oct & Mar, 9.30am-4.30pm Jan, Feb, Nov & Dec), take the steep back stairs to the top, which affords an awesome view down the raked seating to the stage. Designed to seat 10,000 spectators, it's thought to have been built during Augustus Caesar's rule (27 BC–AD 14). The 103m-wide, 37m-high *mur de scène* (stage wall) is the only such Roman structure still standing in the world in its entirety, minus a few mosaics and the roof. A brand-new roof was under construction at the time of research, staking another claim as the only modern enhancement of its kind to an ancient structure. Admission includes a seven-language audioguide.

The admission price is also good for entry to the **Musée d'Orange** (museum only adult/child €4.50/3.50; ⏰ 9.15am-6.45pm Jun-Aug, 9.15am-6.45pm May & Sep, 9.45am-12.15pm & 1.30-5.15pm Mar, Apr & Oct, 9.45am-12.15pm & 1.30-4.15pm Jan, Feb, Nov & Dec)

across the road, with some treasures of its own including segments of the Roman survey registers (essentially the precursor to the tax department), and the friezes that formed part of the theatre's scenery.

Follow montée Philbert de Chalons or montée A Lambert to the top of **Colline St-Eutrope** (St-Eutrope Hill; elevation 97m) for an elevated theatre panorama, where a circular viewing table explains what's what. En route you pass the ruins of a 12th-century **chateau**, the former residence of the princes of Orange.

ARC DE TRIOMPHE

Uncannily like Paris' iconic arch, Orange's 1st-century AD **triumphal arch** stands a proud 19m high and wide, and 8m thick, at the northern end of av de l'Arc de Triomphe, about 450m northwest of the town centre. On its façade, ornate sculptures commemorate the Romans' victories over the Gauls in 49 BC as a not-so-subtle reminder to travellers approaching the city.

Festivals & Events

In June and August Théâtre Antique comes alive with all-night concerts and cinema screenings during the **Les Nocturnes d'Eté** (summer nights) series. During late July and early August, it hosts **Les Chorégies d'Orange** (www.choregies.com), a series of weekend operas, classical concerts and choral performances. Festival tickets (€20 to €200) must be reserved months beforehand. A week-long **jazz festival** swings into town in June.

Sleeping

Hôtel l'Herbier d'Orange (☎ 04 90 34 09 23; www.lherbier dorange.com in French; 8 place aux Herbes; s €25-32, d €30-47, tr €45-52) A groovy choice for style-conscious,

---

IT TAKES A VILLAGE...

It takes a village to raise a child, so the proverb goes, and it takes dedicated international volunteers to restore the ruined medieval village of **St-Victor la Coste**.

If you've dreamed of renovating a Provençal property, volunteering for the lauded **La Sabranenque project** (www.sabranenque.com) can see it to fruition, and help preserve Provence's historic architecture and traditional village way of life into the bargain. Alongside local craftsmen, you'll be involved in anything from cutting stones and dry-walling to tiling or paving in the mornings, with afternoons free to explore the area.

Restoration programmes run between March and September. French isn't a requirement as some project directors speak English, but you must be over 18 and physically fit. Costs (from €530 per week) include accommodation and chef-prepared meals shared around an outdoor communal table. Some programmes include a regional sightseeing tour.

St-Victor is situated 20km west of Châteauneuf du Pape and 27km southwest of Orange.

budget-conscious travellers, this retro-funky pad run by a hip young team has 20 rooms with arctic white walls starkly contrasted with lavender, maroon, yellow or dark chocolate brown. The cheapest rooms come with a sink only but all have TVs, telephones, and fridges to chill Provençal wine.

Hôtel St-Florent (☎ 04 90 34 18 53; fax 04 90 51 17 25; 4 rue du Mazeau; s €27, d €35-75) A trip of a place, the St-Florent has 17 colourful, chintzy rooms with giant murals and antique wooden beds with crushed and studded velvet. Cheapies have toilets outside the rooms. Wear your sunglasses when you head to the breakfast room – a frenzy of iridescent orange tablecloths, a frenzy of fake flowers and blinking Christmas lights.

Le Glacier (☎ 04 90 34 02 01; www.le-glacier.com; 46 cours Aristide Briand; d €47-95; ⊠ ⚤) Cosy and bright, with cute blue and yellow rooms, and in an ultrahandy location near the Théâtre Antique, Le Glacier has a welcoming, kind-hearted staff who can recommend cycling itineraries of the nearby countryside and villages.

Hôtel Arène (☎ 04 90 11 40 40; www.hotel-arene.fr; place des Langes; s €56-64, d €77-140; P ⊠ ☐ ⚤) With a whole floor dedicated to hypoallergenic, ecological rooms, the Arène is privately owned and run with meticulous attention to detail. Furnishings in all 35 rooms, even its whimsically named 'Romantique' and 'Charme' rooms, are modern and streamlined. Downstairs there's a bright bar/breakfast room with Illy coffee and free wi-fi (you might also pick up a signal in your room). Parking costs €8.

Camping Le Jonquier (☎ 04 90 34 49 48; www.avignon -et-provence.com/le-jonquier in French; 1321 rue Alexis Carrel; camping €22.80; ⊠ mid-Mar–Sep; ⚤) Splash in the pool, or play minigolf or tennis at this place near the Arc de Triomphe. Take bus 1 from the République stop (av Frédéric Mistral, 600m from the train station) to the Arc de Triomphe. From there walk 100m back, turn right onto rue des Phocéens and right again onto rue des Étudiants and cross the football field.

Eating

Orange's pedestrianised streets and squares overflow with well-priced, well-patronised restaurants and cafés.

Brasserie Le Palace (☎ 04 90 34 13 51; 7 rue de la République; mains €7; ⊠ 8am-7.30pm Mon-Sat summer, shorter hr winter) Squeeze in with the locals over a drink or casual *plat* at this clattering old-school brasserie with red vinyl booths, a collection of old clocks, and aromatic coffees (€1.30).

La Table d'Angélina (☎ 04 90 30 28 36; 23 rue Victor Hugo; mains €12; ⊠ lunch & dinner Tue-Sat summer, lunch Tue-Sat, dinner Fri & Sat winter) A pastel-pretty place tucked in a 16th-century vaulted dining room, the tiny La Table D'Angélina specialises in cooking up whatever's freshest at the markets.

L'Olivier (☎ 04 90 11 05 22; 12 rue Petite Fusterie; mains €15-19.80; ⊠ closed dinner Wed, lunch Sat & all day Sun winter, closed Sun summer) Remember the name Olivier Teissedre – it won't be the last time you hear of this rising chef, who is creating a buzz at his little French-washed place. Must-tries from the blackboard are Olivier's *tartes* (including vegie ones), *ravioles* (itty-bitty cheese-and-herb local specialities), and his handmade nougat *glacé* (nougat ice cream). The restaurant has wi-fi.

Classic fare stars at the terrace-only **Festival Café** (☎ 04 90 34 65 58; 5 place de la République; mains €8-10; ⊠ lunch & dinner Apr-Oct, closed Nov-Mar), which sets up a marquee in inclement weather; and at **Le Parvis** (☎ 04 90 34 82 00; 55 cours Pourtoules; mains from €17; ⊠ closed Sun dinner & all day Mon), Orange's gastronomic gem.

SELF-CATERING

The town's central streets are lined with stalls each Thursday morning during its weekly market. If you'll need to move your car before the market wraps up, park at the edges of the city.

Getting There & Around

There's no longer a bus station, but buses stop on blvd Édouard Daladier, southwest of the post office, and travel to destinations including Avignon (€5.60, 40 minutes) and Vaison-la-Romaine (€5.10, 45 minutes).

Orange's **train station** (☎ 04 90 11 88 64, 3635; av Frédéric Mistral) has services south to Avignon (€5, 20 minutes), Marseille (€19.50, 1½ hours) and beyond and north including Lyon (€24.30, 2¼ hours).

Le Glacier (☎ 04 90 34 02 01; www.le-glacier.com; 46 cours Aristide Briand) rents bikes (per half/full day €12/16).

VAISON-LA-ROMAINE

pop 5986

This quintessentially Provençal village has a plane-tree–dappled pedestrianised centre and also stretches across the River Ouvèze to the walled Cité Médiévale (mediaeval city) perched on the hilltop.

Vaison has a rich Roman legacy, with the largest archaeological site in France. Originally a Celtic city, it was conquered by the

AVIGNON AREA

Romans in the 2nd century BC. They left a treasure-trove of remains including the picturesque bridge that connects the town's heart with the Cité Médiévale, where the counts of Toulouse built their 12th-century castle.

Situated at the crossroads of Provence, 23km and 47km northeast of Orange and Avignon respectively, and 10km north of Carpentras, Vaison is also a prime staging post for Mont Ventoux mountain forays (p180).

Orientation

The flood-prone River Ouvèze bisects Vaison. The modern centre is on the river's north bank; the Cité Médiévale is on its south side.

Pedestrianised Grand Rue heads northwest from the Pont Romain, changing its name near the Roman ruins to become av du Général de Gaulle.

To get from the bus station to the tourist office, turn left as you leave the station then left again into rue Colonel Parazols, which leads past the Fouilles de Puymin excavations along rue Burrhus.

Information

Post office Opposite place du 11 Novembre. Has an exchange service and Cyberposte.

Tourist office (☎ 04 90 36 02 11; www.vaison-la-romaine .com; place du Chanoine Sautel; ☺ 9am-noon & 2-6.45pm daily Jul & Aug, 9am-noon & 2-5.45pm Mon-Sat, 9am-noon Sun Apr-Jun & Sep–mid-Oct, 9am-noon & 2-5.45pm Mon-Sat mid-Oct–Mar) Just off av du Général de Gaulle.

Sights

GALLO-ROMAN RUINS

The ruined remains of Vasio Vocontiorum, the Roman city that flourished here from the 6th to 2nd centuries BC, are unearthed at two sites covered by a single admission.

At **Puymin** (av du Général de Gaulle; both Puymin & La Villasse adult/child €7.50/4; ☺ 10am-noon & 2-5pm Oct-Dec & early Feb, 10am-noon & 2-6pm Mar, 9.30am-6pm Apr & May, 9am-noon & 6.30pm Jun-Sep, closed Jan-early Feb) you can see **houses**, **mosaics**, the still-functioning **Théâtre Antique** (built around AD 20 for an audience of 6000) and an **archaeological museum** (☺ 10am-noon & 2-5pm Oct-Dec & early Feb, 10am-noon & 2-6pm Mar, 10.30am-6pm Apr & May, 10.30am-6.45pm Jun-Sep, closed Jan-early Feb) with a swag of statues – including the silver bust of a 3rd-century patrician and likenesses of Hadrian and his wife Sabina.

Colonnaded shops and a limestone-paved street with an underground sewer are visible at **La Villasse** (both Puymin & La Villasse adult/child €7.50/4;

☺ 10am-noon & 2-5pm Oct-Dec & early Feb, 10am-noon & 2-6pm Mar-May, 10.30am-noon & 2.30-6pm Jun-Sep, closed Jan-early Feb), to the west of the same road.

Admission includes an audioguide and entry to the 12th-century Romanesque **cloister** (cloister visit only €1.50; ☺ 10am-noon & 2-5pm Oct-Dec & early Feb, 10am-noon & 2-6pm Mar, 10am-noon & 2-6pm Apr & May, 10am-12.15pm & 2-5.45pm Jun-Sep, closed Jan-early Feb) of the **Cathédrale Notre-Dame de Nazareth**, a five-minute walk west across rue du Bon Ange from La Villasse.

From April to September, there are free guided tours in English; check the schedule at the tourist office.

CITÉ MÉDIÉVALE

Across the pretty **Pont Romain** (Roman bridge), cobblestone alleyways carve through the stone walls up to the Cité Médiévale. The highest point is home to an imposing 12th-century **chateau** built by the counts of Toulouse, which was modernised in the 15th century only to be later abandoned. Entry to the chateau is only available by guided tour (in French; €2) – check with the tourist office (left) for schedules.

JARDIN DES NEUF DAMOISELLES

Heading 1km west out of town along the D975 towards Orange brings you to the stone and bamboo garden created by sculptor Serge Boÿer. A memorial to those who died in Vaison's 1992 floods, the **Jardin des Neuf Damoiselles** (Garden of Nine Damsels) centres on a square of nine granite blocks, each representing one of Europe's cities of culture in 2000 and engraved with a short poem of love and peace, written by a native poet of each city. Around it, 72 hefty boulders – each representing a different town in the world with respective inscriptions – spiral outwards to form a monumental sundial.

Festivals & Events

In July dance takes centre stage at Puymin's Théâtre Antique during the two-week **Festival de Vaison-la-Romaine** (www.vaison-festival.com in French) and polyphonic performances can be seen at the Cathédrale Notre-Dame de Nazareth during the **Festival des Choeurs Lauréats**.

Choralies, a two-week choral festival held every three years in August, is Europe's largest. The next take place in 2007 and 2010.

Vaison is one of a dozen villages in the area to partake in the **Festival des Soupes** (Soup Festival; admission free; soup €5-6), held from October to early November. The villages come to life when they take it in turns to host these communal feasts, which the other participating villages attend. Tourist offices sell a festival recipe book (€20) featuring 155 soups to keep you warm throughout winter.

Sleeping

CHAMBRES D'HÔTES

Jade en Provence (☎ 04 90 28 81 60; www.jade-en -provence.com in French; av André Coudray; d incl breakfast €65-75; P ✕ ⊠ ⊠ ⚤) Named after hosts Sabrina and Pierre's young daughter, this family-friendly spot a 500m stroll north of the village centre has five sparkling rooms set at the back of a large garden. Cook in the extensively equipped communal kitchen or book ahead for an all-inclusive table d'hôte (€30).

La Calade (☎ 04 90 46 51 79; www.la-calade-vaison .com; rue Calade, St-Romain-en-Viennois; d incl breakfast €70; ⚤ Easter-Oct) Just 3km northeast of Vaison in the postcard-pretty stone village St-Romain-en-Viennois (worth a trip even if you're not setting down your suitcases here), this sweet little *chambre d'hôte* is furnished with 19th-century family heirlooms and opens to a fountained courtyard. Views across the village and beyond extend from the rooftop terrace. Credit cards are not accepted.

L'Évêché (☎ 04 90 36 13 46; http://eveche.free.fr; rue de l'Évêché; d €70-80, d ste €80-120) Filled with art, antiques, books and fresh flowers, this former 15th-century *évêché* (bishop's residence) in the medieval city has been the ongoing restoration project of hosts Aude and Jean-Loup since they acquired it as a ruin. Three of its five en suite rooms have a separated sitting area, and one has a sun-drenched private terrace. Vehicle access is tricky; it's easier to park in the village and stroll up.

Three heavenly *chambre d'hôte* rooms (€110 to €140 including breakfast) slumber above Vaison's temple to gastronomy, Moulin à Huile (right).

HOTELS

Escapade (☎ 04 90 36 00 78; www.escapade-vacances .com/vaison; av César Geoffray; d with obligatory half-board €38-42; ⚤ closed Dec-Feb) Around 500m southeast of town along the river, this modern family resort is set over peaceful, sprawling grounds with views of Mont Ventoux. This being France, half-board includes wine; breakfast is €5.50.

Hôtel Burrhus (☎ 04 90 36 00 11; www.burrhus.com; 1 place de Montfort; d €44-69, apt €98; ⚤ closed mid-Nov–late Dec, plus Sun Jan & Feb) Right on Vaison's vibrant central square, Burrhus looks like a quaint old-world place from the outside, but inside its 38 rooms have stunning cutting-edge colours (including one vision in all white), funky streamlined furnishings, mosaic bathrooms and dramatic designer lighting. Parking costs €7.

Hostellerie Le Beffroi (☎ 04 90 36 04 71; www.le -beffroi.com; rue de l'Évêché; d €68-130; ⚤ closed late Jan-late Mar; ⚤ ⚤) Within the Cité Médiévale's walls, this 1554-built *hostellerie* is housed over two buildings (the 'newer' one was built in 1690). A fairy-tale hideaway, its 22 rough-hewn stone-and-wood-beam rooms are romantically furnished, and there's a glass-paned breakfast room and summer terrace tumbling onto a rambling rose-and-herb garden with kids' swings. It has been held by the same family since 1904. You can park out the front (spaces are limited and access is tight), or there's a lock-up garage for €8 per day 150m down the hill.

Eating

Le Bateleur (☎ 04 90 36 28 04; 1 place Théodore Aubanel; menus €18-38; ⚤ lunch Tue-Fri & Sun, dinner Tue, Wed & Fri-Sun) In two cosy dining rooms, one of which overlooks the rushing river, this is a convivial place for Provençal fare. Vegan alert: lunchtime mains consist of two choices, meat or fish.

Hostellerie Le Beffroi (☎ 04 90 36 04 71; www.le-beffroi .com; rue de l'Évêché; menus €28-45; ⚤ lunch Sat & Sun, dinner Wed-Mon; ⚤) In the rich red wallpapered dining room of this rambling hotel (see above) or on the summertime terrace, this graciously old-fashioned restaurant serves Provençal specialities such as duck with lavender honey, monkfish in bacon and mushroom sauce, with local wines; and for dessert, a bitter chocolate cake in coffee and walnut sauce.

Moulin à Huile (☎ 04 90 36 20 67; www.robert-bardot .com; quai Maréchal Foch; lunch menu from €40, dinner menu from €60; ⚤ lunch & dinner Tue-Sat, lunch Sun) Master chef Robert Bardot refines and redefines the art of gastronomic cooking at this old clementine-coloured oil mill by the river in the shadow of the Cité Médiévale. Like all great artists (he also paints the watercolour illustrations on the menus), Bardot believes his cooking would be 'insipid if it was not flavoured by a touch of madness'. Sample a cross-section of his creations with his €76 tasting plate.

Other dining recommendations:

Ristorante Gino (☎ 04 90 36 31 05; 1 Grand Rue; mains €12.50-30; ⚤ lunch Mon, Tue, Thu, Fri & Sun, dinner Mon, Thu & Fri-Sun) Atmospheric Italian restaurant in a stone-walled subterranean dining room.

Auberge La Bartavelle (☎ 04 90 36 02 16; 12 place Sus-Auze; mains €16-35; ☺ lunch Tue-Thu, Sat & Sun, dinner Tue-Sun, closed Jan) Popular spot for traditional cuisine such as rabbit-filled ravioli.

Le Brin d'Olivier (☎ 04 90 28 74 79; 4 rue du Ventoux; lunch menus €19-25, dinner menu €38; ☺ lunch & dinner) Near the Pont Romain adjacent to quai Pasteur, specialising in all things truffle.

SELF-CATERING

Wines, honey, jam and nougat are all local specialities available at the tourist office's on-site boutique (p174).

A magnificent market snakes through the central streets Tuesdays from 6.30am to 1pm.

Getting There & Around

Vaison's bus station, where **Lieutard buses** (☎ Vaison 04 90 36 05 22, Avignon 04 90 86 36 75; av des Choralies; ☺ 9am-noon & 2-7pm Mon-Fri, 9am-noon Sat) has an office, is 400m east of the town centre. There are limited services from Vaison to Orange (€5.10, 45 minutes), Avignon (€7.70, 1¼ hours) and Carpentras (€4.30, 45 minutes).

Rent two-wheelers at **Mag 2 Roues** (☎ 04 90 28 80 46; www.mag2roues.com in French; cours Taulignan; ☺ 8.30am-noon & 2-7pm Mon-Sat).

ENCLAVE DES PAPES & AROUND

Shaped like one of the truffles for which the area is famed, the bumpy ball of land constituting the Enclave des Papes has been part of the Vaucluse since 1791 despite being buried within the Drôme *département*. Its extrication today is a result of the refusal of French king Charles VII (r 1422–61) to sell any of his kingdom to the papacy, leaving this enclave, with a diameter of less than 20km, in the hands of the Pope from 1318 until the French Revolution.

Surrounding this anomaly is the area known as Drôme Provençale. East of the enclave is the fabulous foodie town, Nyons (the 's' is pronounced), where ancient groves grow fêted olives.

Information

Nyons tourist office (☎ 04 75 26 10 35; www.paysde nyons.com; place de la Libération; ☺ 9.30am-noon & 2.30-6pm Mon-Sat, 10am-1pm Sun Jun-Sep, 9.30am-noon & 2.30-6pm Mon-Sat Oct-May) Comprehensive information including accommodation options for the region.

Valréas tourist office (☎ 04 90 35 04 71; www .ot-valreas.info; place Aristide Briand; ☺ 9.15am-12.15pm & 2-7pm Mon-Sat Jul & Aug, 9.15am-12.15pm & 2-6pm Mon-Sat Sep-Jun)

Sights

Driving or cycling around the enclave and its environs rewards with visual and gastronomic treats.

Medieval **Valréas** (population 9500; elevation 250m), 29km north of Vaison-la-Romaine, is the primary town here. During the 19th century the town was known for its cardboard production, the history of which unfolds in the world's only **Musée du Cartonnage et de l'Imprimerie** (Cardboard & Printing Museum; ☎ 04 90 35 58 75; musee-cartonnage-imp@cg84.fr; 3 av Maréchal Foch; adult/under 12yr €3.50/free; ☺ 10am-noon & 3-6pm Mon & Wed-Sat, 3-6pm Sun Apr-Oct, 10am-noon & 2-5pm Mon & Wed-Sat, 2-5pm Sun Nov-Mar). Among Valréas' many festivals, including celebrations of its wine, lavender and medieval heritage, the most endearing is the **Nuit du Petit St-Jean**. Each year on 23 June, Valréassiens in traditional dress bear torches and parade through the old-town streets, climaxing with the crowning of a three- to five-year-old boy as the new Petit St-Jean (Little St John).

Lavender fields and treasure troves of truffles hidden underground (see the boxed text, p178) surround Valréas and the fortified villages of **Grillon**, **Visan** and **Richerenches**.

Olive groves stretch across the border to golden-hued **Nyons** (population 7000; elevation 271m). The **Institut du Monde de l'Olivier** (☎ 04 75 26 90 90; www.monde-olivier.com in French; 40 place de la Libération) runs 1½-hour olive workshops with tastings at 3pm on Thursdays between June and September and there are several mills where you can buy Nyons' AOC oil. An easy **Sentier des Oliviers** (Olive Walking Trail) takes in a 4km round-trip circuit, with explanatory panels (in French) along the way. A free brochure outlining the route is available from the tourist office, where the trail begins and ends.

Hop 3km across the enclave's western border to **Suze-la-Rousse** (population 1591) to learn about wine at France's **Université du Vin** (University of Wine; ☎ 04 75 97 21 34; www.universite-du-vin.com in French), inside the magnificent 12th- to 14th-century Château de la Suze.

Sleeping & Eating

Le Mas des Sources (☎ 04 90 41 95 90; www.mas-des -sources.com in French; quartier Lacoste, Visan; d incl breakfast €70; ℗ ☒) In a calm, countrified setting this ochre-coloured *mas* (farmhouse) has three Provençal *chambre d'hôte* rooms, a swimming pool to cool off in and, best of all, host Martine's table d'hôte (€25) with specialities including escargots in garlic butter and truffle omelettes in season. From Visan, take the direction of Vaison-la-Romaine for 200m then take the first turn left, head straight to the crossroad and follow the dirt track to the farmhouse.

Hôtel-Restaurant Colombet (☎ 04 75 26 03 66; www .hotelcolombet.com; 53 place de la Libération; d incl breakfast €66-115; menus from €22; P ✗ ⓖ) Handy for the tourist office and a hop, skip and a jump from Nyons' medieval village, this bright, light-filled, unpretentious hotel has reading rooms, 27 fresh guest rooms in pretty Provençal shades, an outdoor terrace and a decent restaurant. The cheapest rooms have a private toilet outside the room. Garaged parking costs €9.50.

Une Autre Maison (☎ 04 75 26 43 09; www.uneautre maison.com; place de la République; d €60-135; menu €35; ✎ closed early Nov-early Feb; ✗ ⓐ ⓖ) Despite its name, this exquisite place in Nyons' heart is anything but just 'another house'. Its seven artistically decorated rooms are whimsically set around an aromatic cypress- and cicada-filled garden, with an inviting swimming pool and Jacuzzi; its restaurant is also open to non-guests for dinner nightly. Wi-fi is free.

SELF-CATERING
Don't leave Nyons without biting into a *saucisson aux olives de Nyons* (Nyons olive sausage) from *boucheries* (butcher's shops) around town.

Getting There & Around
Taxi Sud Provence (☎ 04 75 46 52 25; www.transports -sudprovence.com) runs a variety of themed tours including lavender roads, vineyard roads, truffle roads and more, and can also customise trips throughout the area.

DENTELLES DE MONTMIRAIL & AROUND
The intricate limestone spires of the Dentelles de Montmirail take their name from the *dentelles* (lace) they resemble. (Some say they're named after the spindly pins on a lace-making board, which has equal visual merit.) Vineyards entwine the lower slopes, and climbers dangle perilously on threaded ropes from the southern face around Gigondas. The rocky terrain, which weaves east to Mont Ventoux (p180), offers spectacular walking and cycling.

See also the itinerary, p155, outlining a day-long cycling/driving loop from Vaison-la-Romaine.

Information
Beaumes de Venise tourist office (Maison des Dentelles; ☎ 04 90 62 94 39; www.ot-beaumesdevenise .com; place du Marché; ✎ 9am-noon & 2-7pm Mon-Sat) Has lists of estates to taste and buy local wines.

Gigondas tourist office (☎ 04 90 65 85 46; ot-gig ondas@axit.fr; place du Portail; ✎ 10am-12.30pm & 2.30-6pm Jul & Aug, 10am-noon & 2-5pm Mon-Sat Sep-Jun) Information on walking and cycling routes in the Dentelles.

Malaucène tourist office (☎ /fax 04 90 65 22 59; ot-malaucene@axit.fr; place de la Mairie; ✎ 10am-noon & 2.30-4.30pm Mon-Sat) Covers the entire Dentelles de Montmirail and Mont Ventoux area including accommodation information.

Sights
In the 14th century Pope Clement V had a residence at **Malaucène** (population 2581; elevation 350m), 10km south of Vaison-la-Romaine. His legacy is the military-style Gothic-Romanesque **Église St-Michel & St-Pierre**, constructed in 1309 on the site of an ancient temple. Coiled around its former fortress (of which only a couple of gates remain) with a beautiful plane tree–lined main street, the town is a central starting point for forays both into the Dentelles and up Mont Ventoux.

Around 6km southwest of Malaucène, little **Le Barroux** (population 574; elevation 325m) tumbles down the hillside from its medieval **Château du Barroux** (☎ 04 90 62 35 21; chateau.barroux .free.fr; adult/child €3.50/free; ✎ 10am-7pm Sat & Sun Apr & May, 2.30-7pm Jun, 10am-7pm Jul-Sep, 2-6pm Oct). **Gregorian chants** are sung at 9.30am (10am Sunday and holidays) by Benedictine monks at Le Barroux's **Abbaye Ste-Madeleine** (☎ 04 90 62 56 31; rte de Suzette), a lavender-surrounded monastery built in Romanesque style in the 1980s. Monk-made bread, cakes and the like are sold in the monastery shop. Hats, miniskirts, bare shoulders and mobile phones are forbidden in the church. With advance reservation, free guided visits are possible at the llama farm, **Ferme Expérimentale d'Élevage de Lamas** (☎ 04 90 65 25 46; rte du Lac du Paty), 1km along the D19 from Le Barroux towards Bédoin.

The sheltered position of **Beaumes de Venise** (population 2070; elevation 126m), 10km southwest of Le Barroux at the crossroads of the D21 and the D90, spares it from the mighty mistral winds. Beaumes' olive oil is sampled and sold at the **Moulin à Huile de la Balméenne** (☎ 04 90 62 93 77; av Jules Ferry; ✎ 8am-noon & 2-6.30pm Mon-Sat, 2-6.30pm Sun Apr-Aug, 8am-noon & 2-6.30pm Mon-Sat Sep-Mar), in business since 1856. But the

AVIGNON AREA

BLACK DIAMONDS

Provence's cloak-and-dagger truffle trade – operated out of a car boot, with payment exclusively by cold, hard cash – is a real black business.

Little known Richerenches, a deceptively wealthy village shielded within the thick walls of a 12th- to 13th-century Templar fortress, is the congruous setting for Provence's leading wholesale market for the far-from-appetising-looking fungus. Once a year villagers celebrate a truffle Mass in the village church, during which parishioners offer up truffles instead of cash donations. The Mass falls on the closest Sunday to 17 January, the feast day of Antoine, the patron saint of truffle harvesters. Contact Richerenches' **Point Tourisme** (☎ 04 90 28 05 34; www.richerenches.fr in French; rue du Campanile; ☯ 2-6.30pm Mon, 9am-12.30pm & 2-6.30pm Tue-Fri, 9.30am-12.30pm Sat) for details.

Crisp, cold Saturday mornings during the truffle season (November to March) see av de la Rebasse – Richerenches' main street – resound with the furtive whisperings of local *rabassaïres* (truffle hunters) selling their weekly harvest to big-time dealers from Paris, Germany, Italy or beyond. Just a handful of dealers attend the weekly market, inspecting, weighing and invariably buying kilos of these black diamonds. Their *courtiers* (brokers) mingle with the truffle hunters to scout out the best truffles and keep tabs on deals being cut by rivals.

Individuals generally have their own dealer whom they telephone to place an order. In the Carpentras area, *trufficulteur* **Jean-François Tourrette** (☎ 06 18 11 32 03, 04 90 66 03 71; jftourrette@wanadoo .fr; Grand rue, Venasque; truffle hunting per person €25; ☯ by appointment) and his family has been in the truffle-hunting business for generations, and Jean-François is now creating a small 'truffle society' dealing with consulting, producing and other truffle-related information, opening up this elusive truffle culture for the public. His truffle-hunting tours run when a minimum of eight people have booked.

Dominique and Eric Jaumard (☎ 04 90 66 82 21; www.truffes-ventoux.com; La Quinsonne), 7km southwest of Carpentras in Monteux, have hunted, harvested and sold truffles from their land for a couple of decades. Between November and March you can go truffle-hunting with them and their dogs (prices arranged on inquiry), or discover the taste of fresh truffles during a truffle-tasting workshop. Year-round they sell (less tasty) frozen or canned truffles as well as truffle juice, truffle vinegar, acacia and truffle honey, truffle olive oil and more.

Truffles can cost upwards of €500 to €1000 per kilogram, making them almost literally worth their weight in gold. The reason for the fluctuating prices, and the mystique surrounding truffles is their inability to be controlled by man alone. *Trufficulteur* Jean-François Tourrette explains: 'The truffles' price depends on the supply and the demand. The demand is always present but the supply, the annual production, depends on the weather. Critical points include spring's water excess, summer's dryness, autumn's water excess, winter's frost etc... According to these elements, as a professional *trufficulteur* I can evaluate if it will be a good, medium or bad season. So it is nature that fixes the general price, followed by the truffles' individual qualities.'

Many a truffle traded at Richerenches market ends up in a can at the world's largest truffle cannery, **Plantin** (☎ 04 90 46 41 44; www.plantin.com; rte de Nyons; ☯ 8am-noon & 1.30-5.30pm Mon-Fri), 7km northeast of Vaison-la-Romaine in Puymeras, where the fungus has been conserved in jars for year-round consumption since 1930. The cannery, which handles between 20 and 30 tonnes of truffles a year, is just west of Puymeras village on the D46/D938 junction.

In season, fresh truffles can also be picked up at general markets in Vaison-la-Romaine (Tuesday), Valréas (Wednesday), Nyons (Thursday) and Carpentras (Friday); and at the truffle-specialist shop in St-Rémy de Provence (p191), inspired by France's top truffle chef, Clément Bruno (see the boxed text, p360). Many restaurants throughout Provence specialise in truffles.

The history of truffles is unearthed in the **Maison de la Truffe et du Tricastin** (House of Truffles; ☎ 04 75 96 61 29; www.maisondelatruffe.com in French; adult/child €3.50/2; ☯ 3-7pm Mon, 9am-noon & 3-7pm Tue-Sat, 10am-noon & 3-7pm Sun Jun-Sep, 3-7pm Mon, 9am-noon & 2-6pm Tue-Sat Oct, Nov & Mar-May, 9am-noon & 2-6pm Tue-Sat, 10am-noon & 2-6pm Sun Dec-Feb), 14km west of Richerenches in St-Paul Troix Châteaux. The village celebrates a **Fête de la Truffe** on the second Sunday in February.

A comprehensive online information source for the region's truffles is www.truffle-and-truffe .com.

village is best known for its **Or Blanc** (white gold) – sweet Muscat wines best drunk young, chilled to 6°C or 8°C, which are the perfect partner for juicy Cavaillon melons (see the boxed text, p223). Shops stock it in town.

Nestled 7.5km southwest of Beaumes de Venise in Sarrians, reached by the D21 then the D52, the ecological farm **Domaine de l'Oiselet** (☎ 04 90 65 57 57; www.oiselet.com; Les Garrigues; programmes incl tastings adult/child from €10/5) regularly throws its gates open for visitors to experience farm life such as cherry-picking in May, and apricot-jam-making in July. Call to find out what's on when. You can also stock up on the farm's red wine made from its century-old vines.

Wines can also be tasted in **Gigondas** (population 648; elevation 282m), 12km northeast of Sarrians. Cellars cram the central square, place du Portail, from where rue du Corps de Garde climbs to Gigondas' ruined chateau, campanile, church and cemetery. Contemporary sculptures en route form **Le Cheminement de Sculptures**; ask for a map of the sculpture trail at the Gigondas tourist office.

Sleeping & Eating

Delicious dining is available at most places listed here.

CHAMBRES D'HÔTES

Many *mas* open their doors to *chambre d'hôte* guests; several are on the northbound D23 to Séguret.

Ferme Le Degoutaud (☎ 04 90 62 99 29; le.degoutaud@wanadoo.fr; rte de Malaucène; d incl breakfast €58-63; P ☒ ﴾) At this authentic working farm dating from the 16th century, you can cosy up in its three rooms (one of which is wheelchair accessible), or soak up the views from the panoramic pool before treating yourself to the tempting table d'hôte (€21). If you're looking to spend longer exploring the area, ask about the farm's self-catering cottages. Ferme Le Degoutaud is 5km north of Malaucène along the D90 to Suzette.

Les Abeilles (The Bees; ☎ 04 90 12 38 96; www.abeilles-sablet.com; 4 rue de Vaison, Sablet; d incl breakfast €60-90; midweek lunch menu €28, menus €38-50; ☒ lunch Tue-Sun, dinner Tue-Sat; P ☒ ﴾) The much-buzzed-about culinary whizzes Johannes and Marlies Sailer have tucked two sweet *chambre d'hôte* rooms above their wonderful restaurant mainly so that diners can indulge in duck breast roasted in honey and lavender, warm cherry soup, and

wonderful local wines without having to rush off. From October to April, one-day cooking courses (€110) include visiting local wine makers, wild herb gardens, markets and more.

Château Juvenal (☎ 04 90 62 31 76; www.chateau-en-provence.com; chemin du Long Serre, St-Hippolyte le Graveyron; d incl breakfast €95-160; P ☒ ﴾) Sprawled within tree-filled gardens amid an ecological wine- and olive-growing estate 5km west of Beaumes de Venise, just four meticulously decorated rooms make up this manor-house–style *chambre d'hôte*. Play billiards, splash in the swimming pool or curl up by the open fire. A table d'hôte (€28) is served on Tuesdays and Thursdays (reserve 48 hours ahead).

HOTELS

Hôtel Montmirail (☎ 04 90 65 84 01; www.hotelmontmirail.com; s/d from €56/77; ☒ mid-May–Oct; P ☒) A 19th-century mansion in a remote spot midway between Gigondas and neighbouring Vacqueyras, the Hôtel Montmirail has a host of thoughtful little touches like dressing gowns

---

A PROVENÇAL CHRISTMAS

Provençal Christmas traditions endure as they have for centuries in the little golden-hued village of **Séguret** (population 892; elevation 250m).

Poised on a rocky outcrop 9km south of Vaison-la-Romaine like a star on a Christmas tree, the village opens its festivities at dusk on Christmas Eve with **Cacho Fio**. During this Provençal ceremony a log – usually cut from a pear, olive or cherry tree – is placed in the hearth, doused with fortified wine, blessed three times by the youngest and oldest family members, and then set alight. The fire must burn until the three kings arrive on 6 January.

Although many still celebrate Cacho Fio at home, it is only in Séguret that villagers gather to bless and burn a log together. This takes place in the Salle Delage, adjoining Chapelle Ste-Thecle on rue du Four. Later, locals wend their way up to Église St-Denis where, during Li Bergié, the Christmas nativity scene is brought to life with real-life shepherds, lambs and a baby in a manger. This *crèche vivant* (living crèche) is followed by midnight Mass in Provençal.

After Mass, families rush home for Caleno vo Careno (see p52).

---

as well as English and German TV channels. Full- and half-board options are available at the on-site restaurant, which spills onto a leafy outdoor terrace.

Le Mas de Magali (☎ 04 90 36 39 91; www.masdemagali .com; quartier Chante Coucou, Le Crestet; half-board per person €68-78; P ❂ ❒) Hidden amid flowers, oak trees and twittering birds, this haven of a hotel-restaurant has magical mountain views. Half-board options provide a fine excuse to dine on the seasonal Provençal cuisine at Magali's restaurant (*menu* €27; open for dinner Thursday to Tuesday), and you can borrow a mountain bike to explore the stunning countryside. Follow the signs from the bottom of the D76 leading up to Le Crestet village

Domaine de Cabasse (☎ 04 90 46 91 12; www .domaine-de-cabasse.fr; rte de Sablet, Séguret; d €98-135; ❂ mid-Mar–Oct; P ❒) Wine connoisseurs will appreciate this wine-producing estate on the plains, 800m south of Séguret village. In addition to 12 sunlit rooms, a pool and tennis courts, there are wines galore to taste from the barrel-lined cellar; best accompanied by taking up the option of half-board, with meals prepared from vegetables grown on the grounds.

HOSTEL & CAMPING

Gîte d'Étape des Dentelles de Gigondas (☎ 04 90 65 80 85; www.gite-dentelles.com in French; dm €12.50, d or tr per person without bathroom €14.50, sheets €3; ❂ Mar-Dec) Next to Gigondas' fire station, this clean, comfortable *gîte* (hostel) has two 13-bed dorms and a handful of two- and three-bed rooms. Join in on a hike or mountain-bike ride (from €9) or a climbing expedition (from €25).

There are several camp sites just north of Bédoin along the D974 east of Le Barroux.

MONT VENTOUX

Visible from as far away as Avignon, at 1909m, Mont Ventoux lords over northern Provence. From its summit, accessible by road between

---

A PICTURE-PERFECT DETOUR

Charge your camera batteries before driving or biking 9km along the wiggly D90 from Malaucène to Suzette to take in the twin-set view of Mont Ventoux (east) and the Dentelles de Montmirail unfolding from the Col de la Chaîne (472m), 4km west, and the Col de Suzette (392m), a further 3km.

May and October, vistas extend to the southern Alps and – on a clear day – as far as the Pyrenees.

Unique species including the snake eagle and an assortment of spiders and butterflies are only found on this isolated peak that marks the divide between northern and southern France's flora and fauna. Shipbuilding in the 17th century felled much of its forests, but since the 1860s reforested tree types such as cedar create a crackling autumnal kaleidoscope of red, yellow and golden brown.

As you ascend the relentless gradients (which regularly feature in the Tour de France), temperatures can plummet by 20°C, and there's twice as much precipitation as on the plains below. The mistral blows here 130 days a year on average, with winds recorded of up to 300km/h. Bring warm clothes and rain gear, even in summer. Snow blankets the areas above 1300m from December to April; in summer it appears snowcapped because of the *lauzes* (broken white stones) covering the top.

Since 1990 the mountain and its environs have been protected by Unesco's Réserve de Biosphère du Mont Ventoux (Mont Ventoux Biosphere Reserve).

Near the southwestern end of the Mont Ventoux massif is the agricultural village of **Bédoin** (population 2657; elevation 295m) and, 4km further east along rte du Mont Ventoux (D974), neighbouring **Ste-Colombe**. Road signs here tell you if the *col* (mountain pass) over the summit is closed.

At the eastern end of the Mont Ventoux massif, the sweet stone village of **Sault** (population 1190; elevation 800m) has sweeping summertime views over the carpet of purple lavender laid out below. In the village, pop into **André Boyer** (☎ 04 90 64 00 23; place de l'Europe) to stock up on lavender honey and almond nougat made by the family since 1887, and to arrange a factory visit. Sault's tourist office has a list of other **artisan industries** throughout the area, which often take visitors behind the scenes.

Information
INTERNET RESOURCES
Destination Ventoux (www.destination-ventoux.com) Comprehensive information on the region.
MAB France (www.mab-france.org) Follow the links to the Réserve de Biosphère du Mont Ventoux.
Mont Ventoux (www.lemontventoux.net in French) Walking and cycling information.

TOURIST INFORMATION

Bédoin tourist office (☎ 04 90 65 63 95; www.bed oin.org; place du Marché; ☻ 9am-12.30pm & 2-6pm Mon-Sat, 9.30am-12.30pm Sun mid-Jun–Aug, 9am-12.30pm & 2-6pm Mon, Tue, Thu & Fri, 9am-12.30pm & 2-5pm Wed, 9.30am-12.30pm Sat rest of year) The meeting point for summertime walks (€6) and children's workshops (€5) run by the Office National des Forêts (ONF; National Forests Office) for the responsible appreciation of the surrounding cedar forest.

Sault tourist office (☎ 04 90 64 01 21; www.saulten provence.com; av de la Promenade; ☻ 9am-12.30pm & 2-6.30pm Mon-Sat, 9.30am-12.30pm Sun Jul-Aug, 9am-noon & 2-6pm Mon-Sat, 9.30am-12.30pm Sun May & Jun, 9am-noon & 2-4pm or 5pm Mon-Sat Sep-Apr) Also a good resource for the Gorges de la Nesque (p188).

Activities

CYCLING

In summer cyclists labour up the sun-baked slopes of Mont Ventoux. Tourist offices distribute *Massif du Mont Ventoux: 9 Itinéraires VTT*, a free booklet detailing nine mountain-bike itineraries ranging from an easy 3.9km (one hour) to a gruelling 56.7km (seven to eight hours) tour of Mont Ventoux.

In Sault, **Albion Cycles** (☎ 04 90 64 09 32; christophe .achard@cegetel.net; rte de St-Trinit; ☻ 9am-12.30pm & 2-7pm Mon-Sat, 9am-12.30pm Sun Jul & Aug, 9am-noon & 3-6.30pm Tue-Sat Sep-Jun) rents bikes for €7.50 to €18 per day, and can arrange to pick them up and drop them off within a 30km radius. **Bédoin Location** (☎ 04 90 65 94 53; www.bedoin-location .com; chemin de la Ferraille) just near Bédoin's tourist office rents road and mountain bikes starting from €14 per half-day (if you've worked up an appetite by the time you get back, it also runs an on-site pizzeria). Both can suggest cycling routes.

FLYING

View the region's most legendary mountain from on high with **Air Ventoux** (☎ 04 90 66 35 81; monsite.wanadoo.fr/airventoux in French). Half-hour flights (adult/child under 12 years €72/36; minimum two passengers) take off from airstrips in Montfavet (near Avignon) and Pernes-les-Fontaines (near Carpentras).

QUADING

Ventoux Quad (☎ 06 19 06 05 92; www.ventoux-quad .com in French; rte de la Madeleine; 1hr/half day/full day €50/90/150) is a quad-hire place in Crillon-le-Brave that organises one-day and weekend quading adventures around Ventoux.

SKIING

December to March, locals ski Ventoux's slopes. **Chalet Reynard** (☎ 04 90 61 84 55; www.chalet-reynard.com in French), at the intersection of the D974 and the eastbound D164 to Sault, is a small ski station (1440m) on the southern slopes. Two *téléskis* (drag lifts) serve two blue runs. A full-day pass costs around €15 and you can hire skis, boots and poles for the same price again per half-/full day. Cross-country skiing is also popular and there is a luge nonskiers can bomb down.

Station de Mont Serein (1400m; www.stationdu montserein.com), 5km west of the summit on the colder northern side, is the main ski station with 12km of downhill pistes served by eight drag lifts. Skis, ski schools, piste maps and ski passes (per afternoon/day €12/15.10) are available from the **Chalet d'Accueil** (☎ 04 90 63 42 02; adpmv@infonie.fr), in the resort centre. **Chalet Liotard** is a midstation, 100m further uphill.

TROUT FISHING

Maurice Paris (☎ 04 75 28 07 66; ☻ Sat & Sun Apr-Jun & Sep, daily Jul & Aug) arranges family-friendly trout fishing including rod rental and bait (by reservation only). Prices depend on the weight of the fish caught.

WALKING

Running from the River Ardèche west, the GR4 crosses the Dentelles de Montmirail before scaling the northern face of Mont Ventoux, where it meets the GR9. Both trails traverse the ridge before the GR4 branches eastwards to the Gorges du Verdon (p234). Continuing on the GR9 takes you across the Monts du Vaucluse and Luberon Range. See p88 for more details.

Bédoin, Sault and Malaucène tourist offices have information on exploring Mont Ventoux on foot, including night-time expeditions up the mountain in July and August (€14; over 15 years only) to watch the celestial sunrise.

The website www.lemontventoux.net (in French) details three walks and 20 cycling routes around Ventoux.

Find out about flora and fauna at Sault's **Centre de Découverte de la Nature** (Nature Discovery Centre; ☎ 04 90 64 13 96; av de l'Oratoire; adult/under 8yr €3/free; ☻ 10am-noon & 2-6pm Mon-Fri Sep-Jun, 10am-noon & 3-7pm Tue-Sun Jul & Aug).

Sleeping & Eating

Places listed under the Dentelles de Montmirail (p179) are also handy for exploring Mont Ventoux.

La Bastide des Bourguets (☎ 04 90 64 11 90; www .bastidedesbourguets.com in French; Les Bourguets, Sault; d incl breakfast €55, gîte per weekend from €148; P) Four floral French-washed rooms (poppy, olive, sunflower and lavender), and a two-bedroom *gîte* are at home amid Sault's lavender fields in this beautiful 19th-century *bastide*, which also serves up a laden table d'hôte (€20) on Monday, Wednesday and Friday by reservation.

La Maison (☎ 04 90 65 15 50; Beaumont du Ventoux; d €60-70; ☼ Mar-Oct; P ✗) This stone house with blue shutters is no longer a restaurant – Michèle Laurelut now concentrates her talents solely on running this charming abode as an intimate *chambre d'hôte*, so the only way to taste her exceptional cooking is at breakfast (€10) with a feast in the courtyard beneath the linden trees.

Hostellerie du Val de Sault (☎ 04 90 64 01 41; www.valdesault.com; rte de St-Trinit; half-board per person from €114; ☼ Mar-early Nov; P ⛱ ♨) 'Gourmet stays' is the elaborate but accurate description of the half-board options at this haven of peace, situated 2km north of Sault along the D950 to Banon. Dine on *menus* (from €37 to €49) such as 'lavender flowers' and 'homage to truffles', then luxuriate in the bubbling Jacuzzi while looking out over Mont Ventoux or swim in the heated pool. It's worth dropping by the restaurant (which is open for lunch and dinner) even if you're not ensconced in one of the whisper-quiet rooms or suites.

Getting There & Away

Mont Ventoux is reached by car from Sault via the D164 or – in summer – from Malaucène or St-Estève via the switchback D974, often snow-blocked until April. For information on bus services in the area, see p185.

CARPENTRAS
pop 27,249 / elev 102m

If you can, plan to be in Carpentras on a Friday morning, when the streets spill over with more than 350 stalls laden with breads, honeys, cheeses, olives, nuts, fruits (especially the area's juicy blood-red strawberries), brittle almond nougat, *nougalettes* (like the nougat but finely crushed), and a rainbow of *berlingots* (Carpentras' striped, pillow-shaped hard-boiled sweets). During winter, there's also a truffle market.

Carpentras' mouthwatering markets aside, this charming agricultural town equidistant from Avignon 25km to the southwest and Orange to the northwest has a handful of architectural treats too. A Greek trading centre and later a Gallo-Roman city, Carpentras became the capital of the papal territory of the Comtat Venaissin in 1320. Pope Clement V was a frequent visitor in the 14th century, during which time Jews who had been expelled from French crown territory took refuge in the Comtat Venaissin under papal protection. The 14th-century synagogue is the oldest still in use in France.

Orientation

A heart-shaped ring of boulevards replaced the city's fortifications in the 19th century; the largely pedestrianised old city sits inside.

If you're arriving by bus, walk northeastwards to place Aristide Briand, a major intersection at the boulevards' southernmost point, where you'll find the tourist office. From here, the pedestrian-only rue de la République, which heads due north, takes you to the 17th-century Palais de Justice and the cathedral. The town hall is a few blocks northeast of the cathedral.

PLATEAU D'ALBION

Until around a decade ago, this uninhabitable moonscape was shrouded in security as the site of France's land-based nuclear missiles, stationed here since 1965. In 1996 President Jacques Chirac ordered the missiles to be deactivated and the military site to be manned by the French Foreign Legion. The last nuclear missile and concrete silo was dismantled in 1998.

France's former biggest secret is riddled with natural potholes and caverns. The plain can be uncovered – above- or belowground – with the **Association Spéléologique du Plateau d'Albion** (☎ 04 90 76 08 33; www.aspanet.net in French; 2 rue de l'Église), a spelunking club in the plain's only real village, **St-Christol d'Albion** (population 555; elevation 850m), 11km south of Sault. Spelunking starts at €60 per day; the association also arranges hikes and mountain-biking expeditions. Basic accommodation (€10/5/25 for dorm bed/breakfast/half-board plus €3.50 for sheets) is available in the club's *refuge* (hut).

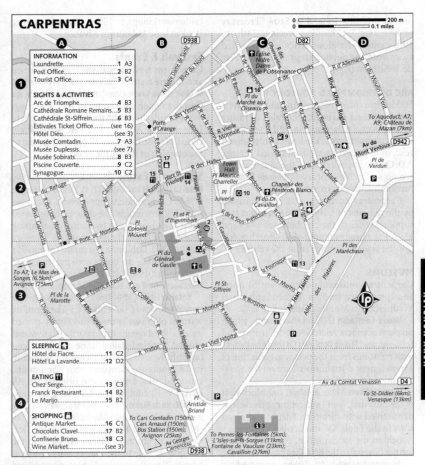

CARPENTRAS

INFORMATION
Laundrette.....................1 A3
Post Office.....................2 B2
Tourist Office..................3 C4

SIGHTS & ACTIVITIES
Arc de Triomphe................4 B3
Cathédrale Romane Remains.....5 B3
Cathédrale St-Siffrein.........6 B3
Estivales Ticket Office......(see 16)
Hôtel Dieu...................(see 3)
Musée Comtadin................7 A3
Musée Duplessis.............(see 7)
Musée Sobirats................8 B3
Piscine Couverte..............9 C2
Synagogue....................10 C2

SLEEPING
Hôtel du Fiacre...............11 C2
Hôtel La Lavande..............12 D2

EATING
Chez Serge....................13 C3
Franck Restaurant.............14 B2
Le Marijo.....................15 B2

SHOPPING
Antique Market................16 C1
Chocolats Clavel..............17 B2
Confiserie Bruno..............18 C3
Wine Market.................(see 3)

AVIGNON AREA

Information

There are commercial banks on central place Aristide Briand and blvd Albin Durand.

Laundrette (118 rue Porte de Monteux; ⌚7am-8pm)

Post office (65 rue d'Inguimbert)

Tourist office (☎ 04 90 63 00 78; www.tourisme .fr/carpentras; place Aristide Briand; ⌚9am-7pm Mon-Sat, 9.30am-1pm Sun Jul & Aug, 9.30am-12.30pm & 2-6pm Mon-Sat Sep-Jun) Sells regional maps and guides, and hands out a free English-language *Discovery Circuit* brochure, corresponding with a walking circuit of signposts marked with *berlingots*.

Sights & Activities

SYNAGOGUE

The centre of Jewish life for centuries and still a place of worship today, Carpentras' moving

synagogue (☎ 04 90 63 39 97; place Juiverie; admission free; ⌚10am-noon & 3-5pm Mon-Thu, 10am-noon & 3-4pm Fri) was founded here in 1367. Rebuilt between 1741 and 1743 and restored in 1929 and 1954, on the 1st-floor wood-panelled sanctuary you can see 18th-century liturgical objects; below, there's an oven used until 1904 to bake *matzo*, Passover's unleavened bread. It's inconspicuously situated opposite the town hall; look for the stone plaque inscribed with Hebrew letters.

CATHÉDRALE ST-SIFFREIN

Église St-Siffrein, once Carpentras' **cathedral** (⌚10am-noon & 2-6pm Tue-Sat), was built in the Méridional (southern French) Gothic style between 1405 and 1519 and is topped by a distinctive contemporary bell tower. Sadly, due to theft, its **Trésor d'Art Sacré** (Treasury of Religious Art) holding precious 14th- to 19th-century religious relics is now salted away from the public except during the Fête de St-Siffrein (right).

ARC DE TRIOMPHE & AQUEDUCT

Hidden in a corner off rue d'Inguimbert – next to the cathedral and behind the Palais de Justice in an episcopal palace built in 1801 – what's left of this **triumphal arch** is the town's only Roman relic, built under Augustus in the 1st century AD. On the opposite side of the square are the remains of a 7th-century **Cathédrale Romane**, predominantly destroyed in 1399.

Carpentras' northern outskirts are crossed by the remains of a 10km-long **aqueduct** that supplied water to the city between 1745 and 1893. For a heady glimpse of all 48 arches, follow the signs to Orange from the centre.

MUSEUMS

Carpentras' museums open 10am to noon and 2pm to 4pm (to 6pm April to September) Wednesday to Monday. Admission is €2.

Musée Comtadin (243 blvd Albin Durand), which displays artefacts related to local history and folklore, and **Musée Duplessis** (243 blvd Albin Durand), with paintings from the personal collection of Monseigneur d'Inguimbert, are on the western side of the old city.

Musée Sobirats (112 rue du Collège), one block west of the cathedral, is an 18th-century private residence filled with furniture, faïence and *objets d'art* in the Louis XV and Louis XVI styles.

Behind the tourist office, the 18th-century former hospital in the **Hôtel Dieu** (place Aristide Briand; ☽ by arrangement with tourist office) has an incredibly preserved **pharmacy** and a **chapel**. Guided tours in English run at 3.30pm on Wednesday between June and late September (€4).

SWIMMING

Art Deco fans can dive into the 1930-built, geometric **piscine couverte** (covered swimming pool; ☎ 04 90 60 92 03; rue du Mont de Piété; adult/3–15yr €2/1.50; ☽ in-season hr vary, closed end Jun–mid-Sep). Built by the Caisse d'Épargne in 1930 it has a water temperature of 20°C; but, unfathomably, it's closed in summer.

Tours

The tourist office organises fabulous tours costing between €3 and €10, including city tours, nature treks, *berlingot* factory tours (free), wine-

tasting workshops, truffle hunts and farm trips. Book at least 24 hours in advance.

Festivals & Events

Carpentras hosts a two-week music, dance and theatre festival, **Estivales** (☎ ticket office 04 90 60 46 00; estivales@ville-carpentras.fr; 4 place aux Marché aux Oiseaux), in open-air venues in July. The town has a wonderful **Jewish music festival** from late July to early August. The **Fête de St-Siffrein** (Feast of St Siffrein) on 27 November marks the opening of the truffle season.

Sleeping & Eating

Hôtel La Lavande (☎ 04 90 63 13 49; 282 blvd Alfred Rogier; d €30-40) La Lavande has nine cheerful, cheap-as-*frites*, frill-free rooms (the cheapest have shared bathrooms), accessed by staircases running between the floors at random angles. There's a bustling, old-fashioned restaurant (*menus* €11 to €15) dishing up home cooking and good deals on half-board. It's on the left just past the intersection of rue Porte de Mazan.

Hôtel du Fiacre (☎ 04 90 63 03 15; www.hotel-du-fiacre.com; 153 rue Vigne; d €62-90; P ✗) The genuine warmth of the welcome at this family-owned hotel is like staying with favourite relatives. Set around a central walled stone courtyard in a beautifully restored 18th-century mansion, its 18 rooms are furnished with floral quilts, canopied beds, antiques and original art. All have TVs (including BBC). Parking costs €5.

Château de Mazan (☎ 04 90 69 62 61; www.chateaude mazan.fr; place Napoléon; d €95-270, ste €320-400; ☽ Mar-Dec; P ✗ ☐ ☎ ⚘) This magnificent castle 7km east of Carpentras in Mazan belonged to the Marquis de Sade in the 18th century. Today it houses 30 regal rooms and suites in an orchard of colours. Gastronomic bliss is dished up at the refined restaurant, l'Ingénue (*menus* €35 to €75; closed Tuesday in summer and Monday and Tuesday in winter). Chef Iris Enrich also whets young appetites with a gourmet children's *menu* (€27.50). Parking is free.

Le Mas des Songes (☎ 04 90 65 49 20; www.mas dessonges.com in French; 1631 impasse du Perrusier; d €140-180; P ✗ ☐ ☎ ⚘) This stunning five-room *maison d'hôte* has contemporary flair – lots of light and air – and breathtaking views from the pool. Prices include afternoon tea. Breakfast is an extra €6 and there are regular *tables d'hôtes* (€30 to €40). Find it 6.5km west of Carpentras in the truffle land of Monteux.

Le Marijo (☎ 04 90 60 42 65; 73 rue Raspail; mains €14.50-16.50; ☽ lunch & dinner Mon-Fri, dinner Sat, lunch Sun)

Behind green timber-framed windows, this local favourite has rich regional fare like goats cheese marinated for 15 days in herbs and olive oil. Proof just how sweet a tooth Carpentras has, the list of desserts, like nougat and honey ice cream, runs longer than the choice of mains.

Chez Serge (☎ 04 90 63 21 24; 90 rue Cottier; lunch menus from €15, dinner menus from €27.50; ☯ lunch & dinner Mon-Sat; ☖) Paris meets Provence by way of Armenia at this legendary bistro where Serge serves up culinary creations like cider-braised salmon and honey-glazed duck, and pizzas (also available to take away) piled high with wood-oven-grilled garlic, olive oil and herbs. There's a well-priced children's *menu* (€6.60), as well as a truffle *menu* (€35).

Franck Restaurant (☎ 04 90 60 75 00; 30 place de l'Horloge; lunch menus from €20, dinner menus from €26.50; ☯ lunch & dinner Thu-Mon) Flanked by a sophisticated, low-lit bar area, this newly opened burgundy-and-stone dining room opening to an elegant white-tableclothed terrace is frequented by those in the know for Franck's seasonal gastronomic cooking, including a heavenly truffle *menu* (€92).

Shopping
MARKETS
Rue d'Inguimbert, most of av Jean Jaurès and often the streets splitting off are the site of Carpentras' fantastic Friday-morning food market (the town gets *very* quiet in the long lunch hours following).

In winter, Carpentras' 'black diamonds' (see the boxed text, p178) are traded at the **truffle market** (place Aristide Briand; ☯ 9-10am Fri, late Nov-Mar), attended by brokers, merchants and wholesalers from all over France. In July and August, drop by the wine market outside the tourist office.

Treasures are jumbled among the trash at the **antique market** (place du Marché aux Oiseaux; ☯ 8am-noon Fri Apr-Oct).

SWEET SHOPS
A Hansel and Gretel fantasy, **Chocolats Clavel** (☎ 04 90 63 07 59; 30 Porte d'Orange; ☯ Mon-Sat) has spectacularly sculptured sweets.

Berlingots have been available from **Confiserie Bruno** (☎ 04 90 63 04 99; www.confiseriebono.fr; 280 allée Jean Jaurès) since 1925.

Getting There & Away
The train station is served by goods trains only, so buses operated by Cars Comtadins and Cars Arnaud provide Carpentras' only intercity

public transport. The **bus station** (place Terradou) is 150m southwest of place Aristide Briand.

Schedules are available from **Cars Comtadins** (☎ 04 90 67 20 25; 192 av Clemenceau) across the square and from **Cars Arnaud** (☎ 04 90 63 01 82; 8 av Victor Hugo).

There are hourly services to Avignon (€4.20, 45 minutes) and infrequent runs to Vaison-la-Romaine (€4.30, 45 minutes) via Malaucène and Bédoin (€3.40, 40 minutes) at the southwestern foot of Mont Ventoux, Cavaillon (€5.10, 45 minutes) and L'Isle-sur-Sorgue (€3.70, 20 minutes), 7km west of Fontaine de Vaucluse.

AROUND CARPENTRAS
Water, water everywhere. See the itinerary, p156, for a day trip through this water-filled wonderland.

Pernes-les-Fontaines
pop 10,309
A former capital of the Comtat Venaissin, Pernes-les-Fontaines, 5km south of Carpentras, is named for the 40 fountains that spring from its stone walls and squares. Upon the discovery of the Font de Bouvery source in the 18th century, the mayor furnished the town with monumental fountains like the grandiose, moss-covered **Fontaine du Cormoran**, **Fontaine Reboul** and **Fontaine du Gigot**. Pick up a free fountain map at the **tourist office** (☎ 04 90 61 31 04; www.ville-pernes-les-fontaines.fr in French; place Gabriel Moutte; ☯ 9am-12.30pm & 2.30-7pm Mon-Fri, 9am-12.30pm & 2.30-6pm Sat Jul & Aug, 9am-noon & 2-6pm Mon-Sat May, Jun, Sep & Oct, 9am-noon & 2-5pm Mon-Sat Nov-Apr).

Le Mas des Abricotiers (☎ 04 90 66 19 16; www.bleu-provence.com; 193 chemin des Terres Mortes, St-Didier; d incl breakfast €63-98; ☯ call for winter opening information; P ☒ ☒ ☒), an 18th-century 'apricot farm' 5km east of Pernes-les-Fontaines, creates the prettiest of Provençal scenes with its warm apricot-coloured walls, cooling wooden shutters and flowerbeds framing the pool. There's a two-night minimum stay. An apartment is also available starting from €450 per week for two people.

At **Mas La Bonoty** (☎ 04 90 61 61 09; www.bonoty.com; chemin de la Bonoty, Pernes-les-Fontaines; d incl breakfast €72-90; ☯ closed Jan-mid-Feb; P ☒ ☒) rooms named after the flowers that fill the gardens are light-filled and lovely. This farmhouse hotel also has an appealing Provençal restaurant (*menus* €22 to €55). In cooler weather, there's a stone-and-wood dining room; in summer, dine under the cool, fragrant pine trees.

Scoot around Pernes-les-Fontaines on a bike rented from **Vélo & Oxygène** (☎ 04 90 61 37 37; 284 rue Émile Zola).

L'Isle-sur-la-Sorgue
pop 18,000

Creaking wooden water wheels trailing strands of moss churn the waterways encircling L'Isle-sur-la-Sorgue's ancient old town.

L'Isle, 11km south of Pernes-les-Fontaines, dates from the 12th century, when fishermen, who harpooned their catch from flat-bottomed gondola-like boats, built huts on stilts above what was then a marsh. By the 18th century canals ploughed by giant wheels (17 of which still turn today) powered thriving paper mills and silk factories. Since the latter half of last century, bustling antiques villages have seen a further resurgence of the town's prosperity.

Scattered around the edges of the canals, car parks allow the narrow laneways meandering through the historic centre to remain largely vehicle-free.

INFORMATION

Maghreb Taxi Phone (☎ 04 90 20 03 28; 3 rue Danton; per hr €3; ☼ 9am-1pm & 3-10pm Mon-Sat, 9am-10pm Sun) Internet access.

Tourist office (☎ 04 90 38 04 78; www.oti-delasorgue .fr; place de la Liberté; ☼ 9am-12.30pm or 1pm & 2pm or 2.30-6pm or 6.30pm Mon-Sat, 9.30am-12.30pm or 1pm Sun) In the centre of the old town.

SIGHTS

Graced by a lunar calendar on its façade, the **Collégiale Notre Dame des Anges** (Our Lady of Angels; place de la Liberté; ☼ 10am-noon & 3-6pm daily Jul-Sep, 10am-noon & 3-5pm Tue-Sat Oct-Jun) has a spectacular baroque interior with the heads of no less than 222 angels, and a magnificent 1648-built organ (the real one is on the left as you face the altar; opposite, a faux organ is purely for symmetry).

Museums include the quaint **Musée du Jouet & de la Poupée Ancienne** (Ancient Toy & Doll Museum; ☎ 04 90 20 97 31; 26 rue Carnot; adult/child €3.50/1.50; ☼ 10am-6.30pm Tue-Sun, call for winter opening times); and one dedicated to native poet René Char (1907–88), housed in the 18th-century private mansion, the **Hôtel Donadeï de Campredon** (☎ 04 90 38 17 41; 20 rue du Docteur Tallet; adult/child €6/5; ☼ 10am-12.30pm & 2-5.30pm Tue-Sun), which also mounts temporary exhibitions.

The tourist office has details about following in the footsteps of the town's **former Jewish community**, which lived here under papal protection from the 14th century until the French Revolution.

About 1km west of the old town towards Fontaine de Vaucluse, the River Sorgue splits in two at the **partage des eaux** (parting of the waters) – a serene spot for watching wildlife like kingfishers, beavers and herons. There are cafés with views of the water.

ANTIQUES & ART

Disused factories along the town's southern quays contain 10 **antiques villages** (☼ 10am-6pm Sat-Mon), which between them house hundreds of antiques dealers and traders. Bargains are a better bet at the two giant four-day **antiques fairs** held in August and over Easter.

Artists galleries – nine to date – proliferate throughout the old town.

SLEEPING & EATING

Moulin Font de Capelle (☎ 04 90 02 39 01; www.moulin decapelle.com; place St-Roch, Le Thor; d incl breakfast €70-85; ☼ Mar–mid-Dec; **P**) Should you be arriving by canoe, you can pull up right at the dock of this *chambre d'hôte* housed in a restored old mill in the little village of Le Thor, 5km west of L'Isle-sur-la-Sorgue. The mill's three rooms are unpretentiously but appealingly themed 'Provençal', 'Moroccan' and 'Romantic'. Breakfast is served on the riverside terrace; and you can swim or fish in the Sorgue. Parking is free.

La Prévôté (☎ 04 90 38 57 29; http://laprevote.site.voila .fr in French; 4bis rue Jean-Jacques Rousseau; d incl breakfast €90-170; menus €25-60; ☼ closed late Feb-early Mar & mid-Nov–early Dec; **☒**) Straddling a burbling waterway in L'Isle-sur-la-Sorgue's old town, this *chambre d'hôte*, pretty as a box of chocolates, has five rich, chocolaty toned rooms, and a spa, Jacuzzi and solarium on the roof. It's an easy amble downstairs to one of the region's finest gastronomic restaurants (closed Tuesday in August, plus Wednesday from September to July), where chef Jean-Paul Alloin concocts fare like foie gras ravioli and thyme and rosemary chocolate accompanied by pear sorbet.

La Maison dur la Sorgue (☎ 04 90 20 74 86; www .lamaisonsurlasorgue.com; 6 rue Rose Goudard; d incl breakfast €180-230; **P ☒ ☒ ☒**) A beautiful 17th-century private mansion is today this luxurious *chambre d'hôte* in L'Isle-sur-la-Sorgue's charming old town, accessed via a glassed-in interior courtyard. Start your day with breakfast beneath a sycamore tree, and spend the evening snuggled up in the cherry red lounge room before the roaring open fire. Ask hosts Marie-Claude and

AVIGNON AREA

Frédéric to let you in on the mansion's intriguing history. Parking costs €10 by reservation.

In-town dining includes sun-kissed southern flavours at **Le Paradis de la Sorgue** (☎ 04 90 21 15 78; La Distillerie, 53 rte de Carpentras; lunch menus €10-12.50, dinner menus €18-25; 🕑 lunch Tue-Sun, dinner Tue-Sat); and gastronomic delights like smoked eel with glazed apple or roasted rabbit with artichoke ravioli at **Le Vivier** (☎ 04 90 38 52 80; 800 cours Fernande Peyre; menus from €28; 🕑 lunch Tue-Fri & Sun, dinner Tue-Sat).

GETTING THERE & AROUND

L'Isle-sur-la-Sorgue train station is not served by passenger trains.

From Avignon **Voyages Arnaud** (☎ 04 90 38 15 58) runs buses to/from L'Isle-sur-la-Sorgue (€3.50, 40 minutes, three to four daily), and between Carpentras and L'Isle-sur-la-Sorgue (20 minutes).

Watch out if you're driving: L'Isle-sur-la-Sorgue is easily confused with the entirely separate, uninspiring town of Sorgues.

For bike hire try **Christophe Tendil** (☎ 04 90 38 19 12; 10 av Julien Guigue; per day adult/child €14/10; 🕑 closed Sun & Mon).

Gliding 8km of waterways by canoe is the most peaceful way to reach L'Isle-sur-la-Sorgue from Fontaine de Vaucluse (see p188). **Canoë Kayak** (☎ 04 90 38 33 22; adult/child €18/10) runs two-hour trips that include a bus ride to Fontaine before canoeing back to L'Isle-sur-la-Sorgue.

Fontaine de Vaucluse
pop 661

All of the rain that falls around Apt, as well as melting snow, gushes out here in Fontaine de Vaucluse (Vau-Cluso La Font in Provençal), 7km east of L'Isle. The world's fifth most powerful spring – and France's most powerful – Fontaine (meaning fountain) is where the River Sorgue surges surfaceward from its subterranean course. Jacques Cousteau was one of many who attempted unsuccessfully to plumb the spring's depths before an unmanned submarine touched base (315m down) in 1985. It's at its most dazzling after heavy rain, when the water is an azure, almost violet, blue.

The spring's crystalline waters flow through the pretty village of Fontaine de Vaucluse about 1km downstream…as do the 1.5 million or more tourists that pour through here each year. Aim to arrive early in the morning before the trickle of visitors becomes a deluge.

INFORMATION

Tourist office (☎ 04 90 20 32 22; www.oti-delasorgue.fr; chemin de la Fontaine; 🕑 9.30am-5.30pm Tue-Sat) Southeast of central place de la Colonne on the way to the spring.

SIGHTS & ACTIVITIES

Most visitors, of course, come to see the spring, but this tiny village also has an eclectic collection of museums including the **Musée d'Histoire 1939–1945** (☎ 04 90 20 24 00; adult/child €3.50/1.50; 🕑 10am-noon & 2-6pm Sat & Sun Mar, 10am-noon & 2-6pm Wed-Mon Apr-Jun, 10am-7pm Wed-Mon Jul & Aug, 10am-noon & 2-6pm Wed-Mon Sep & Oct, 10am-noon & 2-5pm Sat & Sun Nov & Dec), which showcases the Resistance movement during WWII.

Beautiful flower-encrusted paper made as it was in the 16th century is sold in the adjoining boutique and art gallery of the reconstructed **Moulin à Papier** (paper mill; ☎ 04 90 20 34 14; chemin de la Fontaine; admission free; 🕑 9am-12.30pm & 2-5pm Mon-Sat, 10.30am-12.30pm & 2-5pm Sun Sep-Jun, 9am-7pm Jul & Aug) on the river.

Musée Pétrarque (☎ 04 90 20 37 20; admission €3.50; 🕑 10am-noon & 2-6pm Wed-Mon Apr-Sep, 10am-noon & 2-5pm Oct) is devoted to the Italian Renaissance poet Petrarch, who lived in Fontaine de Vaucluse from 1337 to 1353, expressing in verse his futile love for Laura, wife of Hugues de Sade.

Midway between Fontaine and Lagnes on the D24, **Passerelles des Cimes** (☎ 04 90 38 56 87; adult/child from €18/12; 🕑 9am-6pm Jul-Aug, Sat & Sun Mar-Jun, Sep & Oct) is an adventure park filled with rope courses through the trees. You'll need to reserve ahead.

SLEEPING & EATING

L'Isle-sur-la-Sorgue (opposite) makes a good alternative base for visiting Fontaine. Restaurants are sprinkled around Fontaine.

Auberge de Jeunesse (☎ 04 90 20 31 65; fax 04 90 20 26 20; Chemin de la Vignasse; dm €11; 🕑 reception 8-10am & 5.30-9pm, closed mid-Nov–Jan) In a lovely old farmhouse south of Fontaine de Vaucluse in the direction of Lagnes, this peaceful hostel is popular with families and hikers. From the bus stop, walk 800m uphill.

Hôtel du Poète (☎ 04 90 20 34 05; www.hoteldupoete .com; r €70-240; 🕑 closed late Dec–mid-Feb; 🐾 🖳) On the right-hand side of the road as you enter the village, on the riverbank, the peach-tinged Hôtel du Poète has 23 lyrically categorised rooms like 'melody' and 'symphony' with creamy furnishings, a poolside terrace to feast on fresh fruit at breakfast (€17), and can recommend nearby dining options.

AVIGNON AREA

Les Sources (☎ 04 90 20 31 84; rte de Cavaillon; menus €22-35; 🕑 lunch Tue-Sun, dinner daily early Apr–mid-Nov) Regional cuisine is at its freshest from Les Sources, an almond-coloured place with sage green shutters flanked by potted palms.

GETTING THERE & AROUND

Fontaine de Vaucluse is 21km southeast of Carpentras and 7km east of L'Isle-sur-Sorgue. From Avignon, **Cars Arnaud** (☎ 04 90 82 07 35) has a bus (€4.60, one hour, two or three daily) with a stop at Fontaine de Vaucluse.

Fontaine is most easily reached by car, but you'll have to fork out for the privilege of parking. (Don't duck down the little lane opposite the pay parking area instead – it dead-ends with nowhere to turn around, and reversing out is tricky. Trust us, we tried.)

Canoe companies operating guided tours along the river to L'Isle-sur-la-Sorgue include **Canoë Évasion** (☎ 04 90 38 26 22; rte de Fontaine de Vaucluse; 🕑 late Apr-early Nov), next to Camping de la Coutelière on the D24 from Fontaine de Vaucluse towards Lagnes, with an on-site picnic area. **Kayak Vert** (☎ 04 90 20 35 44; www.canoefrance .com; 🕑 late Apr-Oct) in Fontaine de Vaucluse also rent canoes and organises river expeditions. A canoe or kayak with guide costs €17 to €18 per person.

Pays de Venasque

The hilltop villages around **Venasque** (population 980; elevation 320m), 13km southeast of Carpentras, form the seldom-explored yet beautiful 'Venasque Country'. The Venasque **tourist office** (☎ 04 90 66 11 66; www.venasque.fr; Grande Rue; 🕑 10am-12.30pm & 3-7pm Mon, Tue, Thu & Fri, 3-7pm Wed Jul & Aug, 10am-noon & 2-6pm Mon, Tue, Thu & Fri, 2-6pm Wed Apr-Jun, Sep & Oct, closed Oct-Mar) has information on the entire area.

SIGHTS & ACTIVITIES

On an exposed rocky spur at the mercy of the elements, when the winter mistral blows through the village of Venasque, it *howls*. Weathering the winds, Venasque's ancient **baptistry** (☎ 04 90 66 62 01; adult/under 12yr €3/free; 🕑 9.15am-noon & 1-5pm or 6pm Jan–mid-Dec), built in the 5th century on the site of a Roman temple, is one of France's oldest structures. At Le Mas des Lavandes (right), be spellbound during a guided stroll (adult/child €6/3) along an **ethnobotanical walking trail**, listening to stories of the plants' magical powers.

The fortress village of **Le Beaucet** (population 354; elevation 300m) perches 6km south

via the winding D314. Two kilometres south along chemin des Oratoires (the D39A) in the hamlet of **St-Gens** is a small Romanesque basilica, rebuilt in 1884. The hermit Gens, who lived with wolves and performed rain-making miracles, died here in 1127.

The **Forêt de Vénasque**, crossed by the GR91 walking trail, lies to the east of Venasque. Heading across the Col de Murs (627m) mountain pass to the pretty village of **Murs** (population 420), 5km east, you can see remains of **Le Mur de la Peste** (plague wall).

Continuing north, the GR91 leads to the steep **Gorges de la Nesque**, from where Sault and the eastern edges of the Ventoux can be accessed. Frédéric Mistral described its ruggedness as a 'dark anfractuous gorge'. Deep in the canyon, built into a rock shelter, is a 12th-century chapel restored in 1643. On the **Col des Abeilles**, north of the gorges on the D1, you can hire a donkey to accompany you along the gorges or up Mont Ventoux at **Les Ânes des Abeilles** (☎ 04 90 64 01 52; anesdesabeilles@wanadoo.fr; Col des Abeilles). Donkeys carry up to 40kg and amble along at 3km to 4km an hour; a day/ weekend costs €40/80. Sault's tourist office is also a fount of information on the gorge.

SLEEPING & EATING

Les Oliviers Venasque (☎ 06 18 11 32 03, 04 90 66 03 71; www.lesoliviersvenasque.com; Grand rue; d incl breakfast €50-68; **P**) The family farm of *trufficulteur* Jean-François Tourrette (p42), this sweet *chambre d'hôte* has three sun-filled guest rooms with checked bedspreads and a lovely, leafy garden to enjoy breakfast while listening to the birds.

Auberge La Fontaine (☎ 04 90 66 02 96; www.auberge -lafontaine.com; place de la Fontaine, Venasque; d €125; menu €38; **P** 👶) In the heart of the village, this ivy-draped stone inn runs regular intensive three-day cooking courses (€80 per person per day including lunch) and occasional, ambient concerts. Wild asparagus, truffles, locally picked raspberries, and herb-fed rabbit feature at the restaurant (open for dinner Thursday to Tuesday). Parking is free.

Le Mas des Lavandes (☎ 04 90 66 00 58; www.mas -des-lavandes.com in French; Fonnsargoule; gîte per week €305-500; 🕑 closed Jan-Mar; **P** 👶) Each of these two light, airy, self-catering *gîtes* sleeps up to seven people, with cheaper rates for weekends and midweek stays outside June to September. The *mas* is on the edge of Venasque, on the left as you follow the signs south to Le Beaucet.

LES ALPILLES

Strung between the Rivers Durance and Rhône, south of Avignon, the silvery Chaîne des Alpilles is a chain of limestone rocks glinting with heady herbal garrigue and olive groves. St-Rémy de Provence to the north and Maussane-les-Alpilles to the south are linked by the Vallée des Baux where AOC olive oil (p45) is milled.

Les Alpilles' ridge is traversed by the GR6 walking path.

ST-RÉMY DE PROVENCE

pop 10,007

Foodies flock to this chic town in the Alpilles, which has exceptional olive oil, celebrated chefs and one of France's best chocolate makers in its fold, as well as some exquisite places to sleep.

Before St-Rémy garnered gourmands, the Greeks then the Romans inhabited the settlement of Glanum on the city's southern edge, which remains a rich archaeological site. Centuries on, the philosopher Nostradamus (1503–66) was born in a house on rue Hoche. Van Gogh painted some of his best-known works between 1889 and 1890 while hospitalised here. And for all its flair, St-Rémy's inherent charm remains rooted in age-old traditions.

Information

The privately run websites www.alpilles.com and www.alpilles.fr (in French) list information on the region.

Tourist office (☎ 04 90 92 05 22; www.saintremy-de -provence.com; place Jean Jaurès; ⊙ 9am-noon & 2-7pm Mon-Sat, 9am-noon Sun mid-Jun–mid-Sep, 9am-noon & 2-6pm Mon-Sat mid-Sep–mid-Jun) Runs numerous guided tours in English and French (adult/child €6.50/3.70) between Easter and October, including nature forays in the Alpilles.

Sights

GLANUM

Excavated remains from the Gallo-Greek (3rd to 1st centuries BC) to the Gallo-Roman (1st century BC to 3rd century AD) eras can be seen at the vast **Site Archéologique de Glanum** (archaeological site; ☎ 04 90 92 23 79; rte des Baux; adult/ under 18yr €6.50/4.50; ⊙ 9.30am-6.30pm, last tour 5.30pm). Among the finds uncovered are parts of Glanum's temple, public baths dating from 50 BC and the forum.

AVIGNON AREA

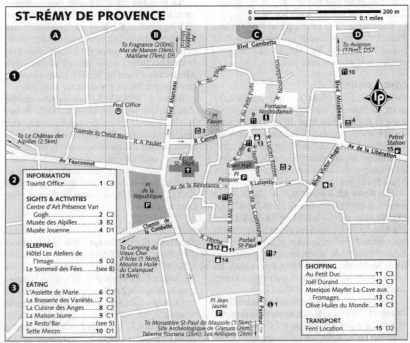

ST–RÉMY DE PROVENCE

0 — 200 m
0 — 0.1 miles

To Fragrance (200m);
Mas de Manon (3km);
Maillane (7km); D5

To Avignon
(17km); D57

Post Office

Fontaine
Nostradamus

To Le Château des
Alpilles (2.5km)

Traversée du Cheval Blanc

Petrol
Station

Église
St-Martin

Town Hall

To Camping du
Vieux Cher
d'Arles (1.5km);
Moulin à Huile
du Calanquet
(4.5km)

Portail
St-Paul

Pl Jean
Jaurès

To Monastère St-Paul de Mausole (1.5km);
Site Archéologique de Glanum (2km);
Taberna Romana (2km); Les Antiques (2km)

INFORMATION	
Tourist Office	1 C3

SIGHTS & ACTIVITIES	
Centre d'Art Présence Van Gogh	2 C2
Musée des Alpilles	3 B2
Musée Jouenne	4 D1

SLEEPING	
Hôtel Les Ateliers de l'Image	5 D2
Le Sommeil des Fées	(see 8)

EATING	
L'Assiette de Marie	6 C2
La Brasserie des Variétés	7 C3
La Cuisine des Anges	8 C2
La Maison Jaune	9 C1
Le Resto'Bar	(see 5)
Sette Mezzo	10 D1

SHOPPING	
Au Petit Duc	11 C3
Joël Durand	12 C3
Monique Mayfer La Cave aux Fromages	13 C2
Olive Huiles du Monde	14 C3

TRANSPORT	
Ferri Location	15 D2

Impossible to miss, Glanum is situated opposite **Les Antiques**, a spectacular pair of Roman monuments comprising a **triumphal arch** (AD 20) and **mausoleum** (30–20 BC), just south of the centre on the southbound D5.

VAN GOGH SIGHTS

Van Gogh admitted himself to the asylum **Monastère St-Paul de Mausole** (☎ 04 90 92 77 00; maison.sante.st.paul@wanadoo.fr; adult/under 12yr €3.80/2.80; ✆ 9.30am-7pm Apr-Oct, 10.15am-4.45pm Nov-Mar), where he accomplished 100 drawings and about 150 paintings, including his famous irises. A prison camp during WWI, the building is once again a clinic (these days for women only). Its Romanesque cloister and a reconstruction of Van Gogh's room are open to visitors.

From the monastery entrance, colour panels mark a **walking trail** of various Van Gogh subjects. Unlike the trail in Arles (p142), panels here aren't located in the spots where Van Gogh set up his easel (confined to the asylum, he painted from his mind's eye and previous forays into the Provençal countryside).

In town, his life and work are depicted at the **Centre d'Art Présence Van Gogh** (☎ 04 90 92 34 72; 8 rue Lucien Estrine; adult/student €3.80/2.80; ✆ 10.30am-12.30pm & 2.30-6.30pm Tue-Sun late Mar-Dec).

The tourist office runs a **guided Van Gogh tour** (€6.50; ✆ by reservation depending on numbers, Easter-Oct).

For more about Van Gogh's time in Provence see the boxed text, p143.

OTHER SIGHTS

Provençal and other natural landscapes painted from a contemporary perspective hang in the **Musée Jouenne** (☎ 04 32 60 00 51; www .michel-jouenne.com in French; 20 blvd Mirabeau; adult/under 12yr €4/free; ✆ 10am-12.30pm & 3-7pm Tue-Sun), a hybrid museum, art gallery and cultural centre showcasing oil-on-canvas works by French hotshot Michel Jouenne (b 1933).

The **Musée des Alpilles** (☎ 04 90 92 68 24; 1 place Favier; adult/child €3/2; ✆ 10am-12.30pm & 2-7pm Tue-Sat Jul & Aug, 10am-noon & 2-6pm Tue-Sat Mar-Jun, Sep & Oct, 2-5pm Tue-Sat Jan, Feb, Nov & Dec, plus 1st Sun each month) has comprehensive coverage of both the natural and manmade landscapes of the Alpilles, from fossils through to the present day. Its inner courtyard is watched over by an Ossip Zadkine–sculpted bust of Van Gogh.

The brother-and-sister-run **Moulin à Huile du Calanquet** (☎ 04 32 60 00 50; www.moulinducalanquet.fr; Vieux Chemin d'Arles; ✆ 9am-noon & 2.30-7pm), 4.5km southwest of St-Rémy, offers tastings of olive oil grown and pressed on the premises, and incorporates the cooking school Moulin des Chefs, featuring top chefs in its upstairs kitchen.

Festivals & Events

Painters and sculptors transform the town streets into an open-air art gallery on four Sundays each year, in May, June, August and September during the **Fête de Peintres**.

Herds of sheep extending as far as the eye can see overtake the streets on Pentecost Monday morning during the **Fête de la Transhumance** as they're shepherded to high-altitude summer pastures. Mid-August sees a 'running of the bulls' as part of the four-day **Féria Provençale**.

Sleeping

CHAMBRES D'HÔTES

Le Sommeil des Fées (Sleepiness of Fairies; ☎ 04 90 92 17 66, 06 14 41 41 31; www.alpilles-delices.com; 4 rue du 8 Mai 1945; d incl breakfast €55-75; ✆) This storybook *chambre d'hôte* drowsing in the town centre has five dreamy rooms named after fairies, wizards and elves overlooking a pretty patio and garden; and an enchanting restaurant (opposite).

Mas de Manon (☎ 04 32 60 09 86; www.masdemanon .com; chemin des Lônes; d incl breakfast €62; P ✆) You can play *pétanque* in the leafy garden of this small and simple 18th-century farmhouse 3km north of St-Rémy, with four bright rooms. From May to October there's a self-catering kitchen (with a dishwasher!) and barbecue terrace. From the town centre, follow the signs for Maillane.

Fragrance (☎ 04 90 92 35 77; www.fragrance-saintremy .com; 2 rue Emile Daillan; d incl breakfast €70-75; P ✆) A 200m stroll from the town centre, this sparkling *chambre d'hôte* filled with crisp white linens and fresh flowers is run by host Chantal Vallette, whose thoughtful touches like heart-shaped soaps in the bathrooms win guests' hearts. Take a dip in the inviting timber-decked pool and breakfast on homemade pastries and cakes.

HOTELS

Hôtel Les Ateliers de l'Image (☎ 04 90 92 51 50; www .hotelphoto.com; 36 blvd Victor Hugo; d from €165, ste from €250; P ✆ ✆ ✆ ✆) A darkroom allows photographers staying at this flash 'photography hotel' to develop prints; photography workshops enhance your skills; and regular photographic exhibitions provide inspiration. The hotel's grounds (including a hedge maze) also inspire, as do the glossy rooms (our favourite: No 28 with a drawbridge to a private treehouse). Internet use is €5 for 45 minutes, parking is free.

Le Château des Alpilles (☎ 04 90 92 03 33; www .chateaudesalpilles.com; D31; d from €170; P 🅿 📶 🐕) Grandeur reigns at this soaring antique-filled chateau sprawled in a park of centuries-old trees. Staff cater to every conceivable whim, and can arrange bicycle rental, horse riding and golf passes. The property's 'cypress farm' shelters apartments and lofts, and there's a collection of small, self-catering cottages. The chateau is 2.5km from the centre; take the Tarascon/Nîmes/Arles exit, turn left on the little road to Rougadou which becomes the D31 and the chateau is 2km along the road on your right.

CAMPING
Camping du Vieux Chemin d'Arles (☎ 04 90 92 27 22; campingstremy@free.fr; Vieux Chemin d'Arles; 2 adults, caravan/tent & car €10; 🕐 Dec–mid-Nov) There are just six spots to pitch your tent at this family-run farm that also has a couple of swings and a seesaw for little kids. The farm is 1.5km down a country lane from St-Rémy's place de la République.

Eating & Drinking
La Cuisine des Anges (☎ 04 90 92 17 66; 4 rue du 8 Mai 1945; lunch menu €12.50, menu €25; 🕐 lunch & dinner daily Jun-Aug, lunch & dinner Tue-Sun Sep-Oct & Dec-May, closed Nov) Attached to the cute-as-pie *chambre d'hôte* Le Sommeil des Fées, at the 'kitchen of angels' Helene Ricard cooks up light, summery Provençal dishes like grilled sea bass and honey-glazed duck.

L'Assiette de Marie (☎ 04 90 92 32 14; 1 rue Jaume Roux; menu €30; 🕐 lunch & dinner Fri-Wed) As in a big farmhouse country kitchen, knick-knacks from past eras clutter this old-world bistro, known for its delicious traditional dishes like Provençal lamb casserole and stuffed vegetables along with contemporary creations.

La Maison Jaune (☎ 04 90 92 56 14; 15 rue Carnot; menus €34-62; 🕐 lunch & dinner Wed-Sun, dinner Tue summer, lunch Tue-Sun winter, closed Jan & Feb) Home to the most buzzing tables in town since being awarded a Michelin star in 2006, the best way to taste chef François Perraud's winning creations like saffron-roasted free-range chicken is his five-course Provençal dégustation *menu* (€52).

Le Resto'Bar (☎ 04 90 92 51 50; www.hotelphoto .com; 36 blvd Victor Hugo; menu €39, sushi €4-47; 🕐 restaurant lunch & dinner, sushi bar dinner Tue-Sun, cocktail bar

5pm-12.30am daily) Flowing from a funky Austin Powers–style cocktail bar, the vegetable patch at the Hôtel Les Ateliers de l'Image grows the ingredients for this slick restaurant, with contemporary angles on classics like loin of Alpilles lamb in herbs and black-olive juice. Its sushi bar offers a takeaway service.

Also recommended:

Sette Mezzo (☎ 04 90 92 59 27; 34 blvd Mirabeau; lunch menu €17, dinner menu €31; 🕐 lunch & dinner daily Jul & Aug, Tue-Sat Sep-Jun) Mediterranean and Italian specialities include *primo* pastas (with truffles in season).

Taberna Romana (☎ 04 90 92 65 97; www.taberna -romana.com; rte des Baux; menus €11-22; 🕐 9am-7pm Apr-Sep) Savour a drink or a Roman-inspired lunch along with a free panorama of Glanum.

Shopping
St-Rémy's shops sell scrumptious gourmet goodies to go:

Au Petit Duc (7 blvd Victor Hugo) Historical biscuits baked by food historian Anne Daguin using old Roman, Renaissance, Alpine and Arlésien recipes.

Joël Durand (3 blvd Victor Hugo) One of France's top 10 chocolate makers, utilising Provençal herbs and plants like lavender, rosemary, violet and thyme, along with out-of-the-box flavours such as Earl Grey, and coffee-and-barley.

Monique Mayfer: La Cave aux Fromages (1 place Joseph Hilaire) Fabulous cheese shop with a 12th-century ripening *cave* (cellar).

Olive: Huiles du Monde (16 blvd Victor Hugo) Taste 30 different oils at its *bar à huiles* (oil bar).

Terre de Truffes (16 blvd Victor Hugo) Classy truffle boutique.

THE AUTHOR'S CHOICE

Hôtel Gounod (☎ 04 90 92 06 14; www.hotel -gounod.com; 18 place de la République; d incl breakfast €99-115; P 🅿 📶 🐕) St-Rémy's oldest hotel has been totally transformed to house 37 beautiful, individually decorated rooms in romantic shades like olive, lilac and rose, and public areas decorated with antique religious icons. It was renamed in honour of composer Charles Gounod (1818–93) who stayed at the hotel in 1863 while composing his opera *Mireille,* based on Frédéric Mistral's poem. The ground-floor courtyard and dining room house an equally beautiful *salon-de-thé* (open from 7.30am to 9pm daily) serving bruschetta, homemade cakes and Illy coffee to the strains of Gounod's music.

AVIGNON AREA

Getting There & Around

Buses to Tarascon and Nîmes operated by **Cévennes Cars** (☎ 04 66 29 27 29) depart from place de la République. Avignon-bound buses run by **Sociétés Rapides du Sud-Est** (☎ 04 90 14 59 00) leave from blvd Victor Hugo.

Ferri Location (☎ 04 90 92 10 88; 35 av de la Libération; ⏰ 7.30am-noon & 1.30-7.30pm Mon-Fri, 8am-noon & 2-6pm Sat), inside the Total petrol station, rents mountain bikes for €18 a day. Helmets/child seats cost €1.50/2.30.

AROUND ST-RÉMY DE PROVENCE

Vineyards, olive groves and heady, herbal garrigue wreathe St-Rémy.

Les Baux de Provence

pop 443 / elev 185m

Along a twisting, turning road 10km south of St-Rémy, Les Baux de Provence was vividly rendered – albeit from a distance – by Van Gogh during his time in St-Rémy.

Clawing precariously to a 245m-high grey limestone *baou* (Provençal for 'rocky spur'), this fortified town gave its name to bauxite, the chief ore of aluminium first mined here in 1822. The ancient outcrop is one of the most visited villages in France – aim to arrive after the caterpillar of tourist coaches has crawled back downhill.

Thought to date back to the 10th century, the town's high-point attraction, the **Château des Baux** (☎ 04 90 54 55 56; www.chateau-baux-provence .com; adult/student €7.50/5; ⏰ 9am-8.30pm Jul & Aug, 9am-6.30pm Mar-Jun & Sep-Nov, 9am-5pm Dec-Feb) was largely destroyed during the reign of Louis XIII in 1633. Audioguides in several languages detail the history of the ruined castle, village

and region, and demonstrations of medieval warfare frequently feature in summer.

Castle apart, Les Baux is on taste-conscious travellers' maps for the two Michelin stars glittering at the legendary 15th-century **L'Ousta de Baumanière** (☎ 04 90 54 33 07; www.oustaude baumaniere.com; d €225-310, apt €360-490; menus €110-150; ⓟ ⓧ 🖵 🖳 🅰), spread over a collection of buildings, and serving rarefied cuisine including a (*très* gourmet) vegetarian *menu*. A minimum of two diners is required. Head chef and owner Jean-André Charial's domain also includes the renowned one Michelin-starred restaurant and luxury rooms of La Cabro d'Or. Reservations are imperative for both.

The **tourist office** (☎ 04 90 54 34 39; www.lesbaux deprovence.com; ⏰ 9.30am-1pm & 2-6pm Mon-Sat) also has information on Les Baux's handful of accommodation options.

There's metered but no free parking within 800m of the village, but free parking is available at **Cathédrale d'Images** (www.cathedrale-images.com; adult/child €7.30/3.50; ⏰ 10am-7pm Apr-Sep, 10am-6pm Oct-early Jan, closed early Jan-Feb), which screens large-scale sound-and-light projections flickering against the backdrop of a former quarry cave a few minutes' stroll north of the village.

Maussane-les-Alpilles & Around

pop 2000

Maussane-les-Alpilles, 3km south of Les Baux on the Alpilles' southern edge, has some of Provence's best-known *moulins d'huile* (oil mills), where five different types of freshly harvested olives are pummelled and pressed into silken oil.

Moulin Jean-Marie Cornille (☎ 04 90 54 32 37; www .moulin-cornille.com; rue Charloun Rieu; ⏰ shop 9am-6pm Mon-Sat), a 17th-century mill run as a cooperative since 1924, sells its oil direct to the public, though depending on the year's yield, oil can sell out by mid-August. New stock comes in mid-December. Between June and September, you can also take a guided tour of the mill (€1.50, 10.30am Tuesday and Thursday).

Stunning views of the sheer, silver-ridged Alpilles unfold along the eastbound D78 from Maussane. A 6km drive southeast along the D17 brings you to **Mouriès** (population 2525). Pop in for a taste of exceptional olive oil milled at its **Moulin Coopératif** (☎ 04 90 47 53 86; www.moulin coop.com; Quartier Mas Neuf; ⏰ 9am-12.30pm & 2-7pm Mon-Sat, 3-7pm Sun Jun-Sep, 9am-noon & 2-6pm Mon-Sat, 2-6pm Sun Oct-May). The village celebrates a **Fête des Olives Vertes** (green olive festival) in mid-September

---

AVIGNON AREA

ALPILLES AMBROSIA

Fine Alpilles dining isn't confined to St-Rémy, with a smorgasbord of countryside options.

- **Le Bistrot du Paradou – Chez Jean Louis** (☎ 04 90 54 32 70; lunch/dinner menus €42/44; ☯ lunch & dinner Mon-Sat Apr-Sep, lunch Mon-Sat Oct-Mar) At his stone house beneath the plane trees, Jean-Louis is fêted for his single fixed Provençal *menus*, around which locals plan their week. Book ahead. It's 3km west from Maussane-les-Alpilles on the D17 to Paradou.
- **Ferme Auberge de Barbegal** (☎ 04 90 54 63 69; Raphèle les Arles; menus €20-23; ☯ year-round, reserve 48hr ahead; 🔧) Lamb doesn't get any more tender than at this 18th-century sheep farm 5km south of Fontvieille. Ask about its *chambre d'hôte* rooms (prices arranged on booking).
- **Le Saint-Georges** (☎ 04 90 92 44 62; www.valmouriane.com; Domaine de Valmouriane, petit rte des Baux; lunch menu €27.50, dinner menus €32-75; ☯ closed mid-late Nov; 🔧) Should you find you can't move after St-George's magnificent *menu dégustation à l'huile d'olive* (olive oil tasting *menu*), this idyllic country estate 6km west of St-Rémy has guest rooms (doubles from €125). Packages including a three-hour painting class for two people plus one night's accommodation and half-board cost €215 per person.
- **Le Château des Alpilles** (p191; menus from €38; ☯ lunch Fri-Tue, dinner Thu-Tue) Dine like royalty in this castle's stately crimson-coloured dining room.

---

and the arrival of the year's new oil with a **Fête des Huiles Nouvelles** in December.

Eyguières (population 5392), 15km further east, is dominated by the Alpilles' highest point (493m).

Nearby in **Eygalières** (population 1850; elevation 134m), take time out in the **Jardin de l'Alchimiste** (☎ 04 90 90 67 77; www.jardin-alchimiste.com; Mas de la Brune; adult/student €6/4, guided visit with drink €9; ☯ 10am-7pm May-Sep), an alchemist's garden of blossoming herbs and plants. The village is also home to the incomparable **Le Bistrot de L'Eygalières** (☎ 04 90 90 60 34; rue de la République; menus €85-100; ☯ restaurant lunch Wed-Sun, dinner Tue-Sun; ☒), where you can savour mind-blowing flavours like cream of foie gras with fig confit and saffron mousse in Wout and Suzy Bru's cosy dining room (twin Michelin-starred, no less), and retreat to four stunning *chambre d'hôte* doubles (from €115) and suites (from €160).

Orgon (population 2268), 9km north of Eygalières is guarded by **Notre Dame de Beauregard** (1878), a church perched up high on a needle of rock with eagle's-eye views of the Alpilles.

Tourist offices with information on the area:

Maussane-les-Alpilles (☎ 04 90 54 52 04; www.maussane.com; place Laugier de Monblan; ☯ 9.30am-12.30pm & 3-7pm Mon-Sat Jul & Aug, 9.30am-12.30pm & 2-6pm Mon-Sat May, Jun, Sep & Oct, 9am-noon Mon-Sat Nov-Apr)

Mouriès (☎ 04 91 13 84 13; www.mouries.com; 2 rue du Temple; ☯ 9am-12.30pm & 2-6.30pm Tue-Sat Apr-Sep, 2-5pm Mon, 9am-noon & 2-5pm Tue-Fri, 9am-noon Sat Oct-Mar)

Orgon (☎ 04 90 73 09 54; www.orgon-tourisme.com in French; place de la Liberté; ☯ 8.30am-6.30pm Mon-Sat, 8.30am-4.30pm Mon, Tue, Thu & Fri Sep-Jun)

Fontvieille
pop 3566

At Frédéric Mistral's invitation, Alphonse Daudet found his way to Fontvieille, 10km west of Maussane along the D17, and later immortalised the town in his short stories *Lettres de mon Moulin* (Letters from my Windmill; 1869). Born in Nîmes, Daudet spent most of his life in Paris but shared a strong spiritual affinity with Provence and is regarded as a Provençal writer.

Le Moulin de Daudet (Daudet's Windmill), which dates back to 1814 and houses the **Musée de Daudet** (adult/6-12yr €2.50/1.50, parking €2; ☯ 9am-7pm Jun-Sep, 10am-noon & 2-5pm Nov, Dec & Feb-May), is not the windmill where the writer spent hours sunk in literary thought. From the windmill-museum, there is a 1½-hour trail that leads to Daudet's true haunt, the **Moulin Tissot-Avon**. Fontvieille's **tourist office** (☎ 04 90 54 67 49; www.fontvieille-provence.com; 5 rue Marcel Honorat; ☯ 9am-noon & 2-6pm Mon-Sat, 9am-noon Sun Jun-Sep, 9am-noon & 2-6pm Mon-Sat Oct-May) has information.

Farm-fresh dining in the area includes the Ferme Auberge de Barbegal (see the boxed text, above).

The most scenic way to reach Fontvieille is by diesel train from Arles (see the boxed text, p146).

Maillane to the Rhône

Frédéric Mistral (p67) hailed from **Maillane** (population 1891), 7km northwest of St-Rémy. Born in 1830 in a farmhouse on its outskirts, the poet moved into the centre of the village with his mother following the death of his father. Upon marrying, 46-year-old Mistral left home, only to move with his 19-year-old wife into the **house** (☎ 04 90 95 74 06; 11 av Lamartine; adult/student €3.50/1; ☉ 9.30-11.30am & 2.30-6.30pm Tue-Sun Apr-Sep, 10-11.30am & 2-4.30pm Tue-Sun Oct-Mar) opposite his mother's, where he lived until his death in 1914. Today the house is a museum, and runs writing workshops in Provençal. Mistral is buried in the village cemetery.

Continuing 3km north, you hit **Graveson** (population 3190) with its garden-graced 19th-century farmhouse containing the **Musée des Arômes et du Parfum** (Museum of Aromas & Perfumes; ☎ 04 90 95 81 55; www.viearome.com in French; petite rte du Gès; adult/under 12yr €4/free; ☉ 10am-noon & 2-6pm, to 7pm summer); **Les Figuières du Mas de Luquet** (☎ 04 90 95 72 03; www.lesfiguieres.com; chemin du Mas de la Musique), an orchard growing over 150 varieties of figs; and **Musée Auguste Chabaud** (☎ 04 90 90 53 02; www.museechabaud.com in French; cours National; adult/student €4/2; ☉ 10am-noon & 1.30-6.30pm Jun-Sep, 1.30-6.30pm Oct-May), dedicated to the Nîmes-born fauvist painter who lived in Graveson for most of his life.

From Graveson the D81 meanders through the undulating **Massif de la Montagnette**. Hidden in its rolling hills is **Abbaye St-Michel de Frigolet**, a neogothic abbey (1863–66) with vast grounds and a tower-topped **hotel-restaurant** (☎ 04 90 90 52 70; www.frigolet.com; d €46-57; menu €13, picnic basket €8; ℗).

Medieval **Barbentane** (population 3780) is dominated by the 28m-tall **Tour Anglica** (1385) and classical 17th-century **chateau** (visitable from Easter to October), and has a particularly lovely *chambre d'hôte* framed by pine trees, **Le Mazet de la Dame** (☎ 04 90 90 91 73; www.la-dame.com; d incl breakfast around €100; ℗ 🖃).

TARASCON & BEAUCAIRE

Provençal lore comes to life in the streets of **Tarascon** (population 12,991) during June's **Fête de la Tarasque**, a Chinese-style dragon parade celebrating St Martha's slaying of Tarasque, a dragon legend says once lurked in the Rhône. Rearing up from the riverbank, **Château de Tarascon** (☎ 04 90 91 01 93; adult/child €6.50/4.50; ☉ 9am-7pm Apr-Sep, 9am-noon & 2-5pm Tue-Sun Oct-Mar) was built by Louis II in the 15th century

to defend Provence's political frontier and richly decorated under King René (1434–80), but later stripped and used as a mint and then as a prison until 1926.

Facing the chateau, across the Rhône in **Beaucaire** (population 14,000), the ruined 11th-century **Château de Beaucaire** (☎ 04 66 59 26 72; www.aigles-de-beaucaire.com; place du Château; adult/5-11yr €9/6; ☉ 3 or 4 afternoon shows mid-Mar–mid-Nov) can only be entered during falconry displays; when visitors can also take advantage of the castle's shaded picnic area. Bulls stampede through Beaucaire's streets heralding the week-long **Foire de Beaucaire** in mid-July.

Southwest of Beaucaire on the D38 towards Bellegarde is the **Mas des Tourelles** (☎ 04 66 59 19 72; www.tourelles.com; adult/5-16yr €4.80/1.50; ☉ 10am-noon & 2-7pm Mon-Sat, 2-7pm Sun Jul & Aug, 2-6pm Apr-Jun, Sep & Oct, 2-6pm Sat Nov-Mar), a farm where you can learn how the Romans made wine. In the cellar, taste farm-made Roman *mucsum* (honeyed wine) and *defrutum* (grape juice).

Tourist offices with information on the towns:

Beaucaire (☎ 04 66 59 26 57; www.ot-beaucaire.fr; 24 cours Gambetta; ☉ 8.45am-12.15pm & 2-6pm Mon-Fri, 9.30am-12.15pm & 3-6pm Sat, 9.30am-12.30pm Sun Jul; 8.45am-12.15pm & 2-6pm Mon-Fri, 9.30am-12.15pm & 3-6pm Sat Aug-Oct & Easter-Jun, 8.45am-12.15pm & 2-6pm Mon-Fri, 9.30am-12.15pm Sat Nov-Easter)

Tarascon (☎ 04 90 91 03 52; www.tarascon.org; 59 rue des Halles; ☉ 9am-noon & 2-7pm Mon-Sat, 9.30am-12.30pm Sun Jul & Aug, 9am-noon & 2-6pm Mon-Fri, 9am-noon & 2-5pm Sat, 9.30am-12.30pm Sun Jun & Sep, 9am-noon & 2-6pm Mon-Fri, 9am-noon & 2-5pm Sat Oct-May)

ACROSS THE RIVER RHÔNE

Roman relics loom large across the Rhône with a resplendent amphitheatre in Nîmes and an enormous aqueduct on the River Gard. Although no longer a part of Provence proper (these sights are located in the Languedoc-Roussillon *région*) both make a striking day trip from Nîmes.

NÎMES

pop 137,740

Ironically for a city on neither a river nor the sea, Nîmes' coat of arms is a crocodile, chained to a palm tree. The shield's insignia harks back to Nîmes' Roman history, recalling the retiring Roman legionaries who fought with Caesar during his River Nile campaign, and were granted land as their reward.

The Roman Colonia Nemausensis reached its zenith in the 2nd century, receiving its water supply from an aqueduct system that included the still-standing Pont du Gard (p200), 23km to the northeast. The sacking of the city by the Vandals in the early 5th century began a downward spiral in fortunes.

The crocodile emblem, redesigned by French style master Philippe Starck, bridges the city's ancient origins with its cutting-edge urban evolution. Starck also designed a bus stop (Abribus) on av Carnot. Other striking contemporary public spaces include Norman Foster's Carrée d'Art and Niçois painter Martial Raysse's fountained square, place d'Assas.

Nîmes' name (well, part of it) is a household one, thanks to Bavarian tailor Levi Strauss who struck gold during the California rush by outfitting miners with durable trousers made from the traditional blue *serge de Nîmes*, nowadays known as denim.

A lesser-known claim to fame is Nîmes' native son Jean Nicot (1530–1600), who was born on place d'Horloge, and imported tobacco into France from Portugal in 1560, hence the word 'nicotine'. Ironically too, Nicot was a doctor by profession.

Orientation

Everything, including traffic, revolves around Les Arènes. Just north of the amphitheatre, the fan-shaped, largely pedestrianised old city is bounded by blvd Victor Hugo, blvd Amiral Courbet and blvd Gambetta. North of place aux Herbes, one of the main squares, lies the Îlot Littré, the preserved dyers' quarter.

Southeast of Les Arènes is esplanade Charles de Gaulle, a large open square, from where av Feuchères leads southeast to the train and bus stations.

Information

INTERNET RESOURCES

Nîmes (www.nimes.fr in French) Official city website.
Sortir a Nîmes (www.sortiranimes.com in French) Indispensable city-entertainment guide.

MEDICAL SERVICES

A list of pharmacies open at night is posted in the window of the tourist office on weekends.

SOS Médecins (☎ 08 20 33 24 24; ☉ 24hr) Call-out doctor service.

MONEY

Commercial banks line blvd Amiral Courbet and the western side of blvd Victor Hugo.

POST

Main post office (1 blvd de Bruxelles)

TOURIST INFORMATION

Comité Départemental du Tourisme du Gard
(☎ 04 66 36 96 30; www.tourismegard.com; 3 rue de la Cité Foulc; ☉ 8am-8pm Mon-Fri, 9.30am-noon Sat Jul & Aug, 8.45am-6pm Mon-Fri, 9.30am-noon Sat Sep-Jun) Information on the Gard *département*.
Tourist office (☎ 04 66 58 38 00; www.ot-nimes.fr; 6 rue Auguste; ☉ 8am-8pm Mon-Sat, 10am-6pm Sun Jul & Aug, 8.30am-7pm Mon-Sat, 10am-5pm or 6pm Sun Sep-Jun) City information.

Sights

LES ARÈNES

Impressively intact, Nîmes' dramatic Roman **amphitheatre** (places des Arènes; adult/10-16yr €7.70/5.60; ☉ 9am-7pm Jun-Aug, 9am-5.30pm Mar-May, Oct & Sep, 9.30am-4.30pm Nov-Feb) was built around AD 100 to seat 24,000 spectators – marginally more than its counterpart in Arles, though Arles' is a smidge bigger in size. Unlike Arles, Nîmes' amphitheatre retains its upper storey. The interior has four tiers of seats and a system of exits and passages designed so that patricians attending the animal and gladiator combats never had to rub shoulders with the plebs up top.

Covered by a hi-tech removable roof October to April, year-round Les Arènes stages plays, music concerts and bullfights (for ticket details see p199).

MAISON CARRÉE & CARRÉE D'ART

Also remarkably preserved, the rectangular, Greek-style temple known as the **Maison Carrée** (Square House; place de la Maison Carrée; adult/11-16yr €4.50/3.60; ☉ 9am-7pm Jun-Aug, 9am-5.30pm Mar-May, Oct & Sep, 9.30am-4.30pm Nov-Feb) was built around AD 5 to honour Augustus' grandsons (whom he adopted and raised), Gaius and Lucius. It survived the centuries as a meeting hall (during the Middle Ages), a private residence, a stable (in the 17th century), a church and, after the Revolution, an archive. Six symmetrical Corinthian columns stand guard at its entrance.

AVIGNON AREA

NÎMES

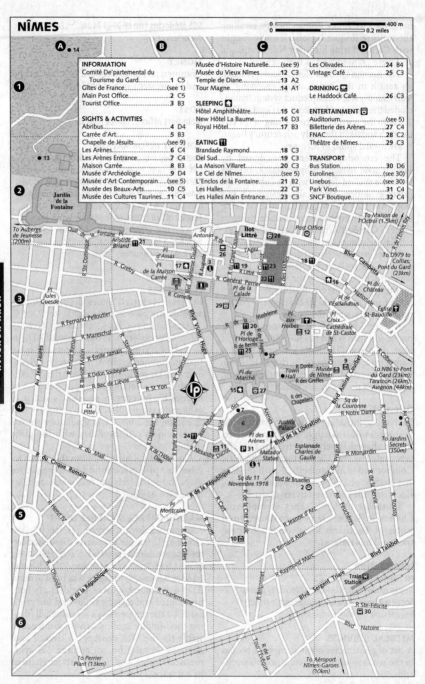

INFORMATION	
Comité De'partemental du	
Tourisme du Gard	1 C5
Gîtes de France	(see 1)
Main Post Office	2 C5
Tourist Office	3 B3

SIGHTS & ACTIVITIES	
Abribus	4 D4
Carrée d'Art	5 B3
Chapelle de Jésuits	(see 9)
Les Arènes	6 C4
Les Arènes Entrance	7 C4
Maison Carrée	8 B3
Musée d'Archéologie	9 D4
Musée d'Art Contemporain	(see 5)
Musée des Beaux-Arts	10 C5
Musée des Cultures Taurines	11 C4

Musée d'Histoire Naturelle	(see 9)
Musée du Vieux Nîmes	12 C3
Temple de Diane	13 A2
Tour Magne	14 A1

SLEEPING	
Hôtel Amphithéâtre	15 C4
New Hôtel La Baume	16 D3
Royal Hôtel	17 B3

EATING	
Brandade Raymond	18 C3
Del Sud	19 C3
La Maison Villaret	20 C3
Le Ciel de Nîmes	(see 5)
L'Enclos de la Fontaine	21 B2
Les Halles	22 C3
Les Halles Main Entrance	23 C3

Les Olivades	24 B4
Vintage Café	25 C3

DRINKING	
Le Haddock Café	26 C3

ENTERTAINMENT	
Auditorium	(see 5)
Billetterie des Arènes	27 C4
FNAC	28 C2
Théâtre de Nîmes	29 C3

TRANSPORT	
Bus Station	30 D6
Eurolines	(see 30)
Linebus	(see 30)
Park Vinci	31 C4
SNCF Boutique	32 C4

AVIGNON AREA

Contrasting yet complementing the temple, directly opposite is the glass-and-steel **Carrée d'Art** (Square of Art; ☎ 04 66 76 35 77; 15 place de la Maison Carrée). Home to the municipal library, *mediathéque* and Musée d'Art Contemporain (see below), the beautiful airy building is the brainchild of British architect Sir Norman Foster (1935–93).

JARDIN DE LA FONTAINE

Adorned with statues lining its green waterways, the **Fountain Garden** was laid out around the Source de la Fontaine (the site of a spring, temple and baths in Roman times). Don't miss the **Temple de Diane**, to the left of the main entrance.

A 10-minute walk uphill through the terraced garden brings you to the crumbly white shell of **Tour Magne** (adult/child €2.70/2.30; ⊙ 9am-7pm Jun-Aug, 9am-5.30pm Mar-May, Oct & Sep, 9.30am-4.30pm Nov-Feb), the largest of the many towers that ran along the city's 7km-long Roman ramparts. A spiral staircase of 140 steps leads to the top.

MUSEUMS

Nîmes' museums open from 10am to 6pm Tuesday to Sunday.

A wonderful Roman mosaic uncovered in 1883 is displayed in the **Musée des Beaux-Arts** (Fine Arts Museum; ☎ 04 66 67 38 21; musee.beauxarts@ville-nimes.fr; 20-22 rue de la Cité Foulc; adult/11-16yr €4.90/3.60) along with more run-of-the-mill Flemish, Italian and French works.

The **Musée d'Art Contemporain** (Contemporary Art Museum; ☎ 04 66 76 35 80; carreart@mnet.fr; place de la Maison Carrée; adult/11-16yr €4.90/3.60) on the 2nd floor of the Carrée d'Art features some ingenious works from the 1960s to 1990s, and is a great excuse to take in this stunning building from the inside out.

The city's 17th-century former Jesuit college now houses the **Musée d'Archéologie** (Archaeological Museum; ☎ 04 66 76 74 80; 18bis blvd Amiral Courbet; admission free), displaying columns, mosaics and sculptures from the Roman and pre-Roman periods; along with the **Musée d'Histoire Naturelle** (Natural History Museum; ☎ 04 66 76 73 45; 13bis blvd Amiral Courbet; adult/10-16yr €4.45/3.20). There's also the **Chapelle des Jésuits** (13bis blvd Amiral Courbet), sacred host to cultural happenings.

Even if you don't catch a bullfight you can gem up on bovine history and culture at the **Musée des Cultures Taurines** (Museum of Bullfighting

---

> **HISTORICAL MONUMENT COMBO**
>
> Save on Nîmes' big three – Les Arènes, La Maison Carrée and Tour Magne – with a **combination ticket** (adult/child €9/7).

Culture; ☎ 04 66 36 83 77; musee.taureau@ville-nimes.fr; 6 rue Alexandre Ducros; adult/10-16yr €4.65/3.40).

Less fascinating (but free) is the **Musée du Vieux Nîmes** (☎ 04 66 76 73 70; musee.vieux-nimes@ville-nimes.fr; place aux Herbes; admission free), a history museum in a 17th-century episcopal palace where among the eccentric collections, pin-ups of jeans-clad Elvis, James Dean and Marilyn Monroe showcase the famous fabric *de Nîmes*.

Tours

The tourist office runs two-hour city tours (€5.50) in French at 10am on Tuesday, Thursday and Saturday in summer, and 2.30pm on Saturday the rest of the year.

Sit back and let someone else worry about Nîmes' merry-go-round traffic aboard **Taxi TRAN** (☎ 04 66 29 40 11), which offers tours of the city (from €25 per hour for up to six people; pickup by arrangement) with recorded commentary in English. Inquire at the tourist office.

Festivals & Events

Nîmes' Spanish spirit comes to the fore during its *férias*, including the five-day **Féria de Pentecôte** (Pentecost Festival) in June, and the three-day **Féria des Vendanges** marking the start of the grape harvest on the third weekend in September. These *corridas*, which see bulls bred to be aggressively killed in a bloody spectacle involving picadors, *toreadors*, matadors and horses, and *novilladas* (fights with bulls less than four years old) are feverishly popular. Reserve tickets several months ahead via the Billetterie des Arènes or FNAC (see p199).

Courses Camarguaises (see the boxed text, p148) are also on show during the bullfighting season. The best bulls are rewarded with a couple of bars from Bizet's opera *Carmen* as they leave the arena.

Every Thursday between 6pm and 10.30pm in July and August, artists, artisans and food stalls selling local delicacies fill the main city squares during **Les Jeudis de Nîmes**.

Sleeping

Accommodation prices fluctuate wildly during *férias*.

AVIGNON AREA

A FIZZY DETOUR

Lift the lid on perennially popular Perrier water (400 million bottles a year are sold in France alone) by heading 13km southwest of Nîmes to the **Perrier plant** (☎ 04 66 87 61 01; adult/child €6/3; ⏰ tours by advance reservation 9.15am-5pm daily Jul & Aug, 9.30am-4pm Mon-Fri Feb-Jun & Sep-Dec). One-hour behind-the-scenes factory tours (in French) take in the manufacturing of Perrier's iconic green bottles, its bottling line and a tasting. From Nîmes, take the A9 or A54 and exit at Gallargue; the plant is on the RN113 in Vergèze.

CHAMBRES D'HÔTES

Maison de l'Octroi (☎ 04 66 27 15 95; www.bed-breakfast-nimes.com; 209 chemin de Russan; d incl breakfast €60-70; P X &) Host Nicole Crès keeps her two *chambre d'hôte* rooms spick-and-span and serves delicious breakfasts overlooking a 5000-sq-metre garden filled with oak and lime trees. (If you stay three or more nights, she also gives you a bottle of wine.) The house is 1.5km north of the city centre; parking is free.

Jardins Secrets (☎ 04 66 84 82 64; www.jardinssecrets.net; 3 rue Gaston Maruéjols; d €190-260; P X &) Palm trees, clambering plants and a profusion of flourishing flowers grace the 'secret garden' at this fashionable *chambre d'hôte*, a five-minute stroll from Les Arènes. Inside, rooms glow with polished floorboards and rich colours, with luxurious touches like tassel-curtained bathtubs. Breakfast is an additional €20; parking also costs €20.

HOTELS

Hôtel Amphithéâtre (☎ 04 66 67 28 51; hotel-amphitheatre@wanadoo.fr; 4 rue des Arènes; s €34-39, d €44-61; ⏰ Feb-Dec; X &) Just up the road from its namesake, this friendly, family-run hotel is snugly at home within a former pair of 18th-century mansions. Each of its 15 rooms is named after a writer or painter and a couple have balconies overlooking pedestrian place du Marché. Paul Valéry, Diderot and Beaumarchais on the 3rd floor have air-con.

Royal Hôtel (☎ 04 66 58 28 27; rhotel@wanadoo.fr; 3 blvd Alphonse Daudet; s €45-65, d €60-85) New owners have preserved the arty atmosphere of this hotel. The huge dove cage still sits beside reception and the local intelligentsia continue to discourse over coffee in La Bodeguita (open

6pm to late Monday to Saturday), its *très Espagnol* (or rather, *mismo Español*) café. Some of the artistically furnished rooms overlook place d'Assas, itself a work of modern art.

New Hôtel La Baume (☎ 04 66 76 28 42; www.new-hotel.com; 21 rue Nationale; s/d €95/120; X X 🖳 &) In true Nîmes style, traditional décor including stone staircases adorned in shades of ochre, beige and cream pairs perfectly with contemporary wrought iron and glass furnishings at this 34-room hotel wrapping around a beautiful interior courtyard. Wi-fi costs €9.50 for two hours; or you can use the internet point via a credit card for €0.35 per minute.

HOSTEL

Auberge de Jeunesse (☎ 04 66 68 03 20; www.hinimes.com; 257 chemin de l'Auberge de Jeunesse, la Cigale; dm €11.65, d/q €27.30/46.60; P 🖳) You'll find everything from dorms to cosy cottages for two to six in this botanical park 3.5km northwest of the train station. As well as a children's playground, self-catering facilities and bike hire (per day €14) there's limited camping (per person €5.85). Take bus I (direction Alès or Villeverte) to the Stade stop; it's a 500m walk uphill.

Eating & Drinking

Place aux Herbes, place du Marché with its crocodile and vast palm tree, and the western side of place de la Maison Carrée buzz with café life. Several cosy dining spots are hidden away on place de l'Esclafidous.

Vintage Café (☎ 04 66 21 04 45; 7 rue de Bernis; lunch menus €11-17, dinner menus €17-23; ⏰ lunch Tue-Fri, dinner Tue-Sat) Exhibitions by local artists add to the ambience of this buzzing little bistro. An intimate spot for authentic Languedoc cuisine like smoked haddock, it's also a cosy, convivial place to discover the region's fine vintages.

Le Haddock Café (☎ 04 66 67 86 57; 13 rue de l'Agau; menus €13-18; ⏰ 11am-3pm & 7pm-1am Mon-Sat; &) A highlight of Nîmois nightlife, this alternative café-bar hosts changing art exhibitions and concerts, and has an affordable and atmospheric restaurant with brimming bowls of *moules et frites* (mussels and fries) on Wednesdays at both lunch and dinner for €10.

Les Olivades (☎ 04 66 21 71 78; 18 rue Jean Reboul; lunch/dinner menu €11/26; ⏰ lunch & dinner Tue-Fri, dinner Sat) First and foremost this is a wonderful wine shop well worth dropping by in its own right to pick up a Costières de Nîmes from the pebble-sprinkled vineyards to the south. But make your way beyond the bottles to the cosy dining area out the back, which dishes up flavoursome regional fare.

Del Sud (☎ 04 66 67 22 50; 10 rue Littré; lunch/dinner menu €12/21; ☺ lunch & dinner Tue-Sat) Views of otherwise-hidden *hôtels particulier* can be savoured along with traditional Mediterranean cuisine in the 15th- to 18th-century courtyard of this popular spot, which has live music (and sometimes theatre) on Wednesdays.

Le Ciel de Nîmes (☎ 04 66 36 71 70; place de la Maison Carrée; mains €12/25; ☺ lunch & dinner Tue-Sun, until 2am Thu-Sat; ☖) Beneath a metallic-covered terrace with a stunning view of Nîmes' Roman temple, this chic rooftop hang-out at the Carrée d'Art is much favoured by fashionable Nîmois for its exemplary cuisine and has good wheelchair access.

L'Enclos de la Fontaine (☎ 04 66 21 90 30; www .hotel-imperator.com in French; quai de la Fontaine; menu €60, mains €22-28; ☺ lunch & dinner) At Nîmes' most beautiful garden restaurant, chef Patrick Chalamet delights with creations like marinaded venison with hazelnut sauce, followed by a mouthwatering selection of farm-fresh *fromage* (cheese). Afterwards the literary-minded can pop into the Hemingway Bar, and the romantically minded can head upstairs to the grand old rooms (doubles from €121) of the Hôtel Imperator Concorde.

SELF-CATERING

The vast covered food market **Les Halles** (rue Guizot, rue Général Perrir & rue des Halles; ☺ 6.30am-1pm) dating to 1885 is the city's 'gourmet soul'.

Caladons – Nîmes' honey and almond-studded biscuits – are sold at most patisseries. Rival *croquants Villaret* – rock-hard finger-shaped almond biscuits – have been baked by the Villaret family at **La Maison Villaret** (cnr rue de la Madeleine & place de l'Horloge) since 1775.

Veteran delicatessen **Brandade Raymond** (☎ 04 66 67 20 47; 34 rue Nationale) has made Nîmes' traditional salted-cod paste, *Brandade de Nîmes*, since 1879.

Entertainment

What's-on listings fill the fortnightly publication *À Nîmes*, available from the **tourist office** (☎ 04 66 58 38 00; www.ot-nimes.fr; 6 rue Auguste; ☺ 8am-8pm Mon-Sat, 10am-6pm Sun Jul & Aug, 8.30am-7pm Mon-Sat, 10am-5pm or 6pm Sun Sep-Jun).

Tickets for bullfights and cultural events are sold at outlets including FNAC, inside La Coupole des Halles indoor shopping centre; at the **Billetterie des Arènes** (☎ 04 66 02 80 90; www .arenesdenimes.com in French; 4 rue de la Violette; ☺ 9.30am-noon & 1.30-6pm Tue-Fri, 10am-1pm Sat); and on the latter's website.

Plays, ballet, modern dance and music recitals take place in the **Théâtre de Nîmes** (☎ 04 66 36 65 00; 1 place de la Calade). Documentaries and films (French only) are screened in the **auditorium** (☎ 04 66 76 35 36) inside the Carrée d'Art.

Getting There & Away

AIR

Aéroport Nîmes-Garons (☎ 04 66 70 49 49) is 10km southeast on the A54 to Arles. At press time, it was served only by Ryanair flights to/from England.

BUS

From the **bus station** (☎ 04 66 29 52 00; rue Ste-Félicité) bus services include Pont du Gard (€6.20, 45 minutes, six daily).

International bus operators **Eurolines** (☎ 04 66 29 49 02) and **Linebùs** (☎ 04 66 29 50 62) have offices at the far end of the terminal. SNCF buses head to Aigues-Mortes (€6.30, one hour) in the Camargue.

TRAIN

The city's **train station** (blvd Talabot) is at the southeastern end of av Feuchères. In town, tickets are sold at the **SNCF Boutique** (11 rue de l'Aspic; ☺ 8.30am-6.50pm Tue-Sat). Destinations include Avignon Centre (€7.50, 45 minutes, 10 or more daily) and Arles (€6.70, 30 minutes, nine daily). A number of SNCF trains head to Aigues-Mortes (€6.30, 40 minutes).

Getting Around

TO/FROM THE AIRPORT

An airport bus (€4.50, 30 minutes), leaving from the train station, meets all flights. Ring ☎ 04 66 29 52 00 to confirm times. Bus drivers sell tickets.

BICYCLE

Motorists parked in **Park Vinci** (place des Arènes; ☺ 24hr) can pick up a bike for free.

Véloland (☎ 04 66 36 01 80; 4 rue de la République; ☺ Tue-Sat & Mon am) rents mountain bikes (per half-/full day €9/15).

AROUND NÎMES

A short side trip from Nîmes brings you to the mighty Pont du Gard, straddling the wild

A SWEET DETOUR

From the Pont du Gard, drive 14km along the D981 to the **Musée du Bonbon** (☎ 04 66 22 74 39; Pont des Charrettes, Uzès; adult/5-15yr €4.50/2.50; ☑ 10am-7pm Jul & Aug, 10am-1pm & 2-6pm Tue-Sun Sep-Jun), a sweets museum where you can identify smells in the Espace Arôme, take part in a treasure hunt, and learn how many millions of jelly bears and kilometres of liquorice wheels are made each day by German sweet maker Haribo. Free sweets are doled out at reception, with trolleyloads for sale at wholesale prices.

river. For *chambre d'hôte* and self-catering accommodation contact **Gîtes de France** (☎ 04 66 36 96 30; www.tourismegard.com; Comité Départemental du Tourisme du Gard, 3 rue de la Cité Foulc; ☑ 8am-8pm Mon-Fri, 9.30am-noon Sat Jul & Aug, 8.45am-6pm Mon-Fri, 9.30am-noon Sat Sep-Jun) in Nîmes.

PONT DU GARD

The Romans didn't do anything on a small scale, and this awe-inspiring three-tiered aqueduct is no exception.

A Unesco World Heritage site, the exceptionally intact Pont du Gard was once part of a 50km-long system of canals built around 19 BC by Agrippa, Augustus' deputy and son-in-law (and the late father of Augustus' adoptive sons), to bring water from the Eure Springs in Uzès, 25km northwest, to Nîmes. The 35 arches of the 275m-long upper tier, running 50m above the River Gard, contain a 1.2m by 1.75m watercourse that, for a century and a half, carried 35,000 cu metres of water a day. Construction spanned 15 years and the aqueduct remained in use until the 3rd century.

From giant **car parks** (€5; ☑ closed 1am-6am) either side of the River Gard, you can walk along the road bridge, built in 1743, which runs parallel with the aqueduct's lower tier. The best view is from upstream, beside the river, where you can swim.

Visitor numbers reach a punishing 15,000 or so daily in July and August. Admission to the site is free; parking is reimbursed if you purchase a **combination ticket** (adult/child €10/8) or **family ticket** (2 adults & up to 4 children under 17yr €20). Combination and family tickets also cover the **museum** (admission €6), a 25-minute **film** (with English version €3) and the **Ludo** (admission €4.50), a fun and informative children's centre. The **Accueil du Pont du Gard** (☎ 08 20 90 33 30; www.pontdugard.fr; Le Portal, rte du Pont du Gard; ☑ 9.30am or 10am-5.30pm or 7pm, closed Mon morning) has information and sells tickets.

It's worth purchasing an explanatory booklet (€4, in English) for the 1.4km-long **Mémoires de Garrigue** (☑ 9.30am-6pm Apr–mid-Oct) walking trail through typical Mediterranean bush, scrubland and olive groves. A spectacular free **light show** (nightly Jul & Aug, Fri & Sat Jun & Sep) beams out into the summer night sky. From mid-June to mid-September, depending on numbers, it's possible to walk the bridge's topmost tier (€6) with a guide.

River Gard

The unpredictable River Gard descends from the Cévennes mountains. Torrential rains can raise the water level by as much as 5m in a flash, whereas during long dry spells it can almost disappear.

The river has sliced itself a meandering 22km gorge (Les Gorges du Gardon) through the hills from **Russan** to the village of **Collias**, about 6km upstream from the Pont du Gard. The GR6 trail runs beside it most of the way.

In Collias, 4km west of the D981, **Kayak Vert** (☎ 04 66 22 80 76; www.canoefrance.com/gardon) and **Canoë Le Tourbillon** (☎ 04 66 22 85 54; www.canoe-le-tourbillon.com), both based near the village bridge, rent out kayaks and canoes.

You can paddle 7km down to the Pont du Gard (€18 per person, two hours), or arrange to be dropped upstream, wending back through watery Gorges du Gardon (€30, full day), usually possible only between March and mid-June, when the river is high enough.

Getting There & Away

The Pont du Gard is 21km northeast of Nîmes and 26km west of Avignon. Buses to/from each (three to five daily) normally stop 1km north of the bridge. In summer, some make a diversion to the Pont du Gard car park.

Marseille & Around

TONY WHEELER

Les Calanques (p115) on Marseille's coast

JEAN-BERNARD CARILLET

Façades in Le Panier quarter (p97), Marseille

GREG ELMS

Bouillabaisse (p108) in Marseille

Sunflowers on a market stall, Aix-en-Provence (p123)

DIANA MAYFIELD

The Camargue

Gardians (Camargue cowboys; p148) during Feria Pascale, Arles

The Camargue's stunning pink flamingos (p137)

Austere architecture in the Camargue (p133)

Roman amphitheatre (p140), Arles

Avignon & Around

Palais des Papes (p161), Avignon

Pont d'Avignon (p159), Avignon

Brightly coloured buildings in Orange (p171)

Hunting for truffles (p178)

The Luberon

The hilltop village of Roussillon (p215)

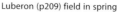
Luberon (p209) field in spring

Driving around the Luberon (p228)

Vineyard and cherry trees near Roussillon (p215)

Haute-Provence

Sisteron (p245)

Walking in the Parc National du
Mercantour (p248)

Lavender field in Banon (p249)

Morning mist in the Vallée du Haut Verdon (p251)

Nice & Around

Hotel Negresco, promenade des Anglais (p265), Nice

Carnaval de Nice parade float, place Masséna (p266), Nice

Crowded 17th-century buildings in Nice's old town (p265)

Nice from Parc du Château (p265)

Cannes & Around

Fortified monastery (p310) on Île St-Honorat, Îles de Lérins

Stone alley lined with art galleries, St-Paul de Vence (p319)

Façade of the Hôtel Majestic Barrière, boulevard de la Croisette (p301), Cannes

Flower market in Grasse (p325)

St-Tropez & Monaco

Palais Princier (p387), Monaco

Chestnuts in Collobrières (p360)

Café de Paris (p392), Monte Carlo

Sunset at the old port (p343), St-Tropez

The Luberon

The picture-perfect area that makes up the Luberon region might take the shape of a rectangle on the map. But navigating its bucolic rolling hills, golden-hued perched villages and hidden valleys is a little like fitting together a jigsaw puzzle.

Part of the Vaucluse *département* (administrative area), the Luberon is named after the main range – culminating with a 1100m-high summit – much of which is protected by the Parc Naturel Régional du Luberon. Split by the Combe de Lourmarin, with the Petit Luberon to the west and Grand Luberon to the east, the Luberon's lush landscapes are crisscrossed by a rambling network of country roads, way-marked walking tracks and signposted cycling routes.

Orchards bowed by blood red cherries, fertile fields of melons and crops, ribboned vineyards, olive groves and aromatic wild herbs buzzing with bees and fluttering butterflies envelop honey-coloured *mas* (Provençal farmhouses) in the lower altitudes. Beneath a canopy of oaks, the upper slopes shelter Bronze Age *bories* (beehive-shaped huts); while nearby, ochre-rich earth creates a powdery sunset-coloured palette. Lavender blazes on the plains around Buoux. Capped by chateaux, the massif's Mediterranean southern side around Pays d'Aigues is bordered by the rushing River Durance.

Cavaillon, to the west, and Apt, in the centre, are the region's two main towns. Both act as engine rooms driving the area's agricultural economy. At the Luberon's eastern edge, industrial Manosque creates natural cosmetics, shipping the scents of Provence to the world.

The Luberon's heady hues, fragrances and flavours subtly transform in tune with the seasons, and exploring even a piece of this picturesque region provides an ever-changing spectacle.

THE LUBERON

HIGHLIGHTS

- Drift up, up and away in the still morning air on a sunrise balloon flight in **Joucas** (p216)
- Get to the essence of Provence's perfusive purple flowers at the lavender museum at **Coustellet** (p223)
- Admire the opulent interiors of **Château d'Ansouis** (p229)
- Take a free behind-the-scenes winery tour and tasting at the Cave des Vignerons in **Pierrevert** (p230)
- Cling to the rugged rocks on a climbing expedition in **Buoux** (p226)

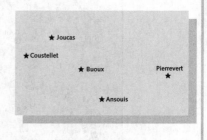

ITINERARIES

STUNNING STONEWORK   One Day / North of the N100

Sojourning at the former-foundry-turned-*chambre d'hôte,* **La Forge** (p218) on the edge of **Rustrel** (**1**; p217) provides the perfect stepping stone for an early-morning walk through the fiery-ochre rock formations of the **Colorado Provençal** (see the boxed text, p220). Then swing your handlebars or steering wheel west to the Luberon's capital, **Apt** (**2**; p212) to learn about its 18th-century earthenware production at the **Musée de l'Aventure Industrielle du Pays d'Apt** (p212).

After lunching on Serge Peuzin's candied creations at **Auberge du Luberon** (see the boxed text, p216), whiz west to Gargas to visit Europe's only operational **ochre quarry** (see the boxed text, p220). Continue west to rust-coloured **Roussillon** (**3**; p215) to amble along its **ochre trail** and take an **ochre workshop** (see the boxed text, p220).

Wiggle your way further west to **Gordes** (**4**; p216) for a glimpse of the village tiered over the valley. North of Gordes, marvel at the masonry skills of 12th-century monks at the **Abbaye Notre-Dame de Sénanque** (p217). Just west of Gordes, more stunning stonework is on view at the **Village des Bories** (**5**; p217), where the concentration of limestone-sliver huts creates spectacular sunlit patterns. For dinner, head southeast to cosy up in the stone dining room of chef Patrick Payet in **Goult** (**6**; p216), then snuggle up in one of his village-view *chambre d'hôte* rooms (or book in for a weeklong cooking course), before traversing the hilltops back towards Apt, or scooting south.

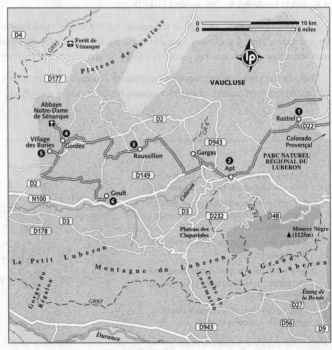

PETIT PROVENCE

Two to Three Days / Le Petit Luberon

A *petit* road trip between Cavaillon and Lourmarin packages up some of Provence's most toy-townlike hilltop villages with panoramas over the patchwork countryside.

Discover the delights of the small city of **Cavaillon** (**1**; p223) including its **melon-filled markets** (see the boxed text, p223), moving **Jewish Museum** (p223) and tantalising **gourmet shops** (p225); and dine in style at one of Provence's best restaurants, **Prévôt** (p225). Set off east in the morning for the rocky hilltop ruins of **Oppède-le-Vieux** (**2**; p222). Continue east to **Ménerbes** (**3**; p221), calling in to the quirky **corkscrew museum** (p222) before charting a course through the higgledy-piggledy village to learn about **wine and truffles** (p222) and feasting on Laurent Jouin's fare at his vaunted new restaurant, **Véranda** (p222). Then push east to **Lacoste** (**4**; p221) to gaze out over the former chateau of the **Marquis de Sade** (p221), where you can tour its ruins undergoing restoration, or catch an open-air concert.

Wind your way around the hillsides east to **Bonnieux** (**5**; p219) to scuttle up 86 steps to its **12th-century church** (p219), and stroll in its protected **cedar forest** (p219). Break your journey at Bonnieux's village-centre *chambre d'hôte*, **Le Clos du Buis** (p220) or live it up at Edouard Loubet's blissful **bastide** (country manor; p221). The following day, sluice through the deep **Combe de Lourmarin** (**6**; p226) to reach its namesake town, the former home of Albert Camus and Henri Bosco, whose trails can be followed on a **literary walking tour** (p228).

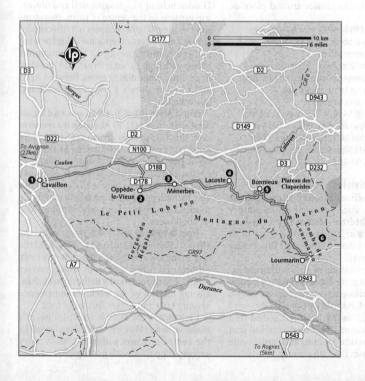

NORTH OF THE N100

Losing yourself in the lush Luberon hills is the ultimate way to absorb the area's charms. The N100, running through the area's capital, Apt, is the main delineation between its northern and southern regions.

APT

pop 11,500 / elev 250m

At the centre of the Luberon's cherry-laden orchards is its capital, Apt. The agricultural town's festive spirit comes alive at its Saturday-morning market, brimming with cherries, grapes, and candied and crystallised fruits; and peaks during its **wine festival**, held on the Ascension (May or June), when up to 30 chateaux show off their wares.

Apt is a handy pit stop for cyclists and walkers: the Luberon en Vélo cycling itinerary (see p81) passes through, as does the GR9 long-distance walking track.

Information

Commercial banks cluster around place de la Bouquerie.

Infotelec (☎ 04 90 04 46 40; www.luberon.org in French; 44 quai de la Liberté; per hr €5; ☻ 9am-noon & 3-7pm Mon-Sat) Internet access.

Laundrette (4 av Victor Hugo; ☻ 7am-8pm)

Luberon News (www.luberon-news.com) Information and what's-on listings for the entire region.

Post office (105 av Victor Hugo)

Tourist office (☎ 04 90 74 03 18; www.ot-apt.fr in French; 20 av Philippe de Girard; ☻ 9am-7pm Mon-Sat, 9.30am-12.30pm Sun Jul & Aug, 9am-noon & 2-6pm Mon-Sat, 9.30am-12.30pm Sun May, Jun & Sep, 9am-noon & 2-6pm Mon-Sat Oct-Apr)

Sights & Activities

Apt's tourist office has information on strolls around town, some passing the 11th-century **Ancienne Cathédrale Ste-Anne** (rue Ste-Anne; ☻ 8.30am-6pm Mon-Sat), where the relics of St Anne hold and illuminated 11th- and 12th-century manuscripts rest.

Gain an appreciation of Apt's artisan and agricultural roots at the **Musée de l'Aventure Industrielle du Pays d'Apt** (Industrial History Museum; ☎ 04 90 74 95 30; 14 place du Postel; adult/under 12yr €4/free; ☻ 10am-noon & 3-6.30pm Mon-Sat, 3-7pm Sun). In an old candied-fruit factory, the museum interprets the candied-fruit trade as well as ochre mining and earthenware production from the 18th century.

Thirty tonnes of cherries a day are candied at the **Confiserie Kerry Aptunion** (☎ 04 90 76 31 43; www.kerryaptunion.com; rte Nationale 100, quartier Salignan; ☻ shop 9am-noon & 2-6pm Mon-Sat), the world's largest crystallised-fruits factory, 2.5km west of town. Free guided factory tours are possible by reservation.

Sleeping & Eating

Many eating and sleeping options throughout this chapter are easily accessible by car from Apt.

Le Couvent (☎ 04 90 04 55 36; www.loucouvent.com in French; 36 rue Louis Rousset; d incl breakfast €75-120; ☒ ☙) Hidden behind a high stone wall and flowering gardens in the centre of town, this stunning *maison d'hôte* occupies a 17th-century convent and offers exceptional value for what you get; namely one of just five sumptuous rooms with high-speed internet, and breakfast in a vaulted stone dining room. Between April and October there's a two-night minimum at weekends.

Hôtel L'Aptois (☎ 04 90 74 02 02; www.aptois.fr.st; 289 cours Lauze de Perret; d €32-56) Above an inexpensive café, this surprisingly stylish cyclist-friendly hotel rents guests bikes that can be dropped off at points along the Luberon – Vélo bike routes, and does repairs. The cheapest rooms have toilets only, but they're all done out with chic fuchsia, purple and red taffeta and funky touches like designer lamps and slimline vases of silk flowers.

Thym, te Voilà (☎ 04 90 74 28 25; 59 rue St-Martin; mains €10; ☻ 11.30am-6pm Tue-Sat) Head to this sweet little spot in the town centre any time but especially on Saturday when a fresh-as-it-gets market soup bubbles aromatically in the open kitchen. During the rest of the week, the homemade savoury tarts and sugary flans are a treat.

L'Intramuros (☎ 04 90 06 18 87; 120 rue de la République; menus €14-27; ☻ lunch & dinner Tue-Sat) In the centre of town within a 19th-century grocery shop filled with nostalgic bric-a-brac

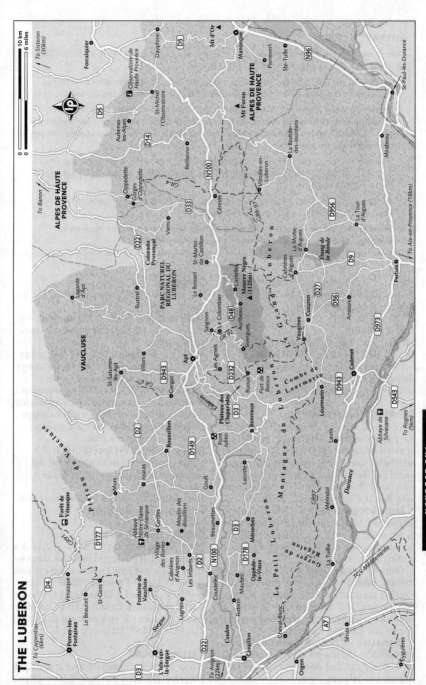

THE LUBERON

LITERARY LUBERON

There's more on the list than the classic *A Year in Provence* (Peter Mayle), regaling the Mayles' move to the Luberon and renovation of a *mas* in Ménerbes (p221).

▪ *Confessions of a French Baker* (Peter Mayle and Gerard Auzet) The secret behind successful breadmaking, revealed by Cavaillon-based baker Auzet (p224) and his English novelist mate.

▪ *Hotel Pastis* (Peter Mayle) Set in Bonnieux, this departure from autobiography sees Mayle delve into fiction with equal passion for Provençal life. *A Good Year*, Mayle's novel-turned-film about a British financier who inherits a Luberon vineyard is likewise a fictional romp through this neck of the woods.

▪ *Village in the Vaucluse* (Lawrence Wylie) Published in the mid-1970s, Wylie wrote this amusing account of life in red-rock Roussillon in the 1950s, decades before all and sundry jumped on the travelogue bandwagon.

▪ *The Luberon Garden* (Alex Dingwall-Main) An English garden designer uproots his family from London to landscape a secret garden in Ménerbes.

▪ *The Man Who Planted Trees* (Jean Giono) A jewel-like short story from this much-loved Manosque writer, many of whose works are available in English.

---

like old coffee grinders, this simple little family-run place is beloved by locals for its 'instinctive Provençal' cooking.

SELF-CATERING

Markets aside (see the boxed text, p217), try **L'o à la Bouche** (98 rue St-Pierre) or **Via Domitia** (19 quai Léon Sagy), two *épiceries fines* (upmarket grocery shops). Directly across from the tourist office is Apt's best boulangerie (bakery).

Drinking & Entertainment

Place de la Bouquerie abounds with cafés like the gregarious **Grand Café Grégoire** (☎ 04 90 04 93 69; place de la Bouquerie; menus from €13.50; ☼ restaurant lunch Thu-Tue, dinner Thu-Mon, bar 6am-1am daily), which opens out the back to a terraced garden filled with umbrellas, and with a billiards table inside. Rue St-Pierre is another hot spot.

Brasserie St-John's (☎ 04 90 74 58 59; place St-Pierre; ☼ closed Sun) Also lively is the pavement terrace at Brasserie St-John's, which has energetic young owners, a fun, friendly vibe and good music (sometimes live).

Pâtisserie Rousset (☎ 04 90 74 14 34; 196 rue des Marchands; dishes €5-9.50; ☼ Tue-Sun) Although the word on the streets of Apt is that this *salon de thé* (tearoom) isn't the 'it' spot it once was, it's worth dropping by for the perennially popular cherry-and-lavender ice cream.

Cinema César (☎ 08 92 68 69 20; www.cinemacesar.fr.tc in French; rue Scudery) screens (often nondubbed) art-house flicks and documentaries as well mainstream releases.

Shopping

For souvenirs with style, pop into the following shops:

Abotis Création (☎ 04 90 04 56 86; www.abotis.com; 494 av Viton) Unusual handcrafted furniture stained with natural pigments.

Atelier Buisson Kessler (☎ 04 90 04 89 61; 20 place du Septier) Small *poterie* (pottery) workshop specialising in contemporary, big 'n' bold bowls, plates and tiles.

Cave du Septier (☎ 04 90 04 77 38; www.vcommevin .com in French; place du Septier) For many, the region's best-stocked wine cellars; rare and highly sought-after vintages.

Confiserie Marcel Richaud (48 quai de la Liberté) Candied figs, cherries and other fruits.

Faïences Atelier du Viel Apt (☎ 04 90 04 03 96; 61 place Carnot) Earthenware featuring the gold- and mud-coloured marbled finish that was all the rage in 18th-century Apt.

La Bonbonnière (57 rue de la Sous-Préfecture) Another place for candied figs, cherries and other fruits.

Getting There & Away

From the **bus station** (☎ 04 90 74 20 21; 250 av de la Libération) east of the centre there are buses to/from Avignon (€7.90, 1¼ hours, three or four daily), to Aix-en-Provence (€9.40, 1½ hours, two daily), Digne-les-Bains (€7.30, two hours, one or two daily), Cavaillon (via Coustellet; €4.80, 40 minutes, two or three daily) and Marseille (€10.90, 2½ hours, two daily).

Getting Around

Equip yourself with pedal power at **Sport 2000** (☎ 04 90 04 30 00; 669 av Victor Hugo; ☼ 10am-12.30pm &

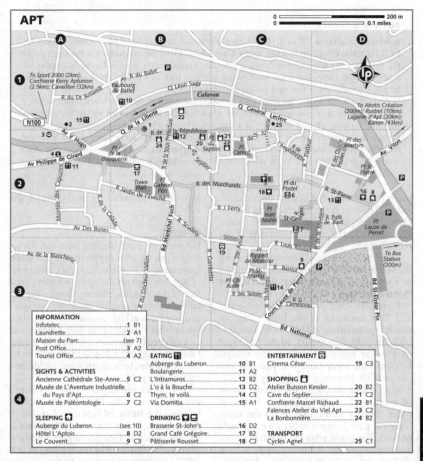

APT

0 ————— 200 m
0 ————— 0.1 miles

To Sport 2000 (2km);
Confiserie Kerry Aptunion
(2.5km); Cavaillon (32km)

N100

To Abotis Création
(200m); Rustrel (10km);
Lagarde d'Apt (20km);
Banon (43km)

To Bus
Station
(200m)

INFORMATION		
Infotelec	1	B1
Laundrette	2	A1
Maison du Parc	(see 7)	
Post Office	3	A2
Tourist Office	4	A2

SIGHTS & ACTIVITIES		
Ancienne Cathédrale Ste-Anne	5	C2
Musée de L'Aventure Industrielle du Pays d'Apt	6	C2
Musée de Paléontologie	7	C2

SLEEPING		
Auberge du Luberon	(see 10)	
Hôtel L'Aptois	8	D2
Le Couvent	9	C3

EATING		
Auberge du Luberon	10	B1
Boulangerie	11	A2
L'Intramuros	12	B2
L'o à la Bouche	13	D2
Thym, te voilà	14	C3
Via Domitia	15	A1

DRINKING		
Brasserie St-John's	16	D2
Grand Café Grégoire	17	B2
Pâtisserie Rousset	18	C2

ENTERTAINMENT		
Cinema César	19	C3

SHOPPING		
Atelier Buisson Kessler	20	B2
Cave du Septier	21	C2
Confiserie Marcel Richaud	22	B1
Faïences Atelier du Viel Apt	23	C2
La Bonbonnière	24	B2

TRANSPORT		
Cycles Agnel	25	C1

2.30-7pm Mon-Sat), a vast sports shop with a bike-rental outlet 1km west of the tourist office. Rental starts at €12/115 a day/week, including helmet and puncture-repair kit.

Similar rates are charged at **Cycles Agnel** (☎ 04 90 74 17 16; 86 quai Général Leclerc; ⏱ 8.30am-noon & 2.15-7pm Tue-Fri, 8.30am-12.15pm & 2.15-5.30pm Sat).

AROUND APT

On the N100's northern side, there are two worthwhile circuits from Apt. One takes you northwest to Roussillon, Gordes and the Abbaye Notre-Dame de Sénanque returning via the pretty villages of **Joucas** (population 321), St-Saturnin-lès-Apt and hilltop **Villars** (population 700). Alternatively, heading northeast, Provence's 'Colorado' (see the boxed text,

p220) makes for a colourful trip. If time is of the essence, both loops can be covered (at a cracking pace) in the same day – see the itinerary, p210.

Sights & Activities

Some of Provence's most quintessential sights – impossibly pretty villages, ochre-rich earth, beehive-shaped *bories*, lavender fields and a stunning Cistercian abbey – are all just a few kilometres apart in this picturesque patch around Apt.

ROUSSILLON

Some two millennia ago, the Romans used the ochreous earth around the village of Roussillon (population 1190; elevation 360m), set in

THE LUBERON

THE LUBERON

AUTHOR'S CHOICE

Auberge du Luberon (☎ 04 90 74 12 50; www.auberge-luberon-peuzin.com; 8 place Faubourg du Ballet, Apt; d €58-118, menus €29-62; ✆ restaurant lunch & dinner; Ⓟ Ⓧ) This cosy inn just a few footsteps across the river from the historic town centre of Apt has 14 guest rooms in warm Provençal colours like (aptly enough) cherry red; some have added comforts such as minibars. Hotel parking costs €7 (or you'll usually find a free spot on the adjacent quay).

Among Luberon locals, the inn is best known as the home of Apt's finest restaurant, which is the magnum opus of chef Serge Peuzin. Hot news from the kitchen: when we last visited, Serge was busy building what he describes as a *'cuisine professionnelle pour des amateurs'* ('professional kitchen for amateurs') where he'll share the secrets of his sweet sauces, jams, glazed fruits and *tapenades* (pastes) using candied fruits during cooking courses. Check the website or with Apt's tourist office (☎ 04 90 74 03 18; www.ot-apt.fr in French) for schedules.

---

the valley between the Plateau de Vaucluse and the Luberon range, for producing pottery glazes. These days the whole village – even gravestones in the cemetery – is built of the reddish stone.

From the town, take a 45-minute walk along the **Sentier des Ocres** (see the boxed text, p220) or a workshop at the **Conservatoire des Ocres et Pigments Appliqués** (see the boxed text, p220).

Roussillon – which is 9km east of Gordes and 7km northeast of the little village of Goult (population 1310) – is inaccessible by public transport. Motorists must park in car parks (€2) outside the village, a 300m walk away (and yes, you will still see tourists brazenly blockading the miniscule village streets, to the consternation of locals and amid the tooting horns of other tourists attempting to do the same – the car park is much easier on everyone's nerves). The **tourist office** (☎ 04 90 05 60 25; www.roussillon-provence.com in French; place de la Poste; ✆ 10am-noon & 2-5.30pm Mon-Sat) has in-

---

DOWN THE TRACK

Trains ceased operating to Apt in the 1960s, but the disused railway tracks are now, slowly, being turned into an extensive **cycleway** that will allow cyclists to steer completely clear of traffic. At press time 6km of the route was open west from Apt's former train station, but 2008 should see the completion of a 70km stretch from Cavaillon to Forcalquier. Further down the track, the cycleway will extend into Italy. Ask at Apt's **tourist office** (☎ 04 90 74 03 18; www.ot-apt.fr in French; 20 av Philippe de Girard) for the latest.

---

formation on walks in and around the village.

GORDES

Forming an amphitheatre over the Rivers Sorgue and Calavon, the tiered village of **Gordes** (population 2127; elevation 372m), 20km west of Apt, sits high on the white, southern rock face of the Vaucluse plateau. Gordes has top billing on many tourists' must-see lists (particularly those of high-profile Parisians). High season sees a cavalcade of tour coaches and cars ushered by attendants into parking bays. Early evenings, the village is theatrically lit by the setting sun, turning the stone buildings a shimmering gold.

Apart from celebrity-spotting, the village's star attraction is its 11th-century chateau housing the **Musée Pol Mara** (☎ 04 90 72 02 75; place du Château; adult/10-17yr €4/3; ✆ 10am-noon & 2-6pm), dedicated to Flemish painter Pol Mara, who lived in Gordes. The **tourist office** (☎ 04 90 72 02 75; www.gordes-village.com; place du Château; ✆ 9am-12.30pm & 2-6pm Jun-Sep, 9am-noon & 2-5pm Oct-May) is in the guards hall of the chateau.

Just outside Gordes, 6km northeast in Joucas, you can take off for a blissful balloon flight over the Luberon with **Hot-Air Ballooning Provence** (☎ 04 90 05 74 39; www.avignon-et-provence.com/ballooning; 1½hr flights from €230, sunrise flights €305).

Heading 3.5km south along rte de St-Pantaléon (D148) you hit the **Moulin des Bouillons** (☎ 04 90 72 22 11; rte de St-Pantaléon; adult/10-17yr €4.50/3; ✆ 10am-noon & 2-5pm or 6pm Feb-30 Oct), an oil mill with a Gallo-Roman 10m-long press weighing seven tonnes, said to be the oldest in the world.

Buses operated by Cavaillon-based **Les Express de la Durance** (☎ 04 90 71 03 00) link Gordes with Cavaillon up to three times daily between Monday and Saturday. Motorists must park in the car park (€3) opposite the bright blue piece of monumental art by Hungarian sculptor Victor de Vasarely (an honorary citizen of Gordes) at the bottom of the village.

VILLAGE DES BORIES

You'll spot beehive-shaped *bories* while you're buzzing around Provence (1610 have been counted to date), but the **Village des Bories** (☎ 04 90 72 03 48; adult/child €5.50/3; ⏰ 9am-8pm Jun-Sep, 9am-5.30pm Oct-May) has hoards of them.

Reminiscent of Ireland's *clochàn*, these one- or two-storey dry-walled huts constructed from slivers of limestone were first built in the area in the Bronze Age. Up until the 18th century, they were lived in, renovated and even built from scratch. Their original purpose isn't known (shelter would seem most likely), but over time they've also been used as workshops, wine cellars and storage sheds. This 'village' contains about 20 *bories*, best visited early in the morning or just before sunset for the interplay of light and shadows.

The village is 4km southwest of Gordes in the direction of Cavaillon. Getting here is easiest with your own wheels, but buses from Gordes to Cavaillon can drop you 1.5km from the village.

ABBAYE NOTRE-DAME DE SÉNANQUE

Framed by fields of lavender in July, this picture-postcard Cistercian **abbey** (☎ 04 90 72 05 72; www.senanque.fr in French; guided tour in French adult/6-18yr €6/2.50; ⏰ by reservation), 4km northwest of Gordes off the D177, was founded in 1148 and is inhabited by a few young monks today. Mass is celebrated at noon on weekdays and 9am Sunday.

ST-SATURNIN-LÈS-APT

Rooftop views of St-Saturnin-lès-Apt (population 2393), 9km north of Apt, and the surrounding Vaucluse hilltops can be enjoyed from the **17th-century windmill**, 1km north of the village off the D943 to Sault. Follow signs for Le Château Les Moulins.

In the village, discover how olives are turned into oil at the **Moulin à Huile Jullien** (☎ 04 90 75 45 80; 1 rue Albert Trouchet). Its boutique can be visited year-round but the mill can only be visited during the December olive harvest.

MARKET DAY

The Luberon's fresh, fabulous food markets take place from around 8am to 1pm unless otherwise noted.

Monday Cadenet, Cavaillon and Lauris
Tuesday Apt, Cucuron, Gordes, Lacoste, La Tour d'Aigues, St-Saturnin-lès-Apt
Wednesday Coustellet (from 5.30pm June to September), Mérindol, Pertuis
Thursday Ansouis, Céreste, La Tour d'Aigues (mid-May to September)
Friday Bonnieux, Cavaillon, Lourmarin, Pertuis, Roussillon
Saturday Apt, Cadenet (farmers market May to October), Lauris (2pm to 5pm winter, 5pm to 8pm summer), Manosque, Oppède-le-Vieux, Pertuis, Vaugines
Sunday Coustellet (April to December), Vaugines

OBSERVATOIRE SIRENE

In Lagarde d'Apt, 20km northeast of Apt, the **Sirene Observatory** (☎ 04 90 75 04 17; www.obs-sirene.com in French; day/night visit €8/40; ⏰ by reservation year-round) lets you learn about astronomy amid the lavender fields by day, but the best time to visit is during an all-night star-gazing session sustained by coffee and goats cheese.

Lagarde d'Apt is also home to a lavender trail (see the boxed text, p226).

RUSTREL & AROUND

The russet red village of **Rustrel** (population 621), 10km northeast of Apt, is the threshold to the otherworldly ochre formations of the **Colorado Provençal** (see the boxed text, p220). For aerial views, take off with paragliding school **Rustr'aile Colorado** (☎ 04 40 04 96 53; www.parapente.biz in French; Le Stade), signposted on the D112. Baptism flights cost €70 to €100.

The eastbound D22 and D33 link Rustrel with **Viens** (population 500), a starting point for forays into the limestone canyon **Gorges d'Oppedette**. From Viens the 3km-long **Circuit des Bories** takes afternoon strollers past several *bories;* yellow markers flag the footpath. In Roman times the Via Domitia passed through **Céreste** (population 1045; elevation 380m), 8km south. Just outside Céreste on the D31, visit the family-run lavender farm **Le Frigoulet** (☎ 04 92 79 05 87; humannfrigoulet@aol.com; ⏰ by reservation).

From Céreste the N100 travels east to Haute-Provence. Lavender fields link these two regions along the scenic northbound D14. Céreste's **tourist office** (☎ 04 92 79 09 84; www .cereste.fr in French; place de la République; ⏱ 10am-noon & 3-6.30pm Mon-Sat, 10am-noon Sun) has information for the area.

Sleeping & Eating

Tourist offices, including in Apt, have information about seasonal camp sites.

La Forge (☎ 04 90 04 92 22; www.laforge.com.fr; Notre-Dame des Anges, Rustrel; d incl breakfast €86-199, picnics & tray meals by reservation €15; P ✗ ☎) Deep within the Colorado Provençal, bordered by forest, this 1840-built former iron and steel foundry has been transformed by artist Dominique Berger-Ceccaldi and her husband Claude into an incredible *maison d'hôte*. Dominique's stylised paintings grace the four rooms and breakfast is served beneath a vine-trailed trellis by the pool. A heartfelt note in the bathrooms alerts guests to indelible stains from ochreous earth (ie don't wipe your shoes on the towels).

La Mas de la Beaume (☎ 04 92 72 02 96; www .labeaume.com; Gordes; d incl breakfast €105-165; P ☎) Behind a stone wall at the top of the road leading to Gordes, this potpourri-scented five-room *maison d'hôte* is the pride and joy of hosts Wendy and Miguel. Beneath a wood-beamed ceiling, the 'blue room' has views of Gordes' chateau and bell tower from the bed. Homegrown produce from the garden arrives on your plate at breakfast and at the twice-weekly table d'hôte (literally 'host's table'; in set courses with little or no choice).

Le Mas Perréal (☎ 04 90 75 46 31; www.masperreal .com; Lieu-dit la Fortune, St-Saturnin-lès-Apt; d incl breakfast €110-125; P ✗ ☎) If you're keen to *améliorer votre Français* (improve your French), Perréal's charming hostess, Elisabeth, a longtime French teacher, offers lessons of all levels to guests (€25 per hour for one or two people) in the shade of the property's vineyards and cherry orchards. When the winter chill sets in, breakfast is served in the cosy farmhouse kitchen. Find the *mas* 1.5km southwest of St-Saturnin-lès-Apt.

Patrick Payet's Chambres de Village (☎ 04 90 72 22 35; www.famous-provence.com; place de l'Ancienne Mairie, Goult; d incl breakfast €81; menu €26; ⏱ dinner Tue-Sun) Picture yourself staying in a charming 18th-century 'room in the village' of Goult with chateau views, creating culinary masterpieces alongside a Provençal chef. Patrick Payet provides intimate and entertaining weeklong programs from €2600 per person including accommodation, meals and visits to surrounding villages. The cosy stone restaurant and guest rooms are open to non-program participants, but you'll need to book ahead.

La Bastide Saint Joseph (☎ 04 90 04 97 80; www .bastide-saint-joseph.com; rte de Banon (D22), Rustrel; d incl breakfast €120-160; P ☎) Phenomenal views of the Colorado Provençal's flame red ochre cliffs unfold from three of the four guest

---

PARC NATUREL RÉGIONAL DU LUBERON

Egyptian vultures, eagle owls, wild boars, Bonelli's eagles and Etruscan honeysuckle are among the species that call the 1650-sq-km **Luberon Regional Park** home. Created in 1977 and recognised as a Biosphere Reserve by Unesco in 1997, the park encompasses 67 villages with a combined population of 155,000, dense forests and unexpected gorges. The GR6, GR9, GR92 and GR97 walking trails all cross it, as does a 230km-long **cycling route** (see p81). For amblers, there is a **sentier botanique** (botanical trail) through the park's oldest cedar forest (Bonnieux; opposite); a trail around **ochre cliffs** (Roussillon; see the boxed text, p220); and a **bories discovery path** (Viens; p217).

Information, maps and guides are available at the **Maison du Parc** (☎ 04 90 04 42 00; www .parcduluberon.fr in French; 60 place Jean Jaurès, Apt; ⏱ 8.30am-noon & 1.30-7pm Mon-Sat Jul-Sep, 8.30am-noon & 1.30-6pm Mon-Fri Oct-Mar). Between March and August, you can join a thematic nature work-shop-walk (French only; adult/under 18 years €5/free). The Maison du Parc's on-site **Musée de Paléontologie** (Palaeontology Museum; adult/child €1.50/free; ⏱ 8.30am-noon & 1.30-7pm Mon-Sat Jul-Sep, 8.30am-noon & 1.30-6pm Mon-Fri Oct-Mar) provides a historical framework, with prehistoric flora and fauna displays.

Guides sold at the Maison du Parc include topoguide *Le Naturel Régional Parc du Luberon à pied* (PN07; in French; €11.90), detailing 24 walks including the GR trails; and the topoguide *Walks in Provence* (PN04; €11.95), which outlines 24 shorter walks (3km to 20km).

Lonely Planet's *Walking in France* also suggests Luberon routes.

rooms at this contemporary *chambre d'hôte* 1km east of Rustrel. In addition to a bountiful breakfast, rates include afternoon drinks and poolside canapés.

Les Grands Camps (☎ 04 90 74 67 33; Le Chêne, Gargas; menu incl wine & coffee €24; ☒ lunch Sun, dinner Mon, Wed, Fri & Sat Jul & Aug, lunch Sun, dinner Fri & Sat Sep-Jun) This unpretentious *ferme auberge*, not far from Gargas' ochre quarry (see the boxed text, p220), cooks up meat, meat and more farm-fresh meat (and sometimes poultry).

Le Mas Tourteron (☎ 04 90 72 00 16; chemin de St-Blaise, Les Imberts; menu €57; ☒ lunch Sun, dinner Wed-Sun Mar-Oct) Dining at the lilac-clothed tables in the stone dining room or amid the flourishing gardens of Chef Elisabeth Bourgeois-Baique and her sommelier husband Philippe's welcoming *mas* is like eating at the home of friends. Elisabeth's seasonally changing *menus* of beautifully presented dishes garnished with sprigs of herbs and lavender and her legendary desserts marry with wines hand picked by Philippe from over 200 vintages in their cellar. The *mas* sits 3.5km south of Gordes village.

SOUTH OF THE N100

To the south of the N100 artery, the deep Combe de Lourmarin carves a north–south divide through the Luberon massif. Bonnieux sits on the western 'little Luberon' side, while Buoux, less than 10km east, is in the Grand Luberon (p226).

LE PETIT LUBERON

The rocky landscape of Le Petit Luberon is sprinkled with cake-decorationlike *villages perchés* overlooking thick cedar forests and Côtes du Luberon vineyards. Bonnieux's tourist office (right) has regional information including lists of estates where you can taste and buy wines and the other local nectar, honey (see the boxed text, p224). At the region's western edge, Cavaillon's tourist office (p223) also has comprehensive information.

Bonnieux & Around
pop 1436 / elev 425m

Bonnieux burst onto cinema screens in late 2006 as the village where Russell Crowe's character Max Skinner, a British finance broker, finds *joie de vivre* in the vineyards of Provence. Based on the 2004 novel *A Good Year* by Peter Mayle and directed by Ridley

Scott, its filming was a good year for Crowe and his wife, whose second child, so locals proudly proclaim, was conceived in Bonnieux (apparently the mayor has offered baby Crowe honorary citizenship).

Navigating Bonnieux, 11km southwest of Apt and 26km east of Cavaillon, is a little jigsaw puzzle in itself. The village straddles several levels, making it easy to miss the **tourist office** (☎ 04 90 75 91 90; www.tourisme-en-luberon .com in French; 7 place Carnot; ☒ 9.30am-12.30pm & 2-6pm Mon-Sat) hiding high above a stone wall – the adjacent restaurant Le Fournil (p221) acts as a handy landmark. From place de la Liberté, 86 steps lead to the 12th-century **Église Vieille du Haut**, while the history of bread-making is raised at the **Musée de la Boulangerie** (☎ 04 90 75 88 34; 12 rue de la République; adult/12-18yr €3/1.50; ☒ 10am-noon & 2.30-6pm or 6.30pm Wed-Mon Apr-Oct), a former bakery.

South of Bonnieux is **Forêt des Cèdres** (1861), a protected cedar forest through which runs a **sentier botanique** (botanical trail). Heading north, taste and buy local wine in the village cooperative, **Caves des Vignerons de Bonnieux**

NATURE'S PAINT PALETTE

Although ochre has been used in the Luberon since Roman times, it wasn't until 1785 that large deposits of the hydrated oxidised iron-and-clay sands were mined industrially. In 1929 – the peak of the ochre industry – some 40,000 tonnes of ochre were mined around Apt, 90% of which was exported to other parts of Europe and America.

Traditionally used as a pigment to colour pots and buildings, ochre comes in some 25 shades ranging from delicate yellow to vivid orange and fire red. Discover these vibrant hues first-hand along short walking trails in Rustrel's **Colorado Provençal** (☎ 04 32 52 09 75; 9am–dusk), a savage landscape of red-ochre sand with rock formations like the fiery upright **Cheminée de Fée** (Fairy Chimney). The extraordinary formations were part of a quarry where ochre was mined from the 1880s until 1956. Today the area is in the process of being listed as a heritage site.

Colour-coded trails for two of the most dramatic trails – the 'blue' **Sentier de Cheminée de Fée** (1km) and the 'red' **Sentier du Sahara** (1.5km) – can be picked up in the Parking des Mille Couleurs car park, signposted south of Rustrel village off the D22 to Banon. Parking costs €3.50 (free November to March), including a trail map.

An equally dramatic discovery is at **Colorado Aventures** (☎ 06 78 26 68 91; www.colorado-aventures .com in French; adult/child €18/14; closed Jan), a Tarzan-style obstacle course rigged between red rocks in a forest. The site, signposted off the D22, is a rocky 15-minute walk from the car park. Kids need to be 150cm tall. Rustrel is the closest town. Call for annual schedules.

Westwards, in Gargas (population 3000; elevation 280m), 4km northwest of Apt, Europe's last remaining **ochre quarry**, run by **Sociétés Ocres en France** (www.ocres-de-france.com), can be visited by guided tour on Friday mornings, with exhibitions (€3) on Monday, Tuesday and Friday from 9am to noon and 4pm to 6pm. The quarry produces around 1000 tonnes of ochre a year, 45% of which is exported. Tours must be booked through the **Gargas mairie** (town hall; ☎ 04 90 74 12 70; info@ville-gargas.fr; adult/under 16yr €6/free) and include a visit to the village's **ochre exhibition** (place des Jardins; adult/under 16yr €1.50/1; 9am–noon & 4-6pm Mon, Tue & Thu, reduced hr in winter).

In rust-coloured Roussillon you can take a 45-minute walk along the **Sentier des Ocres** (Ochre Trail; admission €2; 9.30am-5.30pm Mar-11 Nov). Within fairy-tale groves of chestnuts, maritime pines and scrub the trail leads you through nature's powdery sunset-coloured paint palette of ochre formations created by erosion and winds over centuries. Don't wear white!

Workshops (some in English), exploring the colouring properties of ochre, and factory tours are held at the **Conservatoire des Ocres et Pigments Appliqués** (Applied Pigment & Ochre Conservatory; ☎ 04 90 05 66 69; www.okhra.com in French; rte d'Apt; guided tours adult/student €5/3; office 9am-7pm daily Jul & Aug, to 6pm Tue-Sun Sep-Jun), on the D104 east towards Apt. Guided tours depart every half-hour between 10am to noon and 2pm to 6pm in July and August; call for tour times the rest of the year.

If that's not enough, there's the **Ocres en Vélo cycling trail** (see p82).

(☎ 04 90 75 80 03; www.cave-bonnieux.com; La Gare de Bonnieux; 9am-12.30pm & 2.30-6.30pm Mon-Sat), and stop by the three-arched Roman bridge, **Pont Julien** (27 BC–AD 14), 6km north on the D149.

SLEEPING & EATING

Seasonal camp sites are pitched around the village.

Le Clos du Buis (☎ 04 90 75 88 48; www.leclosdubuis .fr; rue Victor Hugo; d incl breakfast €84-112, cottages per week from €300; P 🐾 🖳) Smack-dab in the village, this stone townhouse *chambre d'hôte* spills out to a vast garden. The dining room serves up panoramic views along with tables d'hôtes (by reservation), and there's a self-catering

kitchen for guests. One of its six rooms is wheelchair accessible, and parking and wi-fi are free. Hosts Lydia and Pierre also rent out three cottages in the Luberon countryside.

La Bouquière (☎ 04 90 75 87 17; www.labouquiere .com; d incl breakfast €90-120; P 🖳) Down a meandering country lane through the cherry trees, at this remote *chambre d'hôte* all four airy rooms open onto gardens filled with chirping birds and the fluttering wings of bees and butterflies, and at night a glittering sea of stars. From Bonnieux village, follow the D3 in the direction of Apt for 2km, then turn left (there's a small sign) onto the chemin de Gardioles for 1km, then turn right (there's a *very* small sign) and traverse the bumpy track to the house.

Auberge de l'Aiguebrun (☎ 04 90 04 47 00; www .aubergedelaiguebrun.com; d cabanon €134, d €140-240; lunch/dinner menu €35/55; P ⊠ ⊠) Sleep in a *cabanon* (wooden chalet) by the river or in the main house, dine at stone tables on a cobbled terrace with rustic views, and stroll through gardens graced with peacocks, a greenhouse and dovecote. The inn is hidden in the dramatic heart of the Combe de Lourmarin, 6km southeast of Bonnieux off the D943.

La Bastide de Capelongue (☎ 04 90 75 89 78; www .capelongue.com; d from €160, menus €121-160, mains from €42; ⊠ closed mid-Nov–mid-Mar; P ⊠ ⊠ ⊡ ⊠) Those *menu* prices make you look twice until you realise that this magnificently restored *bastide* high above Bonnieux is the brand-new bastion of wunderkind chef Édouard Loubet who moved here with his two Michelin stars from Lourmarin, though he still has a hand over there too (see p228). Impeccably decorated by Edouard's mother, his grandmother is the inspiration for many of his renowned recipes; pick up his cookbooks at reception.

Le Fournil (☎ 04 90 75 83 62; 5 place Carnot; lunch/dinner menu €20/37; ⊠ lunch & dinner Wed, Thu, Fri & Sun, dinner Tue & Sat) The Bakehouse is a cut above the average village restaurant – literally. Its glass-and-steel interior is sliced into a rock face, with a fountain in front. Service can be temperamental, but creations like courgette cake with tiny prawns, thyme-dressed shoulder of lamb or *soupe de cerise au vin rouge* (cherry and red-wine soup) are consistently first-rate.

GETTING THERE & AROUND
Buses to/from Apt and Marseille stop in Bonnieux. **Mountain Bike Luberon** (☎ 04 90 75 89 96, 06 83 25 48 07; rue Marceau; ⊠ 8.30am-noon & 1.30-6.30pm Mon-Fri) rents bikes for €14/25/74 per day/ weekend/week. It also has children's seats (€3 per day) and trailers (€5 per day) for hire, and delivers bikes within a 15km radius (free).

Lacoste
pop 417 / elev 320m
Its name may be unrelated to the crocodile-emblem clothing label, but Lacoste, 6.5km west of Bonnieux, does have couturier connections. Earlier this decade, designer Pierre Cardin purchased the 9th-century **Château de Lacoste**, where the notorious Marquis de Sade (1740–1814) retreated when his writings became too scandalous for Paris.

The erotic novels penned by the Marquis (who gave rise to the term 'sadism'), including *120 Journées de Sodome* (120 Days of Sodom; 1785), were only freely published after WWII. De Sade spent chunks of his childhood in Provence where his family had owned Château de Lacoste since 1627. In 1771 he moved here with his wife and three children, engaging in a salacious lifestyle before he was tried on charges of sodomy and attempted poisoning; he spent 27 years in prison. The chateau was looted by revolutionaries in 1789, and subsequently seized and sold.

The 45-room palace, once maintained by 20 servants, remained an eerie ruin until Cardin transformed it into a 1000-seat theatre and opera stage hosting July's month-long **Festival de Lacoste**. In the village, **Espace La Costa** (☎ 04 90 75 93 12) sells festival tickets (€40 to €140) and has information on guided tours of the chateau site (including the incredible old Roman quarry beneath the chateau).

Upping the town's tiny population are students of the US-based art school Savannah College of Art & Design.

A couple of inexpensive cafés are tucked away in the little village centre. For a slice of rural life, at **Ferme de l'Avellan** (☎ 04 90 75 85 10; chemin de St-Jean; d incl breakfast from €54, menu €18; ⊠ Easter-Nov), a working farm filled with vines and cherry orchards, Danielle Ravoire serves *bio* (organic) meals with an abundance of herbs, as well as her homemade wine. Find it 1km from Lacoste village, at the end of an unpaved track signposted off the road to Ménerbes. Advance bookings are essential.

Ménerbes
pop 1007 / elev 230m
Ménerbes, 6km west of Lacoste, captured the attention of millions of armchair travellers when it was memorably rendered by Peter Mayle. The British author's light-hearted, lavishly detailed books *A Year in Provence* and *Toujours Provence* recount renovating a *mas* just outside the village in the late 1980s. Their spectacular success spawned a still-booming genre of expat travel tales – and a spectacular number of tourists traipsing by. Mayle subsequently sold up and moved abroad, though the Luberon's charm has recently lured him back to Lourmarin. His former home, 2km southeast of Ménerbes on the D3 to Bonnieux, is the second house on the right after the football pitch.

Scaling the steep streets to the boat-shaped village moored on the hilltop rewards with uninterrupted views. The maze of streets conceals the 12th-century village **church** and the **Maison de la Truffe et du Vin** (House of Truffle & Wine; ☎ 04 90 72 52 10; www.vin-truffe-luberon.com; place de l'Horloge; ☼ 10am-1pm & 2-6pm daily Jul & Aug, 10am-1pm & 2-6pm Thu-Sat Apr-Jun, Sep & Oct, 3-7pm Thu-Sat Nov-Mar), housed in the former hospice (called Hôtel d'Astier de Montfaucon) on the cobbled square. In July and August it organises a series of two-hour wine-tasting sessions (€40 including lunch) and a couple of truffle workshops (€65); and sells wines at cellar-door prices.

The best Côtes du Luberon wines are nothing but ornaments without a corkscrew – something that's not lost on Ménerbes' mayor, Yves Rousset-Rouard, who created a shrine to the gadgets, the **Musée du Tire-Bouchon** (Corkscrew Museum; ☎ 04 90 72 41 58; www.musee-tirebouchon.com; adult/under 15yr €4/free; ☼ 10am-noon & 2-7pm Apr-Oct, 10am-noon & 2-5pm Mon-Sat Nov-Mar). Situated in the Domaine de la Citadelle, a wine-producing estate on the D3 to Cavaillon, you can sample Côtes du Luberons and marvel over 1000 different corkscrews. Prior to becoming mayor, Rousset-Rouard, who resides in Ménerbes' crow's-nest chateau, was a French MP and film producer whose works include the soft-porn *Emmanuelle* (1974).

Some 30,000-odd gastropods live on the family-run **Parc aux Escargots** (☎ 04 90 72 22 26, 06 61 14 48 84; www.leparcauxescargots.com in French; Les Grès; 1hr guided visit adult/5-16yr €4/3; ☼ 9am-7pm May-Oct), signposted off the D24, which specialises in snail cuisine.

SLEEPING & EATING

La Magnanerie (☎ 04 90 72 42 88; www.magnanerie.com; rte de Bonnieux, Lieu-dit le Roucas; d incl breakfast €85-95; ☼ mid-Mar–mid-Nov & mid-Dec–early Jan; P ⛽ ♿) At this welcoming *maison d'hôte*, guests can barbecue meals in the summer kitchen; there's a fridge to stash drinks; and of its six stylish rooms, the peach room with mezzanine up top and terrace below is ideal for families. A poolside *pétanque* pitch lets you enjoy a lazy late-afternoon game, and you can borrow a bike for a countryside spin. Credit cards aren't accepted. Find La Magnanerie 200m down a single-track unpaved lane, signposted off the D103.

La Bastide de Marie (☎ 04 90 72 30 20; www.labastide demarie.com; rte de Bonnieux, quartier de la Verrerie;

with half-board d from €435, ste €620; ☼ late Apr-early Nov; P ⛽ ♿ 🖥 🛁 💧 ♿) Splashed across *Tatler*, *Cosmopolitan*, *Town & Country* et al, this blue-shuttered 18th-century *bastide* amid vineyards stuns. Soft golds, creams, coffees and slates accentuate the designer interiors, and the tiered, turquoise swimming pool trickled by fountains is paradise found. Prices include everything (breakfast, afternoon tea, dusk-time apéritif, dinner with wine) except lunch. From Ménerbes, follow the eastbound D103 for 4km.

Café du Progrès (☎ 04 90 72 22 09; place Albert Roure; menus €13-16; ☼ lunch, bar 6am-midnight) The village's tobacconist-newsagent-bar run by good-humoured local Patrick hasn't changed since the days before Peter Mayle put Ménerbes on the map, and not much since it opened a century ago. This atmospheric and utterly authentic spot is great for a lunchstop in the dining room out back taking in a spectacular sweep of the countryside, or downstairs on the outdoor terrace.

Véranda (☎ 04 90 72 33 33; 104 av Marcellin Poncet; breakfast & lunch dishes €7.50-13, dinner menu €35; ☼ 10am-9.30pm Fri-Tue) Well-travelled chef Laurent Jouin is doing impressive things in the kitchen of his brand-new establishment high up in the village. Kitchen dressers displaying Provençal fabrics, olive oils and jams still line the walls of this former boutique, where you can now dine on delicious à la carte breakfasts and lunches, tea and cakes between mealtimes, and magnificent evening meals built from seasonal fresh fruit and vegetables.

Oppède-le-Vieux
pop 20 / elev 300m

Tipped as 'the next Les Baux' (so get here before the crowds descend), this medieval hilltop village 6km southwest of Ménerbes was abandoned in 1910 by villagers who moved down the valley to the cultivated plains to earn their living. A handful of artists lives here today. From the car parks (€2) a precarious path leads to the hillside **ruins**. The 16th- to 18th-century **church**, under constant restoration, hosts concerts during August and celebrates mass in honour of Oppède's patron saint (St Laurent) on 10 August.

Signs also direct you from the car parks to the **Sentier Vigneron d'Oppède**, a 1½-hour wine-growers' trail through olive groves, cherry orchards and vineyards. Panels interpret grape varieties, how to train a vine 'lyre' style etc.

THE LUBERON

Oppède-les-Poulivets (or just Oppède), the new village (population 1246), is 1km north of Oppède-le-Vieux.

Coustellet

The main reason to visit Coustellet, on the noisy N100, is its **Musée de la Lavande** (Lavender Museum; ☎ 04 90 76 91 23; www.museedelalavande .com; adult/under 15yr €5/free; �),10am-noon & 2-6pm or 7pm Feb-Dec). Visits include an audioguide, and a short video (in English), that explains how the purple flowers are harvested and distilled (see the boxed text, p244), and you can see stills used to extract the sweet scent and buy lavender-scented products at its boutique.

On Sunday mornings, Luberon locals gather for the **market** (cnr N100 & D2; �),Apr-Dec), where only farmers from a 10km radius are allowed to sell their produce.

Cabrières d'Avignon & Around

pop 1431 / elev 167m

Cabrières d'Avignon, 5km north of Coustellet, was one of the most unfortunate Waldensian villages (see the boxed text, p227). Its privately owned 12th-century chateau (closed to visitors) has since been restored and the old *moulin à huile* (oil mill) is now a wine-tasting school.

Pine and cedar forests, crisscrossed with paths and picnic tables, shroud the northern village fringe. Herbs and flowers are used to flavour honey made at the village *miellerie* (honey house; see the boxed text, p224) and the dishes cooked up at **Le Vieux Bistrot** (☎ 04 90 76 82 08; Grande Rue; d €64-110; lunch menu €16, dinner menus €35-42; �),lunch & dinner Tue-Sun; ☒ ☝), formerly Le Bistrot à Michel. Upstairs are six cosy *chambre d'hôte* rooms; two with private terraces with village views, of which one is endearingly called *chez nous* (our place).

In yellow-brick **Lagnes** (population 1509; elevation 110m), 5km west, enjoy a quintessential Provençal sleeping and eating experience at **Le Mas des Grès** (☎ 04 90 20 32 85; www.masdesgres .com; rte d'Apt; d with half-board €80-269; ☐ ☒ ☝), a farmhouse with 14 rooms in warm hues of rust, ochre and gold. On Thursday nights, nonguests can also take a seat at Nina and Thierry's table d'hôte (€50). Thierry runs a range of cooking courses between April and October (prices vary depending on duration and theme), including fun classes for kids (€50 for two-day courses with lunch).

CAVAILLON

pop 25,058

In France and beyond, Cavaillon is tantamount to its sweet cantaloupe melons, often referred to simply as 'Cavaillons', regardless of where they're grown. As a result, Cavaillon is in the process of establishing its own AOC to protect the melons' prized reputation and ensure quality control.

Masses of melons fill Cavaillon's early-morning Monday market from May to September and abound during the four-day **Fête du Melon** in July. The **tourist office** (☎ 04 90 71 32 01; www.cavaillon-luberon.com in French; place François Tourel; 3hr tour adult/under 12yr €6/free; �),9am-12.30pm & 2-6.30pm Mon-Sat mid-Mar—mid-Oct plus 10am-noon Sun Jul & Aug, 9am-noon & 2-6pm Mon-Fri, 10am-noon Sat mid-Oct—mid-Mar), which has comprehensive information on all of the western Luberon, arranges melon-tasting tours.

But there's more to this appealing and often-bypassed little city 28km southeast of Avignon than merely melons, with a rich history and outstanding gourmet shops in its quaint old town. In March 2007, Cavaillon should have featured on cinema screens as the backdrop for Rowan Atkinson's *Mr Bean II*.

Sights

An **arch** (place François Tourel) built by the Romans in the 1st century BC frames the square in front of the tourist office, at the western end of cours Bournissac, Cavaillon's main shopping street. Three blocks north the 12th-century **Cathédrale Notre Dame et St-Véran** (�),8.30am-noon & 2-6pm Mon-Fri Apr-Sep, 9am-noon & 2-5pm Mon-Fri Oct-Mar) boasts a fine Roman cloister.

Cavaillon's beautiful **synagogue** (1772–74) houses the **Musée Juif Comtadin** (Jewish Museum; ☎ 04 90 76 00 34; rue Hébraïque; adult/under 12yr €3/free;

THE LUBERON

MELON-SHOPPING SECRETS

At the street-side markets, Cavaillon locals shared their top tips for choosing from the mountains of melons:

■ Look for a sticky dark orange resinlike residue on the stalk, indicating the melon's ripeness when it was cut.

■ Test the melon's weight – too light means it's filled with water, not sugar.

■ Follow your nose: the sweeter a melon smells, the more *magnifique* it will taste.

(Y) 9.30am-12.30pm & 2.30-5.30pm Wed-Mon May-Oct, 9am-noon & 2-5pm Mon & Wed-Sat Nov-Apr), inside the former bakery of the Jewish community (women worshipped beneath the synagogue's wooden floor in the bakehouse). The same ticket is also good for the **Hôtel-Dieu** (☎ 04 90 76 00 34; porte d'Avignon; (Y) 9.30am-12.30pm & 2.30-5.30pm Wed-Mon May-Oct, 9am-noon & 2-5pm Mon & Wed-Sat Nov-Apr), at the old town's northern edge, which covers Cavaillon's former Celtic settlement and has archaeological exhibits.

Tours

The **tourist office** (☎ 04 90 71 32 01; www.cavaillon -luberon.com in French; place François Tourel) takes bookings for a bounty of guided tours, including two-hour tours of one of the many nearby hilltop villages (€3); and wine-tasting sessions with farmhouse brunch (€35). Or tour a melon farm (see p51).

Enjoy a customised sightseeing tour in chauffer-driven comfort with **Luberon Taxi** (☎ 04 90 76 70 08; www.taxi-luberon.com); prices are according to individual itinerary.

Sleeping

Campers can pitch up at sites in Robion, 6km east of Cavaillon, and Maubec, 9km east.

Hôtel Toppin (☎ 04 90 71 30 42; 70 cours Léon Gambetta; d €38-44, tr €50-54, q €57-68; (P) (X) (🖳) (♿)) Cyclists are well catered for at this character-filled old hotel in Cavaillon's heart, with a huge breakfast of dried and fresh fruit, cereal and bread (€7.50) and free bike storage (and free parking for cars). The pick are rooms 7 and 8 with private terraces, or there's a communal sun terrace with retro furniture for an evening picnic. Half-board (€14) sees you dining at a choice of nearby restaurants. Wi-fi is €3 per half-hour and there's a free online computer at reception.

Mas des Amandiers (☎ 04 90 06 29 60; www.mas -des-amandiers.com in French; 48 chemin des Puits Neufs; s/d incl breakfast from €70/75, table d'hôte Tue, Thu & Sat €25; (Y) Feb-Nov; (P) (X) (🖳) (♿)) This 'farmhouse of almond trees' is the haven of artist Jean-Claude Lorber, whose official commissions during his career have included portraits of Princess Grace of Monaco, Queen Elizabeth II and Pope John-Paul II. Appropriately, the *mas'* garden-view *chambre d'hôte* rooms are named Monet, Michelangelo and Cézanne. If you're inspired, Jean-Claude teaches painting in a studio attached to the house – lessons start from €30 for half a day's tuition.

Domaine Faverot (☎ 04 90 76 65 16; cottagesfaverot .com; 771 rte de Robion, Maubec; d per week from €650; (P) (X) (🖳) (♿)) Just west of Maubec on the road to Robion, this former silk farm now houses a medal-winning winery and four attached, two-storey *gîtes* (cottages) looking out across the vineyards. The Domaine produces 25,000 bottles a year which guests (and anyone passing by) can snap up before they're exported around the world. If it's quiet, Sally and François can also give you a behind-the-scenes tour. Prices can be negotiated for stays of two nights. Breakfast is €18 by advance reservation and the *gîtes* have fully equipped kitchens.

Eating

Chez Auzet (☎ 04 90 78 06 54; 61 cours Bournissac; plat du jour €8.50; (Y) 7am-7.30pm Wed-Mon) Fifth-generation baker Gerard Auzet turns out dozens of varieties of bread including walnut, Roquefort, olive and onion, along with sandwiches and *plats* (dishes) such as duck with raspberries and zucchini flowers with basil, tomato and thyme at his wonderful bakery-café. Recently he shared his 'Confessions of a French Baker' in the book of the same name which he co-authored with his longtime friend, Peter Mayle (see the boxed

---

HONEY HOUSES

Bees collect the nectar from dozens of different flowers including *bruyerè* (heather), *tilleul* (linden), *châtaignier* (chestnut), *garrigue* (aromatic ground cover) and *lavande* (lavender) to make the area's many *miels* (honeys).

Tourist offices throughout the Luberon have lists of **mielleries** (honey houses), and you'll see signs by the roadside reading '*miel*' where you can pull over to stock up, and in some cases have an informal stickybeak. Sweet honey houses include **Le Mas des Abeilles** (☎ 04 90 74 29 55; Col du Pointu, Bonnieux; (Y) 9am-12.30pm & 2.30-7pm Mon-Sat, 2.30-7pm Sun), a farmhouse shop on the Col du Pointu (at the junction of the D943 and D232), with 10 honey types, honey sweets and vinegar; and **Miel de Cabrières** (☎ /fax 04 90 76 83 52; chemin de la Pourtalette & rue du Château, Cabrières d'Avignon; (Y) variable).

THE LUBERON

WINERY-MAKING

Before making wine, London expat Sally Faverot de Kerbrech and her French husband François first had to make over their newly acquired ruined winery, which proved no small task.

As Sally says: 'We bought the Domaine as a total ruin and run-down vines in 1998. We spent two years going backwards and forwards between London and the Luberon, staying in various *gîtes* and apartments while we made plans for the renovations. We restored and almost totally rebuilt the winery in 1999 and did our first harvest then.

'The renovation work was from the base upwards. There were a few broken-down walls, no roof and some old broken-up cement fermentation vats that we completely restored. We then installed flooring, which had to be tractorproof, and bought three wooden vats from Gigondas for the Grenache aging and storage and 10 oak barrels for the Syrah grapes' aging and storing. But it was worth it.'

Sally and François' first vintage won a gold medal for La Cuvée du Général in Avignon and Orange. Domaine Faverot's wines have since garnered numerous awards, as well as wholehearted approval from their friends and neighbours, for whom the winery is a local gathering spot.

To tour the winery or stay at one of the on-site cottages, see opposite.

---

text, p214). On market days, take in the passing parade from the outdoor terrace.

Côte Jardin (☎ 04 90 71 33 58; 49 rue Lamartine; lunch menus €12.50-14.50, dinner menus €22-27; ☽ lunch Mon-Sat, dinner Tue-Sat Apr-Oct, Wed-Sat Nov-Mar) Behind a melon-coloured wooden façade, this family-run restaurant with sage-coloured wicker chairs and stencilled walls opens to a charming little walled courtyard. Frédéric Toppin's aubergine, tomato and goats-cheese tart is a treat, as is the salmon and St-Jacques accompanied by pureed potatoes drizzled in olive oil and a feather-light vegetable flan.

Prévôt (☎ 04 90 71 32 43; 353 av de Verdun; lunch menus €25-30, dinner menus €35-85; ☽ lunch & dinner Tue-Sat, closed early-late Aug) Melon memorabilia artfully adorns the dining room of Cavaillon's most prestigious address. May to September Jean-Jacques Prévôt conjures up melon-inspired *menus* (€65 to €75). He also works his thematic magic on truffles (January and February), game and chocolate (November and December), asparagus (March and April) and artichokes and aubergines (May to November). See also p42.

SELF-CATERING

Quench your thirst with a taste of Provence: *sirop au mimosa* (a nonalcoholic fizzy mimosa drink), a shot of *crème au melon* (a melon liqueur) or a slow glass of *délice de Cavaillon* (a melon-flavoured apéritif) or *apéritif à la truffe* (a truffle-flavoured apéritif) from *épicerie fine* **Le Clos Gourmand** (☎ 04 90 78 05 22; 8 place du Clos; ☽ 8.15am-12.30pm & 3-7pm Mon-Sat).

Yannick Jaume – *chocolatier-pâtissier-glacier* – also does inventive things with melons, with creations including *melonettes* (melon chocolates) and melon ice cream, available from his shop **L'Étoile du Délice** (☎ 04 90 78 07 51; 57 place Castil-Blaze; ☽ 7am-7.30pm Mon-Tue, Thu-Fri & Sat, to 1pm Sun).

Another fab little *épicerie fine*, **La Régalade** (☎ 04 90 76 15 71; 28 rue Poissonnerie; mains €8.50-11.50; ☽ 9am-3.30pm & 6.30pm-1am Tue-Sat) sells pastis (a 90-proof, anise-flavoured alcoholic drink that turns cloudy when water is added), jams and other Provençal treats, and has an attached restaurant decorated with fantastic '70s kitsch with original furniture and lighting, and retro toys.

Getting There & Away

From the bus stop beside the train station, daily bus services include L'Isle-sur-la-Sorgue (15 minutes, three or four daily) and Aix-en-Provence (1½ hours, three daily).

From the **train station** (place de la Gare) there are trains to/from Marseille (€12.40, 1½ hours, eight or so daily) and Avignon Centre (€5.80, 30 minutes, up to 12 daily).

Getting Around

Cyclix Cavaillon (☎ 04 90 78 07 06; 166 cours Gambetta; ☽ 9am-12.15pm & 3-7pm Tue-Sat) rents tandems for €28/140 per day/week, mountain bikes for €19/92 and road bikes for €16/78, all with helmet, repair kit and mapped itinerary. Bikes can be delivered for €0.61 per kilometre return.

CAVAILLON TO CADENET

Skimming the Petit Luberon's southern boundary, southeast of Cavaillon, the busy D973 delineates the River Durance and the

THE LUBERON

valley it carves. Some 243 species of birds typical of the river banks can be seen from the **Observatoire Ornithologique**, a bird centre run by the Parc Naturel Régional du Luberon (see the boxed text, p218) near the Mérindol–Mallemort dam (signposted 1.5km from the roundabout at the entrance to Mérindol on the D973). Spot herons and great cormorants along the 3km-long **bird sanctuary trail** (1½ hours) marked with yellow blazes.

Mérindol (population 1800; elevation 200m), crossed by the GR6 about 15km east of Cavaillon, was another Waldensian martyr village (see the boxed text, opposite).

Lauris (population 1800; elevation 200m), 10km further east, is a regal hilltop village crowned with an 18th-century **chateau** surrounded by terraced gardens. Tinctorial plants, many rare, grow in the **Jardin Conservatoire de Plantes Tinctoriales** (☎ 04 90 08 40 48; couleur.garance@online.fr; adult/under 10yr €7/free; ❧ 2-5pm Wed-Mon late May & Oct, 3.30-7pm Jun-Sep, by appointment Nov-Mar). Workshops explore dyes traditionally made from these plants. Lauris' **tourist office** (☎ 04 90 08 39 30; ot-lauris@axit.fr; 12 place de l'Église; ❧ 9.30am-12.30pm & 2.30-6pm Mon-Sat) has details on July's **Hot Jazz festival** held around the chateau.

Wickerwork is the mainstay industry of **Cadenet** (population 3937), 7km upstream (east). Learn about the cultivation of *osier* (wicker) on the river banks and its artisan applications in the **Musée de la Vannerie** (☎ 04 90 68 24 44; av Philippe de Giraud; adult/under 12yr €3/free; ❧ 10am-noon & 2.30-6.30pm Wed-Sat, 2.30-6.30pm Sun Apr-Oct).

Abbaye de Silvacane

South of the Durance, 7km southwest of Cadenet, **Silvacane Abbey** (☎ 04 42 50 41 69; adult/child €6.50/4.50; ❧ 10am-6pm Jun-Sep, to 1pm & 2-5pm Wed-Mon Oct-May) is, along with the Abbaye Notre-Dame de Sénanque (p217) and Abbaye de Thoronet (p359), one of a trio of medieval Provençal abbeys built by Cistercian monks in an austere Romanesque style. Constructed between 1175 and 1230, today it hosts classical concerts and three colonies of bats (several hundred in total) in its cloister.

LE GRAND LUBERON

Marking the great divide between Le Petit and Le Grand Luberon, the deep **Combe de Lourmarin** cuts a near-perpendicular swathe through the massif from Bonnieux to Lourmarin. To its east, Le Grand Luberon takes in dramatic gorges and grand fortresses.

Buoux
pop 117

Dominated by the hilltop **ruins of Fort de Buoux**, the tiny village of Buoux (the X is pronounced) sits across the divide from Bonnieux, and less than 8km south of Apt. As a traditional Protestant stronghold, Buoux was destroyed in 1545 (see the boxed text, opposite) and again in 1660. The fort and old village ruins, perilous in places due to loose rocks, can be explored on foot. Painted white arrows mark an optional return route via a spectacular spiralling staircase cut in the rock.

Local climbing club **Améthyste** (☎ 04 90 74 05 92; amethyste1901.free.fr in French) organises rock climbing and walks.

A thrilling 2.5km descent from Buoux village beneath cliffs in the Vallée de l'Aiguebrun is the rambling *gîte d'étape* (hikers accommodation), **Auberge des Seguins** (☎ 04 90 74 16 37; dm with half-board €35, d with shower/shower & toilet with half-board per person €47/52, menus from €26.50; ❧ Mar–mid-

---

A LAVENDER DETOUR

From Buoux an invigorating cycling or driving route takes you north on the D113 to a set of crossroads straddled by lavender fields. From here you can bear west along the D232 to Bonnieux; east along the D48 to Auribeau (4.3km) and Castellet (7km); or northeast to Saignon and Le Boisset (from where you can link up with the N100; for Auribeau, Saignon and Le Boisset see the boxed text, p228). Otherwise you can continue on a northbound lavender trail to Apt.

After passing more lavender fields, the D113 climbs to **Les Agnels**, where lavender, cypress leaves and rosemary are distilled at the 1895-established **Distillerie Agnel** (☎ 04 90 74 22 72; rte de Buoux; free tours daily Jul & Aug, Tue-Sun May, Jun & Sep).

Lavender-lovers should not miss the Musée de la Lavande (p223), 22km west of Apt, and its 800,000-sq-metre lavender farm, **Château du Bois** (☎ 04 90 76 91 23; www. lechateaudubois.com), 25km north of Apt in **Lagarde d'Apt**, where a 2km-long lavender trail blazes from late June until mid-July when the sweet-smelling flower is harvested.

MARTYR VILLAGES

Eleven Luberon villages were brutally massacred on 9 and 10 April 1545 under the terms of the Arrêt de Mérindol, a bill passed by the Aix parliament condemning anyone of Waldensian faith to death. In Cabrières d'Avignon alone more than 700 men were killed in cold blood, and the women of the village were locked in a barn of straw and burnt alive.

The Waldenses (Vaudois) were a minority Protestant group who sought refuge in the Luberon hills (and other remote parts of France and Italy) following the excommunication of their leader Pierre Valdès from the Catholic Church in 1184. The wealthy merchant from Lyon, who rid himself of material possessions in 1176, incurred the wrath of Pope Lucius III for his fervent preaching of a religion based on the gospels and poverty – itself an enigma in the splendidly rich Catholic Church in medieval times.

In 1532 the Waldenses joined the Reformation, ultimately leading to their demise. What remains of the original castrum in Mérindol guards a memorial to the estimated 3000 murdered and 600 sent to the galleys in the two-day massacre. By 1560 there were few Waldenses left in France. In the 1680s large communities reappeared in mountain valleys in Piedmont, northern Italy, where they were granted the right to free worship in 1848. The Waldensian church, a Calvinist form of Protestantism, remains particularly strong there today.

Tours (€3) covering Waldensian history depart from **Mérindol's tourist office** (☎ 04 90 72 88 50; rue du Four; ☷ 9.30am-12.30pm & 2-5.30pm Mon-Sat mid-Mar–Sep, 10am-noon & 2-5pm Oct–mid-Mar) at 9.30am on Thursday, and include a visit to the town's olive-oil mill. **Cavaillon's tourist office** (☎ 04 90 71 32 01; www.cavaillon-luberon.com in French; place François Tourel; ☷ 9am-12.30pm & 2-6.30pm Mon-Sat mid-Mar–mid-Oct plus 10am-noon Sun Jul & Aug, 9am-noon & 2-6pm Mon-Fri, 10am-noon Sat mid-Oct–mid-Mar) also has information.

La Muse (☎ 04 90 72 91 64; 3 rue du Four; ☷ 2.30-5.30pm Sat, 9.30am-noon Wed), in Mérindol, is a Waldensian library and research centre; call in advance to check that someone is there.

Nov; Ⓟ ✕ ☒), where you can dine on *magret de canard* (duck breast) with fresh cherries or peaches on the shaded veranda or loll in the pool gazing out at giant tiger-striped rocks.

Amid flowery gardens, the **Auberge de la Loube** (☎ 04 90 74 19 58; lunch menu €21, dinner menu from €27.50; ☷ closed Mon, Thu & Jan) remains true to its roots serving wicker trays overflowing with *hors d'oeuvres Provençaux* like *tapenade* (olive dip), *anchoïade* (anchovy sauce), quail eggs, melon slices, cherry tomatoes and fresh figs. Leave room for the succulent roast lamb, and allow plenty of time to savour the experience, especially during legendary Sunday lunches. Payment is in cash only (there are no ATMs in Buoux), and reservations are essential.

Plateau de Claparèdes

Purple lavender carpets the area between Buoux (west), Sivergues (south), picture-postcard **Saignon** (north) with its curious vegetable garden (see the boxed text, p228) and **Auribeau** (east). Beyond cycling, walking and scenic motoring, the star attraction of this pretty pocket is its accommodation.

Secluded in a remote valley, the renovated mill **Le Moulin** (☎ 04 90 75 10 63; www.moulindesfondons

.com in French; Auribeau; s/d/tr/q incl breakfast from €42/58/77/92, half-board in gîte d'étape €35, table d'hôte adult/child €12/18.50; Ⓟ ☒ ☒) is a veritable playground, with swings, swimming, horse riding and walks galore. The mill is signposted off the D48, 2.5km west of Auribeau. The final 500m is a partly unpaved, single-track lane.

In the 11th and 12th centuries it was three presbyteries; now **Auberge de Presbytère** (☎ 04 90 74 11 50; www.auberge-presbytere.com; place de la Fontaine, Saignon; d €68-135, menus €26-35; ☷ mid-Feb–mid-Nov, restaurant lunch & dinner Thu-Tue; Ⓟ ✕ ☒) is a village inn with beautiful wood-beamed rooms and an enticing terrace restaurant overlooking the village fountain and wash house.

Husband and wife artists Kamila Regent and Pierre Jaccaud are the creative force behind **Chambre de Séjour avec Vue** (☎ 04 90 04 85 01; www.chambreavecvue.com in French; Saignon; d incl breakfast €80, studio incl breakfast €100; table d'hôte €25) – a 16th-century village house turned *chambre d'hôte/art studio* and stunningly decorated with resident artists' works. Cross a little wooden bridge to the garden where bronze sculptures, terracotta urns and contemporary designer chairs lounge beneath trees. Leaves adorn crisp linen pillows and some rooms have kitchens.

THE LUBERON

Although the isolated **Ferme Auberge Le Castelas** (Chez Gianni; ☎ 04 70 74 60 89; le_castelas@yahoo.fr; Sivergues; menus incl wine €25-30; ✆ lunch & dinner by reservation only Mar-Dec) is well off any track, beaten or not, celebs such as Catherine Deneuve drop in via helicopter to pass around platters at long shared timber tables. Fresh-from-the-farm feasts include bite-sized toast topped with *tomme* (a mild cows-milk cheese). To get here (sans helicopter), follow the only road through the village of Sivergues (ignore the *fin de la route* – end of the road – sign at the village entrance). Continue for 1.5km along the potholed gravel track until you see the black piglets in the field.

Lourmarin

pop 1127 / elev 230m

At the base of the Combe de Lourmarin and, unlike many of the Luberon's precarious hilltop townships, easily accessed, the alluring village of Lourmarin lies alongside its Renaissance **chateau** (☎ 04 90 68 15 23; www.chateau-de-lourmarin .com; adult/student/10-18yr €5.50/3/2.50; ✆ 10am-noon & 2.30-6pm Jul & Aug, Feb-Jun & shorter hr Sep-Dec) – the first of its kind built in Provence.

Today home to author Peter Mayle, charming streets, cafés and a lively Friday morning **market**, Lourmarin was the final home of Nobel Prize–winning writer Albert Camus (1913–60) and his wife, who are buried in the village cemetery. Also buried in the cemetery is the writer Henri Bosco (1888–1976), another Lourmarin local.

The **tourist office** (☎ 04 90 68 10 77; www.lourmarin .com; av Philippe de Girard; ✆ 10am-12.30pm & 3-6pm Mon-Thu & Sat, 10am-1.30pm & 3-6pm Fri) leads guided walks (€4) dedicated to Camus (Tuesday at 10am) and Bosco (Wednesday at 10am) as well as one exploring the village (Friday at 10am).

The use of fragrant plants such as lavender and rosemary at the **Ferme de Gerbaud** (☎ 04 90 68 11 83; adult/child €5/free; ✆ 1½hr guided visits 5pm Tue, Thu & Sat Apr-Oct, 3pm Sat Nov-Mar, boutique 2-7pm) are explained during farm tours in English and French. The farm's owner, Paula, also cooks herb-infused evening meals on Thursdays – call ahead for prices and reservations.

Given its tiny population Lourmarin has a trove of gastronomic gems, unearthed by a stroll around town. Reservations for all restaurants in town are recommended.

Although chef extraordinaire Édouard Loubet is now based in Bonnieux (see p221) he still keeps the wheels turning at **Le Moulin de Lourmarin** (☎ 04 90 68 06 69; www.moulindelourmarin.com; d from €120, ste from €350; menus from €26; ⓟ ⓧ ⓧ ⓛ ⓡ), a restored 17th-century oil mill now housing his Comptoir d'Edouard, a restaurant-*traiteur* (caterers)-*épicerie*-patisserie specialising in foie gras fragranced with plants from the mill's botanical garden, along with dreamy rooms.

In the heart of the village, its oldest bar, the convivial **Café de l'Ormeau** (☎ 04 90 68 02 11; place de l'Ormeau; dishes €4-10; ✆ 6.30am-11.30pm) has a pavement terrace perfect for sipping pastis in the sun.

A CURIOUS DETOUR

A curious little detour starting east of Apt gets you off the busy N100 and onto quiet country lanes.

At the bottom of St-Martin de Castillon, turn left and follow the road up to Castellet. Continue for 2km, driving around a sharp hairpin bend and further uphill to bring you to quaint stone **Auribeau** (elevation 586m). In the village, park on rte Jean Moulin, from where a 5.4km walking trail up Mourre Nègre can be picked up. Nip to the top of the street for a panorama of lavender fields then stroll along rue du Château to the splashing fountain on place de la Fontaine.

Continue out of the village along the same D48, passing a small **private lavender distillery** – where you can buy *miel* (honey) and *extrait traditionnel de lavandin* (lavender extract) on your left (you'll need to knock on the door, as it's not open for tours) – and that field of burnt tree stumps. From here the road snakes uphill for 700m, with a succession of swift glimpses of stone-capped Mont Ventoux as you round several sweeping bends. At the third bend you'll find a picturesque **picnic area**.

Four kilometres further, gasp at the cragtop village of **Saignon** with Mont Ventoux as the backdrop. Drive downhill around the huge hairpin to the village and turn right at the post office, following the signs for **Le Potager d'un Curieux** (☎ 04 90 74 44 68; chemin de la Molière; admission free; ✆ sunrise-sunset Mon & Wed-Fri), 2.6km away. The 'vegetable garden of an inquiring mind' is the creation of Jean-Luc Danneyrolles and his passion for rare and ancient fruits and vegetables.

Vaugines & Cucuron

From Lourmarin the D56 shadows the GR97 walking trail 5km east to **Vaugines** (population 469), where Claude Berri's Pagnol films *Manon des Sources* and *Jean de Florette* (1986) were partly shot with the village's horse-chestnut tree and moss-covered fountain as a backdrop.

Cucuron (population 1792; elevation 350m), 2km further east, is the starting point for walks up **Mourre Nègre** (1125m). Its **tourist office** (☎ 04 90 77 28 37; www.cucuron-luberon.com in French; rue Léonce Brieugne; ☺ 9am-12.30pm & 1.30-6pm Mon-Fri May-Oct, 9am-4pm Mon-Fri Nov-Apr) sells walking/cycling maps and guides.

Pays d'Aigues

Shhhh… the rustic charm of Pays d'Aigues (Aigues Country) remains, for the most part, yet to be 'discovered' by *résidence secondaire* (second-home) owners. For now at least, its peaceful villages and unfolding countryside epitomise timeless Provençal life.

A pretty lake with a beach, **Étang de la Bonde**, 3km south of Cabrières d'Aigues on the D9, is free for the public.

Labelled one of France's 'most beautiful villages' (and it is), **Ansouis** (population 1100), 6km north of Cabrières d'Aigues, shelters the **Musée Extraordinaire** (☎ 04 90 09 82 64; adult/under 16yr €3.50/1.50; ☺ 2-6pm or 7pm), set up by Provençal painter and diver Georges Mazoyer, whose passion for the sea is reflected in the museum's fossilised exhibits and art. Nearby, you can watch *santonnier* Daniel Galli hand-craft *santons* (traditional Provençal figurines) in his **santon workshop** (☎ 04 90 09 87 54; rue du Buis). Right in the village, the palatial **Château d'Ansouis** (☎ 04 90 09 82 70; www.chateau-ansouis.com; adult/6-18yr €6/3; ☺ 2.30-6pm Sun Nov-Easter, 2.30-6pm Wed-Mon Easter-Jun & Oct, 2.30-6pm Jul-Sep) is still inhabited but can be visited by guided tour. Classical-music concerts fill its hedged courtyards in August. For a soothing tea, pop across from the chateau through the art gallery and down a flight of steps to **Les Moissines** (☎ 04 90 09 85 90; Grand Rue; ☺ daily Apr-Sep). And for a delightful dinner, reserve a table at **La Closerie** (☎ 04 90 09 90 54; blvd des Platanes; menus from €21; ☺ lunch Tue-Sun, dinner Tue-Sat). Ansouis' tiny **tourist office** (☎ 04 90 09 86 98; place du Château; ☺ 2-6pm Mon-Fri, 9am-noon & 2-6pm Sat & Sun) stocks local information.

At **Château Val Joanis** (☎ 04 90 79 20 77; www.val joanis.com; rte de Cavaillon; admission free; ☺ shop 10am-7pm Apr-Oct, 2-6pm Tue-Sat Mar & Nov), 8km southeast in

Pertuis, you can take a guided tour of its winery and traditional 19th-century terraced garden with a wine and olive-oil tasting on Thursday at 4pm between April and October.

La Tour d'Aigues (population 4010; elevation 270m), 5km northeast, is dominated by the 12th- to 15th-century **Château de Tour d'Aigues** (☎ 04 90 07 50 33; www.chateau-latourdaigues.com in French; adult/8-18yr €4.50/2; ☺ 10am-1pm & 2.30-6pm Jul–mid-Aug, 2.30-6pm Sun & Mon, 10am-1pm Tue, 10am-1pm & 2.30-6pm Wed-Sat Apr-Jun & mid-Aug–Oct, 2-5pm Sun & Mon, 10am-noon Tue, 10am-noon & 2-5pm Wed-Sat Nov-Mar). It incorporates a **Musée des Faïences** full of 18th-century earthenware. In the chateau, **Provence Luberon** (☎ 04 90 07 30 00; www.provence-luberon.net) provides information on Pays d'Aigues.

MANOSQUE & AROUND

pop 20,309 / elev 387m

Manosque's industrial belt wraps around its cobblestone old town. Provençal writer Jean Giono (1895–1970) was born here, and has an arts centre dedicated to him. To the north, **Mont d'Or** looks out over the town's red-tiled roofs to the hills. **Mont Furon** (600m), 10km west, also has lavish Luberon views.

The town's biggest employer is the natural cosmetics company **L'Occitane en Provence** (☎ 04 92 70 19 50; www.loccitane.com; Zone Industrielle St-Maurice; ☺ boutique 10am-7pm Mon-Sat), on the southeastern outskirts, which utilises Provençal flowers and herbs in its internationally exported products, and runs free one-hour guided visits of its distilling areas, manufacturing facilities, laboratories, and packaging department (if you've ever picked up its perfumes and soaps you'll have felt the Braille text on its labels). Tours must be booked at Manosque's **tourist office** (☎ 04 92 72 16 00; www.manosque-tourisme.com in French; place du Docteur Joubert; ☺ 9am-1pm & 2-7pm Mon-Sat, 10am-noon Sun Jul & Aug, 9am-12.15pm & 1.30-6.30pm Mon-Sat, 10am-noon Sun 15-30 Jun & 1-15 Sep, 9am-12.15pm & 1.30-6pm Mon-Sat 15 Sep-15 Jun), which has regional cycling routes mapped on a board out front.

On Manosque's southwestern fringe, 2km from the centre, the grand manorhouse-turned-*chambre d'hôte* **La Bastide de L'Adrech** (☎ 04 92 71 14 18; www.bastide-adrech.com; av des Serrets; d incl breakfast €68, table d'hôte incl wine & coffee €26; P) languished empty for over a century until its recent resurrection by Géraldine and Robert Le Bozec. Amid heritage-listed trees, its five guest rooms are stocked with L'Occitane products and the sweeping living room hosts tables d'hôtes beside the crackling fireplace. L'Oustau de Baumaniére–trained chef Robert also runs cooking classes (from €30 for three

hours) and gourmet weekends themed around local specialities like truffles.

The **bus station** (☎ 04 92 87 55 99; blvd Charles de Gaulle) is 500m from Manosque's centre. Exit the station, turn left on blvd Charles de Gaulle, then right to av Jean Giono. Frequent buses run by the **Société des Cars Alpes Littoral** (☎ 04 92 51 06 05; ☺ office closed Wed, Sat & Sun) serve Marseille. From the **train station** (place Frédéric Mistral), six south of the centre, there are six daily trains to/from Marseille (€14.80, 1½ hours) and Sisteron (€8, one hour).

Six kilometres southwest of Manosque, the village of **Pierrevert** (population 3500; elevation 420m) is the centre of the Coteaux de Pierrevert AOC. More than 75% of its wine production takes place at the village's co-op, the Cave des Vignerons (☎ 04 92 72 19 06; 1 av Auguste Bastide; ☺ cellar 9am-noon & 3-7pm Mon-Sat mid-Jul–mid-Sep, 9am-noon & 2-6pm Mon-Sat mid-Sep–mid-Jul), where you can have a free tasting and stock up at producers' prices. Call one day ahead for a free behind-the-scenes winery tour.

Twenty-odd kilometres southwest of Manosque adjoining St-Paul-lès-Durance is the nuclear research centre, **Cadarache** – see p77.

Haute-Provence

Haute-Provence's heady mountain ranges arc across the top of the Côte d'Azur to the Italian border, crowning it with snowy peaks and precipitous valleys cradled high in the Alps.

History hangs in the mountains like mist. The route Napoléon, which Bonaparte followed in 1815 en route to Paris after escaping from Elba, passes through the village of Castellane, one of the gateways to the plunging white waters and luminous lakes of Europe's largest canyon, the Gorges du Verdon. The Gorges' alternate gateway, magical little Moustiers Ste-Marie, has a centuries-old gold star strung between its cliffs. Napoleon's footsteps track north to Digne-les-Bains, a curative thermal spa town surrounded by fantastical fossils and serried lavender fields blazing brightly in the pristine air. Rattling on narrow-gauge tracks to Digne from Nice, 'the pine cone train', an enchanting turn-of-the-20th-century railway, stops at fairy-tale mountain villages along the way.

Forging further north, the route Napoléon passes through Sisteron in the Vallée de la Durance and onward through the Alps. Haute-Provence's sparsely populated northern reaches see a smattering of locals ski the glistening slopes and hike the summer trails of the Blanche and Ubaye valleys. The Ubaye plummets east to the Parc National du Mercantour, Provence's largest national park, where iron-rung ladders and steel cables bolted into the sheer mountainsides form high-altitude climbing routes called *via ferrata* (iron way).

Circled by vultures and roamed by wolves, with a 'valley of wonders' sheltering an incredible 36,000 Bronze Age rock carvings, this wild, remote region puts a whole other slant on Provence.

HIGHLIGHTS

- Ponder the planet's evolution at the Centre de Géologie in **Digne-les-Bains** (p242)
- Amble village streets huddled within the formidable fortifications and forested mountains of **Colmars-les-Alpes** (p251)
- Stargaze at St-Michel l'Observatoire's stellar **Observatoire de Haute-Provence** (p248)
- Heliski in the secluded **Vallée de la Vésubie** (p254)
- Discover the Mexican origins of the architecture at the Musée de la Vallée in **Barcelonnette** (p249)

★ Barcelonnette

Colmars-les-★ Alpes

Digne-les-Bains ★

Vallée de la Vésubie ★

★ Observatoire de Haute-Provence

ITINERARIES

GORGE EXPLORER
Two Days / Gorges du Verdon

Yawning gorges cleave the region's mountainous terrain, making it a mecca for hikers, rafters and climbers.

The most cavernous gorge (on the entire continent) is the mighty **Gorges du Verdon** (**1**; p234), often referred to as the Grand Canyon du Verdon. **Cycling or driving** (p235) around the gorges' precarious rimside roads gives you a dramatic introduction to its tortuous topography. Before setting out from **Moustiers Ste-Marie** (**2**; p237), warm up your calf muscles by heading up to its **cliffside chapel** (p237), then give your energy levels a boost with lunch at **Les Comtes** (p239). Afterwards (in the warmer months, when the road's open) take the **route des Crêtes** (**3**; p235) along the northern rim to **Point Sublime** (**4**; p235) for giddying gorge views. If you're planning to **walk** (p236) the gorge in its entirety, pick up the GR4 here for a full two-day trek through the canyon, or tackle a shorter section.

Continue along the route des Crêtes, stopping at the **Belvédère de l'Escalès** (p235) for more heart-lurching views, often with **vultures** (p236) wheeling overhead. Further along the route des Crêtes is **Castellane** (**5**; p236), with a rock-perched **church** (p236) of its own.

After resting up, sign up the next day for **white-water sports** (p236) such as rafting, hot-dogging or aqua-trekking. Or part-swim, part-scramble through the gorges' subterranean depths on a **canyoning expedition** (p236).

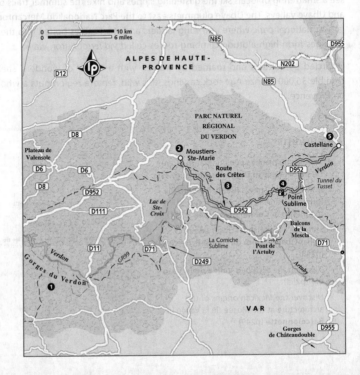

LAVENDER FIELDS FOREVER   One Day / Forcalquier to Digne-les-Bains

Living is easy in Provence when summer brings postcard images to life with row upon serried row of lavender colouring the countryside. To see it at its blooming best, follow this route between late June and mid-July. From mid-July to mid-August you'll see – and smell – the harvest in progress.

Pack a picnic in **Forcalquier** (**1**; p246), then cycle or drive with the windows down to the scented gardens of Mane's beautiful 13th-century priory, **Prieré de Salagon** (p247), and visit its on-site lavender museum.

Cross the River Durance and traverse the little-trafficked D6 along the **Plateau de Valensole** (**2**; p244), where Provence's greatest concentration of farms create purple ribbons intertwined with white-gold wheat. En route you'll pass places to buy lavender honey as well as scenic spots to stop for lunch.

Continue north to **Digne-les-Bains** (**3**; p242); time it right and you could catch the **lavender festival** (p243). Pick up a **walking map** (p242) or organise a **guided hike** (p243) through the wild lavender growing in the mountains surrounding Digne.

Head 20km northwest to Thoard to visit its old-fashioned **distillery** (p244), then have an **afternoon farm tea** (p243) and, for a longer ramble through the lavender-strewn mountains, hire a **donkey** (p243).

If you're a golfer, you can swing a club through lavender fields at Digne's **Hôtel du Golf** (p243). And to immerse yourself, literally, in the heady herbs, take a decadent **lavender bath treatment** (p242).

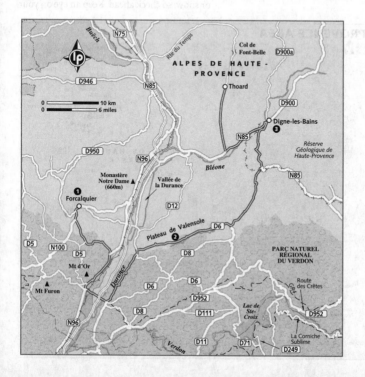

HAUTE-PROVENCE

GORGES DU VERDON

Europe's largest canyon, the plunging Gorges du Verdon, slices a 25km swathe through Provence's limestone plateau. Along with a wealth of white-water sports, there's also breathtaking bird-watching, including the canyon's very own colony of reintroduced griffon vultures.

ORIENTATION

Having been under the protection of the Parc Naturel Régional du Verdon since 1997, the gorges begin at Rougon near the confluence of the Verdon and the Jabron rivers, and then wind westwards until the Verdon's green waters flow into Lac de Ste-Croix. At a dizzying 250m to 700m deep, the gorges' floors are just 8m to 90m wide, and their overhanging rims are from 200m to 1500m apart.

The two main jumping-off points for exploring the gorges are the villages of Castellane, east of Rougon, and Moustiers Ste-Marie.

Maps

You can walk most of the canyon along the often-difficult GR4, a route covered by Didier-Richard's 1:50,000 map No 19, *Haute-Provence-Verdon*.

INFORMATION

Castellane tourist office (☎ 04 92 83 61 14; www .castellane.org; rue Nationale; ☺ 9am-12.30pm & 2-6.45pm Mon-Sat Mar-Oct, also 10am-12.30pm Sun Jul & Aug, 9am-noon & 2-6pm Mon-Fri Nov-Feb)

Moustiers Ste-Marie tourist office (☎ 04 92 74 67 84; www.moustiers.fr; ☺ 10am-12.30pm & 2-5.30pm Mar & Oct, 10am-12.30pm & 2-6pm Apr & May, 10am-12.30pm & 2-6.30pm Jun, 9.30am-12.30pm & 2-7.30pm Jul-Sep, 10am-noon & 2-5pm Nov, 2-5pm Dec-Feb)

DANGERS & ANNOYANCES

The river in the upper part of the canyon can rise very suddenly if the hydroelectric dams upstream are opened, making it difficult, if not impossible, to cross. Check water levels and weather forecasts with the tourist office before you set out.

Roads may be closed due to rock falls and/ or snow, so check ahead. Keep an eye on your

HAUTE-PROVENCE AREA

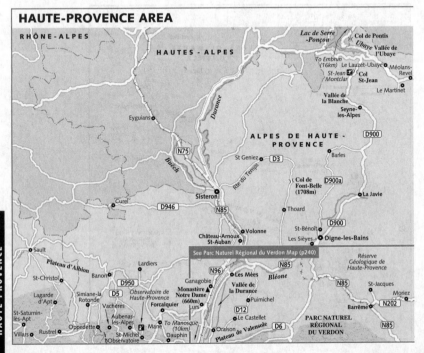

fuel gauge as petrol stations are few and far between.

SIGHTS & ACTIVITIES

High-adrenaline activities abound in and around the canyon. When you need a change of pace, take a stroll around the villages of Moustiers Ste-Marie and Castellane.

The Canyon

The gorges' deep floors are only accessible by foot or raft. Motorists and cyclists can take in staggering panoramas from two vertigo-inducing cliffside roads.

BUNGEE JUMPING & PARACHUTING

Hurtle through the air on a death-defying jump from Europe's highest bungee site, the 182m Pont de l'Artuby, with self-described 'dealers in adrenaline', **Latitude Challenge** (☎ 04 91 09 04 10; www.latitude-challenge.fr in French; €98; ☽ Sat & Sun by reservation). If you're game, second and subsequent jumps on the same day cost €45 (€58 for subsequent jumps on other days). Too tame? Freefall with the company's parachuting programmes. Solo/tandem jumps start from €221/236.

CYCLING & DRIVING

The **route des Crêtes** (the D952 and D23; closed November to February) corkscrews along the gorges' northern rim, past **Point Sublime**, which offers a fish-eye–lens view of serrated rock formations falling away to the river below. The best view from the northern side is from **Belvédère de l'Escalès**. Drive to the third bend and steel your nerves for the stunning drop-off into the gorge. (The belvedere is also one of the best places to spot vultures; see p236.) At its eastern end, the narrow D317 scales 3km to the quaint village of **Rougon** (population 85, elevation 963m).

Also heart-palpitating, **La Corniche Sublime** (the D19 to the D71) twists along the southern rim, taking in landmarks such as the **Balcons de la Mescla** (Mescla Terraces) and **Pont de l'Artuby** (Artuby Bridge), the highest bridge in Europe.

A complete circuit of the Gorges du Verdon involves about 140 unremitting kilometres of driving. Castellane and Moustiers tourist offices have English-language driving itineraries. The only real village en route is **La Palud-sur-Verdon** (population 300, elevation

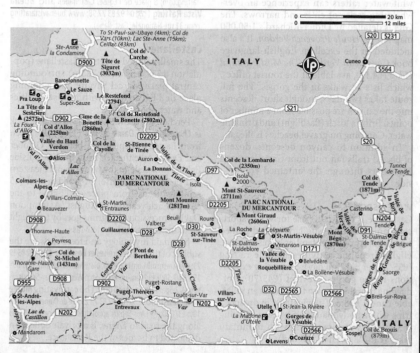

VULTURE CULTURE

Soaring high above the canyon, with a wingspan of 3m, the griffon vulture (Gyps fulvus) is an awe-inspiring sight. Once common in Provence, the species was a useful carrion eater, which helped prevent water pollution. The shotgun and loss of food sources such as the bear and wolf, however, caused its disappearance almost a century ago.

In 1999, 12 young birds were reintroduced into the wild at Rougon. It took them two weeks to learn to fly again, but they eventually settled in the Gorges du Verdon. A total of 90 vultures were released over the following five years and have now formed a breeding colony.

Between June and September half-day vulture-watching walks around Rougon depart from Castellane's tourist office (p234) at 9am (9.30am from Rougon) on Wednesday from June to September (plus Tuesday and Thursday in July and August). Walks cost €6/3 for adults/students (children under 10 free).

The Belvédère de l'Escalès (p235) is one of the best free vantage points to see the vultures in flight.

930m), 2km northeast of the northern bank of the gorges. Traffic on the single-lane roads frequently slows to snail's pace in summer; in winter, roads can be icy. Any time of year watch out for falling (and fallen) rocks.

WALKING

From Point Sublime, the GR4 descends to the bottom of the canyon where walkers and whitewater rafters can experience an overwhelming series of cliffs and narrows. The GR4 is detailed by Didier-Richard's 1:50,000 map No 19, *Haute Provence-Verdon*. It's also included in the excellent English-language book *Canyon du Verdon – The Most Beautiful Hikes* (€4.12), available at the tourist offices, which lists 28 walks in the gorges. The full route takes two days, though short descents into the canyon are possible from a number of points. Bring a torch (flashlight) and drinking water. Camping on gravel beaches is illegal.

In addition to canyon descents, dozens of blazed trails fan out from Castellane and Moustiers through the untamed countryside.

WATER SPORTS

Castellane is the main base for water-sports companies; all offer similarly priced guided trips from April to September by reservation. High-adrenaline activities include rafting (€55/75 per half/full day); canyoning expeditions in the gorges' crevices (€45/70); hot-dogging (bombing down the river in an inflatable canoe; €38 self-navigated); hydrospeed trips with a bodyboard (€45); water trekking (€31); and water-rambling with mountain bikes (€15/22 per half/full day).

For the truly adventurous, **Guides Aventure** (☎ 06 85 94 46 61; www.guidesaventure.com) organises 'floating' (€45/90 per half/full day) – it's like white-water rafting minus the raft, with a buoyancy bag strapped to your back – and also runs a range of canyoning, rock-climbing and rafting trips.

Other water-sports operators include **Aboard Rafting** (☎ 04 92 83 76 11; www.aboard-rafting.com; 8 place de l'Église, Castellane) and **Buena Vista Rafting** (☎ 04 92 83 77 98; www.buenavistarafting.com; 31 rue Nationale, Castellane).

Castellane

The small, cobbled streets of Castellane (population 1539, elevation 723m) surrounding central place Marcel Savaire and adjoining place de l'Église teem with tourist facilities and water-sports shops.

Perched above the town on a needlelike rock is **Chapelle Notre Dame du Roc** (1703). It's open from Easter to September; between October and Easter, take the key from the box outside Église Paroissiale in town (at the northeastern end of place de l'Église). A walking trail (45 minutes) leads from place de l'Église to the chapel. Each year on 15 August (Assumption Day) a procession of pilgrims goes by torchlight up to the rock to celebrate Mass.

Mermaid mythology and fossil facts are the subject of the **Musée Sirènes et Fossiles** (☎ 04 92 83 19 23; www.resgeol04.org in French; place Marcel Sauvaire; adult/7-15yr €4/2.50; 10am-noon & 2-5pm Wed-Sun May-Sep, 9am-noon & 2-5pm Wed-Sun Apr & Oct). The captivating **Musée de la Résistance** (☎ 04 92 83 78 25; rte de Digne; adult/12-18yr €3/1.50; Apr-Sep by appointment), about 1.5km along the road to Digne, is a private collection dedicated to heroes of the Resistance.

Moustiers Ste-Marie

Strung between the two limestone cliffs towering either side of the little village of Moustiers Ste-Marie (population 635, elevation 634m), a 227m-long gold chain bearing a shining star was suspended, so legend claims, by the Knight of Blacas, grateful to have returned safely from the Crusades. Twice a century the weathered chain gives way and the star is replaced.

Beneath the star, clinging to a cliff ledge, is the 14th-century **Chapelle Notre Dame de Beauvoir**, built on the site of an AD 470 temple. A trail climbs up from rue de la Bourgade to the chapel and its waterfall, passing 14 stations of the cross en route; count on at least 30 minutes each way. In July and August, guided tours take place at 10am on Tuesday. On 8 September each year, Mass is held at 5am to celebrate the Virgin Mary's nativity, followed by a communal breakfast on the square.

When silverware was reclaimed by the French kingdom and melted down to mint currency, the village's decorative faïence (earthenware) graced Europe's palaces. Antique masterpieces can be admired in the **Musée de la Faïence** (☎ 04 92 74 61 64; musee-moustiers@wanadoo.fr; rue de la Bourgade; adult/16-18yr €2/1; ✆ 10am-12.30pm & 2-7pm Wed-Mon Jul & Aug, 10am-12.30pm & 2-6pm Wed-Mon Apr-Jun, Sep & Oct) adjacent to Moustiers' *marie* (town hall). After ceasing in 1870, the industry was resurrected in 1927 and found new popularity in the late 1960s. Today there are 15 ateliers in Moustiers, including **Atelier St-Michel** (☎ 04 92 74 67 73; www .faience-ateliersaintmichel.com). Husband-and-wife artisans Martial and Françoise Baudey and their son Sylvain have a shop at the top of the village on place Pomey (closed January), and an atelier at the bottom of the village in the St-Michel quarter where they conduct **workshop tours** (€3) at 11am on Thursday in July and August, showing you step-by-step how they craft the intricate pieces.

SLEEPING & EATING
Castellane & Around

The nearby river is lined with seasonal camping areas (open from April or May until September) charging around €15 to €25 for two adults with a tent and car in high summer. In town, hotels and restaurants cluster around place Marcel Sauvaire and place de l'Église. Hotels recommended here have restaurants.

CHAMBRES D'HÔTES

Gîte de Chasteuil (☎ 04 92 83 72 45; www.gitedechasteuil .com; Hameau de Chasteuil; s/d/t r incl breakfast from €52/59/77; **P** ✆) Walkers will find this *chambre d'hôte* in an old schoolhouse in the 16th-century hamlet of Chasteuil an irresistible stop on the G4, which passes right outside. Host Nancy hand-makes the soaps in the bathrooms, and *tables d'hôtes* (from €20) are served from Monday to Thursday, July to September, with an evening picnic basket available the rest of the year. Chasteuil sits 8km southwest of Castellane.

HOTELS

Ma Petite Auberge (☎ 04 92 83 62 06; fax 04 92 83 68 49; rue de la République; d €46-67, mains from €12; ✆ closed mid-Nov–mid-Mar; **P** ✆) An intimate two-star hotel overlooking Castellane's central square, Ma Petite Auberge has 15 light-filled, airy, elegantly old-fashioned rooms, a peaceful garden shaded by an enormous lime tree, and a bustling restaurant. Parking's free.

WEARABLE ART

Think of faïence pottery, and you would normally think of the plates and serving dishes that served the kings and queens of their day, but artisans Martial, Françoise and Sylvain Baudey are now turning this ancient tradition into a wearable art form.

Madame Baudey explains:

'Faïence jewellery gives an opportunity to wear this traditional art and is fun and different. It's nice because every piece is made by hand. There are no moulds, so every finished item is completely unique in its form and its decoration. It's also easier to take the jewellery to the markets in the region – we don't take the plates to the markets because they're too fragile and expensive, whereas jewellery is easy to transport.'

Twice-fired and glazed for a dazzling brilliance, the jewellery is durable, surprisingly weightless to wear, and makes the ultimate statement in chic for a fashion accessory – individuality.

HAUTE-PROVENCE

Hôtel Restaurant de la Forge (☎ 04 92 83 62 61; http://perso.wanadoo.fr/forge; place de l'Église; d/q from €42/60, menu €18; ☺ closed Dec & Jan) Fronted by a pretty terrace festooned with flowers in summer, this little eight-room place sits at the foot of the Rock. Rooms have dinky wooden shutters and comfy beds and come with TVs and telephones. The restaurant's open for lunch and dinner from Sunday to Friday, with a bargain €10 plat du jour.

Nouvel Hôtel Restaurant du Commerce (☎ 04 92 83 61 00; www.hotel-fradet.com; place de l'Église; d €60-70, tr €75-85, menus €22-29; ☺ closed Oct-Mar; P ♿) Renovated top to bottom in 2006, this exceptionally friendly spot opening to a large, new, private garden – and new, free parking – is best known for its 'rustic-gastronomic' restaurant serving favourites so Provençal that Mistral himself would be proud.

CAMPING

Domaine de Chasteuil Provence (☎ 04 92 83 61 21; www.chasteuil-provence.com; camping €11-16; ☺ May–mid-Sep; ♨) Just south of Castellane, this camping ground has lovely, leafy grounds, optional powered sites, and timber chalets (from €111 for two nights for four people).

Moustiers Ste-Marie & Around

Moustiers has some ultracharming spots to eat and sleep.

GÎTES & FERMES AUBERGE

Le Petit Segries (☎ 04 92 74 68 83; www.gite-segries .fr; Moustiers; d/tr incl breakfast €55/71, table d'hôte incl wine €18, picnic basket €3.50-8; P ♿) At this energetically-run gîte housing six French-washed rooms, guests and nonguests can rent bikes (from €14 per half-day) or sign up for a bike tour (from €65 per half-day) to hidden spots known only to locals such as hosts Sylvie and Noël. By night, join in lively tables d'hôtes at a massive custom-made chestnut table with farm-fresh lamb, rabbit, eggs and mountain honey. Le Petit Segries is 5km northwest of Moustiers village – take the D92 towards Riez and turn right at the top of the hill; it's 300m ahead on your right.

La Ferme Ste-Cécile (☎ 04 92 74 64 18; www.ferme -ste-cecile.com in French; quartier St-Michel; menus €24-46; ☺ closed Mon & mid-Nov–Dec) Fresh fish with roast garlic and fennel ice cream, and anchovies with olive ice cream, are among the delicious culinary surprises served on the terrace of this authentic ferme auberge (farmhouse restau-

rant), 1km out of the village centre along the D952. The last Friday of every month features a wine tasting accompanied by a meal (€50) – book ahead.

HOTELS

Hôtel-Restaurant Le Relais (☎ 04 92 74 66 10; www .lerelais-moustiers.com; place du Couvert; d €50-80, menus €21-29; ☺ closed mid-Nov–Feb; P ♿) With glorious views of the sun rising between Moustiers' star-strung cliffs from the rear east-facing rooms, this apricot-coloured family-run place up in the village has an excellent restaurant (lunch and dinner Saturday to Thursday) specialising in river-caught fish. Parking's free.

Hôtel le Baldaquin (☎ 04 92 74 63 92; place Clerissy; d €60-99; ☺ Mar–mid-Nov; P) Experience heart-warming hospitality at this 17th-century, blue-shuttered place in the village centre. It feels more like a home than a hotel, with seven rooms hung with Renoir and Degas prints. Garaged parking costs €5, and the buffet breakfast (€9) will assuage the heartiest hiker's appetite.

Hôtel Le Clos des Iris (☎ 04 92 74 63 46; www.closdes iris.fr; chemin de Quinson; d €62-67, tr & q €95-110, ☺ closed Dec; P) Down a country lane, this charming house has an untamed, flowery garden dotted with blue ceramic tiled tables. Rooms all have shady private terraces looking onto the lawns. Advance bookings are essential.

La Bastide de Moustiers (☎ 04 92 70 47 47; www .bastide-moustiers.com; d low/high season from €155/180;

AUTHOR'S CHOICE

La Ferme Rose (☎ 04 92 74 69 47; www .lafermerose.fr.fm in French; chemin de Quinson, Moustiers; d €80-145; P ♟) This fabulous converted farmhouse contains quirky collections including antique toys, a Wurlitzer jukebox with 45in records, a display case of coffee grinders, and old telephones, telex machines, theatre lighting and projectors. Its dozen boutique rooms, draped with embroidered white cotton sheets and canopies, are named for the colour dramatising each chic sleeping area and glazed bathroom; and for sun-baskers, the 'almond room' has a private terrace overlooking unfolding paddocks, with reclining lounges and a fibreglass-sculpted boulder. Find 'the pink farm' signposted off the D952 on Moustiers' fringe.

HAUTE-PROVENCE

> **AUTHOR'S CHOICE**
>
> **Les Comtes** (☎ 04 92 74 63 88; rue de la Bour-gade, Moustiers; mains €12-20; ☷ lunch Tue-Sun, dinner Tue-Sat, closed Nov-Feb) Any meal at this low-key, luscious little bistro in Moustiers' village invariably starts with an aperitif from the Vallée de l'Ubaye made from mountain fruits such as blueberries and raspberries. Follow it up with a main course such as squid-ink tagliatelle with saffron; or a 'one-meal plate' laden, for instance, with goat's cheese pie, an aubergine terrine, cherry to-matoes, black-olive *tapenade*, mixed salad, raw fennel and grilled peppers. Meals can be accompanied by a handpicked glass of wine (€2 to €2.50), selected to match indi-vidual dishes. Still going strong? Desserts include a fig and pine-nut pie with fig ice cream. In summer, dine in the sunshine at wooden tables; when the chill sets in, head for the cavelike dining room. Credit cards aren't accepted.

menus €42-57; P ⊠ ⊠ ⊛) Some of France's finest chefs get their start at this bastion be-longing to Alain Ducasse. Inside the rose-draped archways and thick stone walls of this old master-potter's studio are poetic rooms. Outside, baby deer scamper in the grounds, and yes, there's a place to park the helicopter. One room is wheelchair accessible.

CAMPING

Domaine de Le Petit Lac (☎ 04 92 74 67 11; www .lepetitlac.com; route du lac de Ste-Croix; camping incl elec-tricity €14-22.50, 4-person ecocabins per night, min 2 nights, from €45; ☷ camping mid-Jun–Sep, cabins Apr–mid-Oct; ⊠) In a peaceful lakeside spot, this activity-oriented camping ground has new ecocabins with hemp walls, solar hot water and low-output electricity.

Other Moustiers dining recommendations:

Côte-Jardin (☎ 04 92 74 68 91; rue de Lérins; mains €19-27; ☷ closed Wed & dinner Tue, closed Nov & Dec) Dine under the oak trees overlooking the valley.

La Treille Muscate (☎ 04 92 74 64 31; place de l'Église; menus €25-34; ☷ closed Thu & dinner Wed in low season, Wed in high season, closed mid-Nov–Jan) In the heart of the village.

GETTING THERE & AROUND

Public transport to, from, and around the Gorges du Verdon is limited. **Autocars Sumian**

(☎ 04 42 67 60 34) runs buses from Marseille to Castellane (€19.90, 2¼ hours) via Aix-en-Provence (€16.30, 1¾ hours); and from Cas-tellane to Moustiers (€7.30, one hour).

VFD (☎ 04 93 85 24 56, 08 20 83 38 33) operates a daily bus from Grenoble to Nice via Digne-les-Bains and Grasse, stopping en route in Castellane (from Nice €17, 2¼ hours). Tourist offices in Castellane and Moustiers Ste-Marie have schedules.

Castellane and Moustiers tourist offices have information on bike rental. In Castellane, try **Aqua Viva Est** (☎ 04 92 83 75 74; www.aquavivaest .com; 12 blvd de la République). Mountain bikes start from €10/20 per half-/full day.

LACS DU VERDON

Shimmering an unearthly opaque jade green due to their high mineral content, the Verdon lakes appear as timeless as the area's ethe-real gorges. They were, in fact, created by the national electricity company in the second half of the 20th century to provide hydro-electricity, irrigation for cities including Aix and Toulon, and tourism. Today these five mountain lakes offer scenic swimming, water sports and sunbathing on the pebbly shores. Be sure to stick to designated swimming areas as the hydroelectric dams make other sections of the lakes dangerous.

SIGHTS & ACTIVITIES

Charming villages, a storybook castle and a prehistoric cave lie by the Verdon's lakes.

Lac de Ste-Croix

The largest of the lakes, Lac de Ste-Croix, was formed in 1974 and stretches 10km southwest of Moustiers Ste-Marie. Pretty **Bauduen** (popu-lation 276) sits on its southeastern banks. Camp sites dot the lakeside D71 and D249, leading to the village. Bauduen has a small **tourist office** (☎ 04 94 84 39 02; bauduen-sur-verdon .com in French; rue de Juterie), as does the village of **Les Salles-sur-Verdon** (☎ 04 94 70 21 84; www.sallessur verdon.com; place Fontfreye), which has information on the town's lavender distilleries.

Ste-Croix de Verdon (population 103, eleva-tion 525m) is the only village on the western banks of the lake.

By the lake, scads of summertime rentals by the hour include windsurfers, electric boats, canoes and kayaks, as well as paddleboats (not ideal when it's windy as it's difficult to get out onto the lake).

Lac de Quinson

Lac de Quinson, about 1km south of the town of Qunison, sits at the southernmost foot of the lower Gorges du Verdon.

In **Quinson** (population 354), the hi-tech **Musée de la Préhistoire des Gorges du Verdon** (☎ 04 92 74 09 59; www.museeprehistoire.com; rte de Montmeyan; adult/6–18yr/family €7/5/20; ☒ 10am-8pm Jul & Aug, 10am-7pm Wed-Mon Apr-Jun & Sep, 10am-6pm Wed-Mon Feb, Mar & Oct–mid-Dec, closed mid-Dec–end Jan), the creation of British architect Norman Foster, explores the gorges' prehistoric past and archaeological treasures. In July and August it organises expeditions to the **Grotte de la Baume Bonne**, a prehistoric cave discovered by archaeologists in the 1960s.

Fresh truffles are unearthed around quaint **Montagnac** (population 326), 11km north of Quinson off the D11. Eight kilometres west is **Allemagne-en-Provence** (population 384). Contrary to widespread belief, its name isn't German-inspired (despite Allemagne being French for 'Germany'), but is a derivative of the Roman Goddess of fertility, Alemona. Her likeness appears on the village's centrepiece,

the turret-topped 12th- to 16th-century **Château d'Allemagne** (☎ 04 92 77 46 78; guided tours €6; ☒ tours 4pm & 5pm Tue-Sun Jul–mid-Sep, 4pm & 5pm Sat & Sun Easter-Jun & mid-Sep–Oct), a fairy-tale castle where would-be princes and princesses can sojourn (see opposite).

Lacs de Chaudanne & Castillon

At the eastern end of the Gorges du Verdon, Lac de Chaudanne has steep-sided banks, but Lac de Castillon's gently sloping beaches are ideal for swimming and its waters suitable for paddleboating.

From Lac de Castillon, the single-lane D402 cuts into the mountains to the walled **Cité Ste-de Mandarom Shambhasalem** (Holy City of Mandarom Shambhasalem; ☎ 04 92 83 63 83; www.aumisme.org; adult/10–18yr/student €5/2/3; ☒ 10-11.15am & 3-4.30pm Jul & Aug, 3-4.30pm Sat & Sun Sep-Jun), glittering with a 22m Buddha, a giant statue of Christ and temples representing the word's major religions. The 'holy city' is the home of Aumism, founded in 1969 by Gilbert Bourdin (1923–98), aka the Holy Lord Hamsah Manarah, as the 'Religion of the Unity of God's Faces'. Inside the walls, monks in multicoloured robes and mirrored headbands pray for world peace while chant-

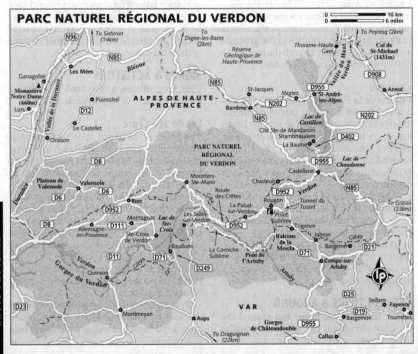

PARC NATUREL RÉGIONAL DU VERDON

MARKET DAY

Market days in the mountains prod sleepy villages and towns into frantic action. Delicacies include wild-boar sausages, fragrant herbs, AOC olive oil, locally made cheeses (including leaf-wrapped Banon; see p249), lavender honey and all the olives your poor stomach can stand. The markets listed below start early in the morning and wrap up at about noon or 1pm.

Monday Forcalquier

Tuesday Breil-sur-Roya, Colmars-les-Alpes, Seyne-les-Alpes

Wednesday Barcelonnette, Castellane, Digne-les-Bains, La Foux d'Allos, La Palud-sur-Verdon, Sisteron, St-André-les-Alpes, Tende

Thursday Allemagne-en-Provence, Allos, Les Salles-sur-Verdon, Montagnac, Sospel

Friday Colmars-les-Alpes, Entrevaux, Moustiers Ste-Marie, Quinson, Seyne-les-Alpes

Saturday Barcelonnette, Castellane, Digne-les-Bains, Sisteron, St-André-les-Alpes

Sunday Bauduen (summer only), La-Palud-sur-Verdon (summer only)

Daily St-Martin-Vésubie

---

ing the holy word 'Aum'. Though it looks for all the world like an outpost of EuroDisney, the compound is revered by its residents; visitors must be dressed modestly.

St-André-les-Alpes (population 832, elevation 914m) is France's leading paragliding centre. Take off with **Aérogliss** (☎ 04 92 89 11 30; www .aerogliss.com; chemin des Iscles), where a five-day beginner's course costs between €445 and €475, and 10-/20-plus minute baptism tandem paragliding sessions cost €60/85. If you can't wait to download those photos for your friends and family to see, there's free wi-fi within a 50m radius of the school.

Also in St-André-les-Alpes, 30 types of sausage are sold at the **Maison du Saucisson** (House of Sausages; ☎ 04 92 89 03 16; place de Verdun; ☒ closed Mon winter), including donkey, ostrich and wild boar. The **tourist office** (☎ 04 92 89 02 39; www.ot-st-andre-les -alpes.fr; place Marcel Pastorelli; ☒ 9am-noon & 2-5pm Mon-Fri, 10am-noon & 2-6pm Sat, 10am-noon Sun mid-Jun–mid-Sep, 9am-noon & 2-5pm Mon-Fri mid-Sep–mid-Jun), in St-André's village centre, has loads of local info.

St-André is linked with eastern Provence and Nice by the narrow-gauge mountain railway (see p245).

SLEEPING & EATING

Camp sites crowd in and around Ste-Croix de Verdon; ask at the Castellane tourist office. St-Andrés tourist office has information about camping in the Lac de Castillon area.

Château d'Allemagne (☎ 04 92 77 46 78; Lac de Quinson; d €80-140; ☒ ☒) Stroll the grounds filled with 100-year-old trees surrounding this magnificent castle, dip in the swimming pool, or just be swept away with the romance of it all in one of just three *chambre d'hôte* rooms

in regal shades such as rich, royal blue and furnished with heavy, dark timber furniture and drapes. Breakfast is provided for stays of three or more nights. In spring and autumn, the five-room caretakers cottage, with a full kitchen and an open fireplace in the lounge room, can be rented starting from €600 per week for six people.

Hôtel Lac et Forêt (☎ 04 92 89 07 38; lacforet@club -internet.fr; rte de Nice; d €40-46, menus €15-22; ☒ ☒) Looking like something from a children's picture book, this red-roofed chalet on the shores of Lac de Castillon has bright, spacious rooms with views of the lake – and of the paragliders from the neighbouring paragliding school dropping from the sky. The restaurant has a good kids menu (€9).

Domaine d'Aiguines (☎ 04 92 34 25 72; fax 04 92 34 29 09; St-Jacques; menus €20-26) Home to hundreds of the birds, this duck farm cooks up farm-made foie gras, pan-fried duck salad and other duck dishes. Follow the N202 for 13km west from St André-les-Alpes and turn left (north) just before Barrême, along the narrow D118 to the hamlet of St-Jacques. Opening hours are variable, so don't just turn up on the off chance.

RÉSERVE GÉOLOGIQUE DE HAUTE-PROVENCE

Footprints of prehistoric birds, outsized ammonites and ram's horn spiral shells are among the amazing fossil deposits found throughout the 1900-sq-km Réserve Géologique de Haute-Provence. You'll need a detailed regional map or *topoguide* (sold at Digne-les-Bains' tourist office) and your own transport to get to the 18 sites, most of which are found around **Barles** (population 114, 24km north of Digne) to the north and **Barrême** (population 442, 28km southeast) to the south. An impressive limestone slab with some 500 ammonites sits 3km north of Digne-les-Bains on the road to Barles. The reserve runs museums in Sisteron (p246) and Castellane (p236).

Find time to visit the fascinating **Centre de Géologie** (☎ 04 92 36 70 70; www.resgeol04.org in French; Parc St-Bénoît; adult/7-14yr €4.60/2.75; ☻ museum 9am-noon & 2-5.30pm Apr-Oct, 9am-noon & 2-5.30pm Mon-Thu, 9am-noon & 2-4.30pm Fri, closed Sat & Sun Nov-Mar, park 8am-7pm Apr-Oct, 8am-7pm Mon-Fri Nov-Mar) in St-Bénoît, 2km north of Digne off the road to Barles. Trails lead to a museum containing aquariums, insect displays, and fossils and plants put into evolutionary context. Take TUD bus 2 from Digne to the Champourcin stop (across the bridge; €1), then follow the road to the left along the signposted 'Musée-Promenade', a dramatic 15-minute clamber up a rocky overhang above the river. Car access is restricted.

DIGNE-LES-BAINS

pop 17,680 / elev 608m

Both wild and cultivated lavender carpet the mountains and plains around Digne-les-Bains, which celebrates the annual lavender harvest with a fragrant festival in August.

Resting at the foot of the Alps, Digne is named for its curative thermal springs, which are visited annually by around 11,000 people seeking cures for rheumatism and other ailments.

In addition to the Réserve Géologique de Haute-Provence's fossil-rich shale, the town has a couple of top museums.

Orientation

Digne hugs the eastern bank of the shallow River Bléone. The major roads into town converge at the Point Rond du 11 Novembre 1918 roundabout, 400m northeast of the train station. The main street, blvd Gassendi, heads northeastwards from the Point Rond and passes the large place du Général de Gaulle, the main square.

Information

INTERNET ACCESS

Cybercafé (☎ 04 92 32 00 19; 48 rue de l'Hubac; per hr €5; ☻ 10am-noon & 2-7pm Tue-Sat) In the centre of town.

LAUNDRY

There are laundrettes, one at 4 place du Marché in the old city (open 8am to 7pm Monday to Saturday) and the other at 99 blvd Gassendi (open 9am to 7pm).

TOURIST INFORMATION

Relais Départemental des Gîtes de France (☎ 04 92 31 30 40; www.gites-de-france.com; ☻ 9am-noon & 1-5pm Mon-Fri, 9am-noon Sat) Adjacent to the tourist office. Can book gîtes in the area from 9am to 11am and 1pm to 4pm.

Tourist office (☎ 04 92 36 62 62; www.ot-dignes bains.fr; place du Tampinet; ☻ 8.45am-12.30pm & 1.30-6.30pm Jul & Aug, 8.45am-noon & 2-6pm Mon-Sat, 10am-noon Sun Sep-Jun) Provides comprehensive regional info including walking and cycling maps; runs seasonal half-day guided tours in English to the lavender distillery in Mézel (€7) by appointment.

Sights

It's worth darting into the **Cathédrale Notre-Dame du Bourg** (av du Camping) at the eastern end of town. Built between the 12th and 13th centuries, it has a simple, clean-cut Romanesque interior and contains some unusual painted murals.

MUSÉE ALEXANDRA DAVID-NÉEL

Tibetan culture is celebrated at the **Fondation Alexandra David-Néel** (☎ 04 92 31 32 38; www .alexandra-david-neel.org; 27 av Maréchal Juin; admission free), in memory of the Paris-born writer and philosopher who made an incognito voyage in the 1900s to Tibet before settling in Digne. Year-round, free two-hour tours (available in English) commence at 10am, 2pm and 3.30pm. Drive 1km along the Nice road or take bus 3 to the Stade Rolland stop.

MUSÉE GASSENDI

Everything from modern art by Andy Goldsworthy to still lifes by 19th-century painter Etienne Martin, natural history, and exhibits on the 16th-century philosopher-scientist-painter Pierre Gassendi are displayed at the **Musée Gassendi** (☎ 04 92 31 45 29; place des Récollets; adult/child €4/2; ☻ 11am-7pm Apr-Sep, 1.30-5.30pm Wed-Mon Oct-Mar) in the town centre.

Activities

Ahhhh...float in the thermal pool, slather yourself in mud and seaweed or luxuriate in a lavender bath at **Établissement Thermal** (☎ 04 92 32 32 92; www.eurothermes.com in French; ☻ Feb-early

---

DONKEY DISCOVERY

Ramble through the lavender-strewn mountains with a donkey from **Lambert Âne** (☎ 04 92 31 60 37; www.lambertane.com; Le Château-Lambert), in the hamlet of La Robine-sur-Galabre, 31km northeast of Thoard, or **Poivre d'Âne** (☎ 04 92 34 87 12; poivre.ane.free.fr; La Bastide des Férauds), northwest of Digne in Thoard.

To discover more about these endearing creatures, Lambert offers **farm visits** (€6.50 to €7.50) where you learn about their breeding and can ask questions during afternoon tea made from farm produce. At Poivre you can stay on the donkey farm in *chambre d'hôte* rooms (double from €51; breakfast €4.70) and feast on farm-fresh tables d'hôtes (€15.50).

Donkey hire starts from €44/80 per one/two days.

Dec), 2km east of Digne's centre. A 20-minute spa or massage starts at €45.

Rando Lavande (☎ 04 92 32 27 44; www.chez.com /randolavande in French; 7 rue de Provence) organises customised walks through the mountains' wild lavender in summer and snowshoeing expeditions in winter (from €20 per person per day).

Festivals & Events

For more than 50 years the five-day **Corso de la Lavande**, starting on the first weekend of August, has heralded the lavender harvest. Musicians flock to town, colourful floats parade through the streets and torch-lit celebrations continue into the night.

The **Journées Tibetaines** (Tibetan Days), an annual celebration of Tibetan culture, is held at the Musée Alexandra David-Néel over three days in August.

Sleeping & Eating

Many of Digne's hotels require half-board in July and August. France's first *gîte* was founded here in 1951; the Relais Départemental des Gîtes de France's headquarters (opposite) has a list of locations.

Hôtel de Provence (☎ 04 92 31 32 19; www.hotel -alpes-provence.com; rte des Thermes; d €43-50, tr €58-60, q €70-72; P ♨) There is only a handful of private parking places for guests at this cheerful Provençal hotel framed by window boxes, but there's plenty of public parking is available nearby. A terracotta-tiled staircase leads to rooms with brightly printed fabrics, and there's an outdoor terrace to soak up the sunshine.

Hôtel du Golf (☎ 04 92 30 58 00; www.golfdigne.com; 57 route du Chaffaut; d €45-68, menus €13-25; ♨ restaurant open lunch year-round, dinner Jul & Aug; P ♨ ♨) Swing a club through fields of lavender. A well-signed 8km southwest of Digne, this resort takes the so-called 'good walk spoiled' *très* seriously,

with packages combining accommodation, dining and golf, multistage lessons, and golf buggy and GPS rental. Rooms are modern, utilitarian arrangements; there's a relaxed restaurant and bar for a postgame pastis.

Hôtel Villa Gaïa (☎ 04 92 31 21 60; www.hotelvilla gaia.fr; 24 rte de Nice; d €85-95, menus €26-39; ♨ Apr-Oct; P) Set in Italianate fountained gardens, this antique-filled 19th-century villa 2km west of town still feels like the private mansion it once was, complete with a tennis court, flowing lounge and guest rooms, a library and a grand dining room.

Also recommended:

Hôtel L'Origan (☎ /fax 04 92 31 62 13; 6 rue Pied de Ville; d €25-35, menus €20-40; ♨ restaurant closed Tue) Great for travellers watching their centimes, with cheap, charmingly comfy rooms and a first-rate regional restaurant.

Hôtel Central (☎ 04 92 31 31 91; www.lhotel-central .com; 26 blvd Gassendi; d €47-57) Overlooking Digne's main café strip (so street rooms can be noisy), with wood-beamed rooms, colourful quilts and accommodating staff.

SELF-CATERING

On Wednesday and Saturday mornings, place du Général de Gaulle overflows with fresh market produce.

The bevy of bakeries in town includes **Boulangerie Patisserie Andre Michel** (16 rue Pied de Ville).

Getting There & Around

BICYCLE

Gallardo (☎ 04 92 31 05 29; 8 cours des Arès; ♨ 9am-noon & 3-7pm Tue-Sat) rents bikes (€15 per day).

BUS

The **bus station** (☎ 04 92 31 50 00; place du Tampinet; ♨ 9am-12.30pm & 3-6.30pm Mon-Sat) is behind the tourist office. Destinations include Nice (2¼ hours, Monday, Tuesday, Friday and Saturday) via Castellane (1¼ hours), Marseille (2½ hours) and Apt (two hours, Monday to Saturday).

THE PERFUME OF PROVENCE

If Provence has a defining colour, it's purple; and a defining fragrance, it's the astringent aroma of lavender (lavande), which flowers for a month prior to harvesting between approximately mid-June and mid-August, depending on the region. Some of the most spectacular fields include those surrounding Abbaye de Sénanque near Gordes, the vast farms sweeping the Plateau de Valensole, and those strewing the arid Sault region.

The aromatic flowers are mechanically harvested in full bloom between 15 July and 15 August on a hot, dry day. Lorry-loads of cut lavender, known as paille (straw), are packed tightly in a steam still and distilled to extract the essential oils.

Authentic lavender farms, all the rage in the 1920s, are a dying breed today. Since the 1950s lavandin (lavendin) – a hybrid of fine lavender and aspic, cloned at the turn of the 20th century – has been mass produced for industrial purposes. Both blaze the same vibrant purple, but lavandin yields five times more oil than fine lavender (which produces 1kg of oil from 130kg of cut straw). Since 1997 huile essentielle de lavande de Haute-Provence – essential lavender oil from Haute-Provence – has been protected by its own appellation d'origine contrôlée (AOC).

Approximately 80% of Provence's 400 lavender farms now produce lavandin. The few remaining traditional lavender farms – like Château du Bois (see p226) – usually colour higher areas. Wild lavender needs an altitude of 900m to 1300m to blossom (unlike lavandin, which sprouts anywhere above 800m) and its more concentrated essences linger longer. Some 80% of essential oils produced in the region's 150 distilleries is exported.

A list of lavender farms, distilleries and scented gardens open to visitors feature in the free brochure Les Routes de la Lavande: La Provence par les Sens (The Lavender Roads: Experiencing Provence through the Five Senses), also available in English from tourist offices or the association **Les Routes de la Lavande** (☎ 04 75 26 65 91; www.routes-lavande.com). In Thoard, 20km northwest of Digne-les-Bains, the old-fashioned **Distillerie du Siron** (☎ 04 92 34 80 33; Quartier le Gazon) offers free guided tours between late July and late August from 10am to noon and 2pm to 5pm on Tuesday, Thursday and at weekends, and sells lavender year-round.

Lavender can be tasted throughout Provence in various guises, including in ice cream, chocolate and honey, and several restaurants offer lavender menus.

Festivals take place in Valensole (3rd Sunday in July), Sault (15 August), and Digne-les-Bains and Valréas (both first weekend in August).

During the ski season and in July and August, two or three buses a week also travel to La Foux d'Allos (two hours); while **Société des Cars Alpes Littoral** (SCAL; ☎ 04 92 51 06 05; www.scal-amv-voyages.com in French) runs a daily bus in either direction between Marseille and Pra Loup (4½ hours) via Digne-les-Bains (2¼ hours) and Barcelonnette (four hours).

TRAIN

Digne's **train station** (☎ 04 92 31 00 67; av Pierre Sémard; ⏰ ticket windows 8.15am-12.30pm & 1-8pm Mon-Fri, 8.15am-12.30pm & 1.45-4.45pm Sat) is a 10-minute walk west of the tourist office. There are daily services to Marseille (€22, 2¼ hours).

Digne-les-Bains is the northern terminus of the **Chemins de Fer de Provence** (☎/fax 04 92 31 01 58; www.trainprovence.com; av Pierre Sémard), which links Digne to Nice via a scenic, narrow-gauge mountain railway. See opposite for highlights.

NORTH OF DIGNE-LES-BAINS

Like a little swatch of Switzerland, the **Vallée de la Blanche** (www.valleedelablanche.com), 50km north of Digne, has more than 110km of ski runs split between three resorts. The main one, well set up for families with amenities including a crèche, is the 1350m **St-Jean Montclar**. Its **tourist office** (☎ 04 92 30 92 01; www.montclar.com; ⏰ call for seasonal opening times) is adjacent to the ski station. The area is the home of Montclar spring water, but you won't need to buy it while you're here – just turn on the tap.

Ski passes for St-Jean Montclar's slopes cost €16 to €18.50 per day. One of the sweetest chambres d'hôtes is **Les Alisiers** (☎ 04 92 35 30 88; fax 04 92 35 02 72; d incl breakfast €48-52, apt €53; ⏰ closed mid-Nov–mid-Dec), 800m past the ski station on your left; with views over the snowy fields from your toasty-warm bed and half-board options.

Between late December and March, there is a bus service from Gap (€11, 45 minutes), which is 47km northwest of here in the Hautes-Alpes; the rest of the year it's best reached by your own wheels.

VALLÉE DE LA DURANCE

At the western edge of Haute-Provence, the impetuous waters of the 324km-long River Durance, an affluent of the Rhône, follow the Via Domitia, the road from Italy that allowed the Romans to infiltrate the whole of France.

The Durance Valley ploughs southwest from Sisteron to the western side of Parc Naturel Régional du Verdon. The three main towns along this 100km stretch are Manosque, on the eastern edge of the Luberon (see p229); industrial **Château-Arnoux St-Auban** (population 5000) with its 16th-century castle on the confluence of the Rivers Durance and Bléone; and Sisteron.

SISTERON

pop 7232 / elev 485m

Sweeping views of Sisteron can be seen from its **citadel**, an imposing 3rd- to 16th-century fortress perched on a rock above the *cluse* (transverse valley), which was strengthened by Vauban in the 18th century to guard against neighbouring Savoy. Open-air classical-music

---

ALONG THE MOUNTAIN RAILWAY

Chugging between the mountains and the sea, narrow-gauge railway *le Train des Pignes* (the pine cone train) is one of Provence's most picturesque trips. Conceived in 1861 and fully inaugurated in 1911, the line was initially serviced by steam train, which still puffs between Puget and Annot in summer. Endearing theories abound (such as pine cones falling into the train one Christmas Eve when it had run out of coal), but no one knows the history behind the name.

Rising to 1000m altitude, with breathtaking views, the 151km track passes through 50 tunnels and over 16 viaducts and 15 metal bridges on its precipitous journey, stopping at villages en route. You can buy direct tickets to the place you want to visit or, if you're travelling the whole route, it's possible to hop out, explore, and join a later train. From Digne-les-Bains, highlights include:

St-André-les-Alpes (€6.60, 50 minutes; see p241)

Thorame-Haute (€8.20, one hour; population 174, elevation 1012m) Despite its pinprick size, this village is a vital bus link between southern Provence and the Allos ski resorts. After Thorame-Haute, the **Col de St-Michel** (1431m) and the ancient shepherds village of Peyresq flash past. The 3.5km-long tunnel here took 400 workers some two years to construct.

Annot (€9, one hour 25 minutes; population 1020, elevation 700m) This sweet old town has a couple of interesting 17th-century chapels, both a short walk from the village. The **tourist office** (☎ 04 92 83 23 03; www.annot.fr in French; blvd St-Pierre) has details.

Entrevaux (€11.15, one hour 50 minutes; population 752, elevation 515m) The 17th-century fortified village tumbles dramatically down the hillside from a Vauban-built citadel. Across the drawbridge is an oil and flour mill that can be visited. The **tourist office** (☎ 04 93 05 46 73; tourisme@entrevaux.info) is inside the old city gate.

Puget-Théniers (€12.15, one hour 55 minutes; population 1624, elevation 405m) The 1909 steam locomotive that gave *Le Train des Pignes* its name is stationed here: from May to October it shunts between Puget and Annot (€6.80 return, 50 minutes). Passengers with appetites fired up by the fresh mountain air should disembark for **Edelweiss** (☎ 04 90 05 01 00; 1 place Adolphe Cornil; menus from €25; ☽ lunch & dinner Thu-Tue Apr-Oct, lunch Thu-Tue, dinner Fri & Sat Nov-Mar) where Christian Recanzone cooks up succulent mountain lamb in lavender pastry. Puget also has a *via ferrata* (see p253).

Touët-sur-Var (€13.20, two hours 10 minutes; population 445) Another stop for gourmands, the perched village's **Auberge des Chasseurs** (☎ 04 93 05 71 11; menus €33-41; ☽ lunch Wed-Sun, dinner Tue-Sun, closed mid-Dec–Mar) is renowned for its seasonal game dishes, especially wild boar. Other treats include a terrine of foie gras with homemade mango chutney.

The entire trip from Digne to Nice takes 3¼ hours (€17.65). There are four to five trains daily. A discount of 20% is available for students, and 50% for children under 12. Bicycles cannot be taken onto the train, but are sent as baggage (€8); contact the railway for information.

Updated schedules are on Chemins de Fer de Provence's website at www.trainprovence.com.

HAUTE-PROVENCE

concerts during the **Festival des Nuits de la Citadelle** (Citadel Nights Festival; www.francefestivals .com/sisteron/indexuk.htm; tickets €36-45) are held here from mid-July to mid-August. The **tourist office** (☎ 04 92 61 12 03; www.sisteron.com; Hôtel de Ville; ☼ 9am-7pm Mon-Sat, 10am-1pm Sun mid-Jul–mid-Aug, 9am-noon & 2-6pm Mon-Sat mid-Aug–Nov & May–mid-Jul, 9am-noon & 2-5pm Mon-Sat Nov-Apr) has information on visiting the citadel, and also conducts 1¼-hour walking tours of the town in July and August (€1).

Time is the essence of the **Musée Terre et Temps** (Museum of Earth & Time; ☎ 04 92 61 61 30; www .resgeol04.org in French; 6 place Général de Gaulle; ☼ 10am-1pm & 3-7pm Jul & Aug, 9.30am-12.30pm & 2-6pm Thu-Mon Apr-Jun, Sep & Oct), inside a former 17th-century chapel. One of a trio of museums (see also Musée Sirènes et Fossiles, p236, and Centre de Géologie, p242) run by the Réserve Géologique de Haute-Provence, time-honoured displays include a Foucalt's Pendulum, sundials and a miraculous water clock.

From the museum, motorists can follow the rte du Temps (Time Rd), a marked itinerary along the eastbound D3 to remote **St-Geniez**, from where it climbs over the Col de Font-Belle (1708m) before swooping south to the medieval fortified village of **Thoard** and Digne-les-Bains. Information panels en route highlight geological sights.

AROUND SISTERON

In **Les Mées** (population 2973), 20km south of Sisteron, is the **Rocher des Mées**, a row of rocky pinnacles that stand 100m tall. They were once a gaggle of monks who were turned to stone for lusting after Saracen women, so legend claims.

Ten kilometres south again in **Ganagobie**, the 10th-century Benedictine **Prieuré de Ganagobie** (☎ 04 92 68 00 04; www.ndganagobie.com in French; ☼ 3-5pm Tue-Sun) showcases an exquisite 12th-century floor mosaic – the largest of its kind in France – in its chapel (the only section of the monastery open to visitors).

Heading 26km west of Sisteron in a secluded valley, the fabulous *ferme auberge* **Danse L'Ombre** (☎ 04 92 62 05 86; Les Remises, Curel; plat du jour €12, menu €22; ☼ by reservation) creates organic feasts from farm-raised meats and farm-grown vegetables and fruits including strawberries, raspberries, apples and pears. Musical-theatrical nights are held on Saturdays (€25). A sign directs you to the farm in the little hamlet of Curel, 200m off the D946 to your left.

PAYS DE FORCALQUIER

Less than a dozen kilometres northeast of its much more famous western neighbour, the Luberon, Pays de Forcalquier (Forcalquier country) is delightfully off mass tourism's radar. The area shelters sweet hilltop villages, wildflower-strewn countryside and gastronomic treats.

Forcalquier

pop 5000 / elev 550m

At the heart of Pays de Forcalquier, the town that bears its name sits atop a rocky perch 19km southwest of Ganagobie. Steep steps lead to the citadel and octagon-shaped chapel at the top of the village, where **carillon concerts** are held most Sundays from 11.30am to 12.30pm.

France's only heritage-listed **cemetery** (place du Souvenir Français; ☼ 9am-6pm) lies 1km north of the centre, distinguished by its age-old yew trees cut to form high, decorative alleys.

Fiery liqueurs such as Bigarade (bitter orange), La Farigoule (thyme), *amandine* (almond) and pastis (see p50) have been distilled at the Distilleries et Domaines de Provences since 1898. Taste and buy at its **Espace Dégustation** (☎ 04 92 75 15 41; www.distilleries-provence.com in French; 9 av St-Promasse; ☼ 9am-7pm Mon-Sat, 9am-noon Sun Jul & Aug, 9am-noon & 2-6pm Mon & Wed-Sat Sep-Jun).

You can also sample local aperitifs at a table d'hôte meal at **Le Lapin Tant Pis** (☎ 04 92 75 38 88; info@lecomptoirdespoivres.com; 10 av St-Promasse; menu €58; ☼ dinner Mon-Sat Jul & Aug, by appointment Sep-Jun), in the atelier of chef and spice-gatherer Gérard Vives. He feeds a maximum of 15 diners, so make sure you book ahead; credit cards are not accepted. To spice up your own cooking, pop into Monsieur Vives' adjoining spice shop.

Taste and stock up on the AOC Haute-Provence olive-oil harvest at **Oliviers & Co** (☎ 04 92 75 00 75; 5 rue des Cordeliers; menus around €18), a shop that dishes up light Mediterranean cuisine in the adjoining bistro.

The **tourist office** (☎ 04 92 75 10 02; www.forcalquier .com; 13 place du Bourguet; ☼ 9am-6pm Mon, 9am-12.30pm & 2-7pm Tue-Sat, 10am-1pm & 3-6pm Sun mid-Jun–mid-Sep, 9am-noon & 2-6pm Mon-Sat mid-Sep–mid-Jun) has information about atmospheric eating and sleeping options throughout Pays de Forcalquier.

Around Forcalquier

There are few more peaceful places in Provence than the 13th-century priory **Prieuré**

A LAKESIDE DETOUR

Straddling the Haute-Provence–Hautes-Alpes border, Europe's largest manmade lake, **Lac de Serre-Ponçon**, sits high in the mountains. Created between 1955 and 1961 to avoid flooding from the River Durance, which caused severe loss of life in the mid-19th century, the lake's construction saw the village of Savines demolished and drowned. The 'replacement' village, **Savines Le Lac**, now sits on the lake's eastern bank overlooking a flotilla of summer sailboats. The lake now seems as if it's been here as long as the mountains surrounding it.

The lake district's main town, **Embrun** (population 6700, elevation 870m), 10km north of Savines Le Lac, was the Roman capital of the Alps and later a bishopric. Its enchanting tangle of cobblestone streets lead to the dramatic black-and-white stone cathedral **Notre Dame du Réal**, which presides 80m above the lake. In town, pack a lakeside picnic from the homemade farm produce at **La Ferme Embrunaise** (☎ 04 92 43 01 98; place Barthelon; ☷ 7.30am-12.30pm & 3-7pm Tue-Sat); and the *chocolatier*-patisserie of **Luc Eyriey** (☎ 04 92 43 01 37; place Barthelon; 8.30am-noon & 3-7pm Tue-Sat, 8.30am-noon Sun), run by his family since 1902. Luc has also opened a small onsite **chocolate museum**. Within a 15th-century Franciscan convent, Embrun's **tourist office** (☎ 04 92 43 72 72; www.ot-embrun.fr in French; place Général Dosse; ☷ 9am-7pm Mon-Sat, 9.30am-noon & 4-7pm Sun Jul & Aug, 9am-noon & 2-6pm Mon-Sat Sep-Jun) has information on a raft of lake and river water sports.

Hidden deep in the forest, 3km uphill from the lake's eastern bank, the beautiful 12th-century **Abbaye de Boscodon** (☎ 04 92 43 14 45; Crots; admission €3.50; ☷ 8.30am-7pm Mon-Sat, 12.15-7pm Sun) fell to ruin and was inhabited by sheep; it has been magnificently resurrected by the community. Next to the abbey, **Le Cellier des Moines** (☎ 04 92 43 00 50; www.gite-boscodon.com in French; d incl breakfast €45-55, menu €21; Ⓟ ♨) has *chambre d'hôte* rooms and shared outdoor tables where meals are served in summer (there's a snug dining room for when it snows). Heading towards Embrun from Savines Le Lac, take the first road on your right.

Other enticing spots to sojourn while exploring the area include **Relais des Ecrins** (☎ 04 92 43 22 01; www.relaisdesecrins.com; Châteauroux-les-Alpes; d €39-46, menu €14; ♨), a charming blue-shuttered village inn 7km north of Embrun, and **Les Peupliers** (☎ 04 92 43 03 47; www.hotel-les-peupliers.com; chemin de Lesdier, Baratier; d €50-57, menus €19-24; Ⓟ ♨), 3km south of Embrun, with dishes such as local trout in pine-tree liqueur with fennel and sweet red peppers. Just nearby is the wonderful farm-*maison d'hôte* **La Fernande** (☎ 04 92 43 81 13; www.gdf05.com in French; champ Rambaud, Baratier; d incl breakfast €64; ☷ May-Nov; Ⓟ ♨), with four sunlit rooms, homemade apple juice, organic tables d'hôtes (€22) and the chance to experience life on a working farm. Embrun's tourist office has information on lakeside camping.

Lake Serre-Ponçon flows into the Ubaye valley. Embrun is 16km north of Col de Pontis, and has a train station with connections to Marseille.

---

de Salagon (☎ 04 92 75 70 50; www.musee-de-salagon .com in French; adult/12-18yr €6/3.60; ☷ 10am-7pm Jun-Aug, 10.30am-12.30pm & 2-6.30pm May & Sep, 2-5pm Oct & Feb-Apr, 2-5pm Sun Nov & Dec, closed Jan), 4km south of Forcalquier in Mane. A multilanguage audioguide lets you ramble at your own pace through the romantic herbs grown in a medieval garden, Provençal perfumes such as lavender, mint, mugwort and sage in its Jardin de Senteurs, a medicinal garden, and a showcase of plants from around the world. Crumbling stone buildings house permanent exhibitions on metal work and lavender.

For a curative little DIY detour, continue a further 800m south of Mane, then turn right for 3km along a bumpy dirt track to the **Église de Châteauneuf**, a remote, centuries-old church on the hillside where the *prêtre* (priest) can concoct a natural remedy for any ailments you might have from his rambling herb garden (you'll need to stop back the next day once he's prepared them). A customised concoction costs around €5. Midmorning is usually a good time to try popping by. Locals swear the cures – for anything from hay fever to arthritis – work wonders.

The scents of the region can be re-created when you get home by way of candles, scented water and mists, incense, essential oils and more at the factory of **Terre d'Oc** (☎ 04 92 79 40 20; www.terredoccreations.com; Zone Artisanale, Villeneuve; ☷ 9am-7pm Mon-Sat), 13km southeast of Forcalquier in Villeneuve, where everything including packaging is done by hand.

HAUTE-PROVENCE

A bunch of villages peeks at Forcalquier from the hilltops west of town: **Vachères** (population 260, elevation 830m), 30km west; **Oppedette** (population 40, elevation 525m) with its lovely gorges crossed by the GR4; **Lurs** (population 381, elevation 600m); and **Simiane-la-Rotonde** (population 532), host to the international music festival **Les Riches Heures Musicales** in August. Tickets (€26) are sold at Forcalquier's tourist office.

ST-MICHEL L'OBSERVATOIRE

The **Observatoire de Haute-Provence** (☎ 04 92 70 64 00; www.obs-hp.fr) is a national research centre situated 10km southwest of Forcalquier at the end of the D305 from the village of **St-Michel l'Observatoire**. It can be visited by a 30-minute **guided tour** (☎ 04 92 76 69 09; adult/6-12yr €2.50/1.50; ☽ tours 2-4pm Wed Jul & Aug, 3pm Wed Oct-Mar); buy tickets from the *billetterie* (ticket office) in the village square. Shuttle buses run every 30 minutes from St-Michel l'Observatoire (2km), which operates a small tourist office from Monday to Friday in July and August.

From St-Michel l'Observatoire, the east-bound D5 flashes past **Centre d'Astronomie** (☎ 04 92 76 69 69; www.centre-astro.fr in French; Plateau du Moulin à Vent), an astronomy centre that organises star-filled multimedia events and educational workshops. Learn how to **watch stars** (adult/6-16yr €8.75/7; ☽ 9pm Fri & Sat Jul & Aug) with the naked eye and telescopes.

Accommodation and food are available in St-Michel l'Observatoire at the friendly **Hôtel-Restaurant l'Observatoire** (☎ /fax 04 92 76 63 62; place de la Fontaine; s/d €41/49, menu €25; ☽ restaurant lunch Tue-Sun, dinner Tue-Sat, closed late Oct-early Nov). The rooms, decorated in warm Provençal colours, are welcoming, the food is great and there's a little bar where you can eavesdrop on the latest village gossip.

Getting There & Around

Buses leave from the **Sisteron bus station** (☎ 04 92 61 22 18) to and from Aix-en-Provence (2½ hours, four daily), Marseille (two hours, four daily) and Nice (3¾ hours, one daily) via Digne-les-Bains (45 minutes).

In Forcalquier, **Voyages Brémond** (☎ 04 92 75 16 32) and **Autocars Sumian** (☎ 04 91 49 44 25) run buses to and from Marseille (two hours, up to five daily). Voyages Brémond also runs buses to Manosque (30 minutes, three per day Monday to Saturday, one Sunday). Daily services to and from Avignon (two hours) and

Digne-les-Bains (one hour) are by **Barlatier** (☎ 04 32 76 00 40). All buses leave from the stop on place Martial Sicard, except on Monday when (because of the market) they depart from in front of the cathedral.

St-Michel l'Observatoire is accessible by one bus a day between Monday and Saturday from Manosque (30 minutes) and Forcalquier (15 minutes).

PARC NATIONAL DU MERCANTOUR

Ringed by a roller coaster of rugged mountains, the Mercantour National Park is Provence at its most majestic. Europe's highest mountain pass, **Col de Restefond la Bonette** (2802m), coils through the Vallée de l'Ubaye, the park's most northerly and wildest area. Ski trails crisscross the Vallées l'Ubaye, du Haut Verdon and de la Tinée. A short hop from the Côte d'Azur, the Vallées de la Vésubie, des Merveilles and de la Roya range around gorges, ageless rocks and white waters.

The Parc National du Mercantour is home to a dazzling array of birds, including the golden eagle and the bearded vulture. Its higher-altitude plains shelter marmot, mouflon and chamois (a mountain antelope), as well as the *bouquetin* (Alpine ibex), reintroduced into the region in the early 1990s. In lower wooded areas, red and roe deer are common. Wild boar roam throughout, and wolves (see p250) are prowling the park once more.

Camping in the park is not allowed.

Orientation

The park's uninhabited heart covers 685 sq km in the northeast of the region and embraces six valleys: (northwest to southeast) Ubaye, Haut Verdon, Tinée, Vésubie, Merveilles and Roya. The park abuts Italy's Parco Naturale delle Alpi Marittime to the east and is surrounded by a 1465-sq-km partially protected and inhabited peripheral zone.

Information

The park's headquarters are in Nice (p268). Permanent Parc National du Mercantour **Maison du Parc** (www.parc-mercantour.fr) offices are in several locations; see information sections for details. All provide detailed information on all aspects of the park and sell maps and guides. Tourist offices in the park's towns also have information.

VALLÉE DE L'UBAYE

Desolate and wild, the Ubaye Valley stretches between the Parc Régional du Queyras (north) and the Parc National du Mercantour (south). Winter skiing and summer white-water rafting are its two main activities. The valley is crossed by the D900, which closely shadows the banks of the River Ubaye.

The valley's only town, **Barcelonnette** (population 3300, elevation 1135m), has a fascinating Mexican heritage, resulting in some exceptional, very unalpine architecture. From the 18th century until WWII, some 5000 Barcelonnettais emigrated to Mexico to seek their fortunes in the silk- and wool-weaving industries, building mansions

---

> **STAR-SPANGLED SCREENINGS**
>
> Summer nights in Haute-Provence see onscreen stars compete with the multitude of stars in the clear night sky during outdoor screenings hosted by a clutch of villages, including Annot, Allemagne-en-Provence, Banon, Castellane, Forcalquier, Moustiers Ste-Marie and Ste-Croix de Verdon. The most breathtaking venue is the Centre d'Astronomie (opposite), near St-Michel l'Observatoire, which features sci-fi flicks.
>
> Screenings start at 9.30pm and cost €4. **Le Cinéma de Pays** (☎ 04 92 78 13 25; cinepays .free.fr in French) runs the Nuits du Cinéma en Plein Air programme; schedules are available online.

throughout the town upon their return. One of the most spectacular now houses the **Musée de la Vallée** (☎ 04 92 81 27 15; musee.vallee@wanadoo.fr; 10 av de la Libération; adult/under 18yr €3.30/1.80; 10amnoon & 3-7pm mid-Jul–Aug, 3-6pm Tue-Sat Jun–mid-Jul & Sep, 2.30-6pm Wed-Sat Oct–mid-Nov & mid-Dec–May), which unravels and explores the town's colourful history.

Information

Barcelonnette's **tourist office** (☎ 04 92 81 04 71; www.barcelonnette.net in French; place Frédéric Mistral; 9am-noon & 2-7pm Jul & Aug, 9am-noon & 2-6pm Mon-Sat Sep-Jun) is a fount of local info.

Stay connected on the town's free wi-fi network (a rarity for Provence).

Activities

CYCLING

The Vallée de l'Ubaye is linked to the outside world by seven mountain passes. Cyclists tough enough to conquer them all, including Col de Restefond la Bonette, are given

---

> **A CHEESY DETOUR**
>
> In the literal sense only. For fabulously authentic *fromage* (cheese), follow the D950 25km northwest from Forcalquier to **Banon** (population 940, elevation 760m), renowned for its *chèvre de Banon* cheese, made from goats milk and wrapped in chestnut leaves. The **Fromagerie de Banon** (☎ 04 92 73 25 03; www.fromages-provence.com; rte de Carniol) sells its cheeses at the Tuesday-morning market on place de la République and at the wonderful cheese-and-sausage shop **Chez Melchio** (☎ 04 92 73 23 05; place de la République; 7.30am-12.30pm & 2.30-7pm Wed-Sun). Banon's **tourist office** (☎ 04 92 73 36 37; banon.accueil@wanadoo.fr; place de la République; 9am-12.30pm & 3-6pm Tue-Sat yearround, also 10am-noon Sun Jul & Aug) has a list of farms in the surrounding countryside where you can sample fresh cheese. In May the town celebrates its annual **Fête du Fromage** (Cheese Fair).

SHADES OF GREY

Sustained hunting over 1000 years led to the eventual disappearance of wolves from France in 1930. But in 1992 two 'funny-looking dogs' were spotted in the Parc National du Mercantour near Utelle. Since then wolves have been making a natural return, loping across the Alps from Italy; there are now upwards of 30 in the park. Summer leaf coverage makes them hard to spot and in warmer weather they usually pad back to Italy.

The grey wolf (canis lupus) is something of a misnomer: its thick, furry coat also comes in shades of black, red, tawny, cinnamon and white. It lives for around 10 years, in packs of two to 12 animals. Howling is its most dramatic form of communication – the sound can travel for 16km in open spaces. As early ecologist Aldo Leopold (1887–1948) put it, 'Only the mountain has lived long enough to listen objectively to the howl of a wolf.'

Unlike the beasts of myths and fairy tales, the wolves are wary animals and will run in the opposite direction if they sniff you – although they do feed on sheep, to the bane of farmers and to the consternation of politicians trying to appease them as well as animal protectionists.

---

a medal; the Maison de la Vallée de l'Ubaye (below) in Barcelonnette has details.

In Le Martinet both white-water-sports bases (see right) rent mountain bikes (€8/26 per hour/day) and arrange guided rides. River has a mini mountain-bike (VTT) course for kids, 20km of forest trails, 1.7km of downhill tracks and a 450m bicross (scramble) circuit for adult riders.

SKIING

Rising 8.5km southwest of Barcelonnette are the twin ski resorts of **Pra Loup 1500** (sometimes called Les Molanes) and **Pra Loup 1600** (which has more infrastructure and nightlife). Both are connected by a lift system with the ski resort of La Foux d'Allos. Pra Loup's 50 lifts are between 1600m and 2600m, with 180km of runs and a vertical drop of almost 1000m. In summer it's a hiker's heaven.

The Pra Loup **tourist office** (☎ 04 92 84 10 04; www.praloup.com; 🕙 9am-noon & 2-6pm Jul & Aug, 9am-noon & 2-6pm Mon-Fri May, Jun & Sep-Nov, 9am-7pm Dec-Apr) and **École de Ski Français** (ESF; ☎ 04 92 84 11 05) are in Pra Loup 1600. Ski passes cost €26.50 per day.

WALKING

Barcelonnette's tourist office has a list of guides who organise walks and cycling and canoeing trips.

Alternatively, contact **Maison de la Vallée de l'Ubaye** (☎ 04 92 81 03 68; www.ubaye.com in French; 4 av des Trois Frères Arnaud, Barcelonnette). The walking and climbing organisation **Club Alpin Français** (☎ 04 92 81 28 18; www.cafubaye.com in French) shares its postal address, but is to be found at the back of the town hall (rue Mairie).

WHITE-WATER SPORTS

Canoe-rental places line the D900 between Le Lauzet-Ubaye and Barcelonnette. In Le Martinet, south off the D900, are **AN Rafting** (☎ 04 92 85 54 90; www.an-rafting.com in French; Pont du Martinet) and **River** (☎ 04 92 85 53 99; www.river.fr in French). Both arrange white-water activities, including two- to three-hour rafting (€37), hot-dogging (€38) and canyoning (€42/60 per half-/full day) expeditions. Other operators charge similar rates.

Sleeping & Eating

In Méolans-Revel, 12km west of Barcelonnette, **Camping du Rioclar** (☎ 04 92 81 10 32; www.rioclar.com; av Georges Pompidou; 2 adults, tent & car €19; 🕙 mid-Jun–mid-Sep; P 🐕) is close to the hamlet's water-sports centre.

The maison d'hôte **Domaine de Lara** (☎ 04 92 81 52 81; www.domainedelara.com; St-Pons de Barcelonnette; d incl breakfast €65-74; P), within a 16th-century bastide (country house) 2km northwest of Barcelonnette in St-Pons, has five Mexican-inspired guest rooms and a stunning raked timber ceiling in the lounge room. It serves piquant Mexican hot chocolate at breakfast.

In Pra Loup, studios and apartments start from around €190 per week in low season, climbing to €650 per week in peak ski season – the tourist office has lists. There's also a handful of hotels, such as the sloped-ceiling, storybook chalet, **Hôtel Le Prieuré** (☎ 04 92 84 11 43; www.prieure-praloup.com; Pra Loup 1500; d winter €60-90, menus €13-27; 🍴 🐕), just across the road from the ski lift, with a restaurant serving alpine fare including fondue and steaming, thick-crusted blueberry pie.

Barcelonnette's place Manuel is ringed by restaurants.

Getting There & Around

The nearest train station is in Gap, 60km to the north; with connections to Marseille (three hours). Buses (usually a couple a day) travel to Pra Loup (1¾ hours) with a change in Barcelonnette.

From Barcelonnette, **Autocars SCAL** (☎ 04 92 81 00 20) runs one bus daily to and from Marseille (four hours) and Digne-les-Bains (1½ hours). During the ski season there's one daily direct bus between Pra Loup and Marseille (4½ hours).

Buses in the Vallée de l'Ubaye are run by **Autocars Maurel** (☎ 04 92 81 20 09). There are three Barcelonnette–Le Martinet buses a day and four daily shuttle buses between Barcelonnette and Le Sauze. Shuttles between Le Sauze (3.5km south of Barcelonnette) and Super-Sauze (5km further south) are free.

VALLÉE DU HAUT VERDON

The dizzying **Col d'Allos** (2250m) links the Vallée de l'Ubaye with the Vallée du Haut Verdon. The mighty River Verdon has its source here at La Tête de la Sestrière (2572m).

Immediately beyond the mountain pass (snow-blocked in winter), 23.5km south of Pra Loup and connected to it by cable car, **La Foux d'Allos** (elevation 1800m) is stacked with concrete buildings and new-fangled timber chalets, but its glistening slopes are pristine. Its **tourist office** (☎ 04 92 83 02 81; www .valdallos.com) is in the Maison de la Foux on the main square. In the upper village you can ski out the front door of the **auberge de jeunesse** (☎ 04 92 83 81 08; la-foux-allos@fuaj.org; dm incl sheets €11; ❧ reception 8-10am & 7-8pm mid-Jun–mid-Sep, 8am-11pm Dec–mid-Apr).

A further 8km south on the D908, family-friendly **Allos** (population 650, elevation 1400m), with a crèche and children's activities, is just as deserted as La Foux d'Allos outside of the ski season, except in July and August when hotels reopen their doors to walkers.

Between the two, 1.8km south of La Foux d'Allos and 5km north of Allos, mountain hospitality will warm your heart at the restored 16th-century working *ferme auberge* **La ferme Girerd-Potin** (☎ 04 92 83 04 76; www.chambredhotes -valdallos.com; rte de la Foux; half-board per person from €38, gîte prices by arrangement; P). Within rough-hewn stone walls, thaw out with hearty casseroles made from farm-raised poultry in the copper pot–lined dining room before an enormous roaring open fire; and snuggle up in three wood-beamed *chambre d'hôte* rooms (two with lofts), or a self-contained three-bedroom *gîte*.

To reach natural mountain lake **Lac d'Allos** (2226m), drive 12km to the end of the bumpy D226, then follow the 40-minute walking trail that leads to the lake from the car park. Route maps and walking information are available from the **Parc National du Mercantour hut** (☎ 06 32 90 80 24) that operates from the car park in July and August.

Lower in the valley is the Vauban-fortified village **Colmars-les-Alpes** (population 385, elevation 1250m). Colmars' maze of quaint streets is tethered between high thick walls, surrounded by magnificent mountainscapes. At the frontier of Savoy in the 14th century, today its Savoy fort can be visited via a little **museum** (place Joseph Girieud; adult/under 10yr €3/free; ❧ 10am-noon & 3-6.30pm Jul–mid-Sep). The **tourist office** (☎ 04 92 83 41 92; www .colmars-les-alpes.fr; Ancienne Auberge Fleurie; ❧ 9am-12.15pm & 2-5.45pm Mon-Sat Sep-Jun, 8am-12.30pm & 2-6.30pm Jul & Aug) has accommodation info.

Getting There & Away

In Colmars-les-Alpes, **Haut Verdon Voyages** (☎ 04 92 83 95 81) runs buses between Digne-les-Bains and La Foux d'Allos (two hours, one daily), stopping at St-André-les-Alpes, Thorame-Haute, Colmars and Allos.

AN ICY DETOUR

If you're averse to the cold, perish the thought. Hardy souls, however, can take the plunge to view frozen trout beneath the ice. **Aqua-Logis** (☎ 04 92 45 00 68; www.aqualogis.com; La Gravière, Ceillac; beginner €50; ❧ office 4-6pm), based in Ceillac, 39km north of St-Paul-sur-Ubaye, runs beginners ice diving during winter.

Diving (15 minutes) takes place at Lac Ste-Anne (2408m), where a hole is cut through the ice; skiers gain access by the Ste-Anne lift, while nonskiers can take the Girardin chairlift, then walk or snowshoe to the lake (1½ hours).

Ski rental and ski pass (€14/17 per half-/full day) aren't included in the price. As with regular diving, you'll need a medical certificate.

On Saturday during the ski season (usually mid-December to early April), direct shuttle buses link La Foux d'Allos with Nice and Marseille airports. You'll need to check fares and schedules, as they change every year.

The mountain railway (p245) from Nice to Digne stops at Thorame-Haute.

VALLÉE DE LA TINÉE

The **Col de Restefond la Bonette** (2802m) links Barcelonnette and the Vallée de l'Ubaye with the tamer, more southern Vallée de la Tinée. In winter, when the snowy pass is closed, the 149km-long valley can only be accessed up its southern leg from Nice. The narrow road (D2205) wiggles along the French–Italian border to **Isola** (875m), where it plummets sharply south towards the coast.

The steep D97 makes an eastbound climb to **Isola 2000** (elevation 2000m), a purpose-built ski resort from where the **Col de la Lombarde** (2350m) crosses into Italy.

Information

Parc National du Mercantour runs information centres in the valley in **Valberg** (☎ 04 93 02 58 23; rue Jean Mineur), **St-Sauveur-sur-Tinée** (☎ 04 93 02 10 33; 11 av des Blavets; ☒ Jul & Aug) and **St-Étienne de Tinée** (☎ 04 93 02 42 27; fax 04 93 02 41 33; quartier de l'Ardon; ☒ Jul & Aug).

Tourist offices in **Isola 2000** (☎ 04 93 23 15 15; www.isola2000.com; Galerie Marchande) and **Valberg** (☎ 04 93 23 24 25; www.valberg.com; place du Quartier) also stock information on various outdoor activities.

Sights & Activities

St-Étienne de Tinée (population 1684) is a lovely Alpine village 15km northwest of Isola village on the D2205. There are endless walking opportunities in summer around the **Cime de la Bonette** (2860m): contact the summer Maison du Parc National du Mercantour information centre (see above) for details. Thrill-seekers can scale new heights at the Via Ferrata La Traditionelle in Auron; see opposite.

South of Isola, the road twists through beautiful gorges to **St-Sauveur-sur-Tinée** (population 459, elevation 490m), a gateway to the Parc National du Mercantour.

From St-Sauveur-sur-Tinée, the spectacular D30 takes you 24km west to tiny **Beuil** (population 334, elevation 1450m), from where you can access the **Gorges du Cians**, carved from burgundy-coloured rock.

Mountain flora can be viewed in the **Arboretum Marcel Kroenlein** (☎ 04 93 57 38 02; fax 04 93 35 00 50; admission free) in Roure, a few hair-raising kilometres west of St-Sauveur off the D30. From the 1920s until 1961, villagers here used a 1850m-long cable to transport their milk and cheese down the mountain and their food provisions up – you can still see the cable today.

Further west is **Valberg** (elevation 1700m), a ski resort that lures walkers and mountain bikers in summer. At the **Espace Valberg Aventure** (☎ 04 93 23 24 25; ☒ Jul & Aug) you can scale trees, cross rope bridges and monkey around dozens more Tarzan-inspired obstacles; routes are graded yellow (ages four to 10; €10), green (beginner; €14, 1½ hours) and blue and red (advanced; €23, three hours). The forested site can be accessed via the Croix du Sapet chairlift; a single ride with/without mountain bike costs €4.10/3.60. Valberg also has a summer luge (one/three rides €3/8).

Guillaumes (elevation 800m), around 13km west of Valberg, is the starting point for forays into the **Gorges de Dalius**, which is chiselled from wine-coloured rock. Thrill-seekers can bungee jump with **Top Jump** (☎ 04 93 73 50 29; topjump.free.fr in French; €60; ☒ 1-5pm Jul & Aug, by reservation on Sun Apr-Jun & Sep) from Pont de la Mariée, an 80m-high stone footbridge across the gorges.

Pont de Berthéou, another bridge 8km south of Guillaumes on the D2202, is the starting point for the scenic **Sentier du Point Sublime** (4km, 1½ hours), an invigorating walk through oak and pine forest and past red rock formations to the panoramic 'sublime point'. Panels on the way interpret flora and fauna. Guillaumes' **tourist office** (☎ 04 93 05 52 73; www.pays-de-guillaumes.com in French; place Napoléon III; ☒ 9am-12.30pm & 1.30-5pm) has information – and a little online webcam so you can check the weather before you arrive.

Sleeping & Eating

Isola 2000 has a stack of flat-pack concrete hotels and apartment blocks.

Hôtel La Renaissance (☎ 04 93 05 59 89; www.hotelrenaissance.fr; 3 place Napoléon; d €35-50, menu €17; ☒ closed mid-Nov–Dec; ☒) In Guillaumes, at the northern mouth of the Gorges de Dalius, is this big, pink, green-shuttered chalet where you can watch the weekly village sheep fair take place at the sheepfolds opposite from your simple but cosy room. Breakfast costs

€5.50, but if you're dining at the restaurant anyway (which is well worth doing), then it's worth taking up the half-pension option for €17 per person, which includes breakfast for free.

Le Valbergan (☎ 04 93 02 50 28; 2 av Valberg, Valberg; menus from €22; ☒ closed Sun dinner & Mon; ♨) The mountain cuisine here is guaranteed to warm your cockles. Specialities include *raclettes* (melted cheese over boiled potatoes, served with pickles and ham), cheese fondues, *fondues bourguignonnes* (beef cubes fried in oil) and fish or meat *pierrades* (meat grilled on a stone slab).

Getting There & Away

Three daily buses run between Nice and Isola 2000 (2½ hours) from December to April, with one or two a day the rest of the year. Call ☎ 04 93 85 92 60 for information. During the ski season, buses serve Nice-Côte d'Azur airport (two hours).

Société Broch (☎ 04 93 31 10 52) operates one daily bus year-round between Nice, Nice-Côte d'Azur airport and Valberg (two hours).

VALLÉE DE LA VÉSUBIE

Signs of civilisation appear in the Vésubie, a dead-end valley accessed from the south, often referred to as 'Nice's Switzerland' due to its proximity to the Côte d'Azur.

The **Gorges de la Vésubie** winds from the valley's south. For a stunning aerial view of the gorge and its surroundings, head for **La Madone d'Utelle** (1181m), a pilgrimage site settled by Spanish sailors in the 9th century and crowned with a chapel (1806). From the mountain village of **St-Jean la Rivière** (on the D2565), a stone bridge crosses the River Var, from where a steep, winding mountain pass (the D32) leads west to **Utelle** (population 489), 6km northeast of La Madone.

About 18km north of St-Jean along the D2565, just past the turning for **La Bollène-Vésubie** (elevation 964m), you arrive at a crossroads. Snake east along the D171 to **Belvédère** (population 495, elevation 820m), a hilltop village where you can learn how milk is made in the **Musée du Lait** (Milk Museum); visits are arranged by the **tourist office** (☎ 04 93 03 51 66; mairie.belvedere@smtm06.fr; 1 place Colonel Baldoni).

VIA FERRATA

During WWI Italian troops moved swiftly and safely through the Dolomites – the natural frontier between Italy and Austria – using iron-rung ladders and steel cables bolted into the rocky mountainside. Today, similar routes known as *via ferrata* (meaning 'iron way' in Italian) allow adventurous tourists to scale Alpine rock faces without knowing the first thing about rock-climbing.

Haute-Provence sports a clutch of *via ferrata* courses, rigged at dizzying heights and guaranteed to get the blood pumping. Anyone (with guts and a good level of fitness) can do it: harnessed climbers are attached to the rock by two lines. To move along the rock-face safely, climbers unclip one karabiner and attach it further along the steel cable, before doing the same with the second.

Courses range in length from 3½ hours to 5½ hours; first-timers can tackle short sections. Giddying elevations of up to 2274m are reached and *ponts Himalayen* (rope bridges with steel cables at waist height), *ponts de singe* (monkey bridges with steel cables above your head) and *tyroliennes* (zip lines, requiring climbers to pull themselves along, legs dangling) are hair-raising features of most.

Climbers need a *casque* (helmet), *mousquetons* (a harness attached to two cables with shock-absorbers and karabiners) and sturdy walking boots with good grip. Gloves also come in handy. Everything but boots and gloves can be hired on-site from €14. Course admission starts from an additional €3 or from €24 for a *carnet* of 10 tickets. Equipment hire and tickets are generally handled by the local tourist office.

There are four *via ferrata* in the northeast of the region: **Baus de la Frema** (☎ 04 93 02 89 54; near La Colmiane, Vallée de la Vésubie); **Les Demoiselles du Castagnet** (☎ 04 93 05 05 05; Puget-Théniers); **La Traditionelle** (☎ 04 93 23 02 66; Auron, Vallée de la Tinée); and the **Circuit des Comtes Lascaris**, which is split across three sites – in La Brigue and Tende in the Vallée de la Roya, and in Peille. Contact the tourist information centres in those towns for details, including local mountain guides if you'd rather not scale new heights alone. The Peille section is not recommended for beginners.

Online, www.viaferrata.org has information as well as a forum for climbers.

The valley's main outdoor-activity base is **St-Martin-Vésubie** (population 1089, elevation 1000m), 13km north of Belvédère. For a panorama of the village, follow the steep D31 up to **Venanson** (elevation 1164m), a hamlet perched on a rock above St-Martin.

Activities

CYCLING

Colmiane Sports and Ferrata Sport (see below) both hire mountain bikes (€6/20 per hour/day) to take on the 215km of trails through the valley.

PARAGLIDING

High-flyers can paraglide in St-Dalmas-Valdeblore (elevation 1350m), 5km west of La Colmiane. The **tourist office** (☎ 04 93 23 25 90; www.colmiane.com in French; ☼ call for seasonal hr) in La Roche, a hamlet 4km west of St-Dalmas-Valdeblore, has a list of paragliding schools.

SKIING

The small ski station of **La Colmiane**, 7km west of St-Martin-Vésubie across Col de St-Martin, has one chairlift. It whisks skiers and walkers up to **Pic de la Colmiane** (1795m), where 30km of ski slopes and several walking and mountain-bike trails can be accessed. A single ascent/descent/10-ride card costs €2.50/2/20. The chairlift runs from 10am to 6pm daily.

Escapade Bureau des Guides (below) offers **heliskiing** (from €210 for two drops).

VIA FERRATA

The **Via Ferrata du Baus de la Frema** (☎ 04 93 02 89 54) is 3km from La Colmiane ski station along an unpaved track. **Colmiane Sports** (☎ 04 93 02 87 00; ferratasport@infonie.fr) and **Ferrata Sport** (☎ 04 93 02 80 56; a.sorridente@wanadoo.fr) both rent *via ferrata* gear.

Escapade Bureau des Guides (below) in St-Martin-Vésubie can help you around the *via ferrata* for €40/55 per half-/full day. It also organises guided climbs (€35) and canyoning (€30 to €60). In La Colmiane, the **Bureau des Guides** (☎ /fax 04 93 02 88 30) charges similar rates.

For more information about *via ferrata*, see p253.

WALKING

In St-Martin-Vésubie, **Escapade Bureau des Guides** (☎ 04 93 03 31 32; www.guidescapade.com; place du Marché; ☼ 10.30am-12.30pm & 4.30-7.30pm Jul & Aug) leads three walks per week into the Vallée des

Merveilles (€30; see below). The **tourist office** (☎ 04 93 03 21 28; www.saintmartinvesubie.fr in French; place Félix Faure; ☼ 9am-7pm Jul & Aug, 9am-noon & 2-6pm Mon-Sat, 2-6pm Sun Sep-Jun) has a list of mountain guides who lead walks and ski tours. Walks are graded from easy to difficult.

A good map for walks in the area is Didier-Richard's No 9 or IGN's Série Bleue map No 3741OT *Vallée de la Vésubie, Parc National du Mercantour*, available at bookshops and national park offices.

Sleeping & Eating

Les Marmottes (☎ 04 93 02 89 04; www.lesmarmottes .com in French; St-Dalmas-Valdeblore; dm/d/tr €14/42/52.50; **P** 🔌) Whether you're a hiker, a couple or a family, this *gîte–chambre d'hôte* in the pretty little stone village of Dalmas makes an ideal base for setting out for mountain walks on your own or in the company of host and mountain guide Bernard. Atmospheric tables d'hôtes (€16) and breakfast (€4) can also be included in half-pension options.

Le Boréon (☎ 04 93 03 20 35; www.hotelboreon.com in French; Le Boréon; d €45-56, menu €18-29; **P** 🔌) Magical mountain views unfold from the timber terrace of this quintessential Snow White chalet 8km north of St-Martin-Vésubie and just an hour due north of Nice. Cosy up in its dozen rooms and watch the snowflakes fall outside while dining on alpine specialities including homemade pasta, terrines and a steaming fondue served by the fire in the beamed dining room.

La Trappa (☎ 04 93 03 21 50; place du Marché, St-Martin -Vésubie; menus from €18; ☼ closed Mon) At this family-run village restaurant you can eat snails in garlic butter, game terrine, herb-infused lamb and other 'mountain' food. It sits in a peaceful square, with the sound of trickling water in the background.

Getting There & Away

Contact Transport Régional des Alpes-Maritimes (☎ 04 93 85 92 60) for seasonal schedules between Nice and La Colmiane (two hours) and a weekend service from La Colmiane via St-Martin-Vésubie (1¾ hours).

VALLÉE DES MERVEILLES

The 'Valley of Wonders' contains one of the world's most stupendous collections of Bronze Age petroglyphs dating between 1800 and 1500 BC, which are thought to originate from a Ligurian cult. Effectively an open-air art gallery, wedged between the Vésubie and Roya Valleys, it shelters more than 36,000 rock engravings of human figures, bulls and other animals spread over 30 sq km around Mont Bégo (2870m).

The main access routes into the valley are the eastbound D91 from St-Dalmas de Tende in the Vallée de la Roya, or the dead-end D171, which leads north to the valley from **Roquebillière** (population 1513) in the Vallée de la Vésubie. Snow-covered much of the year, the best time to visit is July to September. Access is restricted to protect the precious artworks: walkers should only visit with an official guide (see opposite and right).

IGN's Série Bleue map No 3841OT *Vallée de la Roya, Vallée des Merveilles* (€9.50) covers the area in a scale of 1:25,000.

VALLÉE DE LA ROYA

The Roya Valley once served as a hunting ground for King Victor Emmanuel II of Italy, and only became part of France in 1947. The pretty township of **Breil-sur-Roya** (population 2023) sits just 62km northeast of Nice. Panoramic views unfold from the Col de Brouis (879m), which links **Sospel** (population 2937), 21km south, with the Roya Valley.

Gashed into the landscape, the dramatic **Gorges de Saorge**, 9km north of Breil-sur-Roya, lead to fortified **Saorge** (population 398, elevation 520m). The vertiginous village is a maze of tangled streets and 15th- to 17th-century houses.

Immediately north, the **Gorges de Bergue** lead to **St-Dalmas de Tende**, which is the main gateway into the Vallée des Merveilles. From St-Dalmas de Tende, the D91 winds 10km west along the Vallon de la Minière to **Lac des Mesches** (1390m), from where trails lead into the valley past the Refuge des Merveilles (2111m). Alternatively, continue 5km to the mountain resort of **Casterino** to pick up more northern trails.

Equally scenic is the eastbound D143 from St-Dalmas de Tende to **La Brigue** (elevation 770m) and 4km further on to **Notre Dame des Fontaines**, dubbed the Sistine Chapel of the southern Alps, with beautifully preserved frescoes by 15th-century Piedmontese painters Jean Canavesio and Jean Baleison. Contact the tourist office in La Brigue for information.

In **Tende** (population 1890, elevation 830m), 4km north of St-Dalmas de Tende, the **Musée des Merveilles** (☎ 04 93 04 32 50; www.museedes merveilles.com; av du 16 Septembre 1947; adult/14-16yr

€4.55/2.30; ☉ 10am-6.30pm May–mid-Oct, 10am-5pm mid-Oct–Apr, closed mid-late Mar & mid-late Dec) explains the natural history of the valley and exhibits numerous archaeological finds.

Also in Tende, the small but sweet **Maison du Miel et de l'Abeille** (House of Honey & Bees; ☎ 04 93 04 76 22; place Lieutenant Kalck; ☉ Jun-Sep) shows how the region's honey is made. Wonderful cheeses, hams and freshly baked breads are sold at several artisan shops on rue de France and av du 16 Septembre 1947.

In July the valley celebrates **Les Baroquiales**, a baroque art and music festival with period markets, 17th-century restaurant *menus*, street entertainment and a series of concerts.

Just 5km north of Tende, the **Tunnel de Tende** – engineered in 1882 – provides a vital link into Italy.

Information

The Vallée de la Roya has several small tourist offices:

Breil-sur-Roya (☎ 04 93 04 99 76; www.breil-sur-roya .fr in French; place Bianchéri; ☉ 9am-1pm & 2.30-5.30pm Mon-Sat, 9am-1pm Sun May-Sep, 8.30am-12.30pm & 1.30-5.30pm Mon-Fri, 8.30am-12.30pm Sat Oct-Apr)

La Brigue (☎ 04 93 04 60 04; www.labrigue.fr in French; av du Général de Gaulle; ☉ 10am-noon & 2-5pm Wed-Mon)

Sospel (☎ 04 93 04 15 80; www.sospel-tourisme.com in French; 19 av Jean Medecin; ☉ 2.30-6.30pm Mon, 9.30am-12.30pm & 2.30-6.30pm Tue-Sat, 9.30am-12.30pm Sun)

Tende (☎ 04 93 04 73 71; www.tendemerveilles.com in French; av du 16 Septembre 1947; ☉ Tue-Sat)

Activities
VIA FERRATA

The Maison de la Montagne et des Sports (see p256) rents equipment for Tende's dizzying **Via Ferrata des Comtes Lascaris** (for details see p253) and can provide you with a guide (€46). Alternatively, contact the **Bureau des Guides** (☎ 04 93 04 77 85; www.berengeraventures.com in French; Cagnorina) in Tende.

WALKING & CYCLING

Tende's tourist office has information on guided archaeological walks to Mont Bégo (adult/12 to 18 years €10/5) on weekends in June (and May if there's no snow), daily in July and August, and Monday to Friday in September.

In July and August the **Parc National du Mercantour office** (☉ 10am-1pm & 2.15-7pm Fri-Wed mid-Jun–mid-Sep), inside Sospel's old city gate, organises guided walks and distributes a map detailing 19 mountain-biking itineraries. Cycling club **Sospel VTT** (☎ 06 70 76 57 05; www.sospel vtt.net in French; Sospel) rents wheels. In Tende the **Maison de la Montagne et des Sports** (☎ /fax 04 93 04 77 73; mmstende@aol.com; 11 av du 16 Septembre 1947) hires bikes and can give you the inside track on 23 bike trails leading from Tende, Col de Tende, La Brigue and Casterino.

WHITE-WATER SPORTS

Breil-sur-Roya is the premier water-sports base. **Roya Évasion** (☎ 04 93 04 91 46; www.royaeva sion.com in French; 1 rue Pasteur) organises kayaking, canyoning and rafting trips on the River Roya, as well as walks and mountain-bike expeditions. **AET Nature** (☎ 04 93 04 47 64; www.aetcanyoning .com; 392 chemin du Foussa), with a bureau on central place Bianchéri, organises similar trips. A day's canyoning costs between €44 and €60 depending on the level of difficulty, and there are also two-day 'extreme' journeys (€150).

Sleeping & Eating

Le Miramonti (☎ 04 93 04 61 82; fax 04 93 04 78 71; 5-7 rue Vassalo, Tende; d from €35, menus from €15; ☽ restaurant lunch Tue-Sun, dinner Tue-Sat, hotel & restaurant closed Nov)

Rooms at this popular spot in Tende have high ceilings and are awash with natural light. The restaurant, serving Piedmontese specialities, absolutely throngs with people – so book ahead. The Miramonti also organises jeep tours into the Vallée des Merveilles.

Castel du Roy (☎ 04 93 04 43 66; www.casteldu roy.com; rte de Tende; d €60-85, tr €90-100, q €100-110, menu €25; ☽ restaurant dinner daily, hotel & restaurant early Apr–mid-Oct; P ☢ ⅍) Signposted off the Tende-bound N204 from Breil-sur-Roya, this place is famous for its delicious traditional restaurant and cheerful floral guest rooms (some wheelchair accessible) with floor-to-ceiling arched doors and views over five acres of grounds where you can play badminton and fish for trout.

Getting There & Away

Trains run several times per day along the Nice–Turin line through the valley. From Nice, destinations you can travel to include Sospel (€5.90, 45 minutes), Breil-sur-Roya (€7.30, one hour), St-Dalmas de Tende (€9.80, 1½ hours via Breil-sur-Roya) and Tende (€10.80, 1½ hours).

Nice to Menton

What a splendid stretch of coast Nice to Menton is. Crowned by Riviera queen and belle of the ball, Nice, there is far more to this pebbly shoreline than frolicking in the sun or flouncing in a sky-blue chair on Europe's most legendary promenade. Nice itself is a real city that blends old-world opulence with rough'n'tumble modern-day grit, climaxing in an old town by the sea where bustling markets, dimly lit churches and narrow lanes studded with artists' workshops ensure a new experience with every visit. For cosmopolitans who like to dine out (and well), there is no better base from which to explore the Côte d'Azur – unless you're loaded, in which case millionaires' Monaco, with its star-studded hotels and lavish gardens of Menton next door, could be the hedonistic choice.

But if flopping by a pool at the end of the day against a soaring backdrop of majestic scenery and sweet silence (bar cicada song) is for you, stay elsewhere. How about one of the *chambres d'hôtes* that pop up unexpectedly along the three rollercoaster coastal roads, each higher and more hazardous than the last, that link Nice and Menton (and the 30km of towns in between)? Justly celebrated for their breathtaking sea views and luxurious villas, it was along these perilous roads that motorists raced the coastal *Train Bleu* from Paris in the 1920s. Or what about the Niçois hinterland, a spiky maze of hilltop villages and hairpin bends just made for motoring off into the back of beyond?

HIGHLIGHTS

- Make the most of Nice: ogle at its *belle époque* beauties on **promenade des Anglais** (p265) and around Cimiez; visit its **art museums** (p266); and **dine** (p274) exceedingly well.

- Take a coastal walk around a luxuriant cape, far flung from the sun-seeking hordes, on **Cap Martin**, **Cap d'Ail** or **Cap Ferrat** (p280).

- Live like a millionaire: ride a teak-clad air-conditioned funicular for two down the cliff edge to a day of self-pampering at the seaside club of legendary **Grand Hôtel du Cap Ferrat** (p284).

- Revel in Mediterranean botanical splendour at **Villa Ephrussi de Rothschild** (p282) and the gardens of **Menton** (p293).

- Enjoy an eagle's-eye view of the coast – along the **Grande Corniche** (p286) or atop the hilltop villages of the **Niçois hinterland** (p288).

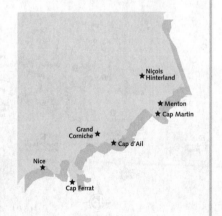

ITINERARIES

ART & ARCHITECTURE
One Day / Nice

No seaside town has a richer trove of art and architecture than Nice (p260). Start the day slowly with an amble around the **cours Saleya markets** (**1**; p273) and *petit dej* at **Le Pain Quotidien** (**2**; p275). Then wind through the narrow old lanes of **Vieux Nice** (**3**; p265) – cut along rue Droite to take in its local **artist workshops** (**4**; p277), then go to **MAMAC** (**5**; p266), an essential port of call for Nice New Realist fans. Don't miss sweeping 360-degree city views from the rooftop sculpture garden or **Sosno's Square Head** (p266) in the modernist concrete gardens below.

For lunch at noon, cut through the Jardin Albert 1er to **promenade des Anglais** (**6**; p265), where lunch in the company of a Niki Saint Phalle statue at **Le 3e** (p274) in the mythical **Palais de la Méditerranée** (p265) is a real treat. Or consider **Karr** (p275) if a post-lunch mooch around the upmarket **art galleries and design shops** (**7**; p277) on rue Dalpozzo appeals. Then it's uphill to Cimiez's **Musée Matisse** (p266), **Musée National Message Biblique Marc Chagall** (p267) and **belle époque architecture** (p268). Late eaters can always squeeze in Cimiez before lunch, and spend the short afternoon devouring the ravishing architecture of Nice's greatest piece of living art, promenade des Anglais.

Make a **big-name dine** (p274) your venue for dinner. If you've nowhere to stay, Nice's **Hôtel Windsor** (**8**; p272), **Hôtel Hi** (**9**; p272) or **Hôtel Beau Rivage** (**10**; p272), where Matisse stayed in Nice, are dead artsy.

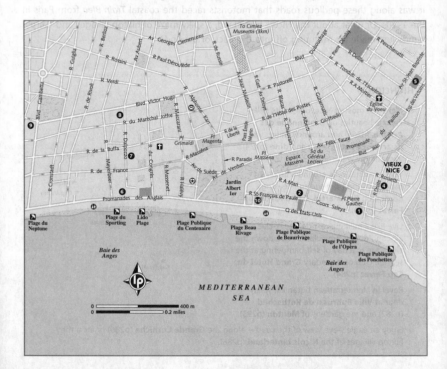

MOUNTAIN ESCAPE
One Day / Nice to Châteauneuf Villevieille

When it all gets too much on the fast-paced, body-packed coast, hit the slow road for a gulp of mountain air in the company of hilltop villages and staggering views: the legendary **Grande Corniche** (1; p286), signposted from Nice port, is your quick exit. Poodle along this magnificent high road, pulling up on the **Col d'Èze** (2; p286) in front of the **Hermitage du Col d'Èze** (p287) for a panoramic coffee break or, if you've brought your own, continuing a tad higher onto the picnic-friendly **Plateau de la Justice** (3; p288). Back on the road, head northeast to the **Fort de la Revère** (4; p288) for an invigorating stroll, then continue along the Grande Corniche to **La Turbie** (5; p287), where **Café de la Fontaine** (p287) is the perfect lunch stop after exploring the village. Not hungry yet? Carry on 15km east (20 minutes) to hilltop **Gorbio** (6; p294) for a quintessential Provençal lunch beneath jasmine.

In the afternoon, wiggle 13km (15 minutes) along the D23, D223 and D22 to **Ste-Agnès** (7; p295), from where the D22 continues in an increasingly alarming manner (hold on tight) to **Peille** (8; p289); pull up on the **Col de la Madone** for the best view of the quaint picture-postcard village. Time it right and you can end up for dinner either in **Peillon** (9; p289) at **Auberge de la Madone** (p289); at **Auberge du Soleil** (p289) in **Coaraze** (10; p288) or – should you decide to kip the night too – around a table shared with jovial *chambre d'hôte* hosts and a dreamy mountain view at **La Parare** in **Châteauneuf Villevieille** (11; p288).

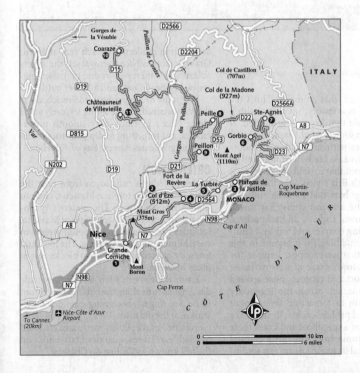

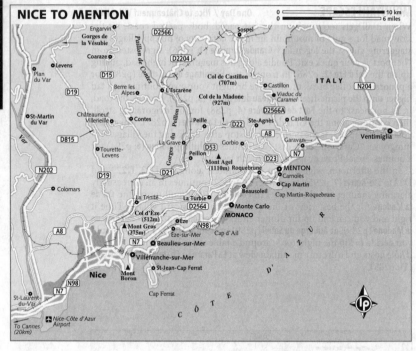

NICE

pop 347,100

Nice is *not* 'nice': what an insult! This Côte d'Azur capital is a sparky, sexy city, with a gritty underside that keeps it grounded. If Nice was a person, it would wear designer cocktail dresses with tatty old army boots (laces undone), cause loads of trouble and be mad as hell about that insipid adjective.

Bursting with Brit-styled pubs that heave, designer lounge bars that sit sleek and cool across from the sea and clubs that throb, Nice *is* party town. Laden with backpackers, romance-seeking couples, old folk and families, there is something for everyone in this seaside town that never stops. Explore the intriguing old-town maze of narrow lanes, discover the port and chateau, nose around the raucous market, stroll the legendary promenade with its fantastical *belle époque* architecture and pebble beaches, fly in the sky from the back of a speedboat and know there is bags more tomorrow. The city's cultural scene buzzes and its museums are extraordin-arily rich in modern art. Each year at Mardi Gras the famous Nice Carnival sets the streets ablaze with a merry-go-round of masked parades, big-head floats and a flower battle.

When the hectic pace gets too much, do as the Victorians did: take a long leisurely stroll along Nice's glorious silky smooth promenades, not forgetting to dip your toes in the sparkling Baie des Anges (Bay of Angels).

ORIENTATION

Av Jean Médecin runs south from near the main train station to place Masséna, close to the beach and old town. The modern city centre, the area north and west of place Masséna, includes the pedestrian shopping streets of rue de France and rue Masséna. The local and intercity bus terminals are two blocks east of place Masséna.

From the airport, 6km west, promenade des Anglais runs along the curving beachfront (Baie des Anges), becoming quai des États-Unis near the old town. Vieux Nice (Old Nice) is crunched into a 500-sq-metre area enclosed by blvd Jean Jaurès, quai des États-Unis and the hill known as Colline du Château.

The wealthy residential neighbourhood of Cimiez, home to several outstanding museums, is north of the centre.

INFORMATION
Bookshops

Cat's Whiskers (☎ 04 93 80 02 66; catswhiskersnice@aol.com; 30 rue Lamartine) New and secondhand English-language novels and guides.
Magellan Librairie de Voyages (☎ 04 93 82 31 81; 3 rue d'Italie) Maps and travel guides (including Lonely Planet) in English.
Papeterie Rontani (☎ 04 93 62 32 43; 5 rue Alexandri Mari) Unsurpassable choice of locally produced guidebooks, reference books on Nice and the Riviera, maps and guides.

Cultural Centres

Holy Trinity Anglican church (☎ 04 93 87 19 83; www.anglican-nice.com; 11 rue de la Buffa) Functions as an Anglophone cultural centre.

Emergency

Central police station (☎ 04 92 17 22 22; 1 av Maréchal Foch; ☸ 24hr) Report lost or stolen passports at the **Foreign Tourist Department** (☎ 04 92 17 20 63; ☸ 9am-5pm) here.

Internet Access

Cyberpoint (☎ 04 93 92 70 63; cybercom_nice@yahoo .fr; 10 av Félix Faure; per 10min €1; ☸ 10am-10pm Mon-Sat, 3-9pm Sun) English keyboards and air-con.
M@il Service Nice (☎ 04 89 92 25 34; 6 rue Meyerbeer; per 10/15/30/60min €1/1.50/2.50/4; ☸ 9.30am-11pm) Quiet, efficient office atmosphere.

Internet Resources

www.nice.fr Official city website.
www.nicerendezvous.com Tours, cooking, Nice Carnival and more.
www.nicetourisme.com Tourist office website.
www.plan-nice.org Interactive city maps.

Laundry

Laundrette (105 rue de France; per 5/16kg wash €3.50/7; ☸ 7am-9pm)
Taxi Lav' (22 rue Pertinax; per 5/7kg wash €2.80/3; ☸ 7am-8pm)

Left Luggage

Gare Nice Ville (av Thiers; manual lockers small/large bag per 24hr €8/10; ☸ 7.10am-10.30pm Mon-Sat, 8.10am-10.30pm Sun; small/medium/large automatic lockers €4/6.50/8.50; ☸ 7am-10.45pm) Luggage lockers at the central train station.

Library

Anglo-American library (12 rue de France; ☸ 10-11am & 3-5pm Tue-Thu & Sat, 3-6pm Fri) Up the passageway opposite 17 rue de France. Short-term membership available.

Medical Services

Hôpital St-Roch (☎ 04 92 03 33 75; www.chu-nice.fr in French; 5 rue Pierre Dévoluy) Has 24-hour emergency service.
Pharmacie Masséna (☎ 04 93 87 78 94; 7 rue Masséna; ☸ 24hr)
Pharmacie Riviera (☎ 04 93 62 54 44; 66 av Jean Médecin; ☸ 24hr)
SOS Médecins (☎ 08 01 85 01 01) Emergency home visits.

LITERARY NICE TO MENTON

Beach reads set in Nice, Menton and the bits in between.

■ *High Season in Nice* (Robert Kanigel) 'How one French Riviera town has seduced travellers for 2000 years' is the tag line of this fascinating portrait of Nice.

■ *The Mystery of the Blue Train* (Agatha Christie) Hercule Poirot investigates a mysterious murder aboard the *Blue Train* to the Riviera.

■ *The Doves' Nest* (Katherine Mansfield) Short story, published the year the tuberculosis-stricken author in Menton died, about a group of lonely women living in a villa on the French Riviera.

■ *The Rock Pool* (Cyril Connolly) Discover 1930s decadence on the French Riviera.

■ *The Long Afternoon* (Giles Waterfield) The tale of the Williamsons and their quest for a quiet retirement, following husband Henry's premature retirement from the Indian Civil Service, in Menton: told through letters, extracts from literature, and travel guides.

■ *Hallucinating Foucault* (Patricia Duncker) Postmodern novel that sees a heterosexual Cambridge postgraduate get entwined in a passionate affair with schizophrenic, homosexual French writer Paul Michel; the novel climaxes in Nice.

NICE

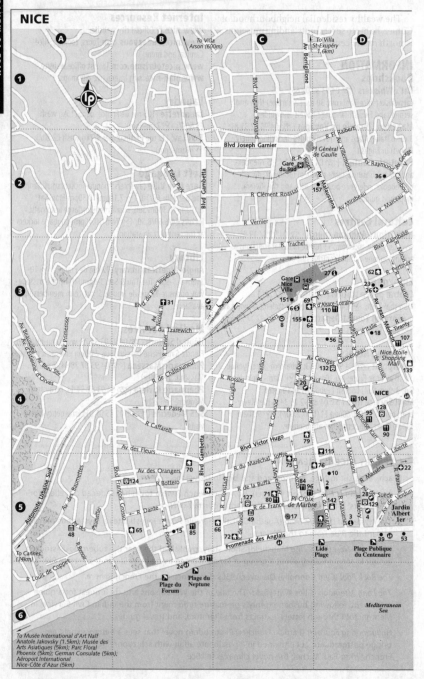

To Villa
Arson (600m)

To Villa
St-Exupéry
1.6km)

Av Borriglione

Blvd Auguste Raymond

Blvd Joseph Garnier

R El Raiberti

Pl Général
de Gaulle

Av Valrimenton

Av Raymond Comboul

Av George

Gare
du Sud

R A Fighet

R Clément Roassal

157

Malausséna

Av Mirabeau

36

R Marceau

R Vernier

R Trachel

Blvd Raimbaldi

Blvd Mari

R Pertinax

Av Primerose

Blvd du Parc Impérial

Blvd du Tzarewich

Av Nicolas II

31

12

Gare
Nice
Ville

149

151

69

R de Belgique

R d'Alsace-Lorraine

110

27

62

23

1

26

Av Jean Médecin

Av Malausséna

R E
Tiranty

R E

107

16

155

8

64

56

R Paganini

R d'Angleterre

R d'Italie

18

Nice Étoile
Shopping
Mall

139

Av Thiers

R de Russie

Blvd du Parc Impérial

R Cluvier

R de Châteauneuf

Blvd du Tzarewich

Av Georges Clemenceau

132

104

NICE

Av Beaulieu

Av Beau Site

Av d'Estienne d'Orves

R F Passy

R Caffarelli

R Rossini

R Berlioz

R Giulia

R Paul Déroulède

20

95

128

90

R Alphonse Karr

Av des Fleurs

R Giulia

R Verdi

R Gounod

Blvd Victor Hugo

79

115

R Maccarani

R de la Liberté

22

Av des Orangers

70

R du Maréchal Joffre

R Meyerbeer

75

76

10

Blvd François Grosso

124

R Bottero

67

R de la Buffa

127

71

84

96

2

R Masséna

R Halévy

28

Suède

129

Av de Verdun

Blvd Gambetta

R Dante

R St Philippe

65

15

85

66

72

R de Rivoli

R de France

49

80

Pl Croix
de Marbre

17

142

3

77

4

Jardin
Albert
1er

R des Brunettes

Av des Brunettes

Autoroute Urbaine Sud

R René

48

Promenade des Anglais

Lido
Plage

Plage Publique
du Centenaire

39

53

To Cannes
(34km)

R Louis de Coppet

83

24

Plage du
Forum

Plage du
Neptune

Mediterranean
Sea

To Musée International d'Art Naïf
Anatole Jakovsky (1.5km); Musée des
Arts Asiatiques (5km); Parc Floral
Phoenix (5km); German Consulate (5km);
Aéroport International
Nice-Côte d'Azur (5km)

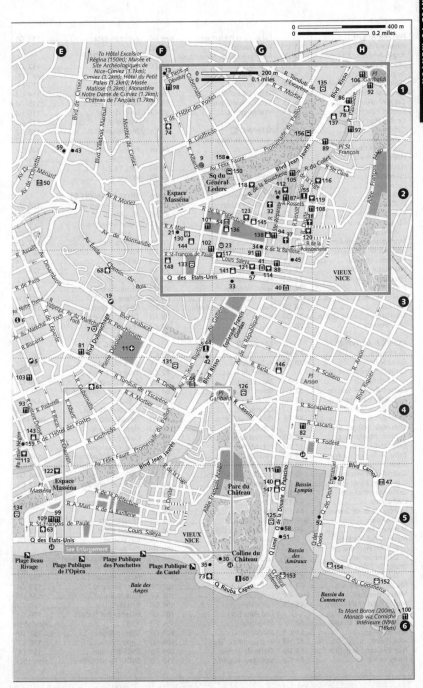

INFORMATION
Alliance Française........................**1** D3
Anglo-American Library............**2** D5
Beachfront Tourist Office...........**3** D5
Belgian Consulate.......................**4** D5
Bibliothèque Louis Nucéra.......(see 44)
Canadian Consulate....................**5** E4
Cat's Whiskers.............................**6** E3
Central Police Station.................**7** E3
Central Post Office......................**8** C3
Cyberpoint..................................**9** F2
Holy Trinity
    Anglican Church...................**10** D5
Hôpital St-Roch.........................**11** F3
Italian Consulate........................**12** B3
Laundrette..................................**13** F1
Laundrette..................................**14** G2
Laundrette..................................**15** B5
Le Change...................................**16** C3
M@il Service Nice......................**17** C5
Magellan Librairie
    de Voyages...........................**18** D3
Monégasque Consulate..............**19** E3
Netherlands Consulate...............**20** C4
Papeterie Rontani.......................**21** F2
Pharmacie Masséna....................**22** D5
Pharmacie Riviera......................**23** G2
Post Office..................................**24** E5
Public Showers............................**25** B6
Taxi Lav'....................................**26** D3
Train Station Tourist Office........**27** D3
US Consulate..............................**28** D5

SIGHTS & ACTIVITIES
3B Plongée.................................**29** H5
Cascade Donjon.........................**30** G5
Cathédral Orthodoxe Russe
    St-Nicolas.............................**31** B3
Cathédrale Ste-Réparate............**32** G2
Centre du Patrimoine.................**33** G3
Chapelle de la Miséricorde........**34** G2
Château Lift...............................**35** F5
Club Alpin Français des
    Alpes-Maritimes...................**36** D2
Église St-Giaume........................**37** G2
Église St-Jacques Le Majeur.......**38** G2
Electric Tourist Train..................**39** D5
Galerie de la Marine..................**40** G3
Galerie des Ponchettes...............**41** G3
Jardin Maréchal Juin..................**42** F3
L'Alhambra................................**43** E2
La Tête Carée de Sosno..............**44** F3
Le Poseidon.............................(see 58)
Matisse's House.........................**45** G3
Musée d'Art Moderne
    et d'Art Humaine de
    Contemporain.......................**46** F4
Musée de Paléontologie
    Terra Amata.........................**47** H5
Musée des Beaux-Arts................**48** A5
Musée Masséna.......................(see 49)
Musée d'Art et d'Histoire...........**49** C5
Musée National Message
    Biblique Marc Chagall..........**50** E2
Nautil Diving.............................**51** G5
Nice Diving................................**52** H5
Nice Le Grand Tour (Bus Stop)...**53** D5
Palais de Justice.........................**54** G2

Palais de la Préfecture............(see 54)
Palais Lascaris...........................**55** G2
Parc National du Mercantour
    Headquarters.......................**56** D3
Roller Station.............................**57** G3
Tour Bellanda.........................(see 35)
Trans Côte d'Azur......................**58** G5
Villa Raphaeli-Surany................**59** E2
War Memorial............................**60** G6

SLEEPING
Auberge de Jeunesse - Les
    Camélias..............................**61** E4
Backpackers
    Chez Patrick.........................**62** D3
Hôtel Beau Rivage.....................**63** E5
Hôtel Belle Meunière.................**64** C3
Hôtel Carlone............................**65** B5
Hôtel Cronstadt..........................**66** C5
Hôtel de la Buffa.......................**67** B5
Hôtel du Petit Palais...................**68** E3
Hôtel Excelsior..........................**69** C3
Hôtel Hi....................................**70** B5
Hôtel Meyerbeer Beach.............**71** C5
Hôtel Négresco..........................**72** C5
Hôtel Suisse...............................**73** F6
Hôtel Wilson..............................**74** F1
Hôtel Windsor...........................**75** C5
Nice Garden Hôtel.....................**76** D5
Palais de la Méditerranée..........**77** D5
Villa la Tour..............................**78** H1
Villa Victoria.............................**79** C4

EATING
11e Art......................................**80** C5
Aphrodite...................................**81** E3
Atelier du Goût...........................**82** G4
Blue Beach.................................**83** B5
Boros...**84** C5
Casitalia....................................**85** B5
Chantecler...............................(see 72)
Chez René Socca.......................**86** H1
Fenocchio..................................**87** G2
Festival de la Moule...................**88** G3
Fish Market................................**89** H2
Fleur de Café.............................**90** D4
Food Market...............................**91** G3
Grand Café de Turin...................**92** H1
Indyana.....................................**93** E4
Juice Bar....................................**94** G2
Karr...**95** G4
Kei's Passion..............................**96** C5
L'Escalinada..............................**97** H1
La Cantine de Lulu.....................**98** F1
La Petite Maison........................**99** E5
La Reserve................................**100** H6
Le 3e.......................................(see 77)
Le Merenda..............................**101** F2
Le Padouk...............................(see 77)
Le Pain Quotidien....................**102** F2
Le Speakeasy...........................**103** E4
Les Viviers...............................**104** D4
Lou Pilha Leva.........................**105** G2
Monoprix.................................**106** H1
Monoprix.................................**107** D3
Restaurant du Gésu..................**108** H2
Terres de Truffes......................**109** E5
Voyageur Nissart.....................**110** D3

Zucca Magica..........................**111** G5

DRINKING
De Klomp.................................**112** G2
L'ybane.................................(see 123)
L'ybane...................................**113** E4
La Casa del Sol........................**114** G3
Le Before.................................**115** D4
Le Water Bar............................**116** H2
Ma Nolan's..............................**117** G3
McMahons Pub.........................**118** G3
O'Hara's..................................**119** H2
Paddy's Pub.............................**120** G2
Thor Pub..................................**121** G3
Villa 14....................................**122** E5
Wayne's...................................**123** G2

ENTERTAINMENT
Blue Boy Enterprise..................**124** B5
Blue Moon................................**125** G5
Cinéma Nouveau
    Mercury.............................**126** G4
Cinéma Rialto..........................**127** C5
FNAC.....................................(see 139)
Le Flag....................................**128** D4
Le Klub....................................**129** D5
Le Liqwid................................**130** F2
Le Smarties..............................**131** F4
Ôdace......................................**132** D4
Opéra de Nice.........................**133** F3
Théâtre de Verdure..................**134** E5
Théâtre National de Nice..........**135** H1

SHOPPING
Antique Market......................(see 91)
Book Market............................**136** G2
Cave de la Tour........................**137** H1
Caves Caprioglio......................**138** G2
Centre Commercial Nice
    Étoile.................................**139** D4
Confiserie Florian....................**140** G5
Flea Market...........................(see 147)
Flower Market..........................**141** G3
Galerie Ferrero........................**142** D5
Galeries Lafayette....................**143** E4
Henri Auer Confiserie...............**144** F2
Jean-Louis Martinetti...............**145** G2
LAC...**146** G4
Les Puces Nice.........................**147** G5
Moulin à Huile
    d'Olive Alziari.....................**148** F3

TRANSPORT
Airport Buses...........................**149** C3
Bus Station..............................**150** G2
Car Rental Agencies
    (Train Station Annexe).........**151** C3
Corsica Ferries Ticket Office....(see 58)
Ferry Terminal 1......................**152** H6
Ferry Terminal 2......................**153** G6
Gare Maritime.........................**154** H5
Holiday Bikes...........................**155** C3
Intercity Bus Station................**156** G1
JLM.......................................(see 155)
Ligne d'Azur............................**157** D2
Ligne d'Azur............................**158** G2
SNCF Boutique........................**159** E4
SNCM Ferries Office..............(see 152)

Money

Banks and ATMs abound city wide.
Le Change (☎ 04 93 88 56 80; 17 av Thiers;
⊙ 7.30am-8pm) Exchange opposite the train station.

Post

Post office (train station 23 av Thiers; Vieux Nice 2 rue
Louis Gassin)

Tourist Information

Tourist offices distribute free city maps and
reserve hotel rooms.
Airport tourist information desk (☎ 08 92 70 74
07; ⊙ 8am-10pm) In the arrivals hall of Terminal 1.
Beachfront tourist office (☎ 04 92 14 48 00; 5 promenade des Anglais; ⊙ 8am-8pm Mon-Sat, 9am-7pm Sun
mid-Jun–mid-Sep, 9am-6pm Mon-Sat mid-Sep–mid-Jun)
Train station tourist office (☎ 04 93 87 07 07; av
Thiers; ⊙ 8am-8pm Mon-Sat, 9am-7pm Sun) Exit the
train station and turn left.

SIGHTS
Vieux Nice

Nice's old town – a mellow-hued rabbit war-
ren – has scarcely changed since the 1700s.
At its northeastern corner lies arcade-lined
place Garibaldi, built during the late 18th century and named after Giuseppe Garibaldi
(1807–82). Born in Nice to a fishing family, Garibaldi went on to become a sailor,
merchant captain, guerrilla fighter, leader
of the Red Shirts and popular hero of Italian
unification. He is buried in the **Parc du Château**
cemetery (see right).

Baroque **Palais Lascaris** (☎ 04 93 62 05 54; 15 rue
Droite; admission free, guided visit €3; ⊙ 10am-6pm Wed-
Mon, guided visit 3pm Fri) was owned by the Lascaris-
Ventimiglia family in the 17th century and is
a frescoed orgy of Flemish tapestries, faïence
and gloomy religious paintings. On the ground
floor is an 18th-century pharmacy.

Parallel **rue Bénoît Bunico** served as Nice's
Jewish ghetto after a 1430 law restricted where
Jews could live. It runs into rue de la Préfecture, the old city's main artery, dominated by
the imposing **Palais de la Préfecture**, the 17th-

NISSART

Nice's traditional hymn, *Nissa la Bella*
(1912) – an ode to '*O la miéu Nissa, regina
de li flou*' (Oh my beautiful Nice, queen of
flowers) – was written in Nissart, the age-
old language of the Niçois.

---

century home of the princes of Savoy; and the
Palais de Justice, the imposing law courts built
in neoclassical style in 1885. Head south to
reach **cours Saleya**, buzzing with restaurants
and markets. Nearby is **Matisse's house** (1 place
Charles-Félix), where he lived in the 1920s. There's
no plaque: look out for the lions.

Sweet-chiming baroque churches in Vieux
Nice include **Cathédrale Ste-Réparate** (place Rossetti), honouring the city's patron saint; blue-
grey and yellow **Église St-Jacques Le Majeur** (place
du Gésu); and **Église St-Giaume** (1 rue de la Poissonnerie),
all dating back to the mid-17th century. The
slightly later **Chapelle de la Miséricorde** (cours Saleya)
was built between 1740 and 1780.

Parc du Château

Vieux Nice's eastern extremity is flanked by
Parc du Château (Castle Park; ⊙ 8am-8pm Jun-Aug, to
7pm Apr, May & Sep, to 6pm Oct-Mar), a towering 92m-
high rock offering a cinematic panorama of
Nice and the Baie des Anges. The 12th-century
castle was razed by Louis XIV in 1706; only the
16th-century **Tour Bellanda**, the round tower you
can see from quai des États-Unis, remains.

The park is fabulous for picnics. Its other
simple attractions include **Cascade Donjon**, an
18th-century artificial waterfall crowned with
a viewing platform; and open-air concerts in
summer. The cemetery containing **Garibaldi's
grave** covers its northwestern section.

To get here, ride the **Chateau Lift** (Ascenseur
du Château; rue des Ponchettes; single/return €0.80/1.10;
⊙ 9am-8pm Jun-Aug, 9am-7pm Apr, May & Sep, 10am-6pm
Oct-Mar) from beneath Tour Bellanda or hike up
the staircases on montée Lesage or the eastern
end of rue Rossetti.

Promenade des Anglais

Palm-lined promenade des Anglais, paid for
by Nice's English colony in 1822, is a fine stage
for a stroll. It's particularly atmospheric in
the evening, with whizzing inline skaters and
epic sunsets over the sea. Don't miss the magnificent façade of **Hôtel Negresco**, built in 1912
for Romanian innkeeper Henri Negresco, or
Art Deco **Palais de la Méditerranée**, the prized
property of American millionaire Frank Jay
Gould and France's top-earning casino until
the 1970s, when his luck changed and the
place closed down.

East towards Vieux Nice, promenade des
Anglais becomes **quai des États-Unis**, named after
the United States in honour of President Wilson's decision in 1917 to join WWI. Modern

art exhibitions are hosted by two former fish halls here: **Galerie des Ponchettes** (☎ 04 93 62 31 24; 77 quai des États-Unis; admission free; ☯ 10am-6pm Tue-Sun), a 19th-century vaulted building that was used as a public *lavoir* (wash house) in the 1840s, then as a fish market until Henri Matisse persuaded the council to revamp it in 1950; and **Galerie de la Marine** (☎ 04 93 91 92 90; 59 quai des États-Unis; admission free; ☯ 10am-6pm Tue-Sun). At the quay's eastern end, a **war memorial** hewn from the rock commemorates the 4000 Niçois who died in both world wars.

At the southern end of av Jean Médecin, Nice's main commercial street, sits **place Masséna**, with early-19th-century, neoclassical arcaded buildings painted in shades of ochre and red. Its western end is dominated by the 19th-century **Jardin Albert 1er**. The giant arc languishing on the lawn was designed by sculptor Bernard Venet to commemorate the centenary of the appellation 'Côte d'Azur', dreamt up by French poet Stéphane Liégeard (1830–1925). **Espace Masséna**, a public square, straddles the eastern side of place Masséna.

Museums
MUSÉE D'ART MODERNE ET D'ART CONTEMPORAIN

European and American avant-garde works from the 1950s to the present are the focus of Nice's don't-miss **Musée d'Art Moderne et d'Art Contemporain** (MAMAC; Museum of Modern & Contemporary Art; ☎ 04 93 62 61 62; www.mamac-nice.org; promenade des Arts; adult/student €4/2.50, guided visit €3; ☯ 10am-6pm Tue-Sun, guided visit 4pm Wed). Highlights among the

---

WHAT'S THAT?

From Nice's port, glance up at Mont Boron, home to celebrities such as Elton John. The pink confection you see is **Château de l'Anglais**, built in 1859 for an English engineer called Robert Smith, renowned at the time as being the only foreigner to live in Nice year-round. Locals quickly dubbed his castle 'Smith's folly'. The historical monument has since been split into private apartments.

---

permanent 2nd- and 3rd-floor exhibits include items wrapped by Christo; a red model-T Ford crunched into a 1.6m-tall block by Marseillais sculptor César; and the mundane objects (rubbish, letters, children's toys) encased in Perspex containers by Nice-born Arman (p61).

Temporary exhibitions fill the ground and 1st floors; art films and cult movies are screened in the auditorium; and atop the building, humpbacked wooden bridges connect the four marble towers, crowned with a rooftop garden and gallery featuring pieces by city son Yves Klein (p61). Outside, the red concrete **Jardin Maréchal Juin** (☯ 10am-8pm Jun-Aug, 10am-7pm Apr, May, Sep & Oct, 10am-6pm Nov-Mar) hugs MAMAC's eastern side and – more spectacularly – frames the giant square head of **La Tête Carrée de Sosno**(2002). The massive 30m-tall sculpture designed by Sacha Sosno (p62) – a 14m-square concrete head sitting on a pair of shoulders – is, in fact a building: the offices of public library **Bibliothèque Louis Nucéra** (2 place Yves Klein) are inside.

MUSÉE MATISSE

Located about 2km north of the centre, **Musée Matisse** (Matisse Museum; ☎ 04 93 81 08 08; www.musee-matisse-nice.org; 164 av des Arènes de Cimiez; adult/under 18yr €4/free; ☯ 10am-6pm Wed-Mon) houses a splendid assortment of works by Matisse (p61). Its permanent collection is displayed in a redochre 17th-century Genoese villa overlooking the olive-tree-studded **Parc des Arènes**. Temporary exhibitions are hosted in the futuristic basement building. The reception hall of the museum is dominated by a colourful, 4.1m by 8.7m paper cutout frieze entitled *Flowers and Fruits*, designed by Matisse for the inner courtyard of a Californian villa in 1953.

Take bus 15, 17 or 22 from the bus station to the Arènes/Musée Matisse stop.

MUSEUMS PASS

Museum fiends can invest in a **Carte Passe-Musées 7 jours** (€6, no concessions) or the **Carte Passe-Musées 1 An** (€18.30, student €9.15), sold at tourist offices. The former allows holders one visit to each of Nice's museums (excluding the privately run Chagall and Asian Arts museums) over seven consecutive days; the latter yields 15 museum visits in the space of a year. Under 18s get into municipal museums in Nice for free – as does everyone on the first and third Sundays of the month (Chagall and Asian Arts museums first Sunday only).

If you're visiting other museums on the Riviera, plump for a **Carte Musées Côte d'Azur** (p403).

MUSÉE NATIONAL MESSAGE BIBLIQUE MARC CHAGALL

The **Musée National Message Biblique Marc Chagall** (Marc Chagall Biblical Message Museum; ☎ 04 93 53 87 20; www.rmn.fr; 4 av Docteur Ménard; adult/18-25yr/under 18 €6.50/4.50/free, plus €1.20 for temporary exhibitions; ☉ 10am-5.50pm Wed-Mon Jul-Sep, 10am-4.50pm Oct-Jun) houses the largest public collection of works by Belarusian painter Marc Chagall (1887–1985), known for his characteristic flying animals, flowers, violinists and kissing couples.

The exuberant swaths of colour used by Chagall to illustrate Old Testament themes are set off by the severity of this purpose-built museum. The main hall contains 12 huge interpretations (1954–67) of stories from Genesis and Exodus. In an antechamber, an unusual mosaic of Elijah in his fiery chariot, surrounded by signs of the zodiac, is viewed through a plate-glass window and reflected in a small pond. Five paintings (1960s) based on the *Song of Songs* form the most startling series, an explosion of passionate red (in contrast to the sea greens, deep purples and blues of the main room) dedicated to his wife Vava.

Take bus 15 to the Musée Chagall stop, or walk (signposted from av de l'Olivetto).

MUSÉE ARCHÉOLOGIQUE DE NICE-CIMIEZ

Nice's little-spoken but lingering language, Nissart, derives most of its vocab from the Roman city of Cemenelum, founded by Augustus in 14 BC. Its ruins form the focus of the **Musée Archéologique de Nice-Cimiez** (Archaeology Museum; ☎ 04 93 81 59 57; 160 av des Arènes de Cimiez; adult/student €4/2.50; ☉ 10am-6pm Wed-Mon). Both the public baths and amphitheatre – the venue for outdoor concerts during the Nice Jazz festival (p270) – can be visited.

Buses 15, 17 and 22 go from the bus station to the Arènes stop.

MUSÉE INTERNATIONAL D'ART NAÏF ANATOLE JAKOVSKY

Over 1000 works of naive art are gathered at the **Anatole Jakovsky International Naive Art Museum** (☎ 04 93 71 78 33; av de Fabron; adult/under 18yr €4/free; ☉ 10am-6pm Wed-Mon), inside 19th-century Château Ste-Hélène, 2km west of the centre. Romanian art critic Anatole Jakovsky (1909–83), who moved to southern France in 1932, kick-started the museum by donating his vast collection. Pieces date from the 18th century to the present day.

Take bus 8, 10, 11 or 12 from the bus station to the Fabron stop, from where it's a 500m walk, or take bus 34 to the Musée Art Naïf stop.

MUSÉE DES ARTS ASIATIQUES

Ornamental treasures from Cambodia, China, India and Japan are showcased in the striking white-marble **Musée des Arts Asiatiques** (Museum of Asian Arts; ☎ 04 92 29 37 00; www.arts-asiatiques.com in French; 405 promenade des Anglais; adult/under 18yr €6/free, 1st Sun of month free; ☉ 10am-6pm Wed-Mon May–mid-Oct, 10am-5pm Wed-Mon mid-Oct–Apr), designed by a Japanese architect, near the airport. Participating in a Sunday afternoon traditional Chinese or Japanese tea ceremony (€10 including museum visit; advance reservations essential) is a highlight. Take bus 9 or 10 from the bus station, or bus 23 from the train station.

MUSÉE DES BEAUX-ARTS

Find Nice's **Musée des Beaux-Arts** (Fine Arts Museum; ☎ 04 92 15 28 28; www.musee-beaux-arts-nice.org; 33 av des Baumettes; adult/under 18yr €4/free, guided tour adult/under 18yr €7/free; ☉ 10am-6pm Tue-Sun) in a fantastic cream-and-apricot villa built in 1878 for Ukrainian princess Elisabeth Vassilievna Kotschoubey. Its decorative stucco friezes and six-column rear terrace overlooking luxuriant gardens make it typical of Nice's *belle époque*.

The collection is a mishmash of absolute gems, like Jan Brueghel's *Allegory of Water* and *Allegory of Earth*, and yawnsome 18th-century portraits. Fauvist appreciators will relish a roomful of works by Raoul Dufy (1877–1953). Also impressive are sculptures by Rodin, and some late impressionist pieces by Bonnard, Monet and Sisley. Local lads Jules Chéret (1836–1932), the 'Father of the Poster', and Alexis Mossa (1844–1926), who painted truly hideous symbolist works, also feature. The latter is more famous for adding wildly decorated floats to the Nice Carnival than for his watercolours.

From the bus station, take bus 38 to the Musée Chéret stop outside.

A BEAUTIFUL DETOUR

Belle époque Nice was beautiful: the wedding-cake mansions, palaces and pastel-painted concrete gateaux that sprang up in abundance were fabulous and fantastical. Take in the cream of these lavish mansions in Cimiez, Nice's wealthy residential district 2.5km northeast of the train station.

From the town centre, follow av Jean Médecin north, beneath the train tracks, and turn right onto av Mirabeau. The **Musée National Message Biblique Marc Chagall** is signposted at the end of the street; follow the signs just past the museum, to blvd de Cimiez. Across this road is the Haussmann-style **Conservatoire de Musique** (8 blvd de Cimiez), built in 1902. At 46 is **L'Alhambra** (1901), an opulent private mansion set on a small, palm-tree-studded mound and surrounded by a high wall, though not high enough to hide the Moorish minarets that rise from the sparkling white building. **Villa Raphaeli-Surany** (1900), opposite at 35, is adorned with intricate mosaic reliefs. The boulevard's crowning jewel is **Hôtel Excelsior Régina** (71 av Régina), built in 1896 to welcome Queen Victoria to Nice (a statue of the queen stands in front). Henri Matisse later lived here. This titanic building houses private apartments and a handful of medical practices today.

MUSÉE DE PALÉONTOLOGIE HUMAINE DE TERRA AMATA

East of the port, this **museum** (☎ 04 93 55 59 93; 25 blvd Carnot; adult/student €4/2.50; ☼ 10am-6pm Tue-Sun) displays objects from a site inhabited 400,000 years ago by the predecessors of *Homo sapiens*. Bus 32 links the local bus station and the museum; alight at the Carnot stop.

MUSÉE D'ART ET D'HISTOIRE

Also called **Musée Masséna** (☎ 04 93 88 11 34; 65 rue de France), this museum was closed for renovation until 2007 at the time of writing, although the marvellous Italianate neoclassical villa (1898) housing the museum is worth a gander.

Cathédrale Orthodoxe Russe St-Nicolas

Step inside this **cathedral** (av Nicolas II; ☼ 9am-noon & 2.30-6pm Mon-Sat, 2.30-6pm Sun) and let the icons and frescoes transport you to 17th-century Moscow. Consecrated in 1912 and crowned by multicoloured onion domes, it is the biggest Russian Orthodox Church outside Russia. Shorts, miniskirts and sleeveless shirts are forbidden.

Monastère Notre Dame de Cimiez

Matisse is buried in the cemetery of the **Monastère Notre Dame de Cimiez** (☎ 04 93 81 00 04; ☼ 8.30am-12.30pm & 2.30-6.30pm). His grave is signposted '*sépulture Henri Matisse*' from the cemetery's main entrance (next to the monastery church on av Bellanda). Raoul Dufy is also buried here.

The monastery itself houses a small **museum** (admission free; ☼ 10am-noon & 3-6pm Mon-Sat) illustrating the everyday lives and activities of its Franciscan monks. Adjoining **Église**

Notre Dame boasts precious medieval art by Louis Bréa, and a monumental 17th-century baroque altar. Surrounding the buildings is **Jardin du Monastère**, filled with cypress trees and an abundance of sweet-smelling roses, and offering a sweeping panorama of the Baie des Anges. The **Nuits Musicales de Nice** (p270) are held in the cloisters in July and August.

Take bus 15, 17 or 22 from the bus station to the Arènes stop.

Villa Arson

Sensational temporary photographic and contemporary art exhibitions are displayed at the **Centre National d'Art Contemporain** (☎ 04 92 07 73 73; www.villa-arson.org in French; 20 av Stéphane Liégeard; admission free; ☼ 2-7pm Wed-Mon Jul-Sep, 2-6pm Wed-Mon Oct-Jun), inside 18th-century **Villa Arson**, 1km north of the town centre.

Take bus 36 to the Villa Arson stop, or bus 4, 7 or 26 to the Fanny stop on blvd de Cessole.

ACTIVITIES

Activities in Nice itself revolve around the water. But head out of town and green foothills quickly kick in. Before venturing out, pick up the scoop from:

Club Alpin Français des Alpes-Maritimes (☎ 04 93 62 59 99; www.cafnice.org in French; 14 av Mirabeau; ☼ 4-8pm Mon-Fri) Walking, paragliding, skiing and most other outdoor sports.

Nice Randonnée (☎ 06 67 22 93 46; www.nice-randonnee.com in French; 29ter blvd de Cimiez) Local walking club.

Parc National du Mercantour Headquarters (☎ 04 93 16 78 88; www.parc-mercantour.fr; 23 rue d'Italie; ☼ 8.30am-noon & 1.45-5pm Mon-Fri) Headquarters of the Mercantour National Park (p248).

Beaches & Boats

If you don't like sand between your toes, Nice's beaches – covered with smooth, round pebbles – are for you. Free public sections of beach with lifeguards, first-aid posts and cold showers alternate with 15 private beaches equipped with restaurants, comfy sun-lounges (obligatory; around €15/day) parasols (optional; €4/day), warm showers and changing rooms. **Plage Publique des Ponchettes**, opposite Vieux Nice, gets the most packed with oiled bodies either baking in the sun or punching a ball on the beach-volleyball court.

Mid-June to mid-September water-sport thrills spill across **Lido Plage** (opposite the Palais de la Méditerranée), **Plage Beau Rivage** (☎ 04 92 47 82 82; 107 quai des États Unis) and **Plage du Neptune** (☎ 04 93 87 16 60; opposite Hôtel Negresco). Take to the air with a parachute strung to the back of a motorboat (*parachute ascensionnel*; one/two people €45/60); be dragged at speed in a rubber ring (*bouée tractée*; €20); water-ski or wakeboard (€25/200 per one/10 turns); have a daredevil blast on a fly fish (€35); or paddle around in a canoe-kayak (€6/10 per 30/60 minutes). Jet skis are only allowed on the far western bit of beach near the airport.

Trans Côte d'Azur (☎ 04 92 00 42 30; www.trans-cote -azur.com; quai Lunel; ⏱ 9am-12.30pm & 1.30-6pm) runs one-hour boat trips along the coast, leaving from the port daily except Monday from March to June (€12.50/7 for adults/four- to 11-year-olds). Mid-June to mid-September it also runs weekly excursions to Île Ste-Marguerite (€34/26), St-Tropez (€49/35) and Monaco (adult/four- to 10-year-olds €26/19). Reservations are essential.

Diving & Snorkelling

Diving shop **3B Plongée** (☎ 04 93 26 09 03; phplus@wanadoo.fr; 3 quai des Deux Emmanuel) sells equipment and offers diving advice. April to October (weekends only March, November and December), portside dive companies **Le Poseidon** (☎ 04 92 00 43 86; www.poseidon-nice.com; quai Lunel), **Nautil Diving** (☎ 04 93 14 66 81, 06 09 55 71 45; www.nautile-diving .com; quai Lunel) and **Nice Diving** (☎ 04 93 89 42 44; www .nicediving.com; 14 quai des Docks) organise courses, expeditions and equipment rental (€40/180 for one/five dives including equipment rental; €290 for a six-day group course).

Inline Skating & Skateboarding

Skaters and boarders speed along the smooth, silky and long cycling track on promenade des Anglais. Hire blades from **Roller Station** (☎ 04 93 62 99 05; 49 quai des États Unis) for €4/6/8 per hour/day/24 hours, or a skateboard or *trottinette* (microscooter) for €3/6/9 per hour/ day/24 hours.

Skating club **Nice Roller Attitude** (☎ 04 93 13 97 64, 06 09 07 57 19; www.nice-roller-attitude.com in French) organises mass skates around town, usually departing from outside Hôtel Beau Rivage (p272) at 9pm on the last Friday of the month (check first; dates are on its website under the 'Randonée' link). In July and August it runs skating courses (€20) for adults and kids.

NICE FOR CHILDREN

Nice works for kids. Its boats and beaches (left) provide hours of fun, and a couple of private beaches, including **Blue Beach** (p272), sport a playground and/or slide-clad paddling pool for younger tots.

On the prom, there are scooters and inline skates to try; an electric tourist train (below) to toot along on; and an open-top double-decker bus (below) to ride. At its far eastern end, **Parc du Château** (p265) makes a relaxed picnic spot, as does playground-equipped **Parc Phoenix** (☎ 04 92 29 77 00; 405 promenade des Anglais: adult/under 12yr €2/free; ⏱ 9.30am-7.30pm Apr-Sep, 9.30am-6pm Oct-Mar) at its western end.

Watching the ferries sail in and out of the port (p278) is always a good activity, as is **Marineland** (p318), a quick flit west by train or car.

TOURS

Chug around the old town and Parc du Château in 40 minutes aboard an **electric tourist train** (☎ 06 16 39 53 51; www.petittrainnice.com; adult/ under 9yr €6/3; ⏱ 10am-5pm, 6pm or 7pm mid-Feb–mid-Nov), departing every 30 minutes (except when it rains) across the street from Jardin Albert 1er on promenade des Anglais.

Or try an open-topped double-decker of **Nice Le Grand Tour** (☎ 04 92 29 17 00; www.nicele grandtour.com; 1-day pass adult/4-11yr/student €18/9/15). Buses go round the port, up to Cimiez, and along promenade des Anglais. Hop on/off at any one of 11 stops, including across the street from the open-air theatre on promenade des Anglais. Drivers and tourist offices sell passes.

Cyclotour (☎ 08 26 10 00 03; 20min tour per 1/2 people €7/10.50; ⏱ 10.30am-7.30 or 8pm Mon-Sat) runs pedal-powered tours around town by three-wheeled rickshaw with driver; telephone bookings only (€1).

Year-round, the tourist office runs an old-town tour in English (adult/five- to 10-year-olds €12/6) departing from the beachfront office at 9.30am on Saturday; you must reserve in advance. Otherwise, walking tours are organised by the **Centre du Patrimoine** (☎ 04 92 00 41 90; centre.patrimoine@ville-nice.fr; 75 quai des États Unis; adult €3). Tours last 1½ to two hours, start at 3pm or 5pm and cover, among other themes, baroque, Art Deco, neoclassical and *belle époque* Nice.

FESTIVALS & EVENTS

The celebrated two-week **Carnaval de Nice** (Nice Carnival; www.nicecarnaval.com) has been held each year around Mardi Gras (Shrove Tuesday) since 1294, and attracts 1.2 million–odd spectators. Highlights include the *batailles de fleurs* (battles of flowers), when hundreds upon thousands of fresh blossoms are tossed into the crowds from passing flower-parade floats; and the ceremonial burning of the carnival king on promenade des Anglais, followed by an enormous fireworks display, at the end of the festivities.

The week-long **Nice Jazz Festival** (www.nicejazz fest.com) jives in July in the olive grove behind Cimiez's Musée Matisse. The two-day **Fête au Château** is an outdoor music festival in Parc du Château in mid-June, and Russian chants meet Mozart's *Requiem* for two weeks in late June during the **Festival de Musique Sacrée** (Festival of Sacred Music). **Les Nuits Musicales de Nice**, a two-week event in early August, brings classical music to the cloisters of **Monastère Notre Dame de Cimiez** (p268).

SLEEPING

Accommodation is of the hotel rather than *chambre d'hôte* variety, but there are a couple of *chambres d'hôtes* with panoramic Nice views on the Corniches (p287) for those seeking peace and tranquillity at the end of a busy day in town.

Only the very best hotels in Nice have sea views. Accommodation can be hard to find in July and August, when most places brandish *complet* (full) signs by 10am.

Budget

HOTELS

Rue Paganini and rue Alsace Lorraine just south of the train station are littered with cheap two-star joints, some more inviting than others.

Hôtel Belle Meunière (☎ 04 93 88 66 15; www .bellemeuniere.com; 21 av Durante; dm with/without shower €22/15, d with washbasin & shared kitchen €36, d €45 with shower & toilet €58, tr with shower & toilet €66; reception 🕑 7.30am-midnight Feb-Nov; 🅿) This bustling place, a minute's walk from the train station, is run by the effervescent Niçoise Marie Pierre, whose family has run the place since 1984. Guests veer towards the younger, backpacking side; the tree-studded garden is great for meeting people and Marie-Pierre will wash your smocks for €5.50 a load (fill the basket up to the line) or stash your suitcase for you (€2). Night owls need a key code to get in after midnight. Rates include breakfast. Parking is €6.50 per night.

Hôtel Meyerbeer Beach (☎ 04 93 88 95 65; www .hotel-meyerbeer-beach-nice.cote.azur.fr; 15 rue Meyerbeer; dm low/high season €15/20, s/d/tr/q high season €60/75/105/135; reception 🕑 24hr Jun-Sep, 8am-8pm Mon-Sat, 8am-6pm Sun Oct-Apr; 🖳 ⊠) Young out-to-party travellers are the primary clientele at this fun and friendly pad, a mere hop, skip and jump from the Med. Reception doubles as a common room with free cordial, instant coffee, tea and biccies, as well as free (but, thanks to the CCTV cameras competing for bandwidth, snail's pace) internet. There are beach mats to borrow and rooms come with a kitchenette hidden behind a roller shutter (€20 deposit).

Hôtel de la Buffa (☎ 04 93 88 77 35; www.hotel-buffa .com; 56 rue de la Buffa; d €25-35; 🅿 🖳 🖳) Character oozes out of this family-run hotel, appropriately accessed via a spiral staircase (no oversized suitcases please!). Ceilings are lofty, furnishings veer on the side of old-fashioned, and a more local-than-local covered food market is its appealing neighbour. Wi-fi access is €10 per 24 hours.

Hôtel Wilson (☎ 04 93 88 95 65; www.hotel-wilson -nice.com; 32 rue de l'Hôtel des Postes; s/d with washbasin €33.50/38, with shower €39.50/45, with shower & toilet €44.50/49) 'Sleep under a beautiful star' is the catchphrase at this unusual one-star hotel – home of bon vivant Jean-Marie Martinez who speaks six languages and shares his convivial dining table, books and classical music with guests. The Matisse room – a sky-blue affair – opens out onto a wrought-iron balcony with wooden chairs overlooking the rooftops. Low-season rates are about €5 less.

HOSTELS

Villa St-Exupéry (☎ 04 93 84 42 83, free phone within France ☎ 08 00 30 74 09; www.vsaint.com; 22 av Gravier; dm €22, s with washbasin €30, s/d/tr with bathroom €32/56/72;

reception (🕑 6.30-2am Jul-Sep, 7am-11pm Oct-Jun; (P) (💻))
Readers rave about this luxurious hostel nestled in an old Carmelite monastery amid a leafy garden on the city fringes – and rightly so! Rooms are clean, fresh and most sport en suite showers; those up top have inspirational sea views (rooms 313, 314 and 315 even open onto a rooftop terrace). It lays on a clutch of free online computers (plus wi-fi); breakfast is a 10-choice cereal feast; and the 24-hour common room rocks as a bar with €1 beer come dusk. St-Exupéry's little prince (p33) would be proud. Find it 2.5km north of the train station. It is serviced by bus 23 to/from the station, bus 1 or 2 to the old town and port, and night bus N3 until 1.10am.

Also recommended:

Auberge de Jeunesse – Les Camélias (☎ 04 93 62 15 54; nice-camelias@fuaj.org; 3 rue Spitalieri; dm incl breakfast €20; (💻)) Flash backpacking in space-age metallic bunks, with two wheelchair-friendly dorms and designer bar to hang in. Rooms locked 11am to 3pm. Wi-fi is €4 per hour.

Backpacker's Chez Patrick (☎ 04 93 80 30 72; www .chezpatrick.com; 1st fl, 32 rue Pertinax; dm/d €21/45; reception (🕑 8am-noon & 5-8pm; (📞)) Central 24-bed place run by cheery Breton Patrick on the 1st floor (not to be confused with the hostel on the 4th floor that's received more than its fair share of complaints).

Midrange

Villa la Tour (☎ 04 93 80 08 15; www.villa-la-tour.com; 4 rue de la Tour; s/d €49/52, with old-town view €72/78, s/d/tr with old-town view & balcony €127/135/145; (📞))
Good service and charm are a given at this hybrid *chambre-d'hôte*–hotel, a convent in the 18th century and the only place to stay in Vieux Nice. Cane garden furniture marks the entrance to a flowery interior, laden with foliage and topped off with a cute little roof patio. Rates are slightly lower November to April.

Hôtel Carlone (☎ 04 93 44 71 61; 2 blvd François Grosso; s/d/tr/q from €50/60/77/90; (P)) This old-style 1950s hotel without air-con is a steal thanks to its prime-real-estate location a stone's throw from the water and spacious balconies with a snippet of sea view. Guests staying a week or so can negotiate cheaper rates. Parking is €7 per night.

Hôtel Cronstadt (☎ 04 93 82 00 30; www.hotelcronstadt .com; 3 rue Cronstadt; s/d/tr €60/80/110; reception (🕑 10am-10pm) Find the Cronstadt hidden inside old-world Palais Adly: enter the building, cross the ravishing Arabian Nights courtyard gar-

den, press the buzzer at the far end, and *don't* be put off by the eccentric and unhelpful owner. Rooms are quiet and graceful, all with garden views, and it's the closest two-star to the sea.

Hôtel du Petit Palais (☎ 04 93 62 19 11; 17 av Émile Bieckert; www.petitpalaisnice.com in French; d low season €80-130, high season €88-150; (P) (💻)) With its quintessential Mediterranean garden and idyllic sea views, this *belle époque* candy-box pink palace in upmarket Cimiez is palatial indeed. Writer, comedian and film-maker Sacha Guitry lived here. Parking is €10 per night.

Villa Victoria (☎ 04 93 88 39 60; www.villa-victoria .com; 33 blvd Victor Hugo; s/d/tr from €75/90/105; (P) (📞) (💻)) The small botanical garden of this apricot villa with sun lounges and a flower-covered gazebo with table beneath is a perfect postcard-writing hide-out. Minibar, trouser press and safety deposit add a big-hotel touch to an otherwise intimate 38-room place to stay. Parking is €10 per day.

Hôtel Suisse (☎ 04 92 17 39 00; hotel.suisse@hotels -ocre-azur.com; 15 quai Rauba Capeu; d low season from €69/ high season €95; (📞)) Teak table and chair–clad wrought-iron balconies strategically placed on five floors overlooking the sweeping Baie des Anges are reason enough to stay at this attractive, three-star hotel on the prom. Service is as crisp and efficient as one would expect of a hotel named Switzerland. Wi-fi access is free.

Hôtel Excelsior (☎ 04 93 88 38 69; www.excelsiornice .com; 19 av Durante; s/d/tr low season €70/100/115, high season €95/140/150; **P** ✕ ▯) Oh-so-aloof Parisian manor in appearance, this handsome bourgeois townhouse dating from 1892 makes a smart choice. Wrought-iron balconies and a trio of enormous French flags front a lush garden with pond, fountain and elevated marble terrace. Parking is free; wi-fi access is €20 per hour.

Hôtel Windsor (☎ 04 93 88 59 35; www.hotelwindsor nice.com; 11 rue Dalpozzo; d with/without balcony low season €150/85, high season €165/110; ✕ ▯ ▯) *Rendez-vous avec l'art* (meeting with art) is how this boutique hotel markets itself – and, indeed, a stay here is just that. Sleep in the company of your favourite artist (Ben makes great bedtime reading) or take your pick from the collection of poster and fresco rooms. White linens show off the original artwork and some rooms have balconies overlooking the true belle of the Windsor ball – a walled garden sprinkled with palm trees, beautifully shaded tables and chairs, and a pool. Free wi-fi.

TOP END

Many upmarket hotels have private beaches so you can bask away from the riffraff.

Hôtel Beau Rivage (☎ 04 92 47 82 82; www.nice beaurivage.com; 24 rue St-François de Paule; d low/mid/high season from €150/240/285; **P** ✕ ▯) Step out of the pulsating summer heat and into this minimalist oasis of cool calm serenity, carved out of sleek designer furnishings and the soft hues of stone, wood, pebble and linen in 2004 by urban architect/interior designer Jean-Michel Wilmotte. Matisse (1916) and Russian playwright Anton Chekhov (1891) stayed here, not that they'd know it now.

Hôtel Hi (☎ 04 97 07 26 26; www.hi-hotel.net; 3 av des Fleurs; d from €190; ✕ **P** ✕ ▯ ▯) A concrete alley links a puritanical 1930s façade with the hi-tech interior of this urban hotel. French Philippe Starck protégé Matali Crasset has designed a hotel that turns convention on its head: baths look like four-poster beds and beds appear as tables in blanket-white White & White rooms; a 'sofablaster' (sofa with integrated sound system) is the *pièce de résistance* of Technocorner rooms; and acid-green Happy Day rooms turn pink come dark. A modish rooftop pool and giant waterbeds crown the 8th floor, and fodder available in the state-of-the-art canteen is strictly or-

ganic. Parking is €24 per 24 hours; wi-fi is €5 per day.

Hôtel Negresco (☎ 04 93 16 64 00; www.hotel-negresco -nice.com; 37 promenade des Anglais; d with courtyard/garden & sea views low season from €280/350, high season from €350/450; **P** ✕ ▯ ▯ ▯) Queen Elizabeth II, Charlie Chaplin, Matisse, Hitchcock, Walt Disney…all and sundry have stayed at this palatial hotel, built for Romanian innkeeper Henri Negresco in 1912. In the most stand-out building on the prom, with its boob-shaped candyfloss-pink dome, opulent rooms range in style from Louis XIII to Art Deco and are loaded with priceless art. At the heart of the hotel sits the stained glass Salon Royale, a Gustave Eiffel creation bearing one of the world's two chandeliers of its kind (16,800 beads of Baccarat crystal weighing over one tonne; the other's in the Kremlin). Jeanne Augier, now in her 80s, has owned the whole lot since 1957.

Palais de la Méditerranée (☎ 04 92 14 77 00; www .lepalaisdelamediterranee.com; 13-15 promenade des Anglais; d low/high season from €280/375, sea view from €550/810; **P** ✕ ▯ ▯) Nice's most historic, story- and celebrity-rich hotel after the Negresco, this stunning nine-storey cruise-ship liner of a building dating from 1929 rose from the ashes in 2004. Nothing more than a crumbling, Art Deco façade a few years back, the palace oozes four-star opulence today.

EATING

Vieux Nice is rammed with restaurants, summer seeing a bounty of hybrid eating-drinking terraces fill its streets and squares: vast cours Saleya, place Pierre Gautier and place Rossetti buzz until well past midnight.

Much of the seashore is backed by beach restaurants offering predictable Mediterranean cuisine and the chance to dip between courses. Food at **Blue Beach** (☎ 04 93 87 10 36; 32 promenade des Anglais; mains €10-15; ☙ lunch year-round, lunch & dinner Jul & Aug) is a cut above the rest, plus it hosts free jamming sessions with musicians performing at the Nice Jazz Festival (p270) as well as interesting dinner conferences on Niçois history and culture in July.

Inland, pedestrianised rue Masséna is lined with unexceptional touristy cafés and restaurants buzzing with business.

Niçois

Restaurant du Gésu (☎ 04 93 62 26 46; 1 place du Gésu; pasta & pizza €8-10; ☙ lunch & dinner Mon-Sat) Locals rave about this no-frills eating house, run with

NIÇOIS NIBBLES

Perfect for filling a hungry moment coming from the beach (or any time of day) are a bunch of battered local specialities, especially common in Vieux Nice where **Chez René Socca** (☎ 04 93 92 05 73; 2 rue Miralhéti; ⏰ Tue-Sun Dec-Oct) and **Lou Pilha Leva** (☎ 04 93 13 99 08; place Centrale; ⏰ 8am-midnight or 1am) dole them out to a merrily munching, family-friendly, fun-loving crowd packed around shared bench seating on the street. Order drinks separately from a passing drinks waiter.

Take your pick while standing in the cacophonous queue. A portion of *beignets d'aubergines* (aubergine slices fried in batter) or *beignets de courgettes* (battered zucchini slices) sets you back €4 (don't expect a china plate), as do *beignets des sardines* (battered sardines) – a guaranteed taste of sea. There are spicy fish cakes, deep-fried whitebait and battered zucchini flowers to choose from, or how about *farcis* (stuffed vegetables), a slice of pizza or *pissaladière* (traditional onion tart topped with black olives and anchovies), or a quintessential *salade Niçoise* (green salad with boiled egg, tuna and anchovy).

Essential tasting for every visiting palate is *socca* (€2), a savoury, griddle-fried pancake made from chickpea flour and olive oil. The *socca* cooked up by the flamboyant **Thérèsa** (Cours Saleya market ⏰ 8am-1pm Tue-Sun) at her market stall (p36) with plastic tables beneath the awning is legendary. Order a glass of rosé with it.

---

dynamism and a huge dose of wit by the most gravelly voiced patron on the Riviera. The menu is simple – Niçois *beignets* (fritters) followed by pizza, escalope or homemade pasta with a choice of sauce, house speciality *sauce daube* (a meaty broth sauce) included. Find Gésu tucked away on an old-town square in the shade of a church.

Voyageur Nissart (☎ 04 93 82 19 60; www.voyageur-nissart.com; 19 rue d'Alsace-Lorraine; menus €12.99, €15.99 & €19.99; ⏰ lunch & dinner Tue-Sat Aug-Jun) No frills, just good solid portions of traditional Niçois fare, served speedily and with a smile, ensure this small three generation–run family bistro near the train station makes it in practically every travel guide. Going strong since 1908, its clientele nonetheless remains fairly local.

La Taca d'Oli (☎ 04 93 80 70 93; 35 rue Pairolière; bagna cauda/pan €16/17.50; ⏰ lunch & dinner Wed-Thu) No wonder the *bagna cauda* (raw mixed veg dipped into a pot of warm tangy anchovy paste known as *anchoïade*) at this tiny old-town bistro dating from 1947 is so legendary: the same chef has been making it here for the past 17 years! A shared portion of *bagna pan* (raw red mullet and sea bream fillets dipped in hot fish soup) ordered alongside it makes a perfect supper for two.

La Cantine de Lulu (☎ 04 93 62 15 33; 26 rue Alberti; starters/mains €10/15; ⏰ lunch & dinner Tue-Fri, lunch Mon Sep-Jul) Lulu – Lucien Brych – is the name behind this illustrious bistro where local specialities and all the great French classics are eaten with vigour by an appreciative, regular crowd. Friday is aïoli, stockfish (€22.50) and *bouillabaisse* (order in advance) day. Lulu's Canteen is small; arrive on the dot.

Le Merenda (4 rue Raoul Bosio; mains €15; ⏰ lunch & dinner Mon-Fri) Simple, solid Niçois cuisine by former Michelin-starred chef Dominique Le Stanc draws the tourist crowds to this pocket-sized bistro with stool seating (rub backs with the person sitting at the table behind you), a tiny open kitchen and the day's menu chalked on the board. Quintessential dishes to try include *tripes à la Niçoise* (tripe) with *panisse* (potato-sized chunks of fried chickpea) and stockfish; ask to taste a smidgen of the latter before ordering, if you're unsure. No credit cards, no telephone; same-day reservations in person only.

L'Escalinada (☎ 04 93 62 11 71; www.escalinada.fr; 22 rue Pairolière; menu €23; ⏰ lunch & dinner daily mid-Dec–mid-Nov) Little has changed at this enchanting old-town *auberge* (inn; think red-and-white checked tablecloths) for decades: all the old Niçois favourites are cooked up here alongside a clutch of more adventurous specialities – pig nose salad and breaded sheep testicles (sweet breads) included. Get here early to snag a table on its candlelit street terrace. No credit cards.

La Petite Maison (☎ 04 93 92 59 59; 11 rue St-François de Paule; mains €13-35; ⏰ lunch & dinner Mon-Sat) A sterling reputation props up this ode to contemporary Niçois cuisine, framed in a stylish clean-cut interior with concrete floor, potted olive trees, crisp white tablecloths and art on the walls. Whet your appetite with a shared

TOP FIVE BIG-NAME DINES

Nice is graced with a handful of already big-name or rapidly rising chefs, so gourmands can dedicate several hours to the simple pleasure of dining decadently well.

- Bruno Clément is the name behind **Terres de Truffes** (☎ 04 93 62 07 68; 11 rue St-François de Paule; menu €40, mains from €18; ☾ lunch & dinner Mon-Sat), an exclusive deli-bistro where the much-acclaimed truffle chef prepares the region's famous fungi in every imaginable form. Truffles star in every dish, most of which you simply won't find anywhere else. Light lunch eaters can always opt for a selection of truffle tapas (€5 a shot) followed by apple pie with truffle caramel!

- A big address houses culinary giant, chef Bruno Sohn, who stuns palates with a cuisine oozing originality at **Le Padouk** (☎ 04 92 14 76 00; 15 promenade des Anglais; lunch starters/mains/desserts €15/23/8, evening starters/mains €25/40, lunch menu €35, dinner menus €50 & €70; ☾ lunch & dinner daily), on the 3rd floor of Palais de la Méditerranée. Be it octopus and red mullet prepared like stockfish, or a sweet feast of almond jelly, roasted apricots, exotic sorbet and basil syrup, Sohn insists on throwing an imaginative twist into his cooking pot. If the sheer length of dish names defeats you before you start (or you simply want to lunch), opt for simpler Le 3e (lunch buffet €24, *plancha* €29), the lounge bar across from the terrace pool where meats are barbecued *à la plancha* (on the griddle).

- His full name is Jouni Tormanen but everyone knows this overtly modern, 30-something Finnish chef, under the wing of Ducasse until branching out on his own, as Jouni. In southern France since 1993, the gastronomic dynamo impresses at his 'taste workshop', **Atelier du Goût** (☎ 04 97 08 14 80; www.jouni.fr; 10 rue Lascaris; menus €30-70; ☾ lunch & dinner Tue-Sat) with a simple choice (but still dead tricky to choose) of three starters, three mains and three desserts. He landed his first Michelin star in 2006 and in early 2007 he breathed new life into Nice's legendary **La Réserve** (☎ 04 97 08 14 80; 60 blvd Franck Pilatte), a *belle époque* building (built in 1876 as a hotel) at the port. Interior décor is pure Art Deco and the contemporary space combines gourmet restaurant with ground-floor lounge and rooftop bar. Watch this space.

- He might only be 26 years old but Japanese hotshot Keisuke Matsushima, alias Kei, makes heads turn at **Kei's Passion** (☎ 04 93 82 26 06; www.keispassion.com in French; place Croix de Marbre, 22ter rue de France; lunch menus €23 & €30, dinner menus €43, €65 & €90; ☾ lunch & dinner), a minimalist space dedicated to gastronomy and crowned with a shiny Michelin star within a year of its opening. Cuisine is overwhelmingly Mediterranean (lots of Italian influence in there) with a subtle dash of the Orient, while the wine cellar, notably, is predominantly organic.

- Inside Hôtel Négresco's Chantecler (p272), chef Bruno Turbot cooks impeccable classic French cuisine with flair at **Chantecler** (☎ 04 93 16 64 00; 37 promenade des Anglais; lunch menus €45 & €60, dinner menus €90 & €130; ☾ lunch & dinner Wed-Sun Feb-Dec). This crimson-coloured place may have lost one of its two Michelin stars (down the back of a Regency sofa?), but remains a mind-blowing extravaganza. Vegetarians get their own evening *menu* (€85).

plate of five/seven Niçois starters (€18/30), followed by a locally caught red mullet or fried snails.

Fishy

A couple of touristy places on cours Saleya serve impressive seafood platters, while you can feast on as many *moules* (mussels) as you can eat at unpretentious, cheerful **Festival de la Moule** (☎ 04 93 62 02 12; 20 cours Saleya).

Grand Café de Turin (☎ 04 93 62 29 52; 5 place Garibaldi; seafood platters €21.10-34.85; ☾ 8am-midnight)

For mountains of fresh-from-the-sea, no-frills shellfish served in an authentic 1900 interior or outside beneath the awning, hit Grand Café de Turin. And yes, the fishmonger opening oysters like there's no tomorrow does do that all day long. Don't miss the sea urchins in season (September to April).

Les Viviers (☎ 04 93 16 00 48; www.les-viviers-nice .com; 22 rue Alphonse Karr; mains €20; ☾ lunch & dinner Mon-Sat Sep-Jul) A magnificent choice of oysters, urchins and other shellfish – not to mention a Breton lobster grilled alive (€69) – are consumed to the sweet tinkle of a piano at this seafood temple. Try the Viviers 1900s-styled bistro next door for something less rarefied.

French

Karr (☎ 04 93 82 18 31; 10 rue Alphonse Karr; mains €21-32; ☿ lunch & dinner Mon-Sat) Hugely popular for lunch with working 30-somethings, this spacious contemporary eating space with crowded street terrace is just the ticket for dining with a difference: think mussel soup, warm oven-baked goat's cheese with honey and almonds, lobster risotto or veal escalope with a stuffed artichoke (in season).

Aphrodite (☎ 04 93 85 63 53; www.restaurant -aphrodite.com; 10 blvd Dubouchage; lunch/dinner menu €23/60; ☿ lunch & dinner Tue-Sun) The uninspired interior might be nothing to write home about (although the tomato plants growing in pots around the glassed-in terrace are a nice touch) but David Faure's food is. Dish names take up at least three lines on the menu, sauces are delicate, there are shoals of fish, and hats off to the chef for his wholly vegetarian *menu* (€35).

11e Art (☎ 04 93 87 57 15; nice11art@yahoo.fr; 11 rue Meyerbeer; plat du jour €12, starters/mains €15/20; ☿ lunch & dinner Wed-Sun, dinner Tue) A relative newbie on the contemporary dining scene, this hybrid lounge-bar–restaurant is a smart, chic affair with steely bar stools out front and sofa seating in an ultracool air-con interior.

World

Boros (☎ 04 93 88 90 75; 4 rue Dalpozzo; lunch platter €12-15, mezze for 1/2/3 people €12/30/45; ☿ lunch Mon-Sun) Don't tell anyone about this oriental *épicerie* (grocery) specialising in Greek, Lebanese, Turkish and Armenian delicacies that serves delicious lunches in the form of generous mixed platters.

Indyana (☎ 04 93 80 67 69; 11 rue Gustave Deloye; mains €21-32; ☿ lunch & dinner Tue-Sat, dinner Mon) Refined and elegant, Indyana lures a dressy set into its lair to nibble on minimalist Asian (tempura and sashimi) and other world cuisines. Pigeon breast in the company of a peachy peach chutney tickled our taste buds.

Cafés & Quick Eats

Quaff beer, coffee and cocktails on shaded café and bar terraces on busy cours Saleya and pedestrian rue Masséna. For unusual freshly squeezed juices and soya milk or yogurt smoothies, hit the **Juice Bar** (16 rue de la Préfecture).

Cheap, quick Vietnamese and Chinese eateries abound in the train station area around rue Paganini, rue d'Italie and rue d'Alsace-Lorraine.

Fleur de Café (☎ 04 93 88 95 25; 7bis rue du Maréchal Joffre; salads €12-14; ☿ 10.30am-6.30pm Tue-Sat) Ice-cream cocktails, infusions, a dizzying choice of freshly squeezed fruit juices and delicious homemade cakes are the trademarks of this sweet café, strung around a small boutique selling nice stuff for the kitchen and home.

Le Pain Quotidien (☎ 04 93 62 94 32; 1 rue St-François de Paule; breakfast €6-8, salads €10.50-13.20, tartines €5.60-8.20; ☿ 7am-7pm) Startlingly good organic (not to mention six other) breakfasts and lavishly topped lunchtime *tartines* (toasted bread) are highlights at this rustic café overlooking the flower market.

Fenocchio (☎ 04 93 80 72 52; 2 place Rossetti; 1-/2-/3-scoop cone €2/3.50/4.50; ☿ 9am-midnight Feb-Oct) Dither too long over the 70-plus flavours of ice cream and sorbet at this unforgettable *glacier* and you'll never make it to the front of the queue. Eschew predictable favourites and indulge in a new taste sensation: black olive, tomato-basil, rhubarb, avocado, rosemary, *calisson* (almond biscuit frosted with icing sugar), lavender, ginger or liquorice. Cone prices are the same whether you lick on the move or order at the counter and then nip inside to help yourself to a jug of iced water before sitting down at a table outside.

Self-Catering

The market adds a whole new dimension to food shopping. Buy the catch of the day at the **fish market** (place St-François; ☿ 6am-1pm Tue-Sun) and fruit, veg, olives, oil and candied fruits at the heaving open-air **food market** (cours Saleya; ☿ 6am-1pm Tue-Sun) wedged between the sea and the old town. Nearby, rue du Collet and its continuation, rue Pairolière, are lined with cheese shops, bakeries, tripe shops and more.

Mainstream supermarkets:

Monoprix (42 av Jean Médecin & place Garibaldi; ☿ 8.30am-8.45pm Mon-Sat)

Casitalia (93 rue de France) Italian supermarket.

DRINKING

Any of the café-terraces on cours Saleya are lovely for an early evening aperitif. Karr (left) lures a local, more sophisticated set and Vieux Nice's bounty of pubs (p277) attracts the noisy, boisterous crowd at the other end of the drinking spectrum.

VEGETARIAN SURPRISE

■ **Zucca Magica** (The Magic Pumpkin; ☎ 04 93 56 25 27; 4bis quai Papacino; lunch/dinner menu €17/27; 🕑 lunch & dinner Tue-Sat; **V**) You'll either love it or you'll hate it…the idea of someone else deciding what you eat. Bursting with vegetarian surprises and guaranteed to thrill, top Italian chef Marco Folicardi moved from Rome to Nice to open this much-vaunted 'veg, egg and cheese restaurant' – the only one of its kind on the Riviera – where one fixed *menu confiance* is served, dictated simply by the market and *la fantasie du chef*. Seating is on a small (traffic-noisy) street terrace or inside amid a fabulous collection of pumpkins. Bring along a gargantuan appetite and an advance reservation at weekends.

■ **Le Speakeasy** (☎ 04 93 85 59 50; 7 rue Lamartine; menus €12-14; 🕑 lunch & dinner Thu & Fri, lunch Mon-Sat) This teeny weeny slice of veggie heaven run by Jane, a former English teacher and an American (hence the name of the place), cooks up unusual organic meals and juices. Takeaways available.

Le Before (☎ 04 93 87 85 59; www.before-nice.com in French; 18 rue du Congrès; 🕑 6pm-midnight Mon-Sat) It's all very hip and trendy at Le Before, chiefly an apéritif bar where a chic crowd gathers for an *apéro dînatoire* (apéritif with food) and background DJ mix.

Villa 14 (☎ 04 93 80 37 82; 14 av Félix Faure; 🕑 lunch & dinner Mon-Sat, dinner Sun) Dining is almost a passing thought at Villa 14, a contemporary eating space (off place Masséna) best known for its superlarge, great-at-any-time-of-the-day terrace beneath a turquoise awning. Lounge DJs kick in on weekends and on summer evenings.

L'ybane (city centre ☎ 04 93 16 26 26; 1 rue de la Liberté; Vieux Nice ☎ 04 93 92 92 32; 9 rue de la Préfecture; lunch platters €10-12; 🕑 lunch & dinner Mon-Sat, dinner Sun) An eating joint too, this sultry lounge bar with food touts a busy street terrace and minimalist interior topped with a glass chandelier. The food is Lebanese.

Le Water Bar (☎ 04 93 62 56 50; 10 rue de la Loge; 🕑 noon-midnight Mon-Sat) Slurp designer bottles of water from around the globe (fancy a Chinese lychee-flavoured water?) to the sound of lounge and electro. Décor is exotic.

La Casa del Sol (☎ 04 93 62 87 28; 69 quai des États Unis; 🕑 Tue-Sat) A former bar turned into a restaurant, new look Casa del Sol is still a busy drinking spot come 11pm, when affluent 30-somethings hang out on sofa seating over cocktails and a dancey DJ mix.

ENTERTAINMENT

Find cinema and theatre schedules online at www.nice.webcity.fr (in French); pick up *Nice Rendezvous* (free) from tourist offices; or buy *Semaine des Spectacles* (€0.80, weekly)

from newsstands. Tickets for most events are sold at FNAC inside the Nice Étoile shopping centre (opposite).

Primary venues for live music are the pubs of Vieux Nice (opposite); for details of sounds and musicians to listen out for, see p70.

Nightclubs

Le Klub (☎ 04 93 16 27 56, 06 60 55 26 61; www.leklub.net; 6 rue Halévy; admission free Wed-Fri & Sun, incl 1 drink up to €15 Sat; 🕑 midnight-5am Wed-Sun) This is not only the hippest gay venue in town; it is simply *the* hippest venue in town *point* (full stop). The best DJs on the Riviera can be heard here while the ever-popular Top 50 nights (every second Sunday) with DJ Max (p308) draw wild crowds.

Blue Moon (☎ 06 29 50 35 56; 26 quai Lunel; admission €12, free before 1am Fri & Sat; 🕑 Wed-Sat 11pm-5am) R & B, rap and house are among the mixed sounds to throb out of this port-side club. Friday is usually themed and Thursday yields various alcohol deals – like as much as Sex on the Beach a girl can drink until 3am.

Ôdace (☎ 04 93 82 37 66; www.odace-club.com; 29 rue Alphonse Karr; admission free; 🕑 7pm-5am Thu-Sat) Lounge bar and club, this huge and happening drinking space is popular both after work and after midnight. Sushi and *nems* (spring rolls) quell hunger pangs.

Le Liqwid (☎ 04 93 76 14 28; www.liqwid-lounge.com; 10 rue Alexandre Mari; admission incl 1 drink €12; 🕑 6pm-midnight Mon-Sat) An exclusive bar-cum-club with food to boot (lunch is served noon to 2pm), Liqwid cooks fusion cuisine in a steely Art Deco interior that, late in the evening, stages some of Nice's best visiting DJs. There's a tough door policy.

Cinema

Cinéma Nouveau Mercury (☎ 08 36 68 81 06; 16 place Garibaldi) and **Cinéma Rialto** (☎ 08 36 68 00 41; 4 rue de Rivoli) screen original-language films.

Gay & Lesbian Venues

The hottest nightclub in town just happens to be gay; see Le Club, opposite.

Le Flag (☎ 04 93 87 29 67; www.le-flag.com; 6 rue Eugène Emmanuel; ⏰ 7pm-1am Wed & Thu, 8pm-2am Fri & Sat) It might be gay (with fabulously gay, as in colourful, interior to boot and a house cocktail called Rainbow), but this modern art gallery and lounge bar has its finger bang on the pulse for pleasing punters of all shapes and sexual orientations.

Le Smarties (☎ 04 93 62 30 75; www.nice-smarties .com; 4 rue Défly; ⏰ 10pm-late Sep-Jul) Nothing to do with chocolate and as mixed as gay, this smart retro *bar de la lounge* behind MAMAC has a 1970s décor, cocktails galore and a great line-up of electro soires. The crowd is wholly local and eclectic.

Blue Boy Enterprise (☎ 04 93 44 68 24; 9 rue Jean-Baptiste Spinetta; admission free, €12 Sat; ⏰ 11pm-4am) Nice's oldest gay club.

Theatre & Opera

Théâtre National de Nice (TNN; ☎ 04 93 13 90 90; contact@theatredenice.org; promenade des Arts; box office ⏰ 2-7pm Tue-Sat & 1hr before performances) Classical music, plays and dance are staged at the city's leading theatre, a modern construction.

Opéra de Nice (☎ 04 92 17 40 79; www.opera-nice .org in French; 4 & 6 rue St-François de Paule; tickets €7-75; box office ⏰ 9.30am-6pm Mon-Sat) From October to mid-June, operas and orchestral concerts are held at this Garnier-designed opera house that was built in 1885.

In summer, performances take to the stage beneath the stars at the atmospheric **Théâtre de Verdure** (promenade des Anglais; tickets €10-30; ⏰ mid-May–mid-Sep); the tourist office has details.

SHOPPING

Mad about markets? Buy blooms at the daily **flower market** (cours Saleya; ⏰ 6am-5.30pm Tue-Sat, 6am-1pm Sun), and jumble goods at the weekly **flea market** (cours Saleya; ⏰ 8am-5pm Mon). On Saturday, browse place du Palais de Justice for **antique books** (1st & 4th Sat of month), **art** (1st, 3rd & 4th Sat) or old **stamps, coins & postcards** (1st, 2nd & 3rd Sat).

Rue Paradis, av de Suède, rue Alphonse Karr and rue du Maréchal Joffre are lined with upmarket boutiques. Mainstream fashion lines av Jean Médecin, with shopping centre **Centre Commercial Nice Étoile** at No 30 and department store **Galeries Lafayette** at No 3.

Art & Antiques

Small-time artists and crafts people labour in a fascinating line-up of *ateliers* (workshops) in Vieux Nice on rue Droite. Bigger prices are commanded by pieces sold in the contemporary galleries and shops on rue Dalpozzo. Top cat is **Galerie Ferrero** (☎ 04 93 88 34 44; www.galerie ferrero.com; 2 rue du Congrès), Nice's most dazzling, dating from 1954 and specialising in works by Arman, César and other Nice New Realists.

PUB TALK

Vieux Nice is loaded with Brit-styled boozers that pull in the punters with a mixed bag of live music, pub quizzes, big-screen-TV sport, Sunday roasts, karaoke, student nights and happy hours lasting three hours. Most open 11am to 2am daily. Best for:

- Fish'n'chips, Irish beef'n'Guinness pie and a hot vibe – bar of the moment, Irish **Ma Nolan's** (☎ 04 93 80 23 87; www.ma-nolans.com; 2 rue St-François de Paule)
- Beach parties, theme nights, meeting other travellers – legend in its own time **Wayne's** (☎ 04 93 13 46 99; www.waynes.fr; 15 rue de la Préfecture)
- Pool table, table football, cheap drinks and karaoke (Tuesday and Thursday) – Irish **McMahon's** (☎ 04 93 13 84 07; www.mcmahonspub.com; 50 blvd Jean Jaurès)
- Live music (chill soloists early on, bands late) – **Thor Pub** (☎ 04 93 62 49 90; www.thor-pub.com; 34 cours Saleya)
- Bottled beer and whisky – Dutch-themed **De Klomp** (☎ 04 93 92 42 85; 6 rue Mascoïnat)
- All-round pub vibe – Irish **Paddy's Pub** (☎ 04 93 80 06 75; 40 rue Droite)
- BBC on the box – **O'Hara's** (☎ 04 93 80 43 22; 22 rue Droite)

GASTRONOMIC SHOP

- Chocolate-coated orange slices, figs and almonds from **Confiserie Florian** (☎ 04 93 55 43 50; www.confiserieflorian.com; 14 quai Papacino)

- Crystallised fruit based on family recipes dating back to 1820 from **Henri Auer Confiserie** (☎ 04 93 85 77 98; www.maison-auer.com; 7 rue St-François de Paule)

- Olive oil fresh from the mill at **Moulin à Huile d'Olive Alziari** (☎ 04 93 85 76 92; 14 rue St-François de Paule); from €9 per litre for extra virgin

- Truffles in every guise (oil, purée, laced in acacia honey) from the boutique of **Terres de Truffes** (p274)

- Wine from *cavistes* (cellarmen) who know what they're talking about: **Cave de la Tour** (☎ 04 93 80 03 31; 3 rue de la Tour), run by the same family since 1947; and **Caves Caprioglio** (☎ 04 93 85 66 57; www.cavescaprioglio.com in French; 16 rue de la Préfecture), since 1910, local wine from €1.60 a litre

- Decadent cakes and chocolates from **LAC** (☎ 04 93 55 37 74; 18 rue Barla)

Shop for antiques under one roof at portside **Les Puces de Nice** (place Robilante; ☷ 10am-7pm Tue-Sat Jun-Sep, 10am-6pm Tue-Sat Oct-May).

GETTING THERE & AWAY

Air

Nice international airport, **Aéroport International Nice-Côte d'Azur** (☎ 08 20 42 33 33, flight information ☎ 08 36 69 55 55; www.nice.aeroport.fr), is 6km west of the city centre on the seafront.

Boat

Ferries to/from Corsica use the **Gare Maritime** (☎ 04 89 88 98 28; www.riviera-ports.com) at the port: **SNCM ferries** (☎ 04 93 13 66 66; ticket counter ☷ 6am-7pm Mon-Fri, 6am-noon & 1-5pm Sat, 6am-10am & 1-5pm Sun) sails in/out of **Terminal 1** (quai du Commerce); **Corsica Ferries** (☎ 08 25 09 50 95; ticket counter ☷ 6-8am & 9am-6pm Mon-Fri, 6-8am & 11am-6pm Sat & Sun) uses **Terminal 2** (quai Amiral Infernet); while the bright orange ships of EasyCruise dock by quai Lunel. See p421 for more details.

Bus

Several bus companies serve the coast and the Niçois hinterland from the **intercity bus station** (☎ 08 92 70 12 06; 5 blvd Jean Jaurès; information counter ☷ 8.30am-5.30pm Mon-Fri, 9am-noon & 1-4pm Sat), including **Intercars** (☎ 04 93 80 08 70), which runs various long-haul services to European destinations (see p419).

Within the Alpes-Maritimes *département*, single bus fares are a flat €1.30 irrespective of distance. Drivers sell tickets. Services are at least hourly Monday to Saturday (less frequent Sunday) to/from Vence (50 minutes), Grasse (1¼ hours), St-Jean Cap Ferrat (30 minutes)

and Èze (20 minutes). Buses to/from Menton (line 100; 55 minutes) and Cannes (line 200; 1¼ hours) stop at most towns en route.

Destinations outside Alpes-Maritimes include Aix-en-Provence (single/day return €23.50/28, 2¼ hours, five daily), Marseille (single/day return €23.50/28, 2¾ hours, five daily), Digne-les-Bains (€23, 2¼ hours, four weekly) and Toulon (single/day return €23/25, 2½ hours, two daily Monday to Saturday) via Hyères.

Ski resorts Valberg (2½ hours, one daily mid-December to mid-April) and Isola 2000 (two hours, one to three daily) command a flat €8 single fare.

Train

Nice's main train station, **Gare Nice Ville** (Gare Thiers; av Thiers) is 1.2km north of the beach. In town, tickets are sold at the **SNCF Boutique** (cnr rue de la Liberté & passage E Negrin; ☷ 8.30am-6.30pm Mon-Sat).

There are fast, frequent services (up to 40 daily in each direction) from Nice to towns along the coast between St-Raphaël and Ventimiglia (Italy), including Antibes (€3.70, 30 minutes), Cannes (€5.60, 40 minutes), Menton

---

POSTCARD HOME

Dear Mum. Pic on the front is a shot of the blue chairs on promenade des Anglais taken by Niçois photographer **Jean-Louis Martinetti** (☎ 04 93 85 61 30; www.martinetti .fr; 17 rue de la Préfecture; ☷ 10am-noon & 3-7pm Tue-Sat). His work is just brilliant. Love N.

(€4.20, 35 minutes), Monaco (€3.10, 25 minutes) and St-Raphaël (€9.80, 45 minutes).

The mountain railway operated by **Chemins de Fer de la Provence** (☎ 04 97 03 80 80; www.trainprovence.com) offers a scenic trip to Digne-les-Bains (€17.65, 3¼ hours, four or five times daily) from Nice's **Gare du Sud** (☎ 04 93 82 10 17; 4bis rue Alfred Binet). See p245 for full details.

GETTING AROUND
To/From the Airport
Bus 99 provides a speedy link between Nice's main train station and the airport (€4, 15 minutes, every 30 minutes between 8am and 9pm), continuing to the port mid-June to mid-September. For the bus station and Vieux Nice, hop aboard bus 98.

From the airport bus station, next to Terminal 1, there are daily buses to destinations including Aix, Avignon, Cannes, Grasse, Isola 2000, Menton, Monaco, Valberg and Vence. Many buses stop at the Terminal 2, too.

A **taxi** (☎ 04 93 13 78 78) from the airport to downtown Nice costs €20 to €30 (cash payment only), depending on the time of day and which terminal you're leaving from.

To/From the Port
Free shuttle buses shunt ferry passengers between the port, train station and several upmarket hotels. Otherwise, buses 1 and 2 link the port with av Jean Médecin.

Bicycle
Holiday Bikes (☎ 04 93 16 01 62; www.holiday-bikes.com; 34 av Auber) and **JML** (☎ 04 93 16 07 00; 34 av Auber; right) as well as Roller Station (p269) rent out road and/or mountain bikes for around €5/10/15 per hour/day/24 hours.

Bus
Local city buses are run by **Ligne d'azur** (☎ 08 10 06 10 06; www.lignedazur.com), with its main hub on sq du Général Leclerc. Time-stamped tickets are valid for one hour and cost €1.30/10 for one/10 rides or €4 for a one-day pass (which covers trips to/from the airport). Passes are sold at **Ligne d'azur agencies** (10 av Félix Faure & 29 av Malausséna; ۞ 7.15am-7pm Mon-Fri, 8am-6pm Sat) and in *tabacs* (tobacconists). Passengers travelling without a ticket/time-stamped ticket risk a €37.80/25.20 on-the-spot fine.

Bus 12 links the train station with promenade des Anglais (15 minutes), and bus 30 is the bus for Vieux Nice.

Car & Motorcycle
All the major car rental agencies are at the airport and snug in a **train station annexe** (12 av Thiers; ۞ 8am-1pm & 2-7pm Mon-Fri, 8am-1pm & 10am-7pm Sat, 8am-noon & 5-7pm Sun).

Opposite the station, Holiday Bikes and JML rent out 50cc scooters/125cc motorcycles for around €40/55 a day.

Parking costs €2-plus per hour and is difficult. Most hotels without private parking have deals with nearby car parks: when making your reservation, ask if the hotel can give you a discount parking card.

Taxi
Call **Central Taxi Riviera Nice** (☎ 04 93 13 78 78) to order a taxi by phone, or pick one up at a rank: in front of the train station; at place Garibaldi; on promenade des Anglais and so on. Journeys are metered and rates (pick-up charge €2.50, plus €1.56/km) must be displayed inside the cab. Night rates (€2.08/km) apply from 7pm and 7am, all day Sunday and on bank holidays. The minimum fare is €5.50.

Tram
At time of writing, the first line of the city's state-of-the-art tramway system was scheduled to be operational from summer 2007: line 1 will run for 8.7km between the north and east of the city. For the latest update, see www.tram-nice.org or call ☎ 08 11 00 20 06.

By 2010 a second line will run from the port, along rue Hôtel des Postes/rue de la Buffa, then along promenade des Anglais and beyond the airport, eventually stretching all the way to Cagnes-sur-Mer.

THE THREE CORNICHES

Three parallel roads offering unparalleled views link Nice and Menton, passing quaint perched villages, epic monuments and the principality of Monaco on the way. The Corniche Inférieure (aka Basse Corniche, the Lower Corniche and the N98) sticks closely to the nearby train line and villa-lined waterfront. The Moyenne Corniche (the N7) is the middle road, clinging to the hillside and affording great views if you can find somewhere to pull over. The Grande Corniche leaves Nice as the D2564 and is the most breathtaking.

The Corniche Inférieure is well served by bus and train from Nice; the two higher roads and the entire Niçois hinterland are practically inaccessible without your own wheels.

CORNICHE INFÉRIEURE

Heading east from Nice to Menton, the Corniche Inférieure, built in the 1860s, passes through the towns of Villefranche-sur-Mer, St-Jean-Cap Ferrat, Beaulieu-sur-Mer, Èze-sur-Mer, Cap d'Ail and Monaco.

This lower coastal road is well served by buses and trains. Bus 100, the fastest line, runs the length of the Corniche Inférieure between Nice and Menton, stopping at all the villages along the way (every 15 minutes from 6am to 8pm), including Villefranche-sur-Mer (eight minutes) and Beaulieu-sur-Mer (11 minutes). The less direct bus 111 serves St-Jean-Cap Ferrat (25 minutes), Villefranche (10 minutes) and Beaulieu (45 minutes). Fares are a flat €1.30.

Nice–Ventimiglia (Italy) trains run along the coast every 10 to 20 minutes between 7am and 6pm, stopping at Villefranche-sur-Mer (€1.40, eight minutes), Beaulieu-sur-Mer (€1.70, 14 minutes), Cap d'Ail (€2.70, 21 minutes), Monaco (€3.10, 25 minutes), Cap Martin-Roquebrune (€3.70, 32 minutes) and Menton (€4.20, 38 minutes).

Villefranche-sur-Mer

pop 6649

Heaped above a picture postcard–perfect harbour, this picturesque village overlooks the Cap Ferrat peninsula and – with its ultra-deep *rade* (harbour) – is prime port of call for Titanic-sized cruise ships (Nice harbour isn't deep enough for the biggest cruise liners so they moor here and passengers get ferried to/from Nice in smaller boats).

Villefranche's 14th-century old town with its tiny, evocatively named streets, broken by twisting staircases and glimpses of the sea, is reason enough to visit. Don't miss eerie arcaded **rue Obscure**, a historical monument a block in from the water.

Above the old fishing harbour, **Port de la Santé**, lies place Amélie Pollonnais, filled by a Sunday **art and antique market**. From here a coastal path runs around the citadel to Port Royal de la Darse, fortified between 1725 and 1737 and sheltering pleasure boats today. En route there are good views of Cap Ferrat and the wooded slopes of the Golfe de Villefranche (Gulf of Villefranche), a Russian naval base in the 19th century during their conflicts with the Turks.

Villefranche was a favourite of Jean Cocteau, who sought solace here in 1924 after the death of his companion Raymond Radiguet.

ORIENTATION & INFORMATION

From Villefranche-sur-Mer train station, follow the signs to the old town, whose main street (rue du Poilu) is on the same vertical level as the station; or take the steps down to quai Amiral Courbet and the shingle beach. To get to rue Obscure from the harbour, walk up the unpromising-looking staircase at 7–9 quai Amiral Courbert (between La Mère Germaine and L'Oursin Bleu) and turn right.

The **tourist office** (☎ 04 93 01 73 68; www.villefranche-sur-mer.com; Jardin François Binon; ⏰ 9am-7pm Jul & Aug, 9am-noon & 2-6.30pm Mon-Sat Jun & Sep, 9am-noon & 2-6pm Mon-Sat Oct-May), a glass-fronted pavilion, is at the top of Villefranche in the newer town. From place Philibert, outside the citadel, follow av du Maréchal Joffre upwards, then bear left onto av du Maréchal Foch. The office is 100m along on your left.

SIGHTS

Chapelle St-Pierre

Neglected 14th-century waterfront **Chapelle St-Pierre** (☎ 04 93 76 90 70; admission €2; ⏰ 10am-noon & 3-7pm Tue-Sun, shorter hrs rest of year, closed mid-Nov–mid-Dec) was used by fishermen to store nets until a 68-year-old Jean Cocteau (1889–1963) transformed it into a mirage of sweeping, mystical frescoes. Scenes of angels, St Peter's life and the Roma of Stes-Maries de la Mer are interspersed with patterns, stars and the apocalyptic Eye of God design. The engraving above the (oddly, inner) door reads 'Enter this building as if it were made of living stone'.

Mass is celebrated here on 29 June, the feast day of St Peter, patron saint of fishermen.

Citadel

The imposing **Fort St-Elme** (place Emmanuel Philibert) was built by the duke of Savoy between 1554 and 1559 to defend the gulf. Nowadays the walls shelter a scattering of cultural doodahs, including the town hall, some well-combed public gardens and a clutch of museum collections: the **Musée Volti** (☎ 04 93 76 33 27; admission free; ⏰ 9am-noon & 2.30-7pm Mon & Wed-Sat, 2.30-7pm Sun Jul & Aug, to 6pm Mon & Wed-Sat Jun & Sep) displays voluptuous bronzes by Villefranche sculptor Antoniucci Volti (1915–89).

Summer ushers in some fine outdoor events, including open-air musical concerts

ITALY FLITS

Titillated by Italianate Nice? Go, taste the real McCoy Italy across the border. Our favourite day trips from Nice (or elsewhere along the coast):

- Lunch in style on the Italian Riviera at **La Réserve** (☎ 0184 26 13 22; Via Arziglia 20, Bordighera; antipasti/pasta €10/15, fish & meat €20-32; ☽ lunch & dinner Tue-Sat, lunch Sun) in Bordighera. Feast on zucchini flower and scallop risotto, followed by a salt-encrusted catch of the day at this design-driven beach restaurant with sun-bathing and swimming decks between the rocks.

- Re-live 1960s bohemia in **Bussana Vecchia**, a medieval village wiped out by an earthquake on 23 February 1887 and rebuilt by artists in the 1960s. The artists moved in and transformed the rubble into the quaint international artists' village Bussana is today. Tempted to stay the night? Eccentric sculptor-turned-writer **Colin Wilmot** (☎ 0184 51 01 14; wilmot@dmw.it; B&B €75) is your man. Wilmot arrived in 1966 to drag his eccentric mother, British socialite Elizabeth Wilmot, back to London – only to fall madly in love with the stunning 360-degree panorama of sea and Alpine foothill enjoyed from the ruins she called home. In 2000 the Italian Cultural Ministry declared Bussana a historical monument, hence state property, and tried to evict Wilmot, among others. The case continues.

- Shop for leather and Italian fashion in **San Remo**, haunt of Europe's social elite in the 19th century. Italy's principal **flower market** (Corso Garibaldi; ☽ 6-8am Jun-Oct) is also here: watch the frantic bidding.

- Ogle at knock-off leather bags, lingerie, clothes, fresh pasta, fruit'n'veg, flowers and a mind-blowing array of other market produce at **Ventimiglia**'s vast, noisy and decades-old **Friday-morning market**. It stretches the length of the seashore.

during July's **Moments Musicaux de Citadelle**. The **Petits Matins de la Citadelle** (Citadel Early Mornings; ☎ 04 93 01 73 68; adult/under 12yr €8/3; ☽ 9am Fri May-Sep) includes a civilised breakfast in the museum garden, followed by a tour of the fortress and old town. Evening attractions include the 15-minute **changing of the guard** (7pm Jul & Aug) and movies screened beneath the stars in the open-air **Théâtre de la Citadelle** (tickets €7; ☽ 9.30pm Jun-Sep).

ACTIVITIES

Dark Pelican (☎ 04 93 01 76 54; www.darkpelican.com; quai Courbet) rents out boats of all shapes and sizes, starting at €60/110 per morning/day for a five-person, no-licence-required Fun Yak 450 (€500 deposit).

Underwater photography is one of the many activities offered by diving school **Aqua Pro Dive** (☎ 04 93 01 71 04; www.apdi-villefranche.com; 16 rue du Poilu). It rents out all the gear and organises baptism dives (€50) and diving courses (€337/407 for seven dives without/with equipment hire).

TOURS

Weekly two-hour boat tours to Monaco (adult/child €15/10, June to September), and one-hour trips around Cap Ferrat (adult/child €10/5, July and August) are organised by **Affrétement Maritime Villefranchois** (☎ 04 93 76 65 65; www.amv-sirenes.com; Port de la Santé; ☽ 9am-noon & 2-6pm Tue-Sun Jun-Sep). Boats leave from Port de la Santé, at the western end of quai Amiral Courbet.

The same company also sells tickets for dolphin- and whale-watching expeditions run by **Acti'Loisirs** (☎ 04 93 62 00 16; www.actiloisirs.com; ☽ Jun–mid-Sep). Boats sail several times weekly and expeditions last four hours.

SLEEPING

Villefranche has no *chambres d'hôtes*.

Hôtel Provençal (☎ 04 93 76 53 53; www.hotelprovencal .com; av Maréchal Joffre; d with garden/sea view low season from €63/89, high season €78/105; ☒) With its warm mustard-coloured façade and rooftop garden, this Logis de France hotel oozes a simple family charm. Over half of its rooms overlook the citadel gardens or harbour, and you can breakfast on a terrace shaded by orange trees. Wi-fi is available.

Hôtel Welcome (☎ 04 93 76 27 62; www.welcome hotel.com; 1 quai Amiral Courbet; d/ste from €132/199; ☽ mid-Dec–mid-Nov; P ☒) Cocteau stayed at this peachy 17th-century convent, which is opposite Chapelle St-Pierre. Every room has a wrought-iron balcony offset by sky-blue shutters overlooking the old port and there's an upmarket wine pier (☎ 04 93 76 27 40) open from 6pm, Tuesday to Sunday, where you can toast the sunset. Parking is €12.20.

EATING

Crack open freshly caught crustaceans on quai Amiral Courbet, a quay lined with restaurants including **Oursin Bleu** (Blue Sea Urchin; ☎ 04 93 01 90 12; 11 quai Amiral Courbet; menu €34) and **La Mère Germaine** (☎ 04 93 01 71 39; 7 quai Amiral Courbet; menu €37), the great-grandmother of Villefranchois cuisine cooking up prized *bouillabaisse* (€63; order 24 hours in advance) since 1938.

La Fille du Pêcheur (☎ 04 93 01 90 09; www.lafilledupecheur.com; 13 quai Amiral Courbet; mains €15, bouillabaisse €45; ☯ lunch & dinner) Shrimps flambéed in pastis, baby octopus cooked in garlic or a simple plate of deep-fried whitebait (€12) are fishy pleasures to be tucked in to with relish at the Fisherman's Daughter…called Krystel.

Beluga (☎ 04 93 80 28 34; www.beluga.eu.com; 3 quai Ponchardier; salads €13-18, mains €25; ☯ lunch & dinner Tue-Sun) This hip DJ bar serves food too – meat and fish grilled *à la plancha* (on a metal plate) – and is a prime spot for lounging over drinks and dinner on soft lounge-style seating. Beluga lives in an old Savoy waterfront palace.

St-Jean-Cap Ferrat
pop 2555

Once a drowsy fishing village, yacht-laden St-Jean-Cap Ferrat sits on the fringe of Cap Ferrat, a stunning wooded peninsula glittering with millionaire mansions framed by high walls and hedges to thwart peeping Toms and paparazzi. Famous former residents read like a *Who's Who* of the 19th and 20th centuries: writer Somerset Maugham owned the luxurious Villa Mauresque (his regular guests included Noël Coward, Ian Fleming and Evelyn Waugh); and Charlie Chaplin, Winston Churchill and Cocteau holidayed here (not together).

Some 14km of eucalyptus-scented walking paths cover the cape; the **tourist office** (☎ 04 93 76 08 90; ot.stjeancapferrat@tiscali.fr; 59 av Denis Séméria; ☯ 8.30am-6pm Mon-Fri, 10am-5pm Sat & Sun) has maps. A coastal path links the fine-shingle **Plage de Passable** on the western side with the café-lined **Port de Plaisance** on the east; the easiest spot to pick it up is from the beach. Walking right round the cape (6km) takes just a few hours and is easily the best way to see the cape.

On the western side of the cape, **Zoo Parc du Cap Ferrat** (☎ 04 93 76 07 60; www.zoocapferrat.com; adult/3-10yr €14/10; ☯ 9.30am-7pm summer, 9.30am-5.30pm winter), a small but well-landscaped botanical park with 300 animals to discover, provides easy entertainment for parents with small children in tow. In town, the tiny portside **Musée des Coquillages** (Shellfish Museum; ☎ 04 93 76 17 61; www.musee-coquillages.com; quai du Vieux Port; adult/under 18yr €2/1; ☯ 10am-12.30pm & 2-6pm Mon-Fri, 2-6pm Sat & Sun) is another crowd-pleaser.

SIGHTS
Villa Ephrussi de Rothschild

It's so extreme you just have to love it. A completely over-the-top *belle époque* confection, **Villa Ephrussi de Rothschild** (☎ 04 93 01 33 09;

TALK TO A FISHERMAN

His father fished alone at sea until the grand old age of 90 – as did his father, and his father. And Jean-Paul Roux, fourth generation fisherman, 60 years old and still going strong, is no exception to the family rule.

'My father fished every single day of his life. He had to eat every day – so he fished every day. That is the essential principle of the fisherman.

'The sea is my passion. It has to be. Fishing is a very hard trade and if you're not passionate about it, you wouldn't do it. I get up at 3am, am at sea from 4.30am until around 10am and work until at least noon sorting out my nets, the boat. There are different nets for every fish; at the moment it's the season for *chapon* and *bouille* (both used in *bouillabaisse*).

'My parents lived in Villefranche; my grandfather did. It is my town, although there are few Villefranchois left – just two or three fishermen like me.'

Jean-Paul can be found every morning from 10am to noon plucking seaweed from his nets aboard his traditional *pointu* (fishing boat), moored next to the quay opposite Hôtel Welcome. Most of the morning's catch goes straight into the kitchen of his daughter's restaurant, the Fisherman's Daughter (above). What's left he sells from a makeshift stall on the quay in front of his boat.

www.villa-ephrussi.com; adult/7-17yr €9.50/7; 10am-7pm Jul & Aug, to 6pm Feb-Jun & Sep & Oct, 2-6pm Mon-Fri, 10am-6pm Sat & Sun Nov-Feb) was commissioned by the eccentric Baroness Béatrice Ephrussi de Rothschild in 1912, and took 40 architects seven years to build. Pink is everywhere (the Baroness' favourite animals were flamingos because of their colour). Fragonard paintings, frilly Louis XVI furniture and flowery porcelain heighten the sugary effect. The 1st floor costs a further €3 to see (tour only), and includes the Monkey Room, decorated with painted monkey friezes on the panelled walls and filled with Béatrice's collection of cheeky porcelain chimps.

Out of this world are the villa's seven themed gardens. Stroll through Spanish, Japanese, Florentine, stone, cactus and pink rose areas, before entering the romantic French garden, landscaped to resemble a ship's deck (the Baroness had her 30 gardeners dress as sailors to complete the effect). A stream flows from the Temple of Love to a pool at the heart of the complex, where musical fountains dance every 20 minutes. Magical.

Bus 111, which links Nice and St-Jean-Cap Ferrat, stops at the foot of the driveway leading to the villa, at the northern end of av Denis Séméria (the D25). By train, get off at Beaulieu-sur-Mer, a 20-minute walk away.

SLEEPING & EATING

Hôtel L'Oursin (04 93 76 04 65; www.hoteloursin.com; 1 av Denis Séméria; d €50-80;) Very chambre d'hôte in mood, the Sea Urchin looks more like an antique shop than a hotel. Breakfast is enjoyed around a shared table in the salon, crammed with period furnishings, and two of the 14 rooms have a sea view. Lou the Alsatian and Rita the French bulldog are permanent residents. Wi-fi access is free.

La Voile d'Or (04 93 01 13 13; www.lavoiledor.fr; av Jean Mermoz; d garden/sea view low season from €229/249, high season from €414/444; menus €80, starters/mains €32/40;) In 1946 when the father of British film-maker Michael Powell bought the

Golden Sail (he sold his farm in Kent to do so), it had 25 rooms and just five bathrooms – that was luxury then. Today this legendary hotel on the water is the place to enjoy the Cap Ferrat good life: luxuries include sauna, two sea-water swimming pools, private beach and palatial rooms fit for a king and the long list of celebrities who've stayed here.

Restaurant du Port (04 93 76 04 46; av Jean Mermoz; menu €17, mains €12; lunch Wed-Mon) It looks so bog standard it scarcely warrants a second glance. But step inside and be stunned by a gregarious local crowd fuelling on excellent quality homemade fare – grilled sardines, steaks, fish carpaccio – courtesy of Richard and Jean-Marie. Sit at the table by the window for a lovely port view (and cooling sea breeze).

Le Sloop (04 93 01 48 63; Port de Plaisance; mains €10-20; lunch & dinner Jun–mid-Sep, lunch & dinner Thu-Tue mid-Sep–May) A blue-and-white nautical décor complements the seafaring spirit of the Sloop, the hot portside address of the moment where moneyed diners feast on seafood and shellfish. Advance bookings recommended.

Beaulieu-sur-Mer
pop 3700

Another popular belle époque resort for Europe's artists, poets and princes. French architect Gustave Eiffel lived at the waterfront Villa Durandy (now converted into luxury holiday apartments) from 1896 until his death in 1923. His next-door neighbour was Théodore Reinach, oddball scholar and originator of the awesome Villa Grecque Kérylos, Beaulieu's main attraction.

Remnants of the resort's golden age include the **Grand Casino** (04 93 76 48 00; www.casinobeaulieu.com; 4 av Fernand Dunan), built in 1928 and still drawing wildcards until sunrise; and neighbouring **La Rotonde** (1899), a wedding cake–white hotel used as a hospital during WWII. Across from the harbour are the **Jardins de L'Olivaie**, venue for a two-week Jazz Parade in August.

Beaulieu's shingle **beach** overlooks the Baie des Fourmis (Bay of Ants). From here, promenade Maurice Rouvier leads southwest beneath a hedgerow of lauriers-roses (oleanders) to the port of St-Jean-Cap Ferrat, a pleasant 2.5km stroll.

For other scenic seaside walks, ask at the **tourist office** (04 93 01 02 21; www.otbeaulieusurmer.fr; place Georges Clemenceau; 9am-12.30pm & 2-7pm Mon-Sat, 9am-12.30pm Sun), in the train station car park.

SIGHTS

Villa Grecque Kérylos

Eccentric and beautiful in equal measure is **Villa Grecque Kérylos** (☎ 04 93 76 44 09; www.villa-kerylos.com; av Gustave Eiffel; adult/7-17yr €8/6; ☯ 10am-7pm Jul & Aug, 10am-6pm Feb-Jun & Sep-Nov, 2-6pm Mon-Fri, 10am-6pm Sat & Sun Nov-Jan), a seven-years-in-the-making mansion designed by scholar-archaeologist Théodore Reinach (1860–1928) and architect Emmanuel Pontremoli (1865–1956) in 1902. Rooms and everything in them are based on ancient Greek models. The result: a perfect reproduction of a 1st-century Athenian villa.

Audio guides lead you from the *balanéion* (bathroom), with its dolphin-decorated marble tub, to the *triklinos* (dining room), complete with Greek-style recliners, frescoes and gold-leaf ceiling. Several hundred square metres of mosaics cover the floors (look out for the wonderful Minotaur), and meticulously made walnut, rosewood, coral, marble and lemonwood furniture fills the rooms. It's all so immaculate, you long to see where Théodore's kids lived (sadly, it's out of bounds).

In the gardens, a botanical trail highlights the ancient uses of plants typical to Greece and the French coast, while the **pottery workshop** (☎ 06 13 27 18 05; www.stonewaves.com; admission from €15; ☯ 1-6pm Thu-Sun term time, 1-6pm daily school holidays, to 7pm Jul & Aug) introduces adults and children to the art of pot decoration and mosaic work.

A combined ticket for the Kérylos and Rothschild villas costs €14.50/10.

SLEEPING & EATING

Hôtel Riviera (☎ 04 93 01 04 92; www.hotel-riviera.fr; 6 rue Paul Doumer; d low/mid/high season from €47/52/56; ☒ ☒) A breath of air in every sense (the place is nonsmoking), this tasteful two-star hotel with Carrara marble staircase, Italian granite floors, wrought-iron balconies and a hibiscus-laden summer patio just perfect for breakfasting really is hard to resist.

Villa Gracia (☎ 04 93 01 03 60; kikou.lacas@laposte.net; montée des Orangers; d/q incl breakfast €90/150; ☒ ☒) Olive, lemon and orange trees – not to mention sky-high palms – add an alluring scent to this delightful *chambre d'hôte* with peach façade, walled-garden and sage-green shutters. Inside the 19th-century villa, a rustic décor with period furnishings, old stone walls and classical music playing in the background shouts 'family house'. Madame Lacas hails from northern France and speaks excellent English; Monsieur speaks Croat.

La Réserve (☎ 04 93 01 00 01; www.reservebeaulieu .com; 5 blvd du Maréchal Leclerc; d with port/sea views from €475/840; ☒ ☒ ☒ ☒) Hard to believe this decadent post-WWII hang-out was a simple fish restaurant in 1880. One of the Riviera's most famed hotels, it has four stars, is very pink and boasts a guestbook to die for – Churchill, Walt Disney and Greta Garbo all stayed here. Hide from the paparazzi on the private pier, in the private saltwater pool and spa, or over champagne in the gourmet restaurant.

Cap d'Ail

pop 4550

Strolling and swimming are the key attractions of unpoetically named Cape of Garlic (actually derived from the Provençal 'Cap d'Abaglio', meaning 'Cape of Bees'). Motion-picture pioneer Auguste Lumière's grand house (1902) still stands among the palm trees and pines at 8 av Charles Blanc, while the spectacular Cocteau-designed **amphitheatre** serves as a youth theatre for the **Centre Méditerranéen**

AUTHOR'S CHOICE

Grand Hôtel du Cap Ferrat (☎ 04 93 76 50 50; www.grand-hotel-cap-ferrat.com; Cap Ferrat; d low/mid/high season pine-tree view from €205/330/480, sea view from €345/515/800; ☒ ☒ ☒ ☒) Wholly aristocratic, you'll know you've made it if you can stay here, a stunning multistarred *belle époque* (1908) wonder bathed in history and brilliantly set well away from the rabble on the tip of Cap Ferrat. Walls are stucco and marble; priceless sculptures stud the vast and lavish gardens tended by an army of 50 gardeners (20 in winter); and the gastronomic creations served in Le Cap (menus €55 & €95) are simply sublime, darling. But forget trying to snag one of the 44 rooms here; they're invariably booked. Rather, lap up the luxury beside the superrich and famous at the Club Dauphin (half/full day Monday to Friday €45/60, weekends €55/70), open from 10am to 7pm from April to September, an exquisitely landscaped club by the sea with pool, poolside restaurant, children's playground and adorable little seaside huts, complete with sun lounges and phone (low/mid/high season €100/130/160 per day). Lebanese diamond dealer and jeweller Robert Mouawad owns the hotel.

(☎ 04 93 78 21 59; www.centremed.monte-carlo.mc; chemin des Oliviers), a language, sports and arts centre.

Smoking and dogs are banned on **Plage Mala**, Cap d'Ail's gravel beach tucked into a cove. From Cap d'Ail train station, walk down the steps to av Raymond Gramaglia, a promenade from where Cap d'Ail's splendid **Sentier du Littoral** (coastal path) can be accessed. Information panels along the way explain the lush flora and plush villas you pass; during rough seas the seaside path is closed. Bear west for a 20-minute amble around rocks to the beach, or east for a more strenuous stroll to Monaco. The **tourist office** (☎ 04 93 78 02 33; www.cap-dail.com; 87bis av du 3 Septembre; ☼ 9am-noon & 2-6pm Mon-Fri, 9am-noon Sat), in the village centre on the N98, has plenty more information on walks.

July kicks off with the three-day **Fête de l'Abeille** (Bee Festival). In August four days of jazz concerts fill the seaside **Amphithéâtre de la Mer** (☎ 04 93 78 02 33; place Marquet), overlooking Cap d'Ail's small port.

Cap d'Ail's stunning seaside hostel **Relais International de la Jeunesse** (☎ 04 93 78 18 58; av Raymond Gramaglia; dm incl breakfast €14, dinner €9, half-/full board €22.50/28; ☼ Apr-Sep) is based in a villa perched above the sea. The downside? Travellers must vacate their rooms between 9.30am and 5pm, and a curfew kicks in at 11pm.

There is nothing more idyllic than a stroll along the Cap d'Ail coastal path to **La Pinède** (☎ 04 93 78 37 10; www.restaurantlapinede.com; 10 blvd de la Mer; menus €27, €37 & €47; ☼ lunch & dinner Thu-Tue Mar-Oct), housed in an old fisherman's hut . Feast on a refined fish lunch then sleep it off on the sea-facing terrace. From the train station, walk down the steps and head straight for the sea.

Cap Martin

Cap Martin – coastal quarter of Cap Martin-Roquebrune (p287) – is a green headland loaded with an incredible treasure trove of sumptuous villas, royal honorary citizens and famous past residents, with Coco Chanel, Winston Churchill, Marlene Dietrich, architect Le Corbusier, designer Eileen Gray and Irish poet WB Yeats among them.

Exploring on foot is pleasurable. Av Le Corbusier follows the coast east, around Baie de Roquebrune to the northern end of the cape where it turns into promenade Le Corbusier. The beach, **Plage du Buse**, is a two-minute stroll from the train station on av de la Gare. The hilltop village of Roquebrune is an hour's walk (2km) – up numerous staircases – from the station, and Monte Carlo is three hours (7km) by foot.

The **tourist office** (☎ 04 93 35 62 87; www.roque brune-cap-martin.com; 218 av Aristide Briand; ☼ 9am-1pm & 3-7pm Mon-Sat, 10am-1pm & 3-7pm Sun Jul & Aug, 9am-12.30pm & 2-6.30pm Mon-Sat Jun & Sep, to 6pm Oct-May), at the northern end of the cape midway between the Carnolès and Cap Martin-Roquebrune train stations, distributes a free map of walking trails around Cap Martin. It also arranges guided tours of Corbusier's seashore studio; see p65.

Le Roquebrune (☎ 04 93 35 00 16; www.leroquebrune .com; 100 av Jean Jaurès; d incl breakfast €135-195; Ⓟ 🖳) might be Cap Martin-Roquebrune's sole *chambre d'hôte*, but it could not be more superbly placed – slap bang on the Lower Corniche above the sky-blue sea. Five rooms poetically named *L'Horizon* (the Horizon), *Ciel et Mer* and so on reflect its stunning location - offset by exquisite furnishings, fresh flowers as a welcome and crisp white tablecloths on the terrace table of each room. Below slumbers sandy Plage du Golfe Bleu (Blue Gulf Beach).

Roquebrune, the medieval counterpart of Cap Martin (see p287), has a couple of delightful eating options.

MOYENNE CORNICHE

Cut through rock in the 1920s, the Moyenne Corniche takes drivers from Nice past the Col de Villefranche (149m), Èze and Beausoleil (the French town bordering Monaco's Monte Carlo).

Èze

pop 2510 / elev 429m

It might be more like toy town than anywhere else on the Riviera, but this rocky little village perched on an impossible peak is undeniably picturesque. After a hard afternoon spent hopping out of the way of other people's photographs and waiting for them to get out of yours, nip down to coastal counterpart Èze-sur-Mer by road or train for a dip in the sea.

When German philosopher Friedrich Nietzsche (1844–1900) stayed here, he started writing *Thus Spoke Zarathustra;* the path that links Èze with Èze-sur-Mer and the beach (45 minutes) is named after him. Walt Disney holidayed in Èze, and U2 guitarist The Edge got hitched on a luxury yacht moored off the coast here.

Visit the **tourist office** (☎ 04 93 41 26 00; www
.eze-riviera.com; place du Général de Gaulle; ⊗ 9am-7pm
Mon-Sat, 10am-1pm & 2-6pm Sun) for the full village
low-down.

SIGHTS & ACTIVITIES

Steep streets lead to the medieval hilltop
village, crammed with dinky art galleries,
boutiques and cafés. Its crowning glory is
the chateau ruins, brightened by a cactus-
laden, oil-scented **Jardin Exotique** (☎ 04 93 41 10
30; adult/11-16yr €5/2.50; ⊗ 9am-8pm or 9pm Jul & Aug,
9am-5pm or 7pm Sep-Jun).

Perfumery Fragonard (p326) has a **factory**
(☎ 04 93 41 05 05; admission free; ⊗ 8.30am-6.30pm
Feb-Oct, 8.30am-noon & 2-6.30pm Nov-Jan) that you can
visit on the eastern edge of Èze, and a small
shop in the village.

SLEEPING & EATING

Hotels here are small, frantically popular and
booked months ahead.

Château Eza (☎ 04 93 41 12 24; www.chateaueza.com;
rue de la Pise; d low/mid/high season €150/230/320; lunch menus
€37 & €47; ⊗ mid-Dec–mid-Nov) The winter residence
(1923–53) of Sweden's Prince William is now
a posh hotel-restaurant with just six rooms,
four suites and a lovely sea-facing terrace and
great views, not that the staff will let you take
a peek unless you absolutely really positively
intend to dine here. Two donkeys called Nani
and Nina tied up in a stable at the foot of the
village serve as a reminder of how the prince's
baggage was carted up to his castle.

Château de la Chèvre d'Or (☎ 04 92 10 66 66;
www.chevredor.com; rue du Barri; d from €270; lunch menu
with/without wine €85/120, dinner menu excl drinks €168;
⊗ Mar–mid-Nov; ⓟ ✗ ⌘) In a class of its own,
this gastronomic temple guarantees to thrill
the most jaded of palates. Hotel facilities are
heavenly too: sauna, hammam (Turkish bath),
fitness centre, spa, infinity-edge swimming
pool…the list is endless!

Getting There & Away

Bus 112, operated by Rapides Côte d'Azur,
serves the Moyenne Corniche, stopping at
Èze village (€1.30, 20 minutes) and Beausoleil (€1.30, 40 minutes) en route to/from
Nice. Buses run seven times a day Monday
to Saturday, and three times daily on Sunday
and holidays.

By train from Nice, get off at Èze-sur-Mer
train station on the Corniche Inférieure, where
shuttle buses transport tourists up and down

the hill from May to October. Failing that, it's
a 3km uphill trudge on foot to Èze village.

GRANDE CORNICHE

Hitchcock was sufficiently impressed by Napoleon's cliff-hanging Grande Corniche to
use it as a film backdrop for *To Catch a Thief*
(1956), starring Cary Grant and Grace Kelly.
Ironically, the Hollywood actress, who met
her Monégasque Prince Charming while making the film, died in 1982 after crashing her
car on this very same road.

SIGHTS

Observatoire de Nice & Astrorama

French architects Gustave Eiffel and Charles
Garnier designed **Nice Observatory** (☎ 04 92 00 31
12; www.obs-nice.fr; guided tours adult/child €5/2.50, park &
observatory tour €7.50), a 19th-century monument
5km northeast of Nice amid 35 hectares of
landscaped parkland atop Mont Gros (375m).
When the observatory opened in 1887, its
telescope – 76cm in diameter – was among
Europe's largest. Guided tours of the observatory take place at 2.45pm on Wednesday and
Saturday, and of the parkland at 9.45am on
Wednesday and 2.15pm on Saturday.

Watch the skies at **Astrorama** (☎ 04 93 41 23
04; www.astrorama.net in French; adult/7-10yr €7/5, 'spectacles aux étoiles' €10/7; ⊗ 6-10.30pm Fri & Sat Sep-Jun,
6-10.30pm Mon-Sat Jul & Aug), a planetarium and
astronomy centre 8km further northeast along
the Grande Corniche in **La Trinité**.

SLEEPING & EATING

Col d'Èze, winding along the Grande Corniche
above hilltop Èze, has some lovely sleeping and
dining options, as does the road that runs east
of the mountain pass off the Grande Corniche
to Astorama and Fort de la Revere (p288).

La Vieille Bergerie (☎ 04 93 41 10 22; www.lavieille
bergerie.com; 585 rte de la Revère; d low/high season €90/120;
ⓟ) This *chambre d'hôte de charme* is charming
indeed. Roselyne Carpentier moved here from
Normandy 30 years ago and spent a good 20 of
them transforming this traditional shelter for
sheep (built in 1860) into a very, *very* romantic
hideaway. Some ceilings are vaulted, walls are
pure stone and furnishings are white, rustic
and a tad flowery. The grounds are less fussy.
Find it 500m from the D46–Grande Corniche
junction, 1.5km before Astorama.

La Bastide aux Camélias (☎ 04 93 41 13 68; www
.bastideauxcamelias.com; 23c rte de l'Adret; d low/high season
€100/120; ⓡ ⓟ) Jacuzzi, hammam, sauna and

olive-tree framed pool are among the lazy-weekend comforts at this lovely *chambre d'hôte* where guests are pampered by Fred and Sylvienne. Four different rooms are named after plants: the Yucca room (€120/100) is a Zen affair with its own garden terrace, while Jasmin is a soft, delicate affair of creams and whites. DVD player, bathrobes, complimentary coffee, tea and infusions, candles and essential oils are beautiful touches. Wi-fi access is free. The Bastide is signposted immediately on your left after turning at the D46–Grand Corniche junction to Astorama and Fort de la Revère.

Hermitage du Col d'Èze (☎ 04 93 41 00 68; www.ezehermitage.fr; 1951 av des Diables Bleus, Grande Corniche, Col d'Èze; s/d low season €59/69, midseason €79/89, high season €99/109, menus €20, €25, €35 & €45; restaurant ⊙ lunch & dinner Thu-Mon, dinner Tue; Ⓟ ☒ ☒) Find this old-style 14-room inn – an apricot affair with lilac shutters – spectacularly set at the top of a mountain pass, 2.5km from Èze village. Food is strictly local fare and delicious to boot – a guaranteed taste of the region. Parking is free.

Camping Les Romarins (☎ 04 93 01 81 64; www.camping-romarins.com; Col d'Èze; 2 adults, tent & car low/mid/high season €22/22.55/23.65; reception ⊙ 7.30am-10.30pm Apr-Sep) This lovely camp site, at the western end of the Col d'Èze, is as close as you'll get to wild camping in this protected neck of the woods. Pitch your tent on the terraced hillside and wake up to the most incredible views ever of Cap Ferrat and the coast.

La Turbie
pop 3150 / elev 480m

La Turbie teeters dramatically on a promontory above Monaco and offers a stunning night-time vista of the principality. By day, enjoy an unparalleled aerial view from the gardens of the **Trophée des Alps** (Trophy of the Alps; ☎ 04 93 41 20 84; 18 av Albert I; adult/under 18yr €5/free; ⊙ 9.30am-1pm & 2.30-6.30pm Tue-Sun mid-May–mid-Sep, 10am-1.30pm & 2.30-5pm Tue-Sun mid-Sep–Mar), a 2000-year-old triumphal monument built by Emperor Augustus in 6 BC on the highest point of the old Roman road. The 45 Alpine tribes he conquered are listed on the inscription carved on the western side of the monument.

La Turbie village is unexciting, bar its small but intact old town neatly packed around the baroque-style **Église St-Michel** (1777), and the stunningly simple but superbly delicious creations cooked with flair by Michelin-starred chef Bruno Cirino at **Café de la Fontaine** (☎ 04 93 28 52 79; 4 av Général de Gaulle; mains €15; ⊙ 6.30am-midnight).

Roquebrune
pop 12,375

Cap Martin-Roquebrune, sandwiched between Monaco and Menton, became part of France in 1861; prior to that it was a free town following its revolt against Grimaldi rule in 1848. The town stretches north from the exclusive suburb of Cap Martin on the coast (see p285) to the hilltop village perched 300m high on a pudding-shaped lump.

A fantastic feudal castle dating from the 10th century crowns medieval Roquebrune. The crenellated mock-medieval **Tour de l'Anglais** (Englishman's Tower) near the entrance was built by wealthy British lord William Ingram, who bought the chateau in 1911. His archaeological vandalism caused such outrage that **Château de Roquebrune** (☎ 04 93 35 07 22; place William Ingram; adult/7-18yr €3.70/1.60; ⊙ 10am-12.30pm year-round, plus 3-7.30pm Jul & Aug, 2-6.30pm Apr-Jun & Sep, 2-6pm Feb, Mar & Oct, 2-5pm Nov-Jan) was immediately classified as a historical monument to protect it from further modification. The four floors are atmospheric, and concerts are held here in July and August.

Of all Roquebrune's steep and tortuous streets, rue Moncollet – with its arcaded passages and stairways carved out of rock – is the most impressive. Architect Le Corbusier (p65) is buried in the cemetery at the top of the village.

PICNIC IN GARRIGUE

Atop the Col d'Èze, head up even higher to the **Plateau de la Justice**; follow the signposted road next to the Hermitage du Col d'Èze. Tree-shaded picnic spots (including a couple of tables and benches) abound amid the heavily scented *garrigue* (typical Mediterranean groundcover of aromatic plants) here.

For even mightier coastal views stretching beyond Cap Ferrat to Cap d'Antibes, the Îles de Lérins and the Ésterel, continue east along the Grande Corniche and at the D46 crossroads turn left (north) along route de la Revère to **Fort de la Revère** (675m).

An orientation table in front of the fort, built on top of the barren rocky outcrop in 1870 to protect Nice, tells you what's what: the panoramic view is the best on the coast. Picnic at tables beneath plane trees here, or follow the footpath around the fort sign-posted 'Maison de la Nature et Animations Nature' into the *garrigue*. On your left, a small rocky path leads to an **observation point**, from which bird enthusiasts can watch more than 80-odd species of migratory birds at work and play, including the osprey and falcon (both late August to mid-October), European bee-eater (mid-August to mid-September) and black stork (mid-October). The observation post faces Mont Agel. Continue downhill along the main footpath to reach the **Maison de la Nature** (☎ 04 93 41 24 36; ☒ variable), painted buttercup yellow. From here, a marked walking trail leads to La Turbie (1¼ hours).

SLEEPING & EATING

Les Deux Frères (☎ 04 93 28 99 00; www.lesdeuxfreres .com; place des Deux Frères; s/d from €75/100, lunch/dinner menu €24/45; restaurant ☒ lunch & dinner Wed-Sat, lunch Sun, dinner Tue; ☒) The stylish restaurant languishing on a terrace above the water certainly steals the show at this beautiful 10-room hotel facing the sea. Waiters wear formal black, and mains come hidden beneath silver domed platters. The lunch menu, including a half-bottle of wine overlooked by a miserable-looking statue of *France Triumphant*, is good value.

Au Grand Inquisiteur (☎ 04 93 35 05 37; 18 rue du Château; menus €14, €26 & €37; ☒ lunch & dinner Wed-Sun) This rock-cave restaurant could be a film set for a movie about mad monks. Meat and fish dishes are the speciality here, carried to your table from the kitchen across the street!

Getting There & Away

Bus 116 to/from Nice stops at La Turbie (€1.30, 35 minutes) en route to Peille (€1.30, one hour, four buses daily Monday to Saturday).

ARRIÈRE-PAYS NIÇOIS

Studded with medieval hilltop villages, the little known Niçois hinterland stretches inland from Nice to Menton. Buses to this remote patch are far from frequent, making your own wheels essential.

CONTES TO COARAZE

Roman **Contes** (population 6600), 16km north of Nice, sits on a ship-shaped rock above the River Paillon de Contes. Before exploring the town, nip into the **tourist office** (☎ 04 93 79 13 99; place A Olivier; ☒ 2-6pm Mon-Fri), level with the river and the D15.

At the northern end of Contes on the D15, olives have been crushed at the still-functioning **Moulin à Huile de la Laouza** (☎ 04 93 79 19 17; www.musee-contes.fr in French; admission €2; ☒ 9.30am-12.30pm & 2-5pm Sat Dec-Oct) since the 13th century. Agricultural tools were made at the **moulin à fer** next door, a 13th- to 14th-century water-powered forge.

Châteauneuf Villevieille (also known as Châteauneuf de Contes), 6km west, sits snug at the foot of the overgrown ruins of the older village, abandoned prior to WWI. Territorial goats aside, the ruins can be freely wandered.

Tourrette-Levens, a particularly dramatic hilltop village 10km southwest via the westbound D815 and southbound D19, is crowned with a **Château Musée** (Castle Museum; ☎ 04 93 91 03 20; www.tourrette-levens.org; place du Château; admission free; ☒ 2-7pm summer, 2-5pm winter) housing an exotic butterfly collection and natural-history museum.

The Provençal words 'coa raza' meaning 'cut tail' gives **Coaraze** (population 659, elevation 650m), 9km north of Contes on the Col St-Roch (D15), its name: a lizard mosaic on place Félix-Giordan illustrates the tale of how villagers caught the devil, leaving Satan with no choice but to slice off his tail to escape. A Jean Cocteau sundial adorns the town hall, and the **tourist office** (☎ 04 93 79 37 47; office .de.tourisme.coaraze@tiscali.fr; 7 place Ste-Catherine) has the key for 14th-century Église St-Jean Baptiste. Futurist works fill the **Musée Figas** (☎ 04 93 79 31 87; www.museefigas.asso.fr; Hameau l'Engarvin Duranas; adult/7–18yr €4/2; ◷ 3-6pm Sat & Sun summer, 2-5pm Sat & Sun winter), designed by painter Marcel Figas (born 1935) and home to his oils.

Sleeping & Eating

L'Alivù (☎ 04 93 80 86 68; www.alivu.com; 816 rte des Baisses, Coaraze; d €100, dinner €29; P ⊠) Hidden among trees, this perfectly manicured suncoloured *mas* (farmhouse) with sage-green shutters and all the mod cons comes as something of a surprise after the 2km-long and narrow, winding lane leading to it. Each of its four rooms exalts a different type of local olive, each has doors leading to a terrace, and the sweeping panorama from the pool is inspirational. Rates include sauna and Jacuzzi, and dinner is a refined treat. To find it, approach the village from the south, turn right immediately after the bridge onto rue de Plan d'Eau and follow the signs. Wi-fi access is free.

Auberge du Soleil (☎ 04 93 79 08 11; 5 camin de la Beguda, Coaraze; d €62, menu €23; ◷ mid-Mar–mid-Nov; ⊠) Tucked right at the top of Coaraze, this family-run inn with 10 lovely double rooms and terrace restaurant is everything a

---

UGLY DUCKLING

Vista Palace (☎ 04 92 10 40 00; www.vistapalace .com; 1551 rte de la Grande Corniche; d with sea view from €215, menus €55 & €75; Vistaero ◷ dinner summer, lunch & dinner winter; ⊠ ▯ P) Never was there a more ugly duckling of a four-star hotel. From the outside the Vista Palace is an unfortunate overdose of concrete and formidable 1970s architecture (it was built in 1978), albeit one that hangs perilously on the edge of the cliff-hanging Grande Corniche. But step inside and be seduced by the most beautiful views of Monaco, its skyline and the rest of the coast. Dinner by candlelight in its sea-facing Vistaero restaurant (named after the original restaurant that wooed diners on this very spot in the 1920s) is a particularly romantic affair.

---

family-run place should be. Friendly, cosy and lacking pretension, it is the ideal spot for village moseying, swimming against a mountain backdrop and lounging in the garden.

PEILLE & PEILLON

Twelfth-century **Chapelle St-Roch** (place Jean Mioul) guards the eastern entrance to quaintly restored **Peille** (population 2055, elevation 630m), probably the hinterland's most intact hilltop village. In its teeny **Musée du Terroir** (◷ 2-6pm summer), captions are written in Pelhasc, a dialect specific to Peille and distinguishable from the Niçois dialect by its absent 'r's and silent 'l's (Peillasques say 'carriea' instead of 'carriera', Niçois for 'street').

Not for the faint-hearted is the **Via Ferrata de Peille**, a difficult course that starts a 10-minute walk from the village and scales the Baous de Caster and Barma de la Sié rock formations with full complement of ladders, monkey bridges and zip lines. The lot takes 3½ hours to conquer, but 45-minute sections can be tackled. Reserve in advance at **Bar l'Absinthe** (☎ 04 93 79 95 75; http://peille.free.fr in French; 6 rue Félix Faure; admission €3, equipment hire €13).

Six kilometres of hairpin bends southwest of Peille on the D53 towards Peillon is **La Grave** (population 500), a blot-on-the-landscape cement works where the hinterland's limestone is turned into cement. The best aerial view of Peille and La Grave is from the **Col de la Madone** (927m), a hair-raising stone-tunnelled mountain pass (the D22) that runs east from Peille to Ste-Agnès.

Peillon (population 1229, elevation 456m), 14km northeast of Nice, is known for its precarious *nid d'aigle* (eagle's nest) location. From the village car park, a footpath leads to the **Chapelle des Pénitents Blancs**, noteworthy for its set of macabre 15th-century frescoes. Longer trails lead to Peille, La Turbie and Chapelle St-Martin. North of Peillon, the **Gorges du Peillon** (D21) cuts through the Peillon Valley to **L'Escarène** (population 2138), an important mule stop in the 17th and 18th centuries for traders working the rte du Sel (Salt Rd) from Nice to Turin in Italy.

Sleeping & Eating

Auberge de la Madone (☎ 04 93 79 91 17; www.auberge -madone-peillon.com; 2 place Auguste Arnulf, Peillon; d €95-200, menus €30 & €65; ◷ Feb–mid-Nov, restaurant closed Wed; P) At the foot of the village of Peillon, this upmarket three-star hotel creates

AUTHOR'S CHOICE

La Parare (☎ 04 93 79 22 62; 67 calade du Pastre, Châteauneuf Villevieille; d incl breakfast low/high season €95/110, dinner €29; Ⓟ Ⓢ) (Swedish) Karin and (French-Dutch) Sydney van Volen are the widely travelled, multilingual couple behind this fabulous *chambre d'hôte*, an 18th-century stone *bergerie* (sheepfold) that they spent 2½ years transforming stone-by-stone into a stunning space framed by terraced olive groves (still to be restored). A contemporary décor tells the tale of their lives – from Paloma Beach on Cap Ferrat where Sydney summered as a child, to Hong Kong where the couple met and lived for 10-odd years. Spacious, stylish rooms sport rich fabrics from China and Thailand, not to mention the odd kimono, and ooze romance: the Chapel room is a suite with a separate dovecote for the kids to sleep in; the Terrace room has a sofa in the bathroom for him to lounge on while she takes a bath; while room 4 – named after the old communal *four* (furnace) that sits outside in the garden, and was used by the village – sports a designer sunken bath overlooking an open fireplace. In keeping with its *'entre Zen et Provence'* (between Zen and Provence) strap line, breakfast is decadently served any time of day, and evening meals are cooked up upon request.

delicious local Peillonnais cuisine that draws diners from far and wide. Rooms and tables need booking well in advance.

MENTON & AROUND

Lemons, lemons, hilltop villages, the most fabulous gardens on the Riviera and more lemons are the main attractions of this privileged coastal pocket, a pebble's throw from Italy.

MENTON
pop 29,200

You'd have thought Eve was in enough trouble. But just before she was chucked out of Eden, she stole one of the garden's Golden Fruits. Upon arriving in lush, subtropical Menton, she was reminded of paradise so much that she instantly planted the fruit's seeds – ensuring a famed and fabulous bounty of lemons for

Menton ever since. Frenzied citrus worship has accompanied the two-week-long Fête des Citrons in February since the 1930s.

Adam and Eve aside, Gustave Flaubert, Guy de Maupassant, Katherine Mansfield and Robert Louis Stevenson all sought solace here. Jean Cocteau lived here from 1956 to 1958, leaving his mark through a couple of fantastic creations. Italians from across the border are the main visitors today, drawn by the town's unassuming magnetic charm, its pretty and precipitous red-hued old town and some of the Riviera's most beautiful gardens.

Historically, Menton, along with neighbouring Cap Martin-Roquebrune, found itself under Grimaldi rule until 1848, when its people rebelled and declared independence. In 1861 the two towns voted to join France, forcing Charles III of Monaco to sell them to Napoleon III for four million francs.

Orientation

The old town and port are wedged between Baie de Garavan (east) and Baie du Soleil, which stretches 3km west to Cap Martin-Roquebrune. Promenade du Soleil and its continuations, quai Général Leclerc and quai de Monléon, skirt the length of Menton's gravel beach. More beaches fringe the coast directly northeast of the old port and east of Port de Garavan, Menton's pleasure-boat harbour.

Information

Find banks on rue Partouneaux and internet access at Café des Arts (p294).

Post office (2 cours Georges V)

Tourist office (☎ 04 92 41 76 76; www.villedementon .com; Palais de l'Europe, 8 av Boyer; Ⓢ 9am-7pm May-Sep, 8.30am-12.30pm & 2-6pm Mon-Fri, 9am-noon & 2-6pm Sat Oct-Apr) Guided tours and garden visits in conjunction with the Service du Patrimoine (p293).

Sights

By the port, the tiny 17th-century seafront bastion crowning the spur of land between Menton's bays shelters the **Musée Jean Cocteau** (☎ 04 93 57 72 30; sq Jean Cocteau; adult/under 18yr/18-25yr/ €3/free/2.25, 1st Sun of month free; Ⓢ 10am-noon & 2-6pm Wed-Mon). Cocteau restored the building himself, decorating the 2m-thick alcoves, outer walls and reception hall with pebble mosaics. Inside are crayon drawings, tapestries and ceramics by the French artist. His gravestone, looking out to sea, reads *Je reste avec vous* (I remain with you).

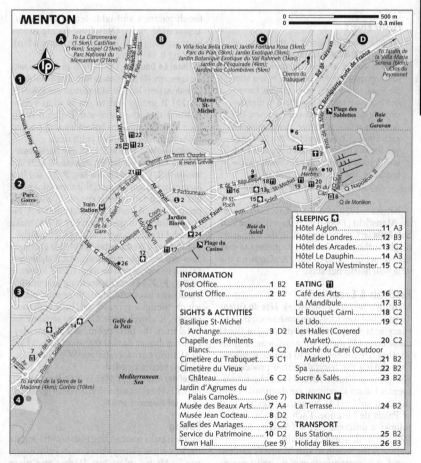

MENTON

0 _____ 500 m
0 _____ 0.3 miles

To La Citronneraie (1.5km); Castillon (14km); Sospel (21km); Parc National du Mercantour (21km)

To Villa Isola Bella (3km); Jardin Fontana Rosa (3km); Parc du Pian (3km); Jardin Exotique (3km); Jardin Botanique Exotique du Val Rahmeh (3km); Jardin de l'Esquirade (4km); Jardins des Colombières (5km)

To Jardin de la Villa Maria Serena (6km); Clos du Peyronnet

Chemin du Trabuquet

Plateau St-Michel

Plage des Sablettes

Baie de Garavan

Parc Gorre

Chemin des Terres Chaudes
R Henri Gréville

Pl aux Herbes

Train Station

Pl de la Gare

R Partouneaux

R de la République

R St-Michel

Pl du Cap

Q Napoléon III

Q de Monléon

Jardins Bioyès

Pl St Roch

Av Félix Faure

Baie du Soleil

Plage du Casino

Golfe de la Paix

Mediterranean Sea

To Jardin de la Serre de la Madone (4km); Gorbio (10km)

INFORMATION
Post Office.....................1 B2
Tourist Office...................2 B2

SIGHTS & ACTIVITIES
Basilique St-Michel
  Archange......................3 D2
Chapelle des Pénitents
  Blancs...........................4 C2
Cimetière du Trabuquet.....5 C1
Cimetière du Vieux
  Château.........................6 C2
Jardin d'Agrumes du
  Palais Carnolès............(see 7)
Musée des Beaux Arts........7 A4
Musée Jean Cocteau.........8 D2
Salles des Mariages...........9 C2
Service du Patrimoine......10 D2
Town Hall.....................(see 9)

SLEEPING
Hôtel Aiglon...................11 A3
Hôtel de Londres.............12 B3
Hôtel des Arcades............13 C2
Hôtel Le Dauphin............14 A3
Hôtel Royal Westminster..15 C2

EATING
Café des Arts..................16 C2
La Mandibule.................17 B3
Le Bouquet Garni............18 C2
Le Lido.........................19 C2
Les Halles (Covered
  Market).....................20 C2
Marché du Carei (Outdoor
  Market).....................21 B2
Spa............................22 B2
Sucre & Salés.................23 B2

DRINKING
La Terrasse....................24 B2

TRANSPORT
Bus Station....................25 B2
Holiday Bikes.................26 B3

In 1957, Cocteau decorated Menton's **Salles des Mariages** (Registry Office; ☎ 04 92 10 50 00; place Ardoïno; adult/under 18yr/18-25yr €1.50/free/1.15; ⏰ 8.30am-12.30pm & 2-5pm Mon-Fri), inside the **town hall**, with scenes of mythological Orpheus' and Eurydice's wedding, galloping horses and starry local lovers.

From place du Cap a ramp leads to Southern France's grandest baroque church, the Italianate **Basilique St-Michel Archange** (place de l'Église St-Michel; ⏰ 10am-noon & 3-5.15pm Mon-Fri) with creamy façade flanked by a 35m-tall clock tower and 53m-tall steeple (1701–03). Up the steps is apricot-coloured **Chapelle des Pénitents Blancs** (place de la Conception; ⏰ 3-5pm Mon), built in 1689, which has an ornate trompe l'oeil cupola inside.

What a shame the occupiers of prime real estate **Cimetière du Vieux Château** (⏰ 7am-8pm May-Sep, 7am-6pm Oct-Apr) can't appreciate the immense views. Walk up montée du Souvenir to reach the main gates of the ornate 19th-century cemetery. Rugby inventor, Reverend William Webb Ellis (1805–72), is buried in the southwest corner. For more grave musing and marvellous vistas, continue north along steep chemin du Trabuquet to **Cimetière du Trabuquet**.

Along the coast, Monaco's royal family summered at 18th-century Palais Carnolès, today the **Musée des Beaux-Arts** (Fine Arts Museum; ☎ 04 93 35 49 71; 3 av de la Madone; admission free; ⏰ 10am-noon & 2-6pm Wed-Mon), surrounded by a fabulous lemon and orange grove studded with sculptures (p293).

FOOD FIGHT

An odd Menton legend is the origin of August's **Fête de Bazaïs**, when everyone gathers round a huge cauldron of bean soup on quai Gordon Bennett. In the Middle Ages, so the story goes, plague, famine and incessant raiding by vicious Barbary pirates threatened to wipe out the town. The surviving residents, rather than turning on each other, clubbed together the food they had left and turned it into a body-and-soul-saving soup. Faced with such unnatural cooperation, the evil marauders fled.

Between 1920 and 1921 novelist Katherine Mansfield (1888–1923) stayed in the **Villa Isola Bella** (av Katherine Mansfield), in the upmarket neighbourhood of Garavan, to attempt to ease her worsening tuberculosis. A plaque on the villa wall marks her stay.

Festivals & Events

Menton's fabulous two-week **Fête du Citrons** (Lemon Festival; www.feteducitron.com in French) in February sees sculptures and decorative floats made from 115 metric tonnes of lemons (plus another five tonnes used to replace damaged fruit during the festival) weave processions along the seafront. Afterwards, the monumental lemon creations are dismantled and the fruit sold off at bargain prices in front of Palais de l'Europe. Each year the festival follows a different theme (Asterix, Alice in Wonderland, world carnivals).

June is the month to visit Menton's gardens (opposite), some private gardens only opening their doors to visitors during the month-long **Rendez-vous aux Jardins.** Mid-July brings contemporary dance and jazz to Menton's gardens (opposite) during the **Rencontres de Danse Contemporaine**. August's classical **Festival de Musique** ushers in classical concerts to Parvis St-Michel (the square in front of Basilique St-Michel Archange).

Sleeping

Hôtel de Londres (☎ 04 93 35 74 62; www.hotel-de-londres.com; 15 av Carnot; s/d with washbasin from €44/55, s/d/tr from €75/88/111; ☸ mid-Jan–Oct; ☒ P) Easily the best in its price range, this reliable Logis de France hotel is set back from the main road 25m from the sea with pretty wooden shutters and a flowery garden. Sun lounges,

beach parasols and table-tennis are much-appreciated perks. Only front-facing rooms have air-con (back-facing rooms have a fan). Parking is €8/49 per day/week.

Hôtel Le Dauphin (☎ 04 93 35 76 37; www.hotel-ledauphin.com; 408 promenade du Soleil; d low/mid/high season with sea view €74/79/92, with mountain view €59/65/73; P ☒) If gazing out to sea is what you're wanting then the three-star Dolphin is for you: bask on wooden balconies and peep at the waves between three palm trees.

Hôtel Aiglon (☎ 04 93 57 55 55; www.hotelaiglon.net; 7 av de la Madone; s low/mid/high season €66/73.50/99.50, d from €86/96/121; ☸ mid-Dec–mid-Nov; P ☒ ☒) In a former merchant's house, this three-star place has a definite air of *belle époque* quality to its pretty façade. A heated pool and upmarket restaurant (lunch/dinner menu €29.90/46) make it a solid family choice. Parking is €6 per day.

Hôtel Royal Westminster (☎ 04 93 28 69 69; www.hotel-royal-westminster-menton.cote.azur.fr; 1510 promenade du Soleil; s/d with sea views low season €75/105, high season €85/133; P ☒) There's something very grandiose about this ornate late-18th-century palace, which, though enormous and busy with tour-groups, is a lovely spot. Gardens separate the hotel from the busy prom, and Wednesday-evening dinner dances transport guests back to Menton's aristocratic pre-WWI days.

Also recommended:

Hôtel des Arcades (☎ 04 93 35 70 62; 41 av Félix Faure; d incl breakfast from €56/65.20) Picturesque option on the old-town edge; no frills.

Eating

Menton lacks outstanding restaurants, despite the line-up of eating places on av Félix Faure, rue St-Michel, place aux Herbes and place du Cap. Pricier terraces with sea views line promenade du Soleil (watch waiters dice with death to bring you a coffee).

Le Bouquet Garni (☎ 04 93 35 85 91; 1 rue Palmaro; plat/menu du jour €11/15; ☸ lunch & dinner Tue-Sat) What you see is what you get at *bouquet garni* (think a bunch of Provençal herbs), a dead-simple bistro and *bar à vins* (wine bar) down an alley off the main pedestrian street. Locals form the bulk of the no-frills-seeking clientele, and the *brochette de volaille à l'estragon* (poultry skewer with tarragon) hits the spot just fine.

Le Lido (☎ 04 93 28 48 71; 24 rue St-Michel; seafood platters for 2 €36-115; ☸ lunch & dinner) Sit on the buzzing terrace at this bustling no-frills seafood bar and feast on piles of *langoustine* (small saltwater lobster), oysters, sea urchins, crab and prawns. Finicky eaters can opt for a bog-standard lasagne.

La Mandibule (☎ 04 93 28 41 95; www.lamandibule .com in French; 1014 promenade du Soleil; mains €10; ☑ lunch

& dinner) Tropical is the tone of this seafront restaurant, which serves a mean cocktail alongside dozens of different rums and good old-fashioned cuisine from the French island

---

GARDENS OF EDEN

Menton's maze of beautiful gardens, each with a different horticultural appeal and historical charm, is a true Eden. But beware: getting into most gardens requires an advance reservation at Menton's **Service du Patrimoine** (☎ 04 92 10 97 10; Hôtel de Daniel d'Aohémar de Lantagnac; 24 rue St-Michel; ☑ 10am-12.30pm & 1.30-6pm). Most of these gardens are a short drive from the town centre.

■ **Jardin d'Agrumes du Palais Carnolès** (☎ 04 93 35 49 71; 3 av de la Madone; admission free, guided tour €5; ☑ 10am-noon & 2-6pm Wed-Mon) Menton's most famous citrus garden in the grounds of Palais Carnolès; 60 different varieties, 400 plants, sprinkled with contemporary sculptures.

■ **Jardin Botanique Exotique du Val Rahmeh** (☎ 04 93 35 86 72; valrahmeh@mnhn.fr; av St-Jacques; admission €5; ☑ 10am-12.30pm & 3.30-6.30pm Wed-Mon Apr-Sep, 10am-12.30pm & 2-5pm Wed-Mon Oct-Mar) Laid out in 1905 for Lord Radcliffe, governor of Malta. The terraces are renowned for their exotic fruit-tree collections and subtropical plants, including the only European specimen of the Easter Island tree *Sophora toromiro*, now extinct on the island.

■ **Jardin Fontana Rosa** (av Blasco Ibañez; admission €5; ☑ tour only 10am Fri) Created by Spanish novelist Vicente Blasco Ibañez in the 1920s and dedicated to writers, its vivid colours are meant to conjure up Spain, but with fanciful benches, pergolas, pools and ceramics the effect is more of a delightful fairyland. Advance reservations at the Service de Patrimoine. Nearby, Parc du Pian (av Blasco Ibañez, admission free) has a 1000-year-old grove of 530 olive trees.

■ **Jardin de la Villa Maria Serena** (21 promenade Reine-Astrid; admission €5; ☑ tour only 10am Tue) France's most temperate garden – known for its palm, olive and citrus trees – framing the white Villa Maria Serena, designed in a grandiose Second Empire style by Charles Garnier in 1866. Advance reservations at the Service du Patrimoine.

■ **Jardin de la Serre de la Madone** (☎ 04 93 57 73 90; www.serredelamadone.com; 74 rte du Val de Gorbio; adult/under 12yr/12-18yr €8/free/4; ☑ 10am-6pm Tue-Sun Apr-Oct, 10am-5pm Tue-Sun Dec-Mar, guided tour 3pm Tue-Sun) It was American gardener Lawrence Johnston who planted dozens of rare plants here, picked up from his travels around the world. Abandoned for decades, it is slowly being restored. Take bus 7 to the 'Serre de la Madone' stop.

■ **Clos du Peyronnet** (☎ 04 93 35 72 15; av Aristide Briand; admission €8; ☑ by appointment only) British artist and garden landscaper Humphry Waterfield's green-fingered triumph, designed around his Italianate villa. These terraced gardens with cypress-tree tunnels, wisteria-shaded porticoes and an incredible series of water pools tumbling down to the Med are exceptional. Pots and pots of rare South African bulbs are a horticultural highlight.

■ **Jardins des Colombières** (rte des Colombières Garavan; admission €8; ☑ tour only Jul–mid-Aug) Olive trees, cypresses, lavender and other nonexotic plants feature here, inspired by different figures in Greek mythology. They were designed in 1919 by Ferdinand Bac (1859–1952), comic writer and the illegitimate son of Napoleon III. Advance reservations at the Service du Patrimoine.

■ **Jardin de l'Esquinade** (☎ 04 93 57 67 28; 2665 rte du Super Garavan; admission free; ☑ by appointment only) Alongside the predictable mimosa, palm and lemon tree grows a rich bounty of vegetables and 120 different types of fruit tree, pomegranate, fig, pistachio and jujube included. Visits arranged directly through the owner.

■ **La Citronneraie** (Colline de l'Annonciade, 69 corniche André Tardieu; admission €5; ☑ tour only) Cultivated by Mentonnais farmers several centuries ago, the Lemon Grove is just that – and more. The 350 citrus trees – think lemons, oranges, clementines, grapefruit – date to the 1950s, but the olive grove is at least 600 years old. Find it hugging Mas Flofaro on a hill above Menton. The tourist office arranges visits.

NICE TO MENTON

of Réunion in the Indian Ocean. The cushioned wicker chairs beneath grass-skirted parasols on the prom have to be the comfiest prom chairs on the Riviera.

Café des Arts (☎ 04 93 35 78 67; 16 rue de République; mains €8-15; ☺ 7.30-10pm Mon-Sat) This unstuffy bistro with stylish traditional-with-a-twist interior and a laid-back staff is a pleasing place to hang, surf, drink or dine on salad and pasta. Internet access costs €1.15 per 15 minutes.

Opposite the bus station, **Sucre & Salés** (8 promenade Maréchal Leclerc) is a contemporary spot to enjoy a coffee, cake or well-stuffed baguette sandwich (€3.80), eat-in or takeaway. The patisserie also serves breakfast (€5).

Picnic shop at **Spa** (8 promenade du Maréchal Leclerc), the daily morning outdoor market **Marché du Carei** (promenade du Maréchal Leclerc) beneath the railway bridge on the same street, or the covered market **Les Halles** (quai de Monléon; ☺ 5am-1pm Tue-Sun) near the water.

Drinking

La Terrasse (☎ 04 92 10 16 16; www.lucienbarriere.com; av Félix Faure; ☺ 7pm-1am) The Terrace, atop the casino, is Menton's only really serious drinking space with sea view. *Ambiance lounge face à la mer* (lounge bar atmosphere facing the sea) is its marketing line. Saturday is disco night.

Getting There & Around

BICYCLE

Holiday Bikes (☎ 04 92 10 99 98; www.holiday-bikes .com; 4 esplanade Pompidou) rents out mountain bikes/50cc scooters for €13/30 per day plus €230/500 deposit.

BUS

From the **bus station** (☎ 04 93 28 43 27; 12 promenade Maréchal Leclerc) there are buses to/from Monaco (30 minutes), Nice (1¼ hours), Ste-Agnès (45 minutes), Sospel (45 minutes) and Nice-Côte d'Azur airport (1½ hours; departures coincide with flight times) via Monaco. Fares are €1.30.

TRAIN

From the **train station** (place de la Gare) frequent trains run to/from Ventimiglia (€2.20, 10 minutes) in Italy. For Côte d'Azur train services see p278.

AROUND MENTON

A string of mountain villages peer down on Menton from the **Col de Castillon** (707m), a hair-raising pass that wends its way up the Vallée

du Carei from the coast to Sospel (21km), the gateway to the Parc National du Mercantour (see p248). The road cuts through **Forêt de Menton**, a thick forest traversed with walking trails, then passes the **Viaduc du Caramel**. In former times the viaduct was used by the old Menton–Sospel tram, which used to trundle along the valley.

One of France's youngest villages, **Castillon** (population 280, elevation 535m), just south of the top of the pass, is a model of modern rural planning. The original village was destroyed by an earthquake in 1887 and bombed in 1944. It was built anew in 1951, perched in true Provençal fashion atop a mountain slope. Castillon has a small **tourist office** (☎ 04 93 04 32 03; www.castillon06.com; rue de la République) and several artist workshops to visit. The Sospel–Menton bus stops in the village.

About 5km northeast of Menton along the D24 is **Castellar** (population 830, elevation 360m). En route you pass **Tempe à Pailla** (1931–34), a glass-and-concrete 1930s building with round windows designed and lived in by Eileen Gray (see p65) until WWII when she was forced to flee further inland. Climb the village's steep narrow streets, scale stairs and cut through tiny covered passages to reach place Clémenceau, at its summit, from where there is a magnificent valley panorama. The GR51 and GR52 walking paths both cross Castellar.

Gorbio

pop 1162 / elev 360m

Flowery hilltop Gorbio, 10km northwest of Menton, is known for its annual **Fête Dieu** (Corpus Christi) feast day in June when villagers light up its medieval streets with snail shells set in pots of sand and filled with burning olive oil during the traditional **Procession aux Limaces**.

Otherwise, exploring its maze of cobbled streets and lunching away several lazy hours at quintessential village inn **Beau Séjour** (☎ 04 93 41 46 15; lunch menus €24, €28 & €38, dinner à la carte; ☺ lunch & dinner Thu-Tue May-Sep) are Gorbio's chief attractions. The stuff of Provençal lunch dreams, Beautiful Stay serves up Provençal fare in a buttermilk house that has peppermint-green shutters and a beautiful jasmine-covered terrace overlooking a fountain and 300-year-old elm tree on the village square. No credit cards.

From Menton, there are a couple of daily buses to/from Gorbio (€1.30, 30 minutes), but having your own wheels makes life substantially easier.

Ste-Agnès
pop 1200 / elev 780m

A 2km-long walking trail leads from Gorbio to Europe's highest 'seaside village'. From montée du Souvenir, 187 rocky steps lead to the rubbly 12th-century **chateau ruins** (admission by donation; ☿ 2-5pm Tue-Sun) with its intriguing flower beds, based on allegorical gardens found in medieval French poetry. Friendly goats graze between the rocks, and coastline views are breathtaking.

The drawbridged entrance to the huge underground **Fort Ste-Agnès** (☎ 04 93 35 84 58; adult/7-14yr €4/2; ☿ 3-6pm Tue-Sun Jul-Sep, 2.30-5.30pm Sat & Sun Oct-Jun) sits at the top of the village. The 2500-sq-metre defence was built between 1932 and 1938 as part of the 240km-long Maginot line, a series of fortifications intended to give France time to mobilise its army if attacked. The fort is in good nick; it was maintained throughout the Cold War as a nuclear fallout shelter!

From Menton there are two or three buses daily to/from Ste-Agnès (€1.30, 45 minutes).

Cannes Area

Glitzy, showbizzy Cannes sets camera flashes popping at its International Film Festival in May, when stars of cinema pose in evening gowns on the red carpet of La Croisette, fine-dine with the famous and drink 'til dawn in the 'magic square'. Hotels and roads are hideously chocka, making Cannes for anyone who doesn't have the right badge heaven (if you get to see your star) or hell (if stars don't do it for you).

But it's the fame of these 10 glorious, short-lived days in which this seaside resort basks for the rest of the year. Elegant architecture on the most photographed prom, parasol-packed sandy beaches and fascinating inhabitants: the town *is* a celebrity – albeit one with few concrete attractions, which can be a disappointing anticlimax for the less starstruck. Beneath its dazzling white smile, though, there are the Îles de Lérins, two Robinson Crusoe islands jam-packed with history in the Baie de Cannes; or the unexpected kaleidoscope of flowery meadows, dashing red rocks and untouristed hilltop villages that unfolds along the slow road out of town. And perfumeries fill the air with scent in Grasse.

Northeast along the coast is beautiful Antibes, a nugget of a medieval harbour with a stunning green cape attached and a wealth of priceless art. Picasso territory, aka Vallauris and Golfe-Juan, sparkles next door. Then there's that extraordinary cluster of inland villages crowned with Matisse's Vence, Chagall's St-Paul de Vence and Renoir's Cagnes-sur-Mer. Art-lovers will love it.

HIGHLIGHTS

- Revel in the glitz and glam of starstruck Cannes: strut along **La Croisette** (p301) and drink and dine on the **sand** (p307) or in the **'magic square'** (p308)

- Take a slow boat to the **Îles de Lérins** (p310) to see where the mysterious Man in the Iron Mask was imprisoned, or explore Cannes' hinterland on a **slow-road itinerary** (p298)

- Learn how roses and jasmine are cultivated and revel in them blooming at a flower farm near **Grasse** (p325)

- View world-famous art à la Matisse in **Vence** (p321), à la Picasso in **Antibes** (p312) and **Vallauris** (p310) and à la Renoir in **Cagnes-sur-Mer** (p318)

- Hang out like an artist in **Mandelieu-La Napoule** (p328): revel in the eccentricity of **Château de la Napoule** followed by a simple or sophisticated **lunch** (p330)

Vence ★

Cagnes-sur-Mer ★

★ Grasse

Antibes ★

Vallauris ★

Cannes ★

Mandelieu-La Napoule ★

★ Îles de Lérins

ITINERARIES

ARTISTS' TRAIL
Three Days / Cagnes-sur-Mer to Antibes

From cutting-edge art spaces to designer chapels, the area around Cannes is essential viewing for anyone crazy about 20th-century art.

Pick up the trail at Renoir's former studio, **Musée Renoir** (p319) in **Cagnes-sur-Mer** (**1**; p318). Then meander north to **St-Paul de Vence** (**2**; p319) where the **Fondation Maeght** (p320) and other outstanding **art galleries** (p322) beckon. Legendary artists' haunt **La Colombe d'Or** (p321) is the hot lunch date; reserve in advance. Afterwards, stroll along the gallery-studded street of the **village** (p319) where Chagall lived: visit his grave, then head back along the ramparts and drive to **Vence** (**3**; p321), home to the Matisse-designed **Chapelle du Rosaire** (p321). Next morning chat art over breakfast with Thierry at **Maison du Frêne** (p323).

Devote day two to Picasso: the scenic westbound D2210 and southbound D3 take you past a couple of inspiring hilltop villages to **Mougins** (**4**; p324) where Picasso lived, worked and was endlessly photographed. Take a side trip to the **Espace de l'Art Concret** (p326) and/or lunch lazily amid priceless art at **Le Moulin de Mougins** (p325); or forget both and push on to Vallauris' **Musée National Picasso** (p311) and **Galerie Madoura** (p312), afterwards grabbing something quick to eat (oysters?) at **Auberge Provençal** (p316) in neighbouring **Antibes** (**5**; p312). Art-lovers in a hurry can squeeze in Antibes' **Musée Picasso** (p313) before dinner at **Hôtel du Cap – Eden Roc** (p314). Otherwise, spend the night – as Picasso, Chagall and other great artists of their time did – at the Riviera legend and savour Antibes' art treasures the next day.

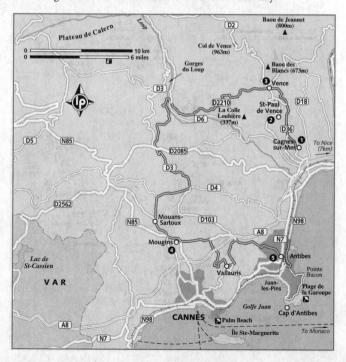

SLOW ROAD
Two Days / St-Raphaël to St-Paul de Vence

It's not all fast-paced, lights-flashing, body-packed coastal madness. Take the slow road inland and a hear-the-silence mirage of pine-scented mountains, cut-throat gorges and flowery meadows guarded by hilltop villages unfurls.

Get into 'go-green' gear in **St-Raphaël** (**1**; p331), from where the eastbound **Corniche d'Or** (p328) skirts the **Massif de l'Estérel** (**2**; p328), a red-rock massif that soars like needles out of the sea. Pull in at the observation point south of **Le Trayas** (**3**; p330) to digest its full majesty, then continue to folly-clad **Mandelieu-La Napoule** (**4**; 328) for lunch in an oasis of green at **L'Oasis** (p331); picnic buddies can buy gourmet supplies here. Spend the afternoon on a boat bound for **Île Ste-Marguerite** (**5**; p310) or push inland for a scenic drive along the wiggly D138 to untouched Auribeau-sur-Siagne and beyond to Cabris where **Le Mas du Naoc** (p327) ensures a peaceful night's sleep.

Next day, breakfast lazily then motor east for an orgy of hilltop villages: stop en route in **Grasse** (**6**; p325) to learn about the perfume industry and visit a **flower farm** (p326). In **Le Bar-sur-Loup** (**7**; p323) follow the 'red' walk to see Corsica, and lunch at **L'Hostellerie du Château** (p324) – in whichever order you fancy. Fill what time you have left with a drive along the **Gorges du Loup** (**8**; p322) or meander east to pretty **Tourrettes-sur-Loup** (**9**; p323) where **Wayne** (p324) tempts with dinner. Spend the night with frogs, squirrels and dragonflies in a tree-house at St-Paul de Vence's **Les Cabanes d'Orion** (p320).

CANNES TO NICE

Heavily developed is an understatement, but the 32km-long wedge of coast between Cannes and Nice is packed with intriguing finds: after WWII, Picasso had a studio in upmarket Antibes, lived in the neighbouring potters' village of Vallauris and lunched with Matisse, Chagall and Fernand Léger in hilltop St-Paul de Vence.

CANNES

pop 68,000

It's the banknotes of the affluent, spent with absolute nonchalance, that keep Cannes' exorbitant hotels, restaurants, fashion boutiques, nightclubs and liner-sized yachts afloat. The wealth is hypnotic, and revelling in it, even if it is secondhand, is a prime pastime: gawping at the unbelievable prices displayed in the windows of Cartier or riding an open-top double-decker bus along the Riviera's poshest promenade can really be quite fun!

For those who simply aren't seduced by Cannes' hedonistic air, there's enough natural beauty to make a trip worthwhile: the harbour, the bay, the clutch of islands off the coast and the old quarter, Le Suquet, all spring into life on a sunny day.

The world over best knows Cannes for its International Film Festival (p302), which sees the city's population treble overnight and packs out every last hotel room. Don't even consider turning up unless you have an advance reservation.

Orientation

Don't expect glitz'n'glamour the second you hop off the train: things don't glam up until rue d'Antibes, the main shopping street a couple of blocks south. Several blocks south again is Palais des Festivals, east of Vieux Port at the start of Cannes' famous promenade, blvd de la Croisette, which follows the shore eastwards along Baie de Cannes to Pointe de la Croisette.

Perched on a hill just to the west of Vieux Port and of the bus station is the old quarter of Cannes: the quaint, pedestrianised Le Suquet.

Information

BOOKSHOPS

Cannes English Bookshop (☎ 04 93 99 40 08; 11 rue Bivouac Napoléon; 🕒 10am-6.30 or 7pm Mon-Sat)

INTERNET ACCESS

Cafe @ to z.net (caféatoz@wanadoo.fr; 46 rue des Serbes; per hr €3; 🕒 10am-10pm Mon-Sat)

Cap cyber (☎ 04 93 38 85 63; 12 rue du 24 Août; per hr €3; 🕒 10am-10pm Mon-Sat)

INTERNET RESOURCES

www.cannes.com Tourist office.

www.palaisdesfestivals.com Festival Palace online.

LEFT LUGGAGE

Train station (rue Jean Jaurès; small/medium/large locker €4/6.50/8; 🕒 8.30am-8.30pm)

MEDICAL SERVICES

SOS Médecins (☎ 04 93 38 39 38; 🕒 24hr) Emergency doctor service.

MONEY

Banks and ATMs stud rue d'Antibes, rue Buttura and elsewhere.

POST

Post office (22 rue Bivouac Napoléon)

MARKET DAY

Monday Cannes, St-Raphaël

Tuesday Antibes (Sep-May), Biot, Cagnes-sur-Mer, Cannes, Fréjus Ville (Jun-Sep), Grasse, Mouans-Sartoux, St-Raphaël, Vallauris, Vence

Wednesday Antibes (Sep-May), Cagnes-sur-Mer, Cannes, Fréjus Ville, Grasse, Mouans-Sartoux, St-Raphaël, Vallauris

Thursday Antibes (Sep-May), Cagnes-sur-Mer, Cannes, Fréjus Ville (Jun-Sep), Grasse, St-Raphaël, Vallauris

Friday Antibes (Sep-May), Cagnes-sur-Mer, Cannes, Fréjus Ville (Jun-Sep), Grasse, St-Raphaël, Vallauris, Vence

Saturday Antibes (Sep-May), Cagnes-sur-Mer, Cannes, Fréjus Ville, Grasse, Mouans-Sartoux, St-Raphaël, Vallauris, Vence

Sunday Antibes (Sep-May), Cagnes-sur-Mer, Cannes, Fréjus Ville (Jun-Sep), Grasse, St-Raphaël, Vallauris, Vence

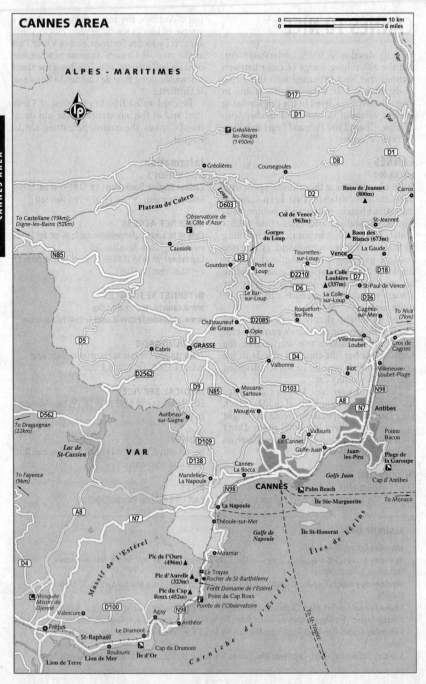

CANNES AREA

0 — 10 km
0 — 6 miles

ALPES - MARITIMES

Var

D17

D1

Var

Gréolières-
les-Neiges
(1450m)

Gréolières

Coursegoules

D8

D1

Baou de Jeannet
(800m)

Carros

D2

Col de Vence
(963m)

St-Jéannet

Plateau de Calern

D603

Observatoire de
la Côte d'Azur

Baou des
Blancs
(673m)

La Gaude

To Castellane (19km);
Digne-les-Bains (52km)

Gorges
du Loup

Tourrettes-
sur-Loup

Vence

D18

N85

Caussols

La Colle
Loubière
(337m)

D7

Gourdon

Pont du
Loup

D2210

St-Paul de Vence

Loup

D6

La Colle-
sur-Loup

D36

Le Bar-
sur-Loup

Cagnes-
sur-Mer

To Nice
(7km)

Roquefort-
les-Pins

Châteauneuf
de Grasse

D2085

D5

Cabris

Opio

D3

Villeneuve-
Loubet

Cros de
Cagnes

GRASSE

D4

Biot

Villeneuve-
Loubet-Plage

D2562

Valbonne

N98

D9

N85

Mouans-
Sartoux

D103

A8

N7

Antibes

To Draguignan
(22km)

Mougins

D562

Auribeau-
sur-Siagne

Vallauris

Pointe
Bacon

Lac de
St-Cassien

VAR

D109

Le Cannet

Golfe-Juan

Juan-
les-Pins

Plage de
la Garoupe

To Fayence
(9km)

D138

Mandelieu-
La Napoule

Cannes-
La Bocca

Golfe Juan

Cap d'Antibes

A8

N7

CANNES

Palm Beach

Île Ste-Marguerite

To Monaco

D4

La Napoule

Golfe de
Napoule

Île St-Honorat

Îles de Lérins

Théoule-sur-Mer

Mosquée
Missiri de
Djenné

Pic de l'Ours
(496m)

Muramar

Massif de l'Estérel

Pic d'Aurelle
(323m)

Le Trayas

Rocher de St-Barthélemy

Valescure

D100

Pic du Cap
Roux (452m)

Forêt Domaine de l'Estérel
Point du Cap Roux

Fréjus

Agay

N98

Pointe de l'Observatoire

St-Raphaël

Le Dramont

Anthéor

Corniche de l'Estérel

To St Tropez

Lion de Terre

Boulouris

Lion de Mer

Île d'Or

Cap du Dramont

CANNES AREA

LITERARY CANNES

- *Perfume* (Patrick Süskind) Evocation of the horrors of the 18th-century perfume industry in steamy Grasse: a quest to create the perfect perfume from the scent of murdered virgins.

- *Tender Is the Night* (F Scott Fitzgerald) A vivid account of life on the Riviera during the decadent 1920s Jazz Age; set on Cap d'Antibes with day trips to Cannes.

- *Bits of Paradise* (F Scott & Zelda Fitzgerald) Twenty-one short stories by one of the Riviera's most notorious couples; Scott's *Love in the Night* (1925), set in Cannes, is the ultimate romance.

- *Perfume from Provence, Sunset House* and *Trampled Lilies* (Lady Fortescue) A lady's life, stretching from the purchase of a house outside Grasse to her final flight back to the UK at the start of WWII.

- *May We Borrow Your Husband* (Grahame Greene) A collection of short 'comedy of sexual life' stories, kicking off with two homosexuals' pursuit of a newly wed groom while honeymooning in Antibes with his virgin wife. Written by Greene in Antibes.

- *Super Cannes* (A G Barrad) Fast-paced action in Edem-Olympia (aka Sophia Antipolis), a work-obsessed technology park on the Med near Cannes; an insightful, satirical, essential read by one of the most important names in contemporary British literature.

TOURIST INFORMATION

Tourist office (☎ 04 92 99 84 22; blvd de la Croisette; ⏱ 9am-8pm Jul & Aug, 9am-7pm Mon-Sat Sep-Jun) On the ground floor of Palais des Festivals.

Tourist office annexe (☎ 04 93 99 19 77; rue Jean Jaurès; ⏱ 9am-7pm Mon-Sat) Next to the train station.

Sights & Activities

People-watching is the primary pastime on the Riviera's poshest prom, palm-shaded **blvd de la Croisette** (aka La Croisette). Start at the eastern end with tea on the terrace of the **Carlton InterContinental** (p305); its twin cupolas, erected in 1912, were modelled on the breasts of the courtesan La Belle Otéro, infamous for her string of lovers – Tsar Nicholas II and Britain's King Edward VII among them.

Continue west and pick yourself a dream mansion (to buy or rent) in the windows of 140-year-old estate agency **John Taylor & Son** (☎ 04 97 06 65 65; www.john-taylor.fr; 55 blvd de la Croisette). Several million euros lighter, walk two blocks to **La Malmaison** (☎ 04 97 06 44 90; 47 blvd de la Croisette; adult/under 18yr/18-25yr €4/free/2; ⏱ 10am-1pm & 3-7pm Tue-Sun Jun-Aug, 10am-1pm & 2.30-6.30pm Tue-Sun Apr, May & Sep, 10am-12.30pm & 2.30-6pm Tue-Sun Oct-Mar), a seaside pavilion in the former games and tea room of Cannes' grandest hotel of the 1860s, the **Grand Hôtel** (opened in 1864, shut in 1950, demolished and rebuilt in the 1960s). Modern art exhibitions fill part of La Malmaison today.

A 400m stroll further along La Croisette is the legendary **Palais des Festivals** (Festival Palace; ☎ 04 93 39 01 01; blvd de la Croisette), a ferociously ugly concrete beast where beauties gather and films are screened during the film festival. Pose for a photograph on the 22 steps leading up to the entrance, then wander along **allée des Étoiles du Cinéma**, a path of celebrity hand imprints in the pavement.

Yachts frame nearby **Vieux Port**, and across the busy street players of *pétanque* (a game like lawn bowls) spin balls on **sq Lord Brougham**. Half the town hangs out here: kids ride the merry-go-round, teens drink shakes outside McDonald's and a **flower market** blooms across the northern side of the square each morning.

Walk diagonally across sq Lord Brougham and join rue Félix Faure. Pass the back of the **Hôtel de Ville** (town hall) to get to the bus station building, jazzed up with the trompe l'oeil fresco, **Cinéma Cannes**, featuring 34 faces from Cannes' cinematic heritage. Across the road, restaurant-crammed rue St-Antoine snakes into hilly **Le Suquet**, the city's oldest quarter. British chancellor Lord Brougham – the first foreigner to live in Cannes – built **Villa Eleanor** (1862) here; locals thought he was crackers when he insisted on laying a pea-green lawn around his abode.

Atop the hill is 12th-century **Église Notre Dame d'Esperance** (⏱ 9am-noon & 3-7pm summer, 9am-noon & 2.15-6pm Tue-Sun autumn & spring, to 4pm Mon winter) and **Musée de la Castre** (☎ 04 93 38 55 26;

adult/under 18yr/18-25yr €3/free/2, 1st Sun of month free; ⊙ 10am-7pm Thu-Tue, 10am-9pm Wed Jul & Aug, 10am-1pm & 2-6pm Tue-Sun Apr, Jun & Sep, 10am-1pm & 2-5pm Tue-Sun Oct-Mar), home to a diverse collection of art, antiquities and ethnographical oddities.

BEACHES

Cannes is blessed with sandy beaches, although much of the stretch along blvd de la Croisette is for guests of top-notch hotels or those prepared to pay for the luxury of having a strip of carpet leading to the water's edge: rates range from €15/19 per half-/full day for a mattress and yellow-and-white parasol on **Plage du Gray d'Albion** (☎ 04 92 99 79 99; ⊙ 10am-6pm) – it has a water-skiing school – to €30/38/44 for a back-row/front-row seat/spot on the pier of exclusive **Carlton Beach**; look for the stylish sand-coloured parasols.

For the ultimate beach experience, flop beneath a pearl-white beach umbrella on **Z Plage** (front row/other rows/pier €28/24/32; ⊙ 9am-6pm),

the beach of Hôtel Martinez. Its Zzzz day package (€88) includes lounger, parasol, a 25-minute massage in a beach cabin and a two-course lunch in its trendy, superstylish beach bar (p307).

This arrangement leaves only a small cheap strip of sand near the Palais des Festivals for the bathing hoi polloi, although free public beaches **Plage du Midi** and **Plage de la Bocca** stretch for several kilometres west from Vieux Port along blvd Jean Hibert and blvd du Midi.

BOAT EXCURSIONS

The Îles de Lérins – a 20-minute skip across the bay – make a fine day out; see p310.

Tours

Le Petit Train (☎ 06 14 09 49 39; www.cannes-petit -train.com; ⊙ 9am-11.30pm Jul & Aug, shorter hours winter) sets off opposite Hôtel Majestic Barrière and chugs along La Croisette and rue d'Antibes

---

STARRING AT CANNES

For 10 days in May, all eyes turn to Cannes, centre of the cinematic universe where more than 30,000 producers, distributors, directors, publicists, stars and hangers-on descend to buy, sell or promote more than 2000 films. As the premier film event of the year, the festival attracts some 4000 journalists from around the world, guaranteeing a global spotlight to anyone with enough looks or prestige to grab it.

At the centre of the whirlwind is the colossal, 60,000-sq-metre Palais des Festivals, on legendary La Croisette, where the official selections are screened. Hand prints and autographs of celebrities frame its stark concrete hulk, dubbed the 'bunker' by locals, who are the first to acknowledge the sheer ugliness of the far-from-fairy-tale Festival Palace.

The palace opened in 1982, replacing the original Palais des Festival – since demolished – built where the Noga Hilton Hotel now sits to accommodate the first Cannes Film Festival. The inaugural festival was scheduled for 1 September 1939, as a response to Mussolini's Fascist propaganda film festival in Venice, but Hitler's invasion of Poland brought the festival to an abrupt end. It restarted in 1946 – and the rest is history.

Over the years the festival split into 'in competition' and 'out of competition' sections. The goal of 'in competition' films is the prestigious Palme d'Or, awarded by the jury and its president to the film that best 'serves the evolution of cinematic art'. Notable winners include Francis Ford Coppola's *Apocalypse Now* (1979), American activist Michael Moore's anti–Bush administration polemic *Farenheight 9/11* (2004) and Ken Loach's *The Wind that Shakes the Barley* (2006).

The vast majority of films are 'out of competition'. Behind the scenes the **Marché du Film** (Film Market; www.marchedufilm.com) sees €150 million worth of business negotiated in distribution deals. And it's this hard-core commerce combined with all the televised Tinseltown glitz that gives the film festival its special magic. For a concentrated dose, don your glad rags, stand up tall and strut into the bar of one of the posh hotels as if you own the place.

Tickets to the Cannes Film Festival are governed by a complex system of passes, and unless you're a high-flyer in the film industry, you're unlikely to get one. What you can get are free tickets to selected individual films, usually after their first screening. Look for the **Cannes Cinephiles** (☎ 04 97 06 44 90; www.cinema-cannes.com in French; ⊙ 9am-5.30pm) ticket booth outside the Palais des Festivals. For the film festival programme, consult the official website, www.festival-cannes.org.

(adult/child three to 10 years old €6/3) or up to Le Suquet (€6/3). Visiting both destinations costs €9/6.

Festivals & Events

The **Festival International du Film** (opposite) lasts 10 days in May. In mid-July classical orchestras and soloists from around the world gather for the 10-day **Nuits Musicales du Suquet**; concerts are held on the square in front of Église Notre Dame d'Esperance.

Sleeping

Hotel prices soar to astronomical, undisclosed rates during the May film festival and congress periods. Snagging a room at these times is near impossible unless you've booked months in advance. The rest of the year, reserve through **Cannes Réservation** (☎ 08 26 00 06 06; www.cannes-reservation.com; 8 blvd d'Alsace; ✆ 7am-7pm Mon-Sat).

Chambres d'hôtes scarcely exist in affluent Cannes: **Cottage Bellevue** (☎ 06 20 02 13 38, 04 93 68 37 29; www.cottage-bellevue.com in French; 7 traverse Sunny Bank; d low/high/festival season €55/80/100; P), a terraced family house on a hill above Cannes, is an option.

BUDGET

Le Chalit (☎ 04 93 99 22 11; www.le-chalit.com; 27 av du Maréchal Galliéni; dm from €20, sheets €3; ✆ reception 8.30am-1pm & 5-8.30pm; 🖳) Around 300m northwest of the station, this private hostel sports a kitchen with food and drinks machine, decent dorms and no curfew. Minimum stay is three nights from July to September.

Le Chantéclair (☎ 04 93 39 68 88; 12 rue Forville; d with shower from €37, with shower & toilet from €50; ✆ Jan–mid-Oct) In the heart of Le Suquet and moments from the market, this sweet 15-room place has an enchanting courtyard garden. There's usually a two-night minimum stay.

Hôtel Atlantis (☎ 04 93 39 18 72; www.cannes-hotel-atlantis.com; 4 rue du 24 Août; d from €45, with air-con from €59; ✖) Run by the friendly Jean-Michel and Christian, the Atlantis has been in the Carre family since 1958 and provides cheerful, basic rooms with hairdryers, telephones and TVs. Unusually for a two-star hotel, there's a sauna and a weights room for guests. Wi-fi access costs €5 a day.

Hotel l'Estérel (☎ 04 93 38 82 82; www.hotellesterel.com; 15 rue du 24 Août; s/d low season €46/58, high season €60/71; ✖) This huge block couldn't be handier for the station, its 55 modern two-star rooms

being spare, simple and unlikely to offend anyone's sensibilities. But breakfast overlooking the rooftops of Cannes in the 6th-floor glass breakfast room with terrace is stunning.

Hôtel des Allées (☎ 04 93 39 53 90; www.hotel-des-allees.com; 6 rue Émile Négrin; s/d low season €49.25/68.50, high season €69.25/88.50; ✖) Annelis and Fritz Wälti-Hoog are the Swiss couple behind this Swiss-clean, comfortable hotel wedged between restaurants on a pedestrian street. Rooms have TV, phone, hairdryer and safety box, and the best have a tiny wrought-iron balcony with snatches of sea view. Wi-fi access is free.

MIDRANGE

La Villa Tosca (☎ 04 93 38 34 40; www.villa-tosca.com; 11 rue Hoche; s/d/tr/q low season €61/75/99/119, high season €89/99/129/149; ✖) This elegant bourgeois townhouse is a great choice for serious shoppers keen to sleep on Cannes' busiest commercial street – fall out of bed and into the shops. Three-/seven-day stays yield a 25/50% discount on the last night.

Hôtel des Orangers (☎ 04 93 39 99 92; www.charmhotel .com; 1 rue des Orangers; s/d/tr low season from €64/71/97, high season €97/109/148; P ✖ ✆) Right in the heart of quaint Le Suquet, this 52-room place has shady gardens and rooms that, though '80s in feel, are decent sized. Some have sea views.

Hôtel Molière (☎ 04 93 38 16 16; www.hotel-moliere .com; 5 rue Molière; s/d low season €72/83, high season €84/104; ✖) Majestic white pillars prop up the pastel-pink wedding-cake façade of this

CANNES AREA

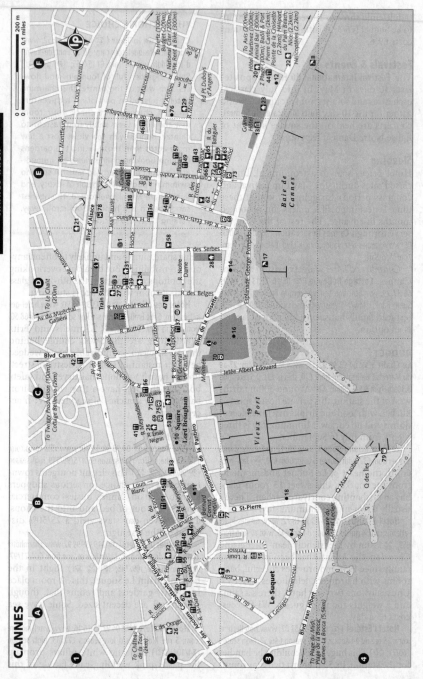

CANNES

regal old pile, crowned by its very own palm- and cypress-tree-studded garden. Decoration inside is as flowery as out; some rooms have balconies. Rates include breakfast.

Hôtel Splendid (☎ 04 97 06 22 22; www.splendid -hotel-cannes.fr; 4 & 6 rue Félix Faure; d low/mid/high season from €124/129/144; 🞕) When the weather's warm, breakfast is served on a terrace plumb above the legendary Palm Square at this glistening white palace with ornate moulded façade. Rates rise the higher you go, peaking with spacious 5th-floor rooms offering Med-facing balcony and the sweet *suite Mansardée* on the 6th. Munch a complimentary *calisson* (frosted almond boat-shaped biscuit from Aix) while checking in/out.

3.14 Hôtel (☎ 04 92 99 72 00; www.3-14hotel .com; 5 rue François Eineasy; d low/mid/high season from €120/170/220; 🅿 🞕 🖳 🞕) A line-up of potted olive trees ushers guests into Trois Quatorze, a dazzling ode (best to keep your sunglasses on) to Pop-Zen design, constructed around the principles of feng shui. Yellow budgies cheep behind reception, a fountain tinkles in the lobby and each perfumed floor whisks guests to a different continent. Parking costs €23 a night.

TOP END

Hôtel Martinez (☎ 04 92 98 73 00; www.hotel-martinez .com; 73 blvd de la Croisette; d low/mid/high season from €260/360/510; 🅿 🞕 🖳 🞕) Arguably the love-liest luxury place to stay, this ultrasmart Art Deco–style hotel opened its doors in 1929, a year before Cannes' first official summer season. Luxurious and vast rooms with all the self-pampering perks are offset by a Gi-venchy spa, fitness centre with sea-facing ter-race, beach (p302) and piano bar (p307). The four-bedroom penthouse suite costs a mere €10,000/15,700/30,000 a night in low/mid/ high season. Parking is €35 a night.

Seafront legends with private beaches:

Carlton InterContinental (☎ 04 93 06 40 06; www .ichotelsgroup.com; 58 blvd de la Croisette; d incl breakfast €200; 🅿 🞕 🖳) Among the world's most photo-graphed hotels.

Hôtel Majestic Barrière (☎ 04 92 98 77 00; www .majestic-barriere.com; 10 blvd de la Croisette; d from €252; 🅿 🞕 🖳 🞕) Art Deco palace with Michelin-starred restaurant.

Hilton (☎ 04 92 99 70 00; www.cannes.hilton.com; 50 blvd de la Croisette; d from €280; 🅿 🞕 🖳 🞕) Big, bold and glassy on the site of the original Palais des Festivals. Rooftop pool.

INFORMATION	
Café @ to z.net	1 D1
Cannes English Bookshop	2 C2
Cap Cyber	3 D1
Laverie du Port	4 B3
Post Office	5 D2
Tourist Office	6 C2
Tourist Office Annexe	7 D1

SIGHTS & ACTIVITIES	
Carlton Beach	8 F3
Chapelle de Ste-Anne	(see 15)
Église Notre Dame d'Esperance	9 A3
Flower Market	10 C2
Grand Hôtel	(see 13)
Hôtel de Ville	11 B2
John Taylor & Son	12 F3
La Malmaison	13 B2
Le Petit Train	14 D3
Musée de la Castre	15 B3
Palais des Festivals	16 C2
Plage du Gray d'Albion	17 D3
Plongée Club de Cannes	18 C3
Vieux Port	19 C3

SLEEPING	
3.14 Hôtel	20 F3
Cannes Réservation	21 D1
Carlton InterContinental	22 F3
Hilton	23 E3
Hôtel Atlantis	24 D2
Hôtel des Allées	25 C2
Hôtel des Orangers	26 A2
Hôtel l'Estérel	27 D1

Hôtel Majestic Barrière	28 D2
Hôtel Molière	29 F2
Hôtel Splendid	30 C2
La Villa Tosca	31 D2
Le Chanteclair	32 B2

EATING	
Astoux & Brun	33 B2
Aux Bons Enfants	34 B2
Barbarella	35 A2
Café Lenôtre	36 C2
Caviar Volga	(see 56)
Citronelle	37 D2
Createurs Café	38 C2
Da Laura	39 D2
Food Market	40 E2
Fromager Ceneri	41 C2
Gusti Italiani	42 C1
Harem	43 E2
kiousk 3.14	44 F3
L'Annexe	45 B2
L'Ardoise	(see 71)
La Cave	46 B2
La Tarterie	47 D2
Le Mesclun	48 B2
Le Riad	49 E2
Mantel	50 B2
Marché Forville	51 B2
Monoprix	52 D1
O'Tchan	53 C2
Oliviers & Co	54 E2
Pacific Express	55 B2
Sun Shine	56 C2
Sushikan	57 E2

DRINKING	
38 The Place	58 D2
Bar des Célébrités	(see 22)
Cantine	59 E2
Carignan	60 A2
Chinks	61 B2
Le 4U	62 E2
Le Living Room	63 E2
Le Must	64 E3
Le Privé	65 E2
Les 3 Portes	66 E2
Twiggy	67 A2

ENTERTAINMENT	
Cat Corner	68 E3
Cinéma Les Arcades	69 C2
Jimmy'z	70 C2
Le 7 of Angels	71 C2
Le Loft	72 E3
Les Coulisses	73 E3
Palais Club	(see 16)
Vogue	74 A2
Zanzibar	75 C2

TRANSPORT	
Bus Azur Information Desk	(see 77)
Compagnie Éstérel Chanteclair	(see 79)
Limousine Services	76 F2
Main Bus Station	77 B2
Small Bus Station	78 E1
Ticket Offices & Embarcation Point for Boat Trips	79 B4
Trans Côte d'Azur	(see 79)

CANNES AREA

CANNES AREA

Eating
RESTAURANTS

Less-expensive restaurants line rue du Marché Forville, and eating options abound along pedestrian rue St-Antoine and rue du Suquet. For informal dining or hybrid drinking-dining with the hip set, hit Cannes' 'magic square' (p308).

Le Riad (☎ 04 93 38 60 95; 6 impasse Florian; dishes €15; ☻ lunch & dinner Tue-Sat) Kacem Laraki, the man behind this opulent Moroccan garden down a car-free dead end, scouted out his chef himself in Fez. A fountain, rose petal–sprinkled pool, mosaic floors, cushioned seating and several eating areas on different levels meet every mood.

Aux Bons Enfants (80 rue Meynadier; menu €17; ☻ closed Sat dinner & Sun Oct-Jun) A people's-choice place since 1935, this old-town bistro cooks up regional dishes such as aïoli *garni* (aïoli with vegetables), marinated herrings, and calf liver with onions and balsamic vinegar, all in a convivial atmosphere. Make no plans for the afternoon after lunching here. No credit cards.

L'Ardoise (☎ 04 93 39 09 02; 5 rue Rouguière; plat/menu du jour €10/20; ☻ lunch Mon-Sat; ☒) The menu changes every fortnight at this 1930s bistro tucked down a pedestrian alley. Fresh red and white roses in vases are about the only excess in the dark wood and red interior where regulars take their pick from four or five market-inspired dishes. No credit cards.

Da Laura (☎ 04 93 38 40 51; 8 rue du 24 Août; pasta €11-15; ☻ lunch Mon-Sat) Cannois flock to this busy trattoria with bustling pavement terrace

---

GASTRONOMIC SHOP

Go on, indulge yourself.

Caviar Volga (☎ 04 92 98 17 12; 5 rue Maréchal Joffre) Caviar emporium; €148/496 for 100g of French/Iranian caviar.

Fromager Ceneri (☎ 04 93 39 63 68; 22 rue Meynadier) Top cheese shop.

Gusti Italiani (3 blvd Carnot) Italian *traiteur* (caterer-delicatessen) with fabulous meat, cheese and ready-made savoury dishes.

Sun Shine (☎ 04 93 39 44 56; 5 rue Maréchal Joffre) Serious wine cellar; sells chilled magnums of champagne.

Oliviers & Co (☎ 04 93 39 00 38; 4 rue Macé) Olive-oil shop, with tastings.

---

for authentic Italian cooking. Pasta portions are larger than traditional *primi* (first course) size – making them a wholesome stand-alone meal – and the star of the show is the largest pepper mill you've ever seen.

La Cave (☎ 04 93 99 79 87; www.restaurant-lacave.com; 9 blvd de la République; lunch menu €22.50; ☻ lunch & dinner Mon-Sat Sep-Jul) The Wine Cellar is a dramatic contrast to most Cannois eating spaces: lace curtains hang at the windows, and roast veal loin with basil tomatoes, calf kidneys and other French classics are served in an intimate, old Parisian bistro setting.

Astoux & Brun (☎ 04 93 39 21 87; www.astouxbrun.com in French; 21 rue Félix Faure; seafood platters €22-92, oysters €9-12 for 6; ☻ lunch & dinner) Every type/size of oyster is available alongside lobster, crab, sea urchins, scallops, stuffed mussels and magnificent seafood platters at this temple to seafood founded in 1953. Chefs draw the crowds by preparing the shellfish out the front in summer.

L'Annexe (☎ 04 93 68 18 71; 5 rue Louis Blanc; ☻ 9am-midnight) Located around the corner from its big brother, Astoux & Brun, L'Annexe offers diners informal *dégustation* (tasting) all hours at the bar.

Mantel (☎ 04 93 39 13 10; noel.mantel@wanadoo.fr; 22 rue St-Antoine; lunch/dinner menus from €25/35; ☻ lunch & dinner Thu-Tue) Discover why Noël Mantel is the hotshot of the Cannois gastronomic scene at his refined old-town restaurant with white tablecloths and silver settings, and homemade jam and chutney tempting diners in the entrance. The bread is also Mantel-baked.

Le Mesclun (☎ 04 93 99 45 19; www.lemesclun-restaurant.com; 16 rue St-Antoine; menu €35; ☻ dinner Mon-Sun, reduced hours winter) The menu here titillates taste buds: wild turbot baked in champagne with summer truffles and mushrooms; langoustine roasted in coriander-flavoured butter and spiced with tomato, courgette, olive and mango; or roast duck breast with spiced honey, a pear in red wine and a peach in olive oil. Dining is refined and artful.

Barbarella (☎ 04 92 99 17 33; 14-16 rue St-Dizier; menu €40; ☻ dinner Tue-Sun) Wok-cooked meat and fish crown the innovative menu at this eye-catching, gay-friendly establishment dressed Philippe Starck–style in Le Suquet.

Bâoli (☎ 04 93 43 03 43; www.lebaoli.com; meals €75; Port Pierre Canto, 50 blvd de la Croisette; ☻ 8pm-5am summer, 8pm-5am Fri & Sat winter) Film-festival stars go crazy about the chic seashore restaurant with dance floor and kitchen cooking up Asian (loads of teppanyaki, sushi and sashimi) and fusion cuisine in an exotic Thai-temple setting.

CAFÉS

kiousk 3.14 (☎ 04 93 39 52 94; 3 rue François Eineasy; breakfast/lunch/afternoon tea €6.50/13/5.50; ☯ 9.30am-8pm; ✗) It's just so design, darling, the café of 3.14 Hôtel (p305) a block down the road. Cream plastic or sofa seating provides a brilliant contrast to the smart emerald-green silk cushions sprinkled around the clean-cut space. It's nonsmoking from noon to 8pm.

Createurs Café (☎ 04 93 39 66 92; www-createurs-café .com; 41bis rue Hoche; starter/plat du jour €5/9, lunch menus €12.80 & €14.80; ☯ 8am-8pm Mon-Sat) Young, innovative and a window on the city's dynamic creative scene, this modern space is half café serving imaginative lunch dishes, half boutique selling limited lines by up-and-coming French designers.

La Tarterie (☎ 04 93 39 67 43; 33 rue Bivouac Napoléon; tart slices €3.50-4, with salad €9; ☯ 8.30am-6.30pm Mon-Fri) Sweet/savoury tarts and *clafoutis* (a batter cake with fruit) ensure there's always a queue at this good-value tart house. You can lunch on delicious homemade fare inside or out.

Citronelle (☎ 06 98 94 36 86; rue Bivouac Napoléon; sandwiches/salads €3.80/4.50; ☯ 10am-8pm Mon-Sat, 10am-3pm Sun) A lime façade sets the fresh tone of this pocket-sized bar serving imaginative and generous salads, sandwiches and freshly squeezed juices (strawberry, kiwi etc) to enjoy on the hoof.

Café Lenôtre (☎ 04 92 92 56 00; www.lenotre.fr; 63 rue d'Antibes; breakfast/lunch from €9/€20; ☯ 9am-6pm) Passionate chefs invest huge effort into exquisite presentation at this classy branch of the Parisian patisserie chain. Savour sublime cakes and pastries in a contemporary setting or learn how to make them during a half-day cake-making workshop.

SELF-CATERING

Food Market (place Gambetta; ☯ daily summer, Tue-Sun winter)

Marché Forville (rue du Marché Forville; ☯ Tue-Sun)

Monoprix (entrances rue Jean Jaurès, rue Maréchal Foch & rue Buttura)

Drinking

Many bars are as much late-night dance venues as drinking holes, staying open until 2.30am or so. Likewise, several eating spaces, particularly in Cannes' 'magic square' (p308),

---

DRINKS ON THE SAND

Z Plage (☎ 04 92 98 73 00; 73 blvd de la Croisette; juice/smoothie €10/8, starters/mains from €9/15, lunch menu €30; ☯ 12.30-4pm & 6-11pm) Lunch at the beach restaurant–bar of Hôtel Martinez is an unforgettable experience. Languish on white-cushioned teak seating beneath white colonial-style umbrellas and sip unusual freshly squeezed juices (fancy a pineapple, litchi and raspberry juice? or how about strawberry, lemon, basil and pineapple, Madame?) and *fusions frappées* (smoothies). The Zen orange and peach purée with chai spices is Zen indeed, as are the Swedish massages (€50/90 per 25/50 minutes) and reflexology sessions (€45 per 25 minutes) that can be indulged in before or after lunch. In July and August, tapas is served in the company of cocktails and electro lounge jazz with DJ Max Léonidas & Sax from 6pm.

---

mutate into trendy bars come dusk. Or you can act like a star (or glimpse one) over an apéritif on the beach (see above) or in a classy hotel bar.

Carignan (☎ 04 93 39 71 14; sommelier.leandre@ wanadoo.fr; 26 rue du Suquet; ☯ 5pm-12.30am) Taste wine safe in the knowledge that Léandre Piquet (a former sommelier at the Majestic) is an authority. Find him behind the bar in his pocket-sized *bar à vins* (wine bar) atop the hill in Le Suquet.

Chink's (☎ 04 92 99 19 09; www.lechinks.com; 88 rue Meynadier; ☯ lunch & dinner) At the foot of Le Suquet on a pedestrian street, this pavement terrace and interior decked out in a cosmopolitan 1950s theme combines Thai cuisine with cocktails, DJs and a trendy bar.

38 The Place (☎ 04 92 99 79 79; 38 rue des Serbes; ☯ 10.30-12.30am) Buzzword of the moment, the Place is the place to chink champagne (€12 a glass). Find it inside Hôtel Gray d'Albion.

Amiral Bar (☎ 04 92 98 73 00; www.hotel-martinez .com; 73 blvd de la Croisette; ☯ 11am-2.30am) A cocktail in the legendary piano bar of Hôtel Martinez is a must when in town. Punters rave about Jimmy the pianist, as much for his hugely amiable manner as for his keyboard skills.

Bar des Célébrités (☎ 04 93 06 40 06; 58 blvd de la Croisette; ☯ 11am-2.30am) The ground-floor bar of the Carlton InterContinental has a sea-facing terrace for all to see and be seen.

THE MAGIC SQUARE

Some of Cannes' hippest haunts hang out in the *carré magique* (magic square), a patch of town bordered by rue Commandant André, rue des Frères Pradignac, rue du Batéguier and rue du Dr Gérard Monod. Places here are informal and trendy, and fuse dining with drinking.

On rue des Frères Pradignac, try lounge bar–cum–Lebanese restaurant **Harem** (☎ 04 93 39 62 70) at No 15; or restaurant–wine bar **Les 3 Portes** (The Three Doors; ☎ 04 93 38 91 70; www.3portes .com) at No 16, a design-led place with seating inside and out and cherry tomatoes on each table. **Le 4U** (☎ 04 93 39 71 21; www.bar4u.com; ✆ 6pm-2.30am) at No 6 is a hot evening venue.

Rue du Batéguier ushers in must-try lounge bar **Le Must** (No 14), where young beauties nibble €6 plates of mixed canapés; chintzy **Le Privé** (☎ 06 66 45 18 92; ✆ 6pm-2.30am), a tiny sushi bar at No 7 with sushi, cocktails and resident DJs; and 'before lounge' (as in before the clubs) **Cantine** (☎ 04 93 38 76 40) next door at No 9.

On rue du Dr Gérard Monod, a low-key American scene fills **Le Loft** (☎ 04 93 39 40 46; ✆ 10.30pm-2.30am) at No 13 while the pace is Zen at **Le Living Room** (☎ 04 93 99 34 82; 17 rue du Dr Gérard Monod; ✆ 6.30pm-2.30am), No 17.

Entertainment

Pick up the free monthly *Le Mois à Cannes*. Tickets for many events are sold at the **box office** (☎ 04 92 98 62 77; ✆ 10am-7pm Mon-Sat), inside the Palais des Festivals tourist office.

NIGHTCLUBS

DJs also mix 'til late in many bars.

Palais Club (☎ 04 92 99 33 33; www.palais-club .com; Palais des Festivals, blvd de la Croisette; admission incl 1 drink €26; ✆ 10pm-5am mid-Jul–late Aug) 'Dance your life' with the world's best DJs is the buzz at this summer club, which has taken Cannes by storm for the past couple of seasons – let's hope it's still around next year. Electronic music and dance is the sound. A 2600-sq-metre dance floor inside and 1500-sq-metre rooftop lounge terrace with glittering views of the Mediterranean is the space, while an affluent crowd of some 2500 clubbers is the set.

GAY & LESBIAN VENUES

Zanzibar (☎ 04 93 39 30 75; www.lezanzibar.com in French; 85 rue Félix Faure; ✆ 6pm-4am) The coast's oldest and most venerable gay bar, going strong since 1885, where people come to dance to house and admire erotic frescoes of well-built sailors.

Le 7 of Angels (☎ 04 93 39 10 36; www.discotheque -le7.com; 7 rue Rouguière; admission free-€20; ✆ 11.30pm-dawn) Known simply as '7' *(sept)*, Cannes' premier gay disco is a high-camp place with drag cabarets etc.

A CANNOIS COUPLE

Name DJ Max and Charlotte.

Passion 70s kitsch.

Occupation Twiggy Production, a boutique with bubblegum-pink façade specialising in 1970s fashion (think snug-fitting T-shirts emblazoned with a slogan of your choice in glittering gold or retro velour) at 35 blvd Carnot, high street of the real Cannes.

Mode of transport A bright orange Vespa with his-and-her Burberry-covered seats.

Best beach Plage du Midi and Palm Beach.

Claim to fame Ran the massively popular, hugely hip Twiggy bar and record shop in Le Suquet from 1996 until 2005 when year-round late-night parties were traded in for a more family-friendly lifestyle shared with daughter Tara, aged seven.

Latest buzz Max has started his own production company: buy the *Chez Twiggy* CD or discover the electronic lounge of Mike with the Twiggy-mixed album, *Castro de Maria*.

Music taste DJ Max is the man behind the legendary 'dig-out-your-platforms' Top 50 (disco with a dash of new wave) and Royal House (retro house 1985–2006) soirees that lured punters for miles around for a good six years or so. From time to time he's still the main man mixing at his…

All-time favourite club Le Klub (p276) in Nice, the best on the coast.

Vogue (☎ 04 93 39 99 18; 20 rue du Suquet; ☾ 8pm-6am Tue-Sun) This ambient bar in Le Suquet draws a young, trendy, predominantly gay crowd into electronic music.

CINEMAS

Catch a movie in English at **Cinéma Les Arcades** (☎ 08 92 68 00 39; 77 rue Félix Faure).

Getting There & Away

AIR

Nice Hélicoptères (☎ 04 93 43 42 42; www.nicehelicopteres.com; blvd de la Croisette; s from Nice/Cannes €94/77, return €157) flies from Nice to Héliport du Palm Beach (free shuttle to La Croisette) in seven minutes.

Otherwise charter a helicopter with **Azur Hélicoptère** (☎ 04 93 90 40 70; www.azurhelico.com) to fly to Nice (one way €330 for one to three passengers) or St-Tropez (€500).

BOAT

Compagnie Estérel Chanteclair (CMC; ☎ 04 93 38 66 33; www.ilesdelerins.com in French) runs trips from Cannes to Monaco (once weekly June to September) and St-Tropez (three weekly May, June and September, six weekly July and August). A return fare to either costs €30/15 per adult/child five to 10 years.

From June to September **Trans Côte d'Azur** (☎ 04 92 98 71 30; www.trans-cote-azur.com; quai Laubeuf) runs boat excursions (note that reservations are essential) to Corniche de l'Estérel (adult/child four to 10 years €17/10); Monaco (€32/16, mid-June to mid-September); and St-Tropez (€36/22).

BUS

The train is quicker and cheaper than buses for coastal journeys. Buses to Nice (€1.30, 1½ hours, every 20 minutes) and Nice-Côte d'Azur airport (€13.70 via A8, 40 minutes; €1.30 via regular road, 1½ hours; hourly 8am to 7pm) leave from the **main bus station** (place Bernard Cornut Gentille).

Buses to/from Grasse (€1.30, 45 minutes) via Mougins (€1.30, 20 minutes), Mouans-Sartoux (€1.30, 25 minutes) and Vallauris (€1.30, 30 minutes) depart every 20 minutes Monday to Saturday (hourly Sunday) from Cannes' **small bus station** (rue Jean Jaurès), next to the train station. **Rapides Côte d'Azur** (RCA; ☎ information office 08 20 48 11 11; www.rca.tm.fr in French; ☾ 7.30am-noon & 1.30-5pm Mon, Tue, Thu & Fri) has an information desk here.

TRAIN

Destinations within easy reach of Cannes **train station** (rue Jean Jaurès) include St-Raphaël (€7.90, 20 minutes, two per hour), from where you can get buses to St-Tropez and Toulon, Marseille (€26.70, two hours) and Nice (€5.60, 25 minutes) via Antibes (€2.40, eight minutes).

Getting Around

BICYCLE

Elite Rent a Bike (☎ 04 93 94 30 34; www.elite-rentabike.com; 32 av Maréchal Juin) rents out wheels (€12/18/22 a day for a road/mountain/electric bike).

Blue.loc (☎ 06 84 07 04 87; www.blueloc.com; ☾ 9am-7pm) rents out *trottinettes* (microscooters) for €10 a day, as well as bikes. It has no office but delivers to your hotel door.

BUS

Cannes and destinations up to 7km away are served by **Bus Azur** (☎ 08 25 82 55 99; www.busazur.com in French; place Bernard Cornut Gentille; ☾ 7am-7pm Mon-Fri, 8.30am-noon & 2-6.30pm Sat), with an information desk at the central bus station. A ticket/10-ticket carnet costs €1.40/9.40.

Bus 8 – served by sleek, open-top double-decker buses – cruises along the coast from quai Max Laubeuf to the port, La Croisette and Palm Beach Casino on Pointe de la Croisette. Departures are hourly 6.45am to 8am then at least every 15 minutes until 8pm. A return ticket valid for one hour on this route costs €2.

Buses 2 and 9 run from the train station, via the bus station, to/from the beaches in Cannes La Bocca, west of the centre. Bus 620 follows the same route but continues further southwest along the coast to Théoule-sur-Mer.

CAR & MOTORCYCLE

Bike-hire companies also rent out 50cc scooters/125cc motorcycles from €35/55 per day. If you absolutely have to get noticed cruising along La Croisette, pick up a chauffeured limo from **Limousine Services** (☎ 04 93 39 60 20; www.limousine-service.fr; 7 rue LaFontaine; ☾ 10am-1pm & 3-7.30pm Mon-Sat). For bog-standard rentals:

Avis (☎ 04 93 94 15 86; 69 blvd de la Croisette)
Budget (☎ 04 93 99 44 04; 160 rue d'Antibes)
Hertz (☎ 04 93 99 04 20; 145 rue d'Antibes)
National Citer (☎ 04 93 43 58 82; 160 rue d'Antibes).

TAXI

Call ☎ 04 93 38 91 91 or ☎ 04 93 49 59 20.

ÎLES DE LÉRINS

The two islands making up Lérins – Île Ste-Marguerite and Île St-Honorat – lie within a 20-minute boat ride of Cannes. Known as Lero and Lerina in ancient times, these tiny, traffic-free oases of peace and tranquillity remain a world away from the glitz, glamour and hanky-panky of cocky Cannes.

Wild camping, cycling and smoking are forbidden on these islands. There are no hotels or camp sites and St-Honorat, the smaller of the two, has nowhere to eat; bring a picnic and a good supply of drinking water.

Beaches are not the reason to come here, although pretty coves can be found on the southern side of Ste-Marguerite (a 45-minute walk from the harbour). On the northern side, sun worshippers lie on rocks and mounds of dried seaweed.

Île Ste-Marguerite

Covered in sweet-smelling eucalyptus and pine, this island, just 1km from the mainland, served as the prison of the enigmatic Man in the Iron Mask in the late 17th century. It makes a great day trip.

Ste-Marguerite is dominated by the 17th-century **Fort Royal**, built by Richelieu to defend the islands from the Spanish (who occupied the fort anyway from 1635 to 1637), with later additions by Vauban. Today it houses **Musée de la Mer** (☎ 04 93 43 18 17; adult/under 18yr/18-25yr €3/free/2, 1st Sun of month free; ◷ 10.30am-1.15pm & 2.15-5.45pm Tue-Sun Apr-Sep, to 4.45pm Oct-Mar), with exhibits on the fort's Greco-Roman history.

A door to the left in the museum's reception hall leads to the **state prison**, built by Louis XIV. Steamboat inventor Claude François Dorothée was imprisoned here between 1773 and 1774; he came up with his idea while watching slaves row the royal galley to the island. Other inmates included six Huguenots, put into solitary confinement for life in 1689 for refusing to renounce their Protestant faith – look at the triple-grilled windows and you'll understand why they went insane.

Ste-Marguerite is encircled and crisscrossed by walking trails. There's also an underwater snorkel trail off the west coast of the island.

GETTING THERE & AWAY

Compagnie Estérel Chanteclair (☎ 04 93 38 66 33; www .ilesdelerins.com in French) and **Trans Côte d'Azur** (☎ 04 92 98 71 30; www.trans-cote-azur.com) run year-round daily ferries at least hourly (7.30am to 5.15pm)

from Cannes to Ste-Marguerite. All charge €10/5 return per adult/child five to 10 years and the journey time is 20 minutes. Ticket offices and boats are on quai Max Laubeuf.

Île St-Honorat

Forested St-Honorat was once the site of a powerful monastery founded in the 5th century. Now it's home to 25 Cistercian monks who own the island but welcome visitors to their monastery and four of the seven chapels dotted around the island, which have drawn pilgrims since the Middle Ages. At 1.5km by 400m, St-Honorat is the smallest (and most southerly) of the two Lérins islands.

The **Monastère Fortifié** (☎ 04 92 99 54 00; www .abbayedelerins.com in French; admission Jul-Sep €2, Oct-Jun free; ◷ 10.30am-4pm mid-Jun–mid-Sep, 10.30am-12.30pm & 2.30-4pm mid-Sep–mid-Jun) guarding the island's southern shores is all that remains of the original monastery. Visits from July to September are by guided tour only. Built in 1073 to protect the monks from pirate attacks, its entrance stood 4m above ground level and was accessible only by ladder (later replaced by the stone staircase evident today). The elegant arches of the vaulted prayer cloister on the 1st floor date from the 15th century, and there's a magnificent panorama of the coast from the donjon terrace.

In front of the donjon is the walled, 19th-century **Abbaye Notre Dame de Lérins**, built around a medieval cloister. In the souvenir shop you can buy the 50% alcohol Lérina, a ruby-red, lemon-yellow or pea-green liqueur concocted by the monks from 44 different herbs.

The Byzantine-inspired **Chapelle de la Trinité** (◷ visits by guided tour only 10.30am-12.30pm & 2.30-4.45pm Mon-Sat, 2.30-4.45pm Sun Jul-Sep) was built between the 9th and 10th centuries on the island's eastern tip.

GETTING THERE & AWAY

Boats to St-Honorat leave from quai des Îles. They are run by the abbey boat service **Planaria** (☎ 04 92 98 71 38; www.abbayedelerins.com; return fare adult/child 5-10yrs €11/5). Boats run almost hourly from 8am to 5.30pm May to September, and every one to two hours from 8am to 4.30pm October to May.

VALLAURIS & GOLFE-JUAN

pop 26,000

Potters' town Vallauris is worth an afternoon for the artistic vestiges left behind by Picasso,

THE MAN IN THE IRON MASK

'More than 60 names have been suggested for this prisoner whose name no one knows, whose face no one has seen: a living mystery, shadow, enigma, problem.'

Victor Hugo

The Man in the Iron Mask was imprisoned by Louis XIV (1661–1715) in the fortress on Île Ste-Marguerite from around 1687 until 1698, when he was transferred to the Bastille in Paris. Only the king knew the identity of the man behind the mask, prompting a rich pageant of myth and legend to be woven around the ill-fated inmate.

Political and social satirist Voltaire (1694–1778) claimed the prisoner was the king's brother – a twin or an illegitimate older brother. In 1751 he published *Le Siècle de Louis XIV*, which attested that Louis XIV's usurped brother, face shrouded in iron, arrived on the island in 1661, was then personally escorted to the Bastille by its new governor in 1690, and died in 1703 aged around 60. His featureless mask was lined with silk and fitted with a spring mechanism at the chin to allow him to eat. Prison guards had orders to kill anyone who dared remove his iron mask.

More than 60 suggested identities have been showered on the masked prisoner, among them the Duke of Monmouth (actually beheaded under James II), the Comte de Vermandois (son of Louis XIV, said to have died from smallpox in 1683), the Duc de Beaufort (killed by the Turks in 1669) and Molière. Some theorists claimed the man in the iron mask was actually a woman.

The storming of the Bastille in 1789 fuelled yet more stories. Revolutionaries claimed to have discovered a skeleton, the skull of which was locked in an iron mask, when plundering the prison, while others focused on a supposed entry found in the prison register that read *détenu 64389000: l'homme au masque de fer* (prisoner 64389000: the man in the iron mask). Others provoked a storm with their allegations that there was *no* iron mask entry in the prison register – just a missing page. In 1855 an iron mask was found in a scrap heap in Langres, north of Dijon, and subsequently displayed in the town museum.

With the 1850 publication of Alexandre Dumas' novel *Le Vicomte de Bragelonne*, the royal crime became written in stone: in 1638 Anne of Austria, wife of Louis XIII (1617–43) and mother of Louis XIV, gives birth to twins; one is taken away from her, leaving her to bear the secret alone until the terrible truth is discovered. Dozens of iron mask films were made last century, including the 1976 version starring Richard Chamberlain and a 1998 film starring Leonardo DiCaprio.

who lived here with Françoise Gilot between 1948 and 1955.

The odd statue of a dour bronze figure clutching a sheep, **L'Homme au Mouton**, on place Paul Isnard (adjoining place de la Libération) was the gift Picasso made to the town after moving his studio here in the 1940s, unwittingly sealing the survival of Vallauris' pottery trade by his actions.

The satellite resort of Golfe-Juan, 2km south on the coast, is where Napoleon landed following his return from exile in 1815. The main reason for visiting today is to catch a boat (summer only) to the Îles de Lérins.

Orientation & Information

Vallauris bus station adjoins place de la Libération, the central square in the northern part of town. From here av George Clémenceau, the main pottery-stuffed street, runs 1.5km south to the **tourist office** (☎ 04 93 63 82 58; www.vallauris-golfe

-juan.fr in French; square du 8 Mai; ⏰ 9am-12.15pm & 1.45-6pm Mon-Sat), in a car park off the D135.

The closest train station is in Golfe-Juan. From Vallauris' tourist office head south along the D135 to Golfe-Juan's central square Nabonnand, then continue south along av de la Gare to Golfe-Juan train station. Golfe-Juan's **tourist office** (☎ 04 93 63 73 12; av des Frères Roustan; ⏰ 9am-7pm Jul & Aug, 9am-12.15pm & 1.45-6pm Mon-Fri Sep-Jun) is past the train station at the seafront.

Sights & Activities

CHÂTEAU MUSÉE DE VALLAURIS

The **Vallauris Castle Museum** (☎ 04 93 64 16 05; contact. musee@ville-vallauris.fr; place de la Libération; adult/under 16yr €3.20/free; ⏰ 10am-12.15pm & 2-6pm Wed-Mon mid-Jun–mid-Sep, 10am-12.45pm & 3-6.45pm mid-Sep–mid-Jun) hosts three museums: the **Musée National Picasso**, based around the Picasso-decorated Chapelle La Guerre et La Paix (War and Peace Chapel); the **Musée Magnelli**, devoted to the works of

Italian artist Albert Magnelli (1899–1971); and the **Musée de la Céramique** (Ceramic Museum), in which the history of Vallauris' age-old craft is unravelled.

Picasso (1881–1973) was 71 when he started work on his *temple de la paix* (temple of peace) in a disused 12th-century chapel. Dramatic murals painted onto plywood panels are tacked to the church's stone walls. In *War*, on the left, a hideous figure clutches a bloody sword, a sack of skulls and a basket of bacteria (representing germ warfare); books are trampled under the hooves of a black horse. The themes are reversed in *Peace*, on the right: figures gather in harmony, a man writes in a book and a child ploughs the sea with a winged white horse.

The museum is next to Vallauris bus station; steps lead from the station to place de la Libération.

GALERIE MADOURA

A handful of licensed copies of ceramics cast by Picasso are on sale at **Galerie Madoura** (☎ 04 93 64 66 39; www.madoura.com; rue Georges et Suzanne Ramié; admission free; ☒ 10am-12.30pm & 3-6pm Mon-Fri), the workshop where Picasso dabbled with clay under the guidance of local potters Georges and Suzanne Ramié in 1946. He consequently granted the Ramiés exclusive rights to reproduce his work, resulting in a limited edition of 633 Picasso pieces cast between 1947 and 1971.

From the bus station, walk south along av George Clémenceau, then west along av Suzanne Ramié.

MAISON DE LA PÉTANQUE

Everything from *pétanque's* invention to its reigning champions is covered in the **Maison de la Pétanque** (Provençal Boules House; ☎ 04 93 64 11 36; www.maisondelapetanque.com; 1193 chemin de St-Bernard; adult/under 18yr €3/free; ☒ 9am-noon & 2-6.30pm Mon-Sat Apr-Sep, Mon-Fri Oct-Mar), a museum dedicated to the region's most popular sport. Amateurs can have a spin on the *pétanque* pitch, and enthusiasts can get their own set of made-to-measure boules.

The museum is 2km north of Vallauris bus station. From the station, head north along av de Grasse and at the roundabout bear east along chemin St-Bernard.

Getting There & Around

Golfe-Juan train station, from where trains serve the coast, is 3km south of Vallauris town,

making bus the most convenient way of getting to/from Vallauris.

From the **bus station** (☎ 04 93 64 18 37; cnr av de la Grasse & av Aimé Berger), buses run to/from Cannes train station (€1.30, every 30 minutes) and Antibes (€1.30, 10 per day). Buses are less frequent on Sundays.

Shuttle buses link Vallauris bus station and Golfe-Juan train station (€1, 11 minutes, every 20 minutes Monday to Saturday, every 35 minutes Sunday).

ANTIBES

pop 72,500

With its boat-bedecked port, 16th-century ramparts and narrow cobblestone streets festooned with flowers, lovely Antibes is the quintessential Mediterranean town. Picasso, Max Ernst and Nicolas de Staël were captivated by Antibes, as was a restless Graham Greene (1904–91) who settled here with his lover, Yvonne Cloetta, from 1966 until the year before his death.

Greater Antibes embraces Cap d'Antibes, an exclusive green cape studded with luxurious mansions, and the modern beach resort of Juan-les-Pins. The latter is known for its seemingly extra-sandy 2km-long beach and nightlife, a legacy of the sizzling 1920s when Americans swung into town with their jazz music and oh-so-brief swimsuits. Party madness peaks during Jazz à Juan, a week-long jazz festival in late July that attracts musicians and music lovers from all over the world.

Orientation

Antibes is divided into three areas: the commercial centre around place du Général de Gaulle, Vieil Antibes (old Antibes) south of Port Vauban and the Vieux Port, and Cap d'Antibes to the southwest, including the contiguous community of Juan-les-Pins.

Av Robert Soleau links Antibes train station with place du Général de Gaulle, where the tourist office is located. From here, Juan-les-Pins is a straight 1.5km walk along blvd du Président Wilson, which runs southwest off Antibes' central square.

Information

BOOKSHOPS

Heidi's English Bookshop (☎ 04 93 34 74 11; 24 rue Aubernon) English books.

Sorbonne (8 av Robert Soleau) The best selection of maps and local/regional guides and reference books.

INTERNET ACCESS

ASA Internet Café (☎ 04 93 34 55 84; 6 rue du Marc; ☼ 10am-1pm & 4-7pm Tue-Sat)

Xtreme Cybercafé (☎ 04 93 34 14 37; Galérie du Port, 8 blvd d'Aguillon; per hr €5; ☼ 10am-8pm Mon-Sat, 10am-4pm Sun) Meet other English-speaking travellers here; there are loads of ads for apartments/jobs etc on the notice board.

LAUNDRY

Laundrette (Av du 24 Août; per 6kg €4.20; ☼ 7.30am-8pm Mon-Sat)

MONEY

Commercial banks dot the length of av Robert Soleau.

POST

Antibes post office (☎ 04 92 90 61 00; place des Martyrs de la Résistance)

Juan-les-Pins post office (sq Pablo Picasso) Cyberposte.

TOURIST INFORMATION

Antibes tourist offices place de Gaulle (☎ 04 92 90 53 00; www.antibes-juanlespins.com; 11 place du Général de Gaulle; ☼ 9am-7pm Jul & Aug, 9am-12.30pm & 1.30-6pm Mon-Fri, 9am-noon & 2-6pm Sat Sep-Jun); train station (☎ 04 92 90 53 00; place Pierre Semard; ☼ 9am-noon & 1.30-5pm Mon-Fri)

Juan-les-Pins tourist office (☎ 04 92 90 53 05; 55 blvd Charles Guillaumont; ☼ 9am-7pm Jul & Aug, 9am-noon & 2-6pm Mon-Fri, 9am-noon Sat Sep-Jun)

Sights & Activities

VIEIL ANTIBES

Because of Antibes' position on the border of France and Savoy, it was fortified in the 17th and 18th centuries, but these fortifications were ripped down in 1896 to give the city room to expand. From the tourist office on place du Général de Gaulle, bear east along rue de la République to **Porte de France**, one of the few remaining parts of the original city walls.

The **Musée Peynet et du Dessin Humoristique** (☎ 04 92 90 54 30; musee.peynet@ville-antibes.fr; place Nationale; adult/under 18yr €3/free; ☼ 10am-6pm Tue-Sun mid-Jun–mid-Sep, to 8pm Wed & Fri Jul & Aug, 10am-noon & 2-6pm Tue-Sun mid-Sep–mid-Jun) features displays of more than 300 pictures, cartoons, sculptures and costumes by Antibes-born cartoonist Peynet, best known for his Lovers series: you'll realise you know him when you see his work. In addition, the museum has good temporary exhibitions by other illustrators and cartoonists.

BARGAIN BOX

If you're visiting all of Antibes' museums, buy a **combined ticket** (€10), valid for seven days, at the tourist office or the six places covered: the Peynet, de la Tour, Archaeology, Picasso and Napoleonic museums, and Fort Carré.

At the southern end of market-busy cours Masséna, 19th-century Tour Gilli houses **Musée de la Tour** (☎ 04 93 34 13 58; 2 rue de l'Orme; admission free; ☼ 4-7pm Wed, Thu & Sat Jun-Sep, 3-5pm Wed, Thu & Sat Oct-May), a small arts and traditions museum.

To the east is **Cathédrale d'Antibes** (rue de la Paroisse), built on the site of an ancient Greek temple. It has an ochre neoclassical façade and its tall, square Romanesque bell tower dates from the 12th century.

Antibes' Greek history is the focus of the **Musée d'Archéologie** (☎ 04 93 34 00 39; Bastion St André; adult/under 18yr €3/free; ☼ 10am-6pm Tue-Sun mid-Jun–mid-Sep, to 8pm Wed & Fri Jul & Aug, 10am-noon & 2-6pm Tue-Sun mid-Sep–mid-Jun), inside the Vauban-built Bastion St-André.

MUSÉE PICASSO

Spectacularly positioned overlooking the sea, 14th-century **Château Grimaldi** served as Picasso's studio from July to December 1946. What is now Antibes' star museum, **Musée Picasso** (☎ 04 92 90 54 20; place Mariejol), will reopen after extensive renovations in late 2007. An excellent collection of Picasso's paintings, lithographs, drawings and ceramics form the main collection, as well as a photographic record of the artist at work. Particularly poignant is Picasso's La Joie de Vivre (The Joy of Life), one in a series of 25 paintings from The Antipolis Suite. The young flower girl, surrounded by flute-playing fauns and mountain goats, symbolises Françoise Gilot, the 23-year-old lover of Picasso, with whom he lived in neighbouring Golfe-Juan.

FORT CARRÉ & PORT VAUBAN

The impregnable 16th-century **Fort Carré** (☎ 06 14 89 17 45; rte du Bord de Mer; guided tour adult/under 18yr €3/free; ☼ 10am-6pm Tue-Sun mid-Jun–mid-Sep, 10am-4.30pm Tue-Sun mid-Sep–mid-Jun), enlarged by Vauban in the 17th century, dominates the approach to Antibes from Nice. **Port Vauban**, one of the first pleasure ports to be

CANNES AREA

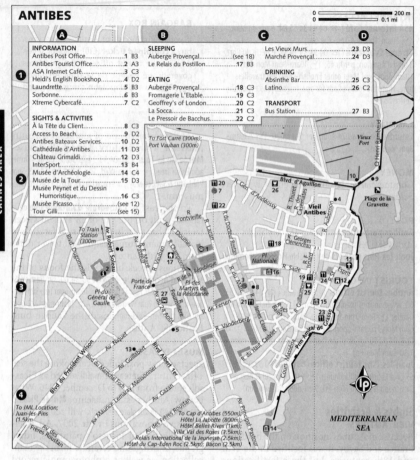

ANTIBES

INFORMATION			
Antibes Post Office	1	B3	
Antibes Tourist Office	2	A3	
ASA Internet Café	3	C3	
Heidi's English Bookshop	4	D2	
Laundrette	5	B3	
Sorbonne	6	B3	
Xtreme Cybercafé	7	C2	
SIGHTS & ACTIVITIES			
À la Tête du Client	8	C3	
Access to Beach	9	D2	
Antibes Bateaux Services	10	D2	
Cathédrale d'Antibes	11	D3	
Château Grimaldi	12	D3	
InterSport	13	B4	
Musée d'Archéologie	14	C4	
Musée de la Tour	15	D3	
Musée Peynet et du Dessin			
Humoristique	16	C3	
Musée Picasso	(see 12)		
Tour Gilli	(see 15)		

SLEEPING			
Auberge Provençal	(see 18)		
Le Relais du Postillon	17	B3	
EATING			
Auberge Provençal	18	C3	
Fromagerie L'Etable	19	C3	
Geoffrey's of London	20	C2	
La Socca	21	C3	
Le Pressoir de Bacchus	22	C2	

Les Vieux Murs	23	D3	
Marché Provençal	24	D3	
DRINKING			
Absinthe Bar	25	C3	
Latino	26	C2	
TRANSPORT			
Bus Station	27	B3	

established on the Med, is between the fort and Vieil Antibes.

Inside the fortress, a pedestrian walkway takes visitors around the stadium hidden within the star-shaped walls. The tourist office has tour details.

CAP D'ANTIBES

You feel like a shrunken Alice in Wonderland on this millionaire's peninsula: pine trees and larger-than-life villas loom at every turn, and the frenzied sound of cicadas (p79) provides an unearthly soundtrack to a cape meander.

Its southwestern tip is crowned by legendary **Hôtel du Cap – Eden Roc** (p317), the Côte d'Azur's most exclusive hotel and the owner of the coast's first open-air swimming pool

(built in 1914 for WWI servicemen). Dating from 1870, it hit the big time just after WWI when a literary salon held here one summer (previous guests had come for the winter season only) was attended by Hemingway, Picasso et al. The icing on the cake was the immortalisation of the hotel (as the thinly disguised, fictional Hôtel des Étrangers) by F Scott Fitzgerald in his novel *Tender Is the Night* (1934).

Other notable names on Cap d'Antibes' guest book include novelist Jules Verne (1828–1905), who lived at **Les Chênes Verts** (152 blvd John F Kennedy), and Cole Porter who, in 1922, rented **Château de la Garoupe**, now owned by one of the many Russian *nouveaux riches* settled on the Côte d'Azur today. Russia's first billionaire, oligarch Boris Berezovski (who amassed his fortune taking control of state assets after communism's collapse), bought the pad for €22 million in 1996.

Immediately northwest of Eden Roc is the **Musée Napoléonien** (☎ 04 93 61 45 32; blvd Kennedy; adult/under 18yr €3/free; ☻ 10am-5.30pm Tue-Sat mid-Jun–mid-Sep, 10am-4.30pm Tue-Sat mid-Sep–mid-Jun), a naval museum inside Tour Sella, which documents Napoleon's return from exile in 1815.

The beautiful **Jardin Botanique de la Villa Thuret** (☎ 04 93 67 88 66; http://jardin-thuret.antibes.inra.fr; 62 blvd du Cap; admission free; ☻ 8am-6pm Mon-Fri Jun-Sep, 8.30am-5.30pm Mon-Fri Oct-May), 3.5 hectares of botanical gardens dating from 1856 and embracing 1600 species, dominates the centre of the cape.

Another lovely garden is the 11-hectare landscaped park around **Villa Eilenroc** (☎ 04 93 67 74 33; av de Beaumont; admission free; ☻ villa 9am-noon & 1.30-5pm Wed Sep-Jun, park 9am-noon & 1.30-5pm Tue & Wed Sep-Jun), on the southern tip of Cap d'Antibes. The villa was designed by Garnier in 1867 for rich Dutchman, Hugh Hope Loudon, who reversed the name of his wife Cornélie to come up with the villa's name. It was not until the 1870s, however, when rich Scotsman James Wyllie bought Eilenroc, that its fabulous gardens were landscaped.

Sweeping views of the coastline from St-Tropez to Italy can be enjoyed from **Chapelle de la Garoupe** (chemin du Phare; ☻ 3-5pm). The neighbouring lighthouse can't be visited. From here steps lead downhill to av Aimé Bourreau; bear right, then turn left along av Guide to get to sandy Plage de la Garoupe. From the far end of the beach, a 2.7km-long scenic coastal path snakes to **Cap Gros**, the cape's southeasternmost tip, and beyond.

BEACHES & BOATS
Antibes has a small sandy beach, **Plage de la Gravette** (quai Henri Rambaud) and the substantially larger beach, **Plage de la Salis**, with unbeatable views of old Antibes, a 20-minute walk along the ramparts towards Cap d'Antibes. For seemingly endless golden beaches that buzz from sunrise to sunset, Juan-les-Pins is the place.

The stretch of coast between Plage de la Salis and Cap d'Antibes, especially the section around **Pointe Bacon**, is fringed with romantic coves and rocks from which snorkellers frolic in clear waters. On the cape itself, **Plage de la Garoupe** was famously first raked clear of seaweed in 1922 by Cole Porter and American artist Gerald Murphy to create a sandy beach. Far from an idyllic paradise today, it is filled with sun-loungers rammed so tightly together that two pontoons have been built to extend body-frying space. Pay €19/21 a day for a lounger on the sand/pontoon run by the two

CANNES AREA

À LA TÊTE DU CLIENT
Holui is a true street artist. The skilled, 50-year-old Shanghai-born sculptor came to France in his early 20s to study fine art in Paris, but subsequently moved to Antibes because 'it was easier to work on the street'.

'I now have my own atelier, but I still go to blvd d'Aguillon in the evening. I have to. I have clients who've known me for 20 years, who I've sculpted from inside their mother's tummy to childhood and so on. People need to know where to find me. So every year, I'm always on the same spot in the same street.'

Holui lures the crowds with a giant pair of silver-painted wooden scissors (secretly embedded with a real pair of scissors), with which he deftly cuts out an uncannily accurate side-profile Chinese shadow of his subject from black paper – in seconds flat.

'The scissors are part of the street act. I made them initially to attract people, but now they're essential to my work. People aren't accustomed to being an artist's model; they need something to look at and also don't like people watching them. So everyone looks at the scissors,' explains Holui, who rings an old microwave bell when his cut-out is done.

And Antibes? What's the best thing about the place?

'There are two things: the *lavoir* (washhouse) and Daniel, Daniel Klemex. If I have a question, I ask him. He is an artist who lives in Antibes and has his studio in Cagnes-sur-mer.'

Find Holui at his studio, **À La Tête du Client** (☎ 04 93 34 62 49; 12 rue James Close; ☻ 10am-1pm & 2-8pm in season) – there's no sign, just look for the scissors – or on blvd d'Aguillon from 8pm 'til late. A postcard-sized, Chinese-shadow portrait costs €5.

adjoining beach restaurants (full of hobnobbing English), or squeeze your bum onto the tiny patch of sand left for nonpaying folk.

In old Antibes, rent a 6cv boat (without licence) at **Antibes Bateaux Services** (☎ 06 15 75 44 36; www.antibes-bateaux.com; quai Henri Rambaud) for €100/140 per half-/full day (plus a €700 deposit).

Enjoy alternative views of wealthy Cap d'Antibes aboard **Visiobulle** (☎ 04 93 67 02 11; www.visobulle.com; pontoon Courbet, blvd Guillaumont; adult/2-11yr €12/6; ☑ Apr-Sep), a glass-bottomed boat that sails around the cape four to seven times daily. Tours last one hour and depart from the jetty opposite the tourist office in Juan-les-Pins.

INLINE SKATING

Hire skates for €12 per day at **InterSport** (☎ 04 93 34 20 14; 10 av Guillabert; ☑ 9.30am-12.15pm & 2.30-7pm Mon-Sat).

Festivals & Events

Cap d'Antibes' premier occasion is **Jazz à Juan** (Festival de Jazz d'Antibes Juan-les-Pins), a week-long festival in late July. There's always a first-rate line-up, and the venues, Juan-les-Pins' **Eden Casino** (☎ 04 92 93 71 71; blvd Édouard Baudoin) and the gardens fronting the beach on sq Gould, are superb.

Sleeping

Unless noted otherwise, the following are in Antibes.

CHAMBRES D'HÔTES

Villa Val des Roses (☎ 06 85 06 06 29; www.val-des-roses.com; 6 chemin des Lauriers; d/tr/q from €160/210/250; ☑ Jan-Oct; Ⓟ ☒ ☐ ☒) This cream, bourgeois villa with marble floors, laptop and flat-screen TV in each room, white walls and a choir of cicadas outside is a 20-minute stroll along the ramparts from the old town. But it's a mere moment from sandy Plage de la Salis, and its walled garden is an oasis of peace. Belgian Filip runs the house; should you fall madly in love with the place, his brother Frederik is opening another Val des Roses by the beach in Kenya! Parking costs €10 a day; breakfast is €16.

HOTELS

Le Relais du Postillon (☎ 04 93 34 20 77; www.relais dupostillon.com; 8 rue Championnet; d €46-85; ☒) This 17th-century coach house has seen better days but its 16 rooms overlooking a quiet courtyard or children's park remain comfortable enough. Rooms on the 1st floor are named after Italian towns and those on the 2nd after German ones, reflecting the owner's travels.

Hôtel La Jabotte (☎ 04 93 61 45 89; www.jabotte .com; 13 av Max Maurey; s/d low season from €63.50/71, high season from €85.50/93; Ⓟ ☒) Beach bunnies will like this hotel, a minute's walk from Plage de la Salis, 1km south of Antibes' old town. Eat your breakfast in the little courtyard, shaded by a handsome orange tree; check in early to snag one of the five free parking spaces out front.

Auberge Provençal (☎ 04 93 34 13 24; www.au bergeprovencale.com; 61 place Nationale; s/d/tr/q low season from €80/95/105/140, high season from €100/110/125/170) Fabulous dining venue (see below) first and foremost, this old Provençal inn – in true coach-inn style – has six romantic rooms up top, each named after a different gal (or guy in the case of Romeo). Ornate canopied or four-poster beds, beamed ceilings, period furnishings and freshly cut flowers mean Juliette will be well pleased.

HOSTELS

Relais International de la Jeunesse (☎ 04 93 61 34 40; 60 blvd de la Garoupe; dm incl breakfast €15, sheets €3; ☑ Mar-Oct, reception 8-11am & 5.30-11pm) Antibes' cheapest option, this hostel is beautifully located on the Baie de la Garoupe (3km south of Antibes' centre) in Cap d'Antibes. It's possible to pitch a tent on site for €8, not including breakfast. Take bus 2A from Antibes' bus station to L'Antiquité stop.

Eating

Terrace restaurants and cafés lace Antibes' old-town streets; blvd d'Aguillon along the ramparts is a gastronomic line-up.

La Socca (☎ 04 93 34 15 00; 1 rue James Close; socca per slice €2.50, salads & pizza €7.50; ☑ lunch & dinner) Otherwise known as Chez Jo, there is no cheaper, more cheerful place than this. Grab a chair and enjoy a quick-eat lunch of Niçois *socca* (chickpea pancake), *pissaladière* (savoury tart) or pizza. Don't be surprised if your neighbour strikes up a conversation with you.

Auberge Provençal (☎ 04 93 34 13 24; www .aubergeprovencale.com; 61 place Nationale; lunch menus €14.50 & €19.50, dinner menus €34.50 & €44.50; ☑ lunch & dinner) The local press has raved about this place, one of Antibes' oldest, since its face-lift at the hands of Sofia and Serge Buga. The teasing oyster bar with a handful of high tables and bar stools at the entrance is hard to resist (six oysters, bread and a glass of wine for €10) but one glimpse of the pretty interior courtyard out the back and you'll be transfixed.

Les Vieux Murs (☎ 04 93 34 06 73; www.lesvieuxmurs .com; promenade Amiral de Grasse; menus €42 & €60, lunch/ dinner mains €20/35; lunch & dinner Jun-Aug, lunch & dinner Wed-Mon mid-Sep–May) The setting of the Old Walls is just that – wedged in the former fortifications of old Antibes, across the street from crashing waves. Its kitchen staff are no slouches, serving up highly rated French and Provençal cuisine.

Bacon (☎ 04 93 61 50 02; blvd de Bacon, Cap d'Antibes; menus €49 & €79; lunch & dinner Wed-Sun, dinner Tue) Nothing to do with pork – rather fish, lots of it, either grilled with fennel, steamed or cooked in a *papillote* (a greased wrapping of parchment paper in which the fish is baked) and dressed in warm olive oil, basil butter, chive butter or broth. *Bouillabaisse* (Marseillais fish stew) is the other dish to revel in at this known-far-and-wide fish restaurant on Pointe Bacon. Hot tip: after lunch, cross the road and sleep off your lunch in one of the rocky coves on the Med.

For self-caterers:

Fromagerie L'Etable (cnr rue Sade & rue Guillaumont) Pongy cheese.

Geoffrey's of London (☎ 04 93 34 55 70; www.geof freysoflondon.com; Galerie du Port, rue Lacan; 9am-7.30pm Mon-Sat) British supermarket: Heinz beans to Walkers salt'n'vinegar crisps.

Le Pressoir de Bacchus (☎ 04 93 74 93 25; 9 rue Fontvieille) Wine cellar.

Marché Provençal (cours Masséna; 6am-1pm Jul & Aug, 6am-1pm Tue-Sun Sep-Jun) Fabulous outdoor food market.

Drinking

Pedestrian blvd d'Aguillon heaves with merrily piddled Anglophones falling out of the busy 'English' and 'Irish' pubs here.

Absinthe Bar (☎ 04 93 34 93 00; 1 rue Sade; 9am-11pm) Flirt with the green fairy at this dedicated absinthe bar, the only one of its kind in France, with an original 1860 zinc bar and five round tables with all the accessories (four-tapped water fountain, sugar cubes etc). Pick from 25 brain-pickling absinthe varieties (€4 per glass).

Latino (☎ 04 93 34 44 22; www.lelatino.com in French; 24 blvd d'Aguillon; tapas platters €13-18; 7pm-2am) Indulge in that essential early-evening apéritif at this busy tapas bar where mixed Mexican, Spanish and vegetarian tapas platters, enchiladas and battered fried squid keep most punters here all night. DJ-spun lounge and house live mixes kick in most weekends.

Getting There & Away
BUS

From Antibes **bus station** (☎ 04 93 34 37 60; information desk 7.30am-7pm Mon-Fri), just off rue de la République, buses leave/arrive every 20 minutes or so between 6am and 8pm to/from Nice (50 minutes), Cagnes-sur-Mer (20 minutes), Golfe-Juan (15 minutes), Cannes (30 minutes), Biot (25 minutes, seven to 10 buses daily) and Vallauris (30 minutes, seven to 10 buses daily). Fares are a flat €1.30.

RIVIERA LEGENDS

Revel in good old-fashioned Riviera glamour and romance at these ravishingly gorgeous seaside villas, loaded with history and loaded guests.

Hôtel Belles Rives (☎ 04 93 61 02 79; www.bellesrives.com; 33 blvd Édouard Baudoin; d low/high season from €130/240, menus €75 & €90;) F Scott and Zelda Fitzgerald stayed at Hôtel Belles Rives – then a house called Villa St-Louis with sea view and untouched beach – in 1926. Three years later a Russian called Boma Estène bought the villa and turned it into a small hotel: much of the original 1930s furniture and Art Deco interior remains today, although the nautical blue carpets, opulent rooms and marbled bathrooms are of a more recent vintage.

Hôtel du Cap – Eden Roc (☎ 04 93 61 39 01; www.edenroc-hotel.fr; blvd Kennedy; s/d low season from €240/350, high season €360/450;) The list of celebrities who've slumbered here is alphabetised and includes names under every letter bar 'X' (name a famous guest beginning with Q). Exquisite and impeccable in taste, the hotel comprises the original Grand Hôtel du Cap (1889) and Eden Roc, the old tearoom built in 1914 around which the world's most beautiful swimming pool was dug from rock. The really truly filthy rich are treated to the Eden Roc suite, with a 250-sq-metre terrace.

CANNES AREA

TRAIN

From Antibes **train station** (place Pierre Semard), at the end of av Robert Soleau, there are frequent trains to/from Nice (€3.70, 30 minutes) and Cannes (€2.40, 15 minutes).

Unlike Antibes, where many TGVs stop, the smaller **train station** (av de l'Estérel) located in Juan-les-Pins is only served by local trains.

Getting Around

City buses are run by **Envibus** (☎ 04 89 87 72 00; www.envibus.fr in French). Tickets valid for one hour cost €1/8 for a one/10-ticket carnet, and a one-day individual/family pass costs €3/5. Buses link Antibes bus station and place du Général de Gaulle with sq du Lys in Juan-les-Pins (15 minutes) every 10 to 20 minutes. Bus 2 from Antibes goes to Eden Roc on Cap d'Antibes (every 30 minutes). Between 15 June and 15 September this bus circles the cape, continuing along the coast from Eden Roc to Juan-les-Pins before returning to Antibes.

BIOT

pop 9000

This charming 15th-century hilltop village perched on an old volcano was once an important pottery-manufacturing centre specialising in large earthenware oil and wine containers. Metal containers brought an end to this, but Biot is still active in handicraft production, especially glassmaking and ceramics. The village was also the one-time HQ (1209–1387) of the Knights Templars, then the Knights of Malta: fragments of their presence remain in the quaint streets. Get here early to beat the hordes.

A list of *verreries* (glass-blowing workshops) is available at the **tourist office** (☎ 04 93 65 78 00; www.biot-coteazur.com; 46 rue St-Sébastien; 10am-7pm Mon-Fri, 2.30-7pm Sat & Sun Jul & Aug, 9am-noon & 2-6pm Mon-Fri, 2-6pm Sat & Sun Sep-Jun).

Sights & Activities

One of the largest of the workshops is **Verrerie de Biot** (☎ 04 93 65 03 00; www.verreriebiot.com; chemin des Combes; admission free, 45min English guided tour €6; 9.30am-8pm Mon-Sat, 10am-1pm & 3-7pm Sun Jul & Aug, 9.30am-6pm Mon-Sat, 10.30am-1pm & 2.30-6.30pm Sun Sep-Jun), 1km from the centre at the foot of the village, where you can watch the glassblowers at work, buy the end results, admire on-site art galleries or have lunch at the terrace restaurant.

In town, the **Musée d'Histoire et de Céramique Biotoises** (☎ 04 93 65 54 54; 9 rue St-Sébastien; adult/under 15yr €2/free, 1st Sun of month free; 10am-6pm Wed-Sun Jul-Sep, 2-6pm Wed-Sun Oct-Jun) displays ancient pottery. A little further along the street, picturesque **place des Arcades**, dating from the 13th and 14th centuries, is worth a peek.

MARINELAND

Down the hill from the village, on the coast, is **Marineland** (☎ 04 93 33 49 49; www.marineland.fr; RN7; adult/3-12yr €34/25; 10am-10.30pm Jul & Aug, 10am-8pm Sep-Dec & Feb-Jun), an impressive water park with killer-whale and dolphin shows, shark tunnels and an aquarium. On the same site, **Aquasplash** (a water park with slides; adult/child €21/17), **La Petite Ferme du Far West** (a cowboy-themed farm with funfair rides and amusements; adult/child €13/10) and **Adventure Golf** (crazy golf; adult/child €10/8) provide additional entertainment, although it's hard to squeeze in more than two parks in a day. Combined tickets for two are available. Child prices are for kids aged three to 12 years.

Take bus 10 from Antibes bus station to the Marineland stop. By train, turn right out of Biot train station, walk 50m along rte de Nice (N7), then turn right along the D4 signposted 'Marineland & Biot'.

Sleeping & Eating

Restaurant des Arcades (☎ 04 93 65 01 04; 16 place des Arcades; d €70-100, mains €25-30; lunch & dinner Tue-Sat, lunch Sun) Dining at this bistro, lovingly run by Mimi and Dédé Brothier as in a bygone era, not only means fabulous regional food: it also snags you a viewing of the Brothier's private collection of art and glass, donated by artists (among them César, Novaro, Vasarely and Folon) as payment for food and lodging. Advance reservations are essential for the restaurant and its 14 period rooms up top. The bistro is on Biot's loveliest and oldest square.

Getting There & Away

Biot village is a steep 4km from Biot train station. From Antibes take bus 10 from the bus station or place du Général de Gaulle to Biot (€1, 25 minutes, seven to 10 buses daily).

CAGNES-SUR-MER

pop 45,000

This is where Renoir spent the last 12 years of his life. His old house and studio have been preserved as a museum dedicated to the artist. Cagnes-sur-Mer is three pockets welded together: Haut de Cagnes, the medieval hilltop town, Cagnes Ville, the modern quarter, and Cros de Cagnes, an age-old fishing village by the beach.

The **tourist office** (☎ 04 93 20 61 64; www.cagnes -tourisme.com in French; 6 blvd Maréchal Juin; ☯ 9am-7pm Mon-Sat, 9am-noon & 3-7pm Sun Jul & Aug, 9am-noon & 2-7pm Mon-Sat Jun & Sep, 9am-noon & 2-6pm Oct-May), just off the A8 in Cagnes Ville, runs annexes in **Haut de Cagnes** (☎ 04 92 02 85 05; place du Château) and **Cros de Cagnes** (☎ 04 93 07 67 08; 20 av des Oliviers).

Sights & Activities
CHÂTEAU-MUSÉE GRIMALDI

Built around 1300 by the Grimaldis, **Château-Musée Grimaldi** (☎ 04 92 02 47 30; place Grimaldi; adult/under 18yr €3/free; ☯ 10am-noon & 2-6pm Wed-Mon), atop the old town, was sold during the French Revolution and bought in 1873 by a doctor who restored it to its 1620s glory. Baroque influences are evident in the grandiose banquet hall and arched galleries, and the old Grimaldi boudoir is filled with a bizarre collection of portraits of Suzy Solidor (1900–85), a Parisian cabaret singer and favourite artists' model who spent the last 25 years of her life living in Cagnes-sur-Mer. Among the 40 portraits are pieces by Brayer, Cocteau, Dufy, Kisling and van Dongen.

The castle also houses a **Musée de l'Olivier** (Olive-Tree Museum) featuring paintings of olive groves and oily paraphernalia and a **Musée d'Art Méditerranéen Moderne** (Museum of Modern Mediterranean Art).

MUSÉE RENOIR

La Domaine des Collettes, today the **Musée Renoir** (☎ 04 93 20 61 07; chemin des Collettes; adult/under 18yr €3/free; ☯ 10am-noon & 2-6pm Wed-Mon summer, to 5pm winter), was home and studio to an arthritis-crippled Renoir (1841–1919), who lived here with his wife and three sons from 1907 until his death. The artist painted, with a brush bandaged to his fingers, in the north-facing, 2nd-floor studio. The chicken wire covering the window protected Renoir from his children's mis-hit tennis balls.

Works of his on display include *Les Grandes Baigneuses* (The Women Bathers; 1892), a reworking of the 1887 original, and rooms are dotted with photographs and personal possessions. The magnificent olive and citrus groves around the Provençal *mas* (farmhouse) and

bourgeois house are as much an attraction as the museum itself.

From Cagnes bus station on place du Général de Gaulle, walk east along av Renoir and its continuation, av des Tuilières, then turn left (north) onto chemin des Collettes. From here the museum is 500m uphill.

Getting There & Around

Cagnes-sur-Mer is served by Le Cros de Cagnes and Cagnes-sur-Mer train stations. Most Cannes–Ventimiglia trains stop at both (they're two to three minutes apart).

Cannes–Nice buses (every 20 minutes) stop outside Cagnes-sur-Mer (52 minutes) and Le Cros de Cagnes (one hour) train stations, and at Cagnes' central bus station on place du Général de Gaulle. The Grasse–Nice bus only stops outside Cagnes-sur-Mer train station (35 minutes, about 10 daily). From Vence, bus 400 departs every 30 minutes for Cagnes-sur-Mer (20 minutes) via St-Paul de Vence. A single fare is €1.30.

A frequent, free shuttle bus trundles tourists up and down between Cagnes Ville bus station and Haut de Cagnes.

ST-PAUL DE VENCE
pop 2900 / elev 125m

Once upon a time St-Paul de Vence, 10km north of Cagnes-sur-Mer, was a small medieval village atop a hill looking out to sea. Walls encircled it in the 16th century, and in the 1960s artists such as Belarusian painter Marc Chagall moved in, marking the start of its new life as art-gallery city. African-American novelist James Baldwin (1924–85) spent the last years of his life here.

When the tourist-clogged village gets too much, flee to the Fondation Maeght, where real nuggets of truly fine modern art lie.

Orientation & Information

Rue Grande, the village's backbone, leads from the main gate to the cemetery.

The **tourist office** (☎ 04 93 32 86 95; www.saint -pauldevence.com; 2 rue Grande; ☯ 10am-7pm Jun-Sep, 10am-6pm Oct-May) is on the right as you enter the walled village.

Sights & Activities
VILLAGE

Strolling the narrow streets is how most visitors pass time in St-Paul. No less than half of its 60-odd **art galleries** are on rue Grande. Steps from rue Grande lead east to place de l'Église, pierced by **Église Collégiale** (containing a hotch-potch of religious icons), adjoining **Chapelle des Pénitents** (with free organ recitals July and August) and the **Musée d'Histoire Locale** (place de l'Église; adult/6-16yr €3/2; ☺ 10am-noon & 2-5.30pm Wed-Sat Dec-Oct), a zoom-in on local history.

Marc Chagall (p61), who moved to St-Paul with his wife, Vava, in 1966, is buried in the **cemetery** at the village's southern end. At the cemetery entrance, turn right, then left to find the couple's simple graves – the third on the left with beach pebbles scattered over them.

Across from the entrance to the fortified village, the **pétanque** pitch, where many a star has had a spin, is the hub of village life. The tourist office rents out balls (€3) and runs one-hour *pétanque* discovery tours (€8).

FONDATION MAEGHT

The region's finest art museum is **Fondation Maeght** (☎ 04 93 32 81 63; www.fondation-maeght.com; adult/under 10yr/10-18yr €11/free/9; ☺ 10am-7pm Jul-Sep, 10am-12.30pm & 2.30-6pm Oct-Jun), inaugurated in 1964 in a purpose-built futuristic building. It hosts an exceptional permanent collection of 20th-century works by Braque, Bonnard, Chagall, Giacometti, Matisse, Miró and Léger, exhibited on a rotating basis, as well as temporary exhibitions. Behind the gallery, the **Miró Labyrinth**, created by Spanish surrealist Joan Miró (1893–1983), zigzags through beautiful terraced gardens studded with gigantic sculptures, comical faces, mosaics and pools of water.

The centre, signposted from rond-point St-Claire, is 800m from the bus stop. A steep driveway leads up to the Foundation. Approaching St-Paul by car, turn left off the D7 from La Colle-sur-Loup.

Sleeping & Eating

Accommodation and dining – often rolled into one – is pricey but classy. Be it pre- or post-lunch, a drink at quintessential village kaf and bar, **Café de la Place** (☎ 04 93 32 80 03; place de Gaulle; plat du jour €9.50; ☺ 7am-midnight summer, 7am-8pm winter), overlooking the *pétanque* pitch, is a must.

CHAMBRES D'HÔTES

Villa St-Maxime (☎ 04 93 32 76 00; www.villa-st-maxime .com; 390 rte de la Colle; d low/high season from €145/160; P ⊠ ⬛ ⬛) James Bond would stay here. Run with a certain American opulence by

Europe veterans Ann and John (they left the USA for Luxembourg 24 years ago and spent holidays in St-Paul since 1983 when they bought a house in the village), this *maison d'hôte* (upmarket *châmbre d'hôte*) is vast, airy and full of architectural flair. No two rooms are on the same level (five marbled steps separate the seven levels); the sky-high lobby with whitewashed stone walls lends the villa a chateaulike air; and the sweeping view of hilltop St-Paul, Cap d'Antibes and the Med from the breakfast terrace, pool and most rooms is unbeatable. But the *pièce de résistance* (actually there are two) is the 007 glass roof that slides open, and the champagne breakfast cooked up by a sabre-wielding John. Guests can buy the art on the walls, and rates include evening apéritifs. Find Villa St-Maxime behind a high green hedge down the hill from the village on the D7 to La Colle-sur-Loup.

Les Cabanes d'Orion (☎ 06 75 45 18 64; www.orionbb .com; impasse des Peupliers, 2436 chemin du Malvan; d from €150; ☺ Apr-Dec; P ⬛ ⬛) At the opposite end of the mood and ethos spectrum is this equally superb, ecological B&B. Dragonflies flit above water lilies in the emerald-green swimming pool (filtered naturally), while guests slumber up top amid a chorus of frogs and cicadas in luxurious cedar-wood tree-houses perched in the trees. Breakfast is served in the shade of a 200-year-old *bergerie* (sheepfold), guests can BBQ their own evening meal, and catching frogs, playing skittles/boules or frolicking with squirrels or black labrador Lucas and his feline friends are childish pleasures. From the village, follow rte des Serres (behind the *pétanque* court) for 2km, turn sharply left onto chemin de la Pounchounière, continue downhill for 500m and after the bridge turn left onto chemin du Malvan. The steep gravel track leading up to Les Cabanes is signed 500m along this road, opposite the traffic mirror.

HOTELS

The list (the tourist office has one) of four-star places is endless.

Hostellerie Les Remparts (☎ 04 93 32 09 88; www .hotel-les-remparts.net; 72 rue Grande; d €54-80, tr/q €80/91, menus from €30; ⬛) The cheapest four-star option. Rooms are named after flowers typical to Provence at this medieval *maison de village* right on St-Paul's main drag. Rates reflect amenities: *Cyclamen* shares a bathroom and *fleur des champs* has no air-con, while *lilas* has air-con and valley-facing balcony. Its terrace restaurant cooks up regional cuisine and has a jaw-dropping panorama.

Getting There & Away

St-Paul de Vence ('St-Paul' on bus timetables and road signs) is served by bus 400 running between Nice (€1.30, one hour) and Vence (€1.30, 15 minutes).

VENCE

pop 17,184 / elev 325m

Vence, a pleasant town 4km north of St-Paul de Vence, has a medieval centre made for strolling, but its most noteworthy feature is out of town: Matisse's otherworldly Chapelle du Rosaire.

Music fills central place du Grand Jardin during July's three-week festival, **Nuits du Sud** (www.nuitsdusud.com in French). A fruit and veg market fills the square several mornings a week (see p299), with antiques on Wednesday.

Orientation & Information

The **tourist office** (☎ 04 93 58 06 38; www.ville-vence .fr in French; 8 place du Grand Jardin; ☼ 9am-1pm & 2-7pm Mon-Sat Jul & Aug, 9am-12.30pm & 2-6pm Mon-Sat Sep-Jun) is on Vence's central square. Rue Marcellin Maurel, which touches its northeastern corner, skirts the medieval city's southern wall. Port du Peyra, the main gate, is at the western end of rue Marcellin Maurel.

Sights & Activities

MEDIEVAL VENCE

Porte du Peyra, the main gate of the 13th-century wall encircling the old city, leads to place du Peyra and its **fountain** (1578). Gate and square are named after the old execution block. Imposing **Château de Villeneuve** and its adjoining 12th-century **watchtower** dominate the western edge of the square. Round the back of the castle is **Fondation Émile Hughes** (☎ 04 93 24 24 23; 2 place du Frêne; adult/12-18yr €5/2.50; ☼ 10am-6pm Tue-Sun Jul-Sep, 10am-12.30pm & 2-6pm Tue-Sun Oct-Jun), a cultural centre with wonderful 20th-century art exhibitions.

Leading east from place du Peyra is narrow rue du Marché, once the stables for the town and now dotted with small food shops. Cut along rue Alsace-Lorraine to reach place Clémenceau, where there's a **market** on Tuesday and Friday mornings. The **Romanesque cathedral** on the eastern side of the square was built in the 11th century on the site of an old Roman temple. It contains Chagall's **mosaic**

of Moses (1979), appropriately watching over the baptismal font.

CHAPELLE DU ROSAIRE

Matisse was 81 when he completed **Chapelle du Rosaire** (☎ 04 93 58 03 26; 466 av Henri Matisse; adult/ 6-16yr €2.80/1.50; ☼ 2-5.30pm Mon, Wed & Sat, 10-11.30am & 2-5.30pm Tue & Thu, plus 2-5.30pm Fri during school holidays, Sunday mass 10am, closed mid-Nov–mid-Dec), floodlit by the most extraordinary stained-glass windows, in 1951.

An ailing Matisse moved to Vence in 1943 where he fell under the care of his former nurse and model Monique Bourgeois, who had since become a Dominican nun. She persuaded him to design the extraordinary chapel for her community: it took Matisse four years to do so and the Dominican nuns of the Rosary still use it today.

From the road, all that you can see are the blue-and-white ceramic roof tiles and a wrought-iron cross and bell tower. Inside, light floods through the glorious stained-glass windows, painting stark white walls with glowing blues, greens and yellows. To achieve this effect, Matisse set up camp 200m down the road at **Le Rêve** (The Dream), a private house opposite 320 av Henri Matisse, so he could visit the chapel site throughout the day and observe the sun's position before signing off on the architectural plans.

THE AUTHOR'S CHOICE

La Colombe d'Or (☎ 04 93 32 80 02; www .la-colombe-dor.com in French; place de Gaulle, St-Paul de Vence; d from €265, mains €25-35; ☼ 12.30-2.30pm & 7.30-10.30pm; P ☒ ☒) The mosaic mural by Fernand Léger, *Les Femmes au Perroquet* (Women with a Parrot), in the courtyard is among the original modern artworks at the Golden Dove, a legendary world-renowned restaurant where impoverished artists Braque, Chagall, Dufy and Picasso paid for meals with their creations – today forming one of France's largest private art collections. Dining is beneath fig trees in a walled courtyard laden with art; a monumental Calder mobile steals the show at the swimming pool; and service is surprisingly uncomplicated. Viewing is strictly for diners or guests staying in one of the luxurious village inn's 26 rooms. Reserve tables and rooms months in advance.

TOP FIVE ART GALLERIES

Vence and St-Paul chalk up at least 100 galleries between them. Our top five:

Fondation Maeght (p320) By far the region's most formidable.

Galerie Catherine Issert (☎ 04 93 32 96 92; www.galerie-issert.com; 2 rte des Serres, St-Paul) Window on the crème of international avant-garde since 1975.

Galerie Guy Pieters (☎ 04 93 32 06 46; www.guypietersgallery.com; chemin des Trious, St-Paul) Contemporary pieces to stagger home with, plus Warhols, Armans etc (not for sale) to ogle at.

Galerie Brettrn.com (☎ 04 93 58 53 55; www.brettrn.com; 6 rue du Peyra, Vence) Pieces by self-taught British painter, sculptor and stained-glass artist Brett Rhodes-Neal (b 1962); dogs all colours of the rainbow were showcased when we visited.

Centre International d'Art Contemporain (☎ 04 93 29 37 97; place Augustin Capel, Carros) Escape the crowds: drive 16km northeast to Carros, a medieval village few seem to know about. Its streets are tourist-free and the modern-art exhibitions inside its hilltop chateau are superb.

A line image of the Virgin Mary and child is painted on white ceramic tiles on the northern interior wall. The western wall is dominated by the bolder *Chemin de Croix* (Stations of the Cross), numbered in Matisse's frenzied handwriting. St Dominic overlooks the altar. Matisse also designed the chapel's stone altar, candlesticks, cross and the way-out priests' vestments (displayed in an adjoining hall).

Find the chapel 800m north of Vence on rte de St-Jeannet (the D2210). From place du Grand Jardin, head east along av de la Résistance then turn right (north) along av Tuby. At the crossroads, turn right onto av Henri Matisse, from where the chapel is signposted.

Sleeping & Eating

Auberge des Seigneurs (☎ 04 93 58 04 24; place du Frêne; d €70, menus €31, €35 & €42; ☼ mid-Mar–mid-Nov) This enchanting little hotel-restaurant, in a 15th-century building, is the only accommodation within the medieval walls. Some rooms have mountain views.

La Maison d'Accueil Lacordaire (☎ 04 93 58 03 26; http://perso.orange.fr/maison.lacordaire; 466 av Henri Matisse; half-/full board per person €30/40; reception ☼ 9am-6pm Mon-Sat) Adjoining the Chapelle du Rosaire, this 24-room house with pretty water garden belongs to the Dominican nuns, who offer beds for the night. Rooms with toilet and shower must be reserved three to eight days in advance and the minimum stay is three nights.

Le P'tit Provençal (☎ 04 93 58 50 64; 4 place Clémenceau; menus €16, €18 & €24.30; ☼ lunch & dinner Wed-Sun) Beside the town hall in the heart of medieval Vence, Little Provençal cooks up local cuisine to thrill on a table-tight pavement terrace. Try pig-cheek stew followed by chocolate pie with cherry marmalade and liquorice ice-cream, or cold peach soup with sweet Muscat, mint and green tea sorbet.

The old town is crammed with touristy restaurants.

Getting There & Away

Bus 400 to and from Nice (€1.30, 50 minutes, at least hourly) stops on place du Grand Jardin.

AROUND VENCE

The northbound D2 from Vence leads to the **Col de Vence** (963m), a mountain pass 10km north offering good views of the *baous* (rocky promontories) typical of this region. At the foot of the pass is the **Baou des Blancs** (673m), crowned by the stony remains of the **Bastide St-Laurent**, inhabited by the Templars in the 13th century. Marked walking trails around the pass follow part of the GR51.

Coursegoules (population 323, elevation 1020m), 6km north along the D2, is a hilltop village with 11th-century castle ruins and fortifications. From here, head west along the D2 to photogenic **Gréolières** (population 455). Walkers can follow the GR4 north to **Gréolières-les-Neiges** (elevation 1450m), a small ski station equipped with 14 lifts on the northern face of Montagne Cheiron; the GR4 scales Cheiron's 1778m-high peak.

From Coursegoules and Gréolières, you can hook up with the dramatic **Gorges du Loup**, 7km south along the D603. The road along the western side of the gorges (the D3) crescendos with the village of **Gourdon** (population 384, elevation 758m). Here Art Deco works, including pieces from designer Eileen Gray's Paris apartment and her seaside villa on Cap

Martin (see p65), can be enjoyed in the **Musée des Arts Décoratifs et de la Modernité** (☎ 04 93 09 68 02; place du Château; admission €10; 🕑 1½hr guided tour by appointment only) in Château de Gourdon (no children). Aspiring 'noses' can see what happens to freshly picked lavender, genista, thyme and orange-tree leaves at **La Source Parfumée** (☎ 04 93 09 68 23; lasourceparfumee@wanadoo.fr; rue Principale; admission free; 🕑 10am-5.30pm), a distillery run by the Galimard perfumery (p326).

Further south along the D3, hilltop **Le Bar-sur-Loup** (population 2540, elevation 320m) pops onto the horizon. Bitter orange trees are cultivated in terraces around the beautifully intact medieval village. One of three marked walks proffers (on clear days) a startling view way down the coast and across to Corsica; ask at the **tourist office** (☎ 04 93 72 72 21; tourisme@lebarsurloup.fr; place Francis Paulet) next to the chateau for the 'three walks' brochure.

Rumbling tummies can lunch chateau-style in Bar or cross the D2085 and continue south to pinprick **Opio** to shop for olive oil at 19th-century **Moulins de la Brague** (☎ 04 93 77 23 03; www.moulin-opio.com; 2 rte de Châteauneuf; 🕑 9am-noon & 2-6pm Mon-Sat) and lunch country-style at Le Mas des Géraniums (p324) instead.

Otherwise, bear east from Bar to **Pont du Loup**; the prime attraction is the sweet **Confiserie Florian Factory** (☎ 04 93 59 32 91; www.confiserie florian.com; 🕑 9am-noon & 2-6pm) where jams, crystallised fruits and flowers are cooked up in a 19th-century flour mill. Free 10-minute tours show you how.

From Pont du Loup the eastbound D2210 snakes east to Tourrettes-sur-Loup, passing goat farm **Ferme des Courmettes** (☎ 04 93 59 31 93; www.chevredescourmettes.com) en route where you can taste/buy organic cheese.

Tourrettes-sur-Loup (population 3900, elevation 400m), dubbed the 'city of violets', is a postcard-perfect 15th-century hilltop village overflowing with art galleries and boutiques selling violet tea, ice cream, melon syrup etc. Its **Fête des Violettes** (Violet Festival) on the first or second Sunday in March closes with a flower battle. The **tourist office** (☎ 04 93 24 18 93; www.tourrettessurloup.com; 2 place de La Libération; 🕑 9.30am-12.30pm & 2.30-6.30pm May & Jun, 10am-6.30pm Mon-Sat, 10am-6pm Sun Jul & Aug, 9.30am-12.30pm & 2.30-6.30pm Mon-Sat Sep-Apr) has details.

From the eastbound D2210 you can also pick up the scenic eastbound D6 to **La Colle-sur-Loup** (population 6670), a less explored village with some interesting sleeping and eating options, the thriving **Maison des Arts** (p60) and an outstanding **tourist office** (☎ 04 93 32 68 36; www .ot-lacolle@atsat.com; 28 rue Maréchal Foch; 🕑 9am-7pm Mon-Fri, 9am-noon & 3-7pm Sat & Sun mid-Jun–mid-Sep, 9am-noon & 2-6pm Mon-Sat mid-Sep–mid-Jun) opposite the church, which stocks the best information on the area.

Sleeping & Eating

Bastide Saint Donat (☎ 04 93 32 93 41; rte du Pont de Pierre, La Colle-sur-Loup; d incl breakfast €65-95; 🅿) Aircon is not a necessity at this stone *bergerie* (sheepfold) where 50cm-thick walls keep things cool. An immaculate garden – scampering ground for Miette the Yorkshire terrier – frames the family house (1850), which comprised four ruined walls when Yvonne and Alphonse Rosso bought it half a century ago. Rooms are beautifully prepared with freshly cut flowers; a pair of olive trees and Monsieur's amber-coloured Fiat 500c marks the entrance. Find it a couple of kilometres from La Colle on the D6 to Grasse.

SLEEP DREAM ART

La Maison du Frêne (☎ 04 93 24 37 83; www.lamaisondufrene.com; 1 place du Frêne, Vence; d low/high season €140/180; 🕑 Feb-Dec; ✂ 💻) This *demeure d'art et d'hôtes* (art guesthouse) is quite astonishing. Yes, that Niki de Saint Phalle is an original. And yes, the César too. The love child of Vence-born Parisian hairdresser Thierry and partner, Guy, this guesthouse across from the Fondation Émile Hughes is an essential sleepover on any true art-lover's itinerary. Thierry and Guy – avid collectors for years (Thierry: 'For 20 years I had no car but I did have a Niki de Saint Phalle') – are passionate about modern art, know everything there is know about the local art scene (did you know Lithuanian-born French expressionist Soutine painted, unusually, their house?) and are happy to chat and chat and chat about their greatest passion in life. Rooms are superbly decorated with contemporary designer furniture, original works of art and plenty of reference books to read up on what's around you. Marilyn dominates the Pop Art suite. Understandably, given the priceless interior, child guests must be at least 12.

WAYNE'S WORLD

Something of a legend in Nice, where the hugely successful pioneering bar he opened all those years ago still trades under his name, Wayne is now a country man. Find him and wife Cécile in Tourrettes-sur-Loup at gastronomic dining spot **Le Relais des Coches** (☎ 04 93 24 30 24; www .lerelaisdescoches.com; 28 rte de Vence; plat du jour €12, lunch menus €16 & €25, dinner menus €38; ☺ lunch & dinner Tue-Sun), an atmospheric medieval house with beautiful village-facing terrace, and happening music club **La Cave du Relais** (☺ dinner Thu-Sat Mar-Aug, event-driven Sep-Feb) in its basement where discerning punters dine to the sound of live soul, jazz, and rhythm and blues.

Those who find Wayne and Cécile truly irresistible can check in to their **Auberge de Tourrettes** (☎ 04 94 59 30 05; www.aubergedetourrettes.fr; 11 rte de Grasse; s/d from €108/120), a charming eight-room boutique inn with contemporary Provençal décor.

Le Mas des Cigales (☎ 04 93 59 25 73; www.lemasdes cigales.com; 1673 rte des Quenières, Tourrettes-sur-Loup; d incl breakfast low/high season €72/92, dinner €20; P ⌘ ☺ ✉) Marc and Davide (who ran a bar in Paris before taking the first step towards retirement in Tourrettes) are the dynamo behind this peaceful *chambre d'hôte*, which induces guests to be dreadfully lazy. Two rooms have gardens out the front and the other three open onto the poolside. A Jacuzzi, tennis courts, bicycles, a flowery garden and dinner cooked by Davide twice a week complete the pretty picture, found 1.6km from Tourrettes village.

L'Hostellerie du Château (☎ 04 93 42 41 10; www .lhostellerieduchateau.com; 6-8 place Francis Paulet, Le Bar-sur-Loup; d low/high season from €100/155; ☺ café & restaurant lunch & dinner Tue-Sun) Château du Bar crowns Bar village; it was in the hands of the counts of Grasse from 1235 until the French Revolution. Lunch around bright-orange bistro tables on the terrace of Café du Château (plat du jour €14, menus €18 to €22) or dine up top in the more formal, very romantic Le Bigaradie (menus €27 to €59), named after the *biga-radie* (bitter orange tree) Bar is known for. Views are sterling and décor is discrete and contemporary.

Le Mas des Géraniums (☎ 04 93 77 23 23; www .le-mas-des-geraniums.com; 7 rte de Nice, Opio; menus €18, €25, €34 & €40; ☺ lunch & dinner Jul & Aug, lunch & dinner Thu-Mon Sep-Jun) Colette and Michel Creusot run this baby-blue shuttered house on a hill overlooking Opio with love and tender care. Dining is country style, alfresco in a vast flowery garden, and parking is in an olive grove. Fresh artichoke hearts, scorpion fish pâté, snails and crayfish are among the mixed bag of market goodies. Reservations essential.

Also recommended is **L'Abbaye** (☎ 04 93 32 68 34; www.hotelabbaye.com; 541 blvd Honoré Teisseire, La Colle-sur-Loup; d low/high season from €80/100, mains €13-20; ☺ restaurant lunch & dinner Tue-Sun; P ⌘ ☒ ✉), a boutique hotel in a 12th-century manor with a 10th-century chapel and cutting-edge restaurant, L541.

Getting There & Away

In short, your own two or four wheels is the only way there, away and around.

INLAND TO GRASSE

From Cannes, an inland journey takes you along the same road Napoleon Bonaparte trod on his return from exile in 1814. From the island of Elba, he landed at Golfe-Juan, from where he and a clutch of faithful followers marched for six days north to Lyons. Now called the rte Napoléon (the N85 today), at that time it was a remote road passing through a couple of medieval villages, including Grasse with its skilled perfumers, then into the mountains of Haute-Provence.

MOUGINS

pop 16,287 / elev 260m

Elite, elegant Mougins prides itself on its arty connections and luxury wining and dining options. Picasso discovered the medieval village in 1935 with lover Dora Marr, and lived here with his final love, Jacqueline Roque, from 1961 until his death. His former house (across the valley from the tourist office) is a private residence and can't be visited, but there are fascinating black-and-white photos of the artist at work and play, snapped by André Villers, in the **Musée de la Photographie** (☎ 04 93 75 85 67; 67 rue de l'Église; adult/child €2/1; ☺ 10am-8pm Jul-Sep, 10am-6pm Mon-Fri, 11am-6pm Sat & Sun Oct & Dec-Jun), inside medieval Porte Sarrazine behind the church bell tower. Celebrated

Riviera photographer Jacques Henri Lartigue (1894–1986) is among the wealth of other famous snappers represented in the small but fabulous photography museum.

Local art can be viewed in the village's 19th-century **lavoir** (washhouse; 15 av Jean-Charles Mallet; admission free; 10am-7pm Mar-Oct) and in the overdose of galleries and artists' workshops filling the village: the **tourist office** (04 93 75 87 67; www.mougins-coteazur.org; Parking Moulin de la Croix; 9am-5.30pm Mon-Fri), in the car park at the foot of the village, and its **seasonal welcome centre** (15 av Jean-Charles Mallet; 5-10pm Mon-Fri, 9am-10pm Sat & Sun Jul & Aug), adjoining the old washhouse, have complete lists.

Motor fiends can ogle over auto art 5km south of town in the **Musée de l'Automobiliste** (04 93 69 27 80; www.musauto.fr.st in French; 772 chemin de Font de Currault; adult/under 12yr/12-18yr €7/free/5; 10am-6pm), a car museum just off the A8 where Bugatti, Rolls-Royce and Ferrari race into gear.

Sleeping

Hotel accommodation is minimum four-star and proffers much fine dining.

CHAMBRES D'HÔTES

The tourist office has a complete list.

Les Rosées (04 92 92 29 64; www.les-rosees.com; 238 chemin de Font Neuve; d low/high season €220/260;) Proof of the pudding that B&B is not necessarily a budget option, this stunning stone manor house with three hugely romantic guest suites, pool and century-old olive trees is a showcase for Danielle's upholstery and interior-design workshop. The Serguey suite with peephole on the open fire in the lounge is stunning. Breakfast is a copious organic affair.

HOTELS

Le Moulin de Mougins (04 93 75 78 24; www.moulin demougins.com; av Notre Dame de Vie; d €140 & €190, ste €300 & €320, lunch menus without wine €48, with wine €58 or €73, dinner menus €98 & €115; restaurant lunch & dinner Tue-Sun;) Alain Lorca's illustrious place is in a 16th-century oil mill with lilac shutters dotted with original Césars and Armans. Spanish Andalusia alongside Provence provides the inspiration in the kitchen, and the menu invites diners to pick from *classique* (traditional), *contemporaine* (new and amazing) or *légère* (natural) creations. Find the mill 2.5km southeast of town off the D3.

Also guaranteed to please is **Le Mas Candille** (04 92 28 43 43; www.lemascandille.com; blvd Clément Rebuffel; d incl breakfast from €320;) Top 18th-century farmhouse with Shiseido spa.

Eating

Dining at the hotels listed above is a memorable experience. Simpler options:

Un Coin à Part (04 93 75 33 70; uncoinapart@voila .fr; 24 rue Honoré Henry; menus €19 & €26; lunch & dinner Fri-Tue) This hip little hole comes as a breath of fresh air in stiff Mougins. Vegetarian and organic creations are a strong feature of the Provençal menu cooked up by formidable team Stéphane and Sébastien. 'Zen attitude' is the house motto.

L'Amandier (04 93 90 00 91; place du Vieux Village; lunch menu €25, dinner menus €34 & €44; 10.30am-10pm) In a rustic 14th-century oil mill, the Almond Tree is a less expensive eating option. Feast on amazing mountain views and traditional Provençal fare from its warm, flower-bedecked stone terraces.

Getting There & Away

Mougins is on the Cannes–Grasse bus route. Buses depart every half-hour (hourly on Sunday) from the bus station next to Cannes train station for Mougins (€1.30, 20 minutes). Grasse is a 20-minute bus ride from Mougins (€1.30).

GRASSE

pop 43,000 / elev 250m

Terracotta roofs rise up pre-Alpine slopes at this old hilltop centre of perfume production surrounded by sprawling suburbs and a profusion of lavender, jasmine, centifolia roses, mimosa, orange blossom and violet fields cultivated to feed its sweet-smelling industry.

Founded by the Romans, Grasse was no more than a small republic exporting tanned hides and oil in the Middle Ages. But with the advent of perfumed gloves in the 1500s (the doing of France's queen, Catherine de Medicis, who detested the smell of raw leather on her hands), it discovered a new wealth. Glove-makers split from the tanners and set up their own perfumeries – a blooming business in the 18th century.

Contemporary Grasse is not glam. Its old city – small, mainly pedestrian and shabby – has seen better days: make a day trip here and overnight in a *chambre d'hôte* in a surrounding village.

ART HOT SPOT

Modern art and architecture lovers will kick themselves if they miss the **Espace de l'Art Concret** (Centre of Concrete Art; ☎ 04 93 75 71 50; www.crdp.ac-nice.fr/eac; place Suzanne de Villeneuve; adult/under 18yr €3/free; ◷ 11am-7pm Jul & Aug, 11am-6pm Tue-Sun Sep-Jun), 4km north of Mougins in Mouans-Sartoux. The contemporary art centre is housed in the 16th-century **Château de Mouans** and in the purpose-built **Donation Albers-Honegger** extension, a brilliant and brilliantly controversial lime-green concrete block ferociously juxtaposed with its historic surroundings. All the old familiars (Eduardo Chillida, Yves Klein, Andy Warhol, César, Philippe Starck) are here, along with lesser-known practitioners and temporary exhibitions.

Information

Tourist office (☎ 04 93 36 66 66; www.grasse.fr; Palais de Congrès, cours Honoré Cresp; ◷ 9am-7pm Mon-Sat, 9am-12.30pm & 1.30-6pm Sun Jul-Sep, 9am-12.30pm & 2-6pm Mon-Sat Oct-Jun) Information on B&Bs and guided walks in the area (walks adult/6-16yr/family €15/7.50/32).

Sights & Activities

PERFUMERIES

Don't expect to sniff out Chanel, Giorgio Beverley Hills or Guerlain here: Grasse's 40 or so *parfumeries* sell their essence to factories or by mail order and are practically unknown. Three allow visitors into their showrooms, where you're taken through every stage of perfume production, from extraction and distillation to the work of the 'nose' (p329). At the end you'll be squirted with scents, invited to purchase any number, and leave under a fragrant cloud. The perfumes are less expensive than store-bought smellies, where 60% of what you pay is for the fancy bottle.

The most convenient perfume house if you're on foot is **Fragonard** (☎ 04 93 36 44 65; www .fragonard.com; 20 blvd Fragonard; admission free; ◷ 9am-6pm Feb-Oct, 9am-12.30pm & 2-6pm Nov-Jan), named in 1926 after painter Jean-Honoàe Fragonard. Visit the upstairs perfume museum then descend for a tour of the former 16th-century tannery. The real perfume production takes place at the modern **Fabrique des Fleurs** (Flower Factory; rte de Cannes; admission free; ◷ 9am-6pm Feb-Oct, 9am-12.30pm & 2-6pm Nov-Jan) on the southbound N85; and at the Fragonard plant in Èze (see p286).

Galimard (☎ 04 93 09 20 00; www.galimard.com; 73 rte de Cannes; admission free; ◷ 9am-6.30pm Jun-Sep, 9am-12.30pm & 2-6pm Oct-May), 3km from Grasse centre on the southbound N85, runs a nearby **Studio des Fragrances** (☎ 04 93 09 20 00; 5 rte de Pégomas; 2hr workshop incl 100ml bottle of perfume €35) where you can create your own unique fragrance (see p329), and a flower distillery in Gourdon, La Source Parfumée (p323).

Ritzier **Molinard** (☎ 04 93 36 01 62; www.molinard .com; 60 blvd Victor Hugo; admission free; ◷ 9am-6.30pm Mon-Sat Jul-Sep, 9am-12.30pm & 2-6pm Mon-Sat Oct-Jun), 1km out of town, was founded in 1849 and displays old copper stills in its former Gustave Eiffel–designed distillery. Molinard likewise runs perfume creation **workshops** (incl 50ml bottle of perfume €40), which last 1¼ hours.

Curious noses can combine a perfumery session with a (literal) field trip in season to see rose and jasmine meadows, cultivated for three generations, at **Domaine de Manon** (☎ 04 93 60 12 76; www.domaine-manon.com; 36 chemin du Servan), a flower farm 15km southeast of Grasse in the village of Plascassier. Guided tours (roses 3pm May to mid-June, jasmine 9am August to October) last an hour and cost €6/free per adult/child under 12.

MUSÉE D'ART ET D'HISTOIRE DE PROVENCE

Everything from faïence pottery to toys, furniture, costumes and paintings evoke the past in this regional **Art & History Museum** (☎ 04 97 05 58 00; www.museesdegrasse.com; 2 rue Mirabeau; adult/10-16yr €3/1.50, during exhibitions €4/2; ◷ 10am-6.30pm Jun-Sep, 10am-12.30pm & 2-5.30pm Wed-Mon Oct & Dec-May), inside Hôtel de Clapiers Cabris. Former owner Jean-Paul de Clapiers loathed his mother, who lived opposite, so much that he had a Gorgon's head carved over his door to leer through her windows.

VILLA-MUSÉE JEAN-HONORÉ FRAGONARD

His paintings shocked and titillated 18th-century France with their licentious love scenes. See why at the **Musee Jean-Honoré Fragonard** (☎ 04 97 05 58 00; www.museesdegrasse .com; 23 blvd Fragonard; adult/10-16yr €3/1.50, during exhibitions €4/2; ◷ 10am-6.30pm Jun-Sep, 10am-12.30pm & 2-5.30pm Wed-Mon Oct & Dec-May) in Grasse, where

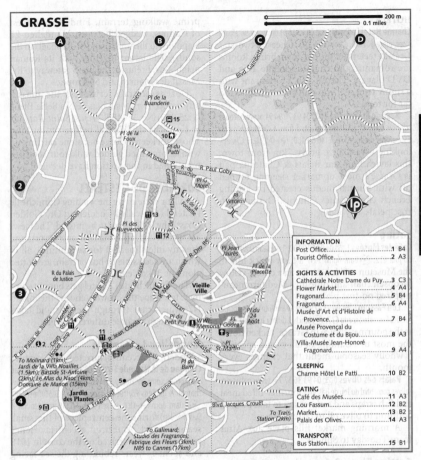

GRASSE

INFORMATION	
Post Office.....................................1	B4
Tourist Office.................................2	A3

SIGHTS & ACTIVITIES	
Cathédrale Notre Dame du Puy.....3	C3
Flower Market.............................4	A4
Fragonard....................................5	B4
Fragonard....................................6	A4
Musée d'Art et d'Histoire de	
Provence..................................7	B4
Musée Provençal du	
Costume et du Bijou.................8	A3
Villa-Musée Jean-Honoré	
Fragonard................................9	A4

SLEEPING	
Charme Hôtel Le Patti................10	B2

EATING	
Café des Musées........................11	A3
Lou Fassum................................12	B2
Market.......................................13	B2
Palais des Olives........................14	A3

TRANSPORT	
Bus Station................................15	B1

the controversial Grasse-born artist Jean-Honoré Fragonard (1732–1806) lived for a year in 1790.

MUSÉE PROVENÇAL DU COSTUME ET DU BIJOU

Lace-capped dummies model 18th- and 19th-century clothes and jewellery in this **Provençal Costume & Jewellery Museum** (☎ 04 93 36 44 65; www .fragonard.com; 2 rue Jean Ossola; admission free; ☼ 10am-1pm & 2-6pm Feb-Oct, 10am-1pm & 2-6pm Mon-Sat Nov-Jan), run by Fragonard.

Festivals & Events

Grasse's two main events are **Exporose** in May, and **La Jasminade**, a jasmine festival held the first weekend in August.

Sleeping

The sweetest options are a short drive away in Mougins and other neighbouring villages.

CHAMBRES D'HÔTES

Le Mas du Naoc (☎ 04 93 60 63 13; www.lemasdunaoc .com; chemin du Migranié, Cabris; d low/high season from €100/120; P ⊠ ⊠) This renovated and vine-covered 18th-century pad in Cabris slumbers in the shade of century-old olive, jasmine, fig and orange trees – and fits the 'quintessentially Provençal' bill perfectly. Soft natural hues dress Sandra and Jérôme Maingret's five lovely rooms, and the coastal panorama from the pool is inspirational. Find signs for the *mas* 4km west of Grasse along the D4 to Cabris. No children under seven.

HOTELS

Charme Hôtel Le Patti (☎ 04 93 36 01 00; www.hotelpatti .com; place du Patti; d from €84; ✿) Cheerful two-star Le Patti teeters on the old-town brink. Rooms are romantic and contain satellite TVs and DVD players. There's also a restaurant with a sunny terrace if you don't want to stray too far for food.

Bastide St-Antoine (☎ 04 93 70 94 94; www.jacques -chibois.com; 48 av Henri Dunant; d from €200; lunch menu €55, dinner menus €130, €140 & €180; ⓟ ✿ 🐾) Overlooking a vast olive grove 2km from town, this lavish four-star Relais & Chateaux pad is Grasse's most upmarket sleeping topped off with sensual menus created by leading French chef Jacques Chibois. Oysters with rose petals, anybody?

Eating

Café des Musées (☎ 04 92 60 99 00; 1 rue Jean Ossola; plat du jour €12; ☯ 8am-6pm) For a tasty quick lunch, the Museum café is best. Sit on a citron-yellow Jacobsen chair and dine on a Mediterranean-inspired no-fuss platter.

Lou Fassum (☎ 04 93 42 99 69; www.loufassum.com; 5 rue des Fabreries; menu €32; ☯ lunch & dinner Tue-Sat) This is the gourmet choice in Grasse, tucked down the most unassuming of alleys and sporting a wholly seasonal menu that changes every month.

Palais des Olives (☎ 04 93 36 57 73; www.palais-des -olives.com; blvd du Jeu de Ballon) Gourmet-filled meat and fish wraps and sandwiches to take away in addition to olive oil to taste or buy.

A morning market fills place aux Aires from Tuesday to Sunday.

Getting There & Around

From the **bus station** (☎ 04 93 36 08 43; place de la Buanderie) there are eight to 10 buses daily to/from Nice (€1.30, 1¼ hours) and Cannes (€1.30, 45 minutes) via Mouans-Sartoux and Mougins.

Grasse train station, 2km south of the centre, is served by trains to/from Cannes (€3.40, 25 minutes) and Nice (€7.70, one hour). Free shuttle buses shunt passengers between the station and the old town.

MASSIF DE L'ESTÉREL

This range of red porphyritic rock scented with pines, oak and eucalyptus trees is one of the coast's most stunning natural features –

prime walking terrain. Find it southwest of Cannes, wedged between Mandelieu-La Napoule (to the north) and St-Raphaël (to the south). The latter, together with its Roman neighbour, Fréjus, is the main gateway to the Massif des Maures and St-Tropez.

Dozens of trails crisscross the massif; buy a decent map such as IGN's Série Bleue (1:25,000) No 3544ET *Fréjus, Saint-Raphaël & Corniche de l'Estérel* before setting out. Those not keen to forge out alone can link up with an organised guided walk: tourist offices mentioned in this section have details.

CORNICHE DE L'ESTÉREL

A walk or drive along the winding Corniche de l'Estérel (also called Corniche d'Or, 'Golden Coast'; the N98) is not to be missed. The views are spectacular, and small summer resorts and dreamy inlets (perfect for swimming), all of which are accessible by bus or train, are dotted along its 30km length.

The Corniche de l'Estérel gets busy in summer: to escape the crowds, choose the inland N7, which runs through the hills and takes you through a whole different world.

Mandelieu-La Napoule

Wonderfully eccentric, turreted, 14th-century **Château de la Napoule** (☎ 04 93 49 95 05; www.chateau -lanapoule.com; av Henry Clews; adult/under 7yr/7-18yr château & gardens €6/free/4, gardens only €3.50/free/3.50; ☯ 10am-6pm Feb-Oct, 2-5pm Mon-Fri, 10am-5pm Sat & Sun Nov-Jan) forms the centrepiece of this small seaside resort. American eccentrics Henry and Marie Clews arrived on the coast in 1918 and spent 17 years rebuilding the sea-facing Saracen tower and decorating it in twisted-fairy-tale style: the effect is Gormenghast-by-the-Sea. Henry Clews' (1876–1937) grave in a tower in the grounds reads 'Poet, Sculptor, Actor, Grand Knight of La Mancha, Supreme Master Humormystic, Castelan of Once upon a Time, Chevalier de Marie'. In a macabre twist, his tomb and Marie's hang open, as though the two corpses have sought each other out after death.

The chateau's interior can only be visited by guided tour (hourly), but the beautiful gardens (with tearooms and treasure hunt for kids), designed by Marie in a classic French formal style, can be wandered freely. Dozens more of Henry's creations sit alongside challenging works by contemporary sculptors in the chateau and gardens. Pride of place in

A HAPHAZARD AFFAIR Nicola Williams

'Perfumery is an art, an innovation. You have to have a vision.'

Jacques Maurel, Galimard perfumer

I don't wear perfume. Never have. The most I can stomach is a quick dash of Clarins' *Eau Dynamisante* before dashing out. Even then, mood depending, the scent makes me nauseous. So creating my own perfume was a prime opportunity to hit upon a scent that didn't make me want to leap in the shower after 10 minutes.

Sitting at my allotted 'organ' faced by a mesmerising line-up of 127 'notes' (miniature ginger-glass bottles of scent), I instantly had to pick two of nine – 'quickly, with no hesitation' explained Galimard perfumer Jacques Maurel. A *nez* (nose) for 43 years and more Grassois than Grasse (his grandfather was a *nez*), Monsieur Maurel entered his first factory when he was 22. Professional noses, of which there are 250 worldwide, combine a natural gift with several years of very hard study and a monklike lifestyle (no alcohol, smoking, coffee, garlic and spicy food) to identify – from no more than a whiff – 6000 or so scents.

My choice of two sealed the 'families' of notes my perfume would be created from: *boisée* (woody) and *fleurie* (flowery). From there on, it was a mere matter of selecting three *fond* (base) notes to fix the fragrance and ensure it lingered, three middle (heart) notes to create its unique and naturally irresistible character, and three top (peak) notes to create that vital first impression when the perfume touches the skin.

On paper, the architecture of a perfume is simple. In reality, I'd clearly smoked far too many cigarettes at university, gorged on too much late-night chicken madras, and drunk way over the odds. After five minutes, my nostrils were reeling: green amber, sandalwood, vanilla, hyacinth, lily of the valley, civet (nose shock or what), hare (unpleasant animal smell, extracted from the secretion of a cat's gland according to the poster on the wall), rose petals (sickly sweet), woody complex, sweet muse, Bavaria mousse. The fact that many of the bottles contained not one, but several scents premixed did little to aid my increasing olfactory bewilderment. At the 'organ' behind me, two little girls were picking names for their perfectly honed perfumes: *Belle* (Beautiful), *Les 2 Princesses* (The Two Princesses), *Les Fées* (The Fairies)…

'Hmm. It's good. Add a rose for fullness' commanded Monsieur Maurel, plucking a bunch of rose-based bottles from my organ and plonking them in front of me. Wild rose, oriental rose, rose petals…my nose felt it had roses coming out of its ears. 'Hmm. It's fuller now,' he observed, 5ml of oriental rose into the glass beaker later, before striding off to leave me floundering in heart notes.

It must have been more straightforward for early perfumers. They quite simply left fresh flower petals to swim in animal fat for three months then mixed the fatty mess with alcohol to extract the essences. Unlike today (synthetic products are used in the main), they created perfumes exclusively from flowers: 600kg of fresh flower petals for every 1L of essence.

'Fresh and fruity with strong amber overtones – very modern' was Monsieur Maurel's analysis of my finished fragrance, which, he informed me, actually contained between 100 and 500 different products, most of which would have macerated for a month already. 'Leave it to rest for another 10 days to complete the maceration process,' he added as I jaunted off with my 100ml glass bottle of exclusively designed, one-of-a-kind perfume that I'd never wear. *Haphazard*, the label read.

the chateau's courtyard is creepy *The God of Humormystics* – Henry's wedding present to his wife!

Outside the chateau wall, coastal paths lead from sandy **Plage du Château** to **Plage de la Raguette** (10 minutes) and **Plage de la Rague** (30 minutes). Inland, a 3.4km-long botanical trail uncovers flora and fauna on **San Peyre**, a hill

above La Napoule; the **tourist office** (☎ 04 93 49 95 31; www.ot-mandelieu.fr; 272 av Henry Clews; ⏰ 10am-12.30pm & 2-6pm Mon-Fri) has details.

From adjacent pleasure-boat harbour Port de la Napoule, **Compagnie Maritime Napouloise** (☎ 04 93 49 15 88; adult/4-6yr return €12/7; ⏰ 1 to 3 daily Apr-Sep) runs seasonal boats to/from Île Ste-Marguerite.

Théoule-sur-Mer

Neighbouring Théoule-sur-Mer, 2.5km south along the coast, is dominated by **Château de la Théoule**, another privately owned folly (and ex-18th-century soap factory) built in the same architectural style as Château de la Napoule. Even more eccentric is bubblelike **Palais Bulles** (think Teletubby house crossed with old diving helmets), hidden amid trees 5km west of the small seaside resort. Hungarian architect Antti Lovag designed it in the 1960s and couturier Pierre Cardin bought it in 1989. Unfortunately, the only chance to get a glimpse of its interior is during July's **Festival International du Palais Bulles** (www.palais bulles.com; tickets €20), which brings concerts and other cultural events to a theatre inside; the **tourist office** (☎ 04 93 49 28 28; www.theoule-sur-mer .org; 1 corniche d'Or; ☽ 9am-7pm Mon-Sat, 10am-1pm Sun) has details.

Le Trayas

Needles of red rock tumble into the sea at Le Trayas, a pretty seaside resort and the highest point of the corniche, 7km south of Théoule-sur-Mer. The road gets more dramatic as it twists and turns along the coastline past the **Forêt Domaine de l'Estérel**. There are several parking areas along this stretch of the corniche where you can stop to picnic, and there are good views of the spectacular **Rocher de St-Barthélemy** (St-Bartholomew's Rock) and **Cap Roux** from the **Pointe de l'Observatoire**, 2km south of Le Trayas.

At the northern end of Le Trayas, a largish beach is tucked in **Anse de la Figueirette**. Stop here to picnic.

Agay

Agay, 10km or so south of Le Trayas, is celebrated for its fine views of the **Rade d'Agay**, a perfect horseshoe-shaped bay embraced by sandy beaches and abundant pine trees. Numerous water sports and boat excursions are offered at busy, central Plage d'Agay. The **tourist office** (☎ 04 94 82 01 85; www.agay.fr in French; place Giannetti; ☽ 9am-noon & 2-6pm Mon-Sat), opposite the beach, has details.

Agay is also a departure point for treks into the Massif de l'Estérel: follow rte de Valescure (which, out of town, turns into the D100) inland, from where various walking trails are signposted, including to **Pic de l'Ours** (496m), **Pic du Cap Roux** (452m) and **Pic d'Aurelle** (323m). All three peaks offer stunning panoramas. Forest rangers lead guided **nature walks** (€10, three hours) into the massif: pick up an itinerary from the tourist office.

Le Dramont

A military semaphore crowns Cap du Dramont, aka Cap Estérel, at the southern end of the Rade d'Agay. From the semaphore there are unbeatable views of the Golfe de Fréjus, flanked by the **Lion de Terre** and the **Lion de Mer**, two red porphyritic rocks jutting out of the sea. Trails lead to the semaphore from **Plage du Débarquement** in Le Dramont on the western side of the cape. In Agay, a path starts from the car park near **Plage du Camp Long**, at the eastern foot of the cape. Both beaches are accessible from the N98.

From Plage du Débarquement you can sail (15 minutes) to **Île d'Or** (Golden Island), a pinprick island uninhabited bar a mock 'medieval' tower. Tintin fans may recognise it: the Île d'Or inspired Hergé's design for *The Black Island*. Catamarans and sailboards can be hired from the wooden hut on the beach here.

Overlooking Plage du Débarquement, 1km west of Boulouris on the Corniche de l'Estérel (N98), is a large **memorial park** (blvd de la 36ème DI du Texas) commemorating the landing of the 36th US Infantry Division on the beach here on 15 August 1944.

Sleeping

Le Relais des Calanques (☎ 04 94 44 14 06; rte des Escalles; d low/high season from €80/100, mains €15; ☽ restaurant lunch & dinner Wed-Sun; P ☒) One of the few places to stay along this dramatic coastal stretch, this old-world inn sits wedged, *les pieds dans l'eau* (feet in the water), between *calanques* (rocky inlets). From the poolside garden with palm and fig trees, or from the leather armchair in reception, views of the red-rocked sea are striking. Find it south of Le Trayas on the N98.

Eating

There are two wildly contrasting, local hot spots in La Napoule.

La Mandarine (☎ 04 93 49 98 83; 18 rue de la Poste; mains €10-15; ☽ dinner Thu-Tue) What you see is what you get at this reader-recommended, lovable eating spot run by a Dutch couple. It's cosy, friendly and cooks up quintessential Provençal fare at prices that keep locals hooked.

L'Oasis (☎ 04 93 49 95 52; www.oasis-raimbault
.com; 6 rue Jean Honoré Carle; menus €80, €120, €145 & €155;
☒ lunch & dinner Tue-Sun, dinner Mon) Two shiny
Michelin stars lure foodies from far and
wide to this gastronomic temple, which is run
with real panache by the Raimbault brothers
(Stéphane cooks, François is the pastry chef).
Dining at this oasis is between century-old
plane trees in a romantic, lantern-lit patio
garden, while the cuisine is Mediterranean
with a generous dash of the Orient. Cakes,
pastries and bread to die for are sold in the
adjoining boutique.

Getting There & Away
BUS
RafaelBus (☎ 04 94 83 87 63) runs the 'Ligne de
la Corniche d'Or' service along the Corniche
de l'Estérel from St-Raphaël to Le Trayas (at
least hourly). From Cannes, buses (five to
eight daily) stop at Boulouris, Cap du Dra-
mont/Le Dramont, Agay and Le Trayas. A
single fare is €1.30.

TRAIN
Train stations at Mandelieu-La Napoule (4km
north of La Napoule), Théoule-sur-Mer, Le
Trayas, Agay and Le Dramont are served by
the Nice–Cannes–St-Raphaël–Fréjus–Les
Arcs-Draguignan train route. Trains run up to
11 times daily between St-Raphaël and Nice,
stopping at all the smaller resort stations.
From Les Arcs-Draguignan to Nice, only two
trains a day stop at the resorts: change in
St-Raphaël.

There are many more trains from Cannes
to St-Raphaël, from where there are regular
buses to the smaller places.

ST-RAPHAËL
pop 31,196

Once upon a time it was a fishing hamlet…
until along came mayor Félix Martin (1842–
99) who took advantage of the new railway to
promote his seaside town and lure in tourists.
It worked. By the 1920s St-Raphaël was a
fabulous place to be seen: F Scott Fitzgerald
wrote *Tender Is the Night* here, while wife
Zelda spent her time drink-diving. During
WWII it was a primary landing base of US
and French troops.

St-Raphaël has lost some teeth and gained
a potbelly since its glamour days. Its old
town was bombed during the war, and the
sprawling seafront suburbs have become

entangled with those of Fréjus, 2km away.
Beaches, water sports and diving – it's one of
France's leading centres – remain its prime
assets.

A two-lane cycling track along the coast
links St-Raphaël with Toulon, a good 100km
away.

Orientation
The old town is off rue de la Liberté, and
the new centre is neatly packed between rue
Waldeck Rousseau and promenade de Lattre
de Tassigny, which leads west to the Vieux
Port. St-Raphaël's beach activities sprawl as
far east as Port Santa Lucia (a modern pleasure port 1.5km along the coast) and 2km
west to Fréjus.

Information
Cyber Bureau (☎ 04 94 95 29 36; cyber.bureau@free.fr;
123 rue Waldeck Rousseau; per 30/60min €4/6; ☒ 9am-
7pm Mon-Fri, 9am-noon Sat) Inside the train-station
shopping centre.
Post office (☎ 04 94 19 52 00; av Victor Hugo)
Tourist office (☎ 04 94 19 52 52; www.saint-raphael
.com; rue Waldeck Rousseau; ☒ 9am-7pm Jul & Aug,
9am-12.30pm & 2-6.30pm Mon-Sat Sep-Jun)

Activities
Pick from sand or shingle: **Plage du Veillat**,
the main beach, has shining golden sand; to
the east, **Plage Beaurivage** is covered in small
pebbles. From June to September you can
water-ski, parascend or ride the waves in a
rubber tyre from most beaches along this
stretch of coastline. **Port Santa Lucia**, a hop
east again, is a water-sports hub with plenty
of places to rent windsurfers, kayaks and
catamarans.

St-Raphaël is a leading diving centre,
thanks to the many WWII shipwrecks off its
coast. Diving club **Club sous l'Eau** (☎ 04 94 95 90
33; www.clubsousleau.com; ☒ 9am-2.30pm Apr-Nov, by
appointment Dec-Mar) at Port Santa Lucia can help
you zoom in.

BOAT EXCURSIONS
Les Bateaux de St-Raphaël (☎ 04 94 95 17 46; www
.tmr-saintraphael.com; quai Amiral Nomy, Vieux Port) organises boat excursions to St-Tropez and Port
Grimaud (p355); the Calanques de l'Estérel
(adult/child two to nine years €13/7); along
the Corniche de l'Estérel (€14/8); and to Île
Ste-Marguerite (full day €23/12, half-day
€16/9).

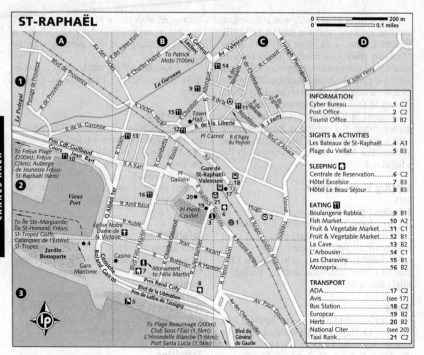

ST-RAPHAËL

INFORMATION

Cyber Bureau	1 C2
Post Office	2 C2
Tourist Office	3 B2

SIGHTS & ACTIVITIES

Les Bateaux de St-Raphaël	4 A3
Plage du Veillat	5 B3

SLEEPING

Centrale de Reservation	6 C2
Hôtel Excelsior	7 B3
Hôtel Le Beau Séjour	8 B3

EATING

Boulangerie Rabbia	9 B1
Fish Market	10 A2
Fruit & Vegetable Market	11 C1
Fruit & Vegetable Market	12 B1
La Cave	13 B2
L'Arbousier	14 C1
Les Charavins	15 B1
Monoprix	16 B2

TRANSPORT

ADA	17 C2
Avis	(see 17)
Bus Station	18 C2
Europcar	19 B2
Hertz	20 B2
National Citer	(see 20)
Taxi Rank	21 C2

Festivals & Events

St-Raphaël's fishing community honours its patron saint, St Peter, every August with a two-day **Fête de la St-Pierre des Pêcheurs**. Local fishermen, dressed in traditional costume, joust Provençal-style from flat-bottomed boats moored in the harbour.

Every year St-Raphaël hosts a number of Provençal **jousting competitions**; members of the Société des Joutes Raphaëloises (Raphaëloises Jousting Society) practise in boats around the Vieux Port.

Sleeping

Book hotel and self-catering accommodation through St-Raphaël's **Centrale de Reservation** (☎ 04 94 19 10 60; reservation@saint-raphael.com; rue Waldeck Rousseau; ⊙ 9am-7pm Jul & Aug, 9am-12.30pm & 2-6.30pm Mon-Sat Sep-Jun).

CHAMBRES D'HÔTES

The tourist office has around eight B&Bs on its books.

L'Hirondelle Blanche (☎ 04 94 11 84 03; www.hiron delle-blanche.fr; blvd de Général de Gaulle; d low/high season from €54/84; ✄ P) The pick of the bunch, an elegant early-20th-century villa is the venue for this six-room *maison d'hôte* with period furnishings and crisp white walls inside and out. Even better, the White Swallow peers out to sea – as do all bar one of the rooms. Find it on the beachfront, a five-minute stroll from Port Santa Lucia.

HOTELS

Hôtel Le Beau Séjour (☎ 04 94 95 03 75; www.hotelbeau sejour.fr; promenade René Coty; s/d/tr/q low season incl breakfast from €45/61/77/96, high season €58/72/87/119; ⊙ Apr-Oct; ✄) Rates quoted are the cheapest rooms in the house at this peppermint-green and red two-star hotel on the seafront. Note: you'll be hard-pushed to squeeze large modern-day suitcases into the rattly old (albeit charming) lift. Superior rooms with sea view are almost twice the price. Parking costs €8.

Hôtel Excelsior (☎ 04 94 95 02 42; www.excelsior -hotel.com; promenade René Coty; d incl breakfast with town/ sea view from €140/160; ✄) Further along the prom is the Excelsior, an elegant old pile near the casino. It's graced with a beautiful tea terrace overlooking the sea, two restaurants and an English-style pub.

HOSTELS

Auberge de Jeunesse Fréjus-St-Raphaël (☎ 04 94 53 18 75; frejus-st-raphael@fuaj.org; chemin du Counillier; dm incl breakfast €15; ☺ reception 8-11am & 5.30-8.30pm Mar–mid-Nov) Set in a seven-hectare park of umbrella pines near Fréjus Ville, this rambling manor house of an HI-affiliated hostel is prime backpacker material. Arriving by train, get off at St-Raphaël (6km away), take bus 7, 10 or 13 to the 'Les Chênes' stop, cross the roundabout and pick up chemin du Counillier.

Eating

Les Charavins (☎ 04 94 95 03 76; 36 rue Charbois; mains €14-24; ☺ lunch & dinner Thu & Fri, lunch Sat & Sun) What a treasure this quaint, old-world wine bar is! Sit around a Parisian bistro table and admire the floor-to-ceiling rows of vintages (300-odd to taste in all), while tucking into delicious *cuisine du marché* cooked to a turn by top Belgian chef (who once ran a Michelin-starred inn) Philippe Furnémont.

La Cave (☎ 04 94 95 79 62; cnr rue de la Thiers & rue Garonne; menus €28 & €38; ☺ lunch & dinner Tue-Sun) A striking modern façade makes the Cellar stand out. Inside, an equally contemporary design frames creative dishes such as *nems de thon rouge* (red tuna spring rolls) and *escalopes de ris de veau en croûte de noisette* (veal sweetbreads encrusted with hazelnuts).

L'Arbousier (☎ 04 94 95 25 00; 4 av Valescure; lunch menu €28, dinner menus €36, €46 & €58; ☺ lunch & dinner Wed-Sun) Its fabulous flowery garden is equal to the reputation of the town's top gastronomic choice. Chef Philippe Troncy cooks up traditional seasonal fare in a staunchly traditional setting – his *carpaccio de langoustines* (wafer-thin slices of raw saltwater lobster) and other shellfish creations are sublime.

Self-catering:

Fruit & Vegetable Markets (place de la République & place Victor Hugo) Daily.

Fish Market (cours Jean Bart) Catch of the day, fresh each morning, at the Vieux Port.

Boulangerie Rabbia (☎ 04 94 95 07 82; 29 rue Allongue) Family bakery since 1885 selling *tarte Tropézienne* and *farinette Niçois* (bread stuffed with olives, bacon bits, anchovy or goat cheese).

Monoprix (58 blvd Félix Martin)

Getting There & Away
BUS

St-Raphaël's **bus station** (☎ 04 94 83 87 63; av Victor Hugo), located behind the train station (accessible via the escalators on the station platforms),

doubles as Fréjus' main bus station. For information on buses to/from Fréjus, see p336.

Services include buses running to and from St-Raphaël and Draguignan (€5, 1¼ hours, hourly Monday to Saturday, six per day Sunday) via Fréjus; along the Corniche de l'Estérel to Le Trayas; and St-Tropez (€10.20, 1¼ hours, six to eight daily) via Grimaud (€8, 55 minutes) and Ste-Maxime (€6, 35 minutes). Services are less frequent in winter.

TRAIN

The Nice–Marseille train line runs through Fréjus and St Raphaël's **Gare de St-Raphaël-Valescure** (rue Waldeck Rousseau). Some trains to/from Nice (€9.60, 45 minutes, every 30 minutes) stop at the villages along the Corniche de l'Estérel. There's also a direct service to Les Arcs-Draguignan.

Getting Around

Patrick Moto (☎ 04 94 53 65 99; 199 av Général Leclerc) rents out mountain bikes (summer only) for around €15 per day. Pick up a taxi in front of the train station or call ☎ 04 94 83 24 24.

Car-rental agencies:

ADA (☎ 04 94 95 01 83; train station)
Avis (☎ 04 94 95 60 42; train station)
Europcar (☎ 04 94 95 56 87; 56 rue Waldeck Rousseau)
Hertz (☎ 04 94 95 48 68; 36 rue Waldeck Rousseau)
National Citer (☎ 04 94 40 27 89; 20 rue Waldeck Rousseau)

FRÉJUS

pop 48,000 / elev 250m

Roman ruins are the trump card of Fréjus, settled by Massiliots (Greek colonists from Marseille) and colonised by Julius Caesar around 49 BC as Forum Julii. Its appealing old town is a maze of pastel buildings, shady plazas and winding alleys, climaxing with extraordinary medieval paintings in an episcopal complex wedged between a trio of market-busy squares. Come dusk, concerts and plays fill the ruins of its Roman theatre with magic during July's Les Nuits Aureliennes.

By the water, sandy Fréjus Plage sits on the fringe of the chic new port, full of seafood restaurants with grossly inflated prices. An evening market spills across the sand most nights in season.

Orientation

Fréjus comprises hillside Fréjus Ville, 3km from the seafront, and Fréjus Plage, on the

Golfe de Fréjus. The modern port is at the western end of blvd de la Libération and its continuation, blvd d'Alger. The Roman remains are mostly in Fréjus Ville.

Information

Post office (264 av Aristide Briand)

Tourist office (☎ 04 94 51 83 83; www.frejus.fr in French; 325 rue Jean Jaurès; ☯ 10am-noon & 2.30-6.30pm Mon-Sat, 10am-noon & 3-6pm Sun Jul & Aug, 10am-noon & 2-6pm Mon-Sat Sep-Jun)

Tourist office kiosk (summer) By the beach, opposite 11 blvd de la Libération.

Sights

GROUPE ÉPISCOPAL

Fréjus' star sight is the **Groupe Épiscopal** (Cathedral Close; ☎ 04 94 51 26 30; 58 rue de Fleury; adult/under 18yr €5/free; ☯ 9am-6.30pm Jun-Sep, 9am-noon & 2-5pm Tue-Sun Oct-May), slap bang in the centre of town on the foundations of a Roman temple. At the heart of the complex is an 11th- and 12th-century **cathedral**, one of the first Gothic buildings in the region (although it retains certain Roman features).

The beautiful carved wooden doors at the main entrance were added during the Renaissance. The octagonal 5th-century **baptistry** (which incorporates eight Roman columns into its structure) is one of the oldest Christian buildings in France, and is exceptionally well preserved.

Stairs from the narthex lead up to the **cloister**, which looks onto a fine courtyard with a well-tended garden and well. Here you'll find the most stunning feature of the complex – its utterly unique 14th- and 15th-century painted **wooden ceiling panels**; 500 of the original 1200 survive. Angels, devils, hunters, acrobats, monsters and a cheery-looking man riding a pig gallivant round the vivid comic-book frames: bring binoculars for a better view or rent a pair at the ticket desk for €1.

ROMAN RUINS

West of the old town, past the ancient **Porte des Gaules**, is the mostly rebuilt 1st- and 2nd-century **Les Arènes** (☎ 04 94 51 34 31; rue Henri Vadon; adult/under 12yr €2/free; ☯ 9.30am-12.30pm & 2-6pm Tue-Sun May-Oct, to 5pm Nov-Apr). It was one of Gaul's largest amphitheatres (seating 10,000 spectators) and is used for concerts today.

At the southeastern edge of the old city is the 3rd-century **Porte d'Orée** (rue des Moulins), the only remaining arcade of monumental Roman thermal baths. North of the old town are the ruins of a **Théâtre Romain** (☎ 04 94 53 58 75; rue du Théâtre Romain; adult/under 12yr €2/free; ☯ 9.30am-12.30pm & 2-6pm Tue-Sun May-Oct, to 5pm Nov-Apr). Part of the stage and the theatre's outer walls are all that remain.

Northeast, towards La Tour de Mare, you pass a section of a 40km-long **aqueduc** (aqueduct; av du 15 Corps d'Armée), which once carried water to Roman Fréjus. Continuing 500m further north, you reach **Villa Aurélienne** (☎ 04 94 52 90 49; av du Général d'Armée Calliès; admission free; ☯ villa 2-5pm during exhibitions, park 9am-7pm Mon-Fri, 9am-noon & 2-7pm Sat & Sun summer, 9am-5pm Mon-Fri, 9am-noon & 2-6pm Sat & Sun winter), a peachy manor built in 1880 that hosts temporary photography and art exhibitions. Its stunning 22-hectare park is crossed by another section – five moss-covered arches – of the aqueduct.

CHAPELLE NOTRE DAME DE JÉRUSALEM

Also known as the **Chapelle Cocteau** (☎ 04 94 53 27 06; av Nicolaï, La Tour de Mare; adult/under 12yr €2/free; ☯ 9.30am-12.30pm & 2-6pm Tue-Sun May-Oct, to 5pm Nov-Apr), this was one of the last pieces of work embarked upon by Jean Cocteau (1889–1963), best known for the fishermen's chapel he decorated in Villefranche-sur-Mer (see p280). Cocteau began work on Chapelle Notre Dame in Fréjus in 1961, but it remained incomplete until the artist's legal heir, Édouard Dermit, finished his former companion's work in 1988. The altar is made from a millstone.

The chapel is about 5km northeast of the old city in the quarter of La Tour de Mare (served by bus 13), on the N7 towards Cannes.

MUSEUMS

Adjoining Fréjus' episcopal complex is the **Musée Archéologique** (☎ 04 94 52 15 78; place Calvini; adult/under 12yr €2/free; ☯ 9.30am-12.30pm & 2-5pm Tue-Sun May-Oct, 9.30am-12.30pm & 2-5pm Tue-Sun Nov-Apr), housing permanent pieces including a two-headed statue of Hermes and a magnificent 3rd-century leopard mosaic. It also puts on temporary exhibitions of finds from archaeological digs.

Local history and traditions are the focus of Fréjus' **Musée d'Histoire Locale et des Traditions** (☎ 04 94 51 64 01; 153 rue Jean Jaurès; adult/under 12yr €2/free; ☯ 9.30am-12.30pm & 2-6pm Tue-Sun May-Oct, to 5pm Tue-Sun Nov-Apr).

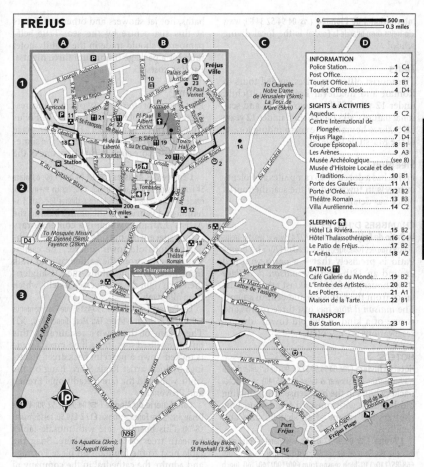

FRÉJUS

INFORMATION
Police Station...........................1 C4
Post Office..............................2 C2
Tourist Office..........................3 B1
Tourist Office Kiosk...................4 D4

SIGHTS & ACTIVITIES
Aqueduc...................................5 C2
Centre International de
  Plongée.................................6 C4
Fréjus Plage............................7 D4
Groupe Épiscopal.....................8 B1
Les Arènes..............................9 A3
Musée Archéologique..........(see 8)
Musée d'Histoire Locale et des
  Traditions...........................10 B1
Porte des Gaules....................11 A1
Porte d'Orée..........................12 B2
Théâtre Romain......................13 B3
Villa Aurélienne.....................14 C2

SLEEPING
Hôtel La Riviéra.....................15 B2
Hôtel Thalassothérapie..........16 C4
Le Patio de Fréjus..................17 B2
L'Aréna................................18 A2

EATING
Café Galerie du Monde...........19 B2
L'Entrée des Artistes..............20 B2
Les Potiers............................21 A1
Maison de la Tarte..................22 B1

TRANSPORT
Bus Station............................23 B1

CANNES AREA

MOSQUÉE MISSIRI DE DJENNÉ

A collection of surprising war memorials and troop-related buildings lies scattered around Fréjus, including this **mosque** (rue des Combattants d'Afrique du Nord), which is a replica of one in Djenné, Mali. It was built in 1930 for the Sudanese troops stationed at a marine base in Fréjus, and lies 5km north of town on the rte de Bagnols-en-Forêt (the D4 towards Fayence).

Activities

Kids never tire of the giant water slides, rubber rings and ride-the-wave madness at **Aquatica** (☎ 04 94 51 82 51; www.parc-aquatica.com; adult/under 12yr €23/16.50; ☀ 10am-7pm Jul & Aug, 10am-6pm Jun & Sep), a giant water park out of town on the southbound N98. Children under 1m tall get in free.

Fréjus Plage, lined with 1950s architectural delights, is an excellent sandy beach. Next door at the new port, built in the 1980s, **Centre**

International de Plongée (☎ 04 94 52 34 99; www .cip-frejus.com; quai de la Foudre) is the local diving school.

Tours

The tourist office organises guided tours of Roman and medieval Fréjus (adult/child under 12 years €5/free, two hours) and seasonal nature walks (adult/child under 12 years €8/5, three hours) in the surrounding forests of the Massif de l'Estérel.

Sleeping

Fréjus has a dozen or so camp sites and plenty of hotels in town and by the sea; the tourist office has details.

CHAMBRES D'HÔTES

Le Patio de Fréjus (☎ 04 94 17 27 43; www.lepatio-frejus .com; 93 rue des Tombades; d incl breakfast €70) The Fréjus Patio is precisely that – a patio wrapped around an 18th-century *maison de village* (townhouse), before-breakfast strolling distance from the cathedral and central square. The *maison d'hôte* has just three rooms and is one of a kind in the old town; advance reservations are essential.

HOTELS

Hôtel La Riviéra (☎ 04 94 51 31 46; 90 rue Grisolle; d with washbasin/shower/shower & toilet €30/35/40) A backpackers hotel in the best sense, this rambling old building with mustard façade and blue shutters has rooms of all shapes, sizes and facilities.

L'Aréna (☎ 04 94 17 09 40; www.arena-hotel.com; 145 rue du Général de Gaulle; s/d/tr/q low season from €68/85/110/110, high season from €90/100/140/160, lunch menu €25, dinner menus €40 & €55; P 🍴 🖳 🎝) A three-star hotel with flower-lined garden terrace and the reliable Logis de France hallmark, L'Aréna is the place to enjoy the most wonderful breakfasts, or to lounge by the pool and indulge in refined, imaginative cuisine in its highly rated restaurant: what about ravioli delicately stuffed with lobster, followed by nougat ice cream with almonds and caramelised ginger? Garage parking costs €10.

Hôtel Thalassothérapie (☎ 04 94 52 55 00; www .hotelthalasso-portfrejus.fr; Port-Fréjus West; d low/mid/high season from €72/88/110; P 🍴 🎝) Cocoon yourself and your kids (the place has a babysitting service and special spa just for teenagers) in a heady whirl of essential-oil massages, seaweed baths, hot jet showers and other treatments at this spa centre by the sea. True self-pamperers should trade in the nightly hotel rates for a package (minimum three nights). Parking costs €5.

Eating

Port Fréjus proffers plenty of cafés and restaurants with bobbing-boat views. In Fréjus Ville try place Paul Albert Février or place de la Liberté for a simple lunch or, for something a tad more sophisticated, try one of the following.

L'Entrée des Artistes (☎ 04 94 40 11 60; 63 place St-François de Paule; plat du jour €10, lunch menu €16, dinner menus €22 & €32; 🕙 lunch & dinner Tue-Sat) Johanna and Fabrice are the names behind the Artists' Entrance, which is a contemporary eating space with outside seating on an inconspicuous old-town square. The easiest way to find it from the cathedral is to walk from place Formigé along rue Désaugiers, then turn right down traverse Castelli, which is an alleyway.

Les Potiers (☎ 04 94 51 33 74; 135 rue Potiers; menus €23 & €34; 🕙 lunch & dinner Thu-Mon, dinner Wed; ✖) The cream of the town's restaurants, this quaint, civilised spot with a lime-green façade is tucked down a peaceful backstreet. Paintings by local artist Regis Sibris hang on the white walls and the fare is traditional French and Provençal.

Café Galerie du Monde (☎ 04 94 17 52 90; 49 rue Désaugiers/place Formigé; menus €12 & €19.50, salads/mains €8/14) This bustling café with mosaic tables beneath trees oozes atmosphere. Snag the table next to the fountain on place Formigé and admire the cathedral in the company of simple but hugely satisfying local fare cooked up by a pair of brothers.

For a picnic stop try Maison de la Tarte (☎ 04 94 51 17 34; 33 rue Jean Jaurès; 🕙 6am-9pm Mon-Sat) for well-filled baguettes and a peachy array of decadent fruit tarts, sold by the slice (around €2).

Getting There & Away

BUS

From Fréjus bus station (AggloBus ☎ 04 94 53 78 46; place Paul Vernet) – a humble series of shelters around a roundabout – bus services run to St-Raphaël (€1.10, 20 to 35 minutes, every 15 or 20 minutes), Draguignan (€5, one hour, hourly), Nice and Marseille. Buses to/from St-Raphaël also stop at Fréjus train station.

TRAIN

The **train station** (rue du Capitaine Blazy) is on the Nice–Marseille train route, although few trains stop here beyond services to/from St-Raphaël (€1.20, two minutes, hourly).

Getting Around

Bus 6 (which leaves hourly) is the service that links the beaches of Fréjus Plage with place Paul Vernet in Fréjus Ville. Bus 13 runs between Fréjus' train station and bus station and Cocteau's Chapelle Notre Dame de Jérusalem. Tickets can be purchased from bus drivers (€1.10/8.40 per ticket/carnet of 10).

Holiday Bikes (☎ 04 94 40 16 62; 238 av de Verdun) rents out bicycles/50cc scooters/125cc scooters for €12/30/55 per day.

St-Tropez to Toulon

Pouting sexpot Brigitte Bardot came to St-Tropez in the '50s to star in *Et Dieu Créa la Femme* (*And God Created Woman; 1956*), with the film's stunning success changing St-Tropez overnight from peaceful fishing village into sizzling jet-set favourite. The Tropeziens have thrived on their glitzy image ever since: millionaires' yachts jostle for the €90,000-per-week moorings, and an infinite number of tourists jostle to admire them.

A battleship-grey blast of reality on this golden stretch of coast fringed by some of France's most beautiful beaches is Toulon, France's most important military port, 20km west of St-Tropez. Continuing west, the pinprick islands off its shores, dubbed the Îles du Fun (Islands of Fun), are not for Robinson Crusoe. In the 1950s pastis millionaire Paul Ricard transformed them into concrete playgrounds, to the joy of many a less-discerning, fun-in-the-sun-seeking tourist.

Between these two towns, fine-sand beaches of buttercream yellow and gold abound: at St-Tropez's 9km-long Plage de Pampelonne; the quiet white coves of Cavalaire-sur-Mer, Le Rayol, Cavalière and Aiguebelle; the resort of Le Lavandou; and La Capte, near pretty palm tree–lined Hyères, a launch pad for day trips to the golden Îles d'Hyères.

Inland, the wild and heavily forested Massif des Maures sprawls west, a hushed, whispering retreat from the crazy Côte d'Azur. Walking and cycling trails radiate around chestnut-sweet Collobrières while further north, around Draguignan, unfolds a maze of solitary hilltop villages with fortified gateways leading to tiny winding streets and sleepy squares.

HIGHLIGHTS

- Star-spot, drink and dance 'til dawn at the beach legends of sexy **St-Tropez** (see the boxed text, p346)

- Take a dramatic cape-to-cape walk around the coast on the **St-Tropez peninsula** (p353)

- Revel in endless sun, sea and sand on the shining islands of the **Îles d'Hyères** (p366)

- Snorkel in clear-blue waters and roam a Mediterranean plant-filled paradise at the **Domaine du Rayol** (p364)

- Lose yourself inside the peace, tranquillity and natural beauty of the village-studded **Haut-Var** (p358)

- Discover the region's **vineyards** (see the boxed text, p373) by pedal power around La Londe

- Gorge out on candied chestnuts in **Collobrières** (p360), black truffles in **Aups** (p358) and Côtes de Provence wines in **Les Arcs-sur-Argens** (p359)

Aups ★
Haut-Var ★
★ Les Arcs-sur-Argens
Collobrières ★
★ St-Tropez
★
Presqu'île de
St-Tropez
Domaine du Rayol ★
★ La Londe
★
Îles d'Hyères

ITINERARIES

BEACH BUM

The fine golden sand beaches on this privileged neck of the coast are the Riviera's finest. Start day one in **St-Tropez** (**1**; p341) with a prebreakfast mooch around the **Place des Lices Market** (p350), followed by a coffee and croissant at Sartre's **Sénequier** (p350). Dynamos can trade in the market meander for an invigorating 12km stroll along St-Tropez's **coastal path** (p346) to **Plage de Tahiti** (**2**; p345), but authentic beach bums can drive. From here, don your best bikini and leg it south to **Plage de Pampelonne** (**3**; p345) in time for an apéritif at **Le Club 55** (see the boxed text, p346) before a sushi lunch at **Kaï Largo** (see the boxed text, p346); find both midway along Pampelonne's divinely sandy 5km-long stretch. Spend the afternoon flopped out on a decadently thick mattress, champagne bucket *à côté*, at **Nikki Beach** (see the boxed text, p346). Come dusk, motor through vineyards to **Plage de Gigaro** (**4**; p353), where **Couleurs du Jardin** (p354) beckons for dinner overlooking the Med. For dance-till-dawn types, the party rages at **La Voile Rouge** (see the boxed text, p346).

Day two, abandon St-Tropez for an island. The curvaceous coastal road to Le Lavandou glides past extraordinary sea gardens at the **Domaine du Rayol** (**5**; p364). Snorkel here then continue southwest to **Chez Jo** (see the boxed text, p365) for *bouillabaisse* (fish stew; order 24 hours in advance) on the beach at noon and swimming in the nude. After lunch, catch a boat from **Le Lavandou** (**6**; p365) to **Île de Port-Cros** (**7**; p369) for an afternoon of gentle walking, or **Île de Porquerolles** (**8**; p366) for scenic cycling beach-to-beach.

ST-TROPEZ TO TOULON

A WINE-LOVER'S TRAIL

Begin at the **Maison des Vins Côtes de Provence** (p359). Gen up on the region's largest appellation, then head out into the field for wine-tasting in situ: try **Château Ste-Roseline** (p359) with its chapel to visit, or **Domaine de la Maurette** (p359), which begs you to lunch in its earthy inn. Alternatively, push northwest to Lorgues where another lunch invitation in the company of truffles and perfectly matched wine is extended by **Chez Bruno** (see the boxed text, p360). Later, wend west past the sober **Abbaye de Thoronet** (**2**; p359) to pinprick **La Celle** (**3**; p359). Taste Coteaux Varois wine at its **Maison des Vins** (p359) and settle down for the night at **Hostellerie de l'Abbaye de la Celle** (p359); again, the wine list is impeccable.

Next morning, head southwest towards the matchless AOC reds of **Bandol** (**4**; p380) and crisp whites of **Cassis** (**5**; p116); or bear southeast instead to **La Londe** (**6**; p371) where the **Route des Vins de la Londe** (**7**; see the boxed text, p373) escorts wine-lovers by pedal-power through vineyards. Between chateaux, picnic on wild boar and hazelnut terrine from the **Domaine de la Sanglière** (see the boxed text, p373) and end the afternoon with a dip in the sea at **Cabasson** (**8**; see the boxed text, p373). As the sun sinks, sail (from Port de Miramar or Le Lavandou) to **Île de Porquerolles** (**9**; p366) for dinner and a night of romance at **Le Mas du Langoustier** (p368), a top-notch hotel and restaurant located on the largest wine-producing estate on the vine-rich island, Domaine de l'Île.

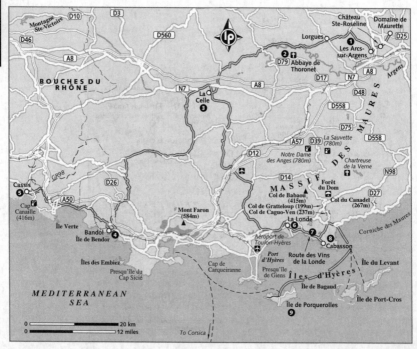

LITERARY ST-TROPEZ

Need a book for the beach? Get into the region with some locally inspired literature:

- *The Hairdressers of St-Tropez* (Rupert Everett) Comedy of hairdressers and talking dogs opening on St-Tropez's Pampelonne beach in 2042.
- *Jigsaw* (Sybille Bedford) An autobiographical novel inspired by the author's years spent in Toulon during the 1920s and 1930s. The author's earlier novel, *A Compass Error* (1968), uses the coast as a backdrop for a love triangle of lesbian and heterosexual encounters.
- *The Rover* (Joseph Conrad) A 1920s novel set in and around Toulon.
- *Travels with Virginia Woolf* (Jan Morris) Entertaining extracts from the playwright's journals, including observations made during visits to her sister's home in Cassis.
- *Houses of St-Tropez* (Marie Bariller) Pick the house of your dreams from 224 glossy pages of utterly gorgeous Tropezien house pics; great beach-fantasy material.

PRESQU'ÎLE DE ST-TROPEZ

Jutting out into the sea, between the Golfe de St-Tropez and the Baie de Cavalaire, is the select Presqu'île de St-Tropez (St-Tropez Peninsula). From swanky St-Tropez on the northern coast, beautiful sandy beaches – easily the loveliest on the Côte d'Azur – ring the peninsula. Inland, Gassin and Ramatuelle charm thousands.

ST-TROPEZ
pop 5754

Guy de Maupassant (1850–93), arriving in St-Tropez in 1887, was mesmerised by its quaint beauty and the 'sardine scales glistening like pearls on the cobblestones'. These days, sleek yachts have chased away the simple fishing boats and those same cobblestones are trampled by 100,000 daily visitors in summer. Don't fight the crowds: go with the flow, window-shop for designer clothes, and

enjoy the spectacle of rich diners aboard their floating palaces, twirling silver knives and forks.

For a glimpse of an older, gentler village, stroll the cobbled lanes of the former fishing quarter of La Ponche or grab a seat at a café on place des Lices and watch *pétanque (boules)* being played under the age-old plane trees. On Tuesday and Saturday mornings, the entire square becomes one enormous food, flower, clothing and antique market – an unforgettable extravaganza.

St-Tropez is at its most seductive, though, from the water. Arriving by boat, the sprawling citadel, glowing terracotta roofs and church tower, with its distinctive Provençal campanile, are postcard-pretty. You don't need your own yacht, either – see p347 and p351 for details on watery ways into town.

Orientation

The old city is packed between quai Jean Jaurès, the main quay of the Vieux Port (Old Port); place des Lices, a vast shady rectangular square a few blocks inland; and the brooding

ST-TROPEZ TO TOULON

MARKET DAY

Monday Bormes-les-Mimosas, Ste-Maxime
Tuesday Bandol, Callas, Fayence, Hyères, Lorgues, St-Tropez, Toulon
Wednesday Bormes-les-Mimosas, Cogolin, Draguignan, La Garde Freinet, Salernes, Sanary-sur-Mer, Toulon
Thursday Aups (November to March truffle market), Bargemon, Callas, Collobrières (July and August), Fayence, Grimaud, Hyères, Le Lavandou, Les Arcs-sur-Argens, Port Grimaud, Ramatuelle, Toulon
Friday Le Rayol (April to October), Ste-Maxime, Toulon
Saturday Cogolin, Draguignan, Fayence, Hyères, St-Tropez, Toulon
Sunday Cavalière (all-day flea market), Collobrières, La Garde Freinet, La Londe, Le Croix Valmer, Port Grimaud, Ramatuelle, Salernes, Toulon

ST-TROPEZ TO TOULON

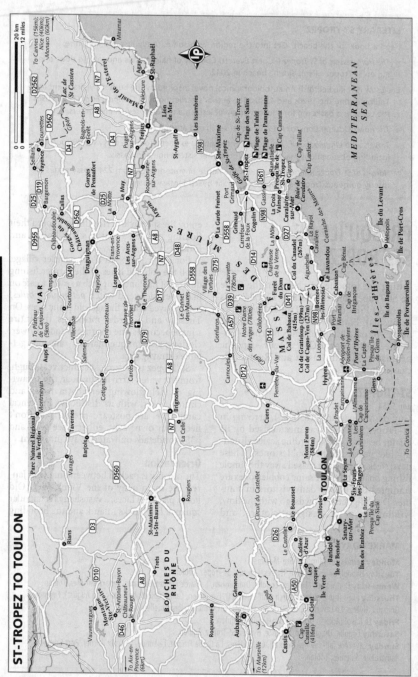

17th-century citadel in the northeast. Yachts like spaceships moor in the old port alongside quai Suffren. The main car park, Parking du Port, is across from the bus station at the Nouveau Port (New Port).

Information
BOOKSHOPS
Librarie du Port (quai Suffren) Newspapers, mags and guidebooks in English.

EMERGENCY
Police station (☎ 04 94 12 70 00; rue François Sibilli)

INTERNET ACCESS
Kreatik Cafe (☎ 04 94 97 40 61; www.kreatik.com; 19 av du Général Leclerc; 1st 10min €2, then per 30min/1hr €4/7; ☉ noon-12.30am Mon, 9.30am-12.30am Tue-Sun)

LAUNDRY
Laverie du Pin (13 quai de l'Épi; per 5.5/16.5kg wash €5.50/13; ☉ 9am-7pm)

MEDICAL SERVICES
Pharmacie du Port (☎ 04 94 97 00 06; 9 quai Suffren; ☉ 8.30am-8.30pm Mon-Sat)
Pôle de Sante (☎ 04 98 12 50 00) Hospital in Gassin, 11km from St-Tropez.
SOS Médecins (☎ 04 94 97 65 65) Emergency medical care.

MONEY
Change Cambio (☎ 04 94 97 80 70; 18 rue Allard; ☉ 9.15am-10pm, shorter hr low season) Charges 3% commission to change travellers cheques; at the Vieux Port.

POST
Post office (place Alphonse Celli)

TOURIST INFORMATION
Tourist office (☎ 04 94 97 45 21; www.ot-saint-tropez .com; quai Jean Jaurès; ☉ 9.30am-8.30pm Jul & Aug, 9.30am-12.30pm & 2-7pm Apr-Jun, Sep & Oct, 9.30am-12.30pm & 2-6pm Nov-Mar, closed Sun Jan & Nov)

Sights & Activities
Weaving your way through the history-laden old city streets is the best way to get a feel for the town's timeless traditions and culture. Start at the **Vieux Port**, the heart of Tropezien life, where a **statue of the Bailli de Suffren** (quai Suffren) cast from a 19th-century cannon peers out to sea. The bailiff (1729–88) was a sailor who fought with a Tropezien crew against Britain and Prussia during the Seven Years' War.

Shrug off the hectic hustle of the port in the charming old fishing quarter of **La Ponche**, northeast of the Vieux Port. From quai Suffren, walk to the northern end of its continuations, quai Jean Jaurès and quai Frédéric Mistral, and at 15th-century **Tour du Portalet**, turn right (east) to the sandy fishing cove. From here, a coastal path (p346) snakes around the peninsula.

From the southern end of quai Frédéric Mistral, place Garrezio sprawls east from 10th-century **Tour Suffren** to place de l'Hôtel de Ville. From here, rue Guichard leads southeast to sweet-chiming **Église de St-Tropez** (place de l'Ormeau), a quintessential St-Trop landmark built in 1785 in Italian baroque style. Inside is the bust of St Torpes, honoured during Les Bravades des Espagnols (p347). Follow rue de Portail Neuf south to **Chapelle de la Miséricorde** (rue de la Miséricorde), built in 1645 with a pretty bell tower and colourful tiled dome.

A block south is legendary **place des Lices**, St-Tropez's loveliest square, studded with plane trees, cafés and (when the market's not on) *pétanque* players. **Chapelle du Couvent** (av Augustin Grangeon) dating from 1757 and **Chapelle Ste-Anne** (av Augustin Grangeon), built in 1618, sit south of here. The marvellous collection of ex-votive paintings and centuries-old miniature boats inside the latter can be viewed just once a year – on St Anne's feast day (26 July).

CITADEL
A 17th-century **citadel** dominates the hillside overlooking St-Tropez to the east. The views (and peacocks!) are great, and its dungeons shelter a **Musée Naval** (☎ 04 94 97 59 43; adult/under 18yr €5.50/free; ☉ 10am-6.30pm), dedicated to the town's maritime history and the Allied landings in August 1944.

MUSÉE DE L'ANNONCIADE
In a gracefully converted 16th-century chapel at the Vieux Port, this famous **art museum** (☎ 04 94 97 04 01; place Georges Grammont; adult/under 12yr €5.50/free; ☉ 10am-1pm & 3-7pm Jul-Sep, 10am-noon & 2-6pm Wed-Mon Oct & Dec-Jun) showcases an impressive collection of modern art infused with the famous Côte d'Azur light. It's also a great opportunity to understand what it was about St-Tropez that captivated so many of these painters: the pointillist collection on the 2nd floor includes Signac's *St-Tropez, L'Orage* (1895), *St-Tropez, Le Quai* (1899) and *St-Tropez, Le Sentier Côtier* (1901). Artists

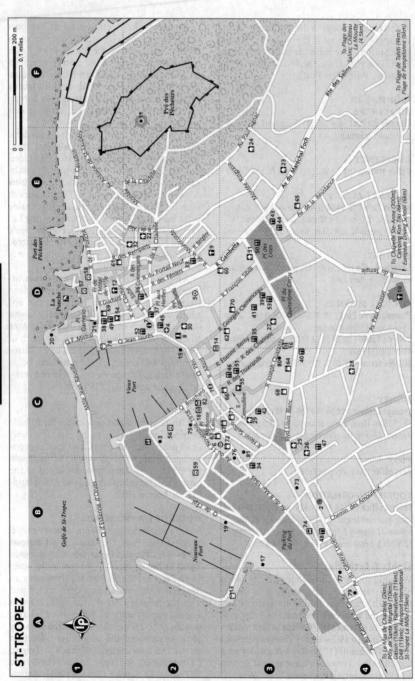

INFORMATION
Change Cambio...........................1 C2
Kreatik Café..............................2 B4
Laverie du Pin...........................3 C2
Librairie du Port....................(see 4)
Pharmacie du Port.....................4 D2
Police Station............................5 D2
Post Office................................6 C2
Tourist Office............................7 D2

SIGHTS & ACTIVITIES
Bailli de Suffren Statue................8 D2
Chapelle de la Miséricorde..........9 D2
Chapelle du Couvent................10 D4
Citadel....................................11 F2
Coastal Path.......................(see 20)
Église de St-Tropez..................12 D1
Excursions Maritimes St-Tropez..13 A3
La Maison des Papillons............14 C2
La Poncho...............................15 C2
Lavoir Vasserot.......................16 D3
Les Bateaux Verts....................17 B3
Musée Naval.......................(see 11)
Musée de L'Annonciade............18 C2
Octopussy...............................19 B3
Tour du Portalet......................20 D1
Tour Suffren............................21 D1

SLEEPING
Baron Lodge............................22 E2
Hôtel Byblos............................23 E3
Hôtel Byblos............................24 E3
Hôtel La Mediterranée..............25 C3
Hôtel La Mistralée....................26 C3

Hôtel Les Palmiers....................27 D3
Hôtel Lou Cagnard...................28 C4
Hôtel Playa..............................29 C3
Hôtel Sube...............................30 D2
La Maison Blanche....................31 D3
Le Yaca...................................32 D2

EATING
Au Caprice des Deux.................33 D2
Boulangerie de l'Olivier.............34 B3
Café Sud.................................35 D3
Chez Fuchs..............................36 D2
Fish Market..............................37 D2
Grand Joseph...........................38 D1
La Table du Marché..................39 D3
La Tarte Tropézienne................40 C3
La Tarte Tropézienne................41 D3
L'Auberge des Maures...............42 C3
Le Bistrot.................................43 E3
Le Café...................................44 E3
Le Gorille................................45 D2
Le Petit Charron.......................46 C3
Monoprix.................................47 C4
Petit Casino.............................48 B4
Petit Joseph.............................49 D1
Place des Lices Market...............50 D3
Salama....................................51 C3
Sénéquier................................52 D2
Spar.......................................53 C3
Spoon Byblos.......................(see 23)

DRINKING
Chez Nano...............................54 D1
La Piscine................................55 C3

ENTERTAINMENT
La Bodega du Papagayo...........56 C2
L'Esquinade.............................57 D1
Le Pigeonnier...........................58 D1
Les Caves du Roy................(see 23)
VIP Room................................59 B2

SHOPPING
Atelier Ivan Hov.......................60 D3
Atelier Ivan Hov.......................61 D1
Atelier Rondini.........................62 D3
De Puta Madre 69....................63 C2
Galerie des Lices......................64 C3
Galerie Nathalie Duchayne.......65 E3
K Jacques................................66 C3
K Jacques................................67 C3
Le Dépôt.................................68 C3
Le Temps des Cerises................69 D1
Poterie Augier..........................70 D3
Vincent Dupontreué..................71 C3
VIP Dog..................................72 C3

TRANSPORT
Avis.......................................73 B3
Bus Station..............................74 B3
Europcar................................75 C2
Hertz......................................76 C3
Holiday Bikes...........................77 A4
Les Bateaux Verts....................78 D1
Lucky Loc................................79 A4
Mas Location 2 Roues..............80 C3
National Citer......................(see 75)
Sixt..81 C3
Taxi Rank...............................82 C2

ST-TROPEZ TO TOULON

such as Vuillard, Bonnard, Maurice Denis and Valloton (the self-named Nabis group) have a room to themselves, and there are wild works by the Fauvists: Matisse spent the summer of 1904 in St-Tropez, starting preliminary studies for *Luxe, Calme et Volupté*. Cubists George Braque and Picasso are also represented.

Summer art exhibitions fill the 19th-century **Lavoir Vasserot** (rue Joseph Quaranta; admission free; ☉ variable), the former communal washhouse.

LA MAISON DES PAPILLONS

Around 4500 butterflies collected by Dany Lartigue, son of Riviera photographer Jacques Henri Lartigue (1894–1986), are pinned to the walls in **La Maison des Papillons** (☎ 04 94 97 63 45; 9 rue Étienne Berny; adult/under 8yr €3/free; ☉ 2.30-6pm Mon-Sat Apr-Oct). Find the House of Butterflies in the former home of Madeleine 'Bibi' Messager, the first wife of Jacques Lartigue (he had three), who remained in St-Tropez after the couple split.

BEACHES

About 4km southeast of town is the start of the magnificent sandy **Plage de Tahiti**, and its

continuation, **Plage de Pampelonne**, studded with some of St-Tropez's most legendary drinking and dining haunts (see the boxed text, p346). To get to here on foot, head out of town along av de la Résistance (south of place des Lices) to rte de la Belle Isnarde and then rte de Tahiti. Otherwise, the bus to Ramatuelle runs about 1km inland along the D93 – from which seven roads lead to the sand.

Closer to St-Tropez, **Plage des Salins** is a long, wide sandy beach 4.5km east of town at the southern foot of Cap des Salins. To get here,

---

A HEADLESS HERO

A grisly legend provided St-Tropez with its name in AD 68. After beheading a Roman officer named Torpes for becoming a Christian, the emperor Nero packed the decapitated body into a small boat, along with a dog and a rooster who were to devour his remains. Miraculously, the body came ashore in St-Tropez unnibbled, and the village adopted the headless Torpes as its saint.

follow rte des Salins to its end. On the way you'll pass **La Treille Muscate** (Wine Trellis), a rambling villa framed with red-ochre columns wrapped in honeysuckle. Here in 1927 Colette wrote *La Naissance du Jour* (Break of Day), which evokes a 1920s unspoilt St-Tropez. She left town in 1938.

At the northern end of Plage des Salins, on a rock jutting out to sea, is the **tomb of Émile Olivier** (1825–1913), who served as first minister to Napoleon III until his exile in 1870. Olivier's 17-volume *L'Empire Libéral* is preserved in the library of **Château La Moutte**, his former home on Cap des Salins, where musical concerts are held in summer. Its unmarked entrance is on chemin de la Moutte.

Olivier's sea-facing tomb looks out towards **La Tête de Chien** (Dog's Head), named after the legendary dog who declined to eat St Torpes' remains. Further south, **Pointe du Capon** is a beautiful cape crisscrossed with walking trails.

Bathers can swim in the buff on aptly named **Plage de la Liberté**, a nudist beach on Pampelonne's northern end; **Plage de la Moutte** on Cap des Salins; or the more secluded **Plage de l'Escalet**, on the southern side of Cap Camarat.

COASTAL WALKS

A scenic coastal path wends its way past rocky outcrops and hidden bays 35km south from St-Tropez, around the Presqu'île de St-Tropez to the beach at Cavalaire-sur-Mer and beyond to Le Lavandou (60km).

In St-Tropez the coastal path, flagged with a yellow marker, starts at **La Ponche**, immediately east of Tour du Portalet at the northern end of quai Frédéric Mistral. From here, trails lead to Baie des Cannebiers (2.7km), La Moutte (7.4km), Plage des Salins (8.5km) and Plage de Tahiti (12km).

Alternatively, drive to the end of rte des Salins, from where it is a shorter walk along the coastal path to Plage de Tahiti (2.7km) and nudist Plage de la Moutte (1.7km) on Cap des Salins.

Ramatuelle **tourist office** (☎ 04 98 12 64 00; www .ramatuelle-tourisme.com in French; place de l'Ormeau) organises *balades nature* (guided nature walks)

TOP FIVE BEACH LEGENDS

Frolic like a sand star at St-Tropez's trendiest beach haunts on (where else?) Plage de Pampelonne:

▪ **Le Club 55** (☎ 04 94 55 55 55; www.leclub55.com; 43 blvd Patch; meals €50; ☽ lunch Mar–mid-Nov) What started out as a simple canteen for the crew of *And God Created Woman* in the 1950s is now the hippest joint on the beach. Dine at tightly packed tables beneath sails strung from trees, drink from plump white sofas on the sand, and be a beach bum on a white cushioned mattress (€16 per day) beneath umbrella (€8 per day) or hip *paillote* (a smart straw shack; €20 a day) on the designer beach. Rumbling tummies with no reservation can opt for a salad or sandwich (€10 to €15) at the twig-topped beach bar nearer the water.

▪ **La Voile Rouge** (Red Sail; ☎ 04 94 79 84 34; rte des Tamaris; ☽ Apr–Sep) Parts of *And God Created Woman* were filmed here followed by the first sightings of topless bathers and later the g-string bikini. The beach club remains hot stuff come dusk today – champagne à gogo, cocktails, dancing on tables and DJ mixes (buy the CD). Find it at the northern end of Pampelonne on Moorea Plage. No credit cards.

▪ **Nikki Beach** (☎ 04 94 79 82 04; www.nikkibeach.com; rte de l'Épi; meals €45-90; ☽ noon-9pm Mon-Thu, noon-1am Fri-Sun May-Sep) Bums are extremely well cushioned at this OTT lap of designer luxury: think king-sized cream mattresses on the sand or up top in colonial-style sun shacks. The bar is hot, there's pool-side service and smart table dining. Feel the vibe at www.nikkinews.com.

▪ **Millesim Beach** (☎ 04 94 97 20 99; www.millesim.net; rte de Tahiti; starters/mains €15/25; ☽ lunch & dinner Jul & Aug, Thu-Tue low season) One of the few to open year-round, this contemporary beach club pampers guests with massages (€70 to €90), manicures (€35) and other Zen relaxants. Cuisine is typically Mediterranean.

▪ **Kaï Largo** (☎ 04 98 12 63 12; www.kailargo.com; 17 blvd Patch; meals €45-80; ☽ lunch & dinner late Jun-Aug, lunch Apr, May & Sep) Flit to Asia at this oasis of exoticism on the sand. Cuisine is a tasty cross of Thai and Indonesian; July and August usher in a sushi bar and the fixtures'n'fittings are predominantly rattan.

to Cap Camarat, Cap Taillat and elsewhere on the peninsula; see p352.

WATER SPORTS

Discover the underworld of St-Tropez with diving schools **Octopussy** (☎ 06 10 25 61 26; www .octopussy.fr; ☼ Apr-Nov), which has a kiosk in the Parking du Port car park at the Nouveau Port; and **European Diving School** (☎ 04 94 79 90 37; www .europeandiving.com; rte des Plages; ☼ mid-Mar–Oct), which is at the Kon Tiki camp site. One/six/12 dives cost €40/220/390, plus equipment charge.

At the northern end of Pampelonne at La Voile Rouge, **Bill Aout Sports** (☎ 06 12 75 11 03) rents out canoes/pedalos/wind surfers for €10/13/13 an hour.

BOAT EXCURSIONS

Boat trips around the glamorous Baie des Cannebiers (dubbed the 'Bay of Stars' after the many celebrity villas dotting the coast) are advertised on boards along quai Suffren: **La Pouncho** (☎ 06 84 07 41 87; www.lapouncho.com; adult/4-10yr €8/4) runs four or five one-hour trips a day around the bay, March to October.

From April to September **Les Bateaux Verts** (☎ 04 94 49 29 39; www.bateauxverts.com) runs various trips departing from quai Jean Jaurès at the Vieux Port including around the Baie des Cannebiers (adult/four to 12 years €8.50/4.50), Calanques de l'Estérel (€16.90/10.20); Caps Camarat, Taillat and Lardier (€16.90/10.20); Cannes (€29/18.50); Îles de Lérins (€29/18.50); Port-Cros (€29/18.50) and Porquerolles (€33/21). The same company also runs shuttle boats between St-Tropez, St-Raphaël, Ste-Maxime and Port Grimaud; see p351 for details.

Excursions Maritimes St-Tropez (EMT; ☎ 04 94 54 53 54; www.emt-golfe-st-tropez.fr) runs weekly trips departing from the *embarcadère*, accessed from Parking du Port, at the Nouveau Port: Caps Camarat, Taillat and Lardier (three hours, adult/child four to 12 years €19/12.50); and Port-Cros and Porquerolles in a day (€36.50/26.50).

Tours

The tourist office (p343) organises 1½- to two-hour **guided walking tours** (adult/under 12yr €2.50/free; ☼ 10.30am Wed Apr-Oct) in French; call to check departure times and to see if an English-speaking guide is available.

Festivals & Events

Guns blaze and flags flutter on 15 June during **Les Bravades des Espagnols**, a festival celebrating St-Tropez's victory over 21 Spanish galleons that attacked the port on 15 June 1637. The colourful processions are led by the town captain.

Celebrated since 1558, the **bravades** (Provençal for 'bravery') on 16, 17 (St Torpes' day) and 18 May see Tropeziens turn out in traditional costume to watch the *capitaine de ville* and an ear-splitting army of 140 musket-firing *bravadeurs* parade through the street carrying a bust of the town's saint.

Sleeping

Seeking a room and breakfast with vineyard view? Head out of town onto the peninsula (p353).

BUDGET

Hôtel La Méditerranée (☎ 04 94 97 00 44; www.hotel mediterranee.org; 21 blvd Louis Blanc; s/d from €50/90; ☒) Get in quick at this old-fashioned, mildly tatty place that needs a face-lift. There is no reception; just head for the bar or courtyard restaurant out the back beneath the trees (mains €16 to €20). Opening hours for both are erratic.

MIDRANGE

Hôtel Lou Cagnard (☎ 04 94 97 04 24; www.hotel-lou -cagnard.com; 18 av Paul Roussel; d low/high season from €48/60; ☼ Jan-Oct; P ☒) That thing of miracles, a decently priced St-Tropez hotel. In an old Provençal house, rooms aren't fancy but they're clean and light, and there's a jasmine-scented old courtyard garden.

Baron Lodge (☎ 04 94 97 06 57; www.hotel-le-baron .com; 23 rue de l'Aïoli; d low/high season from €50/80; P ☒) At the foot of the citadel, the Baron is a unpretentious sort of guy with a clutch of comfy rooms touting sea views or glimpses of the citadel. The best rooms (from €85/115) have a balcony or terrace.

Hôtel Sube (☎ 04 94 97 30 04; www.hotel-sube .com; quai Suffren; d low/high season from €70/90, with sea view €190/290; ☒) Tucked upstairs in an arcade behind the Bailli de Suffren statue, this place is overwhelmingly maritime in spirit. Exquisite wooden sailing boats and nautical knick-knacks decorate public areas, and the bar-restaurant terrace provides an elite eagle's-eye view of the port antics.

Hôtel Playa (☎ 04 98 12 94 44; www.playahotelst tropez.com; 57 rue Allard; d low/high season from €90/128; ☒) A young upstart among the town's list of venerable old hotels, Le Playa still has the unsullied shininess of a brand-new car. Its central rooms are simple but smart, but its best feature is its glass-roofed, palm-filled patio, which doubles as art exhibition space. Luggage fiends note: no lift.

Hôtel Les Palmiers (☎ 04 94 97 01 61; www.hotel-les-palmiers.com; 24-26 blvd Vasserot; d low/high season from €80/102; P ☒) Crisp, no-nonsense décor and a pleasant courtyard, complete with orange trees and sun-lounges, make this hotel a good spot to stay. It's also very central, with prime views of place des Lices' *pétanque* players from rooms overlooking the square.

TOP END

Le Mas de Chastelas (☎ 04 94 56 71 71; www.chastelas.com; quartier Bertaud; d low/mid/high season from €150/240/320; P ☒ ☐ ☒) Guests risk never getting further than the grounds – a luxuriant orgy of flowers and pools – at this beautiful farmhouse hotel bathed in a sea of vines. The mood is classical 18th-century Provence and furnishings are period. Find it a healthy stride away from the humdrum of Tropezien life, signposted off the D98 leading into town.

La Maison Blanche (☎ 04 94 97 52 66; www.hotellamaisonblanche.com; place des Lices; d low/mid/high season from €190/230/270, ste from €350/450/550; P ☒) Design is everything at this cool and elegant town house with a beautiful interior courtyard-turned-summer garden and evening champagne bar that creates an oasis of peace between the hotel and hubbub of St-Tropez's buzzing market-clad square. At the White House, fresh white flowers, wood and natural hues predominate and room No 7 is the star pick.

Hôtel La Mistralée (☎ 04 98 12 91 12; www.hotel-mistralee.com; 1 av du Général Leclerc; d low/mid/high season from €190/330/460; P ☒ ☒) Decorative stained glass, moulded ceilings, marbled floors and other carefully preserved, original 19th-century features are the trademark of this flamboyant 10-room boutique hotel slumbering in the smart town house (1850) where hairdresser to the stars, Alexandre (famously sans surname), lived. Rooms are thematic and range from Chinese and Moroccan to Chanel and Tarzan. Breakfast is served in the glass-paned winter garden or by the mosaic pool.

Le Yaca (☎ 04 94 55 81 00; www.hotel-le-yaca.fr; 1 blvd d'Aumale; d low/mid/high season from €270/335/350; ☽ mid-Apr–mid-Oct; P ☒ ☐ ☒) Utterly without blemish, Le Yaca – a hotel since 1948 – is hushed and understatedly elegant, with a gorgeous courtyard garden and staff so discreet it's like being waited on by charmingly

mannered poltergeists. Colette lived in the early-18th-century town house in 1927 and Orson Welles, Errol Flynn and Greta Garbo all stayed here at varying times.

Hôtel Byblos (☎ 04 94 56 68 00; www.byblos.com; av Paul Signac; d low/high season from €290/330; ☽ mid-Apr–early Oct; P ☒ ☒) It's been the *crème de la crème* of Riviera accommodation for the Paris jet set, movie moguls and superstars since 1967 – and remains elusively exclusive. Pure luxury shrouds its gourmet restaurant (opposite) and nightclub (p351). Parking €30.

Eating

You're dead right: there aren't many greasy spoons in St-Tropez. Café and restaurant prices are, in fact, higher than elsewhere on the coast; the glamour dust sprinkled on fish and chips doesn't come cheap!

Don't leave town without sampling a creamy *tarte Tropézienne*, a decadent sponge cake sandwich filled with custard cream and topped with sugar.

RESTAURANTS

Quai Jean Jaurès is lined with restaurants touting €25 *menus* and a strategic view of the yacht brigade's silverware and champagne. At the northern end of rue des Remparts in the old town, there's a lesser-known cluster of places overlooking Port des Pêcheurs at La Ponche.

Le Petit Charron (☎ 04 94 97 73 78; 6 rue des Charrons; starter/main/dessert from €12/18/8; ☽ dinner Mon-Sat) Sautéed veal with sage or *pintade rôtie à la crème d'ail* (in a garlicky cream sauce) topped off by fig tart are among the classical French dishes served with a refined flourish at this lovely old-town inn.

La Table du Marché (☎ 04 94 97 85 20; www.christophe-leroy.com; 38 rue Georges Clemenceau; menus €18 & €26; ☽ lunch & dinner) With sister 'market tables' in Alpine ski resort Avoriaz and Marrakech, this simple (for St-Trop) yet stylish bistro is something of a success story. Should you want to learn the secrets behind Christophe Leroy's market-driven cuisine, sign up for a session in his *atelier de cuisine* (see the boxed text, p52). Die-hard enthusiasts can also dine at Leroy's Les Moulins de Ramatuelle (p353).

Salama (☎ 04 94 97 59 62; 1 rue des Tisserands; couscous €19-28, mains €22; ☽ dinner Mon-Sun) The smell of cooking wafting down the alley outside Salama is enough to lure you into this hip Moroccan den where St-Tropez's trendiest hang out over cosy exotic furnishings and fresh mint tea.

ST-TROPEZ TO TOULON

Café Sud (☎ 04 94 97 42 52; 12 rue Étienne Berny; plat du jour & starter/dessert €20/18; lunch & dinner May-Oct) French and Italian-inspired cuisine including all things fishy, a fabulous fish risotto and imaginative vegetarian dishes like veg salad with celery ice cream are the order of the day at this tasteful restaurant set in a vine-covered courtyard. Its other restaurant, La Plage des Jumeaux, offers white tablecloth dining on Pampelonne beach (p352).

Grand Joseph (☎ 04 94 97 01 66; www.joseph-saint -tropez.com; 1 place de l'Hôtel de Ville; lunch menu/buffet €18/20, starter/pasta/main €25/28/40; lunch & dinner) Black leather chairs, white tablecloths and steel touches create a cutting-edge feel to this drinking-dining space for St-Tropez beauties. Cuisine is French gastronomic, atmosphere is lounge bar and 'two chefs, two menus' is the buzz: around the corner Petit Joseph (☎ 04 94 97 03 90), at 6 rue Sibille, cooks Asian.

Chez Fuchs (☎ 04 94 97 01 25; 7 rue des Commerçants; menu €35; lunch & dinner mid-Feb–mid-Jan) This casual, unpretentious bar-restaurant is a truly authentic family-run affair where noisy, happy Tropeziens hang out. It's notable for the massive range of cigars it sells, and for its carefully prepared traditional dishes: stuffed courgettes, artichokes *à la barigoule* (traditional Provençal dish of artichokes braised in a tangy white wine broth) and seafood. It positively heaves – book ahead.

Auberge des Maures (☎ 04 94 97 01 50; 4 rue du Docteur Boutin; menu €45; dinner mid-Feb–Nov) The oldest restaurant in town, this favourite serves traditional French cuisine in a quaint Provençal décor (including leafy courtyard). Or opt for the *carte barbecue* – a choice of fish and meats, including tapenade-stuffed shoulder of lamb and honey-caramelised veal shank (both €57 for two).

Spoon Byblos (☎ 04 94 56 68 20; www.spoon.tm.fr; Hôtel Byblos, av du Maréchal Foch; à la carte starter, main & dessert around €70; dinner Fri-Tue) Take your taste buds on a 'grand tour' of the world with Alain Ducasse, following the numbered columns on the menu horizontally for the chef's hot choice or zigzagging to create the culinary unthinkable. Décor is minimal, forks have four prongs, and the cuisine is beyond reproach.

CAFÉS

Le Café (☎ 04 94 97 44 69; www.lecafe.fr; place des Lices; menus €30 & €39; lunch & dinner) Artists and intellectuals have been meeting in St-Tropez's most famous café (originally called Café des Arts) for years. Aspiring *pétanque* players can borrow *boules* from the bar and join the square's illustrious ball-chuckers. Don't confuse this place with the newer, red-canopied Café des Arts on the corner.

Le Bistrot (☎ 04 94 97 11 33; www.bistrot-saint-tropez .com in French; place des Lices; salads €9-11, lunch menu

---

MY ST-TROPEZ

Toulouse-born Nathalie Duchayne fell in love with St-Tropez in 1980, returned four years later to open a small beach restaurant, and in the mid-1990s (following the death of her husband in a car accident) the stunningly elegant entrepreneur switched to art. Her gallery, **Galerie Nathalie Duchayne** (☎ 04 94 97 54 50; www.duchayne.com; 2 rue de la Résistance), is now among France's leading galleries.

'For me St-Tropez is all about the people. Having raised three children here, I feel more St-Tropezien than Toulousian. Many of the same people I knew in my restaurant days are my friends now; they've been very loyal.

'Many forget that St-Tropez was once a place only for artists and intellectuals from St-Germain des Près, real artists who led a very bohemian lifestyle, slept anywhere, all in one flat, shared workshops. It was not a competition before. Now it's very individual, very commercial. It's changed enormously.

'The artists at the old port are part of the city, and there are some incredible personalities. It is a show every day. One painter is an Indian one day, a captain another day; he's very funny and is honest about what he does. It's important to have a place for everybody. If you don't like it, you can always shut your eyes.

'In the evening I like to eat at Salama (opposite) very much and **Au Caprice des Deux** (☎ 04 94 97 76 78; www.aucapricedesdeux.com; 40 rue du Portail Neuf). The other day I went to a tiny restaurant on the beach and it was just like before, with little fairy lights and six tables, very simple. When St-Tropez gets too full I go there.'

€14; ☿ lunch & dinner) A few doors down from Le Café, the Bistro offers all-day dining in a contemporary décor overlooking St-Tropez's busy central square. Fish and shellfish are a gastronomic feature, alongside straightforward hole-filling salads and *tartines* (toast topped with various toppings).

Sénequier (☎ 04 94 97 00 90; quai Jean Jaurès; ☿ 7am-7pm) Sartre wrote parts of *Les Chemins de la Liberté* (Roads to Freedom) at this portside café and hot spot with boaties, in business since 1887. Flop around pillar box–red tables and directors chairs on its terrace and watch the world razz by. Breakfast starts at 7.30am.

Le Gorille (☎ 04 94 97 03 93; www.legorille.com; 1 quai Suffren; ☿ 7am-4am) Another eminent portside bistro, the Gorilla gets it name from its previous owner, the short, muscular and apparently very hairy Henri Guérin! Stop here for a typically French/special/English breakfast (€7.50/10/14) or a postclubbing *croque monsieur* (toasted ham-and-cheese sandwich) and fries (€11.50).

SELF-CATERING

A morning **fish market** (place aux Herbes; ☿ daily summer, Tue-Sun winter) packs out the archway behind the tourist office, while the massive **place des Lices Market** (place des Lices; ☿ 8am-1pm Tue & Sat) – a jam-packed kaleidoscope of everything from fruit and veg to antique mirrors and slippers – is legendary (as the horrendous traffic coming into town on these days attests!).

La Tarte Tropézienne (☎ 04 94 97 19 77; www.tarte-tropezienne.com in French; 9 blvd Louis Blanc & 36 rue Georges Clemenceau) Bakery selling the traditional cream-filled sandwich cake created by *boulanger* (baker) Micka in Cogolin in 1955. Fresh sandwiches, too.

Supermarkets:

Monoprix (9 av du Général Leclerc; ☿ 8am-8.20pm Mon-Sat)

Petit Casino (av du Général Leclerc; ☿ 8am-12.30pm & 3.30-7pm Mon-Sat, 9am-12.30pm & 4-7pm Sun)

Spar (place Georges Clemenceau; ☿ 7.30am-7.30pm Mon-Sat, 9am-7.30pm Sun)

Drinking

St-Tropez's most quintessential cafés (p349) are prime drinking venues, as are the hottest spots on the beach (see the boxed text, p346).

Other bars worth a drink include **Chez Nano** (☎ 04 94 97 72 59; 2 rue Sibille), a high-flyer cabaret bar best known for its raspberry champagne; and **La Piscine** (Swimming Pool; ☎ 04 94 56 51 10; rue Grenouillière), a stark white lounge bar with food.

Entertainment

Clubs open every night during the high season; weekends only September to April. Strict door codes apply; look good to get past the bouncers, pay around €20 to get in and another €15-odd a drink. St-Tropez's trendiest:

La Bodega du Papagayo (☎ 04 94 79 29 50; www.papagayobodega.com; résidence du Nouveau Port, quai

---

MY ST-TROPEZ

Origami sailing boats are the forte of Hungarian-born artist Ivan Hov who fled Budapest for Paris in 1956 and studied art in the capital before moving to St-Tropez in 1968. Today, it is hundreds of tableaux – monumental to minuscule in size and featuring at least one (but invariably thousands) of his signature paper boats – that reflect his life. View them (or buy them – his works sell from anywhere between €20 for a pint-sized piece to €37,800 for a wall-sized work) at his twinset of workshops, **Atelier Ivan Hov** (☎ 06 11 80 12 42; www.ivanhov.com; 20 rue des Remparts & 40 rue Gambetta).

'My work in general is a joy, a pleasure. The day an artist is inspired first by money, he's finished.

'To experience true village life you have to live in it. When I arrived in 1968 I lived right in the heart of the village and loved it. It was like Saturday evening in St-Germain des Près all the time. But now I live 2.5km out of town, in the countryside. We have a little garden, a rabbit, fish. St-Tropez in 1968 was very different to now. Its not the houses, the village, that has changed that much; it's the mentality.

'I eat simply. There is a little pizzeria I discovered only recently and from its terrace, just two steps from port, you raise your head and wow, you see Chapelle Ste-Anne. The place is simple, convivial, friendly, but this view from the terrace is absolutely incredible. It's called **La Tonnelle** (☎ 04 94 54 82 02; Passage Gambetta), off rue Gambetta.'

TOP FIVE UNFORGETTABLE BUYS

- A fluffy pink sweater emblazoned with a rich bitch logo for your pooch from **VIP Dog** (☎ 04 94 79 84 77; place de la Poste).

- A skimpy black bikini with 'playmate' emblazoned in pink sequins, a belt for your jeans with digital display flashing your very own personalised logo and other rebel-yell designs in the brand created by a Columbian drug dealer in a Spanish jail from **De Puta Madre 69** (☎ 06 24 86 61 39; www.deputamadre69.com; Résidence du Port), next to Papagayo.

- A T-shirt starring your portrait in Swarovski crystals (€690), a pair of Dupontreué jeans with a crystal-studded parrot down one leg (€800) or a crocodile-skin bikini by fashion designer **Vincent Dupontreué** (☎ 04 94 44 46 87; 38 rue Seillon).

- Jeans with a 'cherry time' label (€110) from the St-Tropez boutique with the most disconcerting entrance (no, you won't get wet): **Le Temps des Cerises** (☎ 04 94 97 32 58; 1 rue Sibille).

- A giant Provençal urn way too big for any suitcase, or another piece of clay craftmanship, from **Poterie Augier** (☎ 04 94 97 12 55; 19 rue Georges Clemenceau).

Bouchard; menus €25 & €50) Voguish restaurant, nightclub and terrace rolled into one at the Vieux Port.

Le Pigeonnier (☎ 04 94 97 84 26; 13 rue de la Ponche) The least flash with a *'tenue intelligemment négligée'* (trendy casual) dress code.

Les Caves du Roy (☎ 04 94 97 16 02; www.byblos .com; av du Maréchal Foch; ☼ Apr-Oct) 'Beautiful people, Hype, Select' is the strapline: boogie with resident DJ Jack E and celebrities at this legendary club inside Hôtel Byblos.

L'Esquinade (☎ 04 94 97 87 45; 2 rue du Four) Hot, heaving and gay-friendly stuff in the old fishing quarter.

VIP Room (☎ 04 94 97 14 70; www.viproom.fr; av du 11 Novembre 1918) Club at the Nouveau Port, New York–loft style, around for aeons and still VIP-hot.

Shopping

St-Tropez is loaded with voguish boutiques, gourmet food shops and galleries overflowing with bad art. Pick up secondhand designer fashion at **Le Dépôt** (☎ 04 94 97 80 10; 24 blvd Louis Blanc).

Traditional Tropézienne sandals, supposedly inspired by a simple leather pair brought by Colette from Greece to show her cobbler, are all part of the St-Tropez myth. Buy a pair for €94 at **Atelier Rondini** (☎ 04 94 97 19 55; 16 rue Georges Clemenceau), where the strappy footwear has been crafted since 1927; or at **K Jacques** (☎ 04 94 54 83 63, 04 94 97 41 50; www.kjacques.com; 25 rue Allard & 16 rue Seillon), where the family has cobbled since 1933.

Among the plethora of art galleries to visit, Galerie Nathalie Duchayne (see the boxed text, p349) and **Galerie des Lices** (☎ 04 94 97 87 19; www.galeriedeslices.com; 20 blvd Louis Blanc) are outstanding.

Getting There & Away

AIR

The closest airport is **Aéroport International St-Tropez-La Môle** (☎ 04 94 54 76 40; www.st-tropez-airport .com in French), 15km southwest of St-Tropez on the westbound N98 in La Môle. The only scheduled flights are to/from Geneva (May to October) with Swiss budget airline Fly Baboo. Helicopter company **MBH Azur** (☎ 04 50 92 78 00; www.mbh.fr) also lands here.

BOAT

From April to early October, Les Bateaux Verts (see p347) runs shuttleboats to/from Port Grimaud (single/return €6/10.50, 20 minutes, eight to 12 daily). Shuttles to/from Les Issambres (single/return €7/12.50, 20 minutes, eight or nine daily) sail from mid-June to early September, and boats to/from Ste-Maxime (single/return €6.30/11.50, 30 minutes, hourly) sail year-round. Boats depart from the pier off quai Jean Jaurès at the Vieux Port; buy tickets five minutes before departure at the kiosk.

Transports Maritimes Raphaelois (☎ 04 94 95 17 46; www.tmr-saintraphael.com) runs two to six boats daily from St-Tropez to St-Raphaël (adult/two to nine years same-day return €16/8) April to August, and twice-weekly boats in September and October. Boats depart from the Nouveau Port.

See p372 for boats to/from Porquerolles and Port-Cros.

BUS

From the **bus station** (☎ 04 94 97 88 51; av du Général de Gaulle; ☼ information desk 10am-noon & 2-4pm Mon-Fri,

10am-noon Sat), buses to/from Ramatuelle (€3.20, 25 minutes, four daily summer) and Gassin (€3.20, 25 minutes, four daily summer) run parallel to the coast about 1km inland.

There are also buses to/from St-Raphaël (€9.50, 1¼ hours, six to eight daily) via Grimaud and Port Grimaud (€3.50, 15 minutes), Ste-Maxime (€4.70, 40 minutes) and Fréjus (€8.70, one hour).

Buses to Toulon (€18.20, 2¼ hours, seven daily) go inland before joining the coast at Cavalaire-sur-Mer (€4.40, 30 minutes); they also stop at Le Lavandou (€10.30, one hour) and Hyères (€14.90, 1½ hours). Services are less frequent in winter.

Large pieces of luggage command an €0.80 transportation fee on most buses.

CAR & MOTORCYCLE

People who do wrong in life are made to drive to St-Tropez in high season when they die: roads in July and August are chock-a-block and parking costs at least €4 per hour at the Nouveau Port. For your own sanity, try to get here by other means.

Car-rental places:

Avis (☎ 04 94 97 03 10; av du 8 Mai 1945)
Europcar (☎ 04 94 97 15 41; Résidence du Port, av du 11 Novembre 1918)
Hertz (☎ 04 94 55 83 00; av du 8 Mai 1945)
National Citer (☎ 04 94 54 85 19; Résidence du Port, av du 11 Novembre 1918)
Sixt (☎ 04 94 54 22 00; rue Mermoz)

Getting Around
BICYCLE & MOTORCYCLE

Rent a bicycle for €14 a day or a 50cc/125cc scooter for €35/45 a day from **Lucky Loc** (☎ 04 94 97 29 03; av du Général Leclerc), across from Parking du Port. Family firm **Mas Location 2 Roues** (☎ 04 94 97 00 60; 3-5 rue Joseph Quaranta; ☼ Apr-Oct) and **Holiday Bikes** (☎ 04 94 97 09 39; www.holiday-bikes.com; 14 av du Général Leclerc) charge similar rates.

TAXI

Taxi de Mer (☎ 06 09 53 15 47; 5 quartier Neuf) Boat taxi.
Taxi Rank (☎ 04 94 97 05 27; place Georges Grammont) At the Vieux Port.

THE PENINSULA

South of St-Tropez slumbers what many deem to be the Côte d'Azur at its most beautiful – a priceless oasis of peace and tranquillity laced with manicured vineyards, quiet narrow lanes and the odd chateau or charming *chambre*

d'hôte (private bed & breakfast). On its southern side spills the golden sand of France's most chic beach (p345): Pampelonne stretches for 9km from **Cap du Pinet** to **Cap Camarat**, a rocky cape dominated by France's second-tallest **lighthouse** (admission free; ☼ variable), operational since 1831, electrified in 1946 and automated from 1977. The hike up its 84 steps gives fabulous views of St-Tropez, this rich green peninsula and the Med. For fine dining, there's **La Plage des Jumeaux** (☎ 04 94 58 21 80; rte de l'Épi; ☼ lunch Thu-Mon, lunch & dinner Jul & Aug), on the beach.

Cap Lardier, the peninsula's southernmost cape, is protected by the Parc National de Port-Cros (see p366). **Cap Taillat**, 1km northeast, is similarly guarded by the Conservatoire du Littoral (which bought it from Club Med after it tried to turn the precious, nature-rich cape into the world's largest Club Med in the 1970s). The tiny spit of sandy land today supports a range of important habitats, from seashore to wooded cliffs, and hides some of France's rarest plant species as well as a population of Hermann tortoises (see the boxed text, p362). Both can be accessed from Gigaro.

Gassin & Ramatuelle

In medieval **Gassin** (population 2752, elevation 200m), 11km southwest of St-Tropez atop a rocky promontory, narrow streets wend up to the village church (1558). The village's most wowing feature is the 360-degree panoramic view of the peninsula, St-Tropez bay and the Maures forests – don't miss it!

From Gassin, rte des Moulins de Paillas snakes 3km southeast to **Ramatuelle** (population 2174, elevation 136m), an immeasurably picturesque labyrinthine walled village. Its unusual name is thought to come from 'Rahmatu'llah', meaning Divine Gift, a legacy of the 10th-century Saracen occupation. Jazz and theatre fill the tourist-packed streets dur-

---

POLO

Yes, wealthy old St-Tropez even has its very own polo club, the **Polo Club de St-Tropez** (☎ 04 94 55 22 12; www.polo-st-tropez.com; rte de Bourrian, Gassin) with a state-of-the-art club-house designed like a ship, a restaurant and several pro instructors who can help aspiring players saddle up and have a bash at the royal game. The polo season runs April to September.

ing August's back-to-back **Festival de Ramatuelle** (www.festivalderamatuelle.com) and **Jazz Festival** (www.jazzfestivalramatuelle.com), and a Provençal market sets central place du Village abuzz on Thursday and Sunday mornings.

The fruits of the peninsula's vineyards – Côtes de Provence wine – can be tested at various chateaux along the D61; **Ramatuelle tourist office** (☎ 04 98 12 64 00; www.ramatuelle-tourisme.com in French; place de l'Ormeau; ☑ 9am-1pm & 3-7.30pm Jul & Aug, 9am-1pm & 3-7pm Mon-Sat Apr, Jun & Sep, 9am-12.30pm & 2-6pm Mon-Fri Oct-Mar) has a list of estates where you can taste and buy, and organises lovely **guided nature walks** (two hours, adult/under 10 years €8/free) every Thursday through vineyards, along the coast and to the **Moulin de Paillas** (admission free; ☑ 10am-noon Tue Apr-Oct), a restored windmill above the village on the D89.

SLEEPING & EATING

Ferme Ladouceur (☎ 04 94 79 24 95; www.fermeladouceur.com; quartier Les Roullière, Ramatuelle; d €89-96; menu incl wine €38; ☑ dinner) Breakfast in summer beneath a fig tree at this lovely *chambre d'hôte* in a 19th-century *bastide* (country manor) with a rustic restaurant open to anyone who fancies an evening taste of good old-fashioned farm cuisine. Find it north of Ramatuelle, signposted right off the northbound D61 to St-Tropez.

La Vigne de Ramatuelle (☎ 04 94 79 12 50; www.hotel-vignederamatuelle.com; rte des Plages; d low/mid/high season from €95/150/230; ☑ Easter-Oct; P ⊠ ☐ ⊛) The 14 rooms inside this attractive ginger house with olive-green paintwork and a sea of vines outside are booked out months ahead of time. Perhaps the incredible silence that hits you in its manicured gardens or sparkling pool is the reason why. Find it 2km east of the Col de Collebasse on the D93. Parking is €9.90.

Les Moulins de Ramatuelle (☎ 04 94 97 17 22; www.christophe-leroy.com; rte des Plages; d low/mid/high season from €120/195/222; mains/plat du jour €25/15; menu €70; ☑ May-Oct; P ⊠) Five elegant rooms slumber above one of the peninsula's tastiest country-dining restaurants at this old, foliage-covered stone house with perfectly manicured garden and vegetable patch. Christophe Leroy is the culinary hot shot behind it; he runs cooking courses (see the boxed text, p52).

Villa Marie (☎ 04 94 97 40 22; www.villamarie.fr; chemin Val de Rian, rte des Plages; d low/high season from €196/407; ☑ May–mid-Oct; P ⊠) The height of luxury, decadence and sheer romance, this exquisite abode easily makes it to the top of the 'perfect marriage-proposal material' list.

Stylish is an understatement; style is rustic country and the spa is heaven on earth.

Snoozing/lunch recommendations in Ramatuelle village:

L'Ecurie du Castellas (☎ 04 94 79 20 67; www.lecurieducastellas.com; rte des Moulin de Paillas; d low/high season from €76/91, menus €33 & €46) Dining on a flowery terrace with eagle's-eye rooftop view.

Café de l'Ormeau (place du Village) Quintessential village café and bar with vine-covered tables overlooking the village square.

Le Vesuvio (☎ 04 94 79 21 60; 19 av Georges Clemenceau; pizza €8.50-13, pasta €10; ☑ lunch & dinner) Italianate pizza, pasta and seafood kebabs at this 25-year-old firm favourite.

La Croix Valmer & Gigaro

A short distance from the shore, at the southwestern tip of the Presqu'île de St-Tropez, **La Croix Valmer** (population 2846) itself is hardly inspiring but the sleeping and dining gems around the small town are gems. Its **tourist office** (☎ 04 94 55 12 12; www.lacroixvalmer.fr; Esplanade de la Gare) has complete lists.

From the roundabout at the southern end of town, the last exit strikes east to **Gigaro**, a pinprick seaside hamlet with a fine sandy beach and a small water-sports school. From the far end of the beach, a board maps out the **sentier littoral** (coastal path) that wends it way dramatically around the coast to beautiful Plage des Brouïs (1.5km, 40 minutes), Cap Lardier (3.7km, 1½ hours), Plage de Briande (6km, 2¼ hours) and beyond past Cap Taillat to L'Escalet (7.9km, 2¾ hours). Bikes are not allowed along the well-signposted trail.

From Gigaro, the narrow but drop-dead gorgeous D93 winds inland over the Col de Collebasse (129m) to Ramatuelle – a good ride for mountain bikers. **L'Escalet**, accessible by a 2.5km road signposted off the D93, is a pretty little rocky cove with plenty of chanting cicadas and dried seaweed along the shoreline.

SLEEPING & EATING

Options for seaside souls are quite divine in this lesser-known corner of paradise, with something outstanding to suit every budget.

Le Refuge (☎ 04 94 79 67 38; d/tr/studio from €53/69/80; ☑ Apr-Sep; P) Around for 25 years already, this fabulous seaside house with wooden shutters is set back off the sand at the end of a dead-end lane between trees. Inside, 11 humble rooms and four studios with kitchenette provide simple sleeping, opening onto private little tabled terraces. The same people cook up tasty grills at Le Refuge (menus €22 and €28), its restaurant at the start of the coastal path.

La Pinède Plage (☎ 04 94 79 67 38; www.pinedeplage .com; d low/high season from €162/231, menu €50; ☒ Apr-Sep; ℗ ☒ ☒) The orientation of this hotel (plump in a sea of vineyards with its front side facing the water) is towards the Med. Dine on a stylish wooden decking terrace looking out to sea, by the pool or on mellow wicker chairs in a nautical-themed interior. Luxury apartments for four with sea view and terrace start at €469.

Château de Valmer (☎ 04 94 55 15 15; www.cha teauvalmer.com; d low/high season from €201/288, treehouse €320/400, menu €58; ℗ ☒ ☒) If Pinède Plage is for water nymphs, its big sister down the road – a 19th-century wine-producer's mansion – is for nature bods. Sleep above vines in a luxurious *cabane perchée* (treehouse), stroll its heavily scented vegetable and herb gardens, and play hide-and-seek around century-old palm and olive trees.

Couleurs du Jardin (☎ 04 94 79 59 12; starters €12-15, mains €25; ☒ lunch & dinner Apr-Sep) Eclectic and hip, this imaginative beachside space is *the* place to dine and/or drink. Loll on cushioned seating beneath the trees or pick a table on the terrace with nothing between you and the deep blue sea (bar sand). Cuisine is fish- and market-fuelled – grilled sardines or the catch of the

day, followed by strawberry and pineapple soup spiced with a dash of local wine, make a handsome lunch. Reservations are crucial.

Recommended *chambre d'hôte*:
Ferme de l'Audrac (☎ 04 98 12 91 00; s/d incl breakfast €40/77; ☒ Apr-Oct) Four rooms on a vine-covered farm in the middle of nowhere, hugged by vineyards and forest, signposted 1.6km east of the Col de Collebasse.

GOLFE DE ST-TROPEZ

Brash, flash Ste-Maxime dominates the northern end of the bay, while smart aloof Port Grimaud – the 'Venice of Provence' – draws crowds to the southwest with its rainbow of houses straddling manmade waterways. Inland, medieval Grimaud makes a charming if busy retreat from the beaches.

Book accommodation through the **Maison du Tourisme** (☎ 04 94 55 22 00; www.golfe-infos.com; ☒ 9am-7pm Mon-Fri, 9am-6pm Sat, 9am-5.30pm Sun mid-Jun–mid-Sep, earlier closing & closed Sun mid-Sep–mid-Jun), overlooking the busy giant roundabout 2km south of Port Grimaud on the N98 in Carrefour de la Foux.

Ste-Maxime
pop 11,978
Sandy Ste-Maxime, 14km northwest of St-Tropez, screams BEACH RESORT in ever so loud, capital letters. The place is modern,

---

HAPPY CAMPER

Camping on the beach is illegal but 15-odd camp sites (minimum seven-night stays in the high season) on the peninsula compensate, including exceptionally placed:

▪ **Kon Tiki** (☎ 04 94 55 96 96; www.riviera-villages.com; rte des Plages; 2 adults, tent & car low/mid/high season €15/35/40, front-row 4-person Tiki Hutte low/mid/high season €65/105/205; ☒ reception 8am-8pm Apr-Oct; ℗ ▯) Primely placed on the beach next to a diving school at the northern end of Plage de Pampelonne, this site is large and, depending on the spot you plump for, can feel crowded. A front-row beachside 'Tiki Hutte' – a luxurious, ethnic-styled wooden chalet on the sand (marketed as 'the unique experience') – is prime real estate.

▪ **Les Tournels** (☎ 04 94 55 90 90; www.tournels.com; rte de Camarat, Ramatuelle; 2 adults, tent & car low/high season €22/38, 4-person wooden chalet €48/112; ☒ reception 9am-noon & 2-6pm Mar, Nov & Dec, 9am-8pm Apr-Jun, Sep & Oct, 8am-9pm Jul & Aug; ℗ ☒) Green peninsula and blue sea views from this large, happy camper site on a hill between pine trees are unbeatable – a front-row bathroom-clad wooden chalet with terrace is nothing short of idyllic. Facilities cover everything, meaning no cooking (half-board is available should that be your cup of tea) and there's bags to do (tennis, sauna, gym, heated pool – no boxers) from sunrise to sunset.

▪ **Les Eucalyptus** (☎ 04 94 97 16 74; chemin des Moulins, Ramatuelle; 2 adults, tent & car low/high season €16.60/19.90; ☒ late May–mid-Sep) *Camping à la ferme* on this 10-hectare, family-run wine-producing estate is an intimate proposition. Pitch up between olive trees and Plage de Pampelonne is a 450m stroll away through vines. Philippe and Florence also have a handful of rooms in the main house, should bad weather drive you inside.

concrete and crawls with sun-catchers: you'd never guess it was founded by monks in AD 1000. Countless water-sports clubs line the beachfront and there are water slides galore at kid-busy **Aqualand** (☎ 08 92 68 66 13; www.aqualand.fr; adult/child €23/16.50; 🕐 10am-7pm Jul & Aug, to 6pm Jun & Sep) on the edge of town.

Touristy cafés, craft stalls and souvenir shops cram its pedestrian old town, centred around rue Gambetta. Giant pans of paella, fruit stalls and pastry shops line rue Courbet, a cobbled street leading to the town's main market square, place du Marché. Flowers, fish, olives, oil, wine and *tartes Tropéziennes* are sold in the **covered market** (4 rue Fernard Bessy).

The **tourist office** (☎ 04 94 55 75 55; www.sainte-maxime.com; 1 promenade Simon Lorière; 🕐 9am-8pm Mon-Sat, 10am-noon & 4-7pm Sun Jul & Aug, shorter hr & closed Sun Sep-Jun) has information on everything.

BOAT EXCURSIONS

April to September, **Les Bateaux Verts** (☎ 04 94 49 29 39; www.bateauxverts.com; 14 quai Léon Condroyer) runs regular boat excursions from its portside base to Baie des Cannebiers (adult/four to 12 years €12.50/6.50); Gulf of St-Tropez, stopping either in St-Tropez (€14.40/8.20) and/or Port-Grimaud (€20.40/12.50); Calanques de l'Estérel (€16.90/10.20); Caps Camarat, Taillat and Lardier (€16.90/10.20); Cannes (€29/18.50); Îles de Lérins (€29/18.50); Port-Cros (€29/18.50) and Porquerolles (€33/21).

GETTING THERE & AWAY

There are regular buses and shuttleboats between St-Tropez and Ste-Maxime (p351). In Ste-Maxime boats depart from 14 quai Léon Condroyer at the port.

Port Grimaud

Hard to believe pretty little Port Grimaud stands on top of what, in the 1960s, was a 1-sq-km mosquito-filled swamp. Within the high wall that barricades the town from the busy N98, colourful cottages stand gracefully alongside yacht-laden waterways. On Thursday and Sunday mornings a **market** fills place du Marché, from where a bridge leads to Port Grimaud's modernist **church**. Inside, sunbeams shine through a stained-glass window designed by Vasarely, which tends to polarise viewers into lovers and haters. A panorama of red rooftops fans out from the **bell tower** (admission €1).

François Spoerry (1912–99), the Alsatian architect who dreamt up this massive water world,

fought from 1962 to 1966 to get the authorities to agree to his proposal inspired by pictures of prehistoric lagoon towns. Now 400,000 visitors a year come to gape at his work, with its mighty 12km of quays, 7km of canals and mooring space for 3000 luxury yachts. Spoerry, who went on to design Port Liberty in New York, is buried in Port Grimaud's church.

Cars are forbidden (the car park outside charges €2.20 per hour); bronzed residents cruise around in speedboats; and *tenue correcte* (correct dress) is insisted upon, except on the wide sandy beach that can be accessed on foot from Grand Rue.

The **tourist office** (☎ 04 94 56 02 01; quai des Fossés; 🕐 9am-12.30pm & 2.30-6.15pm Mon-Sat Jun–mid-Sep), outside the village on the N98, is next to Porche Ponant, a two-second walk from Porte de Poterne, the main pedestrian entrance into Port Grimaud.

SLEEPING

Chambres d'hôtes just don't exist in exclusive Port Grimaud.

Camping des Mûres (☎ 04 94 56 16 17; www.camping-des-mures.com; 2 people, tent & car low/high season €20/30; 🕐 Apr-Sep) Just outside Port Grimaud, this three-star site has plenty of facilities and safe underground access to the beach. Campers can pay a €4/10 supplement in low/high season to pitch up on the front row – on the beach with no-one between you and the sea. Mobile homes, too.

Le Suffren (☎ 04 94 55 15 05; www.hotellleriedu soleil.com; 16 place du Marché; d low/mid/high/very high season from €90/120/140/155; 🕐 Apr–mid-Sep; 🅿 🌀) A smart mix of Art Deco and modern reds and whites bedecks Port Grimaud's most affordable option. Each of its 19 rooms has a delightful little balcony, overlooking either the market square or the port.

Hôtel Giraglia (☎ 04 94 56 31 33; www.hotelgiraglia.com; place du 14 Juin; d low/high season from €255/285; 🕐 May-Oct; 🅿 🌀 🌀) Upping the ante is this four-star oasis of luxury and romance – definite drop-down-on-your-knee material. Delicious culinary creations are served with a flourish by waiters in dinner jackets at its poolside restaurant. Garage parking is €12.

EATING

Port Grimaud is jam-packed with restaurants, although many leave diners feeling they've paid over the odds for less-than-startling tourist fare.

La Table du Mareyeur (☎ 04 94 56 06 77; www.mare
yeur.com; 10 & 11 place Artisans; seafood platters €46-60, lunch
menu €25; ☑ lunch & dinner Mar-Nov) An exception
to the many tourist traps, those with a soft
spot for all things fishy will adore this highly
regarded seafood restaurant on the edge of
a canal on the road to the beach, near Porte
de Poterne. Oysters, whole red lobsters (from
Brittany or Canada), monkfish with morel
mushrooms – the choice is mouthwatering.

GETTING THERE & AWAY

There are buses between Port Grimaud and
Grimaud (€1.30, 10 minutes, five daily summer) and St-Tropez (€3.20, 15 minutes, six to
eight daily summer).

April to mid-October, an **electric tourist
train** (☎ 04 94 54 09 09; www.nova.fr/petit-train-grimaud)
shunts visitors between Port Grimaud and
Grimaud (single/return €3/5.70, 50 minutes
including tour of Grimaud, five daily). In Port
Grimaud the stop is opposite Porte de Poterne,
the pedestrian entrance to the marine village;
in Grimaud it's on central place Neuve.

March to October, shuttleboats sail to/from
St-Tropez (p351).

GETTING AROUND

Bicycle

L'Amiral (☎ 04 94 43 47 32; www.amiral-immobilier.com; 51
Grand Rue) hires bikes for €5/15 per hour/day.

Boat

Mid-June to mid-September, **Coches d'Eau** (☎ 04
94 56 21 13; 12 place du Marché) runs 20-minute boat
tours of Port Grimaud (adult/three to 12 years
€4/2), departing from place du Marché every
10 minutes between 9am and 10pm daily
(shorter hours outside July and August).

Across the bridge on place de l'Église, hire
a *barque électrique* (electric boat) for €20 per
30 minutes for up to four people, Easter to
mid-November.

Inside Porte de Poterne, **Nautic Location**
(☎ 04 94 56 00 13; www.nautic-location.com; 1 place des
Artisans) hires out speedboats (for licence-hold-
ers; deposit required) and less powerful five-
person cabin boats (for nonlicence-holders)
costing €40/100/120 per hour/half-day/day.

Grimaud

pop 3850 / elev 105m

Port Grimaud's tourist-busy medieval sibling
is an all too picture postcard–perfect, Provençal hilltop village 3km inland. Crowned

with the dramatic shell of **Château du Grimaud**,
its past is bloody – the castle was built in
the 11th century, fortified in the 15th century, destroyed during the Wars of Religion
(1562–98), rebuilt in the 17th century, and
wrecked again during the French Revolution.
Evening concerts held on the stage in the ruins
here during the music festival, **Les Grimaldines**,
in July and August are magical.

In the heart of the village, local lore comes
to life in the small **Musée des Arts et Traditions
Populaires** (☎ 04 94 43 39 29; rte Nationale; admission free;
☑ 2.30-6pm Mon-Sat May-Sep, 2-5.30pm Mon-Sat Oct-Apr),
in an old oil mill. Market day (place Vieille) is
Thursday morning.

Grimaud **tourist office** (☎ 04 94 55 43 83; www
.grimaud-provence.com; 1 blvd des Aliziers; ☑ 9am-12.30pm
& 2.30-6.15pm Mon-Sat), on the D558 at the foot
of the village (a lift connects the two), has
information on village walks with or without
a guide: the **sentier découverte du Vallon du Pont
des Fées** trail takes you past the restored **Moulin
St-Roch** (medieval windmill; admission free; ☑ 9am-1pm &
2.30-7.15pm Mon & Wed-Fri) to the **Pont des Fées** (Fairy
Bridge), a 15th-century aqueduct.

South of the village, along the D61 towards
St-Tropez, enjoy the fruity aroma of local
wine at **Caves des Vignerons de Grimaud** (☎ 04
94 43 20 14; 36 av des Oliviers; ☑ 8.30am-12.30pm & 2-
6.15pm Mon-Sat Mar-Jul), a cooperative where you
can stock up on Vin de Pays du Var or a Les
Grimaldines rosé for €2 a litre.

In summer buses run between St-Tropez
and St-Raphaël (€9.50, 1¼ hours, six to eight
daily) via Grimaud or Port Grimaud (€3.20,
20 minutes).

NORTHERN VAR

What a difference a few miles can make! The
northern half of the Var *département* (generally agreed to be everything north of the
noisy A8 *autoroute*) is vastly different from
its coastal counterpart: in this rural hinterland
there's not a grain of sand or oiled body to be
seen. Instead, peaceful hilltop villages drowse
beneath the midday sun, creating a glorious
vision of unspoilt Provence.

Draguignan is the sore thumb in this romantic area, a gritty, hard-nosed town, where
the French army maintains its largest military
base. From here, the vast Plateau de Canju-
ers sprawls for 30km north to the foot of the
Gorges du Verdon (p234).

East of Draguignan, the green Pays Dracénois is pierced by the perched villages of Fayence and Bargemon. West of Draguignan, numerous little places deal in black truffles and terracotta tiles. Regional wines can be tried and tasted in and around medieval Les Arcs-sur-Argens, to the south.

DRAGUIGNAN
pop 34,814 / elev 187m

France's 'Capital d'Artillerie' is the hard nut at the centre of chocolate-box Provence, and not to everyone's taste. However, you'll almost certainly pass through it when travelling round the Pays Dracénois – a welcome bite of reality for many.

Collect a free town map marked up with a historical walking itinerary from the **tourist office** (☎ 04 98 10 51 05; 2 av Lazare Carnot; ⏱ 9.15am-12.15pm & 1.45-6pm Mon-Sat). The latter has a list of accommodation in town, but sleeping options around Draguignan (p358) are overwhelmingly more charming.

Sights

Old guns, cannons and munitions are among the exhibits in the **Musée de l'Artillerie** (Artillery Museum; ☎ 04 98 10 83 85; musee.artillerie@worldonline.fr; av de la Grande Armée; admission free; ⏱ 9am-noon & 1.30-5.30pm Sun-Wed), inside the artillery school. In the **American cemetery**, a monument pays homage to the combat that occurred around Draguignan during WWII – 9000 American and British soldiers were parachuted in on 15 August 1944.

Traditional Provençal costumes, musical instruments and other ethnographic finds form the **Musée des Arts & Traditions Provençales** (Museum of Arts & Provençal Traditions; ☎ 04 94 47 05 72; 15 rue Roumanille; adult/child €3.50/1.50; ⏱ 9am-noon & 2-6pm Tue-Sat, 2-6pm Sun).

In the last tiny patch of Draguignan's old town, the 18m-tall **tour d'horloge** (clock tower), with it's ornate campanile, is worth a photo.

Getting There & Around

From the **bus station** (☎ 04 94 68 15 34; blvd des Martyrs de la Résistance), there are regular daily buses to/from St-Raphaël (€6, 1¼ hours) and Les Arcs-sur-Argens, home to the closest train station (p360). Services to/from Grasse, Marseille and Toulon are less frequent.

Pick up wheels from **Holiday Bikes** (☎ 04 98 10 63 08; draguignan@holiday-bikes.com; 834 rte de Draguignan). A mountain bike/50cc scooter/125cc motorbike costs around €15/40/60 per day.

A HOUSE IN PARADISE

Dreaming of a house in paradise? Visit **Maison d'Hôtes du Var** (www.mhvprovence.com) to find a clutch of beautiful family homes, farms and castles throughout the Var region that open their doors to B&B (and often dinner) guests.

AROUND DRAGUIGNAN

Draguignan town might not turn you on but its surrounding countryside is among Provence's prettiest – and least populated.

Pays Dracénois

East of Draguignan (along the D562, then the D225 and D25 north) is dinky **Callas** (population 1388, elevation 398m), where the family of Nicole and Serge have cultivated olives to make oil at **Le Moulin de Callas** (☎ 04 94 39 03 20; www.moulindecallas.com; ⏱ 10am-noon & 2-6pm Mon-Sat) since 1928. The mill turns at the southern foot of the village, pressing the freshly harvested olives of 400-odd local olive farmers. Learn about olive oil and buy (€14 a litre) in the on-site shop; for a greater insight, see p50). Afterwards, make your way uphill past the **tourist office** (☎ 04 94 39 06 77; ot.callas@wanadoo.fr; place du 18 Juin 1940; ⏱ 9.15am-12.15pm & 1.45-6pm Mon-Fri, 10am-noon Sat) in the car park, to the central square for a stunning panorama of the redrock Massif de l'Estérel.

Bargemon (population 1217, elevation 416m), 6km north, hit the headlines when the Beckhams bought a pad here in 2004. It has plenty of medieval streets and ramparts to stroll, and a Thursday **market**. Its **tourist office** (☎ 04 94 47 81 73; www.ot-bargemon.fr; av Pasteur; ⏱ 10.15am-1pm & 3-6pm Mon-Fri, 10am-noon Sat) has information on the entire area.

Seillans (population 2115, elevation 365m), a scenic 11km drive east, is an irresistibly pretty, typical Provençal village with cobbled lanes coiling to its crown and a couple of impossibly delicious sleeping and eating options.

Medieval **Fayence** (population 3502, elevation 350m), a scenic motor 5km east, is a picturesque village with an overdose of (English-speaking) estate agents and plenty of resident foreigners in its wealthy population. Climb uphill to its weathered **bell tower** for a fabulous panorama. There is a **tourist office** (☎ 04 94 76 20 08; ot.fayence@wanadoo.fr; place Léon Roux; ⏱ 9am-12.30pm & 2.30-7pm Mon-Sat, 10am-noon Sun).

ST-TROPEZ TO TOULON

SLEEPING & EATING

La Sousto (☎ 04 94 76 02 16; hotel-sousto@wanadoo.fr; place du Paty, Fayence; d/tr €46/53) Something of a dying breed, this six-room hotel unchanged for 20 years or so fills three wonky floors of an old *maison de village* with fountain and pocket-sized public garden in front. For the ultimate in simple grandeur, snag room No 5 with rooftop terrace and fabulous view.

Le Coq qui Chante (☎ 04 94 76 63 40; dami .guiaud@wanadoo.fr; quartier Les Garduelles, Bargemon; d/ tr/q incl breakfast €73.50/94.50/115.50, stays of plus 2 nights d/tr/q incl breakfast €49/63/77; **P**) Delve into life on an olive farm at the Cock who Sings, a 4000-sq-metre olive-producing estate, 2km from Bargemon village, with a cute little stone house – separate from the main house where olive farmers Daniele and Michele live – for B&B guests. Best suited for families, a double and single bed slumbers up top on a mezzanine and there's a sofa bed in the lounge, should you be four. Breakfast is brought to you, and the house has its own little terrace overlooking olive groves.

Hôtel des 2 Rocs (☎ 04 94 76 87 32; www.hoteldeuxrocs .com; 1 place Don't d'Amont, Seillans; small/medium/large d €63/95/125, menus €28 & €35; ☺ restaurant lunch & dinner Tue-Sun) Scipion, knight of the Flotte d'Agout, lived here in the 17th century. Today, the soulful *bastide* is home to Julie and Nicolas Malzac who run this 14-room boutique hotel and restaurant with extraordinary panache (the couple have worked with Alain Ducasse and other big names in the past). Summer dining is alfresco around a fountain beneath trees.

Memorable dining options in Fayence:

La Farigoulette (☎ 04 94 84 10 49; place du Château; menu €34; ☺ lunch & dinner Wed-Sun) Ravioli stuffed with foie gras, duck liver pan-fried with almonds and peaches and other delectable market-driven dishes near the belfry.

Le Temps des Cerises (☎ 04 94 76 01 19; place de la République; menu €37; ☺ lunch & dinner Wed-Fri, Sun & Mon, dinner Sat) French and world cuisine by Dutch chef Louis Schröder beneath a leafy pagoda.

Le Castelleras (☎ 04 94 76 13 80; rte de Seillans; menus €43 & €58; ☺ lunch & dinner Wed-Sun Apr-Feb) The ultimate gastronomic choice.

Haut-Var

West of Draguignan, the rich soil of the Haut-Var region hides earthy black truffles, snouted out November to March. Other gastronomic delights await travellers in a clutch of sleepy, beautifully unspoilt villages teetering on hilltops, although you'll need your own transport to reach them.

Châteaudouble (population 390), north of Draguignan and topped by a chateau no less, and **Tourtour** (population 470, elevation 470m) 16km west along the wiggly D51, are two typically 'eagle nest' villages perched up high. In Tourtour buy oil and, from around 15 December (after the harvest), watch olives being pressed at the village's restored 17th-century **moulin à huile** (oil mill; ☎ 04 94 70 54 74). The vaulted stone building hosts art exhibitions when it's not busy pressing olives. Guided tours of the mill and village are run by the **tourist office** (☎ 04 94 70 59 47; www.tourisme-tourtour.com; montée de St-Dénis; ☺ 9am-noon & 2.30-6pm).

AUPS
pop 1900 / elev 505m

In the truffle season (November to March), those alien-looking nuggets of black fungus can be viewed at the Thursday morning **truffle market**, held on the central square. Truffle hunts and demonstrations of pig-snouting techniques lure a crowd on the fourth Sunday in January, when Aups throws its **Journée de la Truffe** (Day of the Truffle).

SALERNES & AROUND

Handmade terracotta tiles known as *terres cuites* (literally 'baked earth') have been manufactured since the 18th century in **Salernes** (population 3343, elevation 300m), 9km south of Aups along the wiggly D31. Salernes **tourist office** (☎ 04 94 70 69 02; www.ville -salernes.fr in French; place Gabriel Péri; ☺ 9.30am-12.30pm & 2.30-6.30pm Tue-Sat) has a list of local potters and tilemakers (online at www.salernes.com) who open their workshop doors to visitors and can update you on the future **Terra Rossa Maison de la Céramique de Salernes**. Sited in an old factory currently being transformed into a state-of-the-art industrial space, the ceramic museum is slated to open in early 2008.

Cotignac (population 2040, elevation 230m), 11km southwest of Salernes, with its lively morning market; hilltop **Entrecasteaux** (population 850, elevation 156m), a classified historical monument with a 17th-century chateau; and pint-sized **Fox-Amphoux** (population 380, elevation 540m), with an idyllic village inn oozing history in the shape of **Auberge du Vieux Fox** (☎ 04 94 80 71 69; place de l'Église; d €65-100, menu €18; ☺ mid-Jan–mid-Nov, restaurant closed Thu) are other pretty Varois villages well worth the wiggly drive.

Le Thoronet & La Celle

The third in a trio of great Cistercian abbeys (the other two are Silvacane and Notre-Dame de Sénanque), **Abbaye de Thoronet** (☎ 04 94 60 43 90; adult/under 18yr €6.50/free; 10am-6.30pm Mon-Sat, 10am-noon & 2-6.50pm Sun Apr-Sep, 10am-1pm & 2-5pm Mon-Sat, 10am-noon & 2-5pm Sun Oct-Mar), 12km southwest of Lorgues, is remarkable for its ultra-austere architecture: pure proportions, perfectly dressed stone and the subtle fall of light and shadow are where its beauty lies. The chapterhouse, where the monks met to discuss community problems, is more ornate as the only secular room in the complex. Built between 1160 and 1190, early Gothic influences are visible in the pointed arches. Sunday mass is celebrated at noon and concerts are held in summer.

The tiny village of La Celle, some 15km southwest of Thoronet and 2km south of Brignoles, is dominated by **Abbaye de la Celle** (place des Ormeaux), a 12th-century Benedictine abbey that served as a convent from 1225 until its eventual closure in 1657. The church serves the village community today, and hauntingly beautiful **classical concerts** (☎ 04 94 69 10 86; www.soireesmusicales-lacelle.com; tickets €23) fill its cloister in July and August. In the adjoining convent you can taste and buy Coteaux Varois AOC wines at the **Maison des Vins Coteaux Varois** (☎ 04 94 69 33 18; place des Ormeaux; 10am-noon & 2-6pm Mon-Sat).

SLEEPING & EATING

Hostellerie de l'Abbaye de la Celle (☎ 04 98 05 14 14; www.abbaye-celle.com; place du Général de Gaulle, La Celle; d from €205, lunch menus €42, dinner menus €57 & €76; P) Top chefs Bruno Clément and Alain Ducasse are the creative energies behind this fabulous four-star hotel and restaurant in La Celle with 11 country-style rooms and alfresco dining to drool over. If you've got a penchant for bathtubs with legs, pick the Cedar Tree.

Château de Bernes (☎ 04 94 60 43 53; www.chateauberne.com; chemin de Berne, Lorgues; d low/mid/high season from €280/360/410; Mar-Oct; P) Far from intimate, this dynamic wine-growing estate 2km north of Lorgues village offers all kinds of entertainment, including wine tasting, mushroom days, truffle-hunting demos, cooking courses and wonderful jazz picnics. Oh, and it has 16 top-end hotel rooms.

Les Arcs-sur-Argens

pop 6300 / elev 65m

Les Arcs, 11km south of Draguignan, is a perfectly restored old town perched on a hillock, with a bacchanalian House of Wines where you can taste, learn about and buy Côtes de Provence wines.

The **tourist office** (☎ 04 94 73 37 30; www.ville-lesarcs.com; place du Général de Gaulle; 9am-noon & 2-6pm Mon-Fri) is at the foot of the medieval village. Lordly lodgings can be found in the 11th-century castle crowning the village, which shelters the luxurious **Logis du Guetteur** (☎ 04 94 99 51 10; www.logisduguetteur.com; place du Château; d low/high season from €108/130; Mar-Jan; P).

WINE TASTING

The **Maison des Vins Côtes de Provence** (☎ 04 94 99 50 20; www.cotes-de-provence.fr in French; 10am-7pm Mon-Sat, 10am-6pm Sun Apr-Sep, to 6pm Mon-Sat Oct-Mar), 2.5km south of the village on the westbound N7, is the obvious place to start. Sixteen different Côtes de Provence wines are selected for tasting each week (look for the list that tells you the ideal dish to eat with each wine) and over 800 different wines from 230 different wine estates are for sale at producers' prices (starting at €2.85 for a bottle of simple rosé by village cooperative Les Vignerons des Cotignac and peaking at €29 for a bottle of AOC Côtes de Provence Cuvée Guy Da Nine Rosé produced by Château de la Mascaronne in Le Luc). To experience the pleasure of wining *and* dining, lunch at on-site **La Vigne à' Table** (☎ 04 94 47 48 47; starters €15, mains €20-30, menu €34).

A prestigious *cru classé* wine, produced since the 14th century, can be tasted and bought at **Château Ste-Roseline** (☎ 04 94 99 50 30; www.sainte-roseline.com; 9am-6pm), nestled among vineyards 4.5km east of Les Arcs-sur-Argens (on the D91 towards La Motte). A lovely 1975 mosaic by Marc Chagall illuminates the estate's 13th-century Romanesque **Chapelle de Ste-Roseline** (2.30-6pm Tue-Sun), which contains the corpse of St Roseline. Roseline was born at the chateau in Les Arcs in 1263 and became a Carthusian nun. She experienced numerous visions during her lifetime and was said to be able to curtail demons. Upon her death in 1329, her eyes were taken out and separately preserved. Piano recitals and musical concerts are held in the chapel in July and August.

La Motte, the first village in Provence to be liberated after the August 1944 Allied landings, is 3km further east along the D91. For the ultimate Provençal feast, head east out of La Motte along the D47 to **Domaine de la Maurette** (☎ 04 94 45 92 82; rte de Callas; menu incl apéritif

A PERFECT DAY

Create your own perfect day: spend it motoring around the villages of Haut-Var, winding up at these exquisite dinner and overnight author's choices:

- **Chez Bruno** (☎ 04 94 85 93 93; www.restaurantbruno.com; rte de Vidauban; d/ste from €110/306, menus €59, €80, €100 & €120; ☽ lunch & dinner Jun–mid-Sep, lunch & dinner Tue-Sat, lunch Sun mid-Sep–Apr) France's most famous truffle restaurant can be found in a country house 2km east of the tiny backwater of Lorgues, on the D562 towards Les Arcs. In his Michelin-starred restaurant, chef Bruno Clément cooks almost exclusively with those knobbly, pungent delicacies: he gets through an incredible 1000kg of the world's most expensive foodstuff every year. Should you not be able to move after your black diamond feast, Bruno has six lovely rooms up top. Breakfast is continental (€15) or built around truffles (€30).

- **La Sarrazine** (☎ 04 94 73 20 27; www.lasarrazine.com; 375 chemin du Pendedi; d low/mid/high season from €75/88/99; P ☒ ☒) Raved about in the *Sunday Times*, this British-run *chambre d'hôte* languishing in extensive grounds is undeniably lovely. It has tennis courts, flower-bedecked pool and, to preserve the peace of the stately house, no guests under 12 years.

€28.50; ☽ cave 10am-6pm Mon-Sat, restaurant lunch), on the intersection of the D47 and the D25. On this wine estate you can taste and buy wine, and dine on a vine-covered terrace in its *ferme auberge*, a roadside inn where the atmosphere of chattering people dining on wholesome, homemade food is nothing short of electric. Truffle-stuffed ravioli, veal kidneys in red wine and *tournedos façon Rossini* (pan-fried beef tenderloin medallions topped with a slice of foie gras) are tasty highlights.

GETTING THERE & AROUND

Exit Les Arcs-Draguignan train station, turn left, then right at the end of the street. It's a 2km walk straight up this road (av Jean Jaurès) to the town centre.

Les Arcs, on the rail line between St-Raphaël and Toulon, is well served by coastal trains to Nice (€12.90, 1½ hours), Marseille (€18.40, 1¼ hours) and all the stops in between. Les Arcs also serves as the train station for Draguignan.

Les Rapides Varois (☎ 04 94 47 05 05) runs buses every 30 minutes between Les Arcs train station and Draguignan (€3.20, 20 minutes).

MASSIF DES MAURES

Wild boar roam the forests of the Massif des Maures (from the Provençal word *maouro*, meaning dark pine wood), whose hidden towns and villages are little oases of peace. Traditional industries – chestnut harvests, cork production, pipe-making – are their lifeblood, a pleasant surprise in the tourist-economied south of France.

There are superb walking and cycling opportunities, particularly as much of the area is inaccessible by car. The GR91 long-distance trail penetrates the massif at its northern edge, near **Carnoules** (population 2622), wending its way past **Notre Dame des Anges** (780m) and La Sauvette to medieval La Garde Freinet.

The D14 runs through Collobrières, the largest town in the massif and chestnut capital of the universe. This road is particularly popular with cyclists and is graced with fine panoramas. Similarly dramatic is the D39 from Collobrières, which winds and soars up to Notre Dame des Anges before plunging down to Gonfaron. The parallel N98, which skims through vineyards and cork-oak-tree plantations, runs from St-Tropez to Bormes-les-Mimosas and on to Hyères.

The Corniche des Maures is the southernmost extent of the area, where pine trees give way to buckets and spades at Le Lavandou and smaller beach resorts to the east.

COLLOBRIÈRES

pop 1600 / elev 150m

Hidden in the forest 24km west of Grimaud, this leafy village is the self-proclaimed 'capital' of the Maures. Nut lovers will be in seventh heaven: the town is famous for its chestnut produce. Food and drink made from the nuts is sold in summer in front of the tourist office, along with souvenirs made from cork-oak, another local industry. Market day is Thursday (July and August) and Sunday (year-round).

Information

The **tourist office** (☎ 04 94 48 08 00; www.collobrieres.fr in French; blvd Charles Caminat; ☺ 10am-12.30pm & 2-6.30pm Mon-Sat Jul & Aug, 10am-noon & 2-6pm Tue-Sat Sep-Jun) takes accommodation bookings and has details on joining in the October chestnut harvest and participating in guided forest walks (€7). Three short walking trails – including a 200m trail to a *châtaigneraie* (chestnut grove) – are mapped out on the notice board outside.

Sights

Over the 11th-century bridge, **Confiserie Azuréenne** (☎ 04 94 48 07 20) sells a nutty array of products. Sample *glaces aux marrons glacés* (chestnut ice creams), *crème de marrons* (chestnut cream), *marrons au sirop* (chestnuts in syrup), or a shot of *liqueur de châtaignes* (chestnut liqueur). Its small **Musée de la Fabrique** (admission free; ☺ 9.30am-1pm & 2-7pm or 8pm) opposite explains the art of making *marrons glacés* (candied chestnuts).

Festivals & Events

Collobrières cooks up a monstrous-sized *aïoli Provençal complet* (a feast of various vegetables, potatoes, a boiled egg and small shellfish dunked in a pot of garlicky mayonnaise), and makes the place de la Libération fountain spout rosé wine during its annual **Grande Fête des Fontaines** in August. It celebrates a **Fête de la Châtaigne** (Chestnut Festival) on the last three Sundays in October, with craft and home-produce markets, street entertainment and the warming smell of roasted chestnuts drifting over the proceedings. In April the **Fête de la Transhumance** celebrates the seasonal moving of shepherds' flocks.

Sleeping & Eating

Hôtel-Restaurant des Maures (☎ 04 94 48 07 10; 19 blvd Lazare Carnot; d €22) Grab a room at the back of this central hotel overlooking the river and *pétanque* pitch. Its family-friendly, waterside restaurant is good for cheap, filling *menus*, and the downstairs bar sells chestnut ice cream for €3 a bowl.

La Bastide de la Cabrière (☎ 04 94 48 04 31; www .provenceweb.fr/83/cabriere; rte de Gonfaron; d €75-125; **P**) This welcoming five-room *chambre d'hôte*, 6km north of town along the relentlessly winding D39, prepares delicious, seasonal home-grown meals (€35). You can also buy goats' cheese, fruit wine and jams to take away.

Ferme de Peïgros (☎ 04 94 48 03 83; fermedepeigros@ wanadoo.fr; Col de Babaou; menu €22; ☺ lunch daily) Goats and chestnuts are the mainstay of this farm restaurant, 1.8km along a gravel track signposted from the top of the Babaou mountain pass (8km from Collobrières). At different times of year, its menu includes farm-killed goat or poultry, boar, cepes and sometimes farm-made chestnut ice cream. No credit cards.

Getting Around

Cycling is a great way to get around: rent wheels from **Garage BM Varoise** (☎ 04 94 48 01 13; rte de Pierrefeu) at the entrance to the village. A half-/full day's rental costs €6.50/12.

CHARTREUSE DE LA VERNE

Majestic, 12th- to 13th-century **Monastère de la Verne** (☎ 04 94 43 45 51; adult/8-14yr €5/3; ☺ 11am-5pm or 6pm Wed-Mon Feb-Dec) is in a dramatic forest setting 12km southeast of Collobrières. The Carthusian monastery was founded in 1170, possibly on the site of a temple to the goddess

---

A MENHIR DETOUR

With your walking boots firmly laced, set off from the old bridge in Collobrières, walking uphill into town along rue Camille Desmoulins, rue Blanqui and rue Galilée. Follow the signs for the camp site and ruined 15th-century Église St Pons, which will lead you onto the GR90.

It's a steep climb out of town and into the woods, composed of oak trees (including cork-oak), pine, heathers and ferns, then the path ascends more gradually to about 450m above sea level, before levelling off as it reaches Plateau Lambert.

The trail comes out onto a forest road; follow it leftwards for 150m and it will lead you to the *garde forestière* (forest ranger) Ferme Lambert. Ask permission from the forest ranger before crossing the field to see the two biggest **menhirs** in the Var region, now heritage-listed monuments. Each one is over 3m high, and they were raised sometime between 3000 and 2000 BC. Another super sight is the **Châtaignier de Madame**, the biggest chestnut tree in Provence, with a mighty 10.4m circumference.

The walking detour should take you around four hours there and back again.

Laverna, protector of the bandits who hung out in the Maures. The Huguenots destroyed most of the original charterhouse in 1577. Since 1982 the solitary complex has been home to 15 nuns, of the Sisters of Bethlehem.

One of the old monks' cells has been fully restored, complete with a small formal garden, workshop and covered corridor, where the monk would pray as he paced. Other interesting features include the use of serpentine (a stripy green stone) as decoration; it's particularly noticeable in the door arches and vaulted ceiling of the 17th-century church. Various walking trails lead from the monastery into its forested surroundings.

Smoking and revealing clothes are forbidden in the monastery; nor can you steal the nuns' chestnuts from the trees outside. From Collobrières, follow rte de Grimaud (D14) east for 6km, then turn right (south) onto the narrow D214. Follow this road for a further 6km to the monastery; the final section of the single-track road is unpaved.

LA GARDE FREINET

pop 1656 / elev 365m

A stark, rocky spur props up the 13th-century ruins of Fort Freinet (450m), from where there is a fantastic panorama of the small medieval town's red rooftops.

Its tourist office (☎ 04 94 43 67 41; www.lagarde freinet-tourisme.com; Chapelle St-Jean, place de la Mairie;

⊙ 9.30am-12.30pm & 3.30-6.30pm Mon-Sat year-round, plus 9.30am-12.30pm Sun Easter-Oct) has details on walking, wine tasting and chambres d'hôtes in the massif. Village traditions and customs unfold in the adjoining Conservatoire du Patrimoine et du Traditions du Freinet (☎ 04 94 43 08 57; www.conserva toiredufreinet.org; Chapelle St-Jean, place de la Mairie; adult/under 12yr €1.50/free; ⊙ 10am-12.30pm & 3-6pm Tue-Sat). The latter also organises fascinating half-day nature walks, including a two-hour trip (€7) into the forest with a guide to learn how cork is harvested (see the boxed text, p78).

Festivals & Events

Below the ruined fort is a large stone cross where pilgrims pay their respects on 1 May each year during the town's bravades. The relics of St Clément, the village's patron saint, are paraded there, accompanied by the blasting of blunderbusses. The cross is a 20-minute uphill walk from the village centre, signposted from place Neuve.

La Garde Freinet celebrates its traditional Fête de la Transhumance, which marks the seasonal moving of the flocks, in mid-June, and hosts a Fête de la Châtaigne (Chestnut Fair) in mid-October.

Sleeping & Eating

Hôtel La Claire Fontaine (☎ 04 94 43 63 76; 4 place Vieille; d from €45) Out of a trio of midrange places to stay, this is the best value. Half the rooms

---

VILLAGE DES TORTUES

About 20km north of Collobrières on the northern tip of the massif is a tortoise village, where one of France's rarest and most endangered species can be viewed at close quarters. The Hermann tortoise (Testudo hermanni), once common along the Mediterranean coastal strip, is today found only in the Massif des Maures and Corsica. Forest fires in 1990 destroyed 2500 sq km of forest in the massif, reducing the tortoise population further still.

The Station d'Observation et de Protection des Tortues des Maures (SOPTOM; Maures Tortoise Observation and Protection Station) was set up in 1985 by French film-maker Bernaud Devaux and an English biologist to ensure the Hermann's survival.

A well-documented trail (captions in English) leads visitors around the centre: from the tortoise clinic, where wounded tortoises are treated and then released into the Maures; to the quarantine quarter and reproduction enclosures; and to the tropical conservatory, egg hatcheries and nurseries, where the young tortoises (a delicacy for preying magpies, rats, foxes and wild boars) spend the first three of their 60 to 100 years. There's also a great palaeontology trail, where vicious-looking models of the tortoise's ancestors lurk among the bushes.

In summer the best time to see the tortoises is in the morning and late afternoon (they tend to shelter from the heat during the day). Watch tortoises hatch from mid-May to the end of June; from November through to early March they hibernate.

The Village des Tortues (☎ 04 94 78 26 41; www.villagetortues.com in French; adult/5-16yr €9/6; ⊙ 9am-7pm Mar-Nov), about 6km east of Gonfaron, is only accessible by private transport.

overlook a buzzing pedestrianised street, filled with bars and restaurants that can be noisy on summer weekends: ask for a back room if you want to sleep. Cheaper rooms share a toilet on the corridor.

COGOLIN

pop 9181

Industrious Cogolin, 15km south of La Garde Freinet, has a worldwide reputation for clarinet and saxophone reeds. It's also a centre for wooden pipes, cork products and *tapis de Cogolin* (carpets), woven here since the 1920s when Armenian refugees settled here. Its sandy beach and pleasure port is 5km northeast.

Several pipemakers on av Georges Clemenceau welcome visitors; the **tourist office** (☎ 04 94 55 01 50; www.cogolin-provence.com; place de la République; ⏰ 9am-12.30pm & 2-6.30pm Mon-Fri, 9.30am-12.30pm Sat) has a complete list.

Provence's first screen hero, Raimu, is honoured at the **Musée Espace Raimu** (☎ 04 94 54 18 00; www.musee-raimu.com in French; 18 av Georges Clemenceau; adult/11-18yr €3.50/1.75; ⏰ 10am-noon & 3-6pm low season, 10am-noon & 4-7pm high season, closed Sun morning), a museum established by the comic actor's granddaughter in the basement of the arts cinema.

Cycles Évasion (☎ 04 94 54 71 13; www.cycles-evasion.com; 61 av Georges Clemenceau) rents out bicycles for €15/70 per day/week.

Sleeping & Eating

Maison de la Monde (☎ 04 94 54 77 54; www.lamaisondumonde.fr; 63 rue Carnot; small/medium/large low season €70/99/120, high season €95/135/156; 🌂) This apricot boutique hotel with sage-green shutters is like home away from home. Tableau paintings fill the walls, fabrics are from around the world and a tiny path leads through the walled garden to the leafy pool.

Grain de Sel (☎ 04 94 54 46 86, 06 20 98 82 86; rue du 11 Novembre; menu €31; ⏰ lunch & dinner Tue-Sat) This tiny bistro behind the town hall is quality stuff. Feast on age-old Provençal fodder like lamb *pied et paquets* (sheep tripe and trotters) or a dish with a modern twist such as truffle risotto.

La Tarte Tropézienne (☎ 04 94 54 42 59; www.tarte-tropezienne.com; 2 rue Beausoleil) It was here that the sugary *tarte Tropézienne* was created in 1955.

LA MÔLE & AROUND

Tiny La Môle (population 800), 9km southwest from Cogolin along the vineyard-laden

N98, is recognised for three things: Antoine de Saint-Exupéry, author of *Le Petit Prince*, who visited his grandparents here as a boy – their chateau features in the book; its **Boulangerie de la Môle** (⏰ 7am-1pm & 4-7pm Tue-Sun) selling nut and olive breads, on the south side of the N98, towards Cogolin; and its manicured air strip (p351) where the truly wealthy land their private jets. Sample local wine at one of the many wine-producing chateaux on the westbound N98.

From La Môle, narrow route du Canadel (D27) dives dramatically to the coast. All is green serenity until you hit **Pachacaïd** (☎ 04 94 55 70 80; www.pachacaid.com; rte du Canadel; 4-person mobile homes low/high season per week €300/750), a giant camp site full of holidaying families going wild in the neighbouring **Niagara Parc Nautique** (☎ 04 94 55 70 80; www.parcniagara.com; rte du Canadel; adult/5-13yr Jun €12/10, Jul & Aug €14/11.50; ⏰ 10.30am-7pm Jun-early Sep), a water park with seven giant slides.

Sleeping & Eating

Domaine de Ventabren (☎ 04 94 49 51 21; www.le-domaine-de-ventabren.com; chemin des Guiols, La Môle; d low/mid/high season incl breakfast from €81/91/101; ⏰ Feb-Dec; 🅿 🐾) Head out past the village church in La Môle and follow the signs for 3km to uncover this friendly five-room *chambre d'hôte*, a modern house surrounded by oak, cork and pine forest at the end of potholed gravel track. Cross the bridge over the ornamental pond and enter the pool-clad interior courtyard to find hosts Michèle and Emmanuel.

Auberge de La Môle (☎ 04 94 49 57 01; place de l'Église, La Môle; lunch/dinner menu €25/50) Tradition rules at this no-frills village inn, next to the church in La Môle. Once the village petrol station (the old pump outside is stuck on 333), the place fills up quick at lunchtime with hearty appetites eager to feast on its legendary terrines, pâtés and feisty jars of pickles. No credit cards.

FORÊT DU DOM & BORMES-LES-MIMOSAS

Vineyards melt into a rich patchwork of cork-oak, pine and chestnut trees as the N98 continues its path west into the Forêt du Dom, 12km west of La Môle.

From the top of the **Col de Gratteloup** (199m), the steep D41, a popular cycling route, climbs north over the **Col de Babaou** (415m) towards Collobrières. Southbound, the D41 wiggles its way across the **Col de Caguo-Ven** (237m), from where there are good views of **Bormes-les-Mimosas** (population 6399, elevation 180m). This green-fingered 12th-century village is famous for its floral displays, and its **tourist office** (☎ 04 94 01 38 38; www.bormeslesmimosas.com; 1 place Gambetta; ✆ 9am-12.30pm & 3-6.30pm Apr-Sep, Mon-Sat only Oct-Mar) takes bookings for botanical walks (€9) and hikes (€7) with a forest warden in the nearby Forêt du Dom.

CORNICHE DES MAURES

From La Môle, the breathtaking 267m **Col du Canadel** (the D27) offers unbeatable views of the Massif des Maures, the coastline and its offshore islands before plummeting to the Corniche des Maures, a 26km coastal road (D559) stretching southwest from La Croix-Valmer to Le Lavandou. The shoreline is trimmed with sandy beaches ideal for swimming, sunbathing and windsurfing.

The largest **tourist office** (☎ 04 94 01 92 10; www .cavalaire-sur-mer.com; promenade de la Mer; ✆ 9am-7pm mid-Jun–mid-Sep, 9am-12.30pm & 2-6pm Mon-Fri, 9am-12.30pm Sat mid-Sep–mid-Jun) along this stretch is in **Cavalaire-sur-Mer**, from where boats sail to the Îles d'Hyères in season.

Sights & Activities

DOMAINE DU RAYOL

From Le Rayol, a narrow road runs south to the beautiful **Domaine du Rayol** (☎ 04 98 04

La Grande Maison des Campaux (☎ 04 94 49 55 40; www.lagrandemaisondescampaux .com; 6987 rte du Dom, Bormes-les-Mimosas; d €125-150, q €220; ✆ Mar-Nov; (P) (R)) This dreamy 17th-century country house steals the B&B show for miles around. Languishing in the heart of vineyards on the vast 128-hectare Domaine des Campaux, five spacious rooms evoke a bygone era. Beams are sturdy and age-old, a couple of bathtubs have legs, floors are original stone flags or terracotta tiles and linens are crisp white and contemporary bold. Flat-screen TVs are a given and each of the five rooms is named after a wine produced on the estate. Views are strictly green and sensational, as is the terrace out the front from which the wine-producing estate with lake and pool can be surveyed. Find it uphill at the end of a 500m crunchy gravel track, signposted on the N98 some 6km west of La Môle.

---

44 00; www.domainedurayol.org; av des Belges; adult/8-16yr €7/3.50; ✆ 9.30am-12.30pm & 2.30-6.30pm Tue-Sat Apr-Sep, 9.30am-12.30pm & 2-5.30pm Tue-Sat Feb, Mar, Oct & Nov), a 20-hectare botanical garden rescued from abandonment in 1989 and stuffed with plants from around the world. The flowers are at their best in April and May, but it's always worth a visit. The admission includes a 1½-hour guided tour (in French) of the fabulous gardens and, for the truly garden-mad, there are plenty more thematic tours and guided lectures to pick from (€10 to €15; advance reservations required).

In summer you can observe underwater flora and fauna with an experienced guide along a **Sentier Marin** (Marine Trail; adult/8-18yr €15/12; ✆ Jul & Aug). The price includes entrance to the gardens, and your wet suit, flippers, mask and snorkel. Advance bookings essential.

In July and August the estate hosts occasional open-air musical soirees; again, book to ensure a place.

BEACHES

Continuing west, seaside resorts include the tiny hamlets of **Le Rayol**, **Pramousquier**, **Cavalière** and **Aiguebelle**. With the exception of busy **Plage de Cavalière**, a popular family destination, the beaches along this stretch are quiet, sandy and usually tucked in pretty coves. Tiny **Plage du Rayol** and **Plage de l'Escale** are particularly enchanting: they're backed by pine trees and have a restaurant on the sand.

CYCLING

From Cavalière a silky-smooth cycling track wends 4.5km west along the coast to **St-Clair**, the easternmost suburb of Le Lavandou.

Sleeping & Eating

Le Bailli de Suffren (☎ 04 98 04 47 00; www.lebaillide suffren.com; av des Américains, Le Rayol–Canadel-sur-Mer; d low/mid/high season from €160/234/320; (P) (R) (R)) An oh-my-gosh gasp of a place wedged between beaches in an inlet right on the shore. Rooms have rich red terracotta floors, quilted Provençal bedspreads on the romantic four-posters, and spectacular sea views. The hotel has its own private slice of beach, and there are two restaurants, for alfresco lunches and sophisticated evening dinners.

Les Roches (☎ 04 94 71 05 07; www.hotellesroches .com; 1 av des Trois Dauphins, Aiguebelle; d low/high season from €200/240; (P) (R) (R)) The stuff of dreams: Humphrey Bogart, Jean Cocteau and Winston Churchill all stayed at this fabulous four-star

CHEZ JO

Buzzing with bare-footed, overly bronzed, sarong-clad beach lovers with a penchant for bathing in the nod and piercings in the most unexpected of places, this sizzling beach restaurant is hot stuff. Flamboyant, gregarious and not a sign in sight to tell you it's here, beach restaurant **Chez Jo** (☎ 04 94 05 86 06; Plage du Layet, Cavalière; ⏰ lunch May-Sep) is one of those rare 'in the know' addresses, around for a good 30 years already. Dining is around four or five tables on the sand or on a wooden deck above the water; but don't bother dressing up, the regulars don't. Cuisine is straight from the sea and comes out from the shack of a kitchen, snug against rocks, on oversized cork platters: the grilled *langouste* (crayfish) with spaghetti (€135 per kg) and *bouillabaisse* (fish stew; €50) are legendary (order both 24 hours in advance), as is the simple but delicious grilled catch of the day (€65 per kg). Lunch ends with an espresso and a short, sharp (complimentary) shot of Jo's strong house liqueur – intended to enhance the obligatory postlunch siesta on the sand. But what about Jo? He's that bronzed, potbellied bloke with long sea-swept hair, bare chest and blue trousers (no shoes) who strolls the length of the deck every so often.

hotel and restaurant that bears an uncanny resemblance to a majestic liner, moored beneath a cliff looking out to sea. The best view of it is at sea, from one of the boats in the hotel flotilla.

LE LAVANDOU
pop 5508

Once a fishing village, Le Lavandou (from the Provençal 'Lou Lavandou', meaning washhouse) is an appealing beach resort with a seemingly endless (12km) stretch of golden sand, a can't-go-wrong choice of family- and blue rinse–friendly cafés and restaurants, and boats galore yo-yoing across the water to the idyllic Îles d'Hyères.

Concrete blocks dominate the resort to the southwest, but the northeastern old town is beautifully intact. Dramatist Bertolt Brecht and composer Kurt Weill wrote parts of *The Threepenny Opera* while they were holidaying here in 1928.

Orientation & Information

Quai Gabriel Péri and its continuation, quai Baptistin Pins, runs northeast along the beachfront. The port sits at its easternmost end, opposite the old town.

Buses use the shelters either side of the D559. From there, walk one block south then turn left (east) onto av des Martyrs de la Résistance to get to the centre. Its continuation, av du Général de Gaulle, traverses the old town.

The **tourist office** (☎ 04 94 00 40 50; www.lelavandou.com; quai Gabriel Péri; ⏰ 9am-12.30pm & 2.30-7pm Mon-Sat, 10am-12.30pm & 4-6.30pm Sun) is opposite the port.

Boat Excursions

Tickets for *all* boats departing from Le Lavandou's **port** (Gare Maritime; quai des Îles d'Or) are sold at the ticket office 30 minutes before departure. **Vedettes Îles d'Or et Le Corsaire** (☎ 04 94 71 01 02; www.vedettesilesdor.fr; 15 quai Gabriel Péri) runs various trips, including **glass-bottom boat trips** (adult/4-12yr €12/9.20) departing every 40 minutes daily all summer. Destinations include Île du Levant (adult/four to 12 years return €23/19.10, 30 minutes, six daily July and August, two to five daily September to June); Porquerolles (€29.40/23, 50 minutes, one daily July and August, three weekly April, June and September); and Port-Cros (€23/19.10, 40 minutes, seven daily July and August, two to four daily September to June). La Croisiè Bleue (a combined ticket for all three islands) costs €44/36. Boats also sail to St-Tropez (€44/36, two hours, twice weekly June to September).

Sleeping & Eating

Hôtel de l'Îlot Fleuri (☎ 04 94 71 14 82; www.lilotfleuri.com; blvd du Front de Mer; d/tr low season €49/68, high season €63/88, d with sea view low/high season €61/78; ⏰ mid-Apr–mid-Nov; P 🐕) Two-star 'Flowery Islet' with its mimosa-topped balconies looking out to the sparkling blue sea is a real treat. Le Lavandou's oldest hotel, operational since 1928, and it sports secure, free parking – something of a novelty on the Côte d'Azur!

Hôtel Le Rabelais (☎ 04 94 71 00 56; www.le-rabelais.fr; 2 rue Rabelais; d €78 & €85; ⏰ mid-Jan–mid-Dec; 🐕) A rambling building overlooking the port on quai Baptistin Pins. Its pretty-in-pink façade shields a flowery garden, and breakfast is served overlooking the ocean. Streetside rooms don't have air-con.

There are plenty of touristy restaurants on the waterfront, but the best eating places are the terraces in the old town. Recommended:

Chez Mimi (☎ 04 94 71 00 85; 11 quai Gabriel Péri; ☻ mid-Jan–mid-Nov) Breakfast and apéritif spot overlooking the *pétanque* pitch from its portside perch.

La Pignato (☎ 04 94 71 13 02; 13 rue Abbé Hélin; menus €17 & €20) *Cuisine Provençale* has been dished up here for almost 30 years.

La Favouille (☎ 04 94 71 34 29; 9 rue Abbé Hélin; menus €19 & €23; ☻ Mar-Oct) Long list of regional apéritifs, aïoli (€20) every Friday and great sloping tables.

Getting There & Around

Le Lavandou is on the main bus route (up to seven daily) between St-Tropez (€10.30, one hour) and Toulon (€11.60, 1¼ hours). Buses follow the coastal road, also stopping in Le Rayol, Bormes-les-Mimosas, La Londe and Hyères.

Hire wheels from **Holiday Bikes** (☎ 04 94 15 19 99; lavandou@holiday-bikes.com; av Vincent Auriol) for upwards of €10/15/45 per day for inline skates/mountain bike/50cc scooter.

ÎLES D'HYÈRES & ÎLES DU FUN

Legend says gods turned a bunch of swimming princesses into the Îles d'Hyères, and they do have a magical look when viewed from the sea. Their mica-rich rock, which glitters and gleams in the sunlight, gives them their other name, the Îles d'Or (Islands of Gold).

At 7km long and 3km wide, Porquerolles is the largest island; Île de Port-Cros, in the middle, is a national park, while its eastern sister, Île du Levant, is a nudist colony. Wild camping and cars are forbidden throughout the archipelago.

Dubbed the Îles du Fun, Bendor and Embiez, west of the Îles d'Hyères off Toulon's shores, are more sub-Disney than the stuff of myth, but make for a tongue-in-cheek day trip.

Islanders refer to the rest of France as the 'continent'.

ÎLE DE PORQUEROLLES
pop 350

Despite its huge influx of visitors each year, Porquerolles is unspoiled: 10 sq km of its sandy white beaches, pine woods and maquis are protected by the Parc National de Port-Cros. A wide variety of indigenous and tropical flora thrive, including the requien larkspur, which grows nowhere else in the world. In winter blossoming mimosas splash the green island, with colour. April and May are the best months to spot some of its 114 bird species.

Pottering along the island's trails on foot or by bicycle, then flopping on the beach with a picnic, is a delicious way to spend a day. Avoid July and August, when the risk of forest fires makes the interior of the island and its trails inaccessible. This is also the time when the owners of Porquerolles' numerous *résidences secondaires* return to the island, increasing the population sixfold.

Smoking is forbidden outside the village.

Orientation & Information

Boats dock at the port on the island's northern coast. Walk 200m to the tourist office at the end of the jetty, then bear right along rue de la Ferme to place d'Armes, the central village square.

Maison du Parc (☎ 04 94 58 07 24; rte du Phare; ☻ 9.30am-12.30pm & 1.30-5.15pm Mon-Fri Apr-Jun & Sep, 9.30am-12.30pm & 2.30-6.30pm Mon-Fri Jul & Aug) National Park information office; organises 1½-hour guided tours of the island (adult/five to 17 years €4/3).

Post office (place d'Armes)

Société Marseillaise de Crédit (3 rue de la Ferme) ATM and currency exchange.

Tourist office (☎ 04 94 58 33 76; www.porquerolles .com; ☻ 9am-5.20pm Apr-Nov, 9am-1pm Fri-Wed Dec-Mar) Sells island maps (€1) showing the *pistes cyclables* (cycling paths) and *sentiers pédestres* (footpaths), and the plastic *Guide Sous-Marin des Espèces Méditerranéenes* to help snorkellers identify underwater flora (€20).

Sights & Activities

Central **place d'Armes** is dominated by a giant, tree-shaded *pétanque* pitch. In summer, music concerts are held in **Église Ste-Anne**, on the south of the square. Festivities fill the church and the square on 25 July, when islanders celebrate their patron saint's day.

AN ISLAND ROMANCE

Three toasters and a bath-towel set just weren't enough. In 1911 newly married Mrs Fournier received the perfect wedding present from hubby François: the island of Porquerolles!

From place d'Armes, head south along chemin Ste-Agathe to 16th-century **Fort Ste-Agathe** (☎ 04 94 58 07 24; adult/5-17yr €3/1.50; ☯ 10am-12.30pm & 1.30-5pm May-Sep), the only fortification open to visitors. It contains historical and natural-history exhibitions, and the ticket includes access to the tower, with its eye-popping island panorama. Much of the building dates from between 1812 and 1814, when Napoleon had it rebuilt after the British destroyed it in 1739.

From place d'Armes, walk or cycle south along rue de la Ferme and turn right at the crossroads. The **Conservatoire Botanique National Méditerranéen** (☎ 04 94 58 07 24; ☯ by appointment only May-Oct), 700m along this trail, has an open-air exhibition documenting the history of island flora, and a botanical trail that leads visitors through gardens featuring typical plants: 20 types of almond trees, 150 fig types, 83 lauriers rose types and numerous olive trees. The truly dedicated can learn all about palm tree varieties in the nearby **Jardin du Palmier** (☎ 04 94 58 07 24; rte du Phare; ☯ 9.30am-12.30pm & 1.30-5.15pm Mon-Fri Apr-Jun & Sep, 9.30am-12.30pm & 2.30-6.30pm Mon-Fri Jul & Aug), next to the Maison du Parc.

Two kilometres further along rue de la Ferme, on the tip of the cape, is the island's 82m-tall **lighthouse** (☎ 04 94 58 30 78; admission free; ☯ 11am-noon & 2-4pm Apr-Sep). Climb its winding stairs if the weather's clear for a stunning panorama from the top. A military semaphore (142m) northeast of here marks the highest point of the island; it cannot be visited.

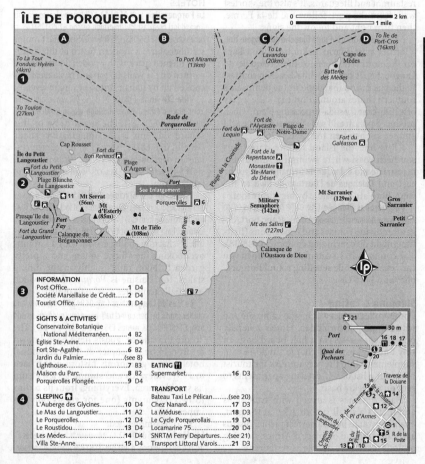

ÎLE DE PORQUEROLLES

INFORMATION
Post Office..............................1 D4
Société Marseillaise de Crédit.....2 D4
Tourist Office..........................3 D4

SIGHTS & ACTIVITIES
Conservatoire Botanique
  National Méditerranéen........4 B2
Église Ste-Anne.......................5 D4
Fort Ste-Agathe.......................6 B2
Jardin du Palmier....................(see 8)
Lighthouse..............................7 B3
Maison du Parc.......................8 B2
Porquerolles Plongée...............9 D4

SLEEPING
L'Auberge des Glycines............10 D4
Le Mas du Langoustier.............11 A2
Le Porquerolles......................12 D4
Le Roustidou..........................13 D4
Les Medes..............................14 D4
Villa Ste-Anne.........................15 D4

EATING
Supermarket............................16 D3

TRANSPORT
Bateau Taxi Le Pélican.........(see 20)
Chez Nanard............................17 D3
La Méduse..............................18 D3
Le Cycle Porquerollais..............19 D4
Locamarin 75...........................20 D4
SNRTM Ferry Departures.......(see 21)
Transport Littoral Varois...........21 D3

Porquerolles' vineyards cover a square kilometre of the western part of the island, and are tended by three wine producers. Each offers *dégustation* (tasting) sessions of their predominantly rosé wines; the tourist office has a list.

BEACHES

Porquerolles' northern coast is laced with beautiful sandy beaches, including **Plage de la Courtade**, signposted 800m east from the port (follow the track uphill behind the tourist office). **Plage de Notre-Dame**, Porquerolles' largest and most beautiful beach, is 2.5km further east along the same track. **Plage d'Argent**, 2km west of the village, is popular with families because of its summer beachside café-restaurant and lifeguards. It's also the shortest walk from the port; follow rue de la Ferme, then turn right and follow the signs.

More secluded is **Plage Blanche du Langoustier**, a former lobster farm 4.5km from the village on the northern shores of the Presqu'île du Langoustier. It's called 'white' beach in contrast to the black sand that darkens the peninsula's southern shores around Port Fay – the legacy of a 19th-century soda-processing plant, which produced potash and soda from sulphuric acid and sea salt between 1828 and 1876.

Cliffs line the island's more dangerous southern coast where swimming and diving is restricted to **Calanque du Brégançonnet** to the east and **Calanque de l'Oustaou de Diou** to the west. Both are accessible by bicycle or foot.

Porquerolles Plongée (☎ 04 98 04 62 22, 06 07 40 25 02; www.porquerolles-plongee.com), at the port, organises diving courses and expeditions (first-time/night dive including equipment €48/38). The company has a catamaran, on which you can breakfast while speeding round Porquerolles and Port-Cros.

Sleeping & Eating

Porquerolles is pricey. It has no camp site and wild camping is forbidden. Hotels generally only accept guests on a half-board basis in July and August, and charge single-person supplements into the bargain. Ask the tourist office for a list of self-catering apartments to rent on a weekly basis.

Place d'Armes is armed with fruit stalls and there's a small supermarket at the port, enabling you to build a perfect picnic. Bistros and cafés abound on place d'Armes; sleeping options listed here double as restaurants.

CHAMBRES D'HÔTES

Le Roustidou (☎ 04 94 58 31 54; www.leroustidou.com; 17 rue du Phare; d incl breakfast low/mid season €95/120, 1 week incl breakfast high season €840-980) Martine and Gilles make great hosts: open the sky-blue wooden shutters to their quintessential Porquerollais cottage and peek at three delightful home-away-from-home rooms (called Orange, Yellow and Blue), a small lush Mediterranean garden and a palm tree–shaded patio to breakfast on.

Also recommended:

Les Pescadous (☎ 06 16 12 46 23; www.lespescadous .com; chemin du Langoustier; d incl breakfast €120; ❂ Mar-Jun & Sep–mid-Nov) Two rooms, rose or green; pretty patio with chairs and flowery garden.

HOTELS

Le Porquerollais (☎ 04 94 12 32 70; www.leporquerollais .com; d incl breakfast low/mid/high season €105/125/145, tr mid/high season €155/185; ❂ Feb-Nov) Six smart rooms slumber above a modern bistro at this nautically themed space, with wooden floors and fish painted on the walls up top and pasta creations cooked up by Italian Bruno at square level.

Villa Ste-Anne (☎ 04 94 04 63 00; www.sainteanne .com; place d'Armes; d low/mid/high season €140/160/190, menus €18 & €23; ✖) The main draw of this square-side inn is the imaginative salads (small/large €8/14) served in its terrace restaurant overlooking the village *pétanque* pitch; staff will lend you a set of *boules* should you fancy a spin.

L'Auberge des Glycines (☎ 04 94 58 30 36; www .aubergedesglycines.net; place d'Armes; d incl breakfast low/ mid/high season from €99/149/249, d per person incl half-board low/mid/high season from €69/99/149; ✖) This absolutely charming village inn, with 11 rooms overlooking the village square and a pretty garden to boot, ranks highly in the dining stakes, too: cuisine is *Porquerollaise*, which essentially translates as 'shoals of fish'.

Le Mas du Langoustier (☎ 04 94 58 30 09; www.lang oustier.com; d per person incl half-board low/mid/high season from €175/198/208, menus €55, €68 & €88; ✖ ❒) The 'to die for' choice: guests have been known to drop in by helicopter at this exceptional hotel with a glamorous history going back to 1931, vineyards and stunning views from its seaside perch. Everything, from its rooms to two restaurants (one for guests only), is impeccable.

Also recommended:

Les Medes (☎ 04 94 12 41 24; www.hotel-les-medes .fr; rue de la Douane; d incl breakfast low/mid/high season

ST-TROPEZ TO TOULON

from €79/99/129; 🔆 🖳) New modern kid on the block with rooms for up to six people on a hotel or self-catering studio basis.

Getting There & Away

Regular boats operated by **Transport Littoral Varois** (TLV; www.tlv-tvm.com) link La Tour Fondue near Hyères (see Boat Excursions, p372) with Porquerolles year-round (adult/four to 10 years return €15.50/13.50). June to September, weekly boats sail to/from Toulon (p377), St-Tropez (p347) and Le Lavandou (p365).

June to September **SNRTM** (☎ 04 94 05 21 14) operates two or three boats daily from Port Miramar, south of La Londe, to Porquerolles.

Getting Around

Two options: foot or bicycle. Bike-rental costs around €12.50/9/29 per day for an adult's bike/child's bike/tandem and €12.50 a day for a *remorque* (buggy) to pedal two kids around in, or €2.30 for a child's bike seat. Outlets include **La Méduse** (☎ 04 94 58 34 27; 🕑 7am-6pm or 7pm Mar-Sep) and **Chez Nanard** (☎ 04 94 58 34 89; 🕑 7am-6pm or 7pm Mar-Sep) at the port; and **Le Cycle Porquerollais** (☎ 04 94 58 30 32; www.cycle-porquerollais .com; 1 rue de la Ferme; 🕑 year-round) in the village.

BOAT

At the port, **Locamarine 75** (☎ 04 94 58 35 84; www .locamarine75.com) rents out 6cv five-person speedboats (no licence required) from €75/80 per half-/full day.

The same company runs a 24-hour boat taxi service, **Bateau Taxi Le Pélican** (☎ 06 09 52 31 19).

ÎLE DE PORT-CROS

pop 40

France's smallest national park, Parc National de Port-Cros (see the table, p76), was created in 1963 to protect at least one small part of the Côte d'Azur's natural beauty from overdevelopment. The park encompasses the 7-sq-km island of Port-Cros and a 13-sq-km zone of water around it. Until the end of the 19th century, the islanders' vineyards and olive groves ensured their self-sufficiency. Today, tourism is their sustenance. Palm trees and tobacco plants imported from Argentina line the pretty port.

The island can be visited all year, but walkers must stick to the 30km of marked trails. Fishing, fires, camping, dogs, motorised vehicles and bicycles are not allowed, and smoking is forbidden outside the portside village.

The national park also manages its westerly neighbour **Île de Bagaud**, the fourth of the Îles d'Hyères. Its 40 hectares of dense vegetation are used for scientific research and are off limits to tourists.

Orientation & Information

Boats dock at the port in the village on the island's northwestern shores.

The **Maison du Parc** (☎ 04 94 01 40 70; 🕑 variable), at the port, has walking, diving and snorkelling information; and sells an island map marked with trails (€3.80) and various guides (in French) to underwater fauna and flora.

Sights & Activities

At the port, Jean-Jacques treats passengers to a 360-degree view of the sea life round Port-Cros aboard his ray-shaped, glass-bottom **Aquascope** (☎ 04 94 05 92 22, 06 08 26 91 99; adult/4-12yr €15/10; 🕑 hourly 9.30am-5pm high season). Trips take 30 minutes.

Plage de la Palud, on the island's northern shores, is a 30-minute walk from the 15th-century **Fort du Moulin**. From the beach, a 35-minute **sentier sous-marin** (underwater trail; 🕑 mid-Jun–mid-Sep) invites snorkellers to discover the park's marine flora and fauna, which include 500 algae species and 180 types of fish. **Sun Plongée** (☎ 04 94 05 90 16; www.sun-plongee .com), at the port, rents out masks, snorkel and flippers for €8/5 per day/half-day and also organises deep-sea dives (€36/28 with/without equipment hire). Minuscule **Îlot de la Gabinière**, an islet off Port-Cros' southern shore, is popular with experienced divers.

WALKING

From the portside post office, a track leads inland, from where 30km of footpaths crisscross the island. The Fort du Moulin is the starting point for a circular, 1½-hour **sentier des plantes** (botanical trail) to Plage de la Palud; it returns along an inland route. This trail also takes in imposing 16th-century **Fort de L'Estissac** (admission free; 🕑 10.30am-12.30pm & 1.30-5.30pm May, Jun & Sep, 10.30am-6pm Jul & Aug), host to summer exhibitions. Climb the tower for a panoramic view of Port-Cros.

The more demanding **sentier des crêtes** (crests trail; three hours) explores the southwestern corner of the island, and the slightly easier **sentier des Port-Man** (Port-Man trail; four hours) takes walkers to Port-Cros' northeastern tip.

Sleeping & Eating

Accommodation is limited and needs booking months in advance. At the port there are six rooms with sea-facing balconies at the **Maison du Port** (☎ 06 80 32 14 16), an idyllic fisherman's house with wooden sea-green shutters. Five restaurants offering sea-inspired cuisine surround the port.

Hostellerie Provençale (☎ 04 94 05 90 43; www .hostellerie-provencale.com; d per person incl half-board low/high season €95/110; ☺ Apr- Nov; ⚇) Run by the island's oldest and largest family since 1921, this bustling *hostellerie* sports five bright rooms with sunny windows facing the port; some have a balcony. Daughter Stéphanie – fourth generation to work here – tends the eye-catching cocktail bar on the waterfront. Look for canary-yellow sun umbrellas.

Le Manoir d'Hélène (☎ 04 94 05 90 52; lemanoir .portcros@wanadoo.fr; d low/high season per person incl half-board from €175/200, menus €43 & €54; ☺ mid-Apr–Sep; ⚇ ⚇) This atmospheric 23-room manor with white turreted façade, an aloof 300m from the port, is the exclusive option. Find it in a sweet-smelling eucalyptus grove with outdoor pool and upmarket restaurant.

Getting There & Away

Le Lavandou (p365) is the main stepping stone to Port-Cros and there are also frequent boats year-round to/from Hyères (p372).

June to September, boats sail several times weekly to/from Toulon (p377) and St-Tropez (p351). There are also crossings in July and August from Port Miramar, La Croix-Valmer and Cavalaire-sur-Mer.

ÎLE DU LEVANT
pop 200

Oddball Île du Levant, an 8km strip of an island, has a split personality. Ninety percent of it is a military camp and strictly off limits, and the remaining pocket of **Héliopolis** (on the island's northeastern tip) has been a nudist colony since the 1930s. Its tiny population increases tenfold in summer, when the village is overrun with bathers baring all.

Boats dock at **Port de l'Ayguade**, home to a summer **tourist information hut** (☎ 04 94 05 93 52; www.iledulevant.com.fr; ☺ 8am-7.30pm Easter–mid-Sep). Central square, place du Village, is 1km uphill along rte de l'Ayguade, the street running along Héliopolis' southern boundary.

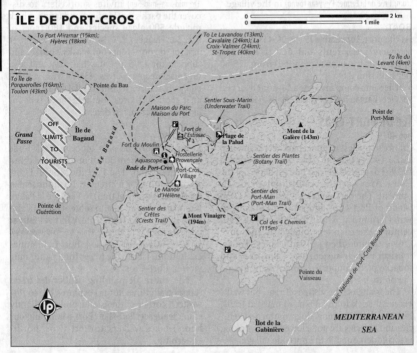

ÎLE DE PORT-CROS

ST-TROPEZ TO TOULON

The post office, cafés and hotels are clustered around this square. The island's camp site, **Colombero** (☎ 04 94 05 90 29; rte de l'Ayguade; camping per person €10; ☺ Easter-Sep), is 150m from the port.

The eastern part of the colony is covered by the **Domaine des Arbousiers**, a nature reservation with rare island plants like *Eryngium tricuspidatum* (a type of thistle). A nature trail leads east from place du Village into the protected area. The tourist office has information on guided tours.

Baring all is not obligatory – except on sandy **Plage Les Grottes**, the main nudist beach east of Port de l'Ayguade. From the port, walk in the direction of Plage de Sable Levant along **sentier Georges Rousseau**, a rocky coastal path. Bold signs reading *'Nudisme Intégral Obligatoire'* mark the moment you are required to strip.

Getting There & Away

Île du Levant is 10 minutes by boat from Port-Cros. Frequent boats sail year-round from Le Lavandou (p365) and Hyères (see p372), and in July and August from Port Miramar (La Londe), La Croix-Valmer and Cavalaire-sur-Mer.

ÎLE DE BENDOR

A place of exile during the 17th century, desolate pinprick Bendor was subsequently abandoned for 250 years. Then in 1951 along came Paul Ricard, a pastis millionaire, who transformed the islet into one of the most sanitised spots on the south coast.

The islet is filled by a leisure centre, which is dominated by larger-than-life Ricard creations, including the **Espace Culturel Paul Ricard** (☎ 04 94 29 44 34; admission free), where art exhibitions are held. There's also the **Exposition Universelle des Vins et Spiritueux** (admission free; ☺ 10am-noon & 2-6pm Tue-Sun), which unravels the history and production of wine and spirits. It's the port itself that's surreal, though, with its shrunken toy-town buildings and meticulously planned alleys and squares. Its shallow-sloping **beach**, with lifeguards, is perfect for tiny kids.

Bendor lies 300m offshore from Bandol, 19km east of Toulon.

Getting There & Away

Boats to Île de Bendor depart from Bandol (adult/four to 12 years return €7/5, seven minutes, every half-hour – fewer in winter – 7am and 2am year-round).

ÎLES DES EMBIEZ

Not content with owning just one island, Paul Ricard also bought the largest of the Embiez islets in 1958 – officially called Île de la Tour Fondue but better known as Îles des Embiez. It's home to the **Institut Océanographique Paul Ricard** (☎ 04 94 34 02 49; www.institut-paul-ricard.org; adult/4-11yr €4/2; ☺ 10am-12.30pm & 1.30-5.30pm Jul & Aug, closed Sat morning Sep-Jun & Wed & Sun morning Nov-Mar), where over 100 Mediterranean species swim around in 27 sea-water aquariums and a marine museum. The rest of the 95-hectare island is occupied by a vast pleasure port, pine forest, maquis scrub and vineyards, apartment blocks and a couple of posh hotels.

The Embiez archipelago lies less than 1km off the Presqu'île du Cap Sicié, between Sanary-sur-Mer and Toulon.

Getting There & Away

Boats (adult/three to 15 years return €10/6, 10 minutes, hourly July to September, less frequent October to June) sail year-round from the small port at Le Brusc, a beach resort adjoining Six-Fours-les-Plages, 5km south of Sanary-sur-Mer.

June to September there are four daily boats to/from Bandol (€10/6 return); see www.les-embiez.com (in French) for updated schedules and fares.

TOULON & AROUND

Relatively unspoilt coastline turns increasingly urban as you head west to Toulon and Marseille. A final pocket of blue and green surrounds **La Londe** (population 8840), midway between Le Lavandou and Hyères. Explore its olive groves, vineyards and flower gardens on guided walks organised by the **tourist office** (☎ 04 94 01 53 10; www.ot-lalondelesmaures.fr; av Albert Roux) or hire a bike and wine-taste by pedal power (see the boxed text, p373).

Two kilometres east, 450 species of tropical birds fly around the **Jardin d'Oiseaux Tropicaux** (☎ 04 94 35 02 15; www.jotropico.org; rte de Valcros; adult/3-12yr €8/5; ☺ 9.30am-7pm Jun-Sep, 2-6pm Oct & Feb-May, 2-5.30pm Nov-Jan), signposted off the N98.

Port Miramar, 3km south of La Londe, is a landing stage for seasonal boats (April to September) to/from Porquerolles (adult/four to 10 years €21/14) and to/from Port-Cros (€23/15).

ST-TROPEZ TO TOULON

HYÈRES

pop 52,000

With its veteran palm trees, colonial air and intact Vieille Ville (Old Town), Hyères retains much of the charm that made it the Côte d'Azur's first resort. Tolstoy took a winter 'cure' here in 1860; Robert Louis Stevenson claimed it was the only place he'd ever been truly happy (he came here in 1886 to work on *Kidnapped*), while Queen Victoria herself breezed through in 1892.

Pink flamingos add a splash of colour to the otherwise barren landscape of **La Capte**, two narrow sand bars supporting saltpans (Les Salins des Presquiers) and a lake (Étang des Presquiers), 4km south of Hyères centre. The spectacular western sand bar road – the **route du Sel** (Salt Rd) – is only accessible in summer. Buses use the eastern bar road (the D42), the northern section of which is graced with a two-lane cycling track that runs for 2km from the beach resort of **L'Ayguade** to the roundabout in front of Toulon-Hyères airport.

At the foot of La Capte sits beach-lined **Presqu'île de Giens**, which briefly became an island in the huge storms of 1811. French poet and 1960 Nobel Literature prize-winner, St-John Perse (1887–1975), is buried in the tiny cemetery off rte Madrague, on the peninsula's northwestern shore.

Orientation

Hyères' medieval Vieille Ville is perched on a hillside north of the new town. The nearest beach is La Capte. Pleasure port, Port d'Hyères, from where boats to Le Levant and Port-Cros depart, is on La Capte's eastern shore. Boats to Porquerolles use La Tour Fondue – the port on the southeastern corner of Presqu'île de Giens.

The train station is 1.5km south of the old town. Walk northeast from the station along av Edith Cavelland to place du 11 Novembre, then north along av Gambetta, the main street into the new town; or catch the bus (p375).

Information

Cyber Espace Genyweb (☎ 04 94 33 43 86; www .genyweb.fr; 4 rue Pierre Brossolette; per 30min/1hr €2/3; ◔ 9am-9pm Mon-Sat)

Post office (av Joseph Clotis)

Tourist office (☎ 04 94 01 84 50; www.ot-hyeres.fr; 3 av Ambroise Thomas; ◔ 9am-6pm Mon-Fri, 10am-4pm Sat)

Sights & Activities

A wonderful jumble of secondhand furniture, floor tiles, clothes, olives and lavender-spiced marmalade fills **place Georges Clemenceau** during the Saturday morning market. Thirteenth-century **Porte Massillon**, on the square's western side, is the main entrance to the Vieille Ville. West along cobbled rue Massillon is beautiful arcaded **rue des Porches**.

Returning to the market square, walk north to 13th-century **Église St-Louis**, a fine example of sober, Romanesque-style architecture. Weave uphill to rue Bourgneuf, then walk west along its continuation, rue St-Esprit, to the limestone arch of **Porte Barruc**. From here, steps pass an iron gate to the rambling hillside grove of **Parc St-Bernard**. Remnants of the 12th-century defensive city wall and Château St-Bernard are visible.

The imposing villa below the walls is **Villa Noailles** (☎ 04 94 01 84 30; ◔ during visiting exhibitions, plus guided tours on request Wed-Mon mid-Jun–mid-Sep), designed by Robert Mallet-Stevens in 1923 for devoted patron of modern art Vicomte Charles de Noailles. Commissioned to build a winter residence 'interesting to inhabit', he created a cubist maze of concrete and glass in a Mediterranean park. The cubist garden was designed by Gabriel Guévrékian in 1925.

Back downhill along rue Barbacane is 12th-century **Porte St-Paul**. The oldest city gate, it frames **Collégiale St-Paul** (◔ 10am-noon Wed-Sat year-round, plus 3-6.30pm Mon & Wed-Sat Apr-Oct), two churches dating from the 12th and 14th centuries joined together perpendicularly. The Gothic section houses a vast collection of predominantly 18th-century, ex-votive paintings.

West of Porte St-Paul, rue St-Paul and rue Ste-Claire lead to **Parc Castel Ste-Claire**, a 17th-century convent converted into a private residence and home to American writer Edith Wharton from 1927. Today the headquarters of the **Parc National de Port-Cros** (☎ 04 94 12 82 30; www.portcrosparcnational.fr; 50 rue Ste-Claire) resides here. The grounds can be freely strolled.

BOAT EXCURSIONS

Boats operated by **Transport Littoral Varois** (TLV; ☎ 04 94 58 21 81; www.tlv-tvm.com) sail from Hyères to the three Îles d'Hyères year-round.

Gare Maritime de La Tour Fondue (☎ 04 94 58 21 81) on the Presqu'île de Giens is the departure point for **glass-bottom boat rides** (☎ 04 94 58 95 14; adult/4-10yr €12/9) that do a nonstop circuit

ST-TROPEZ TO TOULON

PEDAL-POWERED WINE TASTING

From La Londe, follow the main street south, and at the traffic lights turn onto av Général de Gaulle following signs for 'Le Port-les Îles-les Plages-Fort de Brégançon'. Continue for 400m, cross the roundabout, and carry on for 700m to **Syril Bikes** (☎ 04 94 15 92 99; bike/tandem per day €10.50/30; ☺ 9am-noon & 2-7pm) where you can pick up a set of wheels and the start of La Londe's pea-green cycling track. Soon after, scenic views of perfectly kempt, symmetrical rows of vine – a vibrant green against the arid red soil – kick in. At the next roundabout, detour 1km to **Plage d'Argentière** for a dip in the sea and snorkel along an **aquatic nature trail** (☺ May-Sep), or continue east along the D42a following signs for 'Fort de Bregançon'.

You're now plump on the **Route des Vins de la Londe**, with pretty **Château des Bormettes** (☎ 04 94 66 81 35; www.chateaudesbormettes.com; rte de Bregançon), framed by nine sky-high palm trees, your first port of call on this scenic wine trail. The oldest of the 70 hectares of vines at this lumbering chateau, owned by the Faré family (they live in Paris, holiday here), were planted in 1929. Pedal 2km down the silky-smooth lane and you come to another dreamy chateau with sage-green shutters where **Clos Mireille** (☎ 04 94 01 53 50; www.domaines-ott.com; rte de Brégançon), one of the region's most highly regarded wines, has been produced since 1896. Pay €17 to €28 a bottle.

At the next junction bear right towards the fort and Bormes-les-Mimosas. Two needle pines mark the entrance to **Domaine de la Sanglière** (☎ 04 94 00 48 58; www.domaine-sangliere.com; 3886 rte de Léoube), where you can buy tasty wild boar and hazelnut terrine alongside wine. Some 200m further east is the entrance to **Plage du Pellegrin** (€7 per day), the private beach of vast, less personal **Château de Léoube**, 1.7km further down the road. Stock up on fresh seasonal fruit at the fruit stall 700m east of the chateau and carry on 200m to **Parc de l'Esagnot** (☎ 04 94 64 78 76; www.estagnol.com; per car/bicycle €7/0.50) for a picnic on its white sandy beach. Lunch done, leap back on the saddle and pedal for 500m to **Château de Brégançon** (☎ 04 94 64 80 73; www .chateaudebregancon.fr; 639 rte de Léoube), a shabby old chateau with 40-year-old vines covering 52 hectares. Its Reserve du Château white is a brilliant marriage with shellfish.

Don't confuse the chateau with 16th- to 18th-century **Fort de Brégançon**, signposted 500m further east down the road along the D42d on the western side of **Cap de Brégançon**. Once in front of the heavily guarded entrance to the fort where the president of France summers (he's done so since 1968), park up (per car/bicycle €7/2) and flop out on the rocky cape's gorgeous beach, sandy **Plage de Cabasson**.

to Porquerolles and back. There are up to five sailings from Sunday to Friday, May to September.

It's also the departure point for boats to/ from **Porquerolles** (adult/child return €15/13.50). Trips take 20 minutes, leaving every 30 minutes from 7.30am to 6.30pm or 7pm May to September, with six to 10 daily crossings October to April. **Porquerolles/Port-Cros two-island tours** (adult/child return €27/23) depart Monday to Friday in July and August.

Port d'Hyères (Port de la Gavine; ☎ 04 94 57 44 07) on La Capte is the departure point for **Port-Cros trips** (adult/child return €23/20), a one-hour trip that leaves at least once daily year-round with up to four daily in high season; **Île du Levant trips** (adult/child return €23/20), taking 1½ hours, with at least one return sailing daily year-round; and **Île du Levant/Port-Cros two-island tours** (adult/child return €26/22), departing daily July and August.

DIVING

Presqu'île de Giens and Îles d'Hyères are excellent dive sites, with atmospheric shipwrecks sunk around the coast, including the *Donator* and the *Grec*. The tourist office has a list of the eight-odd diving clubs in town, among them **Sub Plongée** (☎ 04 94 58 25 30; www .sub-plongee.com; 109 rte de Giens, allée du Pousset) and **Ulysse Club** (☎ 04 94 58 25 07; www.ulysseclub.com; Port de la Madrague).

SURFING

The beaches at L'Almanarre, at the northern end of the Presqu'île de Giens, are internationally renowned for windsurfing and kitesurfing. For lessons (around €23 for windsurfing, €70 for a maiden kitesurf) and gear rental, **Funboard Center** (☎ 04 94 57 95 33; www.funboardcenter.com; rte L'Almanarre) is your all-year-round man; several other places open in summer.

ST-TROPEZ TO TOULON

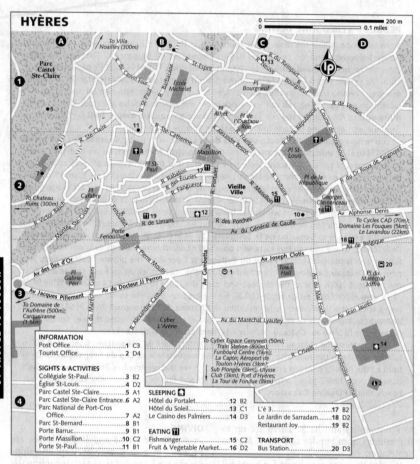

HYÈRES

INFORMATION
Post Office..1 C3
Tourist Office......................................2 D4

SIGHTS & ACTIVITIES
Collégiale St-Paul..............................3 B2
Église St-Louis...................................4 D2
Parc Castel Ste-Claire........................5 A1
Parc Castel Ste-Claire Entrance.......6 A2
Parc National de Port-Cros
    Office...7 A2
Parc St-Bernard..................................8 B1
Porte Barruc.......................................9 B1
Porte Massillon.................................10 C2
Porte St-Paul.....................................11 B1

SLEEPING
Hôtel du Portalet..............................12 B2
Hôtel du Soleil..................................13 C1
Le Casino des Palmiers.....................14 D3

EATING
Fishmonger.......................................15 C2
Fruit & Vegetable Market.................16 D2

L'é 3..17 B2
Le Jardin de Sarradam......................18 D2
Restaurant Joy..................................19 B2

TRANSPORT
Bus Station.......................................20 D3

Sleeping

With nine-odd sites, the Presqu'île de Giens is a camper's delight; the tourist office has a list.

CHAMBRES D'HÔTES

Domaine de l'Aufrène (☎ 04 94 65 45 89; www.aufrene.com; 83 Vieux Chemin de Toulon; d incl breakfast €80-130; **P** **⊠**) It might be a short 1km stroll into town, but the quintessential Provençal charm you'll find oozing out of every last 18th-century stone at this gorgeous *bastide* – which has been in Sylvie and Franck's family since 1880 – more than compensates. Its gardens, not to mention a pool and kids' play area, make it an ideal family choice.

HOTELS

Hôtel du Portalet (☎ 04 94 65 39 40; www.hotel-portalet.com; 4 rue de Limans; s/d/tr €37/42/65) There is not really that much style to this typically Provençal hotel, snug at the bottom of the hill in the Vieille Ville. But rooms are large and airy; triples tout balconies; and there are even a couple of rooms with shared toilet and shower (€33) for those travelling on a shoestring.

Hôtel du Soleil (☎ 04 94 65 16 26; www.hoteldusoleil.com; rue du Rempart; s/d/tr/q low season from €30/40/50/60, high season from €50/70/90/100) Teetering precariously at the top of a vertical medieval street (read: not for the unfit or the suitcase-laden arriving on foot), this two-star, ivy-clad place is easily Hyères' most charming and loveliest hotel – glowingly recommended.

Le Casino des Palmiers (☎ 04 94 12 80 80; www .europe.casinos.com; 1 av Ambroise Thomas; d low/high season from €90/110; **P** ⊠) Top-notch, four-star accommodation with all mod cons and a hint of nostalgia for the resort's golden age is what Hyères' best hotel – inside the town's plush, glass-topped casino – is all about.

Eating
The old town is restaurant-stuffed, peaking with place Massillon – one big terrace restaurant in summer.

L'é3 (☎ 04 94 28 61 02; 3 place Massillon; mains €8-12; ⊙ lunch & dinner) There might be no more than 10-odd dishes to pick from at this superfriendly one-man show, but every one is guaranteed to ooze imagination. Creole platters, clam and mango *brochettes* (kebabs) or a hot box of Camembert are among the colourful world-cuisine temptations. Fun, casual and overtly contemporary is the spirit of the place.

Restaurant Joy (☎ 04 94 20 84 98; 24 rue de Limans; mains €16-29, menus €17, €25 & €29; ⊙ lunch & dinner Mon-Sat high season, lunch & dinner Tue-Sat low season) This modern striking restaurant with a contemporary interior (partly no smoking) and menu to match is a culinary joy. Red, white and steel steal the show alongside several risottos and fantastic cinnamon-spiced foie gras in the company of onions, ginger and pineapple chutney. Cuisine is world inspired.

Le Jardin de Sarradam (☎ 04 94 65 97 53; 35 av de Belgique; tajines from €16; ⊙ closed dinner Sun, plus Mon low season) Mediterranean and Oriental cuisine is served in a flowerpot-filled garden near the bus station. For an Arabian Nights feel, round off your meal with syrupy mint tea poured from a silver pot.

Self-catering:
Fishmonger (rue Massillon; ⊙ morning only)
Fruit & Vegetable Market (place Georges Clemenceau; ⊙ 8am-1pm Sat)

Getting There & Away
AIR
Towards La Capte, **Aéroport de Toulon-Hyères** (Toulon-Hyères airport; ☎ 08 25 01 83 87; http://aero port.var .cci.fr; blvd de la Marine) is 3km south of Hyères.

BUS
From the **bus station** (place du Maréchal Joffre), **Sodetrav** (☎ 08 25 00 06 50; www.sodetrav.fr) runs seven buses daily to/from Toulon (€1.40, one hour), Le Lavandou (€6.50, 30 minutes) and St-Tropez (€14.90, 1¼ hours).

TRAIN
From Hyères **train station** (place de l'Europe), there are around eight local trains per day to/from Toulon (€3.70, 20 minutes). The Marseille–Hyères train (€12.60, 1¼ hours, four daily) stops at Cassis, La Ciotat, Bandol, Ollioules-Sanary and Toulon.

Getting Around
TO/FROM THE AIRPORT
Sodetrav runs shuttle buses between Toulon-Hyères airport and Hyères bus station (€1.40, 10 minutes). During the summer there are also regular daily services from the airport to Toulon and St-Tropez; buses coincide with flight arrivals and departures.

BICYCLE
Rent mountain bikes at **Cycles CAD** (☎ 04 94 65 07 69; 59 av Alphonse Denis) for around €12 per day.

BUS
Buses costing €1.40 link Hyères bus station with the train station (five minutes), Port d'Hyères (15 minutes), La Capte (20 minutes), Giens (30 minutes) and La Tour de Fondue (35 minutes). Buses run almost every 30 minutes between 6.25am and 10pm.

For La Tour de Fondue (boats to Porquerolles), get off at the Tour Fondue stop. For Port d'Hyères (boats to Îles du Levant and Port-Cros), get off at Le Port stop, av de la Méditerranée.

FARM CUISINE

For lunch on the farm – an organic one at that – make a beeline for **Domaine Les Fouques** (☎ 04 94 65 68 19; rte de Hyères, Pierrefeu du Var; adult/child menu €23/11; ⊙ by reservation only dinner Tue & Fri Jul & Aug, lunch Sun Oct-Jun), a wine-producing estate with 19th-century palm tree–framed farmhouse, 45 hectares of vines and a gaggle of chickens, guinea-fowl, capons and ducks running around. Feast on organic farm produce in the company of a Côtes de Provence AOC white, red or refreshing rosé served by hosts Michèle and Yves Gros. Find this *ferme auberge* 5km northeast of Hyères, signposted off the D12 to Pierrefeu du Var.

CAP DE CARQUEIRANNE

Immediately west of Hyères, pretty Cap de Carqueiranne is a partly forested stretch of headland, crisscrossed by tiny lanes. The coastal path that edges its way from the town of Carqueiranne is a particularly scenic means of exploring the cape.

Romantic images are conjured up by the **Site Archaéologique d'Olbia** (☎ 04 94 57 98 28; adult/ under 18yr €5/free; ☑ 9.30am-12.30pm & 3-6pm Thu & Fri, 3-6pm Tue & Sat Apr-Sep), the remnants of a sea port founded by the Greeks in the 4th century BC; there are Roman remains there too. The site is in **L'Almanarre**, at the Presqu'île de Giens' northwesternmost tip.

In **La Garonne** the **Musée de la Mine** (☎ 04 94 08 32 46; www.mine-capgaronne.fr; chemin du Bau Rouge; adult/6-18yr €6.20/3.80; ☑ 2-6pm school holidays, 2-5pm Jul & Aug, 2-5pm Wed, Sat & Sun rest of year) is a disused copper mine where the cape's mineral traditions are delved into. Local bus 91 links Toulon with the mine.

TOULON

pop 168,000

Toulon provokes the reaction a tramp might get in St-Tropez: its seedy rough-cut demeanour just doesn't fit in with the glittering Côte d'Azur. But this is a city on the move. Since becoming mayor in 2002, former government minister and passionate local Hubert Falco has pulled out all the stops to revitalise France's second-largest naval port: the dumpy old bus station has been transformed into a state-of-the-art glass affair, spiffy design-driven bars and bistros are opening, and newly planted palm trees fringe the polished central square, place de la Liberté.

Toulon is no longer so terrible. Some even like this busy port's down-to-earth grit, its buskers and street markets, its tatty bar-laden quarter near the water awash with sailors and locals, and its gaggle of fountains reflecting its watery origins: Toulon is named after Télo, a Celtic-Ligurian goddess of springs.

The city's funniest contemporary product is lovable comic actor Raimu. See his statue on place des Trois Dauphins in the old town.

Orientation

Toulon is built around a *rade*, a sheltered bay lined with quays. To the west is the naval base, and east, the ferry terminal, where boats set sail for Corsica. The city is at its liveliest along quai de la Sinse and quai Cronstadt – from where ferries depart for the Îles d'Hyères – and in the pedestrianised old city. Northwest of the old city is the train station.

Separating the old city from the northern section is a multilane, multinamed thoroughfare (av du Maréchal Leclerc and blvd de Strasbourg as it runs through the centre).

Information

Commercial banks line blvd de Strasbourg.

Cyberespace (☎ 04 98 00 69 11; 61 rue Marquetas; per 15min €0.70; ☑ 10am-10pm)

Hôpital Font-Pré (☎ 04 94 61 60 03; 1208 av Colonel Picot)

Post office (rue Dr Jean Bertholet) Entrance on rue Ferrero too.

Toulon Webcafé (☎ 04 94 22 95 16; http://toulonweb café.free.fr; 33 rue des Boucheries; ☑ 10am-10pm Tue-Sat) Trendy bar with wi-fi, several terminals and DJs mixing from 7pm.

Tourist office (☎ 04 94 18 53 00; www.toulontouris me.com; 335 av de la République; ☑ 9am-6pm Mon & Wed-Sat, 10am-6pm Tue, 10am-noon Sun Jun-Sep, 9.30am-5.30pm Mon & Wed-Sat, 10.30am-5.30pm Tue, 10am-noon Sun Oct-May)

Sights & Activities

An electric **tourist train** (☎ 06 20 77 44 42; adult/ 3-12yr €5/2.50; ☑ 11am & every 30min 2-4pm) chugs from the port to Pointe de la Mître in the beach-rich suburb of Le Mourillon.

MONT FARON

Overlooking the old city from the northern side is Mont Faron (584m), from where you can see Toulon's red-roofed houses and the epic port in its true magnificence. Not far from the hill's summit rises the **Mémorial du Débarquement de Provence** (☎ 04 94 88 08 09; adult/8-18yr €3.80/1.55; ☑ 10am-noon & 2-5.30pm May-Sep, to 4.30pm May-Sep), which commemorates the Allied landings that took place along the coast here in August 1944. Historical displays and a film form part of this fascinating museum.

The Med's only cable car, the **Téléphérique du Mont Faron** (☎ 04 94 92 68 25; adult/4-10yr €5.80/4; ☑ 9.30am-7.45pm Jul & Aug, 9.30am-12.15pm & 2-5.30pm Tue-Sun Feb, to 5.45pm Mar, to 6pm Apr & Oct, to 6.15pm May, to 7pm Jun & Sep, to 5.15pm Nov, closed windy days) climbs the mountain from blvd Amiral Vence. Kids love **Zoo du Faron** (☎ 04 94 88 07 89; adult/4-10yr €8/5; ☑ 10am-6.30pm May-Sep, 2-5.30pm Oct-Apr), a wildcat breeding centre: combination zoo/cable-car tickets cost adult/four to 10 years €11/7.50.

ST-TROPEZ TO TOULON

MAKE A DAY OF IT

'Un petit coin de paradis pour amoureux de simplicité et de convivialité' ('a little corner of paradise for lovers of simplicity and conviviality') is how **Les Oursinières** markets itself – for good reason. Tucked away from the madding crowd on the southwestern shore of Cap de Carqueiranne, the tiny harbour port is picture-postcard delightful. Make a day of its charms by diving with the **Centre de Plongée du Pradet** (☎ 04 94 08 38 09; http://perso.orange.fr/cppradet), followed by lunch at legendary **L'Oursinado** (☎ 04 94 21 77 06; chemin du Pas des Gardéens; menu €39; ⏱ lunch & dinner Thu-Mon, lunch Tue), hidden on a cliff above the boats (by car follow the signs) and famed for its fabulous Toulonnais *bouillabaisse* (fish stew; €38; order 48 hours in advance), which has potatoes in it as well as a shoal of fish. Its tree-framed terrace, where meals are served, looks down onto pounding waves and the huge blue sea.

Local buses 39 and 92 link Toulon with Les Oursinières (€1.40, hourly 6.45am to 6pm), and a two-way cycling track links Toulon and the cape.

To get to the cable car, take bus 40 from place de la Liberté to the *téléphérique* stop. The tourist office has mountains of information on walking and mountain-bike trails on Mont Faron.

MUSEUMS

Top of the 'to-see' list is the **Musée de la Marine** (Marine Museum; ☎ 04 94 02 02 01; place Monsenergue; adult/under 18yr €5/free; ⏱ 10am-5pm Wed-Mon), inside Toulon's lovely 18th-century arsenal building. The seafaring museum contains marvellous models of old sailing ships and paintings illustrating Toulon's history: the city only became part of France in 1481, growing in importance after Henri IV established its arsenal. In the 17th century the port was enlarged by Vauban.

An unexceptional **Musée d'Art** (Art Museum; ☎ 04 94 36 81 00; 113 blvd Maréchal Leclerc; admission free; ⏱ noon-6pm Tue-Sun) and a moth-eaten **Musée d'Histoire Naturelle** (Natural History Museum; admission free; ⏱ 9am-6pm Mon-Fri, 11am-6pm Sat & Sun) share the same Renaissance-style building. Small but of high calibre are the photographic works exhibited at the **Maison de la Photographie** (☎ 04 94 93 07 59; place du Globe; admission free; ⏱ noon-6pm Tue-Sat mid-Jun—mid-Sep, 1-7pm Tue-Sat mid-Jun—mid-Sep) and the temporary art exhibitions hosted by **Hôtel des Arts** (☎ 04 94 91 69 18; 236 blvd General Leclerc; admission free; ⏱ 11am-6pm Tue-Sun).

BOAT EXCURSIONS

Several companies run one-hour **boat trips** (adult/4-10yr €9/5.50) around the bay and Port Militaire with a French-only commentary on events that took place here during WWII. Boats depart from quai Cronstadt.

In July and August **Bateliers de la Rade** (☎ 04 94 46 24 65; quai de la Sinse) runs a daily boat trip to Porquerolles (adult/four to 10 years €22/11) and a weekdays-only circuit of Porquerolles, Levant and Port-Cros (€30/16).

Shuttle boats run by **Réseau Mistral** (☎ 04 94 03 87 03; www.reseaumistral.com) link quai Cronstadt with towns on the peninsula across the harbour, including La Seyne, St-Mandrier-sur-Mer and Sablettes. Tickets for the 20-minute journeys cost €2 at the portside ticket office. Boats sail 6am to 8pm.

Sleeping

There are plenty of cheap options in the old city, though some (particularly those at the western end of rue Jean Jaurès) are rumoured to double as brothels.

Hôtel Molière (☎ 04 94 92 78 35; hotel.moliere@tiscali.fr; 12 rue Molière; s with washbasin €22, s/d with shower €27/32, d with shower & toilet €38-44) Evidence that living is cheap: Molière sits right in the heart of things with tiny balconies looking out onto the opera house and its bustling square. Use of the hallway shower will cost you a pricey €4.

Hôtel Bonaparte (☎ 04 94 93 07 51; 16 rue Anatole France; d €55; 🐾) Completely overhauled a few years back, this charming boutique hotel still gleams. It's well placed for the port, and the huge place d'Armes car park is just opposite. Bedroom walls are sponged yellow, and staff are sweet and cheerful.

Grand Hôtel Dauphiné (☎ 04 94 92 20 28; www.grandhoteldauphine.com; 10 rue Berthelot; s/d/tr €50/56/70; P 🐾) Rooms are large and comfy, and people guard your car for you (€7.80) as you sleep at this reputable midranger, part of the Logis de France chain, to boot. Better still, it's

ST-TROPEZ TO TOULON

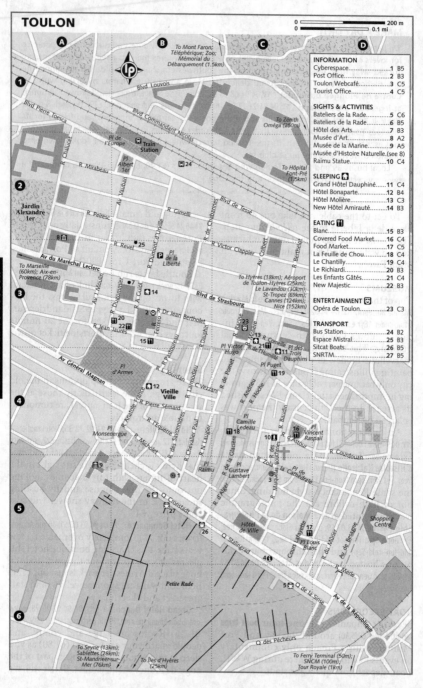

TOULON

| 0 | 200 m |
| 0 | 0.1 mi |

To Mont Faron;
Téléphérique; Zoo;
Mémorial du
Débarquement (1.5km)

To Zénith
Oméga (250m)

Blvd Louvois

Blvd Pierre Toesca

Blvd Commandant Nicolas

Pl de
l'Europe
Train
Station

To Hôpital
Font-Pré
(1.5km)

R. Mirabeau

Pl Albert
1er

R. Vauban

R. Gimelli

Blvd de Tessé

R. Peiresc

R. de Chabannes

R. Victor Clappier

R. Colbert

R. Berthelot

Jardin
Alexandre
1er

Av du Maréchal Leclerc

R. Revel

Pl
de la
Liberté

To Marseille
(60km); Aix-en-
Provence (78km)

R. J. Moulin

R. Dumont d'Urville

To Hyères (18km); Aéroport
de Toulon-Hyères (25km);
Le Lavandou (30km);
St-Tropez (69km);
Cannes (124km);
Nice (152km)

Blvd de Strasbourg

R. A. Guiol

R. Dupleix

R. Ferrero

R. Dr Jean Bertholet

R. Racine

R. Lucre

R. de l'Humilité

Pl des
Trois
Dauphins

R. Corneille

R. Jean Jaurès

R. Pastoureau

R. Dauphin

Pl Victor
Hugo

R. d'Alger

Pl Puget

Av Général Magnan

Pl
d'Armes

R. L. Jourdan

R. de Pomet

R. Andrieu

R. Hoche

Vieille
Ville

R. Anatole France

R. Pierre Sémard

R. l'Équerre

C Vezzani

R. Lamodieu

R. des Savonnières

R. Chevalier Paul

R. N. Laugier

Pl
Camille
Ledeau

R. Baudin

Pl
Vincent
Raspail

R. Courdouan

Pl
Monsenergue

R. Michelet

R. de la Glacière

R. Zola

R. d'Astour

Shopping
Centre

Pl
Raimu

Pl
Gustave
Lambert

R. Maquis Boudrous

Pl de
la Cathédrale

Cronstadt

Av de Bressigne

Hôtel
de Ville

Pl
Louis
Blanc

R. du Mûrier

Cours Lafayette

R. Merle

Q Stalingrad

Av de la République

Petite Rade

Q de la Sirène

To Seyne (13km);
Sablettes (28km);
St-Mandrée-sur-
Mer (76km)

To Îles d'Hyères
(25km)

Q des Pêcheurs

To Ferry Terminal (50m);
SNCM (100m);
Tour Royale (1km)

INFORMATION
Cyberspace	1 B5
Post Office	2 B3
Toulon Webcafé	3 C5
Tourist Office	4 C5

SIGHTS & ACTIVITIES
Bateliers de la Rade	5 C6
Bateliers de la Rade	6 B5
Hôtel des Arts	7 B3
Musée d'Art	8 A2
Musée de la Marine	9 A5
Musée d'Histoire Naturelle	(see 8)
Raimu Statue	10 C4

SLEEPING
Grand Hôtel Dauphiné	11 C4
Hôtel Bonaparte	12 B4
Hôtel Molière	13 C3
New Hôtel Amirauté	14 B3

EATING
Blanc	15 B3
Covered Food Market	16 C4
Food Market	17 C5
La Feuille de Chou	18 C4
Le Chantilly	19 C4
Le Richiardi	20 C4
Les Enfants Gâtés	21 C4
New Majestic	22 B3

ENTERTAINMENT
Opéra de Toulon	23 C3

TRANSPORT
Bus Station	24 B2
Espace Mistral	25 B3
Sitcat Boats	26 B5
SNRTM	27 B5

on a pedestrian street in the old town, meaning no screeching traffic noise.

New Hôtel Amirauté (☎ 04 94 22 19 67; www .new-hotel.com; 4 rue A Guiol; s/d €78/85; 🔀) Indeed a middle-of-the-road, could-be-anywhere-in-the-world chain hotel, but beggars can't be choosers in Toulon. Three stars add a bright, cheerful touch to its 38 rooms where a mix of fancy door handles and strangely shaped bed-heads relieve the business-style blandness.

Eating

Restaurants and bars with occasional live music are abundant along the quays. Another buzzing eating area is in front of the opera house on place Victor Hugo and neighbouring place Puget.

Le Chantilly (☎ 04 94 92 24 37; place Puget; mains €12.50-15; 🕓 7am-8.30pm, lunch served noon-2pm) At the 'tradition' end of the atmosphere spectrum is this century-old institution, an old-fashioned brasserie that seems to have scarcely changed since opening in 1907. Raimu loved the place, as do loyal locals who pack it full for lunch (the only meal served here).

Blanc (☎ 04 94 10 20 40; 51 rue Jean Jaurès; lunch menu incl 50cl wine €14; 🕓 lunch & dinner Wed-Sun) One of a clutch of modern and minimalist dining and drinking spaces that are creating a new buzz in Toulon, White is a bistro run by a young dynamic team, all out to impress.

New Majestic (☎ 04 94 91 61 66; 56 rue Jean Jaurès; 🕓 7am-11pm Mon-Sat) Across the road from Toulon's sleekest address sits this Italian-inspired lounge bar-cum-bistro-cum-space to hang out – perfect for an early morning coffee, lunch, afternoon ice or evening apéritif. A young team are likewise the creative force behind the funky, all-lilac, chandelier-lit interior.

Le Richiardi (☎ 04 94 64 66 39; rue Dugommier; mains €13-22, lunch menu €14.50; 🕓 lunch & dinner Mon-Sat) Ceiling-to-floor windows allow passers-by to see precisely what's going on in this theatrical dining space, kitted out with crushed-velvet opera chairs and modern art on the bright white walls. Make sure you don't miss the old penguin mosaic located above the entrance.

Lovely lunch recommendations:

La Feuille de Chou (☎ 04 94 62 09 26; 15 rue de la Glacière; plat du jour €9.80, lunch menus €15-30; 🕓 lunch Mon-Sat Mar-Jan) Lunch beneath olive trees on a pretty square.

Les Enfants Gâtés (Spoilt Children; ☎ 04 94 09 14 67; 7 rue Corneille; mains €15; 🕓 lunch Mon-Fri low season, lunch & dinner Mon-Fri high season) Literary café serving Provençal dishes and basil-rich Italian suppers.

Self-catering options include the **outside food market** (cours Lafayette; 🕓 morning Tue-Sun) and **covered food market** (place Vincent Raspail; 🕓 Tue-Sun).

Entertainment

Operas and ballets are staged at **Opéra de Toulon** (☎ 04 94 93 03 76, ticket office 04 94 92 70 78; place Victor Hugo; tickets €15-50).

Prime venue for rock, pop and big-band concerts is **Zénith Oméga** (☎ 04 94 22 66 77; www .zenith-omega-toulon.com; blvd du Commandant Nicolas).

Getting There & Away

AIR
Aéroport de Toulon-Hyères (Toulon-Hyères airport; ☎ 04 94 00 83 83; www.toulon-hyeres.aeroport.fr) is 25km east of the city.

BOAT
SNCM (☎ 3260 SNCM; 49 av de l'Infanterie de Marine) sells tickets for ferries to/from Corsica (p422) and Sardinia (p421).

See p372 for boats to or from the Îles d'Hyères.

BUS
Toulon's state-of-the-art glass box **bus station** (☎ 04 94 24 60 00; www.transports.var.fr; blvd de Tessé) is to the left as you exit the train station. Services include to/from Hyères (€1.40, 40 minutes), Le Lavandou (€11.60, 1¼ hours), St-Tropez (€18.20, 2¼ hours, seven daily) and Nice (€25, 2½ hours, two daily Monday to Saturday).

TRAIN
From the **train station** (place de l'Europe) there are frequent connections to numerous coastal cities, including Marseille (€10.20, one hour), St-Raphaël (€13.40, one hour), Cannes (€17.50, 1¼ hours), Nice (€20.80, two hours), Antibes (€18.70, 1½ hours), Monaco (€22.30, 2½ hours) and Menton (€22.30, 2½ hours).

Getting Around

TO/FROM THE AIRPORT
Shuttle buses timed to coincide with flight arrivals/departures link Toulon-Hyères airport with Toulon train station (€1.40, 40 minutes).

ST-TROPEZ TO TOULON

BUS

Local buses are run by **Réseau Mistral** (☎ 04 94 03 87 03; www.reseaumistral.com). Buy tickets (€1.40/9.60 per one/10-ticket carnet) from the **Espace Mistral** (16 rue Revel; ⏰ 7.30am-7pm Mon-Fri, 8am-noon & 1.30-6.30pm Sat), off place de la Liberté. Buses run until 9pm but some night buses exist (€4). Sunday service is limited.

TAXI

Pick up a taxi in front of the train station or call ☎ 04 94 93 51 51.

TOWARDS MARSEILLE

Before hitting sizzling Marseille, take two in a smaller town on the way: Sanary-sur-Mer (as serene as its name suggests) or wine-rich Bandol. Wannabe racers will luurv the Circuit du Castellet, inland.

Sanary-sur-Mer
pop 17,000

Sugary pink-and-white seaside cottages in this quiet resort, 15km west of Toulon, lend Sanary-sur-Mer a settled, mumsy feel. Indeed, novelist Aldous Huxley (1894–1963) called the place home in the early 1930s, as did his biographer Sybille Bedford in the late 1930s and a host of German refugees soon after. Thomas Mann and his brother Heinrich sought refuge here, as did the German painter Feuchtwanger.

Sanary's sandy but shallow beaches get packed in summer. From the small and busy port, **Croix du Sud V** (☎ 06 09 87 47 97; www.croixdusud.com) runs weekly boat excursions west towards Cassis and its *calanques* (rocky inlets; adult/three to 10 years €24/12 for 12 *calanques*, three hours); around the Baies du Soleil (€12/6, 1½ hours) and to Îles des Embiez (€10/5, 15 minutes). Or why not try spotting a dolphin with **Regard du Vivant** (☎ 06 10 57 17 11; www.regard-du-vivant.fr; 26 blvd Henri Fabre, Marseille), an exceptional wildlife-photography outfit that leads full-day dolphin-watching expeditions (for observers and photographers; adult/child under 12 €70/55), setting sail from Sanary-sur-Mer at 9am on Sunday, May to October. See the boxed text, p73) for more information.

Inland, **Ollioules** (population 12,336), 14km north, is known for its October **Fête de l'Olivier** (Olive-tree Festival). Its **tourist office** (☎ 04 94 63 11 74; office-tourisme@ollioules.com; 116 rue Philippe de Hauteclocque) has details.

In Sanary, **Hôtel de la Tour** (☎ 04 94 74 10 10; www.sanary-hoteldelatour.com; quai du Général de Gaulle; d incl breakfast low/high season from €72/75; 🅿), wrapped around a 12th-century tower (hence its name), is a particularly welcoming spot with ab fab views over the port.

Bandol
pop 7975

Ailing foreigners such as DH Lawrence and Katherine Mansfield were drawn to Bandol, 8km west of Sanary, in the 1900s. Now it's windsurfers who pour to its sandy shores to ride the waves, and wine lovers who flock to its terraced vineyards to taste Bandol's famously matchless reds, sold under their own coveted AOC since 1941.

Wine growers celebrate the year's new wine production in early December with a **Fête du Millésime** (Vintage Festival). The **tourist office** (☎ 04 94 29 41 35; www.bandol.fr; allées Vivien; ⏰ 9am-7pm Jul & Aug, 9am-noon & 2-6pm Mon-Fri, 9am-noon Sat Sep-Jun) has a list of cellars where you can taste and buy. Bandol vineyards stretch 15km northwest of town, as far as St-Anne du Castellet.

From Bandol port **Atlantide I** (☎ 04 94 32 51 41; www.atlantide1.com; quai d'Honneur) sails to/from Îles des Embiez (adult/four to 12 years €9/5), Porquerolles (€32/16) and around the *calanques* (six/10/14 *calanques* €16/20/24), from June to September. Easter to September, it runs **glass-bottom boat tours** (€11/6, 35 minutes) around the port. Boats sail year-round to Île de Bendor (see p371).

Les Lecques

The seaside resort of Les Lecques, which is 17km west of Bandol, is unstartling apart from the remnants of two Roman villas displayed in the **Musée Romain de Tauroentum** (☎ 04 94 26 30 46; 131 rte de la Madrague; adult/7-10yr €3/1.50; ⏰ 3-7pm Wed-Mon Jun-Sep, 2-5pm Sat & Sun Oct-May); be warned, parking here is difficult. The museum is arranged around three restored mosaics dating from around AD 1. Archaeologists believe that the Roman town after which the museum is named would have stood somewhere between here and **St-Cyr-sur-Mer**, 2km inland. The **tourist office** (☎ 04 94 26 73 73; www.saintcyrsurmer.com; place de l'Appel du 18 Juin; ⏰ 9am-7pm Mon-Sat, 10am-1pm & 4-7pm Sun Jul & Aug, 9am-6pm Mon-Sat Sep & Jun, 9am-6pm Mon-Fri, 9am-noon & 2-6pm Sat Oct-May) in Les Lecques has more information.

Circuit du Castellet

The calm and tranquillity that caresses the northern Bandol vineyards around the perched village of **Le Castellet** (population 3839, elevation 252m) is smashed with racy aplomb at the **Circuit du Castellet** (www.circuitpaul ricard.com), 2km out of town. The motor-sports racetrack was built by industrialist Paul Ricard in 1970 and sold to F1 racing magnate Bernie Ecclestone in 1999, who went on to transform it into a state-of-the-art HTTT (high-tech test track).

Monaco

Squeezed into just 1.95 sq km, this confetti principality might be the world's second-smallest country (the Vatican's smaller), but what it lacks in size it makes up for in attitude. Glitzy, glam and screaming hedonism, Monaco compels you to let rip. Be it razzing around in a helicopter or Ferrari, risking a little (or a lot) at the casino, sipping designer cocktails by a Med-filled pool or simply revelling in the extraordinary opulence that drips from every last lamp post, this the perfect place to play millionaire.

The stories behind this skyscraper-studded cityscape – a once-impoverished backwater – only add to the glamour: fortunes have been won and lost in the casino in its capital since the *belle époque*. Formula One's showpiece race has ripped around the port since the late 1920s. A Hollywood queen found her prince charming, the late Prince Rainier III, here. And in the 1930s Somerset Maugham famously dubbed this well-known tax haven for astronomical earners 'a sunny place for shady people'. Indeed, with zero natural resources to rely on, this sovereign state has made pampering the super-rich its speciality.

Yet 'decadent hide-out for dodgy characters' is not a designer label reigning monarch Prince Albert II likes. In the wake of his coronation in 2005, the bachelor prince with a couple of illegitimate children dotted around the globe wants to clean things up. Money launderers, shady businessmen et al are *persona non grata* in this fairy-tale kingdom where no-one breaks the rules and practically everyone's a millionaire – for real.

MONACO

HIGHLIGHTS

- Watch the changing of the guard at the Grimaldi's **Palais Princier** (p387)
- Stare nose-to-nose at sharks in the breathtaking **Musée Océanographique** (p386)
- Risk all (or simply sit back and savour the *belle époque* splendour) at **Casino de Monte Carlo** (p388)
- Sip champagne at sunset in the bar of **Columbus Monaco** (p391) or in one of the principality's cutting-edge **designer dines** (p393)
- Jump in an open-topped, cherry-red Ferrari and tear around the **Formula One Grand Prix circuit** (p395)

★ Casino de Monte Carlo

Formula One Grand Prix Circuit ★

Palais Princier ★

★ Musée Océanographique

★ Columbus Monaco

HISTORY

Since the 13th century, Monaco's history has been that of the Grimaldi family whose rule began in 1297 when François 'the Spiteful', disguised as a monk (see a statue of him at the top of the Rampe Major leading up to the palace), begged for shelter at the fortress on Le Rocher. Pitying soldiers let him in, only for François to stab them and open the gates to his followers.

Charles VIII, king of France, recognised Monégasque independence in 1489. But during the French Revolution France snatched Monaco back and imprisoned its royal family. Upon release, they had to sell what few possessions they still owned to survive and the palace became a warehouse.

The Grimaldis were restored to the throne under the 1814 Treaty of Paris. But in 1848 they lost Menton and Roquebrune to France, and Monaco swiftly became Europe's poorest country. In 1860 Monégasque independence was recognised for a second time by France, and a monetary agreement in 1865 sealed the deal on future cooperation between the two countries.

Despite Monaco's 'neutrality' in WWII, Prince Louis II (1870–1949) was a supporter of the Vichy government and turned a blind

---

THE MONÉGASQUES

Citizens of Monaco (Monégasques), of whom there are only 7600, don't pay taxes. They have their own flag (red and white), their national anthem and national holiday (19 November).

The traditional dialect is Monégasque (broadly speaking, a mixture of French and Italian), which children of the 107 different nationalities living in Monaco are taught in schools alongside French, Monaco's official language. Many street signs are bilingual.

Monaco is not quite an absolute monarchy: the ruling prince is assisted by a national council of 18 democratically elected members. Only Monégasques aged 21 or over can vote; elections are held every five years.

---

eye to Jewish 'disappearances' in Monaco. The principality's annual revenues rose from three million francs in 1941 to 80 million in 1943 through money-laundering on the Nazis' behalf.

Rainier III (ruled 1949–2005), nicknamed *le prince batisseur* (the builder prince), expanded the size of his principality by 20% in the late 1960s by reclaiming land from the sea to create the industrial quarter of Fontvieille. In 2004 he doubled the size of the harbour with a giant floating dike (p386) as part of an ambitious project to place Port de Monaco (Port Hercules) among the world's leading cruise-ship harbours. Upon Rainier's death in 2005, son Albert II became prince.

Monaco's economic status is strange. Although not a member of the European Union, because of its continuing special relationship with France, Monaco participates in the EU customs territory (meaning no border formalities crossing from France into Monaco) and uses the euro as its currency. It's been a member of the Council of Europe since 2004.

LITERARY MONACO

Lose yourself in some Monaco-inspired literature.

- *Loser Takes All* (Grahame Greene) Short novel written in 1955 in which a young couple are manipulated into honeymooning at the Hôtel de Paris in Monte Carlo and end up risking all at Monte Carlo casino.

- *Collected Short Stories* (Somerset Maugham) Includes *The Facts of Life,* a short story about a tennis player taking to the gambling tables at Monte Carlo; and *Three Fat Women from Antibes,* inspired by the many years Maugham lived on Cap Ferrat.

- *Mademoiselle of Monte Carlo* (William Le Queux) Who's that woman standing the other side of the roulette table? Drama around Monte Carlo's 'suicide table', written in 1921 by the British writer said to have inspired Fleming's 007.

ORIENTATION

Monaco divides into five: Monaco Ville, a rocky outcrop crowned by the Palace Princier on the southern side of Port de Monaco; Monte Carlo, north of the port; La Condamine, the flat area around the port; Fontvieille, the industrial area southwest of Monaco Ville; and Larvotto, the beach area east of Monte Carlo. The French town of Beausoleil is three streets

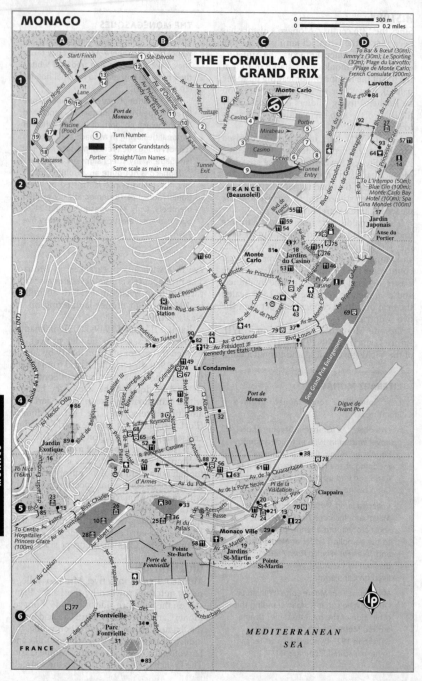

MONACO

0 — 300 m
0 — 0.2 miles

THE FORMULA ONE GRAND PRIX

Start/Finish

Pit Lane

Piscine (Pool)

La Rascasse

Ste-Dévote

Port de Monaco

Monte Carlo

Casino

Mirabeau

Casino

Loews

Portier

Tunnel Exit

Tunnel Entry

① Turn Number
▇ Spectator Grandstands
Portier Straight/Turn Names
Same scale as main map

To Bar & Bœuf (30m);
Jimmy'z (30m); Le Sporting (30m); Plage du Larvotto;
Plage de Monte Carlo;
French Consulate (200m)

Larvotto

FRANCE (Beausoleil)

Blvd de France

Monte Carlo

Jardins du Casino

Train Station

Blvd Princesse

Blvd de Suisse

Pedestrian Tunnel

La Condamine

Port de Monaco

See Grand Prix Enlargement

Digue de l'Avant Port

Jardin Exotique

To Nice (16km)

Jardin Japonais

Anse du Portier

Pl du Casino

Ciappaira

To L'Intempo (50m);
Blue Gin (100m);
Monte-Carlo Bay Hotel (100m); Spa
Gina Mondes (100m)

Pl de la Visitation

Pl d'Armes

Av du Port

Pl du Palais

Monaco Ville

Jardins St-Martin

Pointe Ste-Barbe

Porte de Fontvieille

Pointe St-Martin

To Centre Hospitalier Princess Grace (100m)

Fontvieille

Parc Fontvieille

FRANCE

MEDITERRANEAN SEA

INFORMATION
Canadian Consulate.................(see 1)
Main Post Office......................**1** C3
Notari Cyberspace....................**2** B5
Police Station.........................**3** B4
Post Office............................**4** C5
Post Office............................**5** B5
Scruples...............................**6** B4
Stars 'n' Bars......................(see 61)
Tourist Office........................**7** C3

SIGHTS & ACTIVITIES
Casino de Monte Carlo............**8** D3
Cathédrale de Monaco............**9** C5
Collection de Voitures
    Anciennes.......................**10** A5
Compagnie de Navigation
    et de Tourisme..................**11** C3
Église Ste-Dévote..................**12** B3
Escalator to Monte Carlo Story..**13** C5
Grimaldi Forum.....................**14** D2
Grottes de l'Observatoire.........**15** A5
Jardin Exotique.....................**16** A5
Jardin Japonais......................**17** D2
Jardins du Casino...................**18** C3
Jardins St-Martin...................**19** C5
Ministère d'État.....................**20** C5
Monaco Tours.......................**21** C5
Monte Carlo Story..................**22** C5
Musée d'Anthropologie
    Préhistorique....................**23** A5
Musée de la Chapelle de la
    Visitation.........................**24** C5
Musée des Souvenirs
    Napoléoniens et Archives
    Historiques du Palais...........**25** B5
Musée des Timbres et des
    Monnaies........................**26** B5
Musée National......................**27** D1
Musée Naval.........................**28** A5
Musée Océanographique.........**29** C5
Palais Princier......................**30** B5
Parc Fontvieille.....................**31** B6

Port de Monaco.....................**32** C4
Rampe Major........................**33** B5
Roseraie Princesse Grace.........**34** B6
Stade Nautique Rainier III.........**35** B4
State Apartments....................**36** B5
Thermes Marins de
    Monte-Carlo.....................**37** C3
Yacht Club de Monaco.............**38** C4

SLEEPING
Columbus Monaco..................**39** B6
Hôtel Ambassador...................**40** B5
Hôtel Balmoral......................**41** C3
Hôtel de Paris.......................**42** C3
Hôtel Hermitage.....................**43** C3
Hôtel Miramar.......................**44** B3
Hôtel Villa Boeri....................**45** D2

EATING
Café de Paris........................**46** D3
Carlino's...............................**47** C5
Casino.................................**48** B4
Caves & Gourmandises............**49** B4
Covered Market......................**50** B5
Fuji....................................**51** C3
Fusion...............................(see 61)
Huit Demi.............................**52** B4
Häagen-Dazs.........................**53** C3
Il Terrazzino.........................**54** C2
La Maison du Caviar................**55** C2
La Rascasse..........................**56** C5
La Rose des Vents...................**57** D2
Le Castelroc.........................**58** B5
Louis XV............................(see 42)
Marché 5..............................**59** C2
Polpetta...............................**60** B3
Stars 'n' Bars........................**61** C5
Zebra Square.......................(see 14)

DRINKING
Flashman's............................**62** C3
Karé(ment).........................(see 14)
La Note Bleue......................(see 57)

Quai des Artistes....................**63** C5
Sass Café.............................**64** D2

ENTERTAINMENT
ASM Football Club Pro Shop.....**65** B4
Atrium du Casino..................(see 8)
Auditorium Rainier III.............**66** D3
Automobile Club de Monaco....**67** B4
Boutique Formule 1.................**68** B4
Centre de Congrès
    Auditorium........................**69** D3
Cinéma d'Été........................**70** C5
Cinéma Le Sporting.................**71** C3
Ferrari City Tour.....................**72** B5
FNAC..................................**73** D2
L@Boutique..........................**74** B4
Legend................................**75** D3
Living Room..........................**76** D3
SBM Ticket Office.................(see 46)
Salle Garnier.......................(see 8)
Salles des Princes................(see 14)
Stade Louis II........................**77** A6
Théâtre du Fort Antoine...........**78** D5
Théâtre Princesse Grace...........**79** C3

SHOPPING
Métropole Shopping Centre.....**80** D2

TRANSPORT
Buses to Airport.....................**81** C3
Entrance to Train Station........(see 82)
Gallery to Public Lift................**82** B5
Héliport de Monaco.................**83** B6
Public Lift............................**84** D1
Public Lift............................**85** A5
Public Lift Entrance.................**86** A4
Public Lift Entrance.................**87** B5
Public Lift Entrance.................**88** B5
Public Lift Entrance.................**89** A4
Public Lift Entrance.................**90** B3
Public Lift Entrance.................**91** B3
Public Lift Entrance.................**92** D1
Public Lift Entrance.................**93** D2

up the hill from Monte Carlo, and Moneghetti borders Cap d'Ail's western fringe.

INFORMATION
Bookshops
Scruples (☎ 93 50 43 52; 9 rue Princesse Caroline) English-language bookshop.

Emergency
Ambulance & Fire Brigade (☎ 18)
Police station (☎ 17, 93 15 30 15; 3 rue Louis Notari)

Internet Access
The glass lobby of the Grimaldi Forum (p389) is a Libello **wi-fi hot spot** (2/24hr card €12/24).
Notari Cyberspace (☎ 92 16 17 62; www.notari.mc; 3bis rue Basse; per 30/60min €3/5; ✆ 10am-7pm)
Stars 'n' Bars (☎ 97 97 95 95; www.starsnbars.com; 6 quai Antoine 1er; per 30min €5; ✆ 7.30am-midnight, later in summer, Tue-Sun winter; ✗)

Internet Resources
http://holiday.monacoeye.com Alternative guide to Monaco.
www.gouv.mc The government.
www.monaco-montecarlo.com Five-language site loaded with practical info.
www.monaco-tourisme.com The tourist office.

Media
106.5 Riviera Radio (www.rivieraradio.mc) English-language station with hourly BBC news summaries, on 106.3MHz FM (106.5MHz FM in France).
Radio Monte Carlo (RMC; www.radiomontecarlo.net) French- and Italian-language broadcasts on 98.8MHz FM in Monaco.

Medical Services
Centre Hospitalier Princesse Grace (☎ emergencies 97 98 97 69, switchboard 97 98 99 00; www.chpg.mc in French; 1 av Pasteur)

THINK BIG

With no room for expansion on land, minuscule Monaco is looking to its 12 miles of territorial waters to make more space. Extending Fontvieille still further out to sea is one idea, although the sudden falling away of the sea bed is problematic. A second sky-scraping proposal is to build three offshore islands, each mounted by one leg of a futuristic, 390m-high 'Tour de la Mer'.

Money

Monaco uses the euro. Banks abound near the casino and on blvd Albert 1er.

Change Bureau (Jardins du Casino; ✆ 9am-7.30pm)

Post

Monégasque stamps are only valid for letters sent within Monaco; use a French stamp to send a postcard. Postal rates are the same as those in France.

Main post office (Palais de la Scala, sq Beaumarchais)

Post offices (place de la Mairie)

Telephone

Telephone numbers in Monaco have eight digits and no area code.

Calls between Monaco and France are deemed international calls. When calling Monaco from the rest of France or abroad, dial ✆ 00 followed by Monaco's country code, 377. To call France from Monaco, dial ✆ 00 then France's country code, ✆ 33.

Monaco's public telephones accept Monégasque or French phonecards.

Tourist Information

Tourist office (✆ 92 16 61 16; www.monaco-tourisme .com; 2a blvd des Moulins; ✆ 9am-7pm Mon-Sat, 10am-noon Sun) From June to September additional tourist information kiosks open at the harbour and train station.

SIGHTS

Monaco Ville

Monaco Ville, also called Le Rocher, thrusts skywards on a pistol-shaped rock. The most alluring sights – the Prince's palace, the old town, gardens and museums – are here, and the superb state-wide views help you get your bearings.

The 16th-century red-brick **Rampe Major** provides a steep pedestrian link from the port area of La Condamine to the palace. Alternatively, avoid the sweaty crowd slogging up the ramp and instead take a nautical stroll around the port and up the stairs next to Yacht Club de Monaco onto the **Digue de l'Avant Port**, a record-breaking floating dike, 28m wide, 352m long and weighing 163,000 tonnes, that doubled Monaco port's capacity overnight when it was unveiled in 2004. From its southern end a path winds along the coast and up through the shady Jardins St-Martin to Monaco Ville.

Buses 1 and 2 link the tourist office (via place d'Armes) with Monaco Ville, stopping at place de la Visitation.

MUSÉE OCÉANOGRAPHIQUE & AROUND

Stuck dramatically to the edge of a cliff since 1910, the world-renowned **Musée Océanographique** (Oceanographic Museum; ✆ 93 15 36 00; www.oceano.mc; av St-Martin; adult/6-18yr €11/6; ✆ 9.30am-7.30pm Jul & Aug, 9.30am-7pm Apr-Jun & Sep, 10am-6pm Oct-Mar) – which is a Prince Albert I (1848–1922) creation – is a stunner. Its centrepiece is the 7.5m-long coral reef, with vivid tropical fish on one side and deep-sea predators on the other. Ninety smaller tanks contain a dazzling 450 Mediterranean and tropical species, sustained by 250,000L of freshly pumped sea water per day. The Whale Room, filled with cetacean skeletons and pickled embryos, and fanciful seabird-covered chandeliers, mosaic floors and oak doorframes carved into marine shapes at every turn complete the mesmerising ensemble. Kids will love the **tactile basin** (2-12yr €3; ✆ hourly 10.45am-3.45pm Mon-Fri); tickets for the 30-minute feel-the-fish sessions are sold at the entrance.

Complete the oceanographic trip with a postaquarium stroll around the steep-sided, statue-studded **Jardins St-Martin** (✆ 7am-6pm Oct-Mar, to 8pm Apr-Sep), which run round the coast outside the museum or – the lazy option – a cup of tea in the aquarium's rooftop **brasserie** (mains €10-15; ✆ 10am-5pm).

Ticky-tacky but busy is **Monte Carlo Story** (✆ 93 25 32 33; adult/6-14yr €7/3.50; ✆ 2-5pm Jan-Jun, Sep & Oct, 2-6pm Jul & Aug), a 35-minute film about the Grimaldi dynasty accessed via the escalator in front of the Musée Océanographique.

Opposite, **Monaco Tours** (✆ 92 05 64 38; av St-Martin; adult/2-8yr €7/4; ✆ 10am-5pm Sep-Jun, to 6pm Jul & Aug) runs 30-minute city tours aboard the *Azur Express* tourist train.

PALAIS PRINCIER

Prince Albert and his **palace** (☎ 93 25 18 31; www .palais.mc; place du Palais) are protected by an elite company of 112 guards, the Carabiniers du Prince. In summer they sport bleached hats and uniforms, in winter moody black attire. At 11.55am daily a tourist scrum scrambles to watch the pristine soldiers parade outside the palace during the **changing of the guard**.

If the Grimaldi standard is flying from the palace tower, it means the Prince is at home. Sneak a peak at royal life with an audio-guide tour of the **state apartments** (adult/8-14yr €7/3.50; ☒ 10.30am-6pm Apr, 9.30am-6.30pm May-Sep, 10am-5.30pm Oct); in summer queue for up to 45 minutes to get in.

In the palace's southern wing princely collections of bric-a-brac (medals, coins, uniforms and swords), Napoleon's socks and other fascinating objects of day-to-day life form the **Musée des Souvenirs Napoléoniens et Archives Historiques du Palais** (Museum of Napoleonic Souvenirs & the Palace's Historic Archives; adult/8-14yr €4/2; ☒ 9.30am-6.30pm May-Sep, 10am-5.30pm Oct, 10.30am-5pm Dec, 10.30am-12.30pm & 2-5pm Jan-Apr).

CATHÉDRALE DE MONACO

Visitors flood to this Romanesque-Byzantine **cathedral** (☎ 93 30 87 70; www.cathedrale.mc in French; 4 rue Colonel Bellando de Castro), built in 1875, to view the flower-covered graves of fairy-tale couple Princess Grace (1929–82) and Prince Rainier III.

From September to June, Sunday Mass at 10am is sung by **Les Petits Chanteurs de Monaco** (☎ 93 15 80 88; www.lespetitschanteurs.mc), Monaco's boys' choir, although tours in July and August can take the choir out of town. Organ recit-als are at held at 6pm on alternate Saturdays, from July to September.

MUSÉE DE LA CHAPELLE DE LA VISITATION

Religious artworks by some big-hitters, in-cluding Rubens, Zurbaran and Ribera, are displayed in the enchanting **Musée de la Chapelle de la Visitation** (☎ 93 50 07 00; place de la Visitation; adult/6-12yr €3/1.50; ☒ 10am-4pm Tue-Sun), a 17th-century baroque chapel.

Monte Carlo

The **Jardins du Casino** form the district's green hub. Changing art exhibitions in the central strip add intrigue. For further brushes with

---

HEDONIST MONACO

Go on, spoil yourself. Pretend you're loaded. First stop: the **port** (opposite) with its big-name boats to ogle at and get you in the moneyed mood. Nautical wealth ingested, grab a portside coffee at **La Rascasse** (p392) before revving up a gear with a razz around the Grand Prix circuit in a **Ferrari** (p395). Next, whiz up the rock (cut through the **Jardins St-Martin**; opposite) and pick an unforgettable frock at **Isabelle Kristensen's** (p395) *haute-couture* boutique, then shift to **Monte Carlo** (above) with its glam **designer line-up** (p395). End your shopping spree with apéritifs and Beamer-watching at **Café de Paris** (p392) followed by the lunch of a lifetime at **Louix XV** (see the boxed text, p392).

Fill what's now a short afternoon with a flutter at **Casino de Monte Carlo** (p388) and a drown-your-sorrows session in a 55-minute seaweed bath, caviar facial or old-fashioned shave at the **Thermes Marins de Monte Carlo** (p390). A poolside siesta is mandatory.

Oh dear. It's 5pm. Apéritif time again. Strut north along the coast, savouring a Zen moment in the **Jardin Japonais** (p389) before indulging in a champagne cocktail with sun-drenched sea view at **Karé(ment)** (p392), on the beach with jazz at **La Note Bleue** (p393) or in the extravagant company of gourmet tapas at **Sea Lounge** (p392).

Dinner is a seaside affair at **Bar & Bœuf** (see the boxed text, p393) or **Fuji** (see the boxed text, p393). Then it's drinks with the jet set on the champagne terrace at **Blue Gin** (p392) and dancing 'til dawn at **Jimmy'Z** (p393).

MONACO

DYNASTY

Monaco's longest-ruling monarch, reigning for 56 years, Rainier III (1923–2005), won the heart of a nation with his fairy-tale marriage to Grace Kelly in 1956. The legendary Philadelphia-born actress made 11 films in the 1950s, including Alfred Hitchcock's *Dial M for Murder* (1954), *Rear Window* (1954) and *To Catch a Thief* (1955), in which she played the cool blonde on the coast. The movie took Kelly to Cannes and later to Monaco for a photo shoot where she met Rainier. One year later they wed and the princess retired from film and devoted herself to being Princess of Monaco. Tragically, in 1982, she died in a car crash; a broken-hearted Rainier died 23 years later.

The soap-opera lives of the couple's children – Prince Albert (b 1958), monarch since 19 November 2005, and his two sisters, Caroline and Stephanie – take centre stage today. 'World's most eligible bachelor', 48-year-old Albert lives up to his reputation as athlete and international playboy. He set up Monaco's bobsleigh team in 1986, competing himself in several Olympic Games, is a black belt in judo and played for a while on the national soccer team. Just months after being crowned, he publicly recognised first one (three-year-old Alexandre, son of a former flight attendant from Tongo) and then another (14-year-old Jazmin Grace, daughter of a Californian waitress who had a fling with the Prince while holidaying on the Côte d'Azur) child he'd fathered. The Palace quickly made it clear that neither child – nor any other that pops up out of the woodwork – could be line to the throne.

Indeed, until Prince Albert succeeds first in marrying and second in siring an heir, older sister Caroline (b 1957) remains next in line for the throne. Princess Caroline was widowed in 1990 when her second husband (her marriage to the first was annulled) and father of her three children was killed in a speedboat accident. On her 42nd birthday she wed Prince Ernst of Hanover, a cousin of Britain's Queen Elizabeth.

Wild child Princess Stephanie (b 1965) has been keeping the tabloids in business for more than 20 years, not least because she was in (some say driving) the car during the crash that killed her mother. She wed her bodyguard in 1995, but divorced him a year later after he was snapped frolicking with a Belgian stripper. Her second marriage to Portuguese circus acrobat Adan Peres lasted 10 months; within a couple of weeks of the marriage's end a casino croupier was rumoured to be her latest lover. During the 1980s and early 1990s the entrepreneurial princess launched her own swimwear label (Pool Position) and released a flurry of pop songs, including 'Ouragan' (Hurricane) and 'I am Waiting for You'.

May's Rose Ball, the Summer Ball, the fundraising *Gala de la Croix Rouge* (Red Cross Ball) and the Gala Ball are key events in Monégasque high society – all of which offer a royal chance to glimpse Monégasque royalty.

nature, follow the coastal path (two to three hours) from Monte Carlo to Roquebrune-Cap Martin.

CASINO DE MONTE CARLO

The drama of watching the poker-faced risk all in Monte Carlo's marble-and-gold **casino** (☎ 92 16 20 00; www.casino-monte-carlo.com in French; place du Casino; ☉ from noon Jul & Aug, from 2pm Mon-Fri & noon Sat & Sun Sep-Jun) makes the stiff admission fees, stakes and obligatory cloakroom 'tips' almost bearable. The **Salon Ordinaire** (admission €10) has European roulette (minimum stake €5) and trente et quarante (minimum stake €20); and the **Salons Privés** (admission €20; ☉ from 4pm) offer baccarat, craps, English roulette and chemin de fer.

To enter the casino, you must be at least 18, have a passport for ID, and be dressed relatively smartly (no shorts, trainers etc). A jacket and tie are required to enter the Salons Privés and the Salon Ordinaire in the evening. The one-armed bandits, to the right as you enter, command neither fee nor dress code.

MUSÉE NATIONAL

More innocent pleasures are to be found in Monaco's **Musée National** (National Museum; ☎ 93 30 91 26; www.monte-carlo.mc/musee-national; 17 av Princesse Grace; adult/6-14yr €6/4; ☉ 10am-6.30pm Easter-Sep, 10am-12.15pm & 2.30-6.30pm Oct-Easter), a Garnier-designed villa filled with dolls and mechanical toys (with demonstrations in the afternoons at half past the hour).

JARDIN JAPONAIS

Sandwiched between built-up Monte Carlo, Larvotto and the Mediterranean, the **Jardin Japonais** (Japanese Garden; av Princesse Grace; 9am-dusk) is intended as a piece of paradise. It was blessed by a Shinto high priest, and quiet contemplation and meditation is encouraged.

GRIMALDI FORUM

Monaco's congress and conference centre, the **Grimaldi Forum** (99 99 30 00; www.grimaldiforum.mc; 10 av Princesse Grace), is worth a peak for its architecture – think glass crystal, two-thirds submerged in the sea – and designer dining and drinking spaces. Otherwise, contemporary art exhibitions and cultural happenings add spice to daily Monagésque life.

Fontvieille

Fontvieille – built on 30 hectares of land reclaimed from the sea between 1966 and 1973 – covers the southernmost part of Monaco. From here a 3.5km-long coastal path leads southwest to Cap d'Ail. The lush gardens of **Parc Fontvieille** are equally pleasant for a summer stroll; more than 4000 rose bushes and a small swan-filled lake adorn the **Roseraie Princesse Grace** (Princess Grace Rose Garden),

planted in her memory in 1984. Contemporary sculptures, including works by César and Arman, line the length of the park's **Chemin des Sculptures**. Museum-wise, Fontvieille is Monaco's collector's corner.

COLLECTION DE VOITURES ANCIENNES

Highlights of the 100-odd classic cars displayed in the Palace's regal **Collection de Voitures Anciennes** (92 05 28 56; Centre Commercial de Fontvieille; adult/8-14yr €6/3; 10am-6pm) include a Rolls Royce Silver Cloud, a wedding present from local shopkeepers to Rainier III; a black London cab (Austin 1952) fitted out for Grace Kelly; and the first F1 racing car to win the Monaco Grand Prix – the Bugatti 1929.

MUSÉE NAVAL

An impressive collection of 200-plus model ships fills the **Musée Naval** (Naval Museum; 92 05 28 48; www.naval-museum.mc in French; Centre Commercial de Fontvieille; adult/8-14yr €4/2.50; 10am-6pm).

MUSÉE DES TIMBRES ET DES MONNAIES

The **Museum of Stamps & Coins** (93 15 41 50; Centre Commercial de Fontvieille; adult/12-14yr €3/2; 10am-6pm Jul-Sep, 10am-5pm Oct-Jun) contains Monégasque stamps dating from 1885 and numismatic wonders from 1640.

LOSER RISKS ALL

The beautiful *belle époque* décor of Monte Carlo Casino – Europe's oldest – is as extravagant as those who play in it. The casino was built in several phases, the earliest being the Salon de l'Europe, built in 1865 and splendidly lit with eight 150kg crystal chandeliers from 1898. The second phase saw French architect Charles Garnier, who'd just completed the Paris opera house, move to Monte Carlo to create the luxurious fresco-adorned Salle Garnier in 1878. The main entrance hall, with its 28 marble columns and flurry of gamblers and voyeurs, opened the same year. The third part, the Salle Empire, was completed in 1910.

Monaco's Prince Charles III, who saw the casino as the solution to the principality's financial troubles, was nevertheless concerned about the malign effect of gambling on his subjects. He therefore made it illegal for his family, or any Monégasque, to set foot in the precincts! Money-losing was for rich foreigners only.

Monte Carlo Casino remains in the hands of its founding owner, the **Société des Bains de Mer** (SBM; Sea Bathing Society; www.montecarloresort.com), established in 1863 and Monaco's largest corporation today, owning the principality's priciest hotels, restaurants and spa. Original shareholders included Charles III, and the state remains the leading shareholder today. Despite an initial drop in revenue in 1933 after roulette was legalised in neighbouring France, Casino du Monte Carlo rakes it in.

In 1875, when the then-future Edward VII and Queen Alexandra visited, around 150,000 players per day were frequenting the casino. Shotgun suicides, hot on the heels of a heavy loss at the gaming tables, were still common well into the 1920s. When Charles Deville Wells broke the bank in 1891 – the first and last person to do so – gaming tables were draped in black for three days.

MONACO

Moneghetti

The world's largest succulent and cactus collection tumbles down the slopes of the **Jardin Exotique** (☎ 93 15 29 80; 62 blvd du Jardin Exotique; adult/6-18yr €6.90/3.60; ☺ 9am-7pm mid-May–mid-Sep, 9am-6pm or dusk mid-Sep–mid-May). Seven thousand varieties, from small *echinocereus* to 10m-tall African candelabras, are linked by winding paths and wooden bridges with spectacular views. Keep a firm hold of toddlers – there are some holey fences and unthinkable drops.

Your ticket also gets you a 35-minute guided tour round the **Grottes de l'Observatoire**, a prehistoric cave network stuffed with stalactites and stalagmites, 279 steps down inside the hillside; strangely, it's the only cave in Europe where the temperature rises as you descend. Admission to the **Musée d'Anthropologie Préhistorique** (Museum of Prehistoric Anthropology; ☎ 93 15 80 06), with displays of human artefacts, is also included; it closes 15 minutes before the gardens.

From the tourist office, take bus 2 to the Jardin Exotique stop.

ACTIVITIES
Boats & Beaches

Palatial pleasure crafts bedecked with cinemas, saunas, helicopter pads and lord knows what else dominate the **Port de Monaco**: many of the world's top 100 private yachts (listed at www.powerandmotoryacht.com/megayachts) are frequent visitors here. At the eastern end of quai Antoine 1er, members of the exclusive **Yacht Club de Monaco** (☎ 93 10 63 00; www.yacht-club-monaco.mc in French; 16 quai Antoine 1er) eagerly await a new clubhouse designed by architect Sir Norman Foster.

Lesser mortals should be able to sail in a glass-bottomed catamaran run by the **Compagnie de Navigation et de Tourisme** (☎ 92 16 15 15; www.aquavision-monaco.com; quai des États-Unis), at the quay's northeastern end, from 2007.

The nearest fine-shingle beaches, **Plage du Larvotto** and **Plage de Monte Carlo**, are in Larvotto. Both have private, paying sections where you can hire cushioned sun lounges and parasols for €8/10 per half-/full day. Take bus 4 from the train station or bus 6 from the port to Le Sporting stop.

Pools & Spas

Beautiful swimmers frequent **Stade Nautique Rainier III** (☎ 93 30 64 83; quai Albert 1er; adult/4-12yr €4.50/2.60; ☺ 9am-6pm May, Jun & mid-Sep–Oct, 9am-6pm Mon, 9am-8pm Tue-Sun Jul–mid-Sep), the Olympic-sized outdoor sea-water pool with water slide and sun-loungers/parasols (each €3.90) at the port.

Casino owner SBM runs the prestigious **Thermes Marins de Monte-Carlo** (☎ 92 16 49 46; www.montecarlospa.com; 2 av de Monte Carlo; ☺ 8am-8pm), a spa with 29°C sea-water pool, solarium and other aquatic self-pampering treats. One-/two-day sessions without accommodation start at €188/266.

Spa treatments – Brazilian slimming, Japanese flower baths, Balinese massages et al – span the globe at cutting-edge **Spa Cinq Mondes** (☎ 98 06 01 80; www.cinqmondes.com), inside the Monte Carlo Bay Hotel (opposite).

FESTIVALS & EVENTS

Poor old Ste Dévote, martyred in Corsica in AD 312, was thrown into a boat and left to drift to sea. Miraculously, a dove flew from the dead woman's mouth and blew the boat safely to Monaco, where the inhabitants snapped her up as their patron saint. The **Fête de la Ste-Dévote** on 27 January celebrates her feast day, with a traditional Mass celebrated in Monégasque in **Église Ste-Dévote** (place Ste-Dévote), with a torch-light procession, blessing and symbolic boat-burning in front of the church.

To celebrate midsummer, dancers in folk costume (long, frilly skirts and red-and-white patterned garments) leap around the **St-Jean Bonfires** on place du Palais (23 June) and place des Moulins (24 June).

Early August brings a glittering **International Fireworks Festival** (☎ 93 15 28 63) to the port area, and a carnival spirit fills the streets during the **Fête Nationale Monégasque** – Monaco's national holiday – on 19 November.

SLEEPING

Bar the truly moneyed, few people stay in Monaco; most day-trip it from Nice or elsewhere along the coast. Budget options and *chambres d'hôtes* in the principality are nonexistent.

High-season rates quoted here exclude the Grand Prix and New Year, when prices rocket sky high and most hotels demand a minimum three-night stay.

Midrange

Hôtel Villa Boeri (☎ 04 93 78 38 10; www.hotelboeri.com; 29 blvd du Général Leclerc; s/d/tr low season €49/56/65, high season €54/61/69; ☒) Cross the road to get to blvd de France in Monaco from this appealing

30-room option snug in French Beausoleil.
Trademarks include ultracharming staff, patio
garden to breakfast on and mirrored, plant-
filled public spaces that lend a terrarium feel.
Some rooms have flower-bedecked balconies
with tiny sea view. Use the country code for
France (☎ 00 33) when calling this hotel from
Monaco.

Hôtel Balmoral (☎ 93 50 62 37; www.hotel-balmoral
.mc; av de la Costa; d low/high season from €115/210; ✷)
Built in 1896 and run by the same family ever
since, the Balmoral is set coolly apart from the
clamour of the casino and enjoys inspirational
views over the port and Monaco Ville.

Hôtel Ambassador (☎ 97 97 96 96; www.ambas
sadormonaco.com; 10 av Prince Pierre; s/d/tr low season
€130/150/179, high season €150/180/210; ✷) Clad in
three stars, the Ambassador has a graceful
interior (think carpeted rooms and marble
bathrooms) and lovely Liberty-style restaurant serving Italian cuisine. Breakfast is included and wi-fi is free.

Columbus Monaco (☎ 92 05 90 00; www.columbus
hotels.com; 22 av des Papalins; d from €195; P ✷ ▢ ▣)
Hi-tech urban chic best describes this boutique hotel in Fontvieille – the doing of hugely
successful Glaswegian hotelier Ken McCul-
loch, designer Amanda Rosa and British F1
racing driver David Coulthard (all Monaco
residents today). Its cocktail bar – a designer's
wet dream – is hipper than hip and *the* place
to sip champagne at sunset.

Top End

Monte Carlo Bay Hotel (☎ 98 06 25 25; www
.montecarlobay.com; 40 av Princesse Grace; d from €300;
P ✷ ▢ ▣) Beach babes will enjoy this
waterfront location…not that you're likely

to venture out. A neoclassical interior with
several hip bars and eating spaces, a ravishing lagoonlike pool with waterside cabanas
to hide in, a state-of-the-art spa, and lavish
Mediterranean gardens ensure guests stay
firmly ensconced in this stylish corner of
1930s-cum-21st-century paradise.

Hôtel Hermitage (☎ 92 16 40 00; www.montecarlo
resort.com; sq Beaumarchais; d from €360; P ✷ ▣)
The literary James Bond plumped to stay
here when he was in town. One of many
treasures in the SBM trove, this luxurious
four-star palace with beige-suited doormen
has an Italianate façade, pink-marbled restaurant, stained-glass winter garden designed by
Gustave Eiffel, fabulous rooms in Wedgwood
blues and the full complement of Rolls and
Beamers parked outside.

Hôtel de Paris (☎ 98 06 30 00; www.montecarloresort
.com; place du Casino; d from €395; P ✷ ▣) Monaco's most famous hotel, this magnificent *belle
époque* pad was Monte Carlo's first hotel and
the place where writer Colette spent her last
years. Built between 1859 and 1864, it sits
snug against a gastronomic temple to die
for (see the boxed text, p392). A night in the
Churchill Suite costs a mere €8000.

EATING

Dining in Monaco is overwhelmingly Italian;
even places pertaining to cook Monégasque
(essentially a local adaptation of Niçois cuisine) pepper their menus with a generous
dash of pasta.

But eating here needn't be expensive. There
are cheaper places alongside the star-spangled
whirl of dining legends. Pedestrian rue Princesse Caroline near the port is particularly
well-endowed with affordable, if unmemor-
able, eateries.

Restaurants

La Maison du Caviar (☎ 93 30 80 06; 1 av St-Charles; plat
du jour €16, menu €26; ☾ lunch & dinner Mon-Fri, dinner Sat
Sep-Jul) Going strong since 1950, the House of
Caviar is that – and more. Savour blini with 30
mouth-melting grams of Iranian caviar (€80)
followed by pan-fried beef and caviar (€48)
or homemade gnocchi in a chive and cream
sauce and 20g of the black roe (€60).

Il Terrazzino (☎ 93 50 24 27; www.ilterrazzino.com;
2 rue des Iris; plat du jour €12, menu €37, pasta/meat dishes
€15/18; ☾ lunch & dinner Mon-Sat) Dried sweet-corn
cobs dangle from the ceiling of this colourful
eating space where traditional Neapolitan

fare fuses with Italian charm. Pea-green and turquoise chairs grace the conservatory-style terrace, but the best bit is the eat-as-much-as-you-want antipasti buffet.

Huit et Demi (☎ 93 50 97 02; 4 rue Langlé; pizza €10.50-12.50, pasta €15, meat dishes €16-20; ⌚ closed Sat lunch & Sun) Eight and a Half is a chic, clean-cut place with an industrial interior and pavement terrace filling an entire street running off rue Princesse Caroline. The fare is a mix of Italian (lots of pasta) and local (think *bagna cauda*, or lamb with Sospel olives).

La Rose des Vents (☎ 99 70 46 96; www.larosedesventsmonaco.com; Plage du Larvotto, av Princesse Grace; plat du jour €15, mains €20; ⌚ lunch & dinner) Beach dining at its best. Sit on wooden decking arranged around a century-old palm tree on the sand and enjoy warm baby octopus salad, clams, or the catch of the day simply grilled.

Polpetta (☎ 93 50 67 84; 2 rue Paradis; menu €23; ⌚ lunch & dinner Wed-Fri & Sun, dinner Sat) Craving down-to-earth dining? Then hike uphill to this disarmingly old-fashioned trattoria next to a garage, where eggs and veg are delivered each morning by a man in a little white van. The doing of the Guasco brothers for 20-odd years, Sinatra among others loved Polpetta. We love its osso bucco.

La Rascasse (☎ 93 25 56 90; 1 quai Antoine 1er; starters/mains €10/25, menu €35; ⌚ restaurant lunch & dinner Mon-Sat, bar 10.30am-5am Mon-Sat, from 8pm Sun) It changed its name to Café Grand Prix but the punters just wouldn't have it. It does, after all, sit inside the Rascasse bend of the F1 Grand Prix circuit and throbs with drivers' girlfriends and support teams during the race. The restaurant is on the 1st floor, the bar is on the ground.

Le Castelroc (☎ 93 30 36 68; place du Palais; mains €22-27; ⌚ lunch daily, dinner Tue-Sat May-Sep) Opposite the Palace with an entrance ensnared by T-shirt and souvenir shops it might be, but, incredibly, Le Castelroc is no tourist trap. Spilling out to an al-fresco terrace, its twin dining rooms are the best place around to try authentic Monégasque specialities such as *barbadjuan* (a spinach and cheese–stuffed doughnut) and *pissaladière* (onion and tomato tart; France's version is tomatoless).

Cafés

Café de Paris (☎ 92 16 21 24; place du Casino; starters/salads €15, mains €25-50; ⌚ 8am-2am) A sight in itself, Monaco's best-known café has been in business since 1882 and is *the* place in Monte Carlo to people-watch. A *croque monsieur* (toasted

ham-and-cheese sandwich) on its legendary terrace costs €12.50; a nip to the loo to glimpse the original brasserie interior is a must.

A prime spot for ice cream in a cone or a glass of soda is **Häagen-Dazs** (☎ 93 30 38 30; place du Casino; 1-/2-scoop cone €3.20/4.70, ice-cream soda €5.50) in the Jardins du Casino. Or gorge on tea and cake at 1920s chocolate house **Carlino's** (☎ 97 97 88 88; place de la Visitation).

Self-Catering

Stock up on fruit, veg et al for a picnic at Monaco's indoor and outdoor **market** (place d'Armes; ⌚ 7am-1pm) in La Condamine or at a supermarket:

Casino (17 blvd Albert 1er; ⌚ 8.30am-midnight Mon-Sat summer, 8.30am-10pm Mon-Sat winter) Waterfront supermarket with takeaway pizza (€2.50 to €11.50) and sandwiches (€3.20 to €4).

Caves & Gourmandises (25 blvd Albert 1er) Upmarket grocer.

Marché U (30 blvd Princesse Charlotte)

DRINKING

Much of Monaco's superchic drinking goes on in its designer dines and luxury hotels: the bar in Columbus Monaco (p391) is magical, as is the **Blue Gin** (Monte Carlo Bay Hotel; p391), a cocktail bar with champagne terrace, and the seasonal **Sea Lounge** (av Princesse Grace), with DJ David Parker, in Monte Carlo Beach Hôtel.

Karé(ment) (☎ 99 99 20 20; www.karement.com; 10 av Princesse Grace; ⌚ 9-4.30am Mon-Fri, 6pm-4.30am Sat

& Sun) One glimpse of the stunning waterside terrace and you'll be fighting for a bar stool at this celebrity-cool lounge bar in the Grimaldi Forum. Fashion shows, DJ mixes and cultural happenings are held here.

Quai des Artistes (☎ 97 97 97 77; www.quaides artistes.com; 4 quai Antoine 1er; lunch menu €21.50; ☹ noon-11.30pm) Tucked beneath awning at the port, with a glass façade and terrace overlooking the boats, this Art Deco metropolitan space with Parisian-style metro entrance is a great spot to drink, hang out, chat and dine on seafood. Kitchen closed afternoons.

Sass Café (☎ 93 25 52 00; 11 av Princesse Grace; ☹ 11pm-3am) Hipper-than-cool lounge lizards gather at this piano bar to dine and jive to live jazz.

La Note Bleue (☎ 93 50 05 02; av Princess Grace; ☹ 8am-11pm Feb-Dec) The Blue Note comes in the shape of a jazz lounge with vast decking terrace on the sands of Larvotto.

Flashman's (☎ 93 30 09 03; 7 av Princesse Alice; ☹ 11am-dawn) Down a pint on a pint-sized terrace or mellow out in a steely interior at this English-run disco bar. Bands and DJs let rip Friday and Saturday.

ENTERTAINMENT

Tune in to events with the monthly *Bienvenue* and weekly *Your Week in the Principality* (both free at the tourist office) or online at www.monaco-spectacle.com. Venue box offices sell tickets, as does the *billetterie* at **Fnac** (☎ 93 10 81 81; www.fnac.com/monaco; 17 av des Spélugues; ☹ 10am-7.30pm Mon-Sat) in the Métropole shopping centre.

Nightclubs

Pure hedonism and a total disregard for cost are essential clubbing ingredients. Admission costs €15 to €20, although women often get in for free.

Jimmy'z (☎ 98 06 73 73; Le Sporting, 26 av Princesse Grace; ☹ from 11.30pm Easter-Nov, Wed-Sun Nov-Easter) Part of the SBM empire, the most famous nightclub in town – jet-set den for 30-odd years – comes with Cuban smoking room, top DJs, models and celebrities à gogo.

Living Room (☎ 93 50 80 31; www.mcpam.com; 7 av des Spélugues; ☹ 11pm-dawn) DJ Kriss is the sound man at this hybrid piano bar–nightclub with tough door policy. Dress up nice (jacket required) and be as famous as possible.

TOP FIVE DESIGNER DINES

Hipper than hip, these gastronomic hang-outs are as much drinking as dining haunts for Monaco's jet set. Looking good is key to snagging a table.

Zébra Square (☎ 99 99 25 50; www.zebrasquare.com; 2nd fl, Grimaldi Forum, 10 av Princesse Grace; mains €15-20; ☹ lunch & dinner) The plates, floor and odd lamp are patterned like a zebra at this chic address in the Grimaldi Forum where Monaco trendies mingle with better-known bods on cushion-stacked sofa seating facing the sea. DJs, fashion shows and art happenings add an after-dark buzz.

L'intempo (☎ 93 15 78 50; www.meridien-plaza.monte-carlo.mc; 22 av Princesse Grace; mains €20-30; ☹ 24hr) Hotel restaurants in the principality are not second-best options, as this stunning eating space testifies. Take your pick from one of four dramatically different eating areas stuck in a glass tower on the seashore. Cuisine – some live – is Mediterranean.

Fuji (☎ 93 30 40 11; 4 av de la Madone; sushi €2.50-6.90, sashimi €13-32, menus €15-31; ☹ lunch & dinner Tue-Sat, dinner Mon) With its Zen interior – natural hues broken with the odd splash of lime-green neon – this Japanese restaurant is a sleek crowd-pleaser. Find it beneath the escalator leading down to the Métropole shopping centre and, in July and August, beneath the stars at Le Sporting (26 av Princesse Grace).

Bar & bœuf (☎ 98 06 71 71; www.sbm.mc; Le Sporting, 26 av Princesse Grace; full meal around €150; ☹ 8pm-1am mid-May–mid-Sep) Style-setters hobnob in a minimalist wood-and-glass interior designed by Philippe Starck at this Ducasse venture. Bar & bœuf specialises in just that – sea bass (*bar*) and beef (*bœuf*). Fellas note: jacket required.

Stars 'n' Bars (☎ 97 97 95 95; www.starsnbars.com; 6 quai Antoine 1er; salads €13, mains €15-20; ☹ 7.30am-midnight, later in summer, Tue-Sun winter; ☒) This American bar-restaurant just doesn't lose its touch. A long-time hot spot, its portside terrace remains one of Monaco's sexiest – as does its interior plastered with sporting memorabilia. Tex-Mex platters, buffalo wings, burgers and a generous dose of vegetarian dishes plump out a family-friendly menu, while fusion is the essence upstairs at the grown-up sushi and cocktail club Fusion (☎ 97 97 95 90; open 7pm to 2.30am Monday to Saturday).

MY MONACO

British-born Riviera Radio presenter Elizabeth Lewis lives in Nice and works in Monaco. She commutes to the station's portside studio with Monte Carlo view each morning by train.

Why Monaco? Monaco is glam. I love the beauty of the place, the weather, the attitude of the people, the fact you can be in a party with people of five different nationalities, people who have stories to tell. I like being able to speak French and English in the same sentence without sounding pretentious.

Unique trait: You can never be overdressed in Monaco. However dressed up you are, there's always someone more dressed up than you.

The people: The Monégasque are very loyal. They love their prince and his family; they don't gossip. Businesses require the permission of the princely family (an official portrait of the prince is displayed in every office, shop window). When Rainier died, we had to drape a black ribbon on his portrait for the official three-month mourning period, after which the official portrait of Albert went up.

Favourite spot: The market at 6am. There are no tourists; just the same people each morning walking to work like me. It's a taste of the real old Monaco.

Most loved character: Michel at the bar I go to for a coffee on my way to work. He serves me black coffee with an ice cube in it. It's not a trendy bar; it's where all the place d'Armes market-stall holders get their coffee.

For romance: The beach at night, La Note Bleue (p393). Some of the best jazz musicians in the region play here.

Best bar: The Columbus Monaco (p391) for an apéritif; also the Monte Carlo Bay Hotel (p391). They serve foie gras–flavoured crisps that are purple.

Best shop: There's Karen Millen in Monaco. I'm a €15 dress type of gal, though. I can't afford Chanel.

Hot tip: If you want to break the law, it is not the right place for you, Monaco. There's no crime in Monaco and police cameras everywhere. We're probably being watched now.

Legend (☎ 93 50 53 13; www.thelegendmonaco.com; 3 av des Spélugues; ☿ 11pm-dawn Thu-Sun) Resident DJs Pierre and Max spin a mix of sounds at this disco adjoining the Metropole shopping centre. Bikinis are obligatory at beach parties.

Live Music & Ballet

Le Sporting (☎ 92 16 36 36; www.sportingmontecarlo.com; 26 av Princesse Grace; tickets incl drink/dinner from €40/85) is Monaco's prime pop-concert and cabaret-show venue. Buy tickets at the **SBM Ticket Office** (☎ 98 06 36 36; place du Casino; ☿ 10am-5pm) adjoining Café de Paris or at Fnac.

The Salle Garnier (1892), a confection of neoclassical splendour adjoining Monte Carlo Casino, is the permanent home of the renowned **Opéra de Monte Carlo** (☎ 92 16 22 99; www.opera.mc; place du Casino). The **Monte Carlo Philharmonic Orchestra** (1863; www.opmc.mc) often plays at the Auditorium Rainier III inside the **Centre de Congrès Auditorium** (☎ 93 10 85 00; tickets €10-40; blvd Louis II). In July and August its venue shifts to the star-topped Cour d'Honneur (Courtyard of Honour) at the Palais Princier. Tickets (€18 to €80), sold at the **Atrium du Casino** (☎ 92

16 22 99; place du Casino; ☿ 10am-5.30pm Tue-Sun) in the casino, are like gold dust.

The **Monte Carlo Ballet** (1985; www.balletsdemontecarlo.com) and orchestra perform in the Salles des Princes at the **Grimaldi Forum** (☎ 99 99 30 00; www.grimaldiforum.mc; tickets €25; 10 av Princesse Grace).

Jacket and tie for men is obligatory at all performances (except Le Sporting pop concerts).

Cinemas

Cinéma Le Sporting (☎ French number 08 36 68 00 72; www.cinemasporting.com; place du Casino) shows non-dubbed films daily.

From late June to the end of July films are screened in English at the open-air **Cinéma d'Été** (☎ 93 25 86 80; Parking des Pêcheurs, chemin des Pêcheurs), on a car-park roof. The show kicks off daily at 9.15pm; the programme is online at www.cinemasporting.com.

Theatre

Grace Kelly designed the interior of **Théâtre Princesse Grace** (☎ 93 25 32 27; www.tpgmonaco.com; 12 av d'Ostende; tickets around €40).

Watching an open-air performance at **Théâtre du Fort Antoine** (☎ 93 15 80 00; Jardins St-Martin, av de la Quarantaine) makes for a fabulous evening out. July and August ushers in a rash of free plays and musical concerts.

Sport

FOOTBALL

Football team **AS Monaco** (www.asm-foot.mc) plays at the **Stade Louis II** (Louis II Stadium; ☎ 92 05 40 00; 3 av des Castelans) in Fontvieille; buy match tickets from the ticket office inside or view the stadium as part of a 20-minute **guided tour** (adult/under 12yr €4/2; ⏰ 10.30am, 11.30am, 2.30pm & 4pm Mon, Tue, Thu & Fri); just turn up at the respective time and buy a ticket. **ASM Football Club Pro Shop** (☎ 97 77 74 74; 16 rue Grimaldi) sells all the club gear.

MOTOR SPORT

January's **Monte Carlo Rally** is a high-octane three-day series of timed stages, starting and finishing at the port and ripping through Haute-Provence in between. The traditional night stage and the concentration run, where drivers set off from various European cities to meet in Monte Carlo (like Disney's on-screen VW Beetle Herbie in the 1970s), were scrapped in 1997.

The scent of singed tyres also fills the air at May's **Monaco Formula One Grand Prix** (p396).

From mid-July to the end of August speed fiends can put their foot down in a cherry-red Ferrari during a **Ferrari City Tour** (☎ 92 05 54 20; www.livenupmonaco.com) around the Monaco Grand Prix circuit. A lap takes 15 to 20 minutes and costs €35 in the passenger seat or €70 if you drive (someone comes with you to tell you when to accelerate, change gear etc). Look for the red Ferrari parked near the Rascasse bend at the port.

SHOPPING

Tool up on designer clothes at a dizzying array of big-name couturiers, listed in the annual 150-page *Monaco Shopping* guide, free at the tourist office. From mid-July to mid-August boutiques are open on Sunday too.

Should arranging your own shopping spree be too much of a chore, **Monte Carlo Accueil** (☎ 97 70 89 12; 3hr tailored shopping tour €30) can do it for you (minimum three people). Or take along a **fashion consultant** (Isabelle Ughes; ☎ 06 78 63 83 63; www.make-it-perfect.com; from €160).

Monte Carlo's legendary 'Golden Circle' is the spot to (window) shop. Get going on av des Beaux Arts, on the southern side of the casino gardens, where you can swirl through Chanel, Christian Dior, Céline, Louis Vuitton, Yves St-Laurent and Sonia Rykiel. Bow down at the altar of Italian fashion house Prada, and pay homage to Salvatore Ferragamo inside Hôtel Hermitage. Nearby, av de Monte Carlo is a short, chic street with a luxury line-up: Gucci, Valentino, Hermès, Lalique (crystal) and Prada. Tucked beside the casino is Parisian jeweller Van Cleef & Arpels while Kenzo, Marina Rinaldi, D&G and Christian Lacroix hide alongside more affordable names in the indoor **Métropole Shopping Centre** (Centre Commercial Le Métropole; cnr av de la Madone & av de Spélugues), on the northern side of the casino gardens.

Atop Le Rocher, Danish-born designer and former top model **Isabelle Kristensen** (☎ 97 70 41 94; 18 rue Princess Marie de Lorraine) designs ball gowns and evening wear to die for.

A glimpse in the window of **Quatre Pattes** (18 rue Grimaldi) is a giggle.

GETTING THERE & AWAY

There are no border formalities upon entering Monaco from France.

Air

Monaco's helicopter companies are **Héli-Air Monaco** (☎ 92 05 00 50; www.heliairmonaco.com in French) and **Monacair** (☎ 97 97 39 00; www.monacair .mc in French), based at **Héliport de Monaco** (☎ 92 05 00 10; av des Ligures). They can whirl you anywhere along the coast, including to/from Nice airport (€80/96 one way departing from Monaco/Nice, €166 return including airport taxes; at least 20 daily March to October).

Bus

Bus 100 runs along the Corniche Inférieure (p280) between Nice and Menton, stopping in Monaco. Buses to/from Nice-Côte d'Azur airport (€14.40, 45 minutes) depart hourly from the Casino stop on blvd des Moulins.

Car & Motorcycle

The Corniche Moyenne (N7) links Monaco to the A8. For Italy, look for signs indicating Gênes (Genoa; Genova in Italian).

Well-signposted public car parks are scattered liberally around the principality, including at the train station and Monte Carlo Casino. The first hour is free, the second costs €2.40, and every subsequent 20 minutes is €0.60.

MONACO

THE FORMULA ONE GRAND PRIX *Tony Wheeler*

If there's one trophy a Formula One driver would like to have on the mantelpiece, it would have to be from the most glamorous race of the season, the Monaco Grand Prix. This race has everything. Its spectators are the most sensational: the merely wealthy survey the spectacle from Hôtel Hermitage, the really rich watch from their luxury yachts moored in the harbour, while the Grimaldis see the start and finish from the royal box at the port. Then there's the setting: the cars scream around the very centre of the city, racing uphill from the start/finish line to place du Casino, then downhill around a tight hairpin and two sharp rights to hurtle through a tunnel and run along the harbourside to a chicane and more tight corners before the start/finish. To top it all off there's the race's history: it was first run in 1929, and the winners' list features a roll-call of racing greats right down to Michael Schumacher's five victories between 1994 and 2001.

But despite its reputation, the Monaco Grand Prix is not really one of the great races. The track is too tight and winding for modern Grand Prix cars, and overtaking is virtually impossible. The Brazilian triple world champion Nelson Piquet famously described racing at Monaco as like 'riding a bicycle around your living room'. Piquet clearly rides a much faster bicycle than most of us; Monaco may be the slowest race on the calendar, but the lap record is still over 160km/h and at the fastest point on the circuit cars reach 280km/h. Even the corner in the gloom of the tunnel is taken at 250km/h (over 150mph).

Over the years the race has featured some unexpected surprises. In 1955 Alberto Ascari's Lancia was about to take the lead from Englishman Stirling Moss' silver Mercedes when the Italian arrived at the chicane travelling too fast, shot through the straw bales (this was more than 20 years before modern Armco barriers arrived on the scene) and plunged straight into the harbour. Seconds later the twice world champion bobbed to the surface with only minor injuries. Remarkably, the feat was repeated 10 years later at exactly the same spot. That time it was Australian driver Paul Hawkins who drove into the harbour in his Lotus. If spinning into the harbour was still possible the unlucky driver probably wouldn't have to walk too far to find some dry clothes – typically 10 to 12 (of the 20 to 24) Grand Prix drivers actually live in Monaco.

The track may be slow and overtaking difficult, but the circuit has still seen some great races, particularly in 1961 when Stirling Moss (the greatest driver never to win a world championship) held off the might of Ferrari in his underpowered Lotus. I've been to the Monaco Grand Prix just once, but fortuitously I also chose a classic year. In 1970 Austrian driver Jochen Rindt overtook Australian Jack Brabham on the final corner of the race. Later in the year Rindt was killed at the Italian Grand Prix at Monza, but no-one could surpass his points total and he became Formula One's only posthumous world champion.

The 78-lap race happens on a Sunday afternoon in late May, the conclusion of several days of practice, qualifying and supporting races. Tickets (€50 to €300) are available from **Automobile Club de Monaco** (ACM; ☎ 93 15 26 24; www.acm.mc; 23 blvd Albert 1er) and the official T-shirt, loo seats et al from **L@Boutique** (☎ 97 70 45 35; laboutique@acm.mc; 46 rue Grimaldi) and **Boutique Formule 1** (☎ 93 15 92 44; 15 rue Grimaldi).

Train

Monaco's **train station** (www.monaco-gare.com; blvd Princesse Charlotte) – a glam subterranean marble affair – can be accessed via pedestrian tunnels and escalators from 6 av Prince Pierre de Monaco, pont Ste-Dévote (blvd Princesse Charlotte), place Ste-Dévote and blvd de la Belgique.

Trains run by France's SNCF (p427) run east to Menton (€1.70, 15 minutes) and Ventimiglia (Vintimille in French; €3.10, 25 minutes) in Italy, and west to Nice (€3.10, 20 minutes) and beyond (see p278).

GETTING AROUND
Bus

Monaco's urban bus system has five lines, bizarrely numbered one to six without the three. Line 2 links Monaco Ville to Monte Carlo and then loops back to the Jardin Exotique. Line 4 links the train station with the tourist office, the casino and Plage du Larvotto. A one-way ticket/one-day pass costs €1.50/3.60. Alternatively, buy a four-/eight-ride magnetic card (€3.60/5.70) from the bus driver or from vending machines at most bus stops. Buses run roughly every 11 minutes between 7am and 9pm (every 20 minutes from 7.30am on Sunday).

Lift

A system of escalators and public lifts links the steep streets. They operate either 24 hours or 6am to midnight or 1am.

Taxi

Call ☎ 93 15 01 01.

Directory

CONTENTS

Accommodation	398
Activities	400
Business Hours	400
Children	401
Climate Charts	401
Courses	402
Customs	402
Dangers & Annoyances	402
Discount Cards	403
Embassies & Consulates	404
Festivals & Events	405
Food & Drink	405
Gay & Lesbian Travellers	407
Holidays	407
Insurance	408
Internet Access	408
Legal Matters	408
Local Government	409
Maps	409
Money	410
Photography & Video	410
Post	410
Shopping	411
Solo Travellers	411
Telephone	411
Time	412
Toilets	412
Tourist Information	412
Tours	413
Travellers with Disabilities	413
Visas	414
Volunteering	415
Women Travellers	415
Work	415

ACCOMMODATION

Budget options in this guide command between €40 and €70 a night for a double room in a hotel with private shower and toilet. Bar the odd few that lurk on the coast, few hotels these days have shared bathroom facilities on the corridor. Midrange options cover the €70 to €149 price range, and top end entails anything upwards of €150. With the exception of prices for *chambre d'hôte* and *maison d'hôte* accommodation, rates in this guide don't include breakfast unless noted otherwise. Hotels charge anything from €7 to €30 per person for breakfast.

In July and August don't even contemplate the coast unless you have a reservation or are prepared to pay a fortune for the few rooms available. The exception is rock-bottom budget accommodation, especially in Nice, which rarely gets booked up weeks in advance – but is full most days by noon. Tourist offices can tell you where rooms are available. Some midrange hotels only accept reservations accompanied by a credit-card number. Most budget joints demand payment upon arrival.

Local authorities impose a *taxe de séjour* (tourist tax) on each visitor in their jurisdiction, usually only enforced in the high season (Easter to September). At this time prices charged are €0.20 to €1.50 per person higher than posted rates.

Camping

The region has camp sites galore, most open March or April to September or October.

Stars reflect facilities and amenities. Separate tariffs are charged for people, tents or caravans, and vehicles. Many places have *forfaits* (fixed-price deals) for two people with tent and car. Camp-site receptions are often closed during the day; the best time to call is early morning or evening.

Camping à la ferme (camping farm) is co-ordinated by Gîtes de France (p400).

Camping sauvage (wild camping) is illegal but tolerated in some places. The odd hostel allows travellers to pitch in the back garden.

Chambres & Maisons d'Hôtes

The best way to sleep, eat and dream Provence! A *chambre d'hôte* is a B&B, the most

---

BOOK ACCOMMODATION ONLINE

For more accommodation reviews and recommendations by Lonely Planet authors, check out the online booking service at www.LonelyPlanet.com. You'll find the true, insider low-down on the best places to stay. Reviews are thorough and independent. Best of all, you can book online.

PRACTICALITIES

- France uses the metric system for weights and measures.

- Plugs have two round pins (bring an international adapter), and the electric current is 220V at 50Hz AC.

- Videos in France work on the PAL system.

- Pick up regional news, views, chat and gossip with the Monte Carlo-based, English-language Riviera Radio (106.3MHz FM in Monaco, 106.5MHz FM in France; www.rivieraradio.mc); and the BBC World Service with Radio France Internationale (RFI; 100.5MHz FM and 100.9MHz FM; www.rfi.fr).

- French radio stations include Radio Provence (103.6MHz and 102.9MHz FM), Radio Vaucluse (100.4MHz FM), Radio Luberon (88.6MHz FM) and Cannes Radio (91.5MHz FM). On the coast, music-charged Nice Music (102.3 FM) is the sound.

- Read regional news in French in *Nice Matin* (www.nicematin.fr) and *La Provence* (www.la provence-presse.fr); and in English in the *Riviera Reporter* (www.riviera-reporter.com) and *Riviera Times* (www.rivieratimes.com).

- Switch on the box with private French TV stations TF1 and M6; or state-run France 2, France 3 and 5 (Arte after 7pm).

---

upmarket and/or stylish of which are increasingly tagging themselves as a *maison d'hôte*. A feast of a breakfast is included in the price, and many serve a delicious dinner of several courses around a shared table (known as *table d'hôte*) for €15 to €30, usually including apéritif and wine. Many are in beautiful chateaux, age-old *mas* (Provençal farmhouses) or *moulins* (mills) and are highly sought-after.

Dozens of *chambres d'hôtes* and *maison d'hôtes* are listed in this guide; otherwise, tourist offices keep lists, contact Gîtes de France (p400) or try:

Allo Chambres d'Hôtes (☎ 08 91 16 22 22) The number to call for last-minute vacancies.

Avignon & Provence (www.avignon-et-provence.com) Exceptional online accommodation guide.

Fleurs de Soleil (www.fleursdesoleil.fr) Quality label awarded to *chambres d'hôtes;* national guide online and in print (€12).

Maisons d'Hôtes de Charme (www.guidesdecharme .com) France-specific guidebook featuring properties with bags of charm, published annually online and in print (€22).

Chateaux

In the Côtes de Provence wine region, there are several *domaines viticoles* (wine-growing estates) – invariably arranged around a gorgeous chateau – where you can stay. In addition to a comfortable bed, hearty breakfast and, upon request, an evening meal of fabulous proportions, many let you taste wine and

tour their vineyards. The Maison des Vins in Les Arcs-sur-Argens (p359) has a list.

Should you wish to buy or dream about a chateau or *domaine viticole* of your own, contact oenologist Stéphane Paillard at **Le Bureau Viticole** (☎ 04 90 92 48 74; www.bureauviticole.fr; 10 blvd Mirabeau, 13210 St-Rémy de Provence), a specialist estate agent run by upmarket real-estate agent **Émile Garcin** (www.emilegarcin.fr), with offices in St-Rémy de Provence and Ménerbes.

The Riveria's *belle époque* follies, celebrity real estate and various other properties of dreamy proportions are handled by **John Taylor** (www.john-taylor.fr).

Hostels

There are a fair few hostels sprinkled along the coast, including at Cap d'Antibes, Cap d'Ail, Cassis, Fréjus, Marseille, Nice and near Stes-Maries de la Mer; in the mountains at La Foux d'Allos; and towards the west in Avignon, Aix-en-Provence, Arles, Nîmes and Fontaine de Vaucluse.

You can expect to pay between €11 and €22 per night (occasionally this includes breakfast and/or sheets), plus €3/3.50/10 for sheets/breakfast/dinner. Not all hostels have kitchen facilities. Most don't accept telephone reservations.

Affiliates of the **Fédération Unie des Auberges de Jeunesse** (FUAJ; www.fuaj.org) and the **Ligue Française pour les Auberges de Jeunesse** (LFAJ; www .auberges-de-jeunesse.com) require an HI card.

Hotels

Hotels have one to four stars and charge €7 (budget and midrange) to €30 (top end) extra per person for breakfast. Rooms with bathtubs cost more than rooms with showers. Beds usually tout neck-aching, hot-dog-shaped bolsters – you'll find *oreillers* (regular pillows) hidden in a cupboard in the room.

In many hotels single rooms don't exist, as such; rather, doubles are flogged as singles. Triples and quads often have two double beds. Out of season, most hotels close for at least two weeks for their *congé annuel* (annual closure). Ski-resort hotels in Haute-Provence only open for the winter ski season and a couple of months in summer for walkers.

Budget hotels tend to charge the same rates year-round. Move into the midrange price bracket and there are three sets of seasonally adjusted prices: low season (October/November to February/March), midseason (March to May and September/October) and high season (June to September). Certain festivals (Festival d'Avignon; Cannes film festival; the Nîmes *férias*) bump up prices beyond belief. Reliable bets in the midrange price range are hotels affiliated to **Logis de France** (www.logisdefrance.com).

Many four-star hotels languish in traditional properties: farmhouses, *monastères* (monasteries), *moulins à huile* (oil mills), *prieurés* (priories) or restored Cistercian *abbayes* (abbeys). Lakes, rose gardens and olive groves pepper the vast grounds of these exclusive estates where a night's sleep costs anything upwards of €150. **Châteaux & Hotels de France** (www.chateauxhotels.com) and **Relais & Châteaux** (www.relaischateaux.fr) are two umbrella organisations under which these exclusive and expensive hotels often fall.

Refuges & Gîtes d'Étapes

This kind of accommodation studs the Parc National de Mercantour and Haute-Provence, where undeveloped rural areas are rife.

Gîtes d'étapes (basic dorm rooms) tend to be in towns and villages popular with walkers and climbers; *refuges* (simple mountain shelters) are in isolated wildernesses, often accessible only by foot.

Both are basic and equipped with bunks, mattresses and blankets, but not sheets. Nightly rates start at €10 per person. Cooked meals are occasionally available.

To reserve a *refuge* bed, get in contact with the **Club Alpin Français des Alpes-Maritimes** (Map pp262-3;

☎ 04 93 62 59 99; http://cafnice.org in French; 14 av Mirabeau, F-06000 Nice).

Rental Accommodation

Tourist offices have lists of self-catering studios, apartments and villas to rent on a short- (one week) or long-term (several months) basis. The most sought-after properties are booked a year in advance.

Many extra-charming *gîtes ruraux* (self-catering accommodation) – a century-old *mas* in an olive grove or cherry-tree orchard, say, or converted farm stables surrounded by a menagerie of farmyard animals – are represented by **Gîtes de France** (www.gites-de-france-paca .com), an organisation that liaises between owners and renters. Amenities range from basic bathroom facilities and a simple kitchenette (with oven, hot plates and fridge), to a bathroom, fully equipped kitchen, washing machine, TV, telephone, garden and pool. Linen is never provided, but can be rented. *Gîtes panda* are in regional and national parks.

Bookings can be made online or through a regional Gîtes de France office:

Alpes de Haute-Provence (☎ 04 92 31 30 40; www.gites-de-france-04.fr; rond-point du 11 Novembre, F-04000 Digne-les-Bains)

Alpes-Maritimes (Map pp262-3; ☎ 04 92 15 21 30; www.gites-de-france-alpes-maritimes.com; 57 promenade des Anglais, BP 21614, F-06011 Nice)

Bouches du Rhône (☎ 04 90 59 49 39; www .gitesdefrance13.visitprovence.com; Domaine du Vergon, F-13370 Mallemort)

Var (☎ 04 94 50 93 93; www.gites-de-france-var .fr; rond-point du 4 Decembre 1974, BP 215, F-83006 Draguignan)

Vaucluse (Map p160; ☎ 04 90 85 45 00; www.gites-de -france-vaucluse.asso.fr in French; place Campana, BP 164, F-84008 Avignon)

ACTIVITIES

The wealth of outdoor activities on offer in the region is great; see p80.

BUSINESS HOURS

On Sunday, a bakery is usually about all that is open (in the morning only), and public transport services are less frequent. On weekdays, village shops (including bakeries) close for a long lunch between 2pm and 4pm. Hotels, restaurants, cinemas, cultural institutions and shops close for their *congé annuel* (annual holiday) in winter.

Some hotels, museums and *chambres d'hôtes* only open from *Pâques à la Toussaint* (Easter to All Saints' Day, 1 November). Many places to eat and/or drink in Nice and Marseille brandish 'open nonstop' signs. Far from meaning they open 24 hours, it simply means the place doesn't close for lunch.

Standard hours for commercial banks, museums, pharmacies, post offices, shops, restaurants and supermarkets are listed on the Quick Reference page on cover flap of this book. Places to eat close for two consecutive days a week, often Sunday, Monday and/or Tuesday. Opening hours for bars, pubs and clubs fluctuate wildly.

CHILDREN
Practicalities
Most car-hire firms provide children's car seats for around €30 per rental, but the concept of organising a car seat in a taxi is an alien one.

Many hotels can provide cots (free) or an extra bed (€15 to €40), but families travelling with younger children will find *chambre d'hôte* accommodation more hospitable. Pick one that serves evening meals, too, allowing you to dine in peace while the kids sleep upstairs with a baby monitor (bring your own). For kiddie-dining practicalities see p407.

Cobbled streets, ultranarrow pavements in old towns and bumper-to-bumper parked cars can make strolling with a pushchair something of an obstacle course. Supermarkets and pharmacies sell disposable nappies (diapers) and high-factor sun-protection creams.

Tourist offices maintain lists of babysitters and crèches. For region-specific information read *Le Curieux, Monaco-French Riviera for Families*, by Helen Misseri and Elisabeth Moati, a bilingual French-English book by two mothers living on the coast; or the annual bilingual *Family First: Life & Holidays with Children on the French Riviera* (www.familyfirst.fr), an excellent listings guide crammed with useful information for parents, covering everything from kid-friendly hotels and restaurants to pools, parks and playgrounds.

Sights & Activities
Kids are well-catered for: a water park and aquarium with killer whales in Biot (p318); waterslides at the Niagara Parc Nautique near La Môle (p363); and tortoises at the Village des Tortues in the Massif des Maures (p362)

are but some ways to win the heart of a howling child. Museumwise, try Monaco's Musée Océanographique (p386).

The Parc National du Mercantour (p248), the Office National des Forêts (ONF) and tourist offices organise nature walks for children.

Canoeing beneath the Pont du Gard (p200); horse riding in the Camargue (p137); island cycling on Porquerolles (there are pedal-powered chariots for kids too small to pedal themselves; p369); snorkelling off Port-Cros' shores (p369) or along an underwater nature trail at the Domaine du Rayol (p364); in-line skating in Nice and Marseille (p269 and p103); or skiing in Haute-Provence (p248) are all outdoor thrills.

CLIMATE CHARTS
Mistral aside (p72), the region enjoys a temperate climate with mild winters. For climatic considerations see p20.

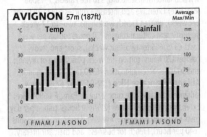

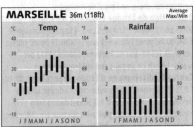

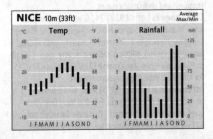

DIRECTORY

COURSES

Art, food, wine, language, film – the best of France is there for the learning. The website www.edufrance.fr/en has information about higher education, and www.studyabroadlinks.com can help you find specific courses and summer programmes.

Arts & Crafts

Painting lavender landscapes is old hat now. Courses these days zoom in on everything from mosaic work to ceramics; see p60.

Cooking & Gardening

For cooking courses, see p52. For gardening courses, see p77.

Language

There are dozens of French language schools; tourist offices have lists.

Alliance Française Marseille (☎ 04 96 10 24 60; www.alliancefrmarseille.org; 310 rue Paradis, F-13008 Marseille) Extensive and intensive courses (six to 20 hours' per week), written French workshops, two- to 12-week linguistic and cultural courses (20 hours tuition per week costs €375/665 for two/four weeks), sport and study courses (20 hours' tuition per week plus sailing or diving); and arranges accommodation (€320 to €550 per month).

Alliance Française Nice (☎ 04 93 62 67 66; www.alliance-francaise-nice.com; 2 rue de Paris, F-06000 Nice) Extensive/intensive courses (2½/four hours' tuition per day costs €430/660 per week), evening classes, private lessons (€40 per hour), French for business, and thematic literary, gastronomic, music and painting workshops.

Association de Langue Française d'Avignon (☎ 04 90 85 86 24; www.alfavignon.com; 4 impasse Romagnoli, F-84000 Avignon) Two-week course with 15 hours' tuition per week (€500) and B&B accommodation (€112 per week); French for au pairs and resident foreigners.

Centre Méditerranéen d'Études Françaises (☎ 04 93 78 21 59; www.centremed.monte-carlo.mc; chemin des Oliviers, F-06320 Cap d'Ail) School dating from 1952, idyllically set in a coastal park with open-air amphitheatre designed by Jean Cocteau (p284); two-week French language and civilisation courses.

Crea Langues (☎ 04 92 77 74 58; www.crealangues.com; Monastère de Segres, F-04360 Moustiers-Ste-Marie) Language training in a cloistered monastery, with hiking, canyoning, cycling, painting and gastronomy options (€130 to €240); one-/two-week course €735/1175 plus €325/715 for full-board monastery accommodation.

International House (☎ 04 93 62 60 62; www.ih-nice.com; 62 rue Gioffredo, F-06000 Nice) One-/two-week courses with 20 lessons (45 minutes) a week cost €215/430, plus €45 enrolment fee; private 45-minute lessons (€50), French for executives and other courses. Arranges half-board accommodation with host family (€186/162 in single/shared room).

Université de Provence (☎ 04 42 95 32 17; www.up.univ-mrs.fr/wscefee; 29 av Robert Schumann, F-13621 Aix-en-Provence) A hot choice in lovely Aix: academic language and methodology courses, as well as writing workshops and basic French classes with painting, cinema, art, song and multimedia options.

Université Nice-Sophia Antipolis (☎ 04 93 37 53 94; http://portail.unice.fr in French; 98 blvd Édouard Herriot, BP 3209, F-06204 Nice) Summer French-language courses at Nice-Sophia Antipolis university; online, follow the 'International' link to get to the Language Institute of the Université Internationale d'Été.

Université Paul Cézanne d'Aix Marseille III (Université d'Aix Marseille III; ☎ 04 42 21 70 90; www.univ.u-3mrs.fr in French; 23 rue Gaston de Saporta, F-13625 Aix-en-Provence) Four-week intensive courses at the university's Institute of French Studies for Foreign Students.

CUSTOMS

Goods brought in and exported within the EU incur no additional taxes, provided duty has been paid somewhere within the EU and the goods are for personal consumption. There is no longer duty-free shopping within the EU; you have to be leaving Europe.

Coming from non-EU countries, duty-free allowances (for adults) are: 200 cigarettes, 50 cigars, 1L of spirits, 2L of wine, 50g of perfume, 250ml of eau de toilette and other goods up to the value of €183. Anything over the limit must be declared and tax may be charged.

DANGERS & ANNOYANCES

Beaches

Larger beaches on the Côte d'Azur have a *poste de secours* (safety post) during the summer season, staffed by lifeguards. In water-sport areas, a section of the sea is always sectioned off for swimmers. Note the colour of the flag flying before diving in: green means it is safe to swim; yellow means bathing is risky; red means that swimming is forbidden; and purple means the water is polluted.

Extreme Weather

During the balmy days of June and the steamy days of July and August, it is hard to believe that the region can be freezing cold when the mistral (p72) strikes.

Thunderstorms in the mountains and on the hot southern plains can be sudden, violent and dangerous. Check the weather report before embarking on a long walk; even then, be prepared for a sudden change in the weather. Storms are common in August and September.

Forest Fires

Forest fires are common in July and August when the sun is hot and the land is dry. Such fires spread incredibly quickly – between 20m and 30m per minute. Between 1 July and the second Sunday in September, forest authorities close high-risk areas. Never walk in a closed zone. Tourist offices can tell you if a walking path is closed. If you come across a fire, call the **fire brigade** (☎ 18).

Forests are crisscrossed with road tracks enabling fire crews to penetrate quickly. These roads, signposted DFCI (*Défense de la Forêt Contre l'Incendie*; Forest Defence against Fire), are closed to private vehicles but you can follow them on foot.

Lighting a campfire is forbidden. Barbecues, even in private gardens, are forbidden in many areas in July and August.

Poisonous Mushrooms

Wild-mushroom picking is a national pastime. Pick by all means, but don't eat anything until it has been positively identified as safe by a pharmacist. Most pharmacies in the region offer a mushroom-identification service.

Rivers & Lakes

Major rivers are connected to hydroelectric power stations operated by the national electricity company, Electricité de France (EDF). Water levels rise dramatically if the EDF opens a dam. White-water sports on the River Verdon of the Chaudanne Dam are forbidden when the water flow is less than 5 cu metres per second. For information on water levels and dam releases call ☎ 04 92 83 62 68.

Swimming is prohibited in lakes that are artificial and have steep, unstable banks (ie Lac de Ste-Croix, southwest of the Gorges du Verdon; and Lac de Castillon and the adjoining Lac de Chaudanne, northeast of the gorges). Sailing, windsurfing and canoeing are restricted to flagged areas.

Theft

Theft – from backpacks, pockets, cars, trains, laundrettes, beaches – is widespread, particularly along the Côte d'Azur. Keep an eagle eye on your bags, especially at train and bus stations, on overnight train rides, in tourist offices and on beaches.

Always keep your money, credit cards, tickets, passport, driving licence and other important documents in a money belt, worn inside your trousers or skirt. Keep enough money for the day in a separate wallet. Theft from hotel rooms is less common but it's still not a great idea to leave your life's belongings in your room. In hostels lock your nonvaluables in a locker provided and cart your valuables along. Upmarket hotels have *coffres* (safes).

When swimming at the beach or taking a dip in the pool, have members of your party take turns sitting with packs and clothes. On the Prado beaches in Marseille, keeping your valuables in one of the free (staffed) lockers provided is a good idea.

Motorists in Marseille, Nice and other larger cities should keep their doors locked when stopped at traffic lights; it is not unheard of for aspiring bandits to open the door to your car, ask you what the time is and, at the same time, scan you and your car for valuables.

DISCOUNT CARDS
Billets Jumelés

Many museums and monuments sell *billets jumelés* (combination tickets), which cover admission to more than one sight and offer a considerable saving. Some cities have museum passes that cut sightseeing costs further.

Carte Musées Côte d'Azur

The Carte Musées Côte d'Azur (French Riviera Museum Pass) gives card-holders unlimited admission to 62 museums along the coast. A one-/three-day pass costs €10/17 (no reduced rates) and a seven-day pass valid for seven days within a 15-day period is €27. Passes are sold at museums, tourist offices and FNAC stores.

Hostel Card

You need an annual Hostelling International (HI) card to stay at official youth hostels, although some let you in with a one-night stamp (€1.50). HI cards costing €10.70/15.25 for those under/over 26 are sold at HI-affiliated hostels and national **Youth Hostelling Associations** (YHA; www.iyhf.org).

Seniors Card

Those aged over 60 or 65 are entitled to discounts on public transport, museum admission fees, public theatres and so on. The Société Nationale des Chemins de Fer (SNCF) issues the Carte Senior (€53; www.senior -sncf.com) to those aged over 60, which gives reductions of 25% to 50% on train tickets, valid for one year.

Student, Youth & Teacher Cards

An International Student Identity Card (ISIC; €12) pays for itself through half-price admissions and discounted air and ferry tickets etc. Many stockists stipulate a maximum age, usually 24 or 25.

If you're under 26 but not a student you can buy an International Youth Travel Card (IYTC; €12), which entitles you to much the same discounts as an ISIC.

Teachers, professional artists, museum conservators and journalists are admitted to some museums for free. Bring proof of affiliation, for example, an International Teacher Identity Card (ITIC; €17) or official press card.

All three cards are administered by the **International Student Travel Confederation** (www .istc.org) and issued by student travel agencies and online at www.carteisic.com. Within the region, try branches of **Voyages Wasteels** (www .wasteels.fr in French; Aix-en-Provence ☎ 04 42 26 68 46; 5bis cours Sextius; Marseille ☎ 04 95 09 30 60; 67 La Canabière; Nice ☎ 04 93 03 60 90; 48 rue de France).

EMBASSIES & CONSULATES
French Embassies & Consulates

France's diplomatic and consular representatives abroad are listed on the website www .france.diplomatie.fr. For some of the following countries, additional consulates exist.

Australia Canberra (☎ 02-6216 0100; www.ambafrance -au.org; 6 Perth Av, Yarralumla, ACT 2600); Sydney Consulate (☎ 02-9261 5779; www.consulfrance-sydney.org; Level 26, St Martin's Tower, 31 Market St, Sydney, NSW 2000)

Belgium Brussels (☎ 02-548 8700; www.ambafrance -be.org; 65 rue Ducale, Brussels 1000); Brussels Consulate (☎ 02-229 8500; www.consulfrance-bruxelles.org; 12a place de Louvain, Brussels 1000)

Canada Ottawa (☎ 613-789 1795; www.ambafrance -ca.org; 42 Sussex Drive, Ottawa, Ont K1M 2C9); Toronto Consulate (☎ 416-925 8041; www.consulfrance-toronto .org; 2 Bloor Est, Suite 2200, Toronto M4W 1A8)

Germany Berlin (☎ 030-590 039 000; www.botschaft -frankreich.de; Pariser Platz 5, Berlin 10117); Munich Consulate (☎ 089-419 4110; www.consulfrance-munich .de; Heimeranstrasse 31, 3rd fl, Munich 80339)

Ireland (☎ 01-277 5000; www.ambafrance-ie.org; 36 Ailesbury Rd, Dublin 4)

Italy (☎ 06-686 011; www.ambafrance-it.org; Piazza Farnese 67, 00186 Rome)

Netherlands The Hague (☎ 070-312 5800; www .ambafrance-nl.org; Smidsplein 1, 2514 BT Den Haag); Amsterdam Consulate (☎ 020-530 6969; www.consul france-amsterdam.org; Vijzelgracht 2, 1017 HR Amsterdam)

New Zealand (☎ 04-384 2555; www.ambafrance -nz.org; 13th fl, Rural Bank Bldg, 34-42 Manners St, PO Box 11-343, Wellington)

South Africa Pretoria Embassy Apr-Jan (☎ 012-425 1600; www.ambafrance-za.org; 250 Melk St, New Muckleneuk, 0181 Pretoria); Pretoria Embassy Feb-Mar (☎ 021-422 1338; 78 Queen Victoria St, 8001 Cape Town)

Spain Madrid (☎ 91-423 8900; www.ambafrance-es.org; Calle de Salustiano Olozaga 9, 28001 Madrid); Barcelona Consulate (☎ 93-270 3000; www.consulfrance-barcelone .org; Ronda Universitat 22, 08007 Barcelona)

Switzerland Berne (☎ 031-359 2111; www .ambafrance-ch.org; Schosshaldenstrasse 46, 3006); Zürich Consulate (☎ 01-268 8585; www.consulatfrance-zurich .org; Signaustrasse 1, 8008 Zürich)

UK London (☎ 020-7073 1000; www.ambafrance-uk .org; 58 Knightsbridge, London SW1X 7JT); London Consu-
late (☎ 020-7073 1200; www.consulfrance-londres .org; 21 Cromwell Rd, London SW7 2EN); London Visa Section (☎ 020-7073 1250; 6a Cromwell Place, London SW7 2EW)

US Washington (☎ 202-944 6000; www.ambafrance -us.org; 4101 Reservoir Rd NW, Washington, DC 20007); New York Consulate (☎ 212-606 3600; www.consulfrance -newyork.org; 934 Fifth Av, New York, NY 10021)

Monégasque Embassies

Monaco's diplomatic missions abroad include the following:

Belgium (☎ 02-347 4987; ambassade.monaco@skynet .be; place Guy d'Arezzo, B-1180 Brussels)

Germany (☎ 30 26 39 033; ambassade.monaco@aol .com; Klingelhöferstr 7, D-10785 Berlin)

Spain (☎ 91 578 20 48; ambmonacomad@hotmail.com; Calle Villanueva 12, ES-28001 Madrid)

Switzerland (☎ 031 356 28 58; ambassademonaco@bluewin.ch; Hallwylstr 34, CP 3000, CH-3005 Berne 6)

USA (☎ 212-286 0500; www.monaco-consulate.com; 565 Fifth Ave, 23rd fl, New York NY 10017)

Consulates in Provence & Monaco

Foreign embassies are in Paris, although some countries have a consulate in Nice, Marseille and/or Monaco:

Belgium Marseille (☎ 04 96 10 11 16; 75 cours Pierre Puget); Nice (Map pp262-3; ☎ 04 93 87 79 56; 5 rue Gabriel Fauré); Monaco (☎ 377-93 50 59 89; 13 av des Castelans)

Canada Nice (Map pp262-3; ☎ 04 93 92 93 22; 10 rue Lamartine); Monaco (Map p384; ☎ 377-97 70 62 42; Palais de la Scala, Bureau No 1178, 1 av Henri Dunant)

France (Map p384; ☎ 377-92 16 54 60; www.consulat france.mc in French); Monaco

Germany Marseille (☎ 04 91 16 75 20; 338 av du Prado) Nice (☎ 04 93 83 55 25; Le Minotaure, 34 av Henri Matisse); Monaco (☎ 377-97 97 49 65; dieter -spaethe@monaco377.com; 2 chemin du Ténao)

Italy Marseille (☎ 04 91 18 49 18; 56 rue d'Alger) Nice (☎ 04 93 14 40 96; 74 blvd Gambetta); Monaco (☎ 377-93 50 22 71; L'Annonciade, 17 av de l'Annonciade)

Monaco (☎ 04 91 33 30 21; 3 place aux Huiles, Marseille)

Netherlands Marseille (☎ 04 91 25 66 64; 139 av de Toulon); Nice (☎ 04 93 87 52 94; 14 rue Rossini); Monaco (☎ 377-92 05 15 02; Aigue Marine, entrance A, 24 av de Fontvieille)

Spain Monaco (☎ 377 93 30 24 98; 20 blvd des Moulins)

Switzerland Marseille (☎ 04 96 10 14 10; 7 rue d'Arcole); Monaco (☎ 377 93 15 58 82; 2 av de Grande Bretagne)

UK Marseille (Map p98; ☎ 04 91 15 72 10; 24 av du Prado); Monaco (☎ 377-93 50 99 54; 33 blvd Princesse Charlotte)

US Marseille (Map p98; ☎ 08 10 26 46 26, 04 91 54 92 00; www.amb-usa.fr; place Varian Fry); Nice (Map p262-3; ☎ 04 93 88 82 61; 7 av Georges V)

FESTIVALS & EVENTS

The region boasts a spicier-than-spicy cultural calendar. Festivals celebrate everything from a historical or folklore tradition to performing art or the region's most beloved pastimes (food and wine).

Destination-specific festivals are listed in the relevant regional chapters. For a complete listing, pick up *Terre de Festivals* (follow the link from www.regionpaca.fr), a meaty 240-page festival-listing guide available for free at most tourist offices, or visit www.cotedazur -en-fetes.com.

Regional festivals:

May & June

May Day Workers' day is celebrated on 1 May with trade-union parades and diverse protests. People give each other *muguet* (lily of the valley) for good luck. No-one works (except waiters and *muguet* sellers).

Fête de la Musique (www.fetedelamusique.culture .fr) Bands, orchestras, crooners, buskers and spectators regionwide take to the streets on 21 June for France's national celebration of music.

Avignon Blues Festival (http://lavoixdublues.free.fr in French) Held from the end of June to mid-August, six weeks of mellow blues in the papal city, Avignon.

Chansons des Pays du Verdon (http://lavoixdublues .free.fr in French) Festival dedicated to traditional Provençal song, dance and chants, held from the end of June to early August in Valensole, Rians and elsewhere around the Verdon.

July

Festival des Nuits de l'Enclave Three weeks of jazz, classical music, theatre and contemporary dance in the Enclave des Papes in July, in and around Valréas.

Les Musicales du Luberon Three-week bonanza of classical music concerts in churches and abbeys in Cavaillon, Ménerbes and other Luberon villages in July.

Festival International de Quators à Cordes du Luberon (www.festival-quators-luberon.com in French) Luberon's international chamber music festival with concerts held in churches in Roussillon, Goult, La Roque d'Anthéron and L'Isle sur la Sorgue and Abbaye de Silvacane in July.

Musiques dans les Vignes Highly atmospheric classical music concerts between vines, from mid-July to early August in Vaucluse.

National Day Fireworks, parades and all-round hoo-ha to mark the storming of the Bastille in 1789, symbol of the French Revolution, celebrated regionwide on 14 July.

Festival Choral International en Provence International polyphony festival held from the end of July to early August, organised by the region's Provençal polyphony group. Held in Var and Bouches du Rhône.

December

Christmas On 25 December, most villages celebrate Noël with midnight Mass, traditional chants in Provençal and a ceremony in which shepherds offer a new-born lamb. Séguret (p179) still celebrates Christmas with Mass and a living crèche.

FOOD & DRINK

For the full low-down on gastronomic Provence see p42.

In the Eating listings in this guide, we indicate the price of a *menu* (two- or three-course meal at a set price); ordering à la carte is generally more expensive.

Budget restaurants serve simple, generally unadventurous meals for €10 or so. Midrange places, of which there are plenty, cook up seasonal specialities accompanied by bags of atmosphere, with *menus* costing €15 to €25 (less at lunchtime). More-formal service, creative cuisine, an unusual and stylish décor, and *menus* costing anything upwards

---

PLAIN OLD WATER

Tap water is safe to drink, but the water spouting from fountains that tout a sign reading *eau non potable* (nondrinking water) isn't.

---

of €30 are distinguishing features of top-end eating spots.

Where to Eat & Drink

Dining *à la provençal* can mean spending anything from €10 in a village bistro to upwards of €75 at a multistarred gastronomic temple. Irrespective of price range, a *carte* (menu) is usually pinned up outside, allowing for a price and dish check.

The most authentic places to eat are invariably in tiny hamlets off the beaten track, touting just one *menu* with *vin compris* (wine included). Coffee, the usual way to end a meal, is served espresso-style – short, black and strong – unless you specify otherwise: *café crème* is an espresso with steamed milk or cream and *café au lait* is hot milk with a dash of coffee. Tea comes in the form of an empty cup and a tea bag (no milk).

Some restaurants in larger towns and with illustrious addresses regionwide get crowded, so it's best to book. Few accept reservations for more than one seating, allowing ample time to linger over coffee and *digestif* (postdinner drink). Some don't accept credit cards.

Standard opening hours for eating places are listed on the Quick Reference page on the front-cover flap of this book. Those deviating from these are listed in the regional chapters.

FERMES AUBERGES & CHATEAUX

Feasting on homemade food on a *ferme auberge* (working farm) or a wine-producing estate is a great way to dine. Typical Provençal cuisine and pace is guaranteed; portions appease the feistiest of appetites and dining is often around shared tables. A four-course *menu*, often with wine, costs €20 to €40.

Maisons des vins (wine houses) have lists of chateaux where you can eat; Gîtes de France (p400) has farm details.

CAFÉS

Cafés – the hub of village life – invariably double as bar and bistro, too. Most serve croissant-and-coffee breakfasts and lunchtime baguettes filled with cheese (around €4) or charcuterie (cold meat). In towns, cafés on grand boulevards or in chic spots such as the Vieux Port in St-Tropez charge more than a place fronting a quiet side street. In fine café tradition Aix-en-Provence's Les Deux Garçons (p129), the region's most famous café, hikes up its prices after 10pm.

QUICK EATS

Crepe makers and ice-cream and *beignet* (doughnut) stalls are rife in seaside resorts, but in inland villages and towns people simply nip into a café for a sandwich, or a *salon de thé* (tea room) or patisserie for a slice of something sweet to munch sitting down or on the move.

SELF-CATERING

When shopping, do as the locals do: buy fresh local produce from the weekly market (market days are listed in regional chapters). Markets are always in the morning (around 7am to noon or 1pm) and – if it's a *marché paysan* (farmers market) or *marché bio* (organic market) – sell produce grown without the aid of pesticides, chemical fertilisers etc. Staple products include fruit and vegetables, olives, olive oil, bunches or woven plaits of *aïl* (garlic), marinated olives and dried herbs in stubby coarse sacks.

Markets aside, buying a baked-that-hour baguette or loaf of *pain aux olives* (olive bread) in the local *boulangerie* (bakery), a *tarte aux fruits* (fruit tart) in the patisserie, cheese in the *fromagerie* (cheese shop), the catch of the day in the *poissonnerie* (fishmongers) and cold meats, seafood salads and so on in the charcuterie can be more expensive – but is definitely more satisfying – than shopping in a supermarket.

Those needing shed-loads of beer, bottled water etc will do no better than Monoprix or one of the *hypermarchés* (Leclerc, Intermarché etc) skirting larger towns.

Vegetarians & Vegans

In a country where *viande* (meat) once meant 'food' too, it comes as no surprise that vegetarians and vegans are not catered for particularly well, if at all: vegetarian restaurants are nonexistent, as are vegetarian *menus*. That said, vegetables form the backbone of many typical Provençal dishes, meaning nonmeat-eaters won't starve (even if it does mean compiling a full meal from a selection of starters), while *produits biologiques* (organic products) are all the rage nowadays, even among carnivores.

Strict vegetarians should note that most cheeses in France are made with *lactosérum* (rennet), an enzyme derived from the stomach of a calf or young goat, and that some red wines are clarified with the albumin of egg whites. Vegetarian wine (clarified using a chemical substitute or not at all) is impossible to find in the region, but *le vin bio* (organic wine) – made from grapes grown without the aid of chemical fertilisers and pesticides and often bottled in recycled glass – is becoming increasingly popular.

Dining with Kids

Children are welcomed in eating establishments, despite the lack of facilities that suggests otherwise. Highchairs are rare and the *menu enfant* (children's *menu*) that ventures away from the €5 to €8 realm of *boeuf haché* (minced beef), *frites* (fries) and *glace* (ice cream) is an exception. That said, *menus* geared to smaller appetites are increasing, with several upmarket places touting *menus* in the €15 range for pint-sized gourmets. For parents with toddlers who can't sit still, less formal *fermes auberges* (opposite) are an attractive option.

Breastfeeding in public is not frowned upon. The choice of baby food, infant formulas, soy and cows' milk and the like is as great in French supermarkets as it is back home; larger pharmacies also sell these products. For grizzly babies cutting teeth, there's nothing better to shut them up than the knobbly end of a baguette!

GAY & LESBIAN TRAVELLERS

There are large gay and lesbian communities in Aix-en-Provence, Nice, Cannes and Marseille, the latter being host to the colourful **Gay Pride march** (www.marseillepride.org in French) in late June or early July and the week-long **Universités Euroméditerranéennes des Homosexualités** (www.france.qrd.org/assocs/ueh/), a Euro-Mediterranean gay and lesbian summer school held in July. Smaller gay groups along the Riviera join forces for the annual **Gay Pride Côte d'Azur** (www.gaypride.fr.st in French), often held in Cannes.

The lesbian scene is as public as its gay counterpart. The region's most active gay and lesbian groups are in Marseille: they include **Act Up Marseille** (☎ 04 91 34 04 14; 1 rue Roussel Doria, 4e);

lesbian group **Centre Évolutif Lilith** (CEL; ☎ 04 91 05 81 41; http://celmrs.free.fr in French; 17 allées Léon Gambetta); and bookshop-café **Les Mots pour le Dire** (☎ 04 91 48 79 10; www.lesmotspourledire.fr in French; 33 rue des Trois Mages), which hosts regular gay-inspired and -driven events (lectures, discussion groups, book readings etc).

Gay Provence (www-gay-provence.org) is an online gay listings guide to the region.

HOLIDAYS
French Public Holidays

Museums and shops (but not cinemas, restaurants or bakeries) and most business shut on the following *jours fériés* (public holidays). When one falls on a Thursday, many people make a *pont* (bridge, ie with the weekend), meaning they don't work the Friday either.

New Year's Day (Jour de l'An) 1 January
Easter Sunday & Monday (Pâques & lundi de Pâques) Late March/April
May Day (Fête du Travail) 1 May
Victoire 1945 8 May – celebrates the Allied victory in Europe that ended WWII
Ascension Thursday (L'Ascension) May – celebrated on the 40th day after Easter
Pentecost/Whit Sunday & Whit Monday (Pentecôte & lundi de Pentecôte) Mid-May to mid-June – celebrated on the seventh Sunday after Easter
Fête Nationale (Bastille Day/National Day) 14 July
Assumption Day (L'Assomption) 15 August
All Saints' Day (La Toussaint) 1 November
Remembrance Day (L'onze Novembre) 11 November – celebrates the WWI armistice
Christmas (Noël) 25 December

Monégasque Public Holidays

Monaco shares the same holidays with France *except* those on 8 May, 14 July and 11 November. Additional public holidays:

Feast of Ste-Dévote 27 January – patron saint of Monaco
Corpus Christi June – three weeks after Ascension
Fête Nationale (National Day) 19 November
Immaculate Conception 8 December

School Holidays

Travelling to/from and around the region during French *vacances scolaires* (school holidays) is not recommended, especially in July and August when French families hit the coast for their annual summer holiday; Saturday is a horrendous day to travel.

Christmas–New Year Schools nationwide are closed 20 December to 4 January.

February–March The 'Feb' holidays last from about 7 February to 5 March; pupils in each of three zones are off for overlapping 15-day periods.

Easter The month-long spring break, which begins around Easter, also means pupils have overlapping 15-day holidays.

Summer The nationwide summer holiday lasts from the tail end of June until very early September.

INSURANCE

A travel-insurance policy to cover theft, loss and medical problems is recommended. Some policies exclude dangerous activities such as scuba diving, motorcycling and trekking up very high mountains.

You may prefer a policy that pays doctors or hospitals directly rather than you having to pay on the spot and claim later. If you have to claim later ensure you keep all documentation. Check that the policy covers ambulances or an emergency flight home. Paying for your airline ticket with a credit card often provides limited travel-accident insurance. Ask your credit-card company what it's prepared to cover.

See p428 for health insurance and p426 for car insurance.

INTERNET ACCESS

Things are improving rapidly for wi-fi users on the coast and in more developed areas inland: wireless access points (some free, some not) can be found in all the region's airports and many hotels, cafés and other public spaces. Check sites such as www.wifinder.com or France-specific www.journaldunet.com/wifi for access points regionwide (389 hot spots in Alpes-Maritimes, 184 in Bouches du Rhône, 135 in the Var, 52 in the Vaucluse and 19 in Alpes de Haute-Provence at the last count).

Internet cafés are fairly abundant in towns and cities; they are listed under Information in the regional chapters. You'll pay €3 to €5 per hour. In museums, tourist offices and other

---

public buildings, you may come across phone-card-operated **Borne internet terminals** (www .netanoo.com in French); a 120-unit France Télécom *télécarte* (€15) gets you two hours online.

Some post offices are equipped with Cyberposte, a card-operated internet terminal for public use. Access cards cost €7.60 for the first hour and €4.60 for a one-hour recharge. Find a list of Cyberposte-equipped post offices at www.cyberposte.com (in French).

On newer SNCF trains an 'office space' next to the luggage compartments between carriages is provided for passengers; it comes complete with desk and plug to hook your laptop into the electricity supply.

If you're using your laptop, check that it is compatible with the 220V current in France; if not, you will need a converter. You'll also need a telephone plug adaptor. Having a reputable global modem will prevent access problems that can occur with PC-card modems brought from home.

If you do not choose a global Internet Service Provider (ISP; such as AOL), make sure your ISP has a dial-up number in France. Local ISPs **Free** (www.free.com), **Tiscali** (www.tiscali .fr) and **Orange** (www.orange.fr in French) have cheap or free short-term membership (look out for free trial membership CD-ROMs).

For useful travel websites, see p22.

LEGAL MATTERS
Police

French police have wide powers of search and seizure, and can ask you to prove your identity at any time. Foreigners must be able to prove their legal status in France (eg passport, visa, residency permit) without delay.

Verbally (and of course physically) abusing a police officer can carry a hefty fine, even imprisonment. You can refuse to sign a police statement, and you have the right to ask for a copy.

People who are arrested are considered innocent until proven guilty, but can be held in custody until trial. The website www.service -public.fr has information about legal rights.

French police are ultrastrict about security. Do not leave baggage unattended at airports or train stations: suspicious objects will be summarily blown up.

Drugs & Alcohol

Contrary to popular belief, French law does not officially distinguish between 'hard' and

---

WHAT THE COMPUTER ICON MEANS

Throughout this guide, only hotels and other types of accommodation that have an actual computer that guests can physically use to access the internet are flagged with a computer icon like this: 🖳 ; those that are wi-fi friendly, but have no computer, are not.

'soft' drugs. The penalty for any personal use of *stupéfiants* (including cannabis, amphetamines, ecstasy and heroine) can be a one-year jail sentence and a €3750 fine. Importing, possessing, selling or buying drugs can get you up to 10 years in prison and a fine of €7,500,000. Being drunk in public places is theoretically punishable with a €150 fine.

LOCAL GOVERNMENT

Provence–Alpes–Côte d'Azur is one of 22 French *régions* (administrative regions). It has an elected *conseil régional* (regional council) based in Marseille.

The *région* is split into six *départements* (departments). This book covers five of them: Alpes de Haute-Provence (04), Alpes-Maritimes (06), Bouches du Rhône (13), Var (83) and Vaucluse (84). Nîmes, on the western bank of the River Rhône, falls into the Gard *département* in the neighbouring Languedoc-Roussillon *région*. *Départements* are known by a two-digit code (listed above), included in postcodes.

France has 96 *départements* (including Corsica). Each *département* has a *préfet* (prefect)

> **LEGAL AGES**
>
> - Age considered minor under anti-child-pornography & child-prostitution laws: 18
> - Age of consent: 15
> - Age of majority: 18
> - Buying alcohol: 16
> - Driving: 18
> - Voting: 18

based in a *préfecture* (prefecture), who represents the national government, and an elected *conseil général* (general council). There's a *préfecture* in Digne-les-Bains (04), Nice (06), Marseille (13), Toulon (83) and Avignon (84).

MAPS

Quality regional maps are widely available outside France. **Michelin** (www.viamichelin.com) and **IGN** (www.ign.fr in French) both have online boutiques where you can purchase maps. Michelin's yellow-jacketed map *Provence and the*

ADMINISTRATIVE RÉGIONS & DÉPARTEMENTS

0 — 50 km
0 — 30 miles

RHÔNE-ALPES 26
07
84
ITALY
LANGUEDOC-ROUSSILLON 84
30 Avignon
04 Digne-les-Bains
06
13
Nice MONACO
83
PROVENCE · ALPES ·
CÔTE D'AZUR
Marseille
Toulon
MEDITERRANEAN SEA

DÉPARTEMENTS
04 Alpes de Haute-Provence
05 Hautes-Alpes
06 Alpes-Maritimes
07 Ardèche
13 Bouches du Rhône
26 Drôme
30 Gard
83 Var
84 Vaucluse

———— International Boundary
———— Regional Boundary
———— Departemental Boundary

Côte d'Azur No 245 covers the area included in this guide at a scale of 1:200,000.

Within the region you can find city maps at *maisons de la presse* (newsagencies) in most towns and cities, at *papeteries* (stationery shops), tourist offices, travel bookshops, and also at many of the mainstream bookshops. Kümmerly & Frey, with its orange-jacketed *Blay-Foldex Plans-Guides* series, and Éditions Grafocarte, with its blue-jacketed *Plan Guide Bleu & Orange,* are the main city-map publishers. A city map typically costs around €4. The free street *plans* (maps) distributed by tourist offices range from the superb to the useless.

For walking and cycling maps see p88 and p81.

MONEY

The euro (€) – Europe's common currency in circulation in 12 Euroland countries since 1 January 2002 – is the only legal tender in France and Monaco.

One euro is divided into 100 cents, also called centimes in France. Coins come in one, two, five, 10, 20 and 50 cents and €1 and €2 denominations; the latter has a brass centre and silvery edges and the €1 has the reverse (silvery centre, brass edges). Euro banknotes, adorned with fictitious bridges (which bear a striking resemblance to the Pont du Gard) are issued in denominations of €5, €10, €20, €50, €100, €200 and the often-unwelcome €500.

Exchange rates are given on the inside front-cover flap of this book. For information on costs see p20.

ATMs

ATMs – *distributeurs automatiques de billets* or *points d'argent* – invariably provide the easiest means of getting cash. Most spit out euro banknotes at a superior exchange rate through Visa or MasterCard, and there are plenty of ATMs in the region linked to the international Cirrus and Maestro networks. If you remember your PIN code as a string of letters, translate it into numbers; French keypads don't show letters.

Credit Cards

This is the cheapest way to pay for things and to get cash advances. Visa (Carte Bleue in France) is the most widely accepted, followed by MasterCard (Access or Eurocard). Amex cards are not very useful except at upmarket establishments, but they do allow you to get cash at certain ATMs and at Amex offices. Travelling with two different credit cards (stashed in different wallets) is safer than taking one.

To report a lost or stolen credit card:
Amex (☎ 01 47 77 72 00)
Diners Club (☎ 08 10 31 41 59)
MasterCard, Eurocard & Access (Eurocard France; ☎ 08 00 90 13 87)
Visa (Carte Bleue; ☎ 08 00 90 20 33)

Tipping

French law requires that restaurant, café and hotel bills include a service charge (usually 10% to 15%), so a tip is neither necessary nor expected. However, most people – except in cases of dire service – do usually leave a euro or two in restaurants.

Travellers Cheques

Most banks cash travellers cheques issued by Amex (in US dollars or euros) and by Visa (in euros) for a charge of around €5 per transaction or a percentage fee.

PHOTOGRAPHY & VIDEO

Photo development in France is of excellent quality but expensive compared with many other countries. Expect to pay around €0.25/0.20 per print for up to 50/100 *tirages numériques* (digital prints). Transferring your images onto a CD usually costs an additional €5, although some photo shops throw a CD in for free.

Colour-print film remains widely available but, again, costly, so stock up ahead of time. For *diapositives* (slides), avoid Kodachrome: it's difficult to process quickly in France and may not be handled correctly. You can easily obtain video cartridges in large towns, but it's good to come with a few from home.

A good companion when on the road is *Travel Photography: A Guide to Taking Better Pictures,* by travel photographer Richard I'Anson.

POST

Postal services are fast (next-day delivery for most domestic letters), reliable and expensive. Post offices are signposted **La Poste** (www .laposte.fr in French). For a pretty postage stamp *(un timbre)* rather than the uninspiring blue sticker *(une vignette)* that comes out of post office coin-operated machines, go to a window marked *toutes opérations* (all services).

Tobacconists and shops selling postcards sell stamps, too. French stamps can be used in Monaco, but Monégasque stamps are only valid in Monaco.

From France and Monaco, domestic letters up to 20g cost €0.53. For international post, there are three zones: a postcard or letter/package under 20g/2kg costs €0.55/12.50 to Zone A (EU, Switzerland, Iceland, Norway); €0.75/14 to Zone B (the rest of Europe and Africa); and €0.90/20.50 to Zone C (North and South America, Asia, Middle East, Australasia).

SHOPPING

For olive oil-shopping tips and tricks see p45.

Many edible products that come from Provence – marrons au sirop (chestnuts in syrup) from the Massif des Maures, calissons (marzipan-like sweets frosted with icing sugar) from Aix-en-Provence and rice from the Camargue – are easy to transport home. But most glass-jar products sold at markets are homemade and rarely contain preservatives. Lavender marmalade from Carpentras market, for example, lasts one month – stored in the fridge – after being opened, while onion chutney from the Luberon – mind-blowingly delicious as it is – won't even survive outside a fridge. The same goes for bread, cheese and fresh truffles. But not for wine.

Less-tasty treats worth a shopping spree include perfumes from Grasse; leather sandals from St-Tropez; colourful wicker baskets and carnations from Antibes; glassware from Biot; Picasso-inspired ceramics from Vallauris; faïence from Moustiers-Ste-Marie; pipes and carpets from Cogolin; soap and santons ('little saints'; p100) from Marseille or Salon de Provence; courgourdons (traditional ornaments made from dyed and hollowed marrows or squash) from Nice; lavender oil, pottery, sundials and wrought-iron pieces from the Luberon; colourful Provençal fabrics from practically anywhere in the region; antiques from L'Isle-sur-la-Sorgue; terracotta and ceramic tiles from Salernes; gallery art from St-Paul de Vence and Mougins, and the latest haute-couture designs from Monaco.

Bargaining

Market shopping is one of the region's greatest joys; market days are listed in each regional chapter. Little bargaining goes on, although it's always worth a try.

SOLO TRAVELLERS

Male or female, travelling solo in the region poses few problems bar the fact that a sizable chunk of hotels don't have single rooms, or charge the same price for a so-called 'single' as a double. Dining alone in restaurants or sipping coffee in cafés is quite common, although lone women might well attract unwanted attention in busier spots on the coast.

TELEPHONE

France and Monaco have separate telephone systems.

French telephone numbers have 10 digits and need no area code; those starting with the digits 06 are mobile-phone numbers. To call anywhere in Provence and the Côte d'Azur from Monaco and abroad, dial your country's international access code, followed by 33 (France's country code) and the 10-digit number, dropping the initial 0. To call abroad from Provence, dial 00 (France's international access code), followed by the country code, area code (dropping the initial 0 if necessary) and local number.

Telephone numbers in Monaco have eight digits and likewise need no area code. To call Monaco from France and abroad, dial the international access code, followed by 377 (Monaco's country code) and the eight-digit number. To call abroad (including France) from Monaco, dial 00, followed by the country code, area code (dropping the initial zero if necessary) and local number.

Mobile Phones

France uses GSM 900/1800, which is compatible with the rest of Europe and Australia but

---

PHONE BOOK

Not sure which number to call? Find the full list of 'help' telephone numbers at ☎ 118 (www.appel118.fr in French):

Directory Inquiries (☎ 118 012; www.118012.fr in French)

France Télécom Customer Service (☎ 08 00 36 47 75, in English)

International Directory Inquiries (☎ 3212; €3 to find two numbers)

International reverse-charge (collect) call (☎ 00-33 plus relevant country code – 11 instead of 1 for the USA and Canada – and telephone number)

not with the North American GSM 1900 or the totally different system in Japan (though some North Americans have GSM 1900/900 phones that do work here). If you have a GSM phone, check with your service provider about using it in France, and beware of calls being routed internationally (very expensive for a 'local' call).

The three major providers of mobile phone access are **SFR** (☎ 08 00 10 60 00; www.sfr.com), **Bouygues** (☎ 08 10 63 01 00; www.bouygtel.com) and France Telecom's **Orange** (☎ 0 800 830 800; www .orange.fr). If you already have a compatible phone, you can buy a 'prepay' phone kit, which gives you a SIM-card with a mobile-phone number and a set number of calls. When these run out you purchase a recharge card at most *tabacs* (tobacconists). You can also get similar 'prepay' deals that include the phone itself.

Card packages, sold at phone shops and branches of FNAC in Avignon, Nice, Nîmes and Marseille, enable you to have your own French mobile-telephone number and make and receive calls at local rates.

Mobile-phone numbers in France always begin with 06. France has a 'caller pays' system, which means that you do not pay to receive a call on your mobile phone unless it is an international call.

Public Phones & Telephone Cards

Public telephones in France are card operated. Most have a button displaying two flags that you push for explanations in English.

Télécartes (phonecards) cost €8 or €15 at post offices, *tabacs* and anywhere that you see a blue sticker reading '*télécarte en vente ici*'. There are two kinds of phonecards, *cartes à puce* (cards with a magnetic chip, that are inserted chip-first into public phones) and *cartes à code* (that you can use from public or private phones by dialling the free access number and then punching in the card's scratch-off code).

Your choice of card will depend on your needs. France Télécom offers different cards suited to national and international dialling. For help in English on all France Télécom's services, see www.francetelecom.com or call ☎ 08 00 36 47 75.

A whole bevy of other cards is available for cheap international calls and most can be used elsewhere in Europe. Compare advertised rates, or ask which one is best for the place you're calling.

TIME

French and Monégasque time is GMT/UTC plus one hour, except during daylight-saving time (from the last Sunday in March to the last Sunday in October) when it is GMT/UTC plus two hours. The UK and France are always one hour apart: when it's 6pm in London, it's 7pm in Nice. New York is six hours behind Nice.

France uses the 24-hour clock and writes time like this: 15h30 (ie 3.30pm). Time has no meaning for many people in Provence.

TOILETS

Public toilets, signposted *toilettes* or WC, are surprisingly few and far between, which means you can be left feeling really rather desperate. Towns that have public toilets generally tout them near the *mairie* (town hall) or in the port area. Many have coin-operated, self-flushing toilet booths – highly disconcerting should the automatic mechanism fail with you inside. These toilets can usually be found in car parks and public squares; they cost €0.20 to enter. Some places sport flushless, kerbside *urinoirs* (urinals) reeking with generations of urine.

Restaurants, cafés and bars are often woefully under equipped with such amenities, so start queuing ahead of time. Bashful males be warned: some toilets are almost unisex; the urinals and washbasins are in a common area through which all and sundry pass to get to the toilet stalls. Older establishments often sport Turkish-style *toilettes à la turque*, a squat toilet with a high-pressure flushing mechanism that can soak your feet if you don't step back in time.

TOURIST INFORMATION
Local Tourist Offices

Every city and town and many villages have an *office du tourisme* (tourist office run by some unit of local government) or *syndicat d'initiative* (tourist office run by an organisation of local merchants). Both are excellent resources and can always provide a local map and information on accommodation.

Regional tourist information is handled by five *comités départementaux du tourisme* (departmental tourist offices), whose websites are invaluable information sources:

Alpes de Haute-Provence (☎ 04 92 31 57 29; www .alpes-haute-provence.com; Maison des Alpes de Haute-Provence, Immeuble François Mitterand, BP 170, F-04005 Digne-les-Bains)

Alpes-Maritimes (Map pp262-3; ☎ 04 93 21 80 95; www
.guideriviera.com; 55 promenade des Anglais, F-06011 Nice)
Bouches du Rhône (Map p98; ☎ 04 91 13 84 13;
www.visitprovence.com; 13 rue Roux de Brignoles,
F-13006 Marseille)
Var (☎ 04 94 50 55 50; www.tourismevar.com in French;
1 blvd Maréchal Foch, BP 99, F-83003 Draguignan)
Vaucluse (Map p160; ☎ 04 90 80 47 00; www
.provenceguide.com; 12 rue Collège de la Croix, BP 147,
F-84008 Avignon)

For tourist information on the principality of
Monaco, contact its national tourist office in
Monte Carlo (see p386).

French Tourist Offices Abroad

There are a number of French tourist offices
abroad (www.franceguide.com), called *mai-
sons de la France*:
Australia (☎ 02-9231 5244; info.au@franceguide.com;
Level 13, 25 Bligh St, Sydney, NSW 2000)
Belgium (☎ 09-028 8025; info.be@franceguide.com; av
de la Toison d'Or 21, 1050 Brussels)
Canada (☎ 514-288 2026; canada@franceguide.com;
1981 McGill College Av, Suite 490, Montreal, Que H3A 2W9)
Germany (☎ 09001 57 00 25; info.de@franceguide.com;
Zeppelinallee 37, 60325 Frankfurt)
Ireland (☎ 01560 235 235; info.ie@franceguide.com;
10 Suffolk St, Dublin 2)
Italy (☎ 899 199 072; info.it@franceguide.com; Via
Larga 7, 20122 Milan)
Netherlands (☎ 0900 11 22 332; info.nl@franceguide
.com; Prinsengracht 670, 1017 KX Amsterdam)
Spain Madrid (☎ 807 117 181; info.es@franceguide.com;
Plaza de España 18, 28008 Madrid); Barcelona (☎ 807 117
181; Fontanella 21-23, 08010 Barcelona)
Switzerland Zurich (☎ 01-211 3085; info.ch@
franceguide.com; Rennweg 42, 8023 Zurich); Geneva
(☎ 0900 900 699; c/o SNCF-Rail Europe, 2 rue de
Lausanne 11, 1201 Geneva)
UK (☎ 09068 244 123; info.uk@franceguide.com;
178 Piccadilly, London W1V 9AL)
USA New York (☎ 514-288 1904; info.us@franceguide
.com; 444 Madison Av, 10022 New York); Los Angeles
(☎ 310-271 6665; info.losangeles@franceguide.com;
9454 Wilshire Blvd, Ste 715, Beverly Hills, CA 90212-2967)

Monégasque Tourist Offices Abroad

Monaco has its own string of tourist offices
(www.monaco-tourisme.com):
France (☎ 01 42 96 12 23; dtcparis@gouv.mc; 73 av des
Champs Elysées, F-75008 Paris)
Germany (☎ 211-323 78 43; monaco_informations
_centrum@gouv.mc; WZ Center, Königsallee 27-31,
D-40212 Düsseldorf)

Italy (☎ 02 8645 8480; principatodimonaco
.milano@gouv.mc; Via Dante 12, I-20121 Milan)
UK (☎ 020-7352 9962; dtc.london@gouv.mc;
206 Harbour Yard, Chelsea Harbour, London SW10 0XD)
USA (☎ 212-286 3330; info@visitmonaco.com; 565 Fifth
Ave, 23rd fl, New York NY 10017)

TOURS

Dozens of enticing half- and full-day tours
available through tourist offices are peppered throughout the regional chapters of
this guide.

Most organised tours are activity-driven,
focusing on the great outdoors (see p87). But
there are lovely ones focusing on art, craft,
food and wine, too:
Arblaster & Clarke (☎ 01730-893344; www.arblaster
andclarke.com; Farnham Rd, West Liss, Hants GU33 6JQ,
UK) Food and wine tour specialists offering different tours
each year, often including a four-night 'Gourmet Provence'
tour, with four-star chateau accommodation, a couple of
meals in two-star Michelin restaurants, cookery demonstrations etc; wine tours, too.
La Provence Verte (☎ 04 94 72 04 21; www
.la-provence-verte.net; Maison du Tourisme, Carrefour
de l'Europe, F-83170 Brignoles) Gastronomy and food
'weekends' (three-night truffle weekends from €259);
'patrimony' sightseeing trips and plenty of outdoor thrills
and spills.
Martin Randall Travel (☎ 020-8742 3355; www
.martinrandall.com; 10 Barley Mow Passage, London W4
4PH, UK) A fabulous wealth of art and architecture tours
led by art historians or experts in their fields. Themes
include 'Art on the Côte d'Azur' (seven days, UK £1370)
and 'Gardens of the Riviera' (six days, UK £1370).
Service Loisirs Accueil Bouches du Rhône (☎ 04
90 59 49 36; www.visitprovence.com; 13 rue Roux de
Brignoles, F-13006 Marseille) A wide range of imaginative
two- to seven-day packages offered by the Bouches du
Rhône tourist board: impressionist-painting courses, chocolate courses, 'discovering Provence', 'pottery in Aubagne'
workshops and mountains of outdoor activity-driven ideas.

TRAVELLERS WITH DISABILITIES

The region is gradually becoming more user-
friendly for *handicapés* (people with disabilities), but kerb ramps remain rare, older public
facilities and budget hotels lack lifts, and the
cobblestone streets typical of hilltop villages
are a nightmare to navigate in a *fauteuil
rouant* (wheelchair).

But all is not lost. Many two- or three-
star hotels are equipped with lifts. On the
coast there are beaches – flagged *handiplages*
on city maps – with wheelchair access in

Cannes, Marseille, Nice, Hyères, Ste-Maxime and Monaco.

Michelin's *Guide Rouge* indicates those hotels with lifts and facilities for people with disabilities, while Gîtes de France (p400) provides a list of *gîtes ruraux* and *chambres d'hôtes* with wheelchair access.

International airports offer assistance to travellers with disabilities. TGV and regular trains are also accessible for passengers in wheelchairs; call the **SNCF Accessibilité Service** (☎ 08 00 15 47 53) for information. Its brochure (with one page in English), *Le Mémento du Voyageur à Mobilité Réduite*, is a useful guide.

Specialised travel agencies abroad include US-based **Wheels Up!** (☎ 1-888 38 4335; www.wheels up.com) and UK-based **Access Travel** (☎ 01942 888 844; www.access-travel.co.uk).

VISAS

Up-to-date visa regulations are posted on the Foreign Affairs Ministry website at www .diplomatie.gouv.fr.

EU nationals and citizens of Switzerland, Iceland and Norway only need a passport or national identity card to enter, and stay in, France.

As tourists, citizens of Australia, the US, Canada, New Zealand, Japan and Israel don't need a visa for stays of up to three months.

As a practical matter, if you don't need a visa to visit France, no-one is likely to kick you out after three months. The unspoken policy seems to be that you can stay and spend your money in France as long as you don't try to work, apply for social services or commit a crime. Staying longer than three months is nonetheless illegal, and without a *carte de séjour* (residence permit) you can face real problems renting an apartment, opening a bank account and so on.

Tourist Visa

Those travellers not exempt need a tourist visa, also known as a **Schengen visa** (www.euro visa.com) after the Schengen agreement that abolished passport controls between Austria, Belgium, Denmark, Finland, France, Germany, Greece, Iceland, Italy, Luxembourg, the Netherlands, Norway, Portugal, Spain and Sweden. A Schengen visa allows unlimited travel throughout this zone for 90 days.

Applications are made with the consulate of the country you are entering first, or of the country that will be your main destination.

Among other things, you will need medical insurance and proof of sufficient funds to support yourself.

If you enter France overland, it is unlikely that your visa will be checked at the border, but major problems can arise later on if you don't have one.

Tourist visas *cannot* be extended except in emergencies (such as medical problems); you'll need to leave and reapply from outside France when your visa expires.

Long-Stay & Student Visa

This is the first step if you want to work or study in France, or stay for more than three months. Long-stay and student visas will allow you to enter France and apply for a *carte de séjour*. Contact the French embassy or consulate nearest your residence, and begin your application well in advance as it can take months. Tourist visas cannot be changed into student visas after arrival. However, shortterm visas are available for students sitting university-entry exams in France.

Working-Holiday Visa

Citizens of Australia, Canada, Japan and New Zealand aged between 18 and 29 years (inclusive) are eligible for a one-year, multiple-entry working-holiday visa, allowing you to travel around France and work at the same time.

You have to apply to the embassy or consulate in your home country, and you must have a return ticket home, insurance and sufficient money to fund the start of your stay. Apply early as quotas do apply.

Once you have found a job in France, you have to apply for an *autorisation provisoire de travail* (temporary work permit), valid for the duration of the employment position offered. The permit can be renewed under the same conditions up to the limit of the authorised length of stay.

Carte de Séjour

Once issued with a long-stay visa, you can apply for a *carte de séjour,* and are usually required to do so within eight days of arrival in France. Make sure you have all the necessary documents *before* you arrive.

EU passport-holders and citizens of Switzerland, Iceland and Norway no longer need a *carte de séjour* to reside (or work) in France. Other foreign nationals must contact the local *préfecture* or *commissariat* (police station) for their permit. Students of all nationalities need a *carte de séjour*.

VOLUNTEERING

Get stuck into a environment-driven volunteering project in the region:

Alpes de Lumière (☎ 04 92 75 22 01; http://alpes-de-lumiere.org; 1 place du Palais, Forcalquier) Brings together 20-odd volunteers in summer to help restore and conserve Haute-Provence's rural heritage; work in the morning, play in the afternoon.

APARE (☎ 04 90 85 51 15; www.apare-gec.org; 25 blvd Paul Pons, Isle-sur-la Sorgue) Volunteer heritage work camps for 16- to 18-year-olds/adults, including 25/35 hours' work a week. Its 2006 list of 23 camps included restoring St-Tropez's citadel walls, a wash house in Vachères or an old dry-stone walled farm near Mont Ventoux; and consolidating the banks of the River Sorgue in Isle-sur-la-Sorgue. Two-/three-week camps command a €95/130 contribution per adult volunteer to cover food and lodging, and €305 for three-week teen camps.

Conservatoire du Patrimoine et Traditions du Freinet (☎ 04 94 43 08 57; www.conservatoiredu freinet.org; Chapelle St-Jean, place de la Mairie, La Garde Freinet) Clear forest areas and shrubland, rebuild dry-stone walls and help out on other *chantiers du patrimoine* (heritage sites) in the Massif des Maures.

Conservatoire Études des Ecosystèmes de Provence-Alpes-Côte d'Azur (CEEP; ☎ 04 42 20 03 83; www.ccep.asso.fr in French; 890 chemin de Bouenhoure haut, Aix-en-Provence) Voluntary *chantiers verts* (green workshops) aimed at discovering nature's ecosystems.

La Sabranenque (www.sabranenque.com) Help restore a Provençal hilltop village between Châteauneuf-du-Pape and Orange; see p172 for details.

Rempart (☎ 01 42 71 96 55; www.rempart.org; 1 rue des Guillemites, Paris) Two- and three-week heritage *chantiers* on endangered sites in France, including several in Provence; volunteers pay €5 to €8 per day, plus €40 insurance and membership.

Village des Tortues (☎ 04 94 78 26 41; www.village tortues.com in French; adult/5-16yr €9/6; ☉ 9am-7pm Mar-Nov) This tortoise village in the Massif des Maures offers a limited number of placements to students aged 17 and over. The centre allows its students to spend 15 days to a month working at the village, March to November. Free board and lodging is included. See p362 for more.

WOMEN TRAVELLERS

French men have clearly given little thought to the concept of *harcèlement sexuel* (sexual harassment). Most still believe that staring suavely at a passing woman is paying her a compliment. Women need not walk around the region in fear, however. Suave stares are about as adventurous as most French men get, with women rarely being physically assaulted on the street or touched up in bars at night.

Unfortunately, it's not French men that women travellers have to concern themselves with. While women attract little unwanted attention in rural Provence, on the coast it's a different ball game. In the dizzying heat of high season, the Côte d'Azur is rampant with men and women of *all* nationalities out on the pull. Apply the usual 'women traveller' rules and the chances are you'll emerge from the circus unscathed. Remain conscious of your surroundings, avoid going to bars and clubs alone at night and be aware of potentially dangerous situations: deserted streets, lonely beaches, dark corners of large train stations, and on night buses in certain districts of Marseille and Nice.

Topless sunbathing – ironically less and less the fashion on Côte d'Azur beaches where it is very much tops on these days – is not generally interpreted as deliberately provocative.

SOS Viol is a voluntary women's group that staffs the national **rape-crisis hotline** (☎ 08 00 05 95 95). Its centre in Marseille is spearheaded by **SOS Femmes** (Map p98; ☎ 04 91 24 61 50; www.sosfemmes .com in French; 14 blvd Théodore Thurner) and in Nice by **Femmes Battues** (☎ 04 93 52 17 81; http://accueilfemmes battues.chez-alice.fr; 81 rue de France, bureau 312).

WORK

EU nationals have an automatic right to work in France. Non-EU citizens need to apply for a work permit, for which they first need a *carte de séjour* or working-holiday visa (see opposite), as well as a written promise of employment. Permits can be refused on the grounds of high local unemployment. That said, work 'in the black' (ie without documents) is possible in the Côte d'Azur's tourist industry and during Provence's grape harvest.

France's national employment service, the **Agence National pour l'Emploi** (ANPE; www.anpe.fr in French), advertises jobs in the region on its website, as does local recruitment agency **Le Cyber Emploi** (☎ 04 97 13 42 80; www.cbyer-emploi.org; place Yves Klein, F-06300 Nice). For those seeking casual, student-style summer work, **La Maison des Étudiants de Nice** (www.cyber-campus.nice.fr in French) in Nice is a handy one-stop shop.

Agricultural Work

To pick up a job in a field, ask around in areas where harvesting is taking place; Provence sees a succession of apple, strawberry, cherry, peach, pear and pumpkin harvests from mid-May to September.

The annual grape harvest happens from about mid-September to mid- or late October. The sun-soaked fruits of the Côtes de Provence vineyards are ready for harvest before those of the more northern Châteauneuf du Pape vineyards. Harvesting is increasingly being done by machine, although mechanical picking is forbidden in some places (such as Châteauneuf du Pape). Once the harvest starts, it lasts just a couple of weeks. The start date is announced up to one week in advance.

Food for *vendangeurs* (grape pickers) is usually supplied but accommodation is often not (which is why most pickers live locally). Tourist offices in the region have a list of local producers who might need an extra pair of hands, as do the different *maisons des vins*.

Au Pair

Under the au pair system, single young people (aged 18 to about 27) who are studying in France live with a French family and receive lodging, full board and a bit of pocket money in exchange for taking care of the kids, babysitting, doing light housework and perhaps teaching English to the children.

Many families want au pairs who are native English speakers, but knowing at least some French may be a prerequisite. **Alliance Française Marseille** (☎ 04 96 10 24 60; www.alliance frmarseille.org; 310 rue Paradis, F-13008 Marseille) places au pairs with families in Marseille, and **Association Familles et Jeunesse** (☎ 04 93 82 28 22; www.afj-aupair.org/apfrance.htm; 4 rue Masséna, F-06000 Nice) is one of dozens of au pair agencies on the Côte d'Azur that arrange placements.

Online, there's an agency directory at www.europa-pages.com/au_pair.

Beach Hawkers & Street Performers

Selling goods and services on the beach is one way to make a few euros, though you've got to sell an awful lot of *beignets* or wrap a lot of hair with coloured beads to make a living.

One good place street musicians, actors and jugglers might try to busk is in Avignon during its July theatre festival.

Crewing on a Yacht

Working on a yacht looks glamorous but the reality is far from cushy. Cannes, Antibes or any other yacht-filled port on the Côte d'Azur are the places to look for work. Antibes, in particular, has a clutch of crew recruitment agencies, including **International Crew Recruitment** (☎ 04 93 34 27 71; 16b av du 24 Août); **YPI Crew** (☎ 04 92 90 46 10; www.ypicrew.com; Les Résidences du Port Vauban, 17 av du 11 Novembre) and **AMPM Crew Solutions** (☎ 04 94 34 06 14; www.ampmcrew.com; 28 av Thiers), which run training courses (safety, yacht management etc) as well as placing crew.

Yacht owners often take on newcomers for a trial period of day-crewing before hiring them for the full charter season, which lasts from March to September on the Mediterranean. By late September long-haul crews are in demand for winter voyages to warmer Caribbean climes.

Ski Resorts

The region's ski resorts – Isola 2000, Pra-Loup and La Foux d'Allos among them – are small and offer few work opportunities. If you contact the ski resort months in advance you might be able to pick up some hospitality work in a hotel or restaurant.

Transport

CONTENTS

Getting There & Away	**417**
Entering the Country	417
Air	417
Land	419
River	421
Sea	421
Getting Around	**422**
Air	422
Bicycle	422
Boat	423
Bus	424
Car & Motorcycle	424
Train	427

GETTING THERE & AWAY

See also p413 and p87 for information on tours to Provence and the Côte d'Azur.

ENTERING THE COUNTRY

European integration means you'll usually cross fluidly between France and other EU countries without passing through customs or border checkpoints. If you're arriving from a non-EU country, you'll have to show your passport (and your visa permit if you need one; see p414) or your identity card if you're an EU citizen, and clear customs.

AIR

International airport departure taxes are included in the price of your ticket.

Airports

A popular tourist destination, Provence has two major airports: Marseille and Nice (although most long-haul destinations still require you to change planes in Paris, London or some other European capital). Avignon, Cannes and St-Tropez-La Môle are very small; the latter two are primarily used by private charter flights. For details on travelling between airports and city centres, see the Getting Around sections in the relevant chapters.

THINGS CHANGE...

The information in this chapter is particularly vulnerable to change. Check directly with the airline or a travel agent to make sure you understand how a fare (and ticket you may buy) works and be aware of the security requirements for international travel. Shop carefully. The details given in this chapter should be regarded as pointers and are not a substitute for your own careful, up-to-date research.

Avignon (code AVN; www.avignon.aeroport.fr/fr in French)
Cannes (code CEQ; www.cannes.aeroport.fr)
Marseille-Provence (code MRS; www.marseille .aeroport.fr)
Nice-Côte d'Azur (code NCE; www.nice.aeroport.fr)
Nîmes-Garons (code FNI; www.nimes.cci.fr in French)
St-Tropez-La Môle (code LTT; www.st-tropez-airport .com in French)
Toulon-Hyères (code TLN; aeroport.var.cci.fr)

Airlines

The following airlines fly to and from Provence and the Côte d'Azur:

Air Algérie (code AH; in Marseille ☎ 04 95 09 31 10, in Nice ☎ 04 93 21 48 20; www.airalgerie.dz; hub Algiers)
Air France (code AF; ☎ 08 20 82 08 20; www.airfrance .com; hub Paris)
Alitalia (code AZ; ☎ 08 20 31 53 15; www.alitalia.it; hub Rome)
bmibaby (code CWW; ☎ 08 90 71 00 81; www .bmibaby.com; hub East Midlands)
British Airways (code BA; ☎ 08 25 82 54 00; www .britishairways.com; hub Heathrow)
Corse Méditerranée (code CCM; ☎ 08 20 82 08 20; www.ccm-airlines.com; hub Paris)
easyJet (code U2; ☎ 08 26 10 26 11; www.easyjet.com; hub London Luton)
Fly Baboo (code BBO; within Europe ☎ 00800 445 445 45, in Switzerland ☎ 0848 445 445; www.flybaboo.com; hub Geneva)
Flybe (code BE; within UK ☎ 0871 700 0535, from outside UK ☎ 4413 922 685 29; www.flybe.com; hub Southampton)
Royal Air Maroc (code AT; in Nice ☎ 04 93 21 40 18; www.royalairmaroc.com; hub Casablanca)

TRANSPORT

CLIMATE CHANGE & TRAVEL

Climate change is a serious threat to the ecosystems that humans rely upon, and air travel is the fastest-growing contributor to the problem. Lonely Planet regards travel, overall, as a global benefit, but believes we all have a responsibility to limit our personal impact on global warming.

Flying & Climate Change

Pretty much every form of motor transport generates CO_2 (the main cause of human-induced climate change) but planes are far and away the worst offenders, not just because of the sheer distances they allow us to travel, but because they release greenhouse gases high into the atmosphere. The statistics are frightening: two people taking a return flight between Europe and the US will contribute as much to climate change as an average household's gas and electricity consumption over a whole year.

Carbon Offset Schemes

Climatecare.org and other websites use 'carbon calculators' that allow travellers to offset the greenhouse gases they are responsible for with contributions to energy-saving projects and other climate-friendly initiatives in the developing world – including projects in India, Honduras, Kazakhstan and Uganda.

Lonely Planet, together with Rough Guides and other concerned partners in the travel industry, supports the carbon offset scheme run by www.climatecare.org. Lonely Planet offsets all of its staff and author travel.

For more information check out our website: www.lonelyplanet.com.

Ryanair (code FR; ☎ 08 92 23 23 75; www.ryanair.com; hub Dublin)

Tunis Air (code TU; ☎ 08 20 04 40 44; www.tunisair .com.tn in French; hub Tunis)

VirginExpress (code TV; ☎ 08 21 23 02 02; www .virgin-express.com; hub Brussels)

Tickets

Air travel is a competitive business, and fares fluctuate wildly according to time of year and general availability: shop around!

The internet makes researching air fares easy. Most airlines have websites listing special offers, and there are some good online ticket agencies that will compare prices for you (eg www.travelocity.co.uk and www.deckchair .com). However, using face-to-face methods like travel agencies can furnish details that are not available on the internet, such as which airlines have the best facilities for children or which travel insurance is most suitable.

Look out for cheap 'no-frills' flights serving Avignon, Marseille, Nice, Nîmes and Toulon.

Africa

Marseille is a hub for flights to and from North Africa.

Air Algérie flies to Algeria. From Marseille there are up to two daily to Algiers and Con-

stantine, five per week to Annaba, up to 14 weekly to Oran, and flights at least weekly to Batna and Bejaia. From Nice there are weekly flights to Algiers, Constantine and Oran.

Royal Air Maroc and Air France codeshare on flights to and from Morocco. From Marseille there are twice-daily flights to Casablanca and direct flights to Oudja nearly daily. There are daily flights most of the time to Casablanca from Nice.

Tunis Air flies to and from Tunis (up to four times daily) and Monastir (up to four flights weekly) from both Nice and Marseille. Air France also flies to both cities.

Australia & New Zealand

Airlines such as Thai Airways International, Malaysia Airlines, Qantas Airways and Singapore Airlines have frequent promotional fares. High-season full-price return fares to Paris cost around A$3000 from Melbourne or Sydney, and around NZ$3500 from Auckland. The following are major agencies for cheap fares:

Flight Centre Australia (☎ 133 133; www.flightcentre .com.au); New Zealand (☎ 0800 243 544; www.flight centre.co.nz)

STA Travel Australia (☎ 1300 733 035; www.statravel .com.au); New Zealand (☎ 0508 782 872; www.statravel .co.nz)

Continental Europe

There are flights two or three times daily between Nice/Marseille and most other European cities. They are cheapest in early spring and late autumn.

There is also a handful of interesting no-frills routes: easyJet offers year-round daily flights between Geneva, Berlin and Nice. Swiss carrier Fly Baboo flies into Nice and St-Tropez. Fares vary enormously depending on travel dates and special offers (from €40 to €180 at the time of research).

VirginExpress flies between Brussels and Nice/Marseille up to four times daily, from where onward connections abound. Again, prices vary hugely.

Across Continental Europe there are many agencies with ties to **STA Travel** (www.statravel.com) from which you can purchase cheap tickets.

UK & Ireland

No-frills airlines have slashed fares between the UK and southern France. Internet bookings are the norm; telephone bookings cost marginally more. Tickets are nonrefundable, but can be changed for a fee.

EasyJet flies to/from Nice and Belfast, Bristol, Liverpool, London Gatwick, London Stansted, London Luton and Newcastle, and to/from Marseille and Bristol, Liverpool and London Gatwick. One-way fares cost anything between UK£20 and UK£155 including airport taxes.

There are bmibaby flights between Nice and Birmingham and London (around UK£60).

Flybe flies three times per week to/from Southampton and Avignon between late May and late October. Flights range from around UK£42 to UK£152.

Dublin-based Ryanair operates low-fare flights between Nîmes-Garons airport and London Luton, as well as between Nîmes and Nottingham East Midlands airport and Liverpool. Ryanair also flies between Marseille and more than a dozen UK, Continental Europe and North African destinations. Flights cost from as little as €10 plus taxes and a checked baggage allowance.

Both Nice and Marseille are served by daily British Airways and Air France flights from London (Gatwick or Heathrow).

Discount air travel is big business in London. Travel-agency ads appear in the travel pages of the weekend broadsheet newspapers, in *Time Out* and in the *Evening Standard*.

Some recommended travel agencies and on-line ticket sites:

Cheap Flights (www.cheapflights.co.uk)
ebookers (☎ 0800 082 3000; www.ebookers.com)
skyscanner (www.skyscanner.net) Offers comparisons between different airlines.
STA Travel (☎ 0870 163 0026; www.statravel.co.uk) Particularly good for travellers under the age of 26.

USA & Canada

Most journeys to Provence from the North American continent entail a change in Paris, London or another European transport hub. A New York–Paris round trip can cost anything from US$400/1000 in the low/high season with Air France or British Airways.

Discount travel agencies are known as consolidators in the USA; track them down through the *Yellow Pages* or the major daily newspapers.

Travel agencies recommended for online bookings:

Expedia (☎ 1 800 397 3342; www.expedia.com)
STA Travel (☎ 1 800 781 4040; www.sta.com)
Travelocity (☎ 1 888 709 5983; www.travelocity.com)

Airlines flying from Canada to France include British Airways, Air France and Air Canada. Flights leave from all major cities including Montreal, Ottawa, Toronto and Vancouver. A Toronto–Paris round trip costs around C$1400 in the high season. Travel agencies specialising in cheap fares include **Flight Centre** (☎ 1877 967 5302; www.flightcentre.com) and **Travel CUTS** (☎ 1 888 359 2887; www.travelcuts.com). **Transat** (www.transat.com) offers travel services and operates low-cost flights between Canada and Europe. **Zoom Airlines** (www.flyzoom.com) is a popular Canadian budget airline serving France.

For online bookings try www.expedia.ca and www.travelocity.ca.

LAND
Continental Europe
BUS

Eurolines (☎ 08 92 89 90 91; www.eurolines.com) is an association of companies forming Europe's largest international bus network. It links Provençal cities such as Nice, Marseille and Avignon with points all over Western and central Europe, Scandinavia and Morocco. Most buses operate daily in summer and several times a week in winter; advance ticket purchases are necessary. Eurolines' website lists representatives in Europe.

The **Eurolines Pass** (15-/30-day pass high season fare late-Jun–mid-Sep €329/439, under 26 €279/359, cheaper mid-Sep–Jun) allows unlimited travel to 40 cities across Europe.

Travelling from Marseille or Toulon, it will cost €170 to Amsterdam and €130/103 to Rome/Florence from Nice, Marseille or Toulon.

Intercars (www.intercars.fr in French) links France with cities in southern and central Europe. In Provence it has a number of **bus-station offices** (Nice ☎ 04 93 80 08 70; nice@intercars.fr; Aix-en-Provence ☎ 04 91 50 57 55; Marseille ☎ 04 91 50 08 66; marseille@intercars .fr; Nîmes ☎ 04 66 29 84 22; nimes@intercars.fr). Sample return fares from Nice include Budapest (€152, 22 hours) and Warsaw (€176, 29 hours). Discounts are available for children, and for those aged under 26 and over 60 (approximately 5% to 10% off a full adult fare).

Linebús (Avignon ☎ 04 90 86 88 67; Nîmes ☎ 04 66 29 50 62; Barcelona ☎ 932 65 07 00; www.linebus.com in Spanish with English sections) links Avignon and Nîmes with Barcelona (€98 and €67, 7½ hours) and other cities in Spain. Children aged four to 12 receive a 50% discount and people under 26 and over 60 are eligible for a smaller reduction.

TRAIN

Paris has connections to cities all over Europe. Within the region, Nice is the major hub, sitting on the busy Barcelona–Rome train line. Day and overnight trains run in both directions. A single 1st-/2nd-class fare from Nice to Rome costs around €85/55 (plus €22 for a couchette) for the 10-hour journey. There are also direct train services between Nice and Milan (€50/33, five hours). Marseille also has trains to destinations all over France with connections across Europe.

A helpful resource is the info-packed website **The Man in Seat 61** (www.seat61.com), which lists train timetables and travel tips for France and beyond.

UK
BUS

Eurolines UK (☎ 0870 514 3219; www.nationalexpress .com/eurolines) runs from London's Victoria coach station via the Dover–Calais channel crossing to Avignon, Marseille, Nice and Toulon. All direct return fares are around UK£100.

CAR & MOTORCYCLE

High-speed shuttle trains operated by **Eurotunnel** (in the UK ☎ 0870-535 3535, in France ☎ 03 21 00 61 00; www.eurotunnel.com) shuttle between Folkestone via the Channel Tunnel to Coquelles, 5km southwest of Calais. Journey time is 35 minutes. Trains run 24 hours a day, every day of the year, with up to five departures an hour. A high-season return fare for a car and passengers costs around UK£200, but there are numerous promotional fares. The fee for a bicycle, including its rider, is UK£32 return; advance reservations are mandatory. LPG and CNG tanks are not permitted, which eliminates many campers and caravans.

TRAIN

The highly civilised **Eurostar** (France ☎ 08 92 35 35 39; www.voyages-sncf.com; UK ☎ 08705 186 186; www .eurostar.com) whisks you between London and Paris in just 2½ hours. There are direct daily services between London and Ashford (Kent) and Paris, Brussels, Lille, Parc Disneyland Paris and Calais-Fréthun. A direct seasonal service operates on Saturday from London and Ashford to Avignon (July to early September).

Eurostar fares vary enormously. A standard 2nd-class one-way ticket from London to Paris costs UK£149; from Paris, the standard fare to London is €223.50. You'll get the best deals if you book a return journey, stay over a Saturday night, book 14 or seven days ahead, if you're under 25 or if you're a student. Student travel agencies may have youth fares not available directly from Eurostar. Eurail pass holders receive discounts. For information about train travel from northern France destinations to Provence & the Côte d'Azur, see below.

Within France
BUS

French transport policy is completely biased in favour of its state-owned rail system: interregional bus services are an alien concept. Take a train.

CAR & MOTORCYCLE

For detailed information on driving, see p424.

TRAIN

France's efficient national rail network is run by the state-owned **Société Nationale des Chemins de Fer** (SNCF; www.sncf.fr).

SNCF's pride and joy is the **Train à Grande Vitesse** (TGV; www.tgv.com) high-speed train service.

TGV Sud-Est links Paris with Dijon and Lyon, from where the TGV Rhône-Alpes continues southeast to Valence. Here, the TGV Méditerranée zips at 310km/h to Avignon where the superfast track splits east to Marseille and west to Nîmes. Avignon and Aix-en-Provence have out-of-town TGV train stations, separate from the town-centre stations used by regional trains. Sample 1st-/2nd-class single TGV fares between Paris and Provence destinations include: Avignon (€110/80, 3½ hours), Marseille (€120/80, three hours), Nice (€160/120, seven hours) and Orange (€120/80, 4½ hours).

The SNCF also operates cheaper, slower rail services. Both *grande ligne* (main line) trains and those operated by **Transport Express Régional** (TER; www.ter-sncf.com) link smaller cities and towns with the TGV network. Many towns not on the SNCF network are linked with nearby railheads by buses.

Under Motorail's Auto Train scheme you can travel with your car on a train. Cars are loaded on the train one hour before departure and unloaded 30 minutes after arrival. This service is available at Avignon, St-Raphaël, Marseille and Nice train stations. Information in the UK is available from Rail Europe (see p425). In France, ticketing is handled by SNCF.

Generally, bicycles are transported free of charge *if* they are packed down into a special 120cm x 190cm transit bag (available from bike shops). Some main-line trains (flagged with a bicycle symbol on timetables) don't make this requirement. On night trains and certain TGV Sud-Est and TGV Méditerranée routes, bikes can only be transported in a four- to six-bicycle wagon, which must be reserved in advance (€10). See the multilingual SNCF brochure *Guide Train & Vélo* (free), available at train stations.

The SNCF baggage service **Sernam** (☎ 08 25 84 58 45) will transport your bicycle door-to-door in France for €49, with bicycles delivered within 48 hours excluding Saturdays, Sundays and public holidays.

European Bike Express (☎ 01642-251 440; www.bike-express.co.uk) transports cyclists and their bikes from the UK to places all over France.

RIVER

Provence is well connected by waterways, thanks to the Rhône. The most popular canal route to Provence is via the Canal du Midi, a 240km waterway that runs from Toulouse to the Bassin de Thau between Agde and Sète, from where you continue northeast to Aigues-Mortes in the Camargue. From Toulouse the Canal du Midi is connected with the Gardonne River leading west to the Atlantic Ocean at Bordeaux.

SEA

Provence has ferry links with Corsica, Italy and North Africa; boats sail to and from Nice, Toulon and Marseille. Rental cars cannot be taken on ferries.

Algeria

Travel in Algeria is considered dangerous for foreign tourists due to ongoing political troubles.

Algérie Ferries (www.algerieferries.com) operates ferries between Marseille and Algiers, Bejaia, Annaba, Skikda and Oran (20 hours). A one-way/return fare on any of these routes costs €280/320 for a *fauteuil* (armchair seat) and €400/470 in a four-bunk cabin, plus port taxes of around €10 each way.

Italy

SNCM (p422) runs two or three car ferries weekly from Marseille or Toulon to Porto Torres on the Italian island of Sardinia (Sardaigne in French). Sailing time is 17 hours.

A one-way passage in a *fauteuil* costs €70/81 in the low/high season (children aged four to 12 €24/37). There are discounts for passengers aged 12 to 25, InterRail Pass holders and those aged over 60. Transporting a car costs an extra €75/109. Motorcycles/bicycles are €43/16 to transport. Allow around €5 per passenger for port taxes plus another €5 per vehicle.

Tickets and information are available from SNCM offices in Provence. In Sardinia, tickets are sold by SNCF agent **Paglietti Petertours** (☎ 079-51 44 77; Corso Vittorio Emanuele 19) in Porto Torres.

Tunisia

SNCM (p422) and Tunisian **CTN** (Compagnie Tunisienne de Navigation; ☎ 216-135 33 31; 122 rue de Yougoslavie, Tunis) together operate car ferries between Marseille/Toulon and Tunis (20 to 22 hours). A one-way *fauteuil* costs €160 (children aged two to 16 €77) year-round. A berth in a cabin starts at €12. If you're taking a vehicle (€364), it's vital to book ahead.

TRANSPORT

UK & Ireland

There are no direct ferries to Provence, but you can take a ferry year-round from Dover to Calais or from Folkestone to Boulogne (the shortest and cheapest crossings). Longer channel crossings include Newhaven to Dieppe, Poole to Cherbourg, and Portsmouth to Cherbourg/Le Havre/Ouistreham/St-Malo. Fares vary crazily according to demand. Some companies and their routes:

Brittany Ferries (www.brittany-ferries.co.uk; France ☎ 0298 292 800; Ireland ☎ 021-427 7801; UK ☎ 08703 665 333) Poole–Cherbourg (4½ hours), Portsmouth–Caen (5¾ hours), Portsmouth–Cherbourg (three hours), Portsmouth–St-Malo (10¾ hours), Plymouth–Roscoff (six hours), Cork–Roscoff (13 hours).

Condor Ferries (www.condorferries.co.uk; France ☎ 08 25 135 135; UK ☎ 0870 243 5140) Weymouth/Poole–St-Malo with change of vessel in Guernsey or Jersey (5½ hours/4½ hours).

Irish Ferries (www.irishferries.ie; France ☎ 02 33 23 44 44; Ireland ☎ 0818 300 400; France ☎ 02 98 61 17 17; UK ☎ 08705 17 17 17) Rosslare–Roscoff (18 hours), Rosslare–Cherbourg (19½ hours).

Norfolk Line (www.hoverspeed.co.uk; France ☎ 03 28 28 95 50; UK ☎ 0870 870 10 20) Dover–Dunkerque (1¾ hours).

P&O Ferries (www.poferries.com; France ☎ 0825 120 156; UK ☎ 0870 5980 333) Dover–Calais (2½ hours).

SeaFrance (www.seafrance.com; France ☎ 0825 0825 05, ☎ 0870 443 1653) Dover–Calais (2½ hours).

Within France

CORSICA

Ferries between mainland France and Corsica are operated by several lines:

Corsica Ferries (☎ 08 25 09 50 95; www.corsicaferries .com) Runs year-round from Nice to Ajaccio, Bastia, Calvi and Île Rousse, and from Toulon to Ajaccio and Bastia.

La Méridionale/CMN (☎ 08 10 20 13 20; www.cmn.fr) An SNCM subsidiary, this company has year-round sailings between Marseille and Ajaccio, Bastia and Propriano.

Société Nationale Maritime Corse-Méditerranée (SNCM; ☎ 08 91 70 18 01; www.sncm.fr) Services from Nice, Marseille and Toulon to Ajaccio, Bastia, Calvi, Île Rousse, Porto Vecchio and Propriano.

Daytime sailings from Nice take around four hours; ferries from Marseille and Toulon are usually overnight.

In summer up to eight ferries depart daily (reservations are essential); in winter as few as eight depart a week and fares are much cheaper. In bad weather, boats can be cancelled at short notice (often on the day of departure).

Fares start at around €24 per adult one way for Nice to Bastia (discount and promotional specials are advertised in low season). Cabins start from an additional €25. Transporting a small car costs upwards of €53 one way. Count on adding from around €18 one way for taxes.

GETTING AROUND

AIR

Air France is the leading carrier on domestic routes, linking Bordeaux, Brest, Clermont-Ferrand, Lille, Lyon, Metz-Nancy, Mulhouse, Nantes, Strasbourg and Toulouse with Avignon, Nice, Nîmes, Marseille and Toulon.

No-frills airline easyJet has cheap fares from Paris to Nice (sometimes as low as €30).

Compagnie Corse Méditeranée (CCM; ☎ 0 820 820 820; www.ccm-airlines.com) flies from Bastia and Ajaccio to Marseille and Nice year-round.

Online agencies include **Nouvelles Frontières** (☎ 08 25 00 07 47; www.nouvelles-frontieres.fr).

There are no scheduled inter-regional plane flights within Provence, but high-fliers can take to the air by helicopter. A handy online source of helicopter information is **Héli Riviera** (www.heliriviera.com).

BICYCLE

Provence – particularly the Luberon – is an eminently cyclable region, thanks to its extensive network of inland back roads with relatively light traffic. They're an ideal way to view Provence's celebrated lavender fields, vineyards and olive groves. On the coast there are also several excellent cycle paths; see individual chapters for information. Cycling in national parks in Provence is forbidden.

By law your bicycle must have two functioning brakes, a bell, a red reflector on the back and yellow reflectors on the pedals. After sunset and when visibility is poor, cyclists must turn on a white light in front and a red one in the rear. Cyclists must ride in single file when being overtaken by vehicles or other cyclists.

See p421 for information about transporting your bicycle by train.

More information of interest to cyclists can be found on p81. A useful resource is the **Fédération Française de Cyclisme** (☎ 01 49 35 69 00; www.ffc.fr in French).

BOAT

Barges such as the beautifully restored **Le Phénicien** (☎ 04 42 41 19 14; www.rhone-croisiere.com) run tours along the Rhône. A six-night trip between Avignon and Aigues-Mortes aboard Le Phénicien including chef-prepared meals, drinks, daily excursions and use of bicycles costs from €2500 per person.

Canal Boat

One of the most relaxing ways to see the region is to rent a houseboat and cruise along the Camargue's canals and rivers. Boats usually accommodate two to 12 passengers and can be rented on a weekly basis. Anyone over 18 can pilot a river boat without a licence: learning the ropes takes about half an hour. The speed limit is 6km/h on canals and 10km/h on rivers.

The following companies rent out boats in Provence. Prices are for July and August; rates drop by around a third in the low season.

Crown Blue Line Camargue (in France ☎ 04 68 94 52 72, in the UK ☎ 0870 160 5634; www.crownblueline.com) Rates around €1690 per week for a six-berth boat.

Rive de France (☎ 08 10 80 80 80; www.rive-de-france .tm.fr) Rates around €1785 per week for a six-berth boat.

Ferry

A plethora of boats plies the waters from the coast to the offshore islands. Ferries also operate to/from St-Tropez to St-Raphaël, Port Grimaud and Ste-Maxime in the warmer months (generally April to October). See the relevant regional chapters For seasonal schedules and prices.

Yacht

One of Europe's largest *ports de plaisance* (pleasure ports) is located at Port Vauban, in Antibes.

Yachts with or without a crew can be hired at most marinas along the coast, including the less-pompous sailing centres at Ste-Maxime and Le Lavandou. A complete list of yacht-rental places is included in the free booklet *Nautisme: Côte d'Azur Riviera* published by the Comité Régional du Tourisme Riviera Côte d'Azur (available from tourist offices).

For up-to-date marina or harbour master information, contact the **Fédération Française des Ports de Plaisance** (FFPP; ☎ 01 43 35 26 26; www .ffports-plaisance.com in French).

TRANSPORT

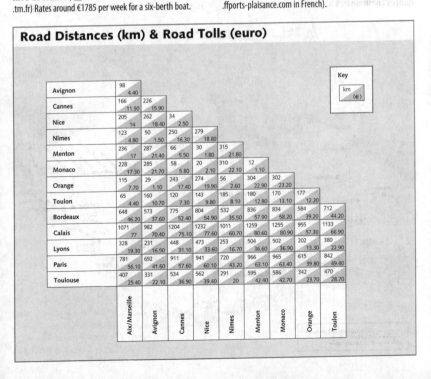

Road Distances (km) & Road Tolls (euro)

Key: km (€)

	Aix/Marseille	Avignon	Cannes	Nice	Nimes	Menton	Monaco	Orange	Toulon
Avignon	98 / 4.40								
Cannes	166 / 11.50	226 / 15.90							
Nice	205 / 14	262 / 18.40	34 / 2.50						
Nimes	123 / 4.80	50 / 1.50	250 / 16.30	279 / 18.80					
Menton	236 / 17	287 / 21.40	66 / 5.50	30 / 1.80	315 / 21.80				
Monaco	228 / 17.30	285 / 21.70	58 / 5.80	20 / 2.10	310 / 22.10	12 / 1.10			
Orange	115 / 7.70	29 / 1.10	243 / 17.40	274 / 19.90	56 / 2.60	304 / 22.90	302 / 23.20		
Toulon	65 / 4.40	160 / 10.70	120 / 7.30	143 / 9.80	185 / 8.10	180 / 12.80	170 / 13.10	177 / 12.20	
Bordeaux	648 / 46.20	573 / 37.60	775 / 52.40	804 / 54.90	532 / 35.50	836 / 57.90	834 / 58.20	584 / 39.20	712 / 44.20
Calais	1071 / 77	982 / 70.40	1204 / 75.10	1232 / 77.60	1011 / 60.70	1259 / 80.60	1255 / 80.90	955 / 57.30	1133 / 66.90
Lyons	328 / 19.30	231 / 16.50	448 / 31.10	473 / 33.60	253 / 16.70	504 / 36.60	502 / 36.90	202 / 13.30	380 / 22.90
Paris	781 / 56.10	692 / 41.60	911 / 57.60	941 / 60.10	720 / 43.20	966 / 63.10	965 / 63.40	615 / 39.80	842 / 49.40
Toulouse	407 / 25.40	331 / 22.10	534 / 36.90	562 / 39.40	291 / 20	595 / 42.40	586 / 42.70	342 / 23.70	470 / 28.70

BUS

Services and routes are extremely limited in rural areas. Bus services are more efficient between towns served by only a few (or no) trains.

Autocars (regional buses) are operated by a muddling host of different bus companies, which usually have an office at the *gare routière* (bus station) in the cities they serve. One company generally sells tickets for all the buses operating from the same station.

CAR & MOTORCYCLE

Having your own wheels is vital to discover the region's least-touched backwaters, with many nooks and crannies impossible to uncover by public transport. Except in traffic-plagued high season, it's easy to drive on the Côte d'Azur.

There are four types of intercity roads, which have alphanumeric designations:

Autoroutes (eg A8) Rapid-transit multilane highways, usually with *péages* (tolls).
Routes Nationales (N, RN) National highways.
Routes Départementales (D) Local roads.
Routes Communales (C, V) Minor rural roads.

Autoroutes in southern France are managed by the **Autoroutes du Sud de la France** (www.asf.fr) and the **Société des Autoroutes Estérel Côte d'Azur-Provence-Alpes** (www.escota.com). The national **Association des Sociétés Françaises d'Autoroutes** (☎ 08 92 68 10 77; www.autoroutes.fr) has masses of traffic-related information online.

The websites www.viamichelin.com and www.mappy.fr plot itineraries between specified departure and arrival points.

Bring Your Own Vehicle

If you bring your own vehicle to France, you'll need registration papers, unlimited third-party liability insurance and a valid driving licence. In the UK, contact the **RAC** (☎ 08705 722 722; www.rac.co.uk) or the **AA** (☎ 0870 600 0371; www.theaa.com) for more advice. In other countries, contact your appropriate automobile association.

Vehicles entering France must display a sticker identifying their country of registration. A right-hand-drive vehicle brought from the UK or Ireland has to have deflectors fitted to the headlights to avoid dazzling oncoming traffic. A reflective warning triangle, to

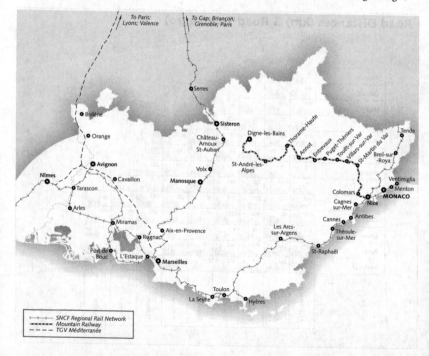

be used in the event of breakdown, must be carried in your car.

Make sure your car is fitted with winter or all-season tyres if there's a chance you'll be driving through snow.

Driving Licence & Documents

All drivers must carry at all times: a national ID card or passport; a valid driver's licence (*permis de conduire*; most foreign licences can be used in France for up to a year); papers of car ownership, known as a *carte grise* (grey card); and proof of third-party (liability) in-surance. If you're stopped by the police and don't have one or more of these documents, you risk a hefty on-the-spot fine.

Fuel & Spare Parts

Be warned that many service stations close on Saturday afternoon and Sunday. Some petrol pumps do stay open after hours, but you have to pay by credit card. *Essence* (pet-rol or gasoline), also known as *carburant* (fuel), is most expensive at the rest stops along the *autoroutes* and is cheapest at super-markets.

TRAIN PASSES & DISCOUNT FARES

The following passes are sold at student travel agencies, major train stations within Europe and the Société Nationale des Chemins de Fer (SNCF) subsidiary **Rail Europe** (in Canada ☎ 1 800 361 7245, in the UK ☎ 0870 5848 848, in the USA ☎ 1 800 438 7245; www.raileurope.com).

SNCF Discount Fares & Passes

Fantastic deals are available on the website www.sncf.com. Last-minute reductions of up to 50% off are published on the site every Tuesday, and Prem's ('early bird deals') are available for online bookings made three months to two weeks in advance. These tickets cannot be exchanged or refunded.

Discounted fares and passes are available at all SNCF stations. Children aged under four travel free of charge; those aged four to 11 travel for half-price. Discounted fares (25% reduction) ap-plies, subject to the trains and conditions of reservation, to: travellers aged 12 to 25, seniors aged over 60, one to four adults travelling with a child aged four to 11, two people taking a return journey together or anyone taking a return journey of at least 200km and spending a Saturday night away.

Guaranteed reductions of 25% to 50% are available with a **Carte 12-25** (€49) aimed at trav-ellers aged 12 to 25; the **Carte Enfant Plus** (€65) for one to four adults travelling with a child aged four to 11; and a **Carte Sénior** (€50) for those aged over 60. A **Carte Escapades** (€99) for those aged 26 to 59 guarantees savings of 25% on a return journey of at least 200km including a Saturday night away.

If you're spending three months to one year in France, ask about *Fréquence* travel cards of-fering savings of up to 50%.

The **France Railpass** entitles nonresidents of France to unlimited travel on SNCF trains for four days over a one-month period. In 2nd class it costs US$229; each additional day of travel costs US$30. The **France Youthpass** entitles holders to four days of travel over a one-month period. In 2nd class it costs US$169, plus US$23 for each extra day. These two passes can be purchased from travel agencies, or online through agencies such as www.raileurope.com.

European Train Passes

If you're planning an extensive European journey, consider buying a **Eurail** (in the USA ☎ 1 888 667 9734; www.eurail.com) pass, available to non-European residents, or a Euro Domino or **InterRail** (www.interrailnet.com) pass, available to European residents. All are valid on the national train network and allow unlimited travel for varying periods of time.

Most train passes must be validated at a train station ticket window before you begin your first journey, in order to begin the period of validity.

There are a number of websites to help you work out whether a pass will be economical for the itinerary you have in mind, including **Railkey** (www.railkey.com).

TRANSPORT

TRANSPORT

If your car is *en panne* (breaks down), you'll have to find a garage that handles your *marque* (make of car). Peugeot, Renault and Citroën garages are common, but if you have a non-French car you may have trouble finding someone to service it in more remote areas.

Hire

Prebooking your vehicle always works out cheaper. If you've left it too late, national French firms like ADA or National-Citer tend to be better value than international companies.

ADA (☎ 08 25 16 91 69; www.ada-sa.fr in French)
Auto Europe (☎ 1 888 223 5555; www.autoeurope .com) US-based online hire company.
Avis (☎ 08 20 05 05 05; www.avis.com)
Budget (☎ 01 41 22 19 89; www.budget.com)
Easycar (in the UK ☎ 0906 33 33 33 3; www.easycar.com)
Europcar (☎ 08 25 82 54 21; www.europcar.com)
Hertz (☎ 08 25 09 13 13; www.hertz.com)
Holiday Autos (☎ 0870 400 4461; www.holidayautos .co.uk) UK-based online hire company.
National-Citer (☎ 08 25 16 12 20; www.citer.com)

Most rental companies require the driver to be over 21 years and have had a driving licence for at least one year. Be sure that you understand what your liabilities are and what's included in the price (injury insurance, tax, collision damage waiver etc), and how many 'free' kilometres you'll get. *Kilométrage illimité* (unlimited mileage) means you can drive to your heart's content. You will probably be asked to leave a signed credit-card slip without a sum written on it as a *caution* (deposit). Make sure that it's destroyed when you return the car.

Note that rental cars with automatic transmission are *very* rare in France. You will usually need to order one well in advance and there's a much more limited (and invariably costlier) range of models to choose from.

All rental cars registered in France have a distinctive number on the licence plate, making them instantly identifiable (including to thieves – never leave anything of value in the car, even in the boot).

Insurance

Unlimited third-party liability insurance is mandatory for all automobiles. If you rent a car, this will be included in the package; however, collision damage waivers (CDW) vary greatly between rental companies. When comparing rates, the most important thing to check is the *franchise* (excess/deductible), which is usually €500 for a small car. If you're in an accident where you are at fault, or the car is stolen or damaged by an unknown party, this is the amount you are liable to pay before the policy kicks in. Some US credit-card companies (such as Amex) have built-in CDW, although you may have to pay up, then reclaim the money when you get home.

Road Conditions

If you're planning to drive along the coast in July or August, be prepared to take hours to move a few kilometres. For traffic reports in English, tune into 107.7MHz FM, which gives updates every 30 minutes in summer.

Road Rules

French law requires that all passengers, including those in the back seat, wear seat belts. Children weighing less than 10kg must travel in backward-facing child seats; children weighing up to 36kg must travel in child seats in the vehicle's rear seat. A passenger car is permitted to carry a maximum of five people. North American drivers should remember that turning right on a red light is illegal in France.

Under the *priorité à droite* rule, any car entering an intersection (including a T-junction) from a road on your right has the right of way, unless the intersection is marked *vous n'avez pas la priorité* (you do not have right of way) or *cédez le passage* (give way). *Priorité à droite* is also suspended on priority roads, which are marked by an up-ended yellow square with a black square in the middle.

Mobile phones may only be used when accompanied by a hands-free kit or speakerphone. British drivers committing driving offences in France can receive on-the-spot fines and get penalty points added to their driving licence.

Riders of any type of two-wheeled vehicle with a motor (except motor-assisted bicycles) must wear a helmet. No special licence is required to ride a motorbike with an engine smaller than 50cc.

In forested areas such as Haute-Provence, the Massif des Maures and the Massif de l'Estérel unpaved tracks signposted DFCI (*défense forestière contre l'incendie*) are for fire crews to gain quick entry in the event of a fire: they are strictly off limits to private vehicles.

ALCOHOL

It is illegal to drive with a blood-alcohol concentration (BAC) of over 0.05% (0.5g per litre of blood). The police conduct frequent random breathalyser tests.

SPEED LIMITS

You will be fined for going 10km/h over the speed limit. Unless otherwise posted, a limit of 50km/h applies in *all* areas designated as built-up, no matter how rural they may appear.

Speed limits outside built-up areas:

- 90km/h (80km/h if it's raining) on undivided N and D highways
- 110km/h (100km/h if it's raining) on dual carriageways (divided highways) or short sections of highway with a divider strip
- 130km/h (110km/h if it's raining, 60km/h in icy conditions) on autoroutes

TRAIN

The SNCF's regional rail network (Map p424) in Provence, served by **TER** (www.ter-sncf.com/paca), is comfortable and efficient. It comprises two routes: one that follows the coast (disappearing inland for the stretch between Hyères and St-Raphaël), with an inland track from Cannes to Grasse; and another that traverses

the interior, running from Marseille through Aix-en-Provence, Manosque and Sisteron before leaving the region northwards. A narrow-gauge railway links Nice with Digne-les-Bains in Haute-Provence (see p245).

It's important that you time-stamp your ticket in a *composteur* (a yellow post at the entrance to the platform) before boarding or you risk a hefty fine.

Reservations

Reservations are not mandatory on most regional trains. However, in summer it's advisable to buy your ticket for any straight-through trains well in advance.

Train Passes

Two regional passes are available to travellers of all ages, from July to September.

Carte Bermuda (€5) One-day pass available weekends and public holidays giving unlimited 2nd-class travel between Marseille and Miramas on the Côte Bleue.

Carte Isabelle (€12) One-day pass allowing unlimited train travel along the coast between Théoule-sur-Mer and Ventimiglia, and inland between Nice and Tende. Cannot be used on TGVs. Allows 1st class travel at no additional cost.

For countrywide SNCF discounts and rail passes, see p425.

Health

CONTENTS

Before You Go 428
Insurance 428
Recommended Vaccinations 428
In Transit 428
Deep Vein Thrombosis (DVT) 428
Jet Lag 428
In Provence & the Côte d'Azur 429
Availability & Cost of Health Care 429
Diarrhoea 429
Environmental Hazards 429
Sexual Health 429
Travelling with Children 429
Women's Health 430

Travel health depends on your predeparture preparations, your daily health care while travelling and how you handle any medical problem that does develop. Provence and the Côte d'Azur are healthy places to travel. Your main risks are likely to be sunburn, foot blisters, insect bites and mild stomach problems from eating and drinking too much.

BEFORE YOU GO

Prevention is the key to staying healthy while abroad. A little planning before departure, particularly for pre-existing illnesses, will save trouble later. See your dentist before a long trip, carry a spare pair of contact lenses and glasses, and take your optical prescription with you. Bring medications in their original, clearly labelled, containers. A signed and dated letter from your physician describing your medical conditions and medications, including generic names, is also a good idea. If carrying syringes or needles, be sure to have a physician's letter documenting their medical necessity.

INSURANCE

If you're an EU citizen or from Switzerland, Iceland, Norway or Liechtenstein, the European Health Insurance Card (EHIC) covers you for emergency health care or in the case of accident while in the region. It will not cover you for nonemergencies or emergency repatriation. Every family member needs a separate card. In the UK, application forms are available from post offices or can be downloaded from the Department of Health website (www.dh.gov.uk).

Citizens of other countries should find out if there is a reciprocal arrangement for free medical care between their country and the country visited. If you do need health insurance, strongly consider a policy that covers you for the worst possible scenario, such as an accident requiring an emergency flight home. Find out in advance if your insurance plan will make payments directly to providers or reimburse you later for overseas health expenditures.

RECOMMENDED VACCINATIONS

No vaccinations are required to travel to Provence and the Côte d'Azur. However, the World Health Organization (WHO) recommends that all travellers should be covered for diphtheria, tetanus, measles, mumps, rubella and polio, regardless of their destination.

IN TRANSIT

DEEP VEIN THROMBOSIS (DVT)

Blood clots may form in the legs during plane flights, chiefly because of prolonged immobility. The longer the flight, the greater the risk. The chief symptom of DVT is swelling or pain of the foot, ankle or calf, usually but not always on just one side. When a blood clot travels to the lungs, it may cause chest pain and breathing difficulties. Travellers with any of these symptoms should immediately seek medical attention.

To prevent DVT developing on long flights you should walk about the cabin, contract the leg muscles while sitting, drink plenty of fluids and avoid alcohol and tobacco.

JET LAG

To avoid jet lag (common when crossing more than five time zones) try drinking plenty of nonalcoholic fluids and eating light meals. Upon arrival, get exposure to natural sunlight and readjust your schedule (for meals, sleep and so on) as soon as possible.

IN PROVENCE & THE CÔTE D'AZUR

AVAILABILITY & COST OF HEALTH CARE

Excellent health care is readily available and for minor illnesses pharmacists can give valuable advice and sell over-the-counter medications. They can also advise when more-specialised help is required and point you in the right direction. The standard of dental care is usually good, however, it is sensible to have a dental check-up before a long trip.

When you ring ☎ 15, the 24-hour dispatchers of the Service d'Aide Médicale d'Urgence (SAMU; Emergency Medical Aid Service) will take details of your problem and send out a private ambulance with a driver or, if necessary, a mobile intensive-care unit. For less serious problems SAMU can dispatch a doctor for a house call. If you prefer to be taken to a particular hospital, mention this to the ambulance crew, because the usual procedure is to take you to the nearest one. In emergency cases (for example, those requiring intensive-care units), billing will be taken care of later. Otherwise, you need to pay in cash at the time.

If your problem is not sufficiently serious to call SAMU, but you still need to consult a doctor at night, call the 24-hour doctor service, operational in most towns in the region. Telephone numbers are listed in the relevant town sections under Medical Services, or see the Quick Reference page on the inside back cover.

DIARRHOEA

If you develop diarrhoea, be sure to drink plenty of fluids, preferably an oral rehydration solution (eg Dioralyte). If diarrhoea is bloody, persists for more than 72 hours or is accompanied by fever, shaking, chills or severe abdominal pain you should seek medical attention.

ENVIRONMENTAL HAZARDS
Hay Fever

Those who suffer from hay fever can look forward to sneezing their way around rural Provence in May and June when the pollen count is at its highest.

Heat Exhaustion

Heat exhaustion occurs following excessive fluid loss with inadequate replacement of fluids and salt. Symptoms include headache, dizziness and tiredness. Dehydration is already happening by the time you feel thirsty – aim to drink sufficient water to produce pale, diluted urine. To treat heat exhaustion, replace lost fluids by drinking water and/or fruit juice, and cool the body with cold water and fans.

Hypothermia

Proper preparation will reduce the risks of getting hypothermia. Even on a hot day in the mountains the weather can change rapidly; carry waterproof garments and warm layers, and inform others of your route.

Acute hypothermia follows a sudden drop in temperature over a short time. Chronic hypothermia is caused by a gradual loss of temperature over hours.

Hypothermia starts with shivering, loss of judgment and clumsiness. Unless rewarming occurs, the sufferer deteriorates into apathy, confusion and coma. Prevent further heat loss by seeking shelter, warm dry clothing, hot sweet drinks and shared bodily warmth.

Insect Bites & Stings

Mosquitoes are found in most parts of Europe. They may not carry malaria but can cause irritation and infected bites. Use a DEET-based insect repellent.

Sand flies are found around the Mediterranean beaches. They usually cause only a nasty itchy bite but can carry a rare skin disorder called cutaneous leishmaniasis.

SEXUAL HEALTH

Emergency contraception is available with a doctor's prescription in the region. Condoms are readily available. When buying condoms, look for a European CE mark, which means they have been rigorously tested, and then keep them in a cool dry place or they may crack and perish.

TRAVELLING WITH CHILDREN

All travellers with children should know how to treat minor ailments and when to seek medical treatment. Make sure the children are up to date with routine vaccinations, and discuss possible travel vaccines well before departure as some vaccines are not suitable for children under a year.

If your child has vomiting or diarrhoea, lost fluids and salts must be replaced. It may be helpful to take rehydration powders for reconstituting with boiled water.

WOMEN'S HEALTH

Emotional stress, exhaustion and travelling through different time zones can all contribute to an upset in the menstrual pattern. If using oral contraceptives, keep in mind that some antibiotics, diarrhoea and vomiting can stop the pill from working and lead to the risk of pregnancy – remember to take condoms with you just in case. Time zones, gastrointestinal upsets and antibiotics do not affect injectable contraception.

Travelling during pregnancy is usually possible but always consult your doctor before planning your trip. The most risky times for travel are during the first 12 weeks of pregnancy and after 30 weeks.

Language

CONTENTS

Provençal	431
French	**431**
Pronunciation	431
Be Polite!	432
Gender	432
Accommodation	432
Conversation & Essentials	433
Directions	433
Health	433
Emergencies	434
Language Difficulties	434
Numbers	434
Paperwork	434
Question Words	434
Shopping & Services	435
Time & Dates	435
Transport	435
Travel with Children	436

Arming yourself with some French will broaden your travel experience, endear you to the locals and, in rural Haute-Provence (where tourism hasn't yet developed enough to persuade people in service industries to speak English), ensure an easier ride around the region. On the coast, practically everyone you are likely to meet speaks basic English (and, in many cases, a rash of other European languages).

Standard French is taught and spoken in Provence. However, travellers accustomed to schoolbook French, or the unaccented, standard French spoken in cities and larger towns, will find the flamboyant French spoken in Provence's rural heart (and by most people in Marseille) somewhat bewildering. Here, words are caressed by the heavy southern accent and end with a flourish, vowels are sung, and the traditional rolling 'r' is turned into a mighty long trill. The word *douze* (the number 12), for example, becomes 'douz-eh' with an emphasised 'e', and *pain* (bread) becomes 'peng'. Once your ears become accustomed to the local lilt you'll soon start picking up the beat.

PROVENÇAL

Despite the bilingual signs that visitors see when they enter most towns and villages, the region's mother tongue – Provençal – is scarcely heard on the street or in the home. Just a handful of older people in rural Provence (Prouvènço) keep alive the rich lyrics and poetic language of their ancestors.

Provençal (*prouvençau* in Provençal) is a dialect of *langue d'oc* (Occitan), the traditional language of southern France. Its grammar is closer to Catalan and Spanish than to French. In the grand age of courtly love between the 12th and 14th centuries, Provençal was the literary language of France and northern Spain and even used as far afield as Italy. Medieval troubadours and poets created melodies and elegant poems motivated by the ideal of courtly love, and Provençal blossomed.

The 19th century witnessed a revival of Provençal after its rapid displacement by *langue d'oïl*, the language of northern France that originated from the vernacular Latin spoken by the Gallo-Romans and that gave birth to modern French (*francés* in Provençal). The revival was spearheaded by Frédéric Mistral (1830–1914), a poet from Vaucluse, whose works in Provençal won him the 1904 Nobel Prize for Literature.

FRENCH

PRONUNCIATION

Most of the letters in the French alphabet are pronounced more or less the same as their English counterparts; a few that may cause confusion are listed below.

c	before **e** and **i**, as the 's' in 'sit'
	before **a**, **o** and **u** it's pronounced as English 'k'
ç	always as the 's' in 'sit'
h	always silent
j	as the 's' in 'leisure'; written 'zh' in the pronunciation guides
r	from the back of the throat while constricting the muscles to restrict the flow of air

n, m   where a syllable ends in a single **n** or **m**, these letters are not pronounced, but the preceding vowel is given a nasal pronunciation; note that in the pronunciation guides, 'un' and 'on' are nasal sounds.

s   often not pronounced in plurals or at the end of words

BE POLITE!

While the French rightly or wrongly have a reputation for assuming that everyone should speak French – until WWI it was the international language of culture and diplomacy – you'll find any attempt you make to communicate in French will be much appreciated.

What is often perceived as arrogance is often just a subtle objection to the assumption by many travellers that they should be able to speak English anywhere, in any situation, and be understood. You can easily avoid the problem by approaching people and addressing them in French. Even if the only phrase you learn is *Pardon, madame/monsieur, parlez-vous anglais?* (Excuse me, madam/sir, do you speak English?), you're sure to be more warmly received than if you stick to English.

An important distinction is made in French between *tu* and *vous,* which both mean 'you'; *tu* is only used when addressing people you know well, children or animals. If you're speaking to an adult who isn't a personal friend, you should use *vous* unless the person invites you to use *tu.* In general, younger people insist less on this distinction, and you will find that in many cases they use *tu* from the beginning of an acquaintance.

GENDER

All nouns in French are either masculine or feminine and adjectives reflect the gender of the noun they modify. The feminine form of many nouns and adjectives is indicated by a silent **e** added to the masculine form, as in *ami* and *amie* (the masculine and feminine for 'friend').

In the following phrases both masculine and feminine forms have been indicated where necessary. The masculine form comes first, separated from the feminine by a slash. The gender of a noun is often indicated by

a preceding article: 'the/a/some,' *le/un/du* (m), *la/une/de la* (f); or one of the possessive adjectives, 'my/your/his/her,' *mon/ton/son* (m), *ma/ta/sa* (f). French is unlike English, in that the possessive adjective agrees in number and gender with the thing in question: 'his/her mother' is *sa mère*.

ACCOMMODATION

I'm looking for a ...	Je cherche ...	zher shersh ...
campground	un camping	un kom-peeng
guesthouse	une pension (de famille)	ewn pon-syon (der fa-mee-ler)
hotel	un hôtel	un o-tel
youth hostel	une auberge de jeunesse	ewn o-berzh der zher-nes

Where can I find a cheap hotel?
Où est-ce qu'on peut trouver un hôtel pas cher?
oo es-kon per troo-vay un o-tel pa shair

What is the address?
Quelle est l'adresse?
kel e la-dres

Could you write the address, please?
Est-ce que vous pourriez écrire l'adresse, s'il vous plaît?
e-sker voo poo-ryay e-kreer la-dres seel voo play

Do you have any rooms available?
Est-ce que vous avez des chambres libres?
e-sker voo-za-vay day shom-brer lee-brer

I'd like (a) ...	Je voudrais ...	zher voo-dray ...
single room	une chambre à un lit	ewn shom-brer a un lee
double-bed room	une chambre avec un grand lit	ewn shom-brer a-vek un gron lee
twin room with two beds	une chambre avec des lits jumeaux	ewn shom-brer a-vek day lee zhew-mo
room with a bathroom	une chambre avec une salle de bains	ewn shom-brer a-vek ewn sal der bun
to share a dorm	coucher dans un dortoir	koo-sher don zun dor-twa

How much is it ...?	Quel est le prix ...?	kel e ler pree ...
per night	par nuit	par nwee
per person	par personne	par per-son

May I see the room?
Est-ce que je peux voir la chambre?
es-ker zher per vwa la shom-brer

Where is the bathroom?
Où est la salle de bains?
oo e la sal der bun

MAKING A RESERVATION

(for phone or written requests)

To ...	À l'attention de ...
From ...	De la part de ...
Date	Date
I'd like to book ...	Je voudrais réserver ...
in the name of ...	au nom de ...
from ... (date) to ...	du ... au ...
credit card	carte de crédit
number	numéro
expiry date	date d'expiration
Please confirm availability and price.	Veuillez confirmer la disponibilité et le prix.

Where is the toilet?
Où sont les toilettes?   oo·son lay twa·let
I'm leaving today.
Je pars aujourd'hui.   zher par o·zhoor·dwee
We're leaving today.
On part aujourd'hui.   on par o·zhoor·dwee

CONVERSATION & ESSENTIALS

Hello.	Bonjour.	bon·zhoor
Goodbye.	Au revoir.	o·rer·vwa
Yes.	Oui.	wee
No.	Non.	no
Please.	S'il vous plaît.	seel voo play
Thank you.	Merci.	mair·see
You're welcome.	Je vous en prie.	zher voo·zon pree
	De rien. (inf)	der ree·en
Excuse me.	Excusez-moi.	ek·skew·zay·mwa
Sorry. (forgive me)	Pardon.	par·don

What's your name?
Comment vous   ko·mon voo·za·pay·lay voo
   appelez-vous? (pol)
Comment tu   ko·mon tew ta·pel
   t'appelles? (inf)
My name is ...
Je m'appelle ...   zher ma·pel ...
Where are you from?
De quel pays êtes-vous?   der kel pay·ee et·voo
De quel pays es-tu? (inf) der kel pay·ee e·tew
I'm from ...
Je viens de ...   zher vyen der ...
I like ...
J'aime ...   zhem ...
I don't like ...
Je n'aime pas ...   zher nem pa ...
Just a minute.
Une minute.   ewn mee·newt

DIRECTIONS

Where is ...?
Où est ...?   oo e ...
Go straight ahead.
Continuez tout droit.   kon·teen·way too drwa
Turn left.
Tournez à gauche.   toor·nay a gosh
Turn right.
Tournez à droite.   toor·nay a drwat
at the corner/at traffic lights
au coin/aux feux   o kwun/o fer

behind	derrière	dair·ryair
in front of	devant	der·von
far (from)	loin (de)	lwun (der)
near (to)	près (de)	pray (der)
opposite	en face de	on fas der

beach	la plage	la plazh
bridge	le pont	ler pon
castle	le château	ler sha·to
cathedral	la cathédrale	la ka·tay·dral
church	l'église	lay·gleez
gallery	la galerie	la galree
island	l'île	leel
lake	le lac	ler lak
main square	la place centrale	la plas son·tral
museum	le musée	ler mew·zay
old city (town)	la vieille ville	la vyay veel
ruins	les ruines	lay rween
sea	la mer	la mair
square	la place	la plas
tourist office	l'office de tourisme	lo·fees der too·rees·mer

HEALTH

I'm ill.
Je suis malade.   zher swee ma·lad
It hurts here.
J'ai une douleur ici.   zhay ewn doo·ler ee·see

EMERGENCIES

Help!	*Au secours!*	o skoor
Call ...!	*Appelez ...!*	a·play ...
a doctor	*un médecin*	un med·sun
the police	*la police*	la po·lees

There's been an accident!
Il y a eu un accident! eel ya ew un ak·see·don
I'm lost.
Je me suis égaré/e. (m/f) zhe me swee·zay·ga·ray
Leave me alone!
Fichez-moi la paix! fee·shay·mwa la pay

I'm ...	*Je suis ...*	zher swee ...
asthmatic	*asthmatique*	(z)as·ma·teek
diabetic	*diabétique*	dee·a·be·teek
epileptic	*épileptique*	(z)e·pee·lep·teek

I'm allergic	*Je suis*	zher swee
to ...	*allergique ...*	za·lair·zheek ...
antibiotics	*aux antibiotiques*	o zon·tee·byo·teek
bees	*aux abeilles*	o za·bay·yer
nuts	*aux noix*	o nwa
peanuts	*aux cacahuètes*	o ka·ka·wet
penicillin	*à la pénicilline*	a la pay·nee·see·leen

antiseptic	*l'antiseptique*	lon·tee·sep·teek
condoms	*des préservatifs*	day pray·zair·va·teef
contraceptive	*le contraceptif*	ler kon·tra·sep·teef
diarrhoea	*la diarrhée*	la de·ya·ray
medicine	*le médicament*	ler me·dee·ka·mon
nausea	*la nausée*	la no·zay
sunblock cream	*la crème solaire*	la krem so·lair
tampons	*des tampons hygiéniques*	day tom·pon ee·zhen·eek

LANGUAGE DIFFICULTIES

Do you speak English?
Parlez-vous anglais? par·lay·voo ong·lay
Does anyone here speak English?
Y a-t-il quelqu'un qui ya·teel kel·kung kee
parle anglais? par long·glay
What does ... mean?
Que veut dire ...? ker ver deer ...
I don't understand.
Je ne comprends pas. zher ner kom·pron pa
Could you write it down, please?
Est-ce que vous pourriez es·ker voo poo·ryay
l'écrire, s'il vous plaît? le·kreer seel voo play
Can you show me (on the map)?
Pouvez-vous m'indiquer poo·vay·voo mun·dee·kay
(sur la carte)? (sewr la kart)

NUMBERS

0	*zero*	ze·ro
1	*un*	un
2	*deux*	der
3	*trois*	twa
4	*quatre*	ka·trer
5	*cinq*	sungk
6	*six*	sees
7	*sept*	set
8	*huit*	weet
9	*neuf*	nerf
10	*dix*	dees
11	*onze*	onz
12	*douze*	dooz
13	*treize*	trez
14	*quatorze*	ka·torz
15	*quinze*	kunz
16	*seize*	sez
17	*dix-sept*	dee·set
18	*dix-huit*	dee·zweet
19	*dix-neuf*	deez·nerf
20	*vingt*	vung
21	*vingt et un*	vung tay un
22	*vingt-deux*	vung·der
30	*trente*	tront
40	*quarante*	ka·ront
50	*cinquante*	sung·kont
60	*soixante*	swa·sont
70	*soixante-dix*	swa·son·dees
80	*quatre-vingts*	ka·trer·vung
90	*quatre-vingt-dix*	ka·trer·vung·dees
100	*cent*	son
1000	*mille*	meel

PAPERWORK

name	*nom*	nom
nationality	*nationalité*	na·syo·na·lee·tay
date/place	*date/place*	dat/plas
of birth	*de naissance*	der nay·sons
sex/gender	*sexe*	seks
passport	*passeport*	pas·por
visa	*visa*	vee·za

QUESTION WORDS

Who?	*Qui?*	kee
What?	*Quoi?*	kwa
What is it?	*Qu'est-ce que c'est?*	kes·ker say
When?	*Quand?*	kon
Where?	*Où?*	oo
Which?	*Quel/Quelle?*	kel
Why?	*Pourquoi?*	poor·kwa
How?	*Comment?*	ko·mon
How much?	*Combien?*	kom·byun

SHOPPING & SERVICES

I'd like to buy ...
Je voudrais acheter ...   zher voo·dray zash·tay ...
I'm looking for ...
Je cherche ...   zhe shersh ...
How much is it?
C'est combien?   say kom·byun
I don't like it.
Cela ne me plaît pas.   ser·la ner mer play pa
May I look at it?
Est-ce que je peux le voir?   es·ker zher per ler vwar
I'm just looking.
Je regarde.   zher rer·gard
It's cheap.
Ce n'est pas cher.   ser nay pa shair
It's too expensive.
C'est trop cher.   say tro shair
I'll take it.
Je le prends.   zher ler pron

Can I pay by ...?
Est-ce que je peux payer avec ...?
es·ker zher per pay·yay a·vek ...
   credit card
   ma carte de crédit   ma kart der kre·dee
   travellers cheques
   des chèques de voyage   day shek der vwa·yazh

more	plus	plew
less	moins	mwa
smaller	plus petit	plew per·tee
bigger	plus grand	plew gron

a bank	une banque	ewn bonk
the ... embassy	l'ambassade de ...	lam·ba·sahd der ...
the hospital	l'hôpital	lo·pee·tal
the market	le marché	ler mar·shay
the police	la police	la po·lees
the post office	le bureau de poste	ler bew·ro der post
a public phone	une cabine téléphonique	ewn ka·been te·le·fo·neek
a public toilet	les toilettes	lay twa·let

TIME & DATES

What time is it?
Quelle heure est-il?   kel er e til
It's (8) o'clock.
Il est (huit) heures.   il e (weet) er
It's half past ...
Il est (...) heures et demie.   il e (...) er e der·mee
It's quarter to ...
Il est (...) heures moins   il e (...) er mwun
le quart.   ler kar
in the morning
du matin   dew ma·tun

in the afternoon
de l'après-midi   der la·pray·mee·dee
in the evening
du soir   dew swar

today	aujourd'hui	o·zhoor·dwee
tomorrow	demain	der·mun
yesterday	hier	yair

Monday	lundi	lun·dee
Tuesday	mardi	mar·dee
Wednesday	mercredi	mair·krer·dee
Thursday	jeudi	zher·dee
Friday	vendredi	von·drer·dee
Saturday	samedi	sam·dee
Sunday	dimanche	dee·monsh

January	janvier	zhon·vyay
February	février	fev·ryay
March	mars	mars
April	avril	a·vreel
May	mai	may
June	juin	zhwun
July	juillet	zhwee·yay
August	août	oot
September	septembre	sep·tom·brer
October	octobre	ok·to·brer
November	novembre	no·vom·brer
December	décembre	day·som·brer

TRANSPORT
Public Transport

What time does À quelle heure   a kel er
... leave/arrive? part/arrive ...?   par/a·reev ...

boat	le bateau	ler ba·to
bus	le bus	ler bews
plane	l'avion	la·vyon
train	le train	ler trun

I'd like a ... Je voudrais   zher voo·dray
ticket. un billet ...   un bee·yay ...

one-way	simple	sum·pler
return	aller-retour	a·lay rer·toor
1st class	de première classe	der prem·yair klas
2nd class	de deuxième classe	der der·zyem klas

I want to go to ...
Je voudrais aller à ...   zher voo·dray a·lay a ...
The train has been delayed.
Le train est en retard.   ler trun et on rer·tar

the first	le premier (m)	ler prer·myay
	la première (f)	la prer·myair
the last	le dernier (m)	ler dair·nyay
	la dernière (f)	la dair·nyair

ROAD SIGNS

Cédez la Priorité	Give Way
Danger	Danger
Défense de Stationner	No Parking
Entrée	Entrance
Interdiction de Doubler	No Overtaking
Péage	Toll
Ralentissez	Slow Down
Sens Interdit	No Entry
Sens Unique	One Way
Sortie	Exit

platform	le numéro	ler new-may-ro
number	de quai	der kay
ticket office	le guichet	ler gee-shay
timetable	l'horaire	lo-rair
train station	la gare	la gar

Private Transport

I'd like to hire	Je voudrais	zher voo-dray
a/an...	louer ...	loo-way ...
bicycle	un vélo	un vay-lo
car	une voiture	ewn vwa-tewr
4WD	un quatre-quatre	un kat-kat
motorbike	une moto	ewn mo-to

Is this the road to ...?
C'est la route pour ...?   say la root poor ...
Where's a service station?
Où est-ce qu'il y a une   oo es-keel ya ewn
station-service?   sta-syon-ser-vees
Please fill it up.
Le plein, s'il vous plaît.   ler plun seel voo play
I'd like ... litres.
Je voudrais ... litres.   zher voo-dray ... lee-trer

petrol/gas	essence	ay-sons
diesel	diesel	dyay-zel

(How long) Can I park here?
(Combien de temps) Est-ce que je peux stationner ici?
(kom-byun der tom) es-ker zher per sta-syo-nay ee-see
I've run out of petrol.
Je suis en panne d'essence.
zher swee zon pan day-sons
I need a mechanic.
J'ai besoin d'un mécanicien.
zhay ber-zwun dun me-ka-nee-syun
The car/motorbike has broken down (at ...)
La voiture/moto est tombée en panne (à ...)
la vwa-tewr/mo-to ay tom-bay on pan (a ...)
The car/motorbike won't start.
La voiture/moto ne veut pas démarrer.
la vwa-tewr/mo-to ner ver pa day-ma-ray

I had an accident.
J'ai eu un accident.   zhay ew un ak-see-don
I have a flat tyre.
Mon pneu est à plat.   mom pner ay ta pla

TRAVEL WITH CHILDREN

Is there a/an ...?
Y a-t-il ...?   ya teel ...
I need a/an ...
J'ai besoin ...   zhay ber-zwun ...

baby change room
d'un endroit pour   dun on-drwa poor
changer le bébé   shon-zhay ler be-be
car baby seat
d'un siège-enfant   dun syezh-on-fon
child-minding service
d'une garderie   dewn gar-dree
children's menu
d'un menu pour enfant   dun mer-new poor on-fon
disposable nappies/diapers
de couches-culottes   der koosh-kew-lot
formula
de lait maternisé   de lay ma-ter-nee-zay
(English-speaking) babysitter
d'une babysitter (qui   dewn ba-bee-see-ter (kee
parle anglais)   parl ong-glay)
highchair
d'une chaise haute   dewn shay zot
potty
d'un pot de bébé   dun po der be-be
pusher/stroller
d'une poussette   dewn poo-set

Do you mind if I breastfeed here?
Cela vous dérange si j'allaite mon bébé ici?
ser-la voo day-ron-zhe see zha-lay-ter mon bay-bay ee-see
Are children allowed?
Les enfants sont permis?
lay zon-fon son pair-mee

Also available from Lonely Planet:
French Phrasebook

Glossary

Word gender is indicated as (m) masculine, (f) feminine; (pl) indicates plural.

abbaye (f) – abbey
anse (f) – cove
AOC – *appellation d'origine contrôlée;* wines and olive oils that have met stringent government regulations governing where, how and under what conditions the grapes or olives are grown and the wines and olive oils are fermented and bottled
arène (f) – amphitheatre
arrondissement (m) – one of several districts into which large cities, such as Marseille, are split
atelier (m) – artisan's workshop
auberge (f) – inn
auberge de jeunesse (f) – youth hostel
autoroute (f) – motorway, highway

baie (f) – bay
bastide (f) – country house
billetterie (f) – ticket office or counter
borie (f) – primitive beehive-shaped dwelling, built from dry limestone around 3500 BC
boulangerie (f) – bread shop, bakery
bureau de location (m) – ticket office

CAF – Club Alpin Français
calanque (f) – rocky inlet
carnet (m) – a book of five or 10 bus, tram or metro tickets sold at a reduced rate
cave (f) – wine or cheese cellar
centre (de) hospitalier (m) – hospital
chambre d'hôte (f) – bed and breakfast accommodation, usually in a private home
charcuterie (f) – pork butcher's shop and delicatessen; also cold meat
chateau (m) – castle or stately home
chèvre (m) – goat
col (m) – mountain pass
comité départemental du tourisme (m) – departmental tourist office
commissariat de police (m) – police station
conseil général (m) – general council
corniche (f) – coastal or cliff road
corrida (f) – bullfight
cour (m) – courtyard
cour d'honneur (f) – courtyard of honour
course Camarguaise (f) – Camargue-style bullfight
cueillette des olives (f) – olive harvest

dégustation (f) – the fine art of tasting wine, cheese, olive oil or seafood
département (m) – administrative area (department)
DFCI – *défense forestière contre l'incendie;* fire road (public access forbidden)
digue (f) – dike
domaine (m) – a wine-producing estate

eau potable (f) – drinking water
église (f) – church
épicerie (f) – grocery shop
étang (m) – lagoon, pond or lake

faïence (f) – earthenware
farandole (f) – a Provençal dance dating from the Middle Ages, particularly popular in Arles today
féria (f) – bullfighting festival
ferme auberge (f) – family-run inn attached to a farm or chateau; farmhouse restaurant
fête (f) – party or festival
flamant rose (m) – pink flamingo
formule (f) – fixed main course plus starter or dessert
fromagerie (f) – cheese shop

galets (m) – large smooth stones covering Châteauneuf du Pape vineyards
gardian (m) – Camargue horseman
gare (f) – train station
gare maritime (m) – ferry terminal
gare routière (f) – bus station
garrigue (f) – ground cover of aromatic plants; see also *maquis*
gitan (m) – Roma; Gypsy
gîte d'étape (m) – hikers' accommodation, often found in the mountains or rural areas
gîte rural (m) – country cottage
golfe (m) – gulf
grand cru (m) – wine of recognised superior quality; literally 'great growth'
grotte (f) – cave

halles (f pl) – covered market; central food market
hôtel de ville (m) – town hall
hôtel particulier (m) – private mansion

jardin (botanique) (m) – (botanic) garden
joute nautiques (f) – nautical jousting tournament

lavoir (m) – communal wash house

mairie (f) – town hall
maison de la France (f) – French tourist office abroad
maison de la presse (f) – newsagent
manade (f) – bull farm
maquis (m) – aromatic Provençal scrub, see also *garrigue*; name given to the French Resistance movement
marais (m) – marsh or swamp
marais salant (m) – saltpan
marché paysan (m) – farmers market
marché Provençal (m) – open-air market
mas (m) – Provençal farmhouse
menu (m) – meal at a fixed price with two or more courses
mistral (m) – incessant north wind
monastère (m) – monastery
Monégasque – native of Monaco
moulin à huile (m) – oil mill
musée (m) – museum

navette (f) – shuttle bus, train or boat
novillada (f) – fight between bulls of less than four years of age

office du tourisme, office de tourisme (m) – tourist office (run by a unit of local government)
ONF – Office National des Forêts; National Forests Office

papeterie (f) – stationery shop
parapente (f) – paragliding
parc national (m) – national park
parc naturel régional (m) – regional nature park
pétanque (f) – a Provençal game, not unlike lawn bowls
phare (m) – lighthouse
pic (m) – mountain peak
place (f) – square
plage (f) – beach
plan (m) – city map
plat du jour (m) – dish of the day
plongée (f) – dive
pont (m) – bridge
porte (f) – gate or door, old-town entrance
préfecture (f) – main town of a *département*
préfet (m) – prefect; regional representative of national government, based in a *préfecture*
presqu'île (f) – peninsula

prieuré (m) – priory
produits du terroir (m) – local food products

quai (m) – quay or railway platform
quartier (m) – quarter or district

rade (f) – gulf or harbour
refuge (m) – hikers' shelter (mountain hut)
région (f) – administrative region
rollers (m) – Rollerblades/inline skates
rond-point (m) – roundabout

salin (m) – salt marsh
santon (m) – traditional Provençal figurine
savon (m) – soap
savonnerie (f) – soap factory
sentier (m) – trail, footpath
sentier de grande randonnée (m) – long-distance path with alphanumeric name beginning with 'GR'
sentier littoral (m) – coastal path
sentier sous-marin (m) – underwater trail
SNCF – Société Nationale des Chemins de Fer; state-owned railway company
SNCM – Société Nationale Maritime Corse-Méditerranée; state-owned ferry company linking Corsica and mainland France
stade (m) – stadium
SRV – *sur rendez-vous;* by appointment only
syndicat d'initiative (m) – tourist office (run by an organisation of local merchants)

tabac (m) – tobacconist (also sells newspapers, bus tickets etc)
taureau (m) – bull
TGV – *train à grande vitesse;* high-speed train or bullet train
théâtre antique (m) – Roman theatre
tour d'horloge (f) – clock tower
trottinette (f) – micro scooter

vendange (f) – grape harvest
vieille ville (f) – old town
vieux port (m) – old port
vigneron (m) – wine grower
vin de garde (m) – a wine best drunk after several years in storage
VTT (m) – *vélo tout terrain;* mountain bike

Behind the Scenes

THIS BOOK

This is the 5th edition of *Provence & the Côte d'Azur*. The first three editions were written by Nicola Williams, who was joined on the 4th edition by Fran Parnell. This edition was written by Nicola Williams and Catherine Le Nevez. Dr Caroline Evans contributed to the Health chapter.

This guidebook was commissioned in Lonely Planet's London office, and produced by the following:

Commissioning Editors Judith Bamber & Tashi Wheeler
Coordinating Editor Gennifer Ciavarra
Coordinating Cartographer Valentina Kremenchutskaya
Coordinating Layout Designer David Kemp
Managing Editor Liz Heynes
Managing Cartographer Mark Griffiths
Assisting Editors Monique Choy, Jackey Coyle, Justin Flynn, Charlotte Harrison, Anne Mulvaney, Joanne Newell, Amy Thomas
Assisting Cartographers Owen Eszeki, Josh Geoghegan, Simon Goslin
Assisting Layout Designers Wibowo Rusli
Cover Designer Karina Dea
Language Content Coordinator Quentin Frayne
Project Manager Chris Love

Thanks to Carol Chandler, Sin Choo, Sally Darmody, Barbara Delissen, Stefanie di Trocchio, Fayette Fox, Mark Germanchis, James Hardy, Nancy Ianni, Laura Jane, Yvonne Kirk, LPI, Trent Paton, Paul Piaia, Averil Robertson, Lauren Rollheiser, Sally Schafer, Phillip Tang, Glenn van der Knijff, Kate Whitfield, Celia Wood

THANKS
NICOLA WILLIAMS

The overwhelming graciousness of the many people I interviewed cannot be emphasised enough: thanks to Louisa Jones, Patricia Wells, Christian Etienne, Brigitte Autier, Sarah-Jane Higgins and Nice *socca* queen Thérèsa, Yvonne Courtière, Bernard Meyssard, Nicole Bérenguier, Fabien Tamboloni, Michel Vivet, Elizabeth Lewis, Jean-Paul Roux, Charlotte and Max, Holui, Jacques Maurel, Ivan Hov and Nathalie Duchayne. Thanks to everyone at LP who tore hairs out over this fabulous project and at home, a flurry of *bisous* to Matthias, Niko and Mischa for kidding around on the beach; Ella, Scott and Auntie Michelle for endless ice cream; and grandparents Christa and Karl-Otto Lüfkens.

CATHERINE LE NEVEZ

Many thanks to all who helped on my journey, including all of the 'unfortunately-too-numerous-to-mention-individually' tourism professionals throughout Provence. Thanks especially to Suzanne in Marseille, Francine in Arles and Corinne in Cavaillon; and to all of the Provençal locals who shared their insights and answered my many, *many* questions. Cheers to Nicola Williams for her inside-out Provence expertise; as well as to Judith Bamber, Fayette Fox for her fantastic transport research, Miles Roddis for Nîmes info, Meg Worby and Tashi Wheeler for giving me the gig, and everyone at LP. Most of all, *merci beaucoup* to my family for their unfailing support.

THE LONELY PLANET STORY

The story begins with a classic travel adventure: Tony and Maureen Wheeler's 1972 journey across Europe and Asia to Australia. There was no information about the overland trail then, so Tony and Maureen published the first Lonely Planet guidebook to meet a growing need.

From a kitchen table, Lonely Planet has grown to become the largest independent travel publisher in the world, with offices in Melbourne (Australia), Oakland (USA) and London (UK). Today Lonely Planet guidebooks cover the globe. There is an ever-growing list of books and information in a variety of media. Some things haven't changed. The main aim is still to make it possible for adventurous travellers to get out there – to explore and better understand the world.

At Lonely Planet we believe travellers can make a positive contribution to the countries they visit – if they respect their host communities and spend their money wisely. Every year 5% of company profit is donated to charities around the world.

OUR READERS

Many thanks to the travellers who used the last edition and wrote to us with helpful hints, useful advice and interesting anecdotes:

James Arthur, Alice Barker, Sue Barnard, Yvonne Beirne, John Busse, Francis Cagney, Romelle Castle, Nadia Collins, Dale Ivens, Hubert Jackie, Soltanhamid Kaykavousi, Andy Killoran, Philip Lukkarinen, Gregory McElwain, Hugh McGlyn, Johannes Sailer, Yvonne Yen

SEND US YOUR FEEDBACK

We love to hear from travellers – your comments keep us on our toes and help make our books better. Our well-travelled team reads every word on what you loved or loathed about this book. Although we cannot reply individually to postal submissions, we always guarantee that your feedback goes straight to the appropriate authors, in time for the next edition. Each person who sends us information is thanked in the next edition – and the most useful submissions are rewarded with a free book.

To send us your updates – and find out about Lonely Planet events, newsletters and travel news – visit our award-winning website: **www.lonelyplanet.com/contact**.

Note: we may edit, reproduce and incorporate your comments in Lonely Planet products such as guidebooks, websites and digital products, so let us know if you don't want your comments reproduced or your name acknowledged. For a copy of our privacy policy visit www.lonelyplanet.com/privacy.

Index

INDEX

A

abbeys & monasteries
Abbaye de la Celle 359
Abbaye de Silvacane 226
Abbaye de Thoronet 359
Abbaye Notre Dame de Lérin 310
Abbaye Notre-Dame de Sénanque 7, 217, 7
Abbaye St-Victor 100
Monastère de la Verne 361-2
Monastère Fortifié 310, 207
Monastère Notre Dame de Cimiez 268
Prieuré de Ganagobie 246
Prieuré de Salagon 246, 7
accommodation 398-400, see also individual locations
camping 398
chambres d'hôtes 21, 398-9
chateaux 399
gîtes d'étapes 400
hostels 399
hotels 400
maison d'hôtes 398-9
refuges 400
rental 400
activities 80-9, 136-8 see also individual activities
administrative regions & departments 409
Agay 330
Aigues Mortes 149-50
aïoli 46
Aix-en-Provence 123-31, 124, 201
accommodation 127-8
activities 125-7
entertainment 129-30
festivals 126-7
food 128-9
history 123
markets 130
sights 125-7
travel to/from 130
travel within 130-1
animals 72-9, 115, 248-9
birds 72, 371
endangered species 73
flamingos 137, 151, 202
tortoises 362
wolves 73, 250
vultures 236
Antibes 312-18, 314
accommodation 316
activities 313-16
drinking 317
festivals 316
food 316-17
internet access 313
sights 313-16
tourist information 313
travel to/from 317-18
travel within 318
antiques 186, 277
Apt 212-15, 215
architecture 62-5
belle époque 27-8, 64, 268, 389
Carrée d'Art 197, 199
Fondation Vasarely 64
Grimaldi Forum 62
Maison Carrée 15, 197, 15
Unité d'Habitation 65, 102
Villa Ephrussi de Rothschild 282-3
Villa Grecque Kérylos 284
Vista Palace 65, 289
Arles 135, 138-46, 139
accommodation 143-4
festivals 142-3
food 144-5
sights 140
tourist information 140
tours 142-3
travel to/from 145-6
travel within 146
Arrière-Pays Niçois 288-95
art 58-62, 297, 315
art galleries see museums & galleries
artists 58-71, 8-9
Cézanne, Paul 9, 60, 126, 131, 8
Chagall, Marc 61, 267, 320, 321, 359
Courbet, Gustave 60
Gauguin, Paul 60, 141, 143
Granet, François Marius 60
Hov, Ivan 350
Klein, Yves 61
Matisse, Henri 9, 61, 265, 266, 268, 321
Picasso, Pablo 9, 61, 131, 311-12, 313, 2
Renoir, Pierre-Auguste 9, 60, 319, 9
Seurat, Georges 60
Signac, Paul 61
Sisley, Alfred 60
Van Gogh, Vincent 9, 60, 135, 138, 141-2, 143, 9
Vasarely, Victor 9, 61
Vernet, Joseph 59
arts 58-71, 266-8, see also individual genres
astronomy 80, 217
Astrorama 286
Haute-Provence 248
Observatoire de Nice 286
ATMs 410
Aubagne 119
Aups 358
Avignon 157-200, 158, 160
accommodation 163-5
activities 163
emergency services 158
entertainment 166-7
festivals 163
food 165-6
history 157
internet access 158-9
itineraries 155-6, 155, 156
literature 157
markets 157
medical services 159
Palais des Papes 161-2, 203
Pont d'Avignon 159-61
sights 159-62
tourist information 159
travel to/from 167
travel within 167-8

B

ballooning 80, 216
Bandol 380
Barcelonnette 249
Bardot, Brigitte 30, 66
bathrooms 412
beach volleyball 80
world championships 104

000 Map pages
000 Photograph pages

beaches 339, 346, 368, **4–5** *see also*
    individual beaches at plage
    Antibes 315
    blue flag 77
    Cannes 302
    Corniche des Maures 364
    Île de Prquerolles 368
    Marseille 102-03
    Monaco 390
    Nice 269
    nudist 85, 147
    Peninsula, the 352
    St-Raphaël 331
    St-Tropez 339, 345-7
Beaucaire 194
Beaulieu-sur-Mer 283-4
belle époque 27-8, 64, 268, 389
Biot 318
birds 72, 371
bird-watching 80, 136-7
    Camargue, the 151
    Observatoire Ornithologique 226
boating 73, 116-17, 118, 150, 347,
    365, 372-3, 390
    Antibes 316
    Marseille 103
    Nice 269
Bonaparte, Napoléon 27, 231
Bonnieux 11, 219-21, **11**
books, *see* literature
bories 122, 217
Bormes-les-Mimosas 363-4
bouillabaisse 44, 45, 108, **201**
boules 39
bullfighting 148, 197
bungee jumping 80, 235
Buoux 226-7
business hours 400-1

C
Cabrières d'Avignon 223
Cadenet 226
Cagnes-sur-Mer 318-19
Calanque d'en Vau 5, 116, **4**
calanques, see Les Calanques
calissons 52, 130
Camargue, the 133-53, **136, 202**
    activities 136-8
    itineraries 134-5, **134, 135**
    tours 138
camping 354
Cannes 296-337, **300, 304, 12, 207**
    accommodation 303-5
    activities 301-2
    cinema 302

drinking 307-9
entertainment 308-9
festivals 303
food 306-7
internet access 299
internet resources 299
itineraries 297-8, **297, 298**
literature 301
markets 299
medical services 299
sights 301-2
tourist information 301
travel within 309
travel to/from 309
canoeing 73, 81, 103, 137, 200
canyoning 81
Cap Couronne 119-20
Cap d'Ail 284-5
Cap de Carqueiranne 376
Cap Martin 285
Carpentras 182-5, **183**
Carry-le-Rouet 119-20
Casino de Monte Carlo 13, 388,
    389, **12**
Cassis 116-19
Castellane 236
cathedrals, *see* churches & cathedrals
Cavaillon 223-5
cell phones 411-12
Cézanne, Paul 9, 60, 126, 131, **8**
Chartreuse de la Verne 361-2
Château d'Allemagne 240, 241
Château d'Ansouis 229
Château d'Avignon 147
Château d'If 102
Château de la Napoule 328
Château de la Théoule 330
Château de l'Anglais 266
Château de Tour d'Aigues 229
Château du Bois 7, 226
Château du Grimaud 356
Château Grimaldi 313
Château La Moutte 346
Château Val Joanis 229
Châteauneuf du Pape 169-71
cheese 45, 249
chefs 43, 44, 52, 274
children, travel with 401, 407, 429-30
    Avignon 163
    Nice 269
churches & cathedrals
    Ancienne Cathédrale Ste-Anne 212
    Basilique Notre Dame de la
        Garde 99-100
    Basilique St-Michel Archange 291

Cathédrale d'Antibes 313
Cathédrale de Monaco 387
Cathédrale Notre Dame et
    St-Véran 223
Cathédrale Orthodoxe Russe
    St-Nicolas 268
Cathédrale Ste-Réparate 265
Cathédrale St-Sauveur 126
Cathédrale St-Siffrein 63, 183
Chapelle Cocteau 334
Chapelle de la Garoupe 315
Chapelle de la
    Miséricorde 265, 343
Chapelle de la Trinité 310
Chapelle de Ste-Catherine 129
Chapelle des Pénitents 320
Chapelle des Pénitents Blancs
    289, 291
Chapelle du Couvent 343
Chapelle du Rosaire 321
Chapelle Notre Dame de
    Jérusalem 334
Chapelle Notre Dame du Roc 236
Chapelle Ste-Anne 343
Chapelle St-Pierre 280
Chapelle St-Roch 289
Collégiale Notre Dame des
    Anges 186
Collégiale St-Paul 372
Église Collégiale 320
Église de Châteauneuf 247
Église de St-Tropez 343
Église des Stes-Maries 147
Église Notre Dame 59
Église Notre Dame d'Esperance 301
Église Ste-Anne 366
Église Ste-Dévote 390
Église Ste-Marie Madeleine 129
Église St-Giaume 265
Église St-Jacques Le Majeur 265
Église St-Louis 372
Église St-Michel 287
Église St-Trophime 141
Église Vieille du Haut 219
Notre Dame des Fontaines 255
Nouvelle Cathédrale de la
    Major 100
Prieuré de Salagon 246-7
cinema 64, 65-6, 67
    Cannes 302
    history 65-6
    Lumière brothers 65
    Musée Jean Cocteau 290
    Nouvelle Vague 66
Circuit du Castellet 381

climate 20, 401, 418
  mistral 72
Coaraze 288
Cocteau, Jean 66, 68, 280,
  290-1, 334
Cogolin 363
Collobrières 360-1, 208
consulates 404-5
Contes 288
Corniche des Maures 364-5
Corniche d'Or 328-31
Corniche Inférieure 280-5
costs 20
Côte Bleue 119-21
Côte d'Azur 29
courses 402
  arts & crafts 402
  cooking 52, 190, 402
  gardening 402
  language 402
  painting & drawing 60
Cousteau, Jacques 187
Coustellet 223
cowboys 152, 202
credit cards 410
customs regulations 402
cycling 81-3, 181, 216, 235-6, 249-50,
  254-6, 155
  Camargue, the 137
  Vallée de Vésubie 254

D

dance 58, 62, 68, 70-1, 129
  ballet 70, 112
  Ballet National de Marseille 71
  contemporary 71
dangers 402-3
  beaches 402
  extreme weather 402-3
  forest fires 403
  poisonous mushrooms 403
  rivers & lakes 403
  theft 403
Daudet, Alphonse 68, 193
Dentelles de Montmirail 177-80
Digne-les-Bains 242-5
Digue à La Mer 150-1
disabilities, travellers with 413-14
diving & snorkelling 83-9, 117, 373
  Marseille 103
  Nice 269

000 Map pages
000 Photograph pages

Domaine du Rayol 364
donkey riding 84, 243
Draguignan 357
drinks 405-7
  liqueurs 246
  pastis 50, 56
  wine 54, 55
driving 21, 235-6

E

economy 23
Eden Roc 314, 13
electricity 399
embassies 404-5
Enclave des Papes 176-7
environment 72-9
Étang de Berre 120-1
events, see festivals
Èze 285-6

F

faïence 237
farms 89, 221
  Danse L'Ombre 246
  Ferme Auberge Le Castelas 228
  Ferme de Gerbaud 228
  organic 75
fashion 99, 395
  bikini 30
  Musée de la Mode 99
festivals 21, 142-3, 405 see also
  individual locations
  Cannes International Film
    Festival 21
  Carnaval de Marseille 104
  Carnaval de Nice 21, 206
  Christmas 179
  Ciné Plein Air festival 104
  Corso de la Lavande 243
  Féria de Pentecôte 197
  Féria des Vendanges 197
  Féria Pascale 142
  Festival Ame Gitane 143
  Festival de Marseille 21, 104
  Festival International d'Art Lyrique
    d'Aix-en-Provence 21, 126
  Festival International du Film 303
  Fête de la Châtaigne 361, 362
  Fête de la Transhumance 21,
    361, 362
  Fête de la Truffe 178
  Fête des Gardians 21, 142
  Fête Nationale Monégasque 390
  film 104, 118
  food 57

Formula One Grand Prix 21, 395, 396
  Journée de la Truffe 358
  Les Chorégies d'Orange 21
  Pèlerinage de la Chandeleur
    100, 104
  Pèlerinage des Gitans 21, 147
film, see cinema
film-makers 66
  Cocteau, Jean 66, 68, 280,
    290-1, 334
  Pagnol, Marcel 66, 97, 119
  Vadim, Roger 66
fishing 84, 181, 282
flying & gliding 84, 181
Fontaine de Vaucluse 187-8
Fontvieille 193, 389
food 42-57, 405-7
  cheese 45-6, 249
  chestnuts 50, 208
  courses 52
  etiquette 49
  fermes auberges 406
  festivals 57
  fish 44-5
  garlic 46-7, 3
  herbs 48-51
  honey 224
  markets 53
  meat 46
  melons 51
  Niçois 272-4
  olive oil 45
  olives 45, 50-1
  organic 375
  red rice 49-50
  self-catering 406
  sweets 52-3, 278, 361
  tomatoes 47, 48
  truffles 42-3, 131-2, 178, 203
  vegetables 48
  vegetarian 276, 406-7
football 395
  Olympique de Marseille 93, 103
Forcalquier 246
Forêt du Dom 363-4
Formula One Grand Prix 21, 395, 396
Fox Amphoux 11, 358
Fréjus 333-7, 335
  accommodation 336
  activities 335-6
  food 336
  tourist information 334
  tours 336
  travel to/from 336-7
  travel within 337

G

galleries, see museums & galleries
gardens & parks 74, 77
    Conservatoire Botanique National
        Méditerranéen 367
    Forêt des Cèdres 219
    Jardin Botanique de la Villa
        Thuret 315
    Jardin Conservatoire de Plantes
        Tinctoriales 226
    Jardin d'Oiseaux Tropicaux 371
    Jardin du Palmier 367
    Jardin Exotique 286, 390
    Jardin Japonais 389
    Jardins de L'Olivaie 283
    Jardins du Casino 387
    Jardins St-Martin 386
    Menton 293
    Parc des Arènes 266
    Parc du Château 265, **206**
    Parc du Mugel 118
    Parc Fontvieille 389
    Parc National de Port-Cros 372
    Parc St-Bernard 372
    Roseraie Princesse Grace 389
    Zoo Parc du Cap Ferrat 282
garlic 46-7, **3**
garrigue 48, 288
Gassin 352
gay & lesbian travellers 112,
    277, 308-9, 407
geography 72
geology 241
Gigaro 353
Glanum 15, 189, **14**
gliding & flying 84, 181
golf 84
Golfe de St-Tropez 354-7
Golfe-Juan 311-12
Gorbio 294-5, **11**
Gordes 216-17, **11**, **10**
Gorges du Verdon 73, 234-9
    accommodation 237-9
    activities 235-7
    Castellane 236
    dangers 234-5
    food 237-9
    La Palud-sur-Verdon 235
    Moustiers Ste-Marie 237
    sights 235-7
    tourist information 234
    travel to/from 239
government, local 409
Grand Hôtel du Cap Ferrat 13, 284
Grande Corniche 286-8

grass skiing 84-5
Grasse 325-8, **327**, **207**
Grimaud 356
gypsy, see Roma

H

Haute-Provence 231-56, **234**, **205**
    itineraries 232-3, **232**, **233**
    markets 241
Haut-Var 358
health 428-30
    children's 429-30
    in Provence & Côte d'Azur 429
    in transit 428-9
    insurance 428
    women's health 430
herbs 48-9, 50, 51
hiking, see walking
history 24-33, 227
    Fête de Bazaïs 292
    French 26-7
    French Revolution 27
    Gallo-Roman 24-5
    industrial 30
    internet resources 25, 31, 32
    medieval 25-6
    modern 29-31
    Nazi Germany 29
    plague, the 26
    popes 26
    prehistory 24, 255
    Treaty of Nice 32
    WWI 28-9
    WWII 29
holidays 20, 407-8
honey 255
horse riding 85
    Camargue, the 137-8, 152-3
Hôtel Martinez 13, 305, **12**
Hyères 372-5, **374**

I

ice diving 85, 251
identity, Provençal 23
Île de Bendor 371
Île de Porquerolles 366-9, **367**
Île de Port-Cros 369-70, **370**
Île des Embiez 371
Île du Levant 370-1
Île du Port-Cros 370
Île Ste-Marguerite 310
Île St-Honorat 310
Îles de Lérins 310
Îles d'Hyères 366-71
Îles du Frioul 102

Îles du Fun 366-71
inline skating 86, 103, 269
insurance 408
    health 428
internet access 408
internet resources 22
Italy, day trips to 281
itineraries
    Avignon 155-6, **155**, **156**
    Camargue, the 134-5, **134**, **135**
    Cannes 297-8, **297**, **298**
    Haute-Provence 232-3, **232**, **233**
    Luberon, the 210-11, **210**, **211**
    Marseille 91-2, **91**, **92**
    Nice to Menton 258-9, **258**, **259**
    St-Tropez to Toulon 339-40,
        329, **340**

J

Jeanneret, Charles Édouard, see
    Le Corbusier
jeep tours 73, 85, 142
jewellery 237

K

kayaking, see canoeing
Kelly, Grace 286, 388, 394
kite-surfing 138

L

L'Estaque 119
L'Isle-sur-la-Sorgue 186-7
La Celle 359
La Ciotat 118-19
La Croix Valmer 353
La Friche La Belle de Mai 59, 64
La Garde Freinet 362-3
La Londe 371
La Môle 363
La Turbie 287
La Canabière 97
Lac de Ste-Croix 239-40
Lacoste 221
Lac de Castillon 240-2
Lac de Chaudanne 240-2
Lac de Quinson 240-1
Lac de Ste-Croix 239-40
Lacs du Verdon 239-41
language 95
    Nissart 265
    Occitan 431
    Pelhasc 289
    Provençal 431
lavender 233, 243, 244, **233**, **6-7** see
    also perfume

INDEX

Le Club 55 13, 346, **13**
Le Corbusier 65, 102, 287
  Unité d'Habitation 65, 102
Le Dramont 330
Le Félibrige 67
Le Grand Luberon 226-9
Le Lavandou 365-6
Le Panier quarter 97, 113, **201**
Le Petit Luberon 219-23
Le Thoronet 359
Le Trayas 330
legal matters 408-9
Les Arcs-sur-Argens 359-60
Les Arènes
  Arles 15, 140, **15**, **202**
  Nîmes 15, 195-7
Les Baux de Provence 192
Les Calanques 115-16, **201**
Les Lecques 380
lesbian travellers 277, 308-9, 407
liqueurs 246
literature 66-8, 93
  Avignon 157
  Camargue, the 138
  Cannes 301
  Luberon 214
  Marseille 93
  medieval 66
  Monaco 383
  Nice to Menton 261
  St-Tropez to Toulon 341
  travel 20-2, 63, 67
Lourmarin 228
Luberon, the 209-30, **213**, **204**
  accommodation 218-19
  food 218-19
  itineraries 210-11, **210**, **211**
  literature 214
  markets 217

M
Maillane 194
Man in the Iron Mask, the 311
Mandelieu-La Napoule 328-9
Manosque 229-30
maps 409-10
markets 53, 185
  Avignon 157
  Camargue, the 145
  Cannes 299
  Haute-Provence 241

Luberon, the 217
Marseille 93
  St-Tropez to Toulon 341
Marseille 90-132, **94**, **98**, **101**,
  106, **114**
  accommodation 104-8
  activities 102-4
  beaches 102-3
  churches & cathedrals 99-100
  coast 100-2
  drinking 111
  emergencies 96
  festivals 104
  food 108-11
  history 93-5
  internet access 96
  itineraries 91-2, **91**, **92**
  literature 93
  markets 93
  medical services 96
  metro 114, **114**
  museums 97-9
  shopping 113-14
  sights 97, 99, 101-02
  tourist information 96
  tours 104
  travel to/from 113-14
  travel within 97, 114-15
Massif de L'Estérel 328-37
Massif des Maures 360-6
Maussane-les-Alpilles 192-3
Mayle, Peter 214, 221, 228
melons 51, 223, see also Cavaillons
metric conversions see front cover flap
Ménerbes 11, 221-2, **10**
Menton 260, 290-5, 291, **291**
  accommodation 292
  drinking 294
  festivals 292
  food 292-4
  literature 261
  sights 290-2
  tourist information 290
  travel within 294
mistral 72
Mistral, Frédéric 67, 68, 194
mobile phones 411-12
Monaco 382-97, **384**, **208**
  accommodation 390-1
  activities 390
  drinking 392-5
  entertainment 393-5
  festivals 390
  food 391-2
  history 383

internet access 385
internet resources 385
literature 383
medical services 385
royalty 388
shopping 395
sights 386-90
telephone 386
tourist information 386
travel to/from 395-6
travel within 396-7
Monaco Ville 386-7
monasteries, see abbeys &
  monasteries
Moneghetti 390
money 20, 403-4, 410, see also front
  cover flap
Mont Faron 376-7
Mont Ventoux 180-2
Montagne Ste-Victoire 131
Monte Carlo 13, 387-9, **208**, **12**
Monte Carlo Casino 13, 388, 389, **12**
Mougins 324-5
Moustiers Ste-Marie 237
Moyenne Corniche 285-6
multiculturalism 32-3, 90
museums & galleries 266-8
  Anatole Jakovsky International
    Naive Art Museum 267
  Astérides 58
  Ateliers Sud Side 58
  Carrée d'Art 195-6
  Centre de Géologie 242
  Centre de la Vieille Charité 97-9
  Centre National d'Art
    Contemporain 268
  Château Musée 288
  Château-Musée de l'Empéri 121
  Château Musée de Vallauris 61,
    311-12
  Château-Musée Grimaldi 319
  Collection de Voitures
    Anciennes 389
  Collection Lambert 162
  Église St-Michel 121
  Espace Culturel Paul Ricard 371
  Espace de l'Art Concret 326
  Espace Simon-Lumière 118
  Espace Van Gogh 142
  Exposition Universelle des Vins et
    Spiritueux 371
  FAI AR 59
  Fondation Émile Hughes 321
  Fondation Maeght 320
  Fondation Vasarely 126

000 Map pages
000 Photograph pages

Fondation Vincent Van
  Gogh 141-2
Galerie d'Art du Conseil Général
  des Bouches du Rhône 126
Galerie de la Marine 266
Galerie des Grands Bains Douches
  de la Plaine 59
Galerie des Ponchettes 266
Galerie Ferrero 277
Galerie Madoura 312
Hôtel des Arts 377
Institut Océanographique Paul
  Ricard 371
La Chambre de Vincent 142
La Cité des Arts de la Rue 58
La Friche La Belle de Mai 59
La Maison des Papillons 345
Lavoir Vasserot 345
Lézarap'art 58
Lieux Publics 58
Maison de la Pétanque 312
Maison de la Photographie 377
Maison de Nostradamus 121
Musée Alexandra
  David-Néel 242
Musée Angladon 162
Musée Archéologique 334
Musée Archéologique de
  Nice-Cimiez 267
Musée Calvet 60, 162
Musée Camarguais 141
Musée Cantini 99
Musée d'Anthropologie
  Préhistorique 63, 390
Musée d'Archéologie 197, 313
Musée d'Archéologie
  Méditerranéenne 63
Musée d'Art et d'Histoire 268
Musée d'Art et d'Histoire de
  Provence 326
Musée d'Art Méditerranéen
  Moderne 319
Musée d'Art Contemporain 99, 197
Musée d'Art Moderne et d'Art
  Contemporain (MAMAC) 266
Musée de la Boulangerie 219
Musée de la Castre 301
Musée de la Céramique 312
Musée de la Chapelle de la
  Visitation 387
Musée de la Marine 377
Musée de la Marine et de
  l'Économie 99
Musée de la Mer 310
Musée de la Mine 376

Musée de la Mode 99
Musée de la Préhistoire des Gorges
  du Verdon 62, 63, 240
Musée de la Résistance 236
Musée de la Torture 150
Musée de la Tour 313
Musée de la Vallée 249
Musée de la Vannerie 226
Musée de l'Annonciade 61, 343-5
Musée de l'Artillerie 357
Musée de l'Automobiliste 325
Musée de l'Aventure Industrielle
  du Pays d'Apt 212
Musée de l'Olivier 319
Musée de Paléontologie Humaine
  de Terra Amata 268
Musée des Alpilles 190
Musée des Arts Asiatiques 267
Musée des Arts et Traditions
  Populaires 356
Musée des Arts et Traditions
  Provençales 357
Musée des Beaux-Arts 59, 60,
  197, 267
Musée des Beaux-Arts
  (Menton) 291
Musée des Coquillages 282
Musée des Docks Romains 99
Musée des Faïences 229
Musée des Merveilles 255
Musée des Souvenirs Napoléoniens
  et Archives Historiques du
  Palais 387
Musée des Timbres et des
  Monnaies 389
Musée d'Histoire de Marseille 99
Musée d'Histoire et de Céramique
  Biotoises 318
Musée d'Histoire Local 320
Musée d'Histoire Locale et des
  Traditions 93
Musée d'Histoire Naturelle 377
Musée d'Orange 172
Musée du Bonbon 200
Musée du Cartonnage et de
  l'Imprimerie 176
Musée du Lait 253
Musée du Riz du Petit
  Manusclat 152
Musée du Terroir 289
Musée du Tire-Bouchon 222
Musée du Vieux Ciotat 118
Musée Espace Raimu 363
Musée Extraordinaire 229
Musée Figas 289

Musée Gassendi 242
Musée Granet 126
Musée Grévin de la
  Provence 121
Musée Jean Cocteau 66, 290
Musée Jouenne 190
Musée Juif Comtadin 223
Musée Lapidaire 162
Musée Magnelli 311
Musée Masséna 268
Musée Matisse 266
Musée Napoléonien 315
Musée National Message Biblique
  Marc Chagall 267
Musée National (Monaco) 388
Musée National Picasso 61, 311
Musée Naval 343, 389
Musée Océanographique
  (Monaco) 386
Musée Paul Arbaud 126
Musée Pétrarque 66
Musée Peynet et du Dessin
  Humoristique 313
Musée Picasso 61, 313
Musée Pol Mara 216
Musée Provençal du Costume et du
  Bijou 327
Musée Réattu 141
Musée Renoir 60, 319
Musée Romain de Tauroentum 380
Musée Sirènes et Fossiles 236
Musée Terre et Temps 246
Musée Volti 280
Museon Arlaten 141
Palais des Papes 63
Palais Longchamp 99
Villa Arson 58
Villa-Musée Jean-Honoré
  Fragonard 326
music 68-70
  festivals 104
  multiculturalism 69
  popular 69
  rap 68

N
Napoleon I, see Bonaparte, Napoleon
national parks 75-7, 136, see
  also regional parks
  Gorges du Verdon 73
  Parc National de Port-Cros 73, 76
  Parc National du Mercantour 73,
    76, 248-56, **205**
naturism 85
news 399

Nice 257-95, 260, 262-4, **262-3**, 206
  accommodation 270-2
  activities 268-9
  drinking 275-6
  emergency 261
  entertainment 276-7
  festivals 270
  food 272-5
  internet access 261
  internet resources 261
  itineraries 258-9, **258**, **259**
  literature 261
  medical services 261
  shopping 277-8
  sights 265-8
  tours 269-70
  tourist information 265
  travel to/from 278-9
  travel within 279
Nîmes 194-9, **196**
  accommodation 197-8
  festivals 197
  food 198-9
  internet resources 195
  medical services 195
  sights 195-7
  tours 197
  tourist information 195
  travel to/from 199
  travel within 199
Northern Var 356-60

O
ochre 216, 220
olive oil 45, 47, 122, 176, 177, 190, 192
olives 45, 50-1
Olympique de Marseille 93, 103
Opéra de Monte Carlo 394
Oppède-le-Vieux 11, 222, **11**
Orange 171-3, **171**, 203

P
Pagnol, Marcel 66, 97, 119
painting 59-62
  courses 60
Palais des Papes 161-2, 203
Palais Princier 387, 208
parachuting 85, 235
paragliding 85
  Haute-Provence 241
  Vallée de Vésubie 254

000 Map pages
000 Photograph pages

Parc National de Port-Cros 73, 76
Parc National du Mercantour 73, 76,
  248-56, 205
passports 417
pastis 50, 56
Pays d'Aigues 229-30
Pays de Pagnol 119
Pays Dracénois 357-8
Peille 289-90
Peillon 289-90
perfume 247, 326, 329
Pernes-les-Fontaines 185-6
Perrier 198
pétanque 39, 320, 13, **13**
  Maison de la Pétanque 312
photography 73, 410, *see also* visual arts
Plage d'Agay 330
Plage de Gigaro 5, **5**
Plage de Notre-Dame 4, **5**
Plage de Piémanson 5, **5**
Plage des Catalans 100
Plage du Layet 5
Plage du Pampelonne 5
planning 20-2, 403-4, 428 *see also*
  itineraries
  holidays 407-8
plants 75, 115
  cork 78
Plateau de Claparèdes 7, 227-8, **6**
Plateau de Valensole 7, 244, **6**
politics 31, 32
pollution 90
  beaches 77
polo 352
Pont d'Avignon 159, 161, 203
Pont du Gard 15, 200, 14
Pont St-Bénézet 159, 161, 203
population 23
Port Grimaud 355-6
postal services 410-11

Q
quading 86, 181

R
radio 68, 95, 399
rafting, *see* water & white-water sports
railway networks **424**
Ramatuelle 352
regional parks 75-7, 136, *see*
  also national parks
  Parc Naturel Régional de Camargue
    76, 136
  Parc Naturel Régional du Luberon
    76, 209, 218

  Parc Naturel Régional du Verdon
    76, **240**
  Parc Régional Marin de la Côte
    Bleue 75, 76
  Réserve de Biosphère du Mont
    Ventoux 76
  Réserve Géologique de Haute-
    Provence 76, 241-5
Richerenches 178
Riviera, French, *see* Côte d'Azur
road distances & road tolls **423**
rock climbing 86
Rognes 131-2
rollerblading, *see* inline skating
Roma 142, 147
Roman sites 63, 138-9
  Arles 15, 140-1, **15**, 202
  Carpentras 184
  Contes 288
  Fréjus 334
  Glanum 15,189, **14**
  Les Alyscamps 141
  Les Arènes 15, 140, **202**
  Musée de l'Arles et de la Provence
    Antiques 140
  Nîmes 15, 195-7
  Orange 171, 172
  Pont du Gard 200
  Site Archéologique d'Olbia 376
  St-Rémy de Provence 189
  Théâtre Antique 140-1
  Thermes de Constantin 140
  Vaison-La-Romaine 174
Roquebrune 287-8
Roussillon 215-16, 204
Rustrel 217-18

S
safety 96-7
sailing 86-7, 254
Ste-Agnès 11, 295
Ste-Maxime 354-5
Stes-Maries de la Mer 146-9
  accommodation 148-9
  festivals 147-8
  food 149
  sights 147
  tours 147
  travel to/from 149
  travel within 149
St-Jean-Cap Ferrat 282-3
St-Paul de Vence 319-21, 207
St-Raphaël 331-3, **332**
St-Rémy de Provence 189-92, **189**
St-Saturnin-lès-Apt 217

St-Tropez 341-52, **342**, **344**, 208
accommodation 347-8
activities 343-7
drinking 350
emergency 343
entertainment 350-1
festivals 347
food 348-50
internet access 343
itineraries 339-40, **339**, **340**
markets 341
medical services 343
shopping 351
sights 343-7
tourist information 343
tours 347
travel to/from 351-2
travel within 352
Salernes 358
Salin de Badon 151
Salin de Giraud 151-2
Salins du Midi 150
Salon de Provence 121-3, **122**
Sanary-sur-Mer 380
santons 100
savonneries 122
sculpture, see visual arts
seasons 20
Seillans 11, 357
senior travellers 404
shopping 411
Sisteron 245-6, 205
skateboarding 86, 103
skiing 87-8, 181, 251
Digne-les-Bains 244
Vallée de l'Ubaye 250
Vallée de Vésubie 254
smoking 23
snorkelling, see diving & snorkelling
snowboarding 87-8
soap factories, see savonneries
solo travellers 411
spas 88, 127, 390
Digne-les-Bains 242
spelunking 88, 182
sport 395
football 395
motor 395
surfing 373-4
sweets 185

T
Tarascon 194
telephone services 411-12
theme parks 318, 335
Aqualand 355
Théoule-sur-Mer 330-1
thermal spas & springs, see spas
time 412
tipping 410
tobacco 195
smoking 23
toilets 412
tomatoes 47, 48
Toulon 376-80, **342**, **378**
tourist information 412-13 see also
individual locations
tours 87, 413
cycling 87
farms 89
jeep 85
walking 87
travel
literature 67
responsible 77-9
travel to/from France 417-22
travel to/from Provence & the Côte
D'Azur 417-22
land 419-21
sea 421-2
travel within Provence & the Côte
d'Azur 422-7
air 422
bicycle 422
boat 423
bus 424
car motorcycle 424-7
train 425, 427, **424**
travellers cheques 410
trekking, see walking
truffles 42-3, 131-2, 178, 203
TV 399

U
Unité d'Habitation 65, 102

V
vacations 407-8
Vaison-la-Romaine 173-6
Vallauris 310-12
Vallée de la Blanche 244

Vallée de la Durance 245-8
Vallée de la Roya 255-6
Vallée de la Tinée 252-3
Vallée de l'Ubaye 249-51
Vallée de Vésubie 253-4
Vallée des Merveilles 254-5
Vallée du Haut
Verdon 251-2, 205
Valréas 176
Van Gogh, Vincent 135, 141-2,
190, **135**
Valruas 176
Vaugines 229
Venasque 188-9
Vence 321-2
via ferrata 86, 253, 254, 255, 289
video 410
video systems 399
Village des Bories 217
Villefranche-sur-Mer 280-2
Villeneuve-lès-Avignon 168-9, **169**
visas 414-15, see also
passports
visual arts 59-62, see also painting,
photography
courses 60, 62
design 63
drawing 60
volunteering 172, 415

W
walking 73, 88-9, 136-7, 181, 236,
254, 255-6, 346-7, 361, 369-72
Camargue, the 151
tours 87, 104, 142
Vallée de Vésubie 254
water & white-water sports 89, 236,
250, 256, 347
weather 20, 72, 401, 418
weights 399
wildlife 72-5, 151, see also
animals
wine 54, 55, 225
wine tasting 117, 163, 169-70, 230,
340, 359-60, 373
women travellers 415
work 415-16

Z
Zidane, Zinadine 36, 103
Zola, Émile 68

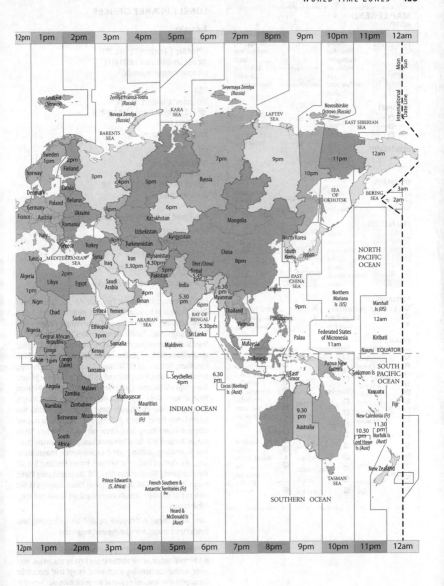

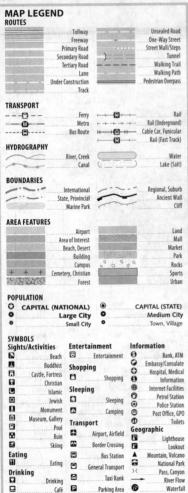

LONELY PLANET OFFICES

Australia
Head Office
Locked Bag 1, Footscray, Victoria 3011
☎ 03 8379 8000, fax 03 8379 8111
talk2us@lonelyplanet.com.au

USA
150 Linden St, Oakland, CA 94607
☎ 510 893 8555, toll free 800 275 8555
fax 510 893 8572
info@lonelyplanet.com

UK
72-82 Rosebery Ave,
Clerkenwell, London EC1R 4RW
☎ 020 7841 9000, fax 020 7841 9001
go@lonelyplanet.co.uk

Published by Lonely Planet Publications Pty Ltd

ABN 36 005 607 983
5th Edition – April 2007
First Published – June 1999

© Lonely Planet Publications Pty Ltd 2007

© photographers as indicated 2007, except:

Cover photograph: Umbrellas at Pampelonne beach, Tania Cagnoni/ Axiom. Internal photographs: p3 Bags of garlic at market, Russell Mountford/Lonely Planet Images; p4 Jean-Bernard Carillet/Lonely Planet Images (top), Palomba/Agence Images/Alamy (bottom); p5 David Martyn Hughes/Images-of-France/Alamy (top), DR-IAP/Agence Images/Alamy (bottom); p6 JLImages/Alamy (top), Boyer/Agence Images/Alamy (bottom); p7 Bill Wassman/Lonely Planet Images (top), Yann/Agence Images/Alamy (bottom); p8 Delderfield/Agence Images/ Alamy (top), Bill Wassman/Lonely Planet Images (bottom); p9 Frances Wysocki/Hemis/Alamy (top), Stella Hellander/Lonely Planet Images (bottom); p10 John Elk III/Lonely Planet Images (top), Barbara Van Zanten/Lonely Planet Images (bottom); p11 David Martyn Hughes/ Images-of-France/Alamy (top), Glenn van der Knijff/Lonely Planet Images (bottom); p12 David Tomlinson/Lonely Planet Images (top), Alex Segre/Alamy (bottom); p13 J Lautier/Agence Images/Alamy (top), Jean-Bernard Carillet/Lonely Planet Images (bottom); p14 Bill Wassman/Lonely Planet Images (top), Bill Wassman/Lonely Planet Images (bottom); p15 Bill Wassman/Lonely Planet Images; p16 Red ochre cliffs of Roussillon beneath stormy sky, David Tomlinson/Lonely Planet Images.

Many of the images in this guide are available for licensing from Lonely Planet Images: www.lonelyplanetimages.com.

Printed by SNP Security Printing Pte Ltd, Singapore